The Legacy of John

Second-Century Reception of the Fourth Gospel

Edited by

Tuomas Rasimus

BRILL

LEIDEN • BOSTON
2010

This book is printed on acid-free paper.

Library of Congress Cataloging-in-Publication Data

The legacy of John : second-century reception of the Fourth Gospel / edited by
Tuomas Rasimus.
    p. cm. — (Supplements to Novum Testamentum ; v. 132)
    Includes bibliographical references and indexes.
    ISBN 978-90-04-17633-1 (hardback : alk. paper)
    1. Bible. N.T. John—Criticism, interpretation, etc.—History—Early church, ca. 30–600.
I. Rasimus, Tuomas. II. Title. III. Series.
    BS2615.52.L44 2009
    226.5'0609015—dc22

                                                                        2009035417

BS
2615.52
.L44
2010

ISSN   0167-9732
ISBN   978 90 04 17633 1

Copyright 2010 by Koninklijke Brill NV, Leiden, The Netherlands.
Koninklijke Brill NV incorporates the imprints Brill, Hotei Publishing,
IDC Publishers, Martinus Nijhoff Publishers and VSP.

PRINTED IN THE NETHERLANDS

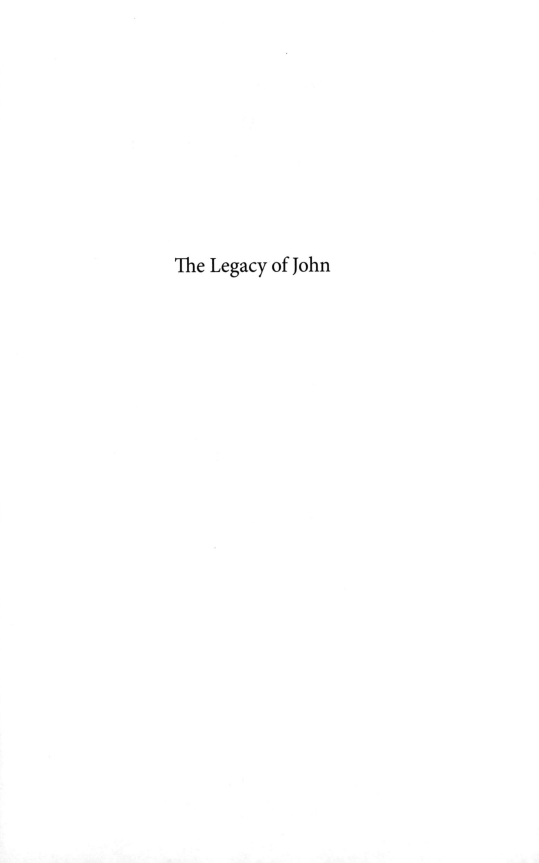

The Legacy of John

˙ Supplements
to
Novum Testamentum

˙VOLUME 132

CONTENTS

LIST OF FIGURES

ABBREVIATIONS

1 Apol.	*First Apology*
1QM	*War Scroll*
1QS	*The Community Rule*
1QSb	*Rule of the Blessings*
2 Apol.	*Second Apology*
4QTest	*Testimonia*
Abr.	*De Abrahamo*
Ad Autol.	*Ad Autolycum*
Adv. haer.	*Adversus haereses*
ANF	Ante-Nicene Fathers
Ap. John	*The Apocryphon of John*
Apoc. Ab.	*Apocalypse of Abraham*
Apoc. Adam	*The Apocalypse of Adam*
Apos. Con.	*Apostolic Constitutions and Canons*
BG	*Berolinensis Gnosticus* = Berlin Codex 8502
Carn. Chr.	*De carne Christi*
CD	The *Damascus Document*
Cels.	*Contra Celsum*
Cher.	*De cherubim*
Cod. Bruc. *Untitled*	*The Untitled Text* in the Bruce Codex
Comm. Jo.	*Commentarii in evangelium Joannis*
Comm. Matt.	*Commentariorum in Matthaeum*
Conf.	*De confusione linguarum*
Cons.	*De consensu evangelistarum*
Contempl.	*De vita contemplativa*
Decal.	*De decalogo*
De princ.	*De principiis*
Dial.	*Dialogue with Trypho*
Div. her. lib.	*Diversarum hereseon liber*
Ecl.	*Eclogae propheticae*
Ep. Apost.	*Epistula Apostolorum*
Ep. Flor.	*Epistula ad Florinum*
Epid.	*Epideixis tou apostolikou kērygmatos*
Ep. Pet. Phil.	*The Letter of Peter to Philip*
EpV&L	*Epistle of Vienne and Lyons*

Ep. Vict.	*Epistula ad Victorem*
Exc. Theod.	*Excerpta ex Theodoto*
Fug.	*De fuga et inventione*
GAJ	*The Gospel of the Acts of John*
GCS	Die griechischen christlichen Schriftsteller der ersten drei Jahrhunderte
Gos. Eg.	*The Gospel of the Egyptians* = *The Holy Book of the Great Invisible Spirit* (NHC III,2; IV,2)
Gos. Pet.	*The Gospel of Peter*
Gos. Thom.	*The Gospel of Thomas*
Gos. Truth	*The Gospel of Truth*
Haer.	*Adversus omnes haereses*
Haer. fab. comp.	*Haereticarum fabularum compendium*
Her.	*Quis rerum divinarum heres sit*
Hist. eccl.	*Historia ecclesiastica*
Hom.	*Pseudo-Clementine Homilies*
In phys.	*In Aristotelis physicorum commentaria*
Interp. Know.	*The Interpretation of Knowledge*
Leg.	*Legum allegoriae*
LR	The long recension (of the *Apocryphon of John*)
Marc.	*Adversus Marcionem*
Mon.	*De monogamia*
Mos.	*De vita Mosis*
Mut.	*De mutatione nominum*
NHC	Nag Hammadi Codex
NRSV	The New Revised Standard Version
O.	Origen, *Commentarii in evangelium Joannis*
Opif.	*De opificio mundi*
Orat.	*Oratio ad Graecos*
Pan.	*Panarion*
PG	Patrologia graeca
Plant.	*De plantantione*
Prax.	*Adversus Praxean*
Princ.	*De principiis*
QG	*Quaestiones et solutiones in Genesin*
Recogn.	*Pseudo-Clementine Recognitions*
Ref.	*Refutatio omnium haeresium* (*Elenchos*)
Sib. Or.	*Sibylline Oracles*
Soph. Jes. Chr.	*The Sophia of Jesus Christ*

Spec.	*De specialibus legibus*
SR	The short recension (of the *Apocryphon of John*)
Strom.	*Stromata*
T. Jud.	*Testament of Judah*
T. Levi	*Testament of Levi*
T. Sim.	*Testament of Simeon*
Trad. ap.	*Traditio apostolica*
Treat. Res.	*The Treatise on the Resurrection*
Trim. Prot.	*Trimorphic Protennoia*
Tri. Trac.	*The Tripartite Tractate*
Val.	*Adversus Valentinianos*
Val. Exp.	*A Valentinian Exposition*
Vir. ill.	*De viris illustribus*

INTRODUCTION

Tuomas Rasimus

University of Helsinki & Université Laval

When one approaches the Gospel of John, one is confronted with beauty and mystery, with almost countless difficulties and controversies, and with a text that has had a tremendous influence on both Christian and Jewish history. One need only think of the impact this gospel has had on the formulation of the Nicene and Chalcedonian Creeds, but also on Christian anti-Semitism that has cast its dark shadow throughout the centuries. The good and evil this "Fourth" or "spiritual" gospel has inspired, is thus a formidable topic to investigate. This volume does not attempt to cover more than a fraction of the effective history of John's Gospel. Instead, the contributions collected here investigate the early, specifically second-century reception of the Fourth Gospel. This is an era when its fortunes are surrounded by silence and mystery. It is often asked, what happened to John's Gospel in the years after its composition and before it was picked up by various Christian theologians in the mid- to late second century. The standard answer, until quite recently, has been that Gnostic and other so-called heterodox groups were the first ones to appreciate this spiritual gospel, and hence the mainstream Christians avoided using it until authors like Theophilus of Antioch and Irenaeus of Lyons, in the last quarter of the second century, rescued it for the church.[1] Lately, this view has been challenged. Several scholars have carefully argued that from early on, there also existed a "catholic" reception of John's Gospel.[2] There have also been advances in the study of heterodox forms of Christianity, especially so-called "Gnostic" ones.[3]

---

[1] See, e.g., Sanders 1943, 86–87; Hillmer 1966, 170–172; Brown 1979, 145ff.; and Haenchen 1984, 18–19.

[2] Hengel 1989; Nagel 2000; Hill 2004.

[3] The category of Gnosticism has been reevaluated by M. Williams (1996); and King (2003); the category of Classic or Sethian Gnosticism has been likewise reevaluated by Layton (1987); Logan (1996); and Rasimus (2009); and a deeper understanding of it has been offered by Pearson (1990) in relation to Jewish traditions, and by J. Turner (2001) in relation to the Platonic tradition. Recent important contributions to Valentinianism have also been made by Thomassen (2006) and Dunderberg (2008).

This has then increasingly led to a desire to abandon the old division between "orthodox" and "heterodox" forms of Christianity as misleading and anachronistic, and to treat all forms of early Christianity in their own right. Additionally, a general, renewed interest in the reception history (or effective history) of the New Testament writings has developed, accompanied by stresses that early exegetes must be studied within their own contexts, that the New Testament writings are indeed open to pluralistic interpretations, and that modern scholarly readings (theories) should not be viewed in isolation from the early exegesis that has sometimes had unrecognized effects on modern views.[4] Therefore, the time seemed ripe for a fresh, comprehensive look at the Fourth Gospel's early reception history.[5]

A natural place to start such an investigation is the Johannine corpus itself. The possible—if not probable—final redactional layer of the gospel, and the Johannine epistles (1–3 John), can be conceived of as representing the earliest reception of the gospel.[6] Whether the gos-

---

Cf. also the recent collection of essays on "Second-Century Christian Heretics" by Marjanen and Luomanen (2005).

[4] On the "history of influence"/"effective history" (*Wirkungsgeschichte*) approach generally, see Luz 1985, 78–82; Räisänen 2001, 263–282; and, of course, Gadamer 1965, e.g., pp. 284ff. Mitchell (2000, 18–22) points out that a reception of a text should not be studied from the point of view of *if* the interpreter understood it correctly, but of *how* the interpreter has interpreted it. Kannengiesser (2004, 3–20) calls for the placing of the ancient interpreters in their own cultural and social contexts. Keefer (2006, 12–20, 81–104), in addition to these emphases, stresses the facts that Biblical texts are open to pluralistic interpretations and that by bringing ancient exegetes into discussion with modern ones, we may gain new insights. Keefer offers, among his other observations, the interesting suggestions that (a) the exegesis of the Valentinian Heracleon is in some ways remarkably similar to those of Käsemann ("naïve docetism"; Käsemann's own reading [1968, 26, 70] can then be seen as naïvely Valentinian!), Meeks, Martyn and Brown ("two-level reading"), and this insight can help us better evaluate the modern discussion; (b) Irenaeus has had much influence on how we view the Fourth Gospel today; and (c) that while we know next to nothing of the first readers of the Fourth Gospel—i.e., the hypothetical construct of the Johannine community—we do get a glimpse of the second-century readers like Heracleon and Irenaeus, and they may be the closest we can get to fleshing out the actual first readers.

[5] Previous scholarship devoted to the second-century reception of the Fourth Gospel includes Sanders 1943; Braun 1959; Hillmer 1966; Kaestli et al. 1990; Nagel 2000; Hill 2004; and Keefer 2006. The older scholarship operated under the old paradigm of early catholic reluctance towards the Fourth Gospel, as well as under the now outdated views on Gnosticism, whereas more recent scholarship—despite all its thoroughness and innovativeness—has not necessarily been able to fully incorporate the latest advances made in the study of heterodox forms of Christianity and/or hermeneutics.

[6] That chapter 21 is a later addition to the gospel, is the standard view today; see, e.g., Brown 1966, xxxii–xxxix; Zumstein 1990; and Koester 2000, 199. Many scholars

pel predates the epistles, and whether they have different authors, are debated issues, but even if the priority of the epistles is assumed, they can be seen to reflect the essential teachings of the Johannine community[7] that became embodied in the gospel. Raimo Hakola's essay investigates the reception and development of the Johannine teachings in the epistles, as well as the nature of the Johannine schism that divided the Johannine community and is reflected in the epistles.

Related to the question of the earliest reception is the question of the gospel's authorship, and, consequently, its title. The gospel is said to have been written by the famous Beloved Disciple (John 21:24), who is just as famously left unnamed. The title of the gospel (*according to John*) is by most accounts a later addition to the manuscript tradition—perhaps necessitated by the circulation of the gospel outside the Johannine community that produced it.[8] However, this then raises questions on the accuracy and origin of the title. Did a John write the gospel, and was the author in reality, or at least via authorial fiction, John the son of Zebedee, one of the twelve? Did the title originate within the Johannine community? Or is the title completely fictitious, secondary and inaccurate? And if so, who invented it?

The manuscript tradition is unanimous: no one other than "John" appears as the author in the titles. Likewise, the church tradition is practically unanimous: apart from the unique third century anti-Montanist tradition, according to which Cerinthus wrote the Revelation, and perhaps also the Gospel,[9] all ancient witnesses assigned the Fourth

---

also assign the prologue—or parts of it—as well as sections from the farewell discourses, to the final redaction. See, e.g., Brown 1966, xxxii–xxxix; Becker 1970; Richter 1975; and Segovia 1981.

[7] For the Johannine community, see especially Meeks 1972; Brown 1979; Martyn 1979; and Kaestli et al. 1990; but also the critical discussions in Bauckham 1998. For a renewed discussion of the role of women in the Johannine community, see Conway 1999.

[8] Cf. Theobald 1996, 250–251; Dunderberg 2006, 120n6. The remark made by E. Turner (1987, 13–14) according to which the gospel title "seems to be a later addition" in the early P66 (Papyrus Bodmer II) appears to pertain only to the *placement* of the title (at the beginning rather than at the end of the gospel), not to the existence of the title itself. On the other hand, the stress on the anonymity of the Beloved Disciple is indeed at odds with the explicit mention of John in the title, which alone suggests that the title does not stem from the evangelist or the redactor(s). Hengel (1989, 26, 74), however, thinks that the title was already part of the original gospel.

[9] Epiphanius (*Pan.* 51.3.6) mentions that the *Alogi* rejected both the Revelation *and* the Fourth Gospel as Cerinthian writings. In addition, some medieval authors—supposedly depending on Hippolytus—made the same claim. However, the reliability

Gospel to John the apostle, who, according to many, would have written at Ephesus during the time of Trajan (98–117 CE).[10] The identification of the earliest known assignment of the Gospel to "John" is debated, but the most common candidates are Papias (ca. 130) and the Valentinian Ptolemaeus (ca. 150).[11] In addition, if at least parts of the *Acts of John* are to be dated as early as the first or second quarter of the second century, then this fragmentary document—which has also sometimes been seen as a product of the schismatic elements of the Johannine community—may even be the earliest document that both identifies the evangelist as John the son of Zebedee, and places him in Ephesus.[12] István Czachesz investigates the relationship of the so-called Gospel-section of the *Acts of John* to the Fourth Gospel.

There did exist an ancient tradition of two different Johns in Ephesus, known to Dionysios of Alexandria and Eusebius, but even these authors assigned only the Revelation to the "other John" (see Eusebius, *Hist. eccl.* 3.39.6; 7.25) while attributing the Gospel and 1 John to the apostle. The theory according to which the "other John"

---

of these traditions concerning the alleged Cerinthian authorship of the gospel is often questioned. See the discussion in Hill 2004, 174–204.

[10] E.g., Irenaeus, *Adv. haer.* 2.22.5; 3.1.1. The dating is more or less in accordance with the scholarly consensus that dates the gospel between 90–125 CE (Brown 1982, 100–103; Moloney 1998, 1–6; Keener 2003, 140–142). A date in the latter half of the second century has sometimes been suggested, but is generally rejected today (see Brown 1966, lxxx; Hengel 1989, 87–88). Suggestions for the place of composition vary more, although the traditional candidate, Ephesus (Irenaeus, *Adv. haer.* 3.1.1; Eusebius, *Hist. eccl.* 4.18.6–8; 5.24.3; 6.14.7), or Asia Minor generally, remains the favored choice (Brown 1966, ciiix–civ; Akin 2001, 27; Keener 2003, 140–149; Köstenberger 2004, 6–8; Trebilco 2004, 241ff.). Syria, Syria-Palestine and specifically Antioch, have also been proposed (Bultmann 1971, 12; Aune 1972, 25; Kümmel 1975, 247; Koester 1990, 245), and less frequently Alexandria (Sanders 1943, 39ff.; Brownlee 1972, 188ff.). On the other hand, the possibility of a transplantation of earlier traditions to the place of composition/publication (e.g., from Palestine to Egypt, Asia Minor or Syria) is considered by several scholars. See Brownlee 1972, 188; Brown 1979, 56–57, 166; Smith 1984, 22; and Beasley-Murray 1987, xlvi.

[11] Hill (2004, 383–396) has suggested that Eusebius has preserved a fragment of Papias in *Hist. eccl.* 3.24.5–17, which assigns the origin of the Fourth Gospel to John, and closely parallels (1) *Hist. eccl.* 2.15.1–2; 3.39.15–16, that discuss the origins of Mark and Matthew, and which sections Eusebius does attribute to Papias; and (2) passages in later authors who are known or suspected to have used Papias' account of the origins of the gospels (e.g., Irenaeus, Clement of Alexandria, the *Muratorian Fragment*, Origen and Victorinus of Pettau). Irenaeus' parallel passage in *Adv. haer.* 3.1.1 relates the origins of all four gospels, and this would, according to Hill, stem from Papias' work.

[12] See now especially Lalleman 1998, e.g., 245–270; and Czachesz in this volume.

wrote the gospel, is a modern one.[13] It is based, among other things, on the fact that Papias elsewhere speaks of two Johns—both "elders"—of whom the first one is associated with the past apostles, and the other one with a present elder Aristion (Papias frg. 3.3–4 Holmes = Eusebius, *Hist. eccl.* 3.39.3–4). Some scholars maintain that the two Johns are, in fact, one and the same, and that John's placement in both groups is due to the fact that while being one of the apostles of the past, he alone of them had lived until the present time, when Papias was making his inquiries into the "sayings of the Lord," and while written down perhaps in the 130s or 140s, Papias may have carried out some of his inquiries much earlier, when John was still alive.[14] However, other scholars think that this passage does indeed refer to two different Johns, the apostle and an elder.[15] Furthermore, the author of 2–3 John identifies himself as an "elder" (2 John 1; 3 John 1), and in the manuscript tradition as well as in the church tradition, he is identified as "John." Given also the facts that several authors in the first and second centuries seem unaware of John the apostle's connection to Ephesus,[16] and that there is a tradition according to which John the apostle was martyred, perhaps already in the first century,[17] some scholars have assumed that it was the "other John," the elder, who was the Beloved Disciple; he then wrote the Fourth Gospel either himself, or left its final composition to his students.[18] That there was a specific Johannine school of authors around the elder/Beloved Disciple that produced the Johannine writings, is a popular theory.[19] Yet some scholars prefer to

---

[13] Brown 1966, xci.

[14] Thus Smalley 1984, 73; Akin 2001, 26; and Köstenberger 2004, 7n17.

[15] Thus Brown 1966, xci; Hengel 1989, 17ff.

[16] Acts 20:18ff. and Eph are silent about John. Ignatius, *Eph.* speaks of Paul but not of John; Papias does not seem to connect John to Ephesus in his surviving fragments; and Polycarp, *Phil.*, does not mention John, although he does cite 1–2 John. See Brown 1966, lxxxviii–lxxxix.

[17] Philip of Side and George Hamartolus affirm that according to Papias (frgs. 5–6 Holmes), John was killed by Jews like his brother James (who was killed in the 40s by Antipas; see Acts 12:2); similarly two martyrologies from Edessa and Carthage. Mark 10:35–40//Matt 20:20–23 can be taken to portray Jesus predicting the martyrdom of both the sons of Zebedee. On the other hand, John need not have been killed at the same time as his brother (cf. Gal 2:9). See Hengel 1989, 158–159n121.

[18] Cf. Brown 1979; Hengel 1989.

[19] See especially Culpepper 1975; as well as Brown 1979; Hengel 1989; and Zumstein 1990. The need to postulate a school is, among other things, due to the "we" passages in the gospel (1:14; 21:24) and 1 John (1:1ff.), as well as to the reference to the death of the Beloved Disciple (John 21:21–23).

think that the Beloved Disciple is a piece of authorial fiction (of the Johannine school), whose figure may or may not be intended to portray John the son of Zebedee.[20] While the ascription of the Fourth Gospel to someone other than John the apostle is common nowadays, there are, nevertheless, many scholars who maintain, in accordance with the church tradition, that the Gospel and the Epistles (perhaps also Revelation) were written by the apostle, the Beloved Disciple himself, at an advanced age in Ephesus.[21]

Whatever the true identity of the gospel's author(s), the figure of the Beloved Disciple has captivated the imagination of many, not just today, but already in the ancient world. Several early Christian writings present a beloved disciple—someone whom Jesus loved more than his other followers—who is then specifically named. These include Mary Magdalene, Judas, Philip and Thomas.[22] Marvin Meyer investigates the various beloved disciples in the second century, as they occur in apocryphal gospels and other early Christian writings.

---

[20] Bultmann (1971, 484–485) considered the Beloved Disciple to be a symbol of gentile Christianity; Kragerud (1959) thinks the character presents the prophetic Johannine community as opposed to the "apostolic Petrine church"; and Dunderberg (2006, 180–198) has argued that the Beloved Disciple is a fictional "anti-James," created to counteract Jewish-Christian appeals to James' authority. On the other hand, Hengel (1989, 129ff.) thinks the Beloved Disciple is a composite figure based on both the son of Zebedee and the elder.

[21] Akin 2001, 26; Keener 2003, 122–139; Köstenberger 2004, 6–8; cf. Osborne 2002, 2–6. For the traditional view, according to which John the son of Zebedee wrote the Gospel, 1–3 John and Rev, see Irenaeus, *Adv. haer.* 3.16.5,8; 4.20.11 (*Adv. haer.* 4.26.3 may contain an allusion to 3 John 9 [thus Hill 2004, 99]); cf. Jerome, *Vir. ill.* 9. That 2–3 John and/or Rev were written by a person other than the evangelist, was an opinion already attested in ancient times (see Eusebius, *Hist. eccl.* 3.39.6; 6.25.9–10; 7.25; Papias, frgs. 5.1–3; 7.5–7 Holmes; cf. Moffatt 1961, 479–481). That the Gospel and 1 John are by different authors was never in doubt in the early church, although it is a common view today (Bultmann 1973, 1; Brown 1982, 19–30; Schnackenburg 1992, 34–42; Painter 2002, 44–74). A church tradition also held that John wrote his gospel with the knowledge of the other three (Clement of Alexandria in Eusebius, *Hist. eccl.*. 6.14.7; Eusebius himself, *Hist. eccl.* 3.24.7–13; Epiphanius, *Pan.* 51.4.11–12; 51.19.1; Augustine, *Cons.* 4.11–20). In modern scholarship, a theory of John's essential dependence on/knowledge of the Synoptics is found, e.g., in Mendner 1957–1958; Neirynck 1979; and Neirynck 1984; cf. Barrett 1978, 42–54. Variants of the theory of essential independence from the Synoptics are found, e.g., in Brown 1966, xliv–xlvii; Schnackenburg 1968, 1:41–43; Smalley 1984, 9–40; and Keener 2003, 42. For John's relationship to the Synoptic Gospels generally, see Smith 1992; and Keener 2003, 40ff.

[22] For the theories of Thomas and John in conflict, see Riley 1995; DeConick 1996; Pagels 1999; DeConick 2001; Pagels 2003; and especially now Dunderberg 2006, 14–46, for relevant discussion.

This brings us to Gnosticism. At least since Bultmann, every student of the Fourth Gospel has had to deal with the question of its
relationship to Gnosticism. Bultmann, of course, argued that parts of
the Fourth Gospel and especially its prologue originated in a Mandean
Gnostic group that held John the Baptist to be their Savior, and whose
ideas were then Christianized to produce the Gospel of John as we
know it.[23] To be sure, Mandeaism, in most scholars' opinion today,
cannot be confidently traced back to the end of the first century (the
probable date of composition of the Fourth Gospel),[24] and in any
case the reconstructed Primal Man myth on which Bultmann largely
built has been shown to be a flawed, artificial construct of the 19th
and early 20th century History-of-Religions school.[25] Another blow
to Bultmann's hypothesis came from the Qumran discoveries that
showed that Johannine dualism finds closer parallels in the Dead Sea
Scrolls (and Jewish apocalyptic) than Mandean sources.[26] However,
the question of the Fourth Gospel's link to Gnosticism, specifically to
some kind of pre-Christian Gnosticism—whose existence in itself is
still maintained by a number of specialists[27]—has ever since captivated
the imagination of many a scholar, and the issue cannot be said to
have been completely resolved.

Some decades ago, Raymond Brown formulated an influential
theory of the hypothetical history of the Johannine community.[28]
Importantly, he suggested that the Johannine schismatics would have
taken the gospel with them on a road that eventually led to Gnosticism
and other heterodox forms of Christianity.[29] This solution shifts the
Gnostic connection to the time after the gospel, in that it was enthusi-
astically adopted by Gnostics from early on. But a more Bultmannian
view is still alive and reasonably well. The Nag Hammadi findings, and
especially the discovery therein of the *Trimorphic Protennoia*, provided
fuel for the fire. This Gnostic document was hailed as the proof of
Bultmann's hypothesis that behind the Fourth Gospel's prologue, there
was an earlier, pre-Christian Gnostic hymn, which was adopted by the

---

[23] Bultmann 1925; 1971, 7ff. Cf. Haenchen 1984, 122ff.
[24] See Buckley 2002, 3ff., 153–160; and Lupieri 2002, 125–126, 165–172. Cf., however, Rudolph 1987, 343–366.
[25] See especially Colpe 1961. Cf. King 2003, 71–148.
[26] See Brown 1966, lii–lxvi; and Charlesworth 1990.
[27] H.-M. Schenke 1981, 607; Pearson 1990, 127–133; J. Turner 2001, 261, 271.
[28] Brown 1979.
[29] Brown 1979, 24.

evangelist.[30] After the early enthusiasm, however, the links between the prologue and *Trim. Prot.* did not seem to prove Bultmann right after all. *Trim. Prot.* was and has been increasingly explained as a corrective reading of John's prologue rather than its source, although it has been argued that both texts independently go back to Jewish Wisdom speculations. However, another Nag Hammadi text, the *Apocryphon of John*, was also discovered to contain a hymn similar not only to *Trim. Prot.*, but also to John's prologue. As this "Pronoia" hymn was even missing from the shorter version of *Ap. John*,[31] many scholars assumed that it was an originally independent hymn based on Jewish Wisdom speculations and was secondarily annexed to *Ap. John*.[32] As this hymn also occurs in a text that claims the authority of John the son of Zebedee, variants of a neo-Bultmannian thesis have been developed, according to which the origins of *Ap. John* and its "Pronoia" hymn lie in the schism that divided the Johannine community.[33] The contributions by Paul-Hubert Poirier and John D. Turner deal with *Trim. Prot.* and *Ap. John*, respectively.

Whatever the relationship between the Gospel and the *Apocryphon* of John, a sure sign of an early adoption of the Fourth Gospel is found in the Valentinian school—although Valentinians are today increasingly dropped from the already problematic category of "Gnosticism."[34] Ptolemaeus put John's prologue to an anti-Marcionite use in his *Letter*

---

[30] G. Schenke 1974, 733–734. See also J. Robinson 1981.

[31] *Ap. John* exists in four Coptic copies from the Nag Hammadi and Berlin codices; two copies are represented by the so-called short recension (NHC III,1; BG 8502,2) and two by the long one (NHC II,1; NHC IV,1). In addition, Irenaeus knew an apparently different version, which he quotes in *Adv. haer.* 1.29.

[32] Cf. J. Turner 2001, 127–155, 214–220; and Perkins 2005, 268.

[33] Tardieu (1984, 10, 37–39) suggests that *Ap. John* was a product of the schismatic "left wing" of the Johannine community. J. Turner (2005, 422ff.; and the essay in the present volume) proposes, by essentially combining the hypotheses of Bultmann and Brown, that the Johannine secessionists joined the ranks of Classic/Sethian Gnostics in the middle of the second century, which then led to the production of *Ap. John*. Rasimus (2009) argues that the Gospel and the *Apocryphon* have undergone connected and parallel literary developments, and stem from the elder's group and some of the schismatics, respectively. The essays by Hakola, Czachesz and Turner in this volume point to the need to pay new attention to the questions concerning the nature of the Johannine schism and the relationship of some of the schismatics to early Gnosticism and the *Acts of John*.

[34] Layton (1987) considers Valentinianism as a reformation of Classic Gnosticism; Markschies (1992; 2000) denies that Valentinus and Ptolemaeus were Gnostics or even proper Valentinians; and Dunderberg (2008, 1–31) wishes to place Valentinianism "beyond Gnosticism," as the title of his book indicates.

to Flora, and either he or his students wrote a commentary on the prologue. Heracleon then wrote a commentary on the gospel itself. These Valentinian authors are a key component in any study of the early reception of the Fourth Gospel, as Ptolemaeus is perhaps the earliest known author to have considered it apostolic, and Heracleon may well be the earliest author to have written a full-scale commentary on a text that was to be included in the New Testament canon. The essays by Tuomas Rasimus and Einar Thomassen discuss the Valentinian use of the Gospel of John.

There is an additional important early document that shows signs of a use of the Fourth Gospel, and which has affinities with both Sethian Gnosticism (represented by *Ap. John* and *Trim. Prot.*) and Valentinianism: *Eugnostos the Blessed*. This text, which is known in two versions and several readaptations,[35] makes heavy use of Jewish Wisdom speculations, and its earliest compositional stages may take us back to the approximate time of the composition of the Fourth Gospel. Anne Pasquier investigates the influence of John's Gospel in the course of the textual history of *Eugnostos*.

The attentive reader will have noticed by now that much of the discussion has revolved around Gnostic and other so-called heterodox evidence. The old paradigm has indeed been that it was such groups that first and foremost used the Johannine gospel in the second century, while the catholic authors avoided it. But this is a distorted picture. First, it relies on the division between orthodoxy and heresy that did not yet clearly exist in the second century—although because much of the scholarship on the early reception of the Fourth Gospel has built on this framework, it may be useful not to discard it here completely, keeping in mind, however, that such a division is an artificial one. Second, there are signs that the "catholic" authors also knew and used the Fourth Gospel in the first half of the second century. In fact, most scholars agree that the works of Ignatius and Justin Martyr, among others, do contain *parallels* to the Fourth Gospel.[36] Opinion

---

[35] *Eugnostos* itself is represented by two Coptic copies in the Nag Hammadi library (III,3; V,1). In addition, much of the text has been incorporated into the *Sophia of Jesus Christ*, a document known from the Nag Hammadi library (III,4), the Berlin Codex (BG 8502,3), as well as from the Oxyrhynchus Papyri (1081). *Eugnostos* probably also lies behind the so-called "Valentinian letter" known to Epiphanius (*Pan.* 31.4.11–6.10) and Irenaeus' refutation of Valentinian views of the first principles in *Adv. haer.* 2.13.1–2. On the relationship between *Eugnostos* and *Ap. John*, see Rasimus 2009.

[36] See, e.g., Sanders 1943, 12ff.; Hillmer 1966, 6ff.; Nagel 2000; and Hill 2004.

is divided, however, when it comes to interpreting these parallels. Those who demand a clear quotation formula or the like, are forced to conclude that since these are not forthcoming in this early catholic evidence, there was no early catholic use of John.[37] The parallels are then explained as going back to an oral tradition that was still alive in the first part of the second century—an oral tradition that also lies behind John.[38] However, once a freer use of a written text (reference, allusion, paraphrase, combination of verses, etc.) is allowed— keeping in mind especially that people in the ancient world did not always cite accurately or provide references[39]—a different picture starts to emerge. Charles E. Hill explores not only the different ways early Christian authors may have quoted/used texts (especially, of course, the Fourth Gospel), but also detects clear signs of a positive and early use of John in the following pre-Irenaean sources, treated in a roughly reverse chronological order: the *Epistle of Vienne and Lyons*, certain Christians known to Celsus, Justin Martyr, the *Epistula Apostolorum*, Polycarp, Aristides of Athens, Ignatius and Papias.

Apart from Justin Martyr, his famous student Tatian also used the Fourth Gospel in his harmony of the gospels, the Diatessaron. The crucial role Tatian gives to the Fourth Gospel in his work speaks, among other things, for an already established reception of the Fourth Gospel, although its significance is often downplayed in scholarship.[40] Nicholas Perrin explores Tatian's use of John in the Diatessaron, and proposes that not only did Tatian give John a hermeneutically privileged position among the gospels, but that Tatian's use of it predates his "lapse into heresy," and rather derives from Justin's church in Rome.

The positive reception of John in Irenaeus, of course, is clear,[41] but the nuances of Irenaeus' use of this gospel have not always been appreciated. Bernhard Mutschler's essay—which essentially summarizes the author's two previous books in German—offers a lucid picture of how Irenaeus was a specifically Johannine theologian, and how he also mined earlier traditions about John to support his own anti-heterodox use of this gospel.

---

[37] Hillmer 1966, 6.
[38] See, e.g., Hillmer 1966, 5–27; and especially Koester 1980, 251ff.; Koester 1990, 244–271; Koester 2000, 182–204; cf. Koester 1957.
[39] See now Inowlocki 2006, e.g., 33ff.
[40] See Hillmer 1966, 51–85; Brown 1979, 148; but also Hill 2004, 298ff.
[41] See, e.g., *Adv. haer.* 2.22.5; 3.1.1; 3.3.4; 3.11.1–2; 3.11.7–9; 5.18.2.

Irenaeus' additional use of Revelation and especially his advocation of its chiliasm caused later authors, such as Eusebius (*Hist. eccl.* 3.39.12–13), to question his sanity and mental abilities. In the second century, however, chiliastic views were not generally considered heretical and they were, in fact, quite common. Papias and Justin Martyr had also been chiliasts,[42] and so were the adherents of the "New Prophecy," a movement later known as Montanism—whose most famous member in the west was to be Tertullian. The role of the apparently Johannine concepts of the "Paraclete" in the movement's spirituality, and "New Jerusalem" in its eschatology,[43] especially in the early evidence, are discussed by Turid Karlsen Seim.

The Gospel of John has also left darker traces behind, since its picture of the Jews as the "children of the devil" (8:44) has directly contributed to Christian anti-Semitism over the centuries.[44] Whatever the evangelist's intentions were in using such language,[45] it had unexpectedly horrific consequences for the centuries to come—alongside verses such as Matt 27:25. For this aspect of John's legacy, the reader is encouraged to consult the recent works by Bieringer et al., Hakola and Reinhartz, among others.[46] Other gaps could have been filled in the composition of this book. Tertullian and Clement, for example, are not treated here more than in passing, but as the crucial question concerns the Fourth Gospel's fortunes in the pre-Irenaean era, it seemed justified to leave these two authors out. Overall, however, it is hoped that this volume offers an approachable, fresh, comprehensive and up-to-date view of the second-century reception of John's Gospel,

---

[42] See Hill 1992.

[43] On this question, see also Heine 1987–1988; Trevett 1996, e.g., 86ff.; and Marjanen 2005.

[44] See especially the essays in Bieringer et al. 2001.

[45] Reinhartz (1998; 2001) and Hakola (2005, 16–22) have recently challenged the prevailing view that the Johannine community was engaged in a hostile conflict with the synagogue, leading to the explusion and killing of Johannine Christians—which would then be reflected in the harsh language of John 8:44. This prevailing view is based especially on a thesis according to which the Fourth Gospel speaks simultaneously about the lives of Jesus and the Johannine community (Martyn 1979, 37ff.; Brown 1979, 40–43; Rensberger 1988, 25ff.; Keener 2003, 194ff.). According to Reinhartz, the Fourth Gospel may well reflect an exaggerated picture of the split between the Johannine and Jewish communities, telling us more about the evangelist and the community's self-definition and exclusivist soteriology than about the actual historical reality.

[46] See the two preceding footnotes.

in a situation where new understandings about various forms of early Christianity and its multiformity have started to emerge.

*

This book could not have seen the light of day without help from several individuals. Thanks are due, first of all, to each one of the contributors to this volume for their time and expertise. Second, they are due to Liesbeth Kanis, Acquisitions Editor at Brill Academic Publishers, for her instrumental role in initiating this project. Gratitude is also extended to Mr. Ivo Romein, Ms. Mattie Kuiper and Ms. Gera van Bedaf, Editors at Brill, for their encouragement and help in preparing the manuscript for publication. Professors Margaret Mitchell and David Moessner read the manuscript and made helpful comments that improved the quality of the volume. Moreover, Margot Stout Whiting and Robert Whiting offered valuable help in improving the English of some of the non-English-speaking contributors. Last, but not least, thanks are due to Risto Auvinen, Ismo Dunderberg, Matti Myllykoski, Louis Painchaud and Päivi Vähäkangas for all their comments and help.

Bibliography

Akin, D., *1, 2, 3 John*, The New American Commentary 38, Nashville: Broadman & Holman, 2001.

Aune, D.E., *The Cultic Setting of Realized Eschatology in Early Christianity*, Supplements to Novum Testamentum 28, Leiden: Brill, 1972.

Barrett, C.K., *The Gospel according to St. John: An Introduction with Commentary and Notes on the Greek Text*, Philadelphia: Westminster, ²1978.

Bauckham, R., ed., *The Gospels for All Christians: Rethinking the Gospel Audiences*, Grand Rapids, Mich.: Eerdmans, 1998.

Beasley-Murray, G., *John*, Word Biblical Commentary 36, Waco, Tex.: Word Books, 1987.

Becker, J., "Die Abschiedsreden Jesu im Johannesevangelium," *Zeitschrift für die neutestamentliche Wissenschaft und die Kunde der älteren Kirche*, 61/3 (1970), 215–246.

Bieringer, R. et al., eds., *Anti-Judaism and the Fourth Gospel: Papers of the Leuven Colloquium, 2000*, Jewish and Christian Heritage Series 1, Assen: van Gorcum, 2001.

Braun, F.-M., *Jean le Théologien et son Évangile dans l'église ancienne*, Paris: Librairie Lecoffre / Gabalda, 1959.

Brown, R.E., *The Gospel according to John (i–xii): Introduction, Translation, and Notes*, The Anchor Bible 29, Garden City, N.Y.: Doubleday, 1966.

—— *The Community of the Beloved Disciple*, New York: Paulist Press, 1979.

—— *The Epistles of John*, The Anchor Bible 30, Garden City, N.Y.: Doubleday, 1982.

Brownlee, W., "Whence the Gospel according to John?" *John and Qumran*, J.H. Charlesworth, ed., London: Chapman, 1972, 166–194.

Buckley, J., *The Mandeans: Ancient Texts and Modern People*, Oxford: Oxford University Press, 2002.

Bultmann, R., "Die Bedeutung der neuerschlossenen mandäischen und manichäischen Quellen für das Verständnis des Johannesevangeliums," *Zeitschrift für die Neutestamentliche Wissenschaft* 24 (1925), 100–146.

—— *The Gospel of John: A Commentary*, G.R. Beasley-Murray, transl., Oxford: Blackwell, 1971.

—— *The Johannine Epistles*, R. O'Hara, L. McGaughy and R. Funk, transl., Hermeneia, Philadelphia: Fortress, 1973.

Charlesworth, J.H., ed., *John and the Dead Sea Scrolls*, Christian Origins Library, New York: Crossroad, 1990.

Colpe, C., *Die religionsgeschichtliche Schule: Darstellung und Kritik ihres Bildes vom gnostischen Erlösermythus*, Forschungen zur Religion und Literatur des Alten und Neuen Testaments 78, Göttingen: Vandenhoeck & Ruprecht, 1961.

Conway, C., *Men and Women in the Fourth Gospel: Gender and Johannine Characterization*, Society of Biblical Literature Dissertation Series 167, Atlanta: Society of Biblical Literature, 1999.

Culpepper, R.A., *The Johannine School: An Evaluation of the Johannine-School Hypothesis based on an Investigation of the Nature of Ancient Schools*, Society of Biblical Literature Dissertation Series 26, Missoula: Scholars Press, 1975.

—— *John, the Son of Zebedee: The Life of a Legend*, Columbia: University of South Carolina Press, 1994.

DeConick, A.D., *Seek to See Him: Ascent and Vision Mysticism in the Gospel of Thomas*, Supplements to Vigiliae Christianae 33, Leiden: Brill, 1996.

—— *Voices of the Mystics: Early Christian Discourse in the Gospels of John and Thomas and Other Ancient Christian Literature*, Journal for the Study of the New Testament Supplement Series 157, Sheffield: Sheffield Academic Press, 2001.

Dunderberg, I., *The Beloved Disciple in Conflict? Revisiting the Gospels of John and Thomas*, Oxford: Oxford University Press, 2006.

—— *Beyond Gnosticism: Myth, Lifestyle, and Society in the School of Valentinus*, New York: Columbia University Press, 2008.

Gadamer, H.-G., *Wahrheit und Methode: Grundzüge einer philosophischen Hermeneutik*, Tübingen: Mohr (Paul Siebeck), ²1965.

Haenchen, E., *John 1: A Commentary on the Gospel of John Chapters 1–6*, R.W. Funk, transl., Philadelphia: Fortress, 1984.

Hakola, R., *Identity Matters: John, the Jews and Jewishness*, Supplements to Novum Testamentum 118, Leiden: Brill, 2005.

Heine, R.E., "The Role of the Gospel of John in the Montanist Controversy," *Second Century* 6 (1987–1988), 1–19.

Hengel, M., *The Johannine Question*, J. Bowden, transl., London: SCM; Philadelphia: Trinity Press International, 1989.

Hill, C.E., *Regnum Caelorum: Patterns of Future Hope in Early Christianity*, Oxford Early Christian Studies, Oxford: Clarendon Press, 1992.

—— *The Johannine Corpus in the Early Church*, Oxford: Oxford University Press, 2004.

Hillmer, M.R., "The Gospel of John in the Second Century," Th.D. dissertation, Harvard University, 1966.

Holmes, M., *The Apostolic Fathers: Greek Texts and English Translations*, Grand Rapids, Mich.: Baker Academic, ³2007.

Inowlocki, S., *Eusebius and the Jewish Authors: His Citation Technique in an Apologetic Context*, Ancient Judaism and Early Christianity 64, Leiden: Brill, 2006.

Kaestli, J.-D., J.-M. Poffet and J. Zumstein, eds., *La communauté johannique et son histoire: La trajectoire de l'évangile de Jean aux deux premiers siècles*, Le monde de la Bible, Geneva: Labor et Fides, 1990.

Kannengiesser, C., *Handbook of Patristic Exegesis: With special contributions by various scholars*, 2 vols., The Bible in Ancient Christianity 1, Leiden: Brill, 2004.

Käsemann, E., *The Testament of Jesus: A Study of the Gospel of John in the Light of Chapter 17*, G. Krodel, transl., London: SCM, 1968.

Keefer, K., *The Branches of the Gospel of John: The Reception of the Fourth Gospel in the Early Church*, Library of the New Testament Studies 332, London: T&T Clark, 2006.

Keener, C.S., *The Gospel of John: A Commentary*, vol. 1, Peabody: Hendrickson Publishers, 2003.

King, K.L., *What is Gnosticism?* Cambridge, Mass.: The Belknap Press of Harvard University Press, 2003.

Koester, H., *Synoptische Überlieferung bei den apostolischen Vätern*, Texte und Untersuchungen zur Geschichte der altchristlichen Literatur 65, Berlin: Akademie-Verlag, 1957.

—— "Gnostic Writings as Witnesses for the Development of the Sayings Tradition," *The Rediscovery of Gnosticism: Proceedings of the International Conference on Gnosticism at Yale New Haven, Connecticut, March 28–31, 1978: Volume One: The School of Valentinus*, B. Layton, ed., Studies in the History of Religions (Supplements to Numen) 41, Leiden: Brill, 1980.

—— *Ancient Christian Gospels: Their History and Development*, London: SCM; Philadelphia: Trinity Press International, 1990.

—— *Introduction to the New Testament: Volume 2: History and Literature of Early Christianity*, Berlin: de Gruyter, ²2000.

Kragerud, A., *Der Lieblingsjünger im Johannesevangelium: Ein exegetischer Versuch*, Oslo: Osloer Universitätsverlag, 1959.

Kümmel, W., *Introduction to the New Testament*, Revised edition, H. Kee, transl., Nashville: Abingdon, 1975.

Lalleman, P.J., *The Acts of John: A Two-Stage Initiation into Johannine Gnosticism*, Studies on the Apocryphal Acts of the Apostles 4, Leuven: Peeters, 1998.

Layton, B., *The Gnostic Scriptures: A New Translation with Annotations and Introductions*, Garden City, N.Y.: Doubleday, 1987.

Logan, A., *Gnostic Truth and Christian Heresy: A Study in the History of Gnosticism*, Peabody, Mass.: Hendrickson, 1996.

Lupieri, E., *The Mandeans: The Last Gnostics*, C. Hindley, transl., Grand Rapids, Mich.: Eerdmans, 2002.

Luz, U., *Das Evangelium nach Matthäus: 1. Teilband Mt 1–7*, Evangelisch-Katolischer Kommentar zum Neuen Testament 1/1, Zürich: Benziger Verlag; Neukirchen-Vluyn: Neukirchener Verlag, 1985.

Marjanen, A., "Montanism and the Formation of the New Testament Canon," *The Formation of the Early Church*, J. Ådna, ed., Wissenschaftliche Untersuchungen zum Neuen Testament 183, Tübingen: Mohr Siebeck, 2005, 239–263.

Marjanen, A. and P. Luomanen, eds., *A Companion to Second-Century Christian 'Heretics,'* Supplements to Vigiliae Christianae 76, Leiden: Brill, 2005.

Markschies, C., *Valentinus Gnosticus? Untersuchungen zur valentinianischen Gnosis mit einem Kommentar zu den Fragmenten Valentins*, Wissenschaftliche Untersuchungen zum Neuen Testament 65, Tübingen: Mohr (Paul Siebeck), 1992.

—— "New Research on Ptolemaeus Gnosticus," *Zeitschrift für Antikes Christentum* 4 (2000), 225–254.

Martyn, J.L., *History & Theology in the Fourth Gospel*, Nashville: Abingdon, ²1979.

Meeks, W., "The Man from Heaven in Johannine Sectarianism," *Journal of Biblical Literature* 91 (1972), 44–72.

Mendner, S., "Zum Problem 'Johannes und die Synoptiker,'" *New Testament Studies* 4 (1957–1958), 282–307.

Mitchell, M.M., *The Heavenly Trumpet: John Chrysostom and the Art of Pauline Interpretation*, Hermeneutische Untersuchungen zur Theologie 40, Tübingen: Mohr Siebeck, 2000.

Moffatt, J., *An Introduction to the Literature of the New Testament*, ³1918, reprinted Edinburgh: T&T Clark, 1961.

Moloney, F., *The Gospel of John*, Sacra Pagina 4, Collegeville, Minn.: The Liturgical Press, 1998.

Nagel, T., *Die Rezeption des Johannesevangeliums im 2. Jahrhundert: Studien zur vorirenäischen Aneignung und Auslegung des vierten Evangeliums in christlicher und christlich-gnosticher Literatur*, Arbeiten zur Bibel und ihrer Geschichte 2, Leipzig: Evangelische Verlagsanstalt, 2000.

Neirynck, F., *Jean et les synoptiques: Examen critique de l'exégèse de M.-É. Boïsmard*, Bibliotheca Ephemeridum Theologicarum Lovaniensium 49, Leuven: Leuven University Press, 1979.

—— "John and the Synoptics: The Empty Tomb Stories," *New Testament Studies* 30 (1984), 161–187.

Osborne, G., *Revelation*, Baker Exegetical Commentary on the New Testament, Grand Rapids, Mich.: Baker Academic, 2002.

Pagels, E.H., "Exegesis of Genesis 1 in the Gospels of Thomas and John," *Journal of Biblical Literature* 118 (1999), 477–496.

—— *Beyond Belief: The Secret Gospel of Thomas*, New York: Random House, 2003.

Painter, J., *1, 2, and 3 John*, Sacra Pagina 18, Collegeville, Minn.: The Liturgical Press, 2002.

Pearson, B.A., *Gnosticism, Judaism, and Egyptian Christianity*, Studies in Antiquity & Christianity, Minneapolis: Fortress, 1990.

Perkins, P., "Gnostic Revelation and Johannine Sectarianism: Reading 1 John from the Perspective of Nag Hammadi," *Theology and Christology in the Fourth Gospel: Essays by the Members of the SNTS Johannine Writings Seminar*, G. van Belle et al., eds., Bibliotheca Ephemeridum Theologicarum Lovaniensium 184, Leuven: Leuven University Press / Peeters, 2005, 245–276.

Rasimus, T., *Paradise Reconsidered in Gnostic Mythmaking: Rethinking Sethianism in Light of the Ophite Evidence*, Nag Hammadi and Manichaean Studies 68, Leiden: Brill, 2009.

Reinhartz, A., "The Johannine Community and its Jewish Neighbors: A Reapprisal," *"What is John?" Volume II: Literary and Social Readings of the Fourth Gospel*, F. Segovia, ed., Society of Biblical Literature Symposium Series 7, Atlanta: Scholars Press, 1998, 111–138.

—— "'Jews' and Jews in the Fourth Gospel," *Anti-Judaism and the Fourth Gospel: Papers of the Leuven Colloquium, 2000*, R. Bieringer et al., eds., Jewish and Christian Heritage Series 1, Assen: van Gorcum, 2001, 341–356.

Rensberger, D., *Johannine Faith and Liberating Community*, Philadelphia: Westminster, 1988.

Riley, G., *Resurrection Reconsidered: Thomas and John in Controversy*, Minneapolis: Fortress, 1995.

Robinson, J.M., "Sethians and Johannine Thought," *The Rediscovery of Gnosticism: Volume 2: Sethian Gnosticism*, B. Layton, ed., Studies in the History of Religions 41 (Supplements to Numen), Leiden: Brill, 1981, 643–662.

Rudolph, K., *Gnosis: The Nature & History of Gnosticism*, R. Wilson, transl., San Francisco: HarperSanFrancisco, 1987.

Räisänen, H., *Challenges to Biblical Interpretation: Collected Essays 1991–2001*, Biblical Interpretation Series 59, Leiden: Brill, 2001.

Sanders, J.N., *The Fourth Gospel in the Early Church: Its Origin & Influence on Christian Theology up to Irenaeus*, Cambridge: Cambridge University Press, 1943.

Schenke, G., "Die dreistaltige Protennoia," *Theologische Literaturzeitung* 99 (1974), 731–746.

Schenke, H.-M., "The Phenomenon and Significance of Gnostic Sethianism," *The Rediscovery of Gnosticism: Volume 2: Sethian Gnosticism*, B. Layton, ed., Studies in the History of Religions 41 (Supplements to Numen), Leiden: Brill, 1981, 588–616.

Schnackenburg, R., *The Gospel According to St John: Volume One: Introduction and Commentary on Chapters 1–4*, K. Smyth, transl., Montreal: Palm, 1968.

—— *The Johannine Epistles: Introduction and Commentary*, R. and I. Fuller, transl., New York: Crossroad, 1992.

Segovia, F., *Love Relationships in the Johannine Tradition: Agapê/Agapan in 1 John and the Fourth Gospel*, Society of Biblical Literature Dissertation Series 58, Chico, Calif.: Scholars Press, 1981.

Smalley, S., *John: Evangelist and Interpreter*, 1978, reprinted Nashville: Nelson, 1984.

—— *1, 2, 3 John*, Word Biblical Commentary 51, Waco, Tex.: Word Books, 1984.

Smith, D.M., *Johannine Christianity: Essays on Its Setting, Sources, and Theology*, Columbia: University of South Carolina Press, 1984.

—— *John Among the Gospels: The Relationship in Twentieth-Century Research*, Minneapolis: Fortress, 1992.

—— *John*, Abingdon New Testament Commentaries, Nashville: Abingdon Press, 1999.

Tardieu, M., *Écrits Gnostiques: Codex de Berlin*, Paris: Cerf, 1984.

Theobald, M., "Der Jünger, den Jesus liebte: Beobachtungen zum narrativen Konzept der johanneischen Redaktion," *Geschichte—Tradition—Reflexion: Festschrift für Martin Hengel zum 70. Geburtstag: Band III: Frühes Christentum*, H. Lichtenberger, ed., Tübingen: Mohr (Paul Siebeck), 1996, 219–255.

Trebilco, P., *The Early Christians in Ephesus from Paul to Ignatius*, Wissenschaftliche Untersuchungen zum Neuen Testament 166, Tübingen: Mohr Siebeck, 2004.

Trevett, C., *Montanism: Gender, Authority and the New Prophecy*, Cambridge: Cambridge University Press, 1996.

Turner, E., *Greek Manuscripts of the Ancient World*, Revised edition, Bulletin Supplement 46, London: University of London Insititute of Classical Studies, [2]1987.

Turner, J.D., *Sethian Gnosticism and the Platonic Tradition*, Bibliothèque Copte de Nag Hammadi, Section: «Études» 6, Québec: Les Presses de l'Université Laval; Leuven: Peeters, 2001.

—— "Sethian Gnosticism and Johannine Christianity," *Theology and Christology in the Fourth Gospel: Essays by the Members of the SNTS Johannine Writings Seminar*, G. van Belle et al., eds., Bibliotheca Ephemeridum Theologicarum Lovaniensium 184, Leuven: Leuven University Press / Peeters, 2005, 399–433.

Williams, M., *Rethinking "Gnosticism": An Argument for Dismantling a Dubious Category*, Princeton: Princeton University Press, 1996.

Zumstein, J., "La rédaction finale de l'évangile selon Jean (à l'exemple du chapitre 21)," *La communauté johannique et son histoire: La trajectoire de l'évangile de Jean aux deux premiers siècles*, J.-D. Kaestli, J.-M. Poffet and J. Zumstein, eds., Le monde de la bible, Geneva: Labor et Fides, 1990, 207–230.

THE RECEPTION AND DEVELOPMENT OF
THE JOHANNINE TRADITION IN 1, 2 AND 3 JOHN

Raimo Hakola
University of Helsinki

The three writings known as the First, Second and Third Epistles of John are related to the Gospel of John in a distinctive way. Scholars have become more and more skeptical about the common apostolic authorship of these writings, but the gospel and the epistles are still universally grouped together and regarded, if not as written by a single hand, then as produced in a common school of thought or community which explains the affinities between them.[1] It is undecided whether it is legitimate to speak about the legacy or reception of the Fourth Gospel in the Johannine epistles at all. There is no agreement among scholars about the sequence in which the gospel and the epistles were written. The question is all the more complicated if we reckon that the gospel itself was composed in different stages. In this case, it could be argued that an early version of the gospel predates the epistles which are, however, contemporary or prior to the final redaction of the gospel (especially John 21 and possibly also John 15–17).

In this essay, I do not intend to ultimately settle the question concerning the sequence in which the gospel and the epistles were written. In my opinion, there is no solid evidence for the view that the epistles predate the gospel, but, for the reasons detailed in the course of this essay, I think we should also be cautious in reading the epistles with a preconception that they presuppose and build upon the finished version of the gospel.[2] Instead of postulating a direct literary relationship

---

[1] It is disputed how closely—or if at all—the Book of Revelation is related to the Johannine corpus. For a detailed discussion of the question, see Frey 1993, 326–429. Because of its remoteness from other writings regarded as Johannine, Revelation has had little—if any—significance in recent reconstructions of the history of Johannine community.

[2] Likewise, one needs to be cautious in assessing the sequence among the three epistles, not least because of the brevity of 2 and 3 John. For the difficulties in fixing a clear sequence among the epistles, see R.E. Brown, 1982, 30–32. Brown thinks that 1 and 2 John were written about the same time, while 3 John comes *logically* after these,

between these writings, I explore how ideas similar to those found in the gospel were received and developed in the Johannine epistles. I will first list the most important of the similarities and then discuss the main differences between the gospel and the epistles. I suggest that these similarities and differences are best understood if we take the gospel and the epistles as independent witnesses of the shared tradition that is developed in different ways in different contexts. The following discussion quite obviously focuses on the Gospel of John and 1 John because 2 and 3 John are so brief that they do not provide much material for the discussion.[3] I finally discuss the theories concerning the opponents in 1 John because these theories have played an important role in how the relationship between the gospel and the epistles has been understood. I also suggest that insights from the Social Identity Perspective could prove helpful in explaining the function of the portrait of the opponents in 1 John and the function and role of John's legacy as it was developed in the epistles.

1. Similarities between the Gospel and the Epistles

Not only are most of the themes that are discussed in the epistles present in the gospel but also the ways of expressing these themes are often similar. A detailed comparison of the vocabulary, grammar, syntax and idioms has revealed that the style of the longest of the epistles, 1 John, has a general similarity to the style of the gospel but this comparison

---

even though we cannot be sure whether it was also *chronologically* the last one. Brown concludes that "the three Johannine epistles were composed about the same time and dealt with ramifications of the same problem throughout the Johannine churches" (p. 32). Cf. also Lieu 2008a, 18. According to Lieu, 2 John is most likely literarily dependant on 1 John and may also draw on 3 John which represents the form of a genuine letter more authentically. In the following, I leave open the internal order of the epistles. I think it is safe to assume that the epistles were written approximately at the same time and that they all bear witness to a similar type of development of the Johannine tradition. It is difficult—if not impossible—to fix a clear date and locale for the composition of the epistles. 2 John 10 and 3 John 9–10 seem to presuppose a situation of various, presumably rather small, groups arranged around individual households, a situation also well known from other Christian sources (cf. White 1990, 103–110). On the basis of the external evidence, the epistles are most commonly placed in Asia Minor, especially in Ephesus, and dated to about 100–110 CE. For a discussion, see R.E. Brown 1992, 100–103.

[3] I have included references to 2 and 3 John whenever they are relevant. It should be noted, however, that there are also differences among the epistles. Cf., e.g., Lieu 1986, 217–221.

also reveals some subtle differences between these two writings.[4] The matters of style, however, are not enough to settle the question concerning the relationship between the gospel and the epistles because, if these writings stem from a common circle or community, we must entertain the possibility that this circle used a distinctive sociolect characteristic not only of a single author but of different members of the circle.[5]

The theological terminology common and, for the most part, distinctive to the gospel and to the epistles provides a more convenient point of departure for a comparison of these writings. In what follows, I list the most important of these common expressions and then proceed to evaluate what they say about the relationship between the gospel and the epistles.[6]

	The Expression	The Epistles	The Gospel
1	the beginning, the word (λόγος)	1 John 1:2 What was from the beginning, what we have heard, what we	John 1:1 In the beginning was the Word John 1:4
	life	have seen with our eyes, what we have looked at and touched with our hands,	in him was life, and the life was the light of all people 1:14
	we have seen and testify	concerning the word of life—this life was revealed, and we have seen it and testify to it	We have seen his glory 3:11 We speak of what we know and testify to what we have seen

---

[4] A classic comparison between the styles of the gospel and 1 John was made by Dodd 1937, 129–156. Dodd pointed out some differences in style in order to argue for the separate authorships of these works. Stylistic criteria, however, have also been used to support the common authorship of the gospel and all three Johannine epistles. Cf. Ruckstuhl and Dschulnigg 1991, 44–54, 245–246.

[5] As R.E. Brown (1982, 21) has remarked, we must take into account the possibility of deliberate copying or "unconscious imitation within a school of writers" before we use stylistic criteria to argue for the common authorship of the Johannine writings.

[6] I have consulted the more complete list in R.E. Brown 1982, 755–759. I have organized the similarities thematically and omitted the cases where the similarity suggested by Brown is not relevant or uncertain. In the table, I have given the Greek forms and quoted the passages when this is significant for the recognition of the similarities and differences. An asterisk (*) denotes an expression that is distinctive in the New Testament to the Gospel of John and 1, 2 and 3 John. For a comparison of the language of the gospel and the epistles in relation to the rest of the New Testament, see Painter 2002, 62–64.

(*cont.*)

	The Expression	The Epistles	The Gospel
2a	light	1 John 1:5 God is light	John 8:12; 9:5; 12:46 I am the light of the world
2b	* light shines (φαινεῖν)	1 John 2:8	John 1:5
2c	* the true light (τὸ φῶς τὸ ἀληθινόν)	1 John 2:8	John 1:9
2d	light vs. darkness	1 John 1:6–7; 2:8–11	John 1:5; 3:19–20; 8:12; 11:9–10; 12:35,46
2e	* walk (περιπατεῖν) in the light/darkness	1 John 1:6–7; 2:11	John 8:12; 11:9 (walk during the day); 11:10 (walk at night); 12:35
3a	* do truth	1 John 1:6	John 3:21
3b	truth being/abiding in a person	1 John 1:8; 2:4; 2 John 2	John 8:44
3c	* know (γινώσκειν/ εἰδέναι) the truth	1 John 2:21; 2 John 1	John 8:32
3d	* be of (ἐκ) the truth	1 John 2:21; 3:19	John 18:37
3e	* the Spirit of truth	1 John 4:6	John 14:17; 15:26; 16:13
4	* know (γινώσκειν) the true one/the only true God	1 John 5:20 know the true one; Jesus is the true God	John 17:3 (cf. also 7:28) know the only true God
5a	* be from (εἶναι ἐκ) God	1 John 3:10; 4:1,2,3,4,6; 5:19; 3 John 11; cf. 1 John 3:16: be from the father	John 8:47
5b	* be born from (ἐκ) God	1 John 2:29; 3:9; 5:1,4,18	John 1:13
5c	* be from (εἶναι ἐκ) the devil	1 John 3:8: cf. 1 John 3:12: be from the evil one	John 8:44 ("You are from your father, the devil")
5d	* be from (εἶναι ἐκ) the world	1 John 2:16; 4:5	John 8:23; 15:19; 17:14,16; 18:36

(cont.)

	The Expression	The Epistles	The Gospel
6a	* conquer (νικᾶν) the world	1 John 5:4–5	John 16:33
6b	* the world hates (μισεῖν) you	1 John 3:13	John 7:7; 15:18
6c	the world did not know God	1 John 3:1	John 17:25
7a	* abide (μένειν) in Jesus/God	1 John 2:6,27,28: 3:6,24; 4:13–16	15:4,6,7
7b	* God/Jesus abides in a believer	1 John 3:24; 4:12–16	John 6:56; 15:5
7c	* word of God abides in you	1 John 2:14	John 5:38
8	children (pl. τέκνον) of God	1 John 3:1,2,10; 5:2	John 1:12; 11:52
9a	keep (τηρεῖν) Jesus'/ God's words/com-mandments	1 John 2:3–5; 3:22,24; 5:3	John 8:51–52,55; 14:15,21,23–24; 15:10,20; 17:6
9b	* new commandment (ἐντολὴν καινήν)	1 John 2:7,8: 2 John 5	John 13:34
9c	* commandment to love one another	1 John 3:23; 4:21; 2 John 5; cf. also 1 John 3:11: the message (ἀγγελία) that we should love one another.	John 13:34; 15:12,17
9d	* to love Jesus/God is to keep his command-ments	1 John 5:2–3; 2 John 6	John 14:15,21; 15:10
10	whatever we/you ask, we/you receive	1 John 3:22; 5:14–15	John 14:13,14; 15:7,16; 16:23
11	* lay down one's life for (τίθημι ψυχὴν ὑπέρ) others	1 John 3:16	John 10:11,15,17,18; 13:37
12	* Jesus takes (αἴρειν) away sins	1 John 3:5	John 1:29
13	* has passed (μεταβαίνειν) from death to life	1 John 3:14	John 5:24

(cont.)

	The Expression	The Epistles	The Gospel
14	stay forever (μένει εἰς τὸν αἰῶνα)	1 John 2:17	John 8:35; 12:34
15	no one has ever seen God	1 John 4:12 (cf. 1 John 4:20)	John 1:18
16	* we have known and believed (ἐγνώκαμεν καὶ πεπιστεύκαμεν)	1 John 4:16	John 6:69 (have believed and known)
17	* water and blood	1 John 5:5–8	John 19:34
18	* joy fulfilled	1 John 1:4; 2 John 12	John 16:24; 17:13; cf. also 3:29; 15:11
19	the purpose of writing	1 John 5:13	John 20:30

With some exceptions, the similarities presented in the list above are unique to the Gospel of John and 1, 2 and 3 John. It is not just a question of similarity of language but in many cases, the idioms betray a common and distinctive view of the world. The language of light and darkness (2a–e) is a characteristic of a dualistic worldview which sees the world divided into the realms of light and darkness. The world is described as a hostile sphere that has not known God (6c) and hates God, his Son and the believers (6b). Only those who are born of God and believe that Jesus is the Son of God can conquer the world (6a). They know the truth (3c) and the true God (4), keep God's or Jesus' commandments and love one another (9a–d) and have passed from death to life (13). The close relationship between God, his Son and the believers is expressed in terms of mutual indwelling (7a–c). The dualistic nature of the worldview common to the gospel and the epistles is best captured in the use of the preposition ἐκ to denote the dichotomy between those who belong to God's realm and those who do not, a unique usage in the New Testament (3d, 5a–d).

Given the similarities not only in the fundamental theological terminology but also in the worldview, it is no surprise that, from early on, especially 1 John and, to a lesser degree, 2 and 3 John, came to be seen in close relationship with the Fourth Gospel. In the early church, this relationship was explained in a tradition that ascribed the gospel and the epistles to the apostle John. There already appear possible echoes of the Johannine epistles in works of several second-century writers but these writers do not identify the source they are using.[7] The first explicit and undisputed citation of the epistles comes from Irenaeus who quotes both 1 John and 2 John but possibly thinks that his quotations stem from the same letter which he assigns to John, the disciple of Jesus (*Adv. haer.* 1.16.3; 3.16.5; 3.16.8).[8] Like Irenaeus, several subsequent writers cite both 1 John and 2 John but show no knowledge of 3 John. It is revealing that the first attestation of the existence of 3 John refers to the disputed position of 2 and 3 John among Christian writers.[9] The position of 2 and 3 John remained disputed especially in Syrian churches where they, along with 2 Peter and Jude, were translated into Syriac only in the sixth century.[10]

The doubts concerning the authenticity of 2 and 3 John notwithstanding, the prevailing view was that the gospel and the epistles were written by a single author who was identified as Jesus' disciple. In modern scholarship, the common authorship of the gospel and the epistles is still supported by some scholars who ascribe these writings either to the apostle John or to the presbyter mentioned in 2 and 3 John (2 John 1; 3 John 1).[11] However, the majority of scholars nowadays think that the gospel and the epistles were not written by a single hand.[12] The reason for this is that despite the similarities in the style and in theology, there are also marked differences which suggest that

---

[7] For possible echoes of the Johannine epistles prior to 175 CE, see R.E. Brown 1982, 6–9. Cf. also the table collected by Hill 2004, 450. The most important parallel to the epistles is in Pol. *Phil.* 7:1: "For every one who shall not confess that Jesus Christ is come in the flesh, is antichrist." These words possibly allude to 2 John 7 and to 1 John 4:2–3; the appearance of the phrase ἐκ τοῦ διαβόλου in the same connection (cf. 1 John 3:8) and the sentence, "Let us...turn back to the word which was delivered to us from the beginning" (cf. 1 John 2:7, 24; 3:11; 2 John 5) in Pol. *Phil.* 7:2 increases the likelihood of this allusion. Cf. Hill 2004, 418–419.

[8] See R.E. Brown 1982, 9–10; Hill 2004, 99; Lieu 2008a, 2, 26.

[9] According to Eusebius (*Hist. eccl.* 6.25.10), Origen said that John was the author of the Gospel, Apocalypse, and an Epistle and then added: "there may also be a second and third but not all say they are genuine."

[10] R.E. Brown 1982, 12; Lieu 2008a, 27.

[11] The apostolic authorship of the gospel and the epistles is defended, for example, by the following scholars: J.B. Lightfoot, A. Schlatter, T. Zahn, B.F. Büchsel, W. Michaelis, A. Wikenhauser, G. Maier, L. Morris and B. Schwank. The presbyter-hypothesis is supported by A. Harnack, W. Bousset, W. Heitmüller, R.H. Charles, B.H. Streeter, E. Käsemann, W.G. Kümmel, E. Ruckstuhl and M. Hengel. See Kim 2001, 4–80, 309–310.

[12] The following scholars postulate two different authors for the gospel and the epistles: H. Windisch, C.H. Dodd, R. Schnackenburg, C.K. Barrett, R.E. Brown, J. Zumstein, H.-J. Klauck and D.M. Smith. Furthermore, many scholars think that the gospel and the epistles were written by at least three different writers: R. Bultmann,

the gospel and the epistles have emerged in different situations and
represent two different renderings of the shared tradition.

2. Differences between the Gospel and the Epistles

The most obvious difference is that the gospel centers around the conflict
between Jesus and "the Jews," while there is no sign of this conflict in
the epistles.[13] The word Ἰουδαῖοι that appears in the gospel seventy-
one times is not used at all in 1, 2 and 3 John. While the gospel deals
extensively with such central aspects of Jewish identity as the temple
and worship (John 2:13–22; 4:20–24), the Sabbath and circumcision
(5:1–18; 7:19–24), the revelation at Sinai, Moses and the law (5:37–47;
6:26–59) and Abraham (8:31–59), these topics do not appear at all in the
epistles where the objects of the attack are those who, from the writer's
perspective, have left the community and deny that Jesus is the Christ
(1 John 2:18–22; 1 John 4:2–3; 2 John 7).[14] This clearly indicates that
the main concerns are quite different in the gospel and in the epistles.
The former seeks to clarify and maintain the identity of the believers
in relation to "the Jews" and Judaism whereas the latter addresses a
community that has experienced an internal division.[15]

In addition to dissimilarity in the main focus of writing, there are
more subtle differences between the gospel and the epistles. Together
with the gospel, the epistles present Jesus as the Son of God who has
been sent to the world (1 John 4:9–10,14) and repeatedly use fixed language when speaking of the Father and the Son (1 John 1:3; 2:22–24;
4:14; 2 John 9). However, the division of labor between the Father and

---

H. Conzelmann, E. Haenchen, E. Lohse, P. Vielhauer, K. Wengst, G. Strecker, U.
Schnelle, K. Berger and M. Labahn. See Kim 2001, 310.

[13] The conflict with "the Jews" in the gospel is quite commonly understood to
reflect an allegedly bitter and violent conflict between the Johannine community and
the post-70 CE emergent rabbinic Judaism. However, the external evidence for this
kind of conflict is meager, which suggests that the scholarly consensus needs to be
reconsidered. See Reinhartz 2001, 37–53; Hakola 2005, 41–46; Hakola and Reinhartz
2007, 131–147.

[14] The lack of terminology related to the scriptures (γραφή, γράφειν, νόμος, see
below) in the epistles reflects this difference.

[15] There may also be some hints of an internal division among believers in the gospel (John 6:66; 8:30–31). These passages may refer to a group of believers who continued to interact with other Jews and found the practice of basic matters of Jewishness
still attractive, which aroused their fierce denunciation by the evangelist. See Hakola
2007a, 192–197.

the Son is slightly different. Many of those images that are used of Jesus in the gospel have God as their focus in the epistles. In the gospel, Jesus is presented as the light of the world (John 8:12; 9:5; 12:46; cf. also 1:5) but in 1 John 1:5, it is God who is light. In the gospel, it is exclusively Jesus who abides (μένειν) in the believers or the believers in Jesus (John 6:56; 15:4–7),[16] while 1 John 3:24 and 4:15 speak of the mutual abiding between God and those who believe.[17] Furthermore, the epistles lack the idea of the mutual indwelling of the Father and the Son that forms a foundation for the indwelling of the believers in God in the gospel (John 14:10–11,20; 17:21). Judith Lieu is right in concluding that the language of indwelling is "both more structured and more restrained" in the gospel than in 1 John which "does not exhibit the discipline of the Gospel."[18]

In the gospel, the knowledge of God is transmitted exclusively through Jesus (John 14:7) but 1 John 4:6–8 allows that everyone who loves God knows God. In the gospel, Jesus' love is presented as a prototype for the mutual love of the disciples (13:34; 15:12); this model appears in 1 John 3:16 but, in addition to this, God is described as love and his love as a model to be imitated (1 John 4:7–11). In the gospel, Jesus repeatedly says to his disciples that to love him is to keep his commandments (14:15,21; 15:10); in the epistles, the same kind of language is used to underscore that to love God is to keep his commandments (1 John 5:2–3; 2 John 6). In the gospel, Jesus promises that he (14:13–14) or the Father (15:7,16; 16:23) will do whatever his disciples ask in his name. The same kind of promise appears in 1 John without the mention that prayers should be said in Jesus' name. Those who obey God's commandments and do what pleases him (1 John 3:22) and who ask anything according to his will (5:14–15), receive whatever they ask.

At some points, ideas that are said of Jesus in the gospel are presented as characteristics of all those who believe. 1 John 5:4–5 states that

---

[16] Cf., however, John 14:23: "Those who love me will keep my word, and my Father will love them, and we will come to them and make our home (μονὴν ποιησόμεθα) with them." This verse probably presents a Johannine reinterpretation (cf. 14:2) of traditional apocalyptic imagery. See, e.g., Lincoln 2005, 389, 396.

[17] Cf. Rensberger (1997, 107) who remarks that "the abiding of God directly in Christians and they in God goes beyond anything that is said in the Gospel of John." 1 John repeatedly uses the vague "abide in him" which means that it is often unclear whether God or Jesus is intended (cf. 2:6, 27–28; 3:6). This vagueness is typical of the epistles (see below).

[18] Cf. Lieu 2008a, 73.

"whatever is born of God" or "our faith" or "the one who believes that Jesus is the Son of God" conquers the world;[19] in the gospel, it is Jesus who has conquered the world (16:33). According to 1 John 2:17, the one who does the will of God stays forever (μένει εἰς τὸν αἰῶνα), while, in the gospel, it is the Son (John 8:35) or the Messiah (12:34) who stays forever. The idea that no one has ever seen God is used Christologically in John 1:18 to set up the idea that the only Son has made God known.[20] In 1 John 4:12, the phrase "no one has ever seen God" paves the way for the conclusion that "if we love one another, God lives in us, and his love is perfected in us." A similar kind of difference can be found with the use of the expression "to pass from life to death." In John 5:24, the phrase is closely linked to Jesus who promises that "anyone who hears my word…has passed (μεταβέβηκεν) from death to life." In 1 John 3:14, the phrase is linked to the mutual love of the believers: "We know that we have passed (μεταβεβήκαμεν) from death to life because we love one another." It seems that the central role played by Jesus in the gospel is, at least partly, absorbed into the idea of community in 1 John.[21]

We have seen that many parallels between the epistles and the gospel betray, at a closer inspection, nuanced differences which show that it is not enough to list parallel expressions without detailing their use. The differences in how Jesus' role in relation to God is portrayed gain more significance because many of the theologically laden terms that are used in the gospel do not appear at all in the epistles:[22] ἀναβαίνειν (16, 5*), καταβαίνειν (17, 9*), ἄνω and ἄνωθεν (8, 5*), οὐρανός (19), ὑψοῦν (5), δόξα (18), δοξάζω (23), κρίνειν (19), κρίσις (11),[23] σώζειν (6), ἀπολλύναι (10), ἀνιστάναι (8), ἀνάστασις (4), ζωοποιεῖν (3), εἰρήνη (3), ἁγιάζειν (4), γραφή (12), γράφειν (10 with reference to the scriptures) and νόμος (14). It is especially noteworthy that the basic elements of the high Christology which is quite commonly seen as distinctive to the gospel do not appear in the epistles. In the gospel, Jesus'

---

[19] According to 1 John 4:4, "you are from God, and have conquered them," which refers to the spirit of the antichrist mentioned in 4:3.

[20] For the following comparisons, see North 2001, 24–25.

[21] Cf. Lieu 1986, 206.

[22] For the list of the terms appearing in the gospel but missing from the epistles, see Dodd 1937, 139–140; and Lieu 1986, 221. In the list that follows, the occurrences of the term in the gospel are given in parentheses and theologically significant usages are marked with an asterisk (*).

[23] κρίσις is found once (1 John 4:17) in the expression ἐν τῇ ἡμέρᾳ τῆς κρίσεως which is not found at all in the gospel.

mission is described as descending from above or from heaven and as ascending to the Father or to heaven. His death is understood as his lifting up or as his glorification and the goal of his mission as salvific or, alternatively, as bringing judgment. The terminology expressing these central Christological beliefs is missing from the epistles that, nonetheless, repeatedly stress the importance of the right confession of Jesus (1 John 2:22–23; 4:2–3,15; 2 John 7). Despite this emphasis on right confession, it is justified to speak about the theocentricity of the epistles in comparison to the gospel.[24]

Another major difference concerns the eschatological thinking in the epistles. One of the characteristics of the gospel is its insistence that God has already revealed himself in Jesus in a definitive form. This conviction does not leave much room for speculation about God's final intervention in the future and makes the gospel a good example of the so-called realized eschatology. Even though some passages in the gospel contain elements of future eschatology, 1 John goes far beyond what is said in the gospel.[25] The writer understands that it is the last hour (ἐσχάτη ὥρα) when the antichrist is coming (2:18), he waits for a future time when Jesus is revealed and when the believers "will be like him" (2:28; 3:2), refers to Jesus' future coming (παρουσία; 2:28) and urges his readers to have boldness on the day of judgment (ἐν τῇ ἡμέρᾳ τῆς κρίσεως; 4:17). These ideas are familiar from other, non-Johannine, Christian sources but hard to connect with the thought of the gospel.[26]

---

[24] Lieu 1991, 78–79, 103. Cf. also Rensberger 1997, 40. Rensberger works with the hypothesis that the epistles presuppose the gospel and says that, in 1 John, "Jesus' role as mediator between Christians and God is reduced. Relationship with Jesus and mediation by him are not eliminated…but the epistles seem to focus primarily on their result, the direct relationship between Christians and God. This shift in focus seems important, but the reason for it is unclear." Rensberger speculates that the author may stress God because the opponents had cast doubt on the role of Jesus or because he is closer than the gospel to non-Johannine Christianity where the "hierarchical relationship from God to Jesus" was not emphasized.

[25] For a discussion of the eschatology of the gospel, see R.E. Brown 2003, 234–248. Brown notes that while he was, earlier in his commentary on John, "attracted by the logic that the same person would scarcely have combined the two eschatologies as John's Gospel does," he has come to realize that "a perspective must be sought from and in which the diverse eschatology of John as it now stands makes sense—a perspective involving some form of complementarity rather than correction" (p. 246).

[26] For a more detailed comparison with the same conclusion, see already Dodd 1937, 142–144.

Unlike the gospel (John 14:16,26; 15:26; 16:7), 1 John does not apply the term παράκλητος to the Spirit but only to Jesus (1 John 2:1). This application is only implied in the gospel where the Spirit is called "another Paraclete" (14:16) which suggests that Jesus is understood as the first Paraclete. The term "Spirit of truth" appears both in the gospel (John 14:16–17; 16:13) and in 1 John 4:6 but the usages are different.[27] In the gospel, there appears only one Spirit called the Spirit, the Holy Spirit, the Paraclete or the Spirit of truth and presented in personal terms with a function that is tightly connected to Jesus. However, as a part of the dualistic framework of 1 John, the Spirit of truth in 1 John 4:6 has as its opposite the Spirit of error (τὸ πνεῦμα τῆς πλάνης). The idea that there are different spiritual beings in the world that act either on the side of God or against God has clear parallels in Jewish apocalyptic and dualistic thinking. The clearest parallels to the juxtaposition of the Spirit of truth and the Spirit of error are found in the doctrine of the two spirits in the Qumran *Community Rule* (1QS 3,7–9) and in *The Testament of Judah* (20:1; cf. also *T. Sim.* 2:7; *T. Jud.* 19:4; *T. Levi* 3:3). The pattern of thought appearing in these sources forms a much closer background to 1 John 4:1–6 than the more refined concept of the Spirit-Paraclete found in Jesus' farewell speeches in the gospel.[28]

The above-mentioned differences suggest that, in spite of the common theological terminology, the theological profiles of the gospel and the epistles are different. The ideas in the gospel related to the central role of Jesus and high Christology, realized eschatology and the role of the Spirit-Paraclete are more structured and distinctive in comparison with the epistles whose ideas are, in many cases, more loosely formulated and akin to other Christian and Jewish sources.[29] We may add to

---

[27] It may be that there are different concepts of the Spirit in the gospel itself. Cf. T.G. Brown 2003, 261–267. Brown concludes that the use of the Spirit outside Jesus' farewell speeches (John 13–17) is different from the concept of the Spirit-Paraclete appearing in the farewell speeches.

[28] Thus Lieu 2008a, 174. For the comparison of 1 John to the Dead Sea Scrolls, see also Boismard 1991, 156–165. Boismard even concludes that "the epistle is addressed to a Christian community whose members to a large extent had been Essenes...If we maintain the traditional idea, according to which the Johannine writings received their final form at Ephesus, we should be able to conclude that there existed at Ephesus an Essene community" (p. 165). However, the parallels between the Johannine literature and the Dead Sea Scrolls can be explained by a common background. See Hakola 2005, 199–200.

[29] Cf. Rensberger (1997, 21) who notes that "the use of terms and concepts not found in the Fourth Gospel but common elsewhere in early Christian literature" is a

the features that are distinctive to the Fourth Gospel but missing from other early Christian sources, including the Johannine epistles, the figure of the Beloved Disciple (John 13:23; 19:35; 20:2; 21:7,20). That the epistles lack many features that are unique to the gospel must be explained in any hypothesis concerning the relationship of the gospel and the epistles. These features pose a serious challenge to the theory that the epistles were written as a reaction to the misinterpretation of the gospel (see below).

3. Common Johannine tradition

That the epistles are, at the same time, closely related to and yet different from the gospel suggests that these writings represent two different forms of the shared tradition. This reinforces the scholarly consensus that sees them as emerging from a distinctive circle or community. Certainly, the consensus that the gospels in general or the Gospel of John in particular emerged in distinctive Christian communities has recently been called into question.[30] This criticism may be justified in the sense that many earlier studies have taken quite a bold leap from the narrative of the gospel to the historical reality behind it.[31] It is also undeniable that the Gospel of John, like the epistles, contains several features that appealed to a wide range of different Christian communities beyond its local area of origin. However, both the evidence concerning the reception of the gospels in the early church and various extra-canonical texts suggest that it is not anachronistic to think that, just as many other early Christian documents, the Johannine writings also reflect, at least to some extent, the experiences and needs of that particular community or a cluster of communities where they were produced.[32]

"major pattern" in 1 John. According to Rensberger, this "may represent an effort to open the Johannine community up to other forms of developing Christianity."

[30] Most notably, see Bauckham 1998, 9–48. Bauckham claims that all the canonical gospels were written for all Christians and not for particular Christian communities. As Bauckham (2001, 101–114) argues for this thesis in the case of the Fourth Gospel, he bypasses almost completely the Johannine epistles that support the community-hypothesis.

[31] For methodological criticism of J.L. Martyn's (2003) two-level reading of John, see Hakola 2005, 18–22.

[32] For patristic counter-evidence for the view that the gospels were written for all Christians, see Mitchell 2005, 36–79. For the reevaluation of Bauckham's proposal in the light of extra-canonical Christian texts, see Kazen 2005, 561–578. For earlier criticisms of Bauckham's views, see Esler 1998, 235–248; and Sim 2001, 3–27.

On purely literary grounds, it is difficult to define the mutual relationship of the gospel and the epistles. Those who think that the epistles presuppose the gospel, often claim that the beginning of 1 John
(1 John 1:1–4) is modeled after the prologue of the gospel (John 1:1–
18).[33] However, the beginnings of the gospel and 1 John, even though
they seem to be surprisingly similar, also show clear differences. The
gospel begins with the statement, "In the beginning was the Word,"
(ἐν ἀρχῇ ἦν ὁ λόγος) which presents Jesus as the preexistent Word
that was with God before Creation. It is not clear, however, that the
phrase "what was from the beginning" (ὃ ἦν ἀπ' ἀρχῆς) in the beginning of 1 John refers to this view. The expression "from the beginning"
can sometimes be used in 1 John to refer either to God or to Jesus.[34]
However, the neuter pronoun suggests that the usage in 1 John 1:1
is related to 1 John 2:24: "Let what you heard from the beginning (ὃ
ἠκούσατε ἀπ' ἀρχῆς) abide in you." Other passages speak of the commandment that the community has had "from the beginning" (1 John
2:7; 2 John 5–6) or of the message (ἀγγελία; cf. the verb ἀπαγγέλλω
in 1 John 1:2 and 3) the community has heard "from the beginning"
(1 John 3:11). Furthermore, the expression "concerning the word of
life" (περὶ τοῦ λόγου τῆς ζωῆς) at the end of 1 John 1:1 suggests that
the term "word" is not used absolutely to refer to God's eternal Word
as in the gospel but means "word" or "message."[35] In 1 John 1:3, the
word κοινωνία denotes the fellowship of the believers with the Father
and the Son, a word not found at all in the gospel. These differences
suggest that 1 John 1:1–4 is not simply a reproduction of John 1:1–18
but that shared tradition has been developed in different ways in these
passages.[36] If we suppose that the prologue of the gospel is reworked

---

[33] Thus R.E. Brown 1982, 91–92; Becker 2004, 39.

[34] Cf. 1 John 2:13 and 14: "You know him who is from the beginning" (τὸν ἀπ'
ἀρχῆς). It is typical of 1 John that it is not totally certain whether this expression
refers to God or to Jesus.

[35] For the discussion whether λόγος in 1 John 1:1 is used absolutely or not, see R.E.
Brown 1982, 164–167. Brown supports with good arguments the impersonal meaning
of λόγος as "word" or "message." Brown notes, in spite of his view that 1 John 1:1–4
is written in imitation of John 1:1–18, that "we cannot totally depend for guidance on
the use of 'word' in the GJohn Prologue."

[36] For more detailed arguments, see Schnelle 1987, 65–67; and Lieu 2008a, 37–46.
The likelihood of this scenario is supported by the fact that most scholars are ready
to acknowledge that the main bulk of John 1:1–18 is based on a traditional hymn. It
is also often argued that 1 John 5:13 is based on the original ending of the gospel in
John 20:31. See, e.g., Painter 2002, 70–72. It is, however, not clear that the function
of 1 John 5:13 is similar to John 20:31. 1 John 5:13 is often taken as the conclusion of

in 1 John 1:1–4 we must assume that the writer has deliberately played down those parts of the prologue that emphasize the revelation of the divine reality as a part of his strategy to counter the claims of his opponents.[37]

Most of the other similarities listed earlier in this essay are common themes or idioms that, while clearly indicating the kinship between the gospel and the epistles, are used in the epistles irrespective of the textual or thematic context in which they appear in the gospel. For example, there appears in 1 John 5:6 the combination of water and blood which is found also, in reversed order, in John 19:34. Both these passages are well-known cruxes of interpretation, and scholars have not reached a definite agreement what these ambiguous references mean. Despite the use of the common symbols, the meaning of which was probably more obvious to the original audience than to us, the passages are different. In 1 John 5:6, Jesus is said "to come by water and blood...not with the water only but with the water and the blood," while in John 19:34, blood and water come out of Jesus' pierced side. According to 1 John 5:6–7, the Spirit is the one who testifies, and the testimonies of the Spirit and the water and the blood agree. The theme of testimony appears in John 19:35 but it is "he who saw this" who testifies; elsewhere in the gospel, this figure is identified as the Beloved Disciple. The theme of the Spirit appears in the crucifixion scene only if the mention, "Then he bowed his head and gave up the spirit," (John 19:30) is taken to refer to Jesus' giving of the Holy Spirit to his followers at the time of his death. Even though common themes appear in both passages, it is by no means self-evident that these themes are used in the same way. Rather, as Judith Lieu has concluded, we have here another example of "divergence in application and reference of shared language and concepts" that is "the main characteristic of the relationship" between the Gospel of John and 1 John.[38]

---

the letter as a whole in which case the passage 5:14–21 is a kind of appendix that is attached somewhat clumsily to the rest of the letter. For the discussion, see Strecker 1996, 197–200. These verses have been taken as a secondary addition to 1 John, e.g., by R. Bultmann, C.H. Dodd., P. Vielhauer and K. Wengst while Strecker here joins R.E. Brown, R. Schnackenburg, E. Stegemann, W.G. Kümmel and M. de Jonge in defending these verses as an integral part of 1 John. As Strecker notes, 1 John 5:13 repeats many of the key words in the preceding section 5:4–12 and follows this section seamlessly. There is no need to think that this verse is literarily dependent on John 20:31. Cf. also Lieu 2008a, 220–222.

[37] Thus R.E. Brown 1982, 180–187. For the problems with this view, see below.

[38] Lieu 2008a, 212.

Some parallels found in the gospel are, on the basis of the internal analysis of the gospel, explicable as stemming from the community tradition. In John 3:11, there appears, quite surprisingly in the middle of the dialogue between Jesus and Nicodemus, a confession in the first person plural that is put in Jesus' mouth: "We speak of what we know and testify to what we have seen." This is quite commonly seen as an example of Jesus representing "the perspective of the evangelist and his community."[39] We also find elsewhere in the gospel and in the epistles similar kinds of "we"-confessions, and they seem to be an established part of the Johannine tradition.[40] Especially the end of the confession in John 3:11 (ὃ ἑωράκαμεν μαρτυροῦμεν) comes close to the words "we have seen and testify" (ἑωράκαμεν καὶ μαρτυροῦμεν) at the beginning of 1 John (1:2). This suggests that not only the "we"-form of the passages but also their common terminology stems from the shared tradition.[41]

The postulation of a common tradition used both in the gospel and in the epistles may help us to explain some sayings which are not completely at home in their present contexts.[42] In 1 John 2:2, Jesus is called "the atoning sacrifice for (ἱλασμὸς περί) our sins, and not for ours only but also for the sins of the whole world." What is significant here is the idea that Jesus has died for the sins of the whole world. Elsewhere in 1 John, the salvific effect of Jesus' mission is usually restricted to "us," that is, the believing community (cf. 1 John 3:1,16; 4:9,16).[43] In 1 John, the dualism of light and darkness is developed more consistently than in the gospel, and it is even stated that "the whole world lies under the

---

[39] Lincoln 2005, 152.

[40] Cf. Lieu 2008b, 818: "It is evident that such evocations of 'our' experience, particularly articulated in frequently anonymous confessional or testimonial formulae, were a familiar strategy within the broader Johannine tradition (John 1:14,16; 3:11; 6:69; 21:24; 3 John 12)."

[41] Another passage where a similar kind of confessional formula in the first person plural appears is Peter's confession in John 6:69: "We have come to believe and know that you are the Holy One of God." Again, it is significant that the language of the confession may reflect a common Johannine formula; an unusual combination "we have come to believe and know" (πεπιστεύκαμεν καὶ ἐγνώκαμεν) is not found elsewhere in John or in the NT but appears, in reversed order, in 1 John 4:16: "We have known and believe (ἐγνώκαμεν καὶ πεπιστεύκαμεν) the love that God has for us."

[42] For the following, cf. North 2001, 34–35.

[43] See especially 1 John 4:9: "God sent his only Son into the world so that we might live through him." This comes close to the idea expressed in John 3:16 with the exception that the world is the object of God's love and salvific intent in the gospel.

power of the evil one" (1 John 5:19).[44] In light of this, the statement
in 1 John 2:2 is surprisingly universal and inclusive.[45] While there are
no parallels for the use of the term ἱλασμός in the gospel, the idea
that Jesus' sacrifice is for the sins of the world is logically close to the
testimony of John the Baptist in John 1:29 (cf. also John 1:36): "Here is
the Lamb of God who takes away (ὁ αἴρων) the sin of the world!" No
matter whether this passage is to be understood as a reference to the
Lord's Suffering Servant (Isa 53) or to the Passover lamb (Exod 12) or
as a combination of both of these images, the significance of Jesus the
Lamb of God is described in universal terms. There are further echoes
of the Baptist's testimony in 1 John 3:5: "He was revealed to take away
sins" (ἐφανερώθη, ἵνα τὰς ἁμαρτίας ἄρῃ). Both the combination of the
verb αἴρω with sins (only here and in John 1:29 in the NT) and the
use of the verb φανερόω for Jesus' mission (cf. John 1:31) connects this
verse to the Baptist's testimony.[46] It is certainly possible to think that
the writer of 1 John has derived these ideas and terminology directly
from John 1:29, but the scattered references found in different parts of
the writing could be explained, at least as reasonably, by postulating a
common tradition that is used both in the gospel and in 1 John.[47] This
hypothesis is also helpful in explaining the appearance of the idea of
atonement in John 1:29 whereas elsewhere in the gospel, Jesus' death
is understood primarily as his lifting up and glorification or as his

---

[44] Cf. Lieu 1991, 100.

[45] However, see also 1 John 4:14: "The Father has sent his Son as the Savior of
the world." Lieu (1986, 183) has noted that 1 John 2:2 and 4:14 "sound like statements which have survived in tradition and they have no effect on the theology of the
immediate context or of the Epistle as a whole." Later Lieu (2008a, 66) has reiterated
this conclusion in the case of 1 John 4:14 but says of 1 John 2:2: "The lack of obvious
parallels makes it more difficult to dismiss 1 John 2:2 as a relic of earlier tradition
with no serious contribution to the thought…1 John 2:2 may, then, offer some hope
to those yet to become members of the community of believers…It is but a slender
thread, however, and does little to change the overall pattern of the letter." Cf. also
Strecker (1986, 41) who says that the Christological atonement sayings (*die christolo-
gische Entsühnungsaussagen*) in 1 John 1:7, 2:2 and 4:10 stem from the tradition used
by the writer.

[46] Cf. R.E. Brown 1982, 401.

[47] Rensberger (1997, 57) thinks that the inclusive statement in 1 John 2:2 is probably derived directly from John 1:29. R.E. Brown (1982, 240) says that the statement
"may have been an echo of the theology of salvific death in the Johannine eucharistic
formula" (John 6:51). For Brown, this is another instance where the author of 1 John
"may be reaching back to the early stages of Johannine tradition…to refute his opponents' reading of the tradition." 1 John 2:2 may indeed represent earlier Johannine
tradition but it is not necessarily used polemically (see below).

return to the Father. Another passage in the gospel where Jesus' death is presented in terms of atonement is John 11:51–52 that is formulated in a way that is close to 1 John 2:2, which is another link between this verse and the gospel.[48]

These examples of scattered and mostly isolated links do not seem to establish a direct literary relationship between the gospel and the epistles. The similarities concern brief idioms, fixed linguistic patterns and common yet differently shaped theological themes which could regularly have been transmitted in catechetical, sermonic or liturgical traditions of the community, whether in oral or in written form. It is fully plausible, therefore, to explain the coexistent similarities and differences between these writings by a common Johannine tradition that is developed in a different way in different situations. This conclusion has been put forward in a number of writings by Judith Lieu, and it is effectively argued by Wendy Sproston North, who has used this hypothesis to explain the formation of the Lazarus story in John 11.[49]

The above conclusion does not represent the majority view among scholars. Conjectures concerning the mutual relationship of the gospel and the epistles are seldom decided on the basis of the assessment of parallels and differences. Many scholars are ready to admit that there

---

[48] John 11:51–52: "Jesus was about to die for the nation and not for the nation only, but also (καὶ οὐχ ὑπὲρ τοῦ ἔθνους μόνον ἀλλ᾽ ἵνα καὶ) to gather into one the dispersed children of God." 1 John 2:2: "He is the atoning sacrifice for our sins, and not for ours only but also (οὐ περὶ τῶν ἡμετέρων δὲ μόνον ἀλλὰ καὶ) for the sins of the whole world."

[49] Lieu 1986, 166–216; Lieu 1991, 98–107; Lieu 2008a, 17–18; North 2001, 17–40. Grayston (1984, 12–13) also defends the independence of the epistles from the gospel but, at the same time, argues for the priority of the epistles. Cf. also Strecker 1986, 40–41; and Strecker 1996, xl. Strecker thinks that the gospel is not used in the epistles and that the gospel and 1 John are independent representatives of the Johannine tradition, even though he dates 1 John prior to the gospel (1986, 47n50). The most disputed part of Strecker's reconstruction, however, is his view that 2 and 3 John were written before the gospel and 1 John and represent the chiliastic idea of an intervening earthly and corporeal messianic reign. Cf. Strecker 1986, 34–40; and Strecker 1996, 232–236. Strecker's interpretation is based to a large extent on the interpretation of the present participle found in 2 John 7: "Who do not confess Jesus Christ coming (ἐρχόμενον) in the flesh." Strecker says that the participle should be understood in the future sense to refer to Jesus' future coming in the flesh, the reality of which the opponents of the presbyter deny. This is grammatically a possible interpretation of the participle but the lack of any other signs of chiliastic thinking in the Johannine tradition—with the exception of Revelation (see footnote 1)—makes Strecker's conclusion unpersuasive. 2 John 7 is probably a combination of 1 John 2:18–19 and 4:2, and the present participle can be explained as a variation of the Johannine tradition where Jesus is repeatedly described using the present participle of ἔρχομαι as the one who comes into the world (e.g., John 1:5; 6:14; 11:27). Cf. Lieu 2008a, 252–255.

is little evidence to suggest a direct literary dependence between these writings but they still think that the epistles build upon the ideas presented in the gospel.[50] This view is largely based on the reconstructions of the schism that is allegedly said to be in the background of the epistles. Therefore, we need to take a look at the theories concerning the opponents in 1 John in order to get a balanced picture of the way the Johannine tradition is developed and received in the epistles.

4. The opponents in *1 John*

Scholars have become increasingly aware of the problems of the so-called mirror-reading that treats polemical texts as mirrors in which we can see a clear picture of the people and the arguments under attack.[51] The historical situation of the epistles is still quite often inferred from the scattered allusions that are taken to directly represent the thinking of the opponents of the writer (1 John 2:18–22; 1 John 4:2–3; 2 John 7). This supposed schism is then used to clarify also those passages where the writer uses quite general and vague expressions that do not, automatically, need to be understood as a response to the claims of his opponents.[52] The circularity of this reasoning is obvious, and, therefore,

---

[50] Cf. R.E. Brown 1982, 33. Brown admits that "no passage in any of the of Epistles is a direct or certain quotation from GJohn, a surprising fact if 1 John was written after GJohn." In his detailed exegesis, however, Brown often assumes the knowledge of the gospel by the writer of 1 John. For a justified criticism of Brown's view, see North 2001, 11–14.

[51] For the problems of mirror-reading, see Barclay 1987, 73–93. Even though Barclay concentrates especially on Paul's epistle to the Galatians, the problems identified by him are also highly relevant for the interpretation of 1 John. It has been too easy "to jump to conclusions about what the conversation is about and, once we have an idea fixed in our minds, we misinterpret all the rest of the conversation" (p. 74). Barclay identifies as special interpretational pitfalls *undue selectivity* when scholars base their interpretations on some isolated individual passages, *overinterpretation* when every statement in a writing is taken as a rebuttal of the counter-argument of the opponents, *mishandling of polemics* when scholars ignore how the opponents might have understood the disagreements, and *latching onto particular words and phrases* that are taken as direct echoes of the opponents' vocabulary and then a whole thesis is hung "on those flimsy pegs." For the problems in the study of antagonists in early Christian sources, see also Thurén 2008, 79–95. In what follows, I give some examples of how these problems have surfaced in the research of 1 John.

[52] For this kind of procedure, see R.E. Brown 1982, 762–763; Painter 1986, 49–71; and Painter 2002, 88–93. For example, some statements concerning sin (e.g., 1 John 1:6,8,10; 3:9–10) are quite often taken to represent the thinking of the opponents. For the problems of this view, see Dunderberg 2008.

we should be cautious in reading the antithetical language in the epistles as a direct reflection of reality.

The majority of scholars think that the alleged schism reflected in the epistles deals with the right interpretation of the Johannine tradition as it is encapsulated in the gospel.[53] It is assumed that the opponents interpreted some elements found in the gospel in a way that was unacceptable to the writer of 1 John who offered what he regarded as the true interpretation of the legacy of the gospel.[54] The schism is often understood in Christological terms and said to concentrate on the meaning of Jesus' earthly life because in 1 John 4:2 it is stated that "every spirit that confesses Jesus Christ having come in the flesh is from God" (cf. also 2 John 7). The use of the perfect in the expression ἐν σαρκί ἐληλυθότα seems to refer not only to the moment of Jesus' incarnation (cf. the aorist used in John 1:14) but to Jesus' completed coming and the resulting remaining *in* the flesh.[55] 1 John 4:2 is often connected to the interpretation of 1 John 5:6–8 ("This is the one who came by water and blood, Jesus Christ, not with the water only but with the water and the blood.") where the word "blood" is taken to refer to Jesus' death. The combined interpretations of 1 John 4:2 and 5:6–8 are then compared to some early Christian writings that polemicize against those who deny that Jesus truly suffered and that are customarily defined as representing some sort of docetism.[56] It is claimed

---

[53] For an alternative view that takes the gospel as a response to the schism mentioned in the epistles, see Strecker 1986, 42; Schnelle 1987, 249–258; and Talbert 2005, 64–65. These scholars think that the gospel was directed, at least in part, against the schismatics identified as docetics in 1 John 4:2. It is not evident, however, whether we can find in the gospel, if it is read in its own right and not in light of later theological discussions, explicit docetic or anti-docetic language. For a discussion see Becker 1991, 745–752; Becker 2004, 126–131. Becker concludes that the question of docetism does not emerge in the gospel but belongs to a later stage in the history of the Johannine community reflected in the epistles. For the problems of finding explicit anti-docetic polemic even in the epistles, see below.

[54] This view is argued most consistently by R.E. Brown (1982, 69–116) even though its basic elements have been presented before. For a similar view with slight variations, see Painter 1986, 48–49; Painter 2002, 16–17; Klauck 1991, 34–42; de Boer 1991, 330–332; Rensberger 1997, 20–25; Culpepper 1998, 48–61; and Ehrman 2006, 242–243.

[55] For example, see Talbert 2005, 36.

[56] Cf. Ehrman 2006, 238–244. Ehrman says that it is not helpful to call the opponents in 1 John simply docetics because there were several quite distinct varieties of docetism in early Christianity. The first, represented by Basilides, claimed that Christ only appeared to suffer because someone else was crucified in his place (Irenaeus, *Adv. haer.* 1.24.3–4). The second, represented by Cerinthus, thought that Jesus and the Christ were actually separate entities (Irenaeus, *Adv. haer.* 1.26.1). The third form appears in the polemic of Ignatius against those who claimed that Jesus suffered only

that the opponents in 1 John took the high Christology of the gospel to its extreme conclusion and thereby obscured the salvific relevance of Jesus' earthly life or death. This is also seen as a reason why the terms that represent the high Christology of the gospel and the "progressive" theology of the opponents do not appear in the epistles.[57]

It is not self-evident, however, whether we should read 1 John 4:2 as an expression of anti-docetic polemic. This conclusion may be an overinterpretation because it puts too great an emphasis on the words ἐν σαρκί ἐληλυθότα as the focus of the right confession. The structure of the sentence ὃ ὁμολογεῖ Ἰησοῦν Χριστὸν ἐν σαρκί ἐληλυθότα suggests that the whole phrase "Jesus Christ having come in the flesh" is the object of the confession, not only its latter part.[58] This is confirmed as the writer describes the wrong confession in 4:3 only by saying that "every spirit that does not confess Jesus is not from God." It seems that the writer is not interested in the facts that are confessed about Jesus or in the erroneous details of the faith of the alleged opponents.[59] A number of early Christian writings connect the word "flesh" to Jesus; while this connection may sometimes appear in polemical contexts (Ignatius), the word is also used in an unpolemical way to refer either

---

in appearance and not truly (Ign. *Smyrn.* 1:1–2; 2:1; 3:1; 4:2; 5:2; Ign. *Trall.* 9:1–2; 10:1). Ehrman concludes that the thought of the opponents in 1 John 4:2 is very close to Ignatius' opponents. Thus also Rensberger 1997, 2–3.

[57] Cf. R.E. Brown 1982, 97–98.

[58] There are basically three ways to the understand the confession in 1 John 4:2: (1) "Confesses Jesus Christ having come in the flesh"; (2) "Confesses Jesus Christ as having come in the flesh"; and (3) "Confesses Jesus as the Christ having come in the flesh." For the arguments for the first one that takes the whole phrase Ἰησοῦν Χριστὸν ἐν σαρκί ἐληλυθότα as the object of the confession, see R.E. Brown 1982, 492–493; and Lieu 2008a, 166–169. As Lieu notes, 1 John 4:2–3 was quite often interpreted in an anti-docetic way in the early church. It is noteworthy that later interpreters sometimes felt the need to change the wording of these verses so that they more clearly appear as a formal confession. In 4:2, the Codex Vaticanus has the infinitive ἐληλυθέναι instead of the participle ἐληλυθότα, a reading that seems to place more emphasis on Jesus' coming in the flesh ("Confesses Jesus Christ *as having come* in the flesh"). The infinitive also appears in Pol. *Phil.* 7:1 which is possibly influenced by 1 John 4:2. In 1 John 4:3, several church fathers read λύει instead of μὴ ὁμολογεῖ, a reading that is also presupposed by the Vulgate and that sometimes has been taken as the original one even though it does not appear in the Greek manuscript tradition. Cf. R.E. Brown 1982, 494–496. Ehrman (2006, 221–246) has shown, however, that λύει is a deliberate variant that is more applicable to the Christological views opposed by several church fathers than the original reading.

[59] Lieu 2008a, 170.

to Jesus' sufferings or to his earthly life in general.[60] Whatever the exact meaning of ἐν σαρκὶ ἐληλυθότα in 1 John 4:2 is, this expression is unspecified and general as compared, for example, to Ignatius' anti-docetic polemic.[61] Therefore, it is not wise to hang the whole recon-struction of the situation behind 1 John on the disputed interpretation of this verse or on the even more disputed interpretation of 5:6.

The above conclusion is confirmed if we read 1 John 4:2 as a part of its immediate context and the whole 1 John. The antithesis between "every spirit that confesses" and "every spirit that does not confess" is only one form of several antitheses found in 1 John 4:1–6.[62] In this series of antitheses, the expression ἐν σαρκὶ ἐληλυθότα describes "Jesus Christ" in the same way as the perfect ἐξεληλύθασιν describes false prophets in the preceding verse ("false prophets have gone out into the world").[63] The use of the analogous forms could be taken to imply the sense of confrontation with the meaning that Jesus who has come in the flesh is greater than false prophets who have gone out into the world or the spirit of the antichrist that is coming and is already in the world (v. 3). Nothing in 4:1–6 suggests that the expression ἐν σαρκὶ ἐληλυθότα is the chief part of the argumentation; on the con-

---

[60] Cf. Dunderberg 2006, 87–88; and Lieu 2008a, 168–169. See the following exam-ples: John 1:14; Rom 8:3; Col 1:22; Eph 2:14; Heb 2:14; 5:7; 1 Tim 3:16; 1 Pet 4:1,18; *Barn.* 5:1,6,10; 6:3,7,9,14; 12:10; *Gos. Thom.* 28. Cf. also Marjanen 2002, 487–498; and Marjanen 2006, 210–219. Marjanen shows that, even though some forms of docetism are quite often connected to writings labeled as "Gnostic," several Nag Hammadi texts, in particular *Gos. Thom.* and *Ep. Pet. Phil.*, contain interpretations of Jesus' flesh, death and sufferings that deviate from docetic views appearing, for example, in Ignatius. The opponents in 1 John have repeatedly been described as some kind of emerging Gnostics. For the history of research, see Painter 2002, 1–26. Painter admits that the Qumran and Nag Hammadi discoveries have "cast doubt on any Gnostic influence" on the Johannine epistles (p. 27) but he still thinks that "the relationship to emerg-ing Gnosticism is more apparent in 1 John [than in the Gospel of John] because the author is specifically confronting the position of his opponents...the author of 1 John is critical of emerging Gnosticism" (p. 58).

[61] Minear (1970, 292) has suggested that the expression "in the flesh" in 1 John 4:2 should be understood as a parallel and synonymous expression for "in you" in 4:4: "The one who is in you is greater than the one who is in the world." Cf. also Lieu (2008a, 168) who says that "in the flesh" may point "to that which the believers also share. Belief is not directed to an isolated event situated in the past but is interlocked with believers' own certainty of divine indwelling as also with their obedience to the commands." Lieu adds that the first readers would also have recognized in the expres-sion "in the flesh" a number of resonances from the shared Johannine tradition (cf. John 1:14; 6:51–56,63).

[62] Cf. Minear 1970, 293–294.

[63] Minear 1970, 294; Lieu 2008a, 167.

trary, it is only a part of the series of contrasts and, "as the number of surrogates for one expression grows, the more flexible must one's thinking become, and the less enslaved to a single formulation."[64]

The rest of 1 John supports the above conclusion. 1 John 4:2–3 is only one of the many passages emphasizing the need for right belief and confession, but there is no interest in Jesus' flesh or blood in these other passages.[65] The role of the passages urging the confession of Jesus as the Christ (2:22) or as the Son of God (4:15) is problematic if we unduly select 1 John 4:12 and 5:6 as the focal points of the confession and think that the author was mainly combating those who denied the relevance of Jesus' humanity and life in the flesh.[66] If we should take up some other confessions in 1 John as the point of departure for our historical reconstructions, the portrait of the alleged opponents would be very different.[67] The diversity of confessional terminology itself "suggests that the author was not interested in the juridical formulation

---

[64] Minear 1970, 294.

[65] 1 John 2:22–23: "Who is the liar but the one who denies that Jesus is the Christ? This is the antichrist, the one who denies the Father and the Son. No one who denies the Son has the Father; everyone who confesses the Son has the Father also." 3:23: "This is his commandment, that we should believe in the name of his Son Jesus Christ." 4:15: "God abides in those who confess that Jesus is the Son of God." 5:1: "Everyone who believes that Jesus is the Christ has been born of God." 5:5: "Who is it that conquers the world but the one who believes that Jesus is the Son of God?" 5:10: "Those who believe in the Son of God have the testimony in their hearts. Those who do not believe in God have made him a liar by not believing in the testimony that God has given concerning his Son."

[66] Rensberger (1997, 23) admits that "it remains unclear how the passages that insist on confession of Jesus as Christ and Son of God fit" the view according to which the opponents devaluated Jesus' physical and human reality. Cf. also Klauck 1991, 233. Klauck resolves the differences in confessional language by assuming that the confessions that demand faith in Jesus as the Christ (2:22) or as the Son of God (4:15) stem from the tradition while the confession in 4:2 is an expansion of these shorter formulae. For Klauck, this expansion directs the interpretation of other confessions.

[67] Cf. Grayston (1984, 12) who says that, from the writer's perspective, the problem of the opponents was not an excessively high Christology but whether "it was necessary to attach any christology to Jesus at all." It was inappropriate for the opponents to call Jesus the Christ and say that he alone could provide access to God (p. 19). In my opinion, this conclusion is on the right track because different forms of confessions suggests that the writer of 1 John wants to depict the opponents as lacking any faith in Jesus at all. We should not, however, take this as an accurate portrait of the faith of the opponents. According to Smalley (1984, xxiii–xxxii), the different confessions reflect two different groups of opponents: those who came from a Jewish background understood Jesus in human terms and had too "low" a Christology, while those who came from a Gnostic background understood Jesus as God and represented too "high" a Christology.

of a single creedal test."[68] This diversity tends to blur any details of the faith of those who do not share what the writer regards as the authentic faith in Jesus. The cumulative force of the varying demands of the right confession is that the opponents simply lack any authentic faith in Jesus and, from the writer's perspective, any authentic faith in God.

There is little evidence in 1 John as a whole that the humanity of Jesus was the main concern of the author. In several cases, the writer uses undefined language as he speaks of God or Jesus and often it is difficult—if not impossible—to determine which of the two the author intends (e.g., 1:9; 2:3–4; 2:29; 3:3,7,24). As Martin de Boer has remarked, this "lack of clarity calls into question the claim that the author wants to *underline* Jesus' humanity against those who hold a docetic christology." De Boer continues, stating that the frequent use of the terms "Son" or "Son of God" suggests that "the author actually wants to emphasize [Jesus'] unique, divine status and origin."[69] At the end of the epistle, the writer even calls Jesus "the true God."[70] It is not obvious, therefore, that there is a deliberate tendency to avoid terms related to Jesus' divine status in 1 John. There is nothing complicated in the way Jesus is described both as divine and as "having come to flesh" as these ideas are presented in 1 John. This combination appears problematic only if we read 1 John with the assumption that the writer had in his mind a clearly defined theological agenda that was directed

---

[68] Minear 1970, 297.

[69] De Boer 1991, 328. De Boer rejects the common understanding that 1 John is directed against docetism as such and revises Raymond Brown's interpretation of the position of the opponents. According to Brown (1982, 76–77), the secessionists "admitted the reality of Jesus' humanity but refused to acknowledge that his being in the flesh was essential to the picture of Jesus *as the Christ*, the Son of God." For the secessionists, Jesus' coming only confirmed Jesus as the Son of God but did not have any salvific value. De Boer develops Brown's view further and claims that 1 John 4:2 as interpreted in light of 5:6 is "*primarily* a claim about the death of Jesus Christ and refers only *secondarily* to his humanity as such." The secessionists value Jesus' earthly career as the divinely authorized baptizer (cf. water in 1 John 5:6), while the author puts the emphasis on Jesus' death (pp. 330, 339). These more and more nuanced ways to reconstruct the position of the alleged opponents illuminate clearly the problems of reading 1 John 4:2 or the whole of 1 John in anti-docetic terms alone. In my opinion, however, these attempts fail to establish a compelling reconstruction of the thinking of the opponents. The evidence we have is simply too shaky and brief because the rhetorical strategy of the writer is not based on theological precision but on generalizations that present the opponents simply as unbelievers.

[70] For the arguments that ὁ ἀληθινὸς θεός in 5:20 refers to Jesus, not to God, see R.E. Brown 1982, 625–626.

against the opponents' misuse of the gospel and that explains the selective use of the gospel material.

Additionally, the role of the Spirit in 1 John is explained as a reaction to the extremist beliefs of the opponents based on the role of the Spirit-Paraclete in the gospel.[71] It is not clear, however, whether the alleged schism can account for the lack of the references to the Spirit as the Paraclete. One of the main functions of the Spirit-Paraclete in the gospel is to remind the disciples of all that Jesus has said when he still was with them (John 14:26). It is emphasized that the Spirit "will not speak on his own" but will glorify Jesus "because he will take what is mine and declare it to you" (John 16:13–14). If the writer of 1 John knew the gospel and its teaching of the Spirit-Paraclete, he would have had a ready model to emphasize the connection between the testimony of the Spirit and the earthly life of Jesus.[72] On the basis of the gospel, however, the juxtaposition of the Spirit of truth and the Spirit of error in 1 John 4:1–6 is something that is not expected even though it is quite regular on the basis of Jewish apocalyptic and dualistic traditions (cf. above).[73]

On the basis of the above observations, it is defensible to conclude that the alleged schism does not explain why certain features distinctive to the Fourth Gospel do not appear in the epistles. The writer of

---

[71] See Painter 2002, 92–93. Cf. also R.E. Brown 1979, 138: "The opponents may have designated themselves as teachers and prophets and have claimed to speak under the guidance of the Spirit." When Brown explains how the writer of 1 John responded to these claims, he says that "truly noteworthy is what he does not say…Presumably the author would not deny that the Spirit was the Paraclete, but he never mentions it. Rather he emphasizes what is only hinted at in the gospel, namely, that Jesus is the Paraclete" (pp. 140–141). In another connection, Brown (1982, 241) remarks that the silence about the Paraclete in the epistles may be "accidental."

[72] Thus also Grayston 1984, 13. Cf. also T.G. Brown 2003, 259. T.G. Brown concludes that the portrayals of the Spirit in the gospel and in 1 John do not "clearly indicate a sequence of the composition of either writing in relation to the other." In spite of this, she is inclined to think that 1 John borrowed some of its ideas from the gospel. She has earlier (pp. 247–248), however, argued with good reasons that it is unlikely that the opponents in 1 John derived their understanding of the Spirit directly from the gospel. T.G. Brown thus rejects the view that is, for example, represented by Raymond Brown and John Painter (cf. the previous note). According to T.G. Brown, we find, in the farewell discourses of the gospel, "a degree of emphasis on the continued significance and presence of Jesus that would seem to contradict the opponents' views on Jesus."

[73] Cf. R.E. Brown 1982, 27: "The treatment of the Spirit of Truth alongside the Spirit of Deceit in I John 4:1–6 is strangely vague about the personal quality of the Spirit." Rensberger 1997, 114: "Placing the Holy Spirit over against the 'Spirit of deceit' is somewhat odd, the result of inserting 'Spirit of truth' into a dualistic framework."

1 John portrays those who, from his perspective, have left the community (1 John 2:19) as lacking any real faith in Jesus which frustrates
our attempts to reconstruct a detailed position of the opponents. If
we are to believe the author and conclude that these opponents once
belonged to the community, it is quite certain that their portrait as
unbelievers is exaggerated. The same kind of sweeping use of language
is seen as the author develops, on the basis of the traditional dualistic
images, the contrast between the children of God who should love
one another and the children of the devil whose deeds are bad and
who are full of hatred (3:7–17). In this connection, the writer uses the
example of Cain to portray those who hate their brothers or sisters
as murderers (3:15), a depiction that is hardly ever taken literally but
seen as hyperbole.[74]

These kinds of contrasts are quite expected if we take seriously
the fact that the Johannine epistles, or any other epistles in the New
Testament, were not written primarily to give an unbiased portrait of
those who are differentiated and devalued as "others" but to persuade
the audience to receive the message of the writer. Therefore, what is
said of the alleged opponents should be seen first and foremost as a
part of the rhetoric of differentiation that strives to reinforce the collective identity of the writer and his audience. According to the Social
Identity Perspective, it is predictable that the negative traits of those
who are perceived as "others" are exaggerated as a group constructs
its social identity.[75] This perspective holds that social categorization is
a fundamental aspect of group behavior. When we define ourselves
in relation to other people, we experience ourselves as similar to one
clearly-defined category of people and therefore as different from
those in other categories. This process helps us to orientate ourselves
in variable social environments by making those environments more
predictable and meaningful. Social categorization, however, results

---

[74] Cf. R.E. Brown 1982, 447: "The reference to murder is hyperbole for maltreat-
ment." Rensberger 1997, 99: "Verse 15 then makes explicit the symbolic meaning of
the example of Cain: the murderer is anyone who hates a brother or sister. This seems,
at first glance, a very sweeping statement...[but] it is not necessary to suppose that
the opponents posed an actual mortal danger to other Christians." However, Painter
(1986, 63) goes significantly far beyond this: "It is possible that the opponents not only
separated from the author and his adherents but were violently antagonistic to them
even to the point of causing their death."

[75] The Social Identity Perspective has increasingly been applied to early Christian
and Jewish sources. For an introduction and application of the theory, see, e.g., Hakola
2007b, 259–276; Hakola 2008, 123–139; and Hakola 2009.

in exaggeration and a polarization of perception whereby individuals belonging to different groups are viewed as being more different from each other than they really are, while individuals belonging to the same group are perceived as more alike. Furthermore, it has been demonstrated that, in the context of intergroup tensions, a clear *linguistic intergroup bias* is discernible because positive ingroup behaviors and negative outgroup behaviors tend to be described in quite abstract and general terms.[76] The use of such abstract adjectives or state verbs as good vs. evil, true vs. untrue, or hate vs. love is especially suitable to induce and communicate a one-dimensional view of the world because general descriptions of behavior are detached from specific situations and thus become too vague to be tested. Generalizations do not invite verification attempts and are relatively immune from falsification.[77]

The way the Johannine tradition is developed in the Johannine epistles, and especially in 1 John, is a good case in point of the above-mentioned intergroup bias. The writer does not try to describe his opponents in any detail but creates an imaginary universe where the children of God are clearly separate and distinguishable from the children of the devil even though the fact that the latter originally "went out from us" (1 John 2:19) suggests that the reality may have been much more complicated and unpredictable.

5. Conclusion

In this essay, I have argued that the Johannine epistles should not be read as a reaction to the alleged schism prompted by the excessive interpretation of the gospel. The detailed comparison of the gospel and the epistles clearly demonstrates the kinship of these writings but also reveals clear differences in how common idioms and themes are developed. The similarities can be explained by the use of the common tradition but they are not enough to establish a direct literary dependence between these writings. The main differences concern some major themes that are distinctive to the gospel but missing from the epistles. The lack of the high Christology and the Spirit-Paraclete in the epistles,

---

[76] Cf. Fiedler and Schmid 2001, 272.
[77] Fiedler and Schmid 2001, 267. The seemingly contradictory statements concerning sin in 1 John also can be taken to reflect the ingroup language of the writer. See Dunderberg 2008.

for example, cannot be explained as an intentional reworking of the gospel material but supports the view that the gospel and the epistles represent the shared Johannine tradition that is developed in different ways in different situations.

The view argued here supports the diversity of the Johannine tradition in its early stages. Not only the differences between the gospel and the epistles but also the fact that there seems to be some kind of dispute—however vaguely described as it is—in the background of the epistles speaks for the dynamic nature of the Johannine tradition.[78] The epistles can be seen as an attempt to come to terms with the fluidity of this tradition in a situation where no external authority solved the disputes among those who believed in Jesus. While the Gospel of John, owing to its refined portraits of Jesus and the Spirit-Paraclete, made a lasting impression on the formulations of later Christological and trinitarian thinking among various Christian groups, the epistles, despite their more mundane theological profile, also influenced later theology. This influence was not achieved through theological precision, but, on the contrary, by creating a visionary space where people are divided into two plain categories on the basis of their faith in Jesus. This vision may already originally have been an overtly simplistic representation of a much more diverse reality but it still provided later Christians with a ready model as they defined themselves in opposition not only to the outside world but also to some—real or imagined—internal threats.[79] While the Johannine epistles testify to the original diversity of the Johannine tradition, they also betray a clear tendency to reduce this diversity into controllable categories. This tentative move from diversity to uniformity may be the most important legacy of the Johannine tradition as it was developed and transmitted in the Johannine epistles.

---

[78] Cf. Black 1986, 147–148. Black argues against the view that the Johannine epistles represent a kind of "early Catholism" and concludes that "it may have been precisely because faith in these communities was so dynamic and fluid that it had shaded into beliefs unacceptable to the presbyter." Black finds "some rudimentary notion of 'orthodoxy'" in operation in how the epistles struggle to establish the criteria by which truth and error are distinguished. Black remarks, however, that these criteria are not enforced in any way.

[79] Cf. Lieu (1986, 33) who gives examples of how 2 John 9–11 was used as a standard proof-text to sanction the fellowship with those regarded as schismatics or heretics. Klauck (1991, 155–156) refers to how 1 John 2:19 authorized the detection of heretics among those who had originally been understood as belonging to the church.

BIBLIOGRAPHY

Barclay, J.M.G., "Mirror-Reading a Polemical Letter: Galatians as a Test Case," *Journal for the Study of the New Testament* 31 (1987), 73–93.
Bauckham, R., "For Whom Were Gospels Written," *The Gospels for All Christians: Rethinking the Gospel Audiences*, R. Bauckham, ed., Grand Rapids, Mich.: Eerdmans, 1998, 9–48.
—— "The Audience of the Fourth Gospel," *Jesus in Johannine Tradition*, R.T. Fortna and T. Thatcher, eds., Louisville, Ky.: Westminster John Knox, 2001, 101–114.
Becker, J., *Das Evangelium nach Johannes*, 2 vols., Ökumenischer Taschenbucher-Kommentar zum Neuen Testament 4, Gütersloh: Mohn; Würzburg: Echter Verlag, ³1991.
—— *Johanneishes Christentum*, Tübingen: Mohr-Siebeck, 2004.
Black, C., "The Johannine Epistles and the Question of Early Catholism," *Novum Testamentum* 28 (1986), 131–158.
Boismard, M.-É., "The First Epistle of John and the Writings of Qumran," *John and the Dead Sea Scrolls*, J.H. Charlesworth, ed., enlarged edition, New York: Crossroad, 1991, 156–165.
Brown, R.E., *The Community of the Beloved Disciple: The Life, Loves, and Hates of an Individual Church in New Testament Times*, New York: Paulist Press, 1979.
—— *The Epistles of John*, The Anchor Bible 30, Garden City, N.Y.: Doubleday, 1982.
—— *An Introduction to the Gospel of John*, F. Moloney, ed., Anchor Bible Reference Library, New York: Doubleday, 2003.
Brown, T.G., *Spirit in the Writings of John*, Journal for the Study of the New Testament Supplement Series 253, London: T&T Clark, 2003.
Culpepper, R.A., *The Gospel and Letters of John*, Nashville: Abingdon, 1998.
de Boer, M.C., "The Death of Jesus Christ and His Coming in the Flesh (1 John 4:2)," *Novum Testamentum* 23 (1991), 326–346.
Dodd, C.H., "The First Epistle of John and the Fourth Gospel," *Bulletin of the John Rylands Library* 21 (1937), 129–156.
Dunderberg, I., *The Beloved Disciple in Conflict? Revisiting the Gospels of John and Thomas*, Oxford: Oxford University Press, 2006.
—— "Sin and Sinlessness in 1 John: Theory and Practice," A Paper Read in the Johannine Literature Section at the Society of Biblical Literature Annual Meeting in Boston, 2008.
Ehrman, B.D., "1 John 4:3 and the Orthodox Corruption of Scripture," *Studies in the Textual Criticism of the New Testament*, New Testament Tools and Studies 33, Leiden: Brill, 2006, 221–246.
Esler, P.F., "Community and Gospel in Early Christianity: A Response to Richard Bauckham's *Gospels for All Christians*," *Scottish Journal of Theology* 51 (1998), 235–248.
Fiedler, K. and J. Schmid, "How Language Contributes to Persistence of Stereotypes As Well As Other, More General, Intergoup Issues," *Blackwell Handbook of Social Psychology: Intergroup Processes*, R. Brown and S. Gaertner, eds., Oxford: Blackwell, 2001, 261–280.
Frey, J., "Erwägungen zum Verhältnis der Johannesapokalypse zu den übrigen Schriften des Corpus Johanneum," M. Hengel, *Die johanneische Frage: Ein Lösungsversuch, mit einem Beitrag von Jörg Frey*, Wissenschaftliche Untersuchungen zum Neuen Testament 67, Tübingen: Mohr Siebeck, 1993, 326–429.
Grayston, K., *The Johannine Epistles*, New Century Bible, Grand Rapids, Mich.: Eerdmans, 1984.
Hakola, R., *Identity Matters: John, the Jews and Jewishness*, Supplements to Novum Testamentum 118, Leiden: Brill, 2005.

—— "The Johannine Community as Jewish Christians? Some Problems in Current Scholarly Consensus," *Jewish Christianity Reconsidered: Rethinking Ancient Groups and Texts*, M. Jackson-McCabe, ed., Minneapolis: Fortress, 2007a, 181–201.

—— "Social Identities and Group Phenomena in the Second Temple Period," *Explaining Early Judaism and Christianity: Contributions from Cognitive and Social Science*, P. Luomanen, I. Pyysiäinen and R. Uro, eds., Biblical Interpretation Series 89, Leiden: Brill, 2007b, 259–276.

—— "Social Identity and a Stereotype in the Making: The Pharisees as Hypocrites in Matt 23," *Identity Formation in the New Testament*, B. Holmberg and M. Winninge, eds., Wissenschaftliche Untersuchungen zum Neuen Testament 227, Tübingen: Mohr-Siebeck, 2008, 123–139.

—— "The Burden of Ambiguity: Nicodemus and the Social Identity of the Johannine Christians," *New Testament Studies*, 2009 [forthcoming].

Hakola, R. and A. Reinhartz, "John's Pharisees," *In Quest of the Historical Pharisees*, J. Neusner and B.D. Chilton, eds., Waco, Tex.: Baylor University Press, 2007, 131–147.

Hill, C.E., *The Johannine Corpus in the Early Church*, Oxford: Oxford University Press, 2004.

Kazen, T., "Sectarian Gospels for Some Christians? Intention and Mirror-Reading in the Light of Extra-Canonical Texts," *New Testament Studies* 51 (2005), 561–578.

Kim, M.G., *Zum Verhältnis des Johannesevangeliums zu den Johannesbriefen: Zur Verfasserschaft der 'johanneisschen' Schriften in der Forschung*, Europäische Hochschulschriften, Reihe 23/761, Frankfurt am Main: Lang, 2001.

Klauck, H.-J., *Der erste Johannesbrief*, Evangelisch-Katolischer Kommentar zum Neuen Testament 23/1, Zürich: Benziger; Neukirchen-Vluyn: Neukirchener Verlag, 1991.

Lieu, J., *The Second and the Third Epistles of John*, Studies of the New Testament and Its World, Edinburgh: T&T Clark, 1986.

—— *The Theology of the Johannine Epistles*, New Testament Theology, Cambridge: Cambridge University Press, 1991.

—— *I, II and III John: A Commentary*, The New Testament Library, Louisville, Ky.: Westminster John Knox, 2008a.

—— "Us or You? Persuasion and Identity in 1 John," *Journal of Biblical Literature* 127 (2008b), 805–819.

Lincoln, A., *The Gospel According to Saint John*, Black's New Testament Commentaries 4, London: Continuum; Peabody, Mass.: Hendrickson, 2005.

Marjanen, A. "The Suffering of One Who Is a Stranger to Suffering: The Crucifixion of Jesus in the Letter of Peter to Philip," *Fair Play: Diversity and Conflicts in early Christianity: Essays in Honor of Heikki Räisänen*, I. Dunderberg, C. Tuckett and K. Syreeni, eds., Supplements to Novum Testamentum 113, Leiden: Brill, 2002, 487–498.

—— "The Portrait of Jesus in the *Gospel of Thomas*," *Thomasine Traditions in Antiquity: The Social and Cultural World of the Gospel of Thomas*, J. Asgeirsson, A.D. DeConick and R. Uro, eds., Nag Hammadi and Manichean Studies 59, Leiden: Brill, 2006, 209–219.

Martyn, J.L., *History and Theology in the Fourth Gospel*, Louisville, Ky.: Westminster John Knox Press, ³2003.

Minear, P.S., "The Idea of Incarnation in First John," *Interpretation* 24 (1970), 291–302.

Mitchell, M.M., "Patristic Counter-Evidence to the Claim That 'The Gospels Were Written for All Christians,'" *New Testament Studies* 51 (2005), 36–79.

North, W.S., *The Lazarus Story within the Johannine Tradition*, Journal for the Study of the New Testament Supplement Series 212, Sheffield: Sheffield Academic Press, 2001.

Painter, J., "The 'Opponents' in 1 John," *New Testament Studies* 32 (1986), 48–71.

—— *1, 2, and 3 John*, Sacra Pagina 18, Collegeville, Minn.: The Liturgical Press, 2002.

Reinhartz, A., *Befriending the Beloved Disciple: A Jewish Reading of the Gospel of John*, New York: Continuum, 2001.

Rensberger, D., *1 John, 2 John, 3 John*, Abingdon New Testament Commentaries, Nashville: Abingdon, 1997.

Ruckstuhl, E. and P. Dschulnigg, *Stilkritik and Verfasserfrage im Johannesevangelium: Die johanneische Sprackmerkmale auf dem Hintergrund des Neuen Testaments and des zeitgenössischen hellenistischen Schrifttums*, Novum Testamentum et Orbis Antiquus 17, Göttingen: Vandenhoeck & Ruprecht, 1991.

Schnelle, U., *Antidoketische Christologie im Johannesevangelium: Eine Untersuchung zur Stellung des vierten Evangeliums in der johanneischen Schule*, Göttingen: Vandenhoeck & Ruprecht, 1987.

Sim, D.C., "The Gospels for All Christians: A Response to Richard Bauckham," *Journal for the Study of the New Testament* 84 (2001), 3–27.

Smalley, S., *1, 2, 3 John*, Word Biblical Commentary 51, Waco, Tex.: Word Books, 1984.

Strecker, G., "Die Anfänge der johanneischen Schule," *New Testament Studies* 32 (1986), 31–47.

—— *The Johannine Letters: A Commentary on 1, 2 and 3 John*, Hermeneia, Minneapolis: Fortress, 1996.

Talbert, C.H., *Reading John: A Literary and Theological Commentary on the Fourth Gospel and the Johannine Epistles*, revised edition, Macon, Ga.: Smyth & Helwys, 2005.

Thurén, L., "Antagonists—Rhetorically Marginalized Identities in the New Testament," *Identity Formation in the New Testament*, B. Holmberg and M. Winninge, eds., Wissenschaftliche Untersuchungen zum Neuen Testament 227, Tübingen: Mohr-Siebeck, 2008, 79–95.

White, L.M., *Building God's House in the Roman World: Architectural Adaptation among Pagans, Jews, and Christians*, Baltimore: Johns Hopkins University Press, 1990.

THE *GOSPEL OF THE ACTS OF JOHN*:
ITS RELATION TO THE FOURTH GOSPEL

István Czachesz
Helsinki Collegium for Advanced Studies & Ruprecht-Karls
Universität Heidelberg

The apocryphal *Acts of John* is one of the so-called major Apocryphal Acts of the Apostles, which date from the second and early third centuries CE and report the mission, miracles and martyrdom of the apostles.[1] Unlike the canonical Acts, each of these writings focuses on the story of one chosen apostle: Paul, John, Peter, Andrew and Thomas, respectively. There are different suggestions about the provenance and date of composition of the *Acts of John*. Earlier, I proposed that the book in its present form probably dates from the late second century and its final revision was made in Alexandria, although much of the material contained in it is earlier and perhaps originates from Asia Minor.[2] In this essay, I will focus on the *Gospel of the Acts of John* (*GAJ*), which is found in chapters 87–105 of the *Acts of John*.[3] The text of the *GAJ* is known from a single manuscript of the Austrian National Library, Codex Vindobonensis historicus graecus 63, dated to 1319 or 1324.[4] These chapters contain a complete gospel narrative, which has been preserved independently of the rest of the book—with clear signs, however, that at some point it formed part of the *Acts of John*.[5] The *GAJ* is connected to the plot of the *Acts of John* by a narrative frame (ch. 87) and begins with a prologue and the calling of John and James at a lake (chs. 88–89). Subsequently, it reports a number of episodes from Jesus' ministry, many of them known from other gospels, such as Jesus' transfiguration (in two versions), a visit at the house of a Pharisee and the multiplication of bread. There are also episodes that do not readily evoke any of the canonical gospel narratives: John watches Jesus on

---

[1] For a recent overview, see Klauck 2008, 1–14.
[2] Czachesz 2007a, 92n1, 120–122, with references to alternative suggestions.
[3] Czachesz 2007a, 102–106; Czachesz 2007b, 92n1, 245–246.
[4] Bonnet, Lipsius and Tischendorf 1898, xxx; Junod and Kaestli 1983, 26–29. References in this essay follow the line numbering of Junod and Kaestli's edition.
[5] Lalleman 1998, 25–30.

several occasions, Jesus never blinks his eyes, leaves no footprints on
the ground, and once pulls John's beard. Jesus and his disciples do not
share a last supper but rather they sing a hymn and celebrate a dance
ritual (chs. 94–96). After a peculiar crucifixion episode, an ascension
scene follows immediately and concludes the narrative (chs. 97–102).
Finally, an exhortation (chs. 103–104) and a closing narrative frame
complete the text of the gospel.

After the publication of the manuscript by M.R. James,[6] scholars'
attention was directed to the possible connections between this text
and the Fourth Gospel. In particular, it has been suggested that the
Fourth Gospel was influenced by the *Acts of John*, a hypothesis that has
been abandoned in subsequent scholarship.[7] During most of the twentieth century, the connection between these sources has not received
much attention from scholars, including the commented edition of
the *Acts of John* by E. Junod and J.-D. Kaestli.[8] In the last two decades,
however, consensus seems to have emerged that the *Acts of John* used
the Fourth Gospel.[9] According to R.I. Pervo, "Most of the material in
AcJn 87–105 may be accounted for as intra-johannine development, as
the result of fresh interpretation of and meditation upon the message
contained in the [Fourth] Gospel."[10] More recently, P.J. Lalleman suggested that the common tradition of the two writings was transmitted
orally,[11] and concluded that "in the AJ [*Acts of John*], John has become
an opponent to the Gospel that bears his own name," attributing particularly the gospel section to an "ultra-Johannine group" which was
"forced to combat the very Gospel [that is, the Fourth Gospel] that was
formative of their thought."[12] In this essay, I will argue for a different
relation between the Fourth Gospel and the *GAJ*. According to my
hypothesis, the Fourth Gospel did not rely on the *GAJ*, as suggested
by Corssen and Hilgenfeld, nor did the *GAJ* use the Fourth Gospel as
a source, as maintained in recent scholarship, but rather the author(s)
of the *GAJ* had access to a (Johannine) gospel tradition that also influenced the Fourth Gospel. In the first part of my essay, I will review the
most important parallels between the *GAJ* and the Fourth Gospel. In

---

[6] James 1897.
[7] Corssen 1896, 118–134; Hilgenfeld 1900.
[8] Junod and Kaestli 1983.
[9] Lalleman 1998, 110–111.
[10] Pervo 1992, 67.
[11] Lalleman 1998, 116.
[12] Lalleman 1998, 122.

the second part, I will discuss evidence that forces us to look beyond the previous research positions. In the third part, I will show how my hypothesis explains the present shape of the sources.

1. The *Gospel of the Acts of John* and the Fourth Gospel: Parallels

As Lalleman already noted, the overall structure of the *GAJ* agrees with that of the canonical gospels, and in particular, with the structure of the Fourth Gospel.[13] This overall resemblance is demonstrated by Lalleman's chart:

	Gospel of John	Acts of John
Introduction	1:1–18	87.1–88.8
public ministry	1:19–12:50	88.9–93.17
private teaching	13–17	94–96
ceremony	13:1–30	94–95
teaching proper	13:31–17:36	96
the glorious cross	18–20	97–102
epilogue	21	103–105

Whereas the basic plot of the narrative agrees with that of all four canonical gospels, the design of the *GAJ* has a particularly Johannine character inasmuch as it emphasizes the self-revelation of Jesus before his disciples. In Bultmann's words, chapters 13–20 of the Fourth Gospel are about Jesus' love for his followers—which can be equally said about *GAJ* 94–102. Another feature of the *GAJ*, however, sets its plot apart from that of all four canonical gospels: this gospel has no resurrection narrative, but rather Christ directly ascends to heaven from the Mount of Olives, while his human appearance is being crucified on Golgotha. This major difference has to do with the Christology of the *GAJ*, according to which "the Lord never was a human being...but he was seen now and then as a divine messenger in a more or less human appearance which should not be confused with a real body."[14]

---

[13] Lalleman 1998, 45.
[14] Lalleman 1998, 46.

The setting of the opening scene of the *GAJ*, the calling of John and James, parallels the synoptic call story found in Mark 1:16–20 and Matt 4:18–22, yet without much agreement in the details. The *GAJ* does not mention that John and James were the sons of Zebedee, had hired workers and were repairing their nets on the shore. Unlike in the synoptic story, the brothers are at sea (we do not know which one) rather than on the shore, Jesus' words to them are reported and Jesus helps them bring the boat onto the shore. The story of the *GAJ* does not include the point of the synoptic story, that "they immediately left the boat and their father, and followed Jesus." The call story of the *GAJ* also shows parallels with an episode from the Fourth Gospel, that is, the post-Easter appearance of Jesus at the Sea of Galilee in John 21,[15] where indeed Jesus stands on the shore whereas the disciples are sailing, and steer the boat to the shore after they recognize Jesus.

The public ministry of Jesus in the *GAJ* is concluded by John's statement, "Now, these things, dear brethren, I speak to you to encourage you in your faith towards him, for we must at the present keep silent about his mighty and wonderful works, inasmuch as they are mysteries and doubtless cannot be uttered or heard" (93.14–17).[16] Lalleman, who accepts Junod and Kaestli's hypothesis that chapters 94–102 and 109 were added to the text at a later point, interprets this sentence as the epilogue to an earlier version of the gospel narrative and calls attention to its similarity with the first epilogue of the Fourth Gospel:[17] "Now Jesus did many other signs in the presence of his disciples, which are not written in this book. But these are written so that you may come to believe that Jesus is the Messiah, the Son of God, and that through believing you may have life in his name" (John 20:30).[18]

Beyond the similarities in the overall structure of the *GAJ* and the Fourth Gospel, respectively, scholars have observed a number of shared lexical features.[19] The Hymn of Christ in *GAJ* 94–95 calls Christ by names that also occur in the Fourth Gospel, such as "word" and "light": Christ was "the word" and the life that was in him was "the light" according to the Johannine prologue (1:1–18); he is "the light of the world," according to one of the Johannine "I am" sayings (John

---

[15] Junod and Kaestli 1983, 480–481; Lalleman 1998, 112–113.
[16] Unless otherwise indicated, citations from the *Acts of John* are adapted from Elliott 1994, 310–338.
[17] Lalleman 1998, 113.
[18] Unless otherwise indicated, biblical citations are adapted from NRSV (1989).
[19] Kaestli 1987; Pervo 1992; Lalleman 1998, 114–116.

8:12, see below). Other expressions in the hymn are also characteristic of the language of the Fourth Gospel: "glory" is an important attribute of Jesus (e.g., John 1:11; 2:11; 17:5,22,24); he possesses "grace" (John 1:14,16,17) and "spirit" (e.g., John 7:39; 14:17,26; 20:22). Several lines of the hymn remind one of the form of the Johannine "I am" sayings (e.g., John 6:35; 8:12; 11:25; 15:1),[20] particularly the closing verses, "I am a lamp to you who see me. Amen. I am a mirror to you who perceive. Amen. I am a door to you who knock on me. Amen. I am a way to you, wayfarer. Amen." The attributes "door" and "way" are ones that occur in the respective Johannine sayings (John 10:9; 14:6). It has to be remarked, however, that whereas in the Fourth Gospel all "I am" sayings begin with the personal pronoun ἐγώ, this is not the case in the parallels of the *GAJ*. Furthermore, whereas the attributes in the Fourth Gospel always have the definite article (ἡ ὁδός, ἡ θύρα), they stand without an article in the *GAJ*. Other attributes from the "I am" sayings appear in the *GAJ* in Jesus' words to John on the Mount of Olives, especially in his explanation about the cross of light (from which Jesus talks to John):

> This cross of light is sometimes called the word by me for your sakes, sometimes mind, sometimes Jesus, sometimes Christ, sometimes *door* [John 10:9], sometimes *way* [John 14:6], sometimes *bread* [John 6:35], sometimes seed, sometimes *resurrection* [John 11:25], sometimes son, sometimes father, sometimes spirit, sometimes *life* [John 11:25, 14:6], sometimes *truth* [John 14:6], sometimes faith, sometimes grace. (*GAJ* 98.8–13)

A substantial verbatim parallel occurs in the transfiguration scene of the *GAJ*, when Jesus rebukes John with the words, "John, be not unbelieving but believing, and not inquisitive" (*GAJ* 90.16), the first part of the sentence (μὴ γίνου ἄπιστος ἀλλὰ πιστός) agreeing verbatim with Jesus' words to Thomas in John 20:27b. Another parallel is found in Jesus' words on the Mount of Olives, "John, to the multitude down below in Jerusalem I am being crucified, and pierced with lances and reeds, and gall and vinegar is given me to drink." The joint occurrence of "lance" (λόγχη) and "to pierce" (νύσσω) agrees with the Johannine crucifixion scene (John 19:34)—which is, however, not the only existing parallel.[21]

---

[20] Pervo 1992, 63.
[21] Lalleman 1998; Czachesz 2007b, 246.

Other similarities between the two texts include common themes and motifs without significant verbatim agreement. In the *GAJ*, John reports, "when I sat at table, he [Jesus] would take me upon his breast (ἐπὶ τὰ στήθη), and I held him" (*GAJ* 89.11). The corresponding passages of the Fourth Gospel mention a single event during the last supper: "One of the disciples, the one whom Jesus loved, was reclining on his breast (ἐν τῷ κόλπῳ)...So while resting on Jesus' breast (ἐπὶ τὸ στῆθος)..." (John 13:23,25). The theme recurs in John 21:20, where John is referred to as "the one who rested on Jesus' breast (ἐπὶ τὸ στῆθος) at the supper."[22] In the Hymn of Christ, Jesus says, "Who I am, you shall know when I go away," which parallels his words in John 8:28, "When you have lifted up the Son of Man, then you will realize that I am (he)" and John 13:7, "You do not know now what I am doing, but later you will understand." The *GAJ* mentions that Jesus loved John (φιλέω, 90.7), as does the Fourth Gospel (ἀγαπάω, John 13:23; 19:26; 20:2). "Light," as we have seen above, is a central theme of the Fourth Gospel,[23] and it becomes a leading motif of the *GAJ*, especially in the appearance of the cross of light (98–101). The idea that Christ "descended" from heaven, mentioned in *GAJ* 100.3, is paralleled in various Johannine passages (John 3:13,31; 6:62), as well as the claim "I am wholly with the Father and the Father with me" (*GAJ* 100.11–12; cf. John 10:38; 14:10–11; 17:21).[24] Finally, the *GAJ* mentions the hour of the crucifixion: "when he was hung upon the cross on Friday, at the sixth hour of the day" (97.6). According to Junod and Kaestli, as well as Lalleman,[25] this is an agreement with John 19:14–16, from where the information was also derived. Scholars have also identified further "allusions" and "echoes" in the two texts (such as the use of the verb χωρέω in *GAJ* 88.4 and John 21:25). However, the identification of such parallels is often quite subjective and is largely motivated by the fact that one already sees a particular relation between the two texts.[26]

---

[22] NRSV translates "next to Jesus/him" all three times.
[23] Bultmann 1948.
[24] Cf. Lalleman 1998, 116.
[25] Junod and Kaestli 1983, 655; Lalleman 1998, 116.
[26] Confirmation bias (Eysenck and Keane 2005, 470–480) is a significant factor that cannot be completely excluded from research. It means that we find it much easier to collect supporting evidence for an existing hypothesis (especially our own) than to identify contradictory evidence.

2. CHALLENGES TO THE PRESENT CONSENSUS

According to the consensus of recent scholarship, cited in the introduction, the similarities reviewed in the previous section resulted from
the use of the Fourth Gospel by the author(s) of the *GAJ* (in a written form or through oral transmission). The two texts were possibly
written and read by the same Johannine community[27] and/or the *GAJ*
criticized the theology of the Fourth Gospel, or at least the interpretation of the writing in a contemporary (proto-orthodox) Christian
circle.[28] My purpose in this section is to cite evidence that requires us
to reconsider the relationship of the two texts.

We begin with comments on some minor details. As we have seen
above, scholars have argued that the *GAJ* mentions the time of the
crucifixion, relying on John 19:14–16. Among the canonical gospels,
information about the hour of the crucifixion is only given in the
Gospel of Mark, where it is "the third hour" (Mark 15:22–26). In all
three synoptic gospels, the "sixth hour" is the time when the darkness over the whole land (or earth) begins (Matt 27:45; Mark 15:33;
Luke 23:44). According to the *Gospel of Peter* 15, darkness fell over
all of Judea at noon (ʾΗν δὲ μεσημβρία). The Fourth Gospel does not
mention the time of either of these events, but rather the time when
Pilate sentences Jesus to death, which takes place "about the sixth
hour" (John 19:14). Now, in the Greek text of the *GAJ*, the "the sixth
hour of the day" either indicates the beginning of the darkness, or the
time of the crucifixion *and* the beginning of the darkness. The word
order of the sentence seems to support the first option: "And when on
Friday he was hung upon the cross[,] at the sixth hour of the day darkness came over all the earth." Junod and Kaestli's as well as Lalleman's
reading is only plausible if we insert a comma before "darkness"—
but such interpunction marks were absent from ancient manuscripts.[29]
The darkness, in contrast, is not mentioned at all in the Fourth Gospel.
Consequently, this gospel agrees with the synoptics as well as with the

---

[27] E.g., Koester 1980, 635–637; Kaestli 1987, 46; Pervo 1992, 68; Lalleman 1998, 244–256.

[28] E.g., Pervo 1992, 68; Lalleman 1998, 122.

[29] Without having access to the only manuscript of the *GAJ*, I cannot determine if this fourteenth-century text contains a comma at this place—which, however, is not important for deciding the question of whether the ancient author borrowed from the Fourth Gospel.

Gospel of Peter 15 on the hour of the darkness, which it *perhaps* also identifies as the moment of the crucifixion.

Another detail that was assumed to have been borrowed from the Fourth Gospel is the mention of "piercing" and "lances" in *GAJ* 97.9. If we look at the whole sentence, we can identify more words that have to be taken into consideration when deciding about textual parallels and sources: "John, to the multitude down below in Jerusalem I am being crucified, and *pierced* with *lances* and *reeds*, and *gall* and *vinegar* is given me to drink." One or more of these motifs occur in various canonical and non-canonical passion narratives.[30] Among these parallels, the *Gospel of Peter* (9 and 16) mentions both piercing "with reed" (in singular) and drinking gall and vinegar, but does not mention "lance"; the Fourth Gospel mentions piercing "with lance" (in singular) and drinking vinegar, but lacks "reeds" and "gall" (John 19:34); Mark has "reed" (15:19) and "gall" (15:36) but none of the other words; Matthew mentions "gall" and "vinegar," but in two different episodes (27:34,48); Luke only mentions vinegar (23:36); finally, the *Epistle of Barnabas* has both vinegar and gall, in the same order as the *GAJ*. Interestingly, most early patristic sources agree with the *Gospel of Peter* rather than with the canonical gospels in respect to the order of drinking gall and vinegar.[31] This is a clear indication that we cannot easily decide which of these sources contains the oldest tradition, and therefore it is difficult to reach a conclusion with regard to who borrowed what from whom. Such diversity in the use of related expressions could be explained in the framework of oral transmission, a perspective that I have pursued elsewhere.[32] Given this general picture, the fact that "lance" is preserved only in the *GAJ* and the Fourth Gospel does not necessarily suggest direct borrowing by either of the authors.[33]

The mention of John leaning on Jesus' breast and the motif of the Beloved Disciple, both of which have parallels in the Fourth Gospel, belong to the major, overarching theme of the *GAJ*. In the *GAJ*, physical intimacy between John and Jesus is not limited to the last supper. "When I sat at table," John says, "he would take me upon his breast and

---

[30] Lalleman 1998, 129–130; Czachesz 2007b, 245–246.
[31] Lalleman 1998, 130n275.
[32] Czachesz 2007b; Czachesz 2009; Czachesz in press.
[33] Lalleman (1998, 130n278) in fact weakens his case when he cites his other observations about John 19 and the *GAJ* as supporting evidence.

I held him" (89.11–12). This habitual physical contact between John and Jesus becomes a source of knowledge about Jesus: "and sometimes his breast felt to me to be smooth and tender, and sometimes hard like stone" (89.12–14). The motif of physical touch occurs once more in the text: "Sometimes when I meant to touch him, I met a material (ὑλώδης, literally "woody") and solid (παχύς literally "thick") body; and at other times when I felt him, the substance was immaterial and bodiless and as if it were not existing at all" (93.1–4). As I have argued elsewhere, the theme of fondness and physical closeness between John and Jesus originates in the Platonic tradition.[34] In the *Symposium*, Socrates arrives for the dinner after waiting outside, deeply immersed in his thoughts. Agathon expresses his wish that Socrates would recline next to him: "Here you are, Socrates. Come and recline next to me; I want to share this great thought that has just struck you in the porch next door" (175c8–d2).[35] Socrates complies with Agathon's wish, reclines next to him and answers: "'My dear Agathon,' Socrates replied as he took his seat beside him, 'I only wish that wisdom were the kind of thing one could share by sitting next to someone—if it flowed, for instance, from the one that was full to the one that was empty, like the water in two cups finding its level through a piece of worsted'" (175d4–d7). In the famous Diotima speech (201d–212b), Socrates speaks about two different effects of Eros. Most people are "fertile in body," turn to women and raise a family, in the hope that they will secure immortality, a memory of themselves, and happiness. They who are "fertile in soul," in contrast, conceive and bear the things of the spirit. They look for beautiful souls, educate them, and procreate more beautiful and immortal children. Socrates then explains how the philosopher proceeds from devoting himself to the beauties of the body to the revelation of absolute beauty:

> And so, when his correct boy-loving has carried our candidate so far that he begins to catch sight of that beauty, he is almost within reach of the final revelation. And this is the way, the only way, he must approach, or be led toward the matters of love. Starting from individual beauties, the quest for the universal beauty must find him ever moving upwards, stepping from rung to rung—that is, from one to two, and from two to every lovely body, from bodily beauty to the beauty of institutions, from institutions to learning, and from learning in general to the special lore

---

[34] Czachesz 2006; Czachesz 2007a, 106–111.
[35] Translation adapted from Hamilton and Cairns 1985, 526–574.

that pertains to nothing but the beautiful itself—until at last he comes
to know what beauty is. (211b5–d1)

Later, Agathon's place next to Socrates is taken by Alcibiades, an exceptionally handsome young man, who earlier invited Socrates to his home
in the hope that he would sleep with him. Socrates explains that the
intimacy between master and disciple, which Agathon and Alcibiades
conceive in erotic terms, must be clean and spiritual. In sum, the relation between Socrates and his disciples in the *Symposium* is similar
to the relation of Jesus and John in the *GAJ*. While the *GAJ* is more
reserved in the use of erotic vocabulary, the overall theme of physical closeness and fondness between master and disciple is still clearly
recognizable. According to the teaching of the *Symposium*, such closeness and fondness provide an opportunity for learning. Furthermore,
according to the Diotima speech, the love of physical bodies is the
first step on the way to absolute beauty—an idea that is elaborated
in another section of the *Acts of John*.[36] What does this imply about
the parallels between the *GAJ* and the Fourth Gospel? In the Fourth
Gospel, the tradition that John is the "Beloved Disciple" is merely
reported as an epithet, without filling it with any content. The content
of this tradition, in turn, becomes clear from the *GAJ*. This leads to
the conclusion that the *GAJ*, rather than borrowing from the Fourth
Gospel, preserved an aspect of Johannine tradition that is only vaguely
recognizable in the Fourth Gospel.

In order to understand the significance of the knowledge that John
gains about Jesus through physical closeness, we have to turn to
another major theme of the *GAJ*, that is Jesus' ability to appear in different forms. This phenomenon has been discussed as the "polymorphy of Christ" in previous scholarship.[37] The calling of John and James
in the *GAJ* 88–89 contains various instances of polymorphy:

> And my brother said, "John, this child on the shore who called to us,
> what does he want?" And I said, "What child?" He replied, "The one
> who is beckoning to us." And I answered, "Because of our long watch
> that we kept at sea you are not seeing straight, brother James: but do
> you not see the man who stands there, fair and comely and of a cheer-
> ful countenance?" But he said to me, "Him I do not see, brother; but let

---

[36] *Acts of John* 113; cf. Czachesz 2006, 67–68; Czachesz 2007a, 111–115.
[37] Peterson 1959, 83–128; Stroumsa 1981; Junod 1982; Stroumsa 1992, 43–63;
Lalleman 1995; Lalleman 1998, 97-118; Garcia 1999; Czachesz 2007c, 127–146; Foster
2007.

us go and we shall see what it means."…And when we left the place, wishing to follow him again, he again appeared to me, bald-headed but with a thick and flowing beard; but to James he appeared as a youth whose beard was just starting. We were perplexed, both of us, as to the meaning of what we had seen.

Another important example of polymorphy occurs in *GAJ* 96–102, where people see Jesus dying on the cross on Golgotha, while he speaks to John from the cross of light on the Mount of Olives. What other passages of the *GAJ* qualify as cases of polymorphy depends on how one defines the concept. In the strictest sense, polymorphy means "a metamorphosis of such a kind that the person or deity can be seen differently by different people *at the same time*."[38] According to Lalleman, this has to be distinguished from "the wider concept of metamorphosis, in which a person…takes several forms *consecutively*."[39] Indeed, in the first example, John and James see Jesus in different forms simultaneously, and this motif recurs in *GAJ* 89. However, in the subsequent episodes, we can see no distinction between synchronic polymorphy and diachronic metamorphosis (that is, subsequent appearances in various forms). Immediately after the second parallel vision of John and James, we read John's report that Jesus' body was sometimes soft, but sometimes hard. In the same section, he recalls that Jesus' eyes were always open, and that he often saw him as a small figure looking upwards to the sky. At his transfiguration on the mountain, Jesus' head reaches to sky (90.13), but when John cries out with fear, Jesus turns around, becomes a small man and pulls John's beard (90.14–16). Reflecting on these events, John speaks about "his unity which has many faces" (πολυπρόσωπον ἑνότητα, 91.6). At (the lake of) Gennesaret (ch. 92), John sees "another one like him" who speaks to Jesus. In *GAJ* 93, we read about Jesus' body again, which felt sometimes solid, but at other times "immaterial and bodiless, as if it were not existing at all." Finally, in the crucifixion episode (chs. 97–102), Jesus is crucified on Golgotha *and* simultaneously appears to John on the cross of light on the Mount of Olives. Even if one can make a distinction between simultaneous and consecutive appearances, such a distinction was not important to the author of the *GAJ*, in which all of these instances

---

[38] Lalleman 1998, 99; emphasis by P. Lalleman.
[39] Lalleman 1998, 102; emphasis by P. Lalleman.

together form the theme of the "polymorphous Jesus."[40] From where did the author(s) of the *GAJ* take the concept of polymorphy? The polymorphy of Christ, according to Lalleman, was introduced first by the *Acts of John*, and the other Apocryphal Acts of the Apostles borrowed the concept from it. The *Acts of John*, in turn, relied on the canonical writings, including the transfiguration scene of Mark 9:2–8 (and its parallels) as well as the post-Easter appearances, particularly in Mark, Luke, and the Fourth Gospel (Mark 16:12; Luke 24; John 20).[41] However, there is one aspect of polymorphy in the Apocryphal Acts that almost certainly excludes this explanation, that is, the polymorphy of the evil. In *Acts of John* 70, the lover of Drusiana is "inflamed by the influence of the polymorphous Satan to the most ardent passions." In *Acts of Thomas* 44, the apostle calls the evil "the polymorphous one" (ὁ πολύμορφος)—referring to the two black demons that attacked the woman and her daughter on the street.[42] A similar story is found in the later *Martyrdom of Matthew*, where the apostle exorcises the king's wife, daughter and son-in-law, but the demon appears again as a soldier. In a number of other, later Acts and apocalyptic texts, Satan and the demons are capable of polymorphy.[43] Whereas the source of the idea of polymorphy in the Apocryphal Acts cannot be decided with absolute certainty, I will outline an alternative proposal.[44]

The most probable solution is that the authors were acquainted with the concept of polymorphy from Greek and Egyptian traditions and combined it with Christological ideas of their communities. Except for one debated occurrence, the noun "polymorphy" (πολυμορφία) does not appear before the fourth century CE, and then it is used mainly in Christian sources.[45] The adjective "polymorphous" (πολύμορφος), in contrast, has been in use since the fifth century BCE, in the meaning of

---

[40] Junod and Kaestli (1983, 466–493) analyze chs. 87-93 and 104–105 as a rhetorical unit, and speak about John's "twelve testimonies" of Jesus' polymorphy. I find the formal rhetorical analysis somewhat forced, but agree with the authors insofar as they do not reduce the theme of polymorphy to the simultaneous appearances.

[41] Lalleman 1995; Foster 2007, 67–77.

[42] Czachesz 2001; Czachesz 2007c, 35–65.

[43] For a list of these passages, see Junod and Kaestli 1983, 473–474n3.

[44] Cf. Czachesz 2007c, 127–146.

[45] Liddell, Scott and Jones 1996, 1140 and Supplement, 254; Thesaurus Linguae Graecae 2009. A possibly earlier occurrence is Pseudo-Longinus, *On the sublime* 39.3.8, dated between the first and third centuries CE.

"having many forms."[46] The mythographer Heraclitus, writing in the first century CE, mentions the "polymorphous Scylla."[47] Lucian, a contemporary of the major Apocryphal Acts, writes about the capacity of Eros to change Zeus into many forms (Δία πολύμορφον ... ἀλλάττειν).[48] Hippolytus of Rome (died in 235) writes about the "polymorphous Attis"[49] and quotes an invocation to "Gorgo, Mormo, Luna, and the Polymorphous One."[50] Which deity is meant by the latter is uncertain, but Horus might be a good candidate (see below). We have to add another Egyptian deity who is called "polymorphous" in Oxyrhynchus papyrus 1380, dating from the early second century CE. In this source, Isis is addressed as "polymorhous" and "of many names."[51] That the epithets in this invocation were permanently associated with Isis is demonstrated by a passage in Apuleius' *Metamorphoses* 11.5,[52] where the deity speaks to Lucius: "My divinity is one, worshipped by all the world under different forms (*multiformi specie*), with various rites, and by manifold names."

This brings us to an important aspect of the term "polymorphous" when used in connection with deities. Zeus, Attis and Isis were undoubtedly popular in the second century CE, worshipped in different forms across the Mediterranean basin.[53] The point is made explicit in *Metamorphoses* 11, where an extensive list is provided of the names under which Isis is worshipped in different countries. The cult of Attis or Cybele plays an important role in another chapter of *Metamorphoses*, where Lucius, in the form of an ass, carries her statue on his back.[54] But whereas Zeus/Jove invaded the Mediterranean basin with the spread of Hellenism and the Roman Empire, and his worship remained tied up with the religion of the state and with the public sphere, Cybele and Isis traveled without such infrastructure.[55] Judaism

---

[46] Hippocrates, *Airs, Waters, Places* 12.32; Aristotle, *Historia animalium* 606b.18; *Eudemian Ethics* 1239b11–12; etc.

[47] Heraclitus, *Allegories* 70.11.1 (date uncertain).

[48] Lucian, *Dialogs of the Gods* 20.1.4.

[49] Hippolytus, *Ref.* 5.9.9. Hippolytus' text may postdate the *Acts of John*, but his usage of polymorphy does not seem influenced by it.

[50] Hippolytus, *Ref.* 4.35.5.

[51] Cf. Lalleman 1995, 112.

[52] Junod 1982, 40; Garcia 1999, 22.

[53] It must be noted that Lucian, *Dialogs of the Gods* 20.1.4 refers to Zeus' adventures in different shapes rather than his worship in many forms.

[54] Apuleius, *Metamorphoses* 8.24–27.

[55] Nock 1933, especially pp. 77–98, "How Eastern Cults Travelled."

was also represented in many places, but its presence was tied up with the presence of the Jewish population. Cybele, Isis, Mithras and several other popular cults of the time relied on their psychological appeal rather than on migration, demographical factors, or political power as they traveled.[56]

In the light of these parallels, I suggest that Christ was called "polymorphous" based on the analogy of Attis and Isis. As Christianity crossed geographical, cultural, and social boundaries, the cult and its deity necessarily followed other popular religions in developing toward polymorphy. In early Christian art and literature, Christ could be identified with a number of well-known figures, such as Apollo, Asclepius, Dionysus, the eagle (bird of Zeus), Hercules, Helios and the shepherd (*kriophoros*).[57] The purpose and extent of identification varied across time and space. The quick spread of Christianity is probably responsible for the fact that Christ did not have a "proper" form. Thus, whereas Christ had many forms, he actually had none. This issue might already be addressed in various passages of the New Testament, where Jesus teaches that he is present in the form of children, the needy, the stranger, the sick, the prisoner, and the apostles.[58] Christ's ambiguous shape is signaled in the post-resurrection appearances, when his disciples fail to recognize him.[59] Finally, the same ambiguity is expressed in passages about Christ's return to earth: "And if anyone says to you at that time, 'Look! Here is the Messiah!' or 'Look! There he is'—do not believe it."[60] Such ambiguities about the appearance of Christ contributed to the formation of a particular image of the polymorphous Christ, one that is different from the polymorphous Isis, whose polymorphy rather consisted of swallowing up the forms of other goddesses. The polymorphy of Christ in the *GAJ* rather means the lack of a proper form, leaving the reader with ever shifting, elusive images.[61] In sum, the concept of polymorphy in the *GAJ* was not inspired by the transfiguration and post-resurrection narratives (such

---

[56] Nock 1933, especially pp. 77–98, "The Appeal of these Cults."

[57] Detschew 1950, 530; Cf. Herzog 1950, 798; Brettman 1985; Molinari 2000, 139; Rutgers 2000; Trombley 2001, 99–108; Czachesz 2004.

[58] Children: Mark 9:37; Matt 18:5; Luke 9:48. Needy, stranger, sick, prisoner: Matt 25:35–36,42–43; Apostles: Matt 10:40; Luke 10:16; John 13:20.

[59] Particularly in Luke 24:15–16,30–32; and John 20:14–16.

[60] Matt 24:23; Mark 13:21.

[61] The elusive shape of Christ was interpreted in terms of a negative theology (apophatism) at a later stage (see below).

as John 20) of the canonical gospels, but rather by the diversity of contemporary Christian worship as well as analogies in the religious context of the author's community.

Yet another general feature of the *GAJ* to be discussed in this context is its intriguing theory of miracles. The *GAJ* contains a series of miracles—in fact, apart from the ritual dance, it mainly focuses on miraculous episodes from Jesus' activity on earth. Most of these episodes, however, are quite different from the miracle stories known from other gospels. The central topic of most of these stories is Jesus' polymorphy (understood in a broad sense). The miracles culminate in the crucifixion episode, accompanied by the interpretation of the event that is related from the cross of light, according to which the Lord did not actually suffer any of the torments which people saw him suffer. The final miracle is Christ's ascent to heaven, which is not seen by anyone in the multitude (*GAJ* 102.1–3). As we have seen above, in the conclusion of the pre-Easter section, John says, "we must at the present keep silent about his mighty and wonderful work" (93.15–16). Since the *GAJ* in fact contains many miracles, this sentence can be interpreted only as an explanation of why some other miracles, known or heard of by the author, were not included in the gospel.

Whereas the majority of the miracles that are reported in *GAJ* are unknown from other gospels, there are three important exceptions: the transfiguration of Jesus (reported in two different versions in *GAJ* 90), the multiplication of bread (93.4–10) and the ascension (102.1–3). Neither the transfiguration of Jesus nor his ascension occurs in the Fourth Gospel. Among the three synoptic versions of the transfiguration scene, Luke's text probably comes closest to the *GAJ*, both containing the information that Jesus took the three disciples to the mountaintop to pray. The *GAJ* reports the ascension with the words, "When he had spoken to me these things and others which I know not how to say as he would have me, he was taken up (ἀνελήφθη), without any of the multitude having seen him." Among the different ascension episodes in the New Testament (Mark 16:19; Luke 24:51; Acts 1:9), the closest parallel is found in the long ending of Mark, "So then the Lord Jesus, *after he had spoken* to them, *was taken up* (ἀνελήμφθη) into heaven and sat down at the right hand of God" (Mark 16:19). The multiplication of bread is the only miracle that occurs in all four canonical gospels. It is remarkable, however, that the *GAJ*, in agreement with all three synoptic versions of the feeding of the five thousand (as well as with the story of the feeding of the four thousand in

Matthew and Mark) uses the verb χορτάζω when it mentions that everyone "was filled" (Mark 6:42; 8:8 parr.),[62] whereas the Fourth Gospel
uses ἐμπίπλημι to express this (John 6:12). Moreover, the *GAJ* sets the
miracle into the episode of a visit to the house of a Pharisee. This scene
has various synoptic parallels, yet the closest ones are found in the
Gospel of Luke.[63] In sum, among the miracles that occur in the Fourth
Gospel, but not in the synoptics, the *GAJ* mentions none, whereas it
does contain miracles (transfiguration and ascension) that occur only
in the synoptics but not in the Fourth Gospel. Finally, when it comes to
miracles found both in the synoptics and John, the account of the *GAJ*
contains no particular reference to the Fourth Gospel's version. The
way the multiplication of bread is presented in the *GAJ* suggests that
the author did not know the miracle stories of the Fourth Gospel.

The *GAJ*'s terminology of miracles also deserves attention. When
describing the unutterable character of Jesus' miracles, the *GAJ* refers
to them as "mighty and wonderful works," in Greek τὰ μεγαλεῖα καὶ
τὰ θαυμάσια (*GAJ* 93.15–16). This terminology is different from the
usage of the Fourth Gospel, which famously calls Jesus' miracles "signs"
(σημεῖα, e.g., John 2:11,23; 20:30), or "signs and wonders" (σημεῖα
καὶ τέρατα, John 4:48). This difference in terminology also challenges
the assumed parallel between the first epilogue of the Fourth Gospel
and the *GAJ*'s conclusion of Jesus' ministry, suggested by Lalleman
(see above). But where does the terminology of the *GAJ* come from?
Both μεγαλεῖα and θαυμάσια occur once in the New Testament, but
not in the Fourth Gospel: μεγαλεῖα is found in Acts 2:11, referring
to God's miracles, whereas θαυμάσια in Matt 21:15 refers to those
of Jesus. Both words occur frequently in the Septuagint, the epilogue
of Deuteronomy containing τὰ θαυμάσια τὰ μεγάλα (Deut 34:12)
next to σημεῖα καὶ τέρατα (34:11). We cannot decide with certainty
whether the *GAJ* created the phrase from earlier (separate) occurrences
of both words, borrowed it from the Septuagint,[64] or the combination
was already part of Christian usage.[65] We can conclude, however, that

---

[62] The exact form, however, is different: ἐχορτάσθησαν in all synoptic passages and
ἐχορτάζετο in *GAJ* 93.9.

[63] Luke 7:36; 11:37; cf. Czachesz 2007a, 103n54.

[64] Lalleman 1933 suggested a couple of Old Testament parallels in the *Acts of John*,
especially with the LXX *Book of Wisdom*. He proposed that such similarities stem
from the general use of Jewish vocabulary in Christian groups.

[65] Both *Acts of Thomas* 141.6–7 and Eusebius, *Hist. eccl.* 1.12 are later occurrences
of the expression.

the *GAJ* did not employ the usual designation of Jesus' miracles in the Fourth Gospel, including the epilogue of John 20:30, and therefore its author(s) probably did not borrow from the epilogue.

To sum up the findings of this section, we have seen that various features of the *GAJ* challenge the majority view that this gospel relied on the Fourth Gospel. In particular, we have shown that the polymorphic Christology of the *GAJ* does not originate in post-resurrection narratives. Furthermore, the theme of intimacy between Jesus and John, the Beloved Disciple, is an elaboration of Platonic traditions and creates a framework for the Christology of the gospel. The presentation of miracles in the *GAJ* also draws on sources other than the Fourth Gospel. Other earlier suggestions about "borrowings" in the crucifixion scene also proved questionable on closer scrutiny. A number of quite interesting parallels, however, remain between the two texts, which I will attempt to explain in the final part of this essay.

3. Proto-John: The Hypothesis of a Common Source Behind the *GAJ* and the Fourth Gospel

We can explain the similarities and differences between the *GAJ* and the Fourth Gospel if we hypothesize the existence of common tradition used by both authors. This tradition was probably accessible to the authors in the form of an oral gospel narrative. This gospel, which I will call Proto-John, was much closer to the present form of the *GAJ* than to the present form of the Fourth Gospel. We can now attempt a tentative reconstruction of the content of Proto-John.

In the previous section I have argued, first, that the themes of polymorphy and the Beloved Disciple in the *GAJ* did not originate in the Fourth Gospel or in other known gospels, and second, that the two themes are intertwined as parts of a larger Christological concept. In particular, the theme of the Beloved Disciple is more consistent in the *GAJ* than in the Fourth Gospel. I suggest that Proto-John featured the apostle John as the intimate disciple of Jesus, who learned about the true nature of Christ through their affectionate relationship. The narrative relied on Socratic tradition (particularly on Plato's *Symposium*) to characterize their relationship, and was not lacking in homoerotic connotations. The background of this tradition within Christianity was the major significance of shared meals, witnessed by the Pauline correspondence and other passages of the New Testament, as well as a whole range of non-canonical literature (including *Didache*, Ignatius and the Apocryphal Acts of the Apostles).[66] In contemporary Greek and Roman culture, private dinners, followed by symposia, traditionally served as the venues of intellectual life and provided important settings for sharing and discussing literature.[67] The occasions created by shared meals in early Christian communities probably served as important *Sitze im Leben* for the transmission of a great deal of literary tradition. Given the importance of the motif of meals in the whole gospel tradition, it would not be surprising if Proto-John reached back to the ideal type of Plato's *Symposium* to epitomize the figure of John and his special role as Jesus' Beloved Disciple.

Whereas the *GAJ* makes no mention of the last supper, as known from Paul or the canonical gospels, it is quite possible that tradition set the ritual dance and the Hymn of Christ (possibly combining more than one hymn) into the framework of a final meal shared by Jesus and his disciples. Greek and Roman symposia could include both songs and dance.[68] In Plato's *Symposium*, it is decided to compose encomia to Eros instead of proceeding with the usual songs (176e–178e). A Christian example of using such an opportunity to praise Christ is provided by *Acts of Thomas* 6–7, where the apostle sings the Hymn of the Bride in the framework of a symposium. In addition to being transmitted as part of a particular last-supper tradition, the Hymn of Christ could also have its *Sitz im Leben* in the meals of the Christians who composed it. That Christians practiced dance as part of their rituals is altogether feasible in light of contemporary analogies.[69] As we have seen above, the hymn of *GAJ* 94–96 mentions a number of Christ's attributes that are also known from the Fourth Gospel. The "I am" sayings that appear in a poetic form here have a different syntax in the Fourth Gospel: of the two versions, probably the uniform syntax of the sayings in the Fourth Gospel is secondary. Moreover, it is quite certain that the long discourses attached to these sayings in the Fourth Gospel are written compositions. I suggest, therefore, that the speeches of the Fourth Gospel containing the "I am" sayings offer written elaborations of elements of the original Hymn of Christ.

---

[66] Bolyki 1998.
[67] Starr 1987; Johnson 2000.
[68] Gross 1979; Binder 1998; Schmitt-Pantel 1998.
[69] Philo, *Contempl.* 83–85; Dio Chrysostomos, *Discourse* 12.33; cf. Klauck 2008, 33–34. For dance in Greco-Roman religions, see Shapiro, Giannotta, von den Hoff, Lesky et al. 2004.

The passion narrative of the *GAJ*, especially the accompanying teaching of Christ from the cross of light, is also a written composition in its present form. Given the Christological views of the preceding sections, it is likely that in an earlier, oral version, Jesus also ascended to heaven without undergoing death and resurrection. One can, in fact, omit the teaching from the cross of light (chs. 98–101) without interrupting the narrative sequence. In Proto-John, Christ could appear to John, who fled to the Mount of Olives, tell him he was not actually suffering as the crowd thought, and ascend to heaven.

How was Proto-John used by the author(s) of the Fourth Gospel? It is not possible to offer a theory of the composition of the whole gospel here. We can identify, however, the most important differences vis-à-vis the *GAJ*, which include the accommodation of its Christology to the Pauline and synoptic views and the integration of John's figure into the same line of tradition. The Fourth Gospel, like Proto-John, contains a great deal of tradition that is unknown from other sources, including a sequence of miracles called "signs," and a number of theological discourses presented as Jesus' speeches. The overall composition of the gospel is such that all of these unique traditions are eventually streamlined to fit into the Pauline tradition of death, resurrection and post-resurrection appearances as well as the synoptic picture of Jesus as a wandering prophet/philosopher and miracle worker. First, let us consider briefly how the Fourth Gospel accommodated the Christology of Proto-John to the Pauline and synoptic view. Three important attributes of Christ in Proto-John, that is, "word," "light," and "glory" become the leading motifs of the Johannine prologue (John 1:1–18). However, the prologue reframes these key terms in such a way that it leaves no doubt about the truly human nature of Jesus ("the word became flesh"), which was denied in Proto-John. Instead of reporting the miracles of Proto-John, which are strongly tied up with its peculiar Christology, the Fourth Gospel relies on the miracles ("signs") found in the so-called *Semeia source*.[70] Although these miracles are often missing from the synoptics, they are, most of the time, fully compatible with synoptic Christology. As we have noted, the transfiguration and ascension of Jesus are reported in Proto-John but not in the Fourth Gospel. This is understandable if we see

---

[70] Van Belle 1994. The existence of the Semeia source is not unanimously accepted by New Testament scholars, but this does not influence my hypothesis.

these episodes as expressions of Proto-Johannine Christology, which was mitigated by the author of the Fourth Gospel. Additionally, this might indicate that the author of the Fourth Gospel was not familiar with the texts of the Synoptic Gospels. The passion narrative reports the *real* suffering, death and resurrection of Jesus, notwithstanding the view of Proto-John. It has to be remarked that John 17 connects the motifs of suffering and glory in ways that are only implied by the Hymn of Christ (*GAJ* 96), where the interpretation of suffering is followed by the closing doxology of the hymn. Second, let us see how the figure of John was altered by the author of the Fourth Gospel. Whereas the themes of dining, love, physical contact and knowledge form a theological and philosophical unity in Proto-John, this particular epistemology and the exclusive position of the apostle is not maintained in the Fourth Gospel, where John's authority is balanced against that of Peter.[71] John is referred to as the Beloved Disciple, yet the exact nature of this "love" is not described. The homoerotic connotations that are evident in Proto-John are downplayed in the Fourth Gospel. This might also reflect the adaptation of a distinctively Greek tradition (with a positive view of certain forms of homosexuality) to a cultural milieu shaped by Jewish conventions (in which homosexuality was unacceptable). The calling of John and James, with its polymorphic theme, is not mentioned, but perhaps its elements are found in the post-Easter appearances of the Fourth Gospel.

Finally, how did the author(s) of the *GAJ* use the text of Proto-John? We cannot decide whether the *GAJ* in its present form existed independently of the *Acts of John*. We can, however, identify a few passages that were probably not in Proto-John but were added when the *GAJ* received its final shape. First, these sections include the references to the unutterable character of Jesus' words and deeds in 88.3–5 and 93.15–17. These passages reflect the philosophical and theological tradition of apophatism, in terms of which human language cannot grasp God, who can be known only through mystical experience.[72] Although parts of the *GAJ* lend themselves to such an interpretation (for example, John often gains knowledge about Jesus through mys-

---

[71] For an attempt to reconstruct the social dynamics behind the characters of John and Peter in the Fourth Gospel, see Theissen 1988; Theissen, Jaillet and Fink 1996, 209–226; and Theissen 1999, 357–358.

[72] Vollenweider 1985, 13–27; Farrow 1998; Widdicombe 2001. For a discussion of the *Acts of John* and apophatism, see Czachesz 2007a, 115–119.

tical experience rather than from words), it is certainly not true of the text as a whole: these interpretations are probably later additions. Second, the teaching from the cross of light, as mentioned above, is a piece of written composition that introduces a complex cosmological imagery, which is not otherwise mentioned in the *GAJ*. Previous scholarship identified a number of characteristically Gnostic themes in this section.[73] It is possible that the author of the *GAJ* wanted to criticize the treatment of Proto-John by the author(s) of the Fourth Gospel. The statements about Jesus' miracles could be directed against the Fourth Gospel's use of "signs": in the opinion of the *GAJ*'s author, these reports should not be included in the gospel narrative, because they cannot capture the unutterable character of Jesus' power. The teaching from the cross of light, in turn, criticizes the Fourth Gospel's use of Christ's attributes found in Proto-John, and reinterprets them in light of the final author's own (docetic) Christology.[74]

What can we say, in conclusion, about the date and provenance of Proto-John? Since it pre-dated the Fourth Gospel, we can provisionally date this gospel to the early second century.[75] The use of ἀρουβάτον as a word for Friday (*GAJ* 97.5) might provide a clue about the place of origin.[76] This evidence, however, does not necessarily point to Syrian Christianity in a strict sense, as suggested by Junod and Kaestli.[77] The word is a transcription of ערובתא, the term used for the day of preparation in Aramaic, except in the dialect of Jerusalem.[78] A Greek-speaking Christian community could have borrowed the word from Aramaic-speaking Jews in one of the multicultural cities of the eastern Mediterranean.[79] As far as the final revision of the *GAJ* is concerned, it could have taken place when the gospel was added to the *Acts of John*, which I earlier located in late second century Alexandria.[80]

---

[73] Luttikhuizen 1995, 133–147. For other opinions about the Gnostic character of chs. 87–105 and 109, see Lalleman 1998, 31–32, 52–61.

[74] In spite of the debates around this term, "docetic" is still the best designation that captures the "apparent" humanity of Christ in the text, Lalleman 1998, 204–212.

[75] I reject the view that the Rylands Papyrus 52 necessitates a first-century date for the Fourth Gospel and accept the conclusion of Nongbri (2005, 46) that the manuscript can be dated anywhere in the "later second and early third centuries."

[76] Hilgenfeld 1900; James 1910.

[77] Junod and Kaestli 1983, 631.

[78] Levy 1881, 2:241.

[79] Cf. Rabin 1976.

[80] Czachesz 2007a, 120–122, with references to alternative proposals.

BIBLIOGRAPHY

Binder, G., "Gastmahl: Rom," *Der Neue Pauly: Enzyklopädie der Antike*, H. Cancik, H. Schneider and A. Friedrich von Pauly, eds., Stuttgart: Metzler, 1998, 803–806.

Bolyki, J., *Jesu Tischgemeinschaften*, Tübingen: Mohr (Paul Siebeck), 1998.

Bonnet, M., R.A. Lipsius and C. Tischendorf, eds., *Passio Andreae. Ex actis Andreae. Martyria Andreae. Acta Andreae et Matthiae. Acta Petri et Andreae. Passio Bartholomaei. Acta Joannis. Martyrium Matthaei*, Acta apostolorum apocrypha 2/1, Leipzig: Mendelssohn, 1898.

Brettman, E.S., *Vaults of Memory: Jewish and Christian Imagery of the Catacombs of Rome: an Exhibition*, Boston: International Catacomb Society, 1985.

Bultmann, R., "Zur Geschichte der Lichtsymbolik im Altertum," *Philologus* 97 (1948), 1–36.

Corssen, P., *Monarchianische Prologe zu den vier Evangelien: ein Beitrag zur Geschichte des Kanons*, Leipzig: Hinrichs, 1896.

Czachesz, I., "The Bride of the Demon: Narrative Strategies of Self-Definition in the Acts of Thomas," *The Apocryphal Acts of Thomas*, J.N. Bremmer, ed., Studies on Early Christianity, Leuven: Peeters, 2001, 36–52.

—— "The Eagle on the Tree: A Homeric Motif in Early Christian and Jewish Literature," *Jerusalem, Alexandria, Rome: Studies in Ancient Cultural Interaction in Honour of A Hilhorst*, F.G. Martínez and G.P. Luttikhuizen, eds., Supplement to the Journal for the Study of Judaism 82, Leiden: Brill, 2004, 87–99.

—— "Eroticism and Epistemology in the Apocryphal Acts of John," *Nederlands Theologisch Tijdschrift* 60 (2006), 59–72.

—— *Commission Narratives: A Comparative Study of the Canonical and Apocryphal Acts*, Leuven: Peeters, 2007a.

—— "The Gospel of Peter and the Apocryphal Acts of the Apostles: Using Cognitive Science to Reconstruct Gospel Traditions," *Evangelium Nach Petrus*, T. Nicklas and T.J. Kraus, eds., Berlin: de Gruyter, 2007b, 245–261.

—— *The Grotesque Body in Early Christian Literature: Hell, Scatology, and Metamorphosis*, Habilitationsschrift, Ruprecht-Karls Universität Heidelberg, 2007c.

—— "Rewriting and Textual Fluidity in Antiquity: Exploring the Sociocultural and Psychological Context of Earliest Christian Literacy," *Myths, Martyrs, and Modernity: Studies in the History of Religions in Honour of Jan N. Bremmer*, J.H.F. Dijkstra, J.E.A. Kroesen and Y.B. Kuiper, eds., Leiden: Brill, 2009 [forthcoming].

—— "Passion and Martyrdom Traditions in the Apocryphal Acts of the Apostles," *Entwicklungen von Passions- und Auferstehungstraditionen im frühen Christentum*, A. Merkt and T. Nicklas, eds., Tübingen: Mohr Siebeck, in press.

Detschew, D., "Apollon," *Reallexikon für Antike und Christentum: Sachwörterbuch zur Auseinandersetzung des Christentums mit der antiken Welt*, T. Klauser, ed., Stuttgart: Hiersemann, 1950, 524–529.

Elliott, J.K., *The Apocryphal New Testament: A Collection of Apocryphal Christian Literature in an English Translation Based on M.R. James*, Oxford: Clarendon Press, 1994.

Eysenck, M.W. and M.T. Keane, *Cognitive Psychology: A Student's Handbook*, Hove: Psychology Press, ^{5}2005.

Farrow, D.B., "Apophatische Theologie," *Religion in Geschichte und Gegenwart: Handwörterbuch für Theologie und Religionswissenschaft*, H.-D. Betz, ed., Tübingen: Mohr Siebeck, 1998.

Foster, P., "Polymorphic Christology: Its Origins and Development in Early Christianity," *Journal of Theological Studies* 58 (2007), 66–99.

Garcia, H., "La polymorphie du Christ dans le christianisme ancien: Remarques sur quelques définitions et quelques enjeux," *Apocrypha* 10 (1999), 16–55.

Gross, W.H., "Symposium," *Der Kleine Pauly: Lexikon der Antike*, K. Ziegler, W. Sontheimer, H. Gärtner and A.F. von Pauly, eds., München: Deutscher Taschenbuch, 1979, 449–450.

Hamilton, E. and H. Cairns, *The Collected Dialogues of Plato Including the Letters*, Princeton: Princeton University Press, 1985.

Herzog, R., "Asklepios," *Reallexikon für Antike und Christentum: Sachwörterbuch zur Auseinandersetzung des Christentums mit der antiken Welt*, T. Klauser, ed., Stuttgart: Hiersemann, 1950, 759–799.

Hilgenfeld, A., "Der gnostische und der kanonische Johannes über das Leben Jesu," *Zeitschrift für wissenschaftliche Theologie* 43 (1900), 1–61.

James, M.R., *Apocrypha Anecdota 2*, Cambridge: Cambridge University Press, 1897.

—— "Notes on Apocrypha," *Journal of Theological Studies* 11 (1910), 288–291.

Johnson, W.A., "Toward a Sociology of Reading in Classical Antiquity," *The American Journal of Philology* 121 (2000), 593–627.

Junod, E., "Polymorphie du Dieu sauveur," *Gnosticisme et monde hellenistique*, J. Ries et al., eds., Louvain-La-Neuve: Universite Catholique de Louvain, 1982, 38–46.

Junod, E. and J.-D. Kaestli, *Acta Iohannis*, Turnhout: Brepols, 1983.

Kaestli, J.-D., "Le mystère de la croix de lumière et le johannisme: Actes de Jean Ch 94–102," *Foi et vie* 86 (1987), 35–46.

Klauck, H.-J., *The Apocryphal Acts of the Apostles: An Introduction*, Waco, Tex.: Baylor University Press, 2008.

Koester, H., *Einführung in das Neue Testament im Rahmen der Religionsgeschichte und Kulturgeschichte*, Berlin: de Gruyter, 1980.

Lalleman, P.J., "Polymorphy of Christ," *Apocryphal Acts of John*, J.N. Bremmer, ed., Kampen: Kok Pharos, 1995, 97–118.

—— *The Acts of John: A Two-Stage Initiation into Johannine Gnosticism*, Leuven: Peeters, 1998.

Levy, J., *Chaldäisches Wörterbuch über die Targumin und einen grossen Theil des Rabbinischen Schriftthums*, 2 vols., Leipzig: Baumgärtner, ³1881.

Liddell, H.G., R. Scott and H.S. Jones, *A Greek-English Lexicon with a Revised Supplement (1996)*, Oxford: Clarendon Press, 1996.

Luttikhuizen, G.P., "A Gnostic Reading of the Acts of John," *Apocryphal Acts of John*, J.N. Bremmer, ed., Kampen: Kok Pharos, 1995, 119–152.

Molinari, A.L., *The Acts of Peter and the Twelve Apostles (NHC 6.1): Allegory, Ascent, and Ministry in the Wake of the Decian Persecution*, Atlanta: Society of Biblical Literature, 2000.

Nock, A.D., *Conversion*, Oxford: Oxford University Press, 1933.

Nongbri, B., "The Use and Abuse of P[52]: Papyrological Pitfalls in the Dating of the Fourth Gospel," *Harvard Theological Review* 98 (2005), 23–48.

Pervo, R.I., "Johannine Trajectories in the Acts of John," *Apocrypha* 3 (1992), 47–68.

Peterson, E., *Frühkirche, Judentum und Gnosis: Studien und Untersuchungen*, Rome: Herder, 1959.

Rabin, C., "Hebrew and Aramaic in the First Century," *The Jewish People in the First Century: Historical Geography, Political History, Social, Cultural and Religious Life and Institutions*, S. Safrai, M. Stern, D. Flusser and W.C. van Unnik, eds., Assen: van Gorcum; Philadelphia: Fortress, 1976, 1007–1039.

Rutgers, L.V., *Subterranean Rome: In Search of the Roots of Christianity in the Catacombs of the Eternal City*, Leuven: Peeters, 2000.

Schmitt-Pantel, P., "Gastmahl: Griechenland," *Der Neue Pauly: Enzyklopädie Der Antike*, H. Cancik, H. Schneider and A.F. von Pauly, eds., Stuttgart: Metzler, 1998, 798–803.

Shapiro, H.A., K. Giannotta, R. von den Hoff, M. Lesky, et al., "Dance," *Thesaurus cultus et rituum antiquorum (ThesCRA), Vol. 2: Purification, Initiation, Heroization,*

Apotheosis, Banquet, Dance, Music, Cult Images, V. Lambrinoudakis and J. Balty, eds., Los Angeles: J. Paul Getty Museum, 2004, 299–343.

Starr, R.J., "The Circulation of Literary Texts in the Roman World," *The Classical Quarterly* 37 (1987), 213–223.

Stroumsa, G.A., "Polymorphie divine et transformations d'un mythologème: l'Apocryphon de Jean et ses sources," *Vigiliae Christianae* 35 (1981), 412–434.

—— *Savoir et salut: traditions juives et tentations dualistes dans le christianisme ancien*, Paris: Cerf, 1992.

Theissen, G., "Autoritätskonflikte in den johanneischen Gemeinden zum 'Sitz im Leben' des Johannesevangeliums," *Diakonia: aphieroma ste mneme Vasileiou Stogiannou*, V.P. Stogiannos, ed., Thessaloniki: Aristoteleio Panepistemio Thessalonikes, Epistemonike Epetrida Theologikes Scholes, 1988, 243–258.

—— *A Theory of Primitive Christian Religion*, London: SCM, 1999.

Theissen, G., I. Jaillet and A.L. Fink, *Histoire sociale du christianisme primitif: Jésus, Paul, Jean*, Geneva: Labor et Fides, 1996.

Thesaurus Linguae Graecae: http://stephanus.tlg.uci.edu, 2009.

Trombley, F.R., *Hellenic Religion and Christianization, c. 370–529*, Leiden: Brill, 2001.

van Belle, G., *The Signs Source in the Fourth Gospel: Historical Survey and Critical Evaluation of the Semeia Hypothesis*, Leuven: Peeters, 1994.

Vollenweider, S., *Neuplatonische und christliche Theologie bei Synesios von Kyrene*, Göttingen: Vandenhoeck & Ruprecht, 1985.

Widdicombe, P., "Justin Martyr's Apophaticism," *Studia Patristica XXXVI: Papers presented at the Thirteenth International Conference on Patristic Studies held in Oxford 1999*, M.F. Wiles et al., eds., Leuven: Peeters, 2001, 313–319.

WHOM DID JESUS LOVE MOST? BELOVED DISCIPLES IN JOHN AND OTHER GOSPELS

Marvin Meyer
Chapman University

Whom did Jesus love most? Once upon a time this question may have been answered with relative confidence and ease, and the typical answer to this question is displayed in much of Christian literature and art: Jesus loved the Beloved Disciple, specifically as presented in the Gospel of John. While the text of the Gospel of John certainly raises a number of questions about the figure of the Beloved Disciple—the disciple whom Jesus loved—in the gospel narrative, the traditional understanding has been that the Beloved Disciple may be none other than John son of Zebedee, taken to be the author of the Gospel of John. Leonardo DaVinci and many others in the history of Christian art thought so, and in DaVinci's "Last Supper" he paints a young John leaning on Jesus as his dear friend and confidant (compare John 13:23–25). In our day, in popular culture, Dan Brown in *The DaVinci Code* also assumes that this figure in the painting is the Beloved Disciple, though he suggests a dramatically different identity of who the person actually might be.

With careful and sometimes innovative study of the Gospel of John, especially in modern times, the complexities of the Gospel of John are becoming increasingly apparent and the identity of the Beloved Disciple is open for renewed discussion.[1] Furthermore, over the past several decades the discovery of new manuscripts, often in the sands of Egypt, has made available a number of previously unknown Christian texts that contribute to the discussion of the Beloved Disciple, or beloved disciples, in the early church. These manuscript discoveries include the (supposed) discovery of the *Secret Gospel of Mark* in the library of the Mar Saba Monastery; the discovery of Berlin Gnostic Codex 8502, perhaps deriving from Akhmim; the discovery of the Nag Hammadi library at the base of the Jabal al-Tarif in Upper Egypt; and the more recent discovery of Codex Tchacos, apparently from the

---

[1] Cf., for example, Schenke 1986; Meyer 2003; and Dunderberg 2006.

region of al-Minya. The study of these texts sheds new light on the quest for the Beloved Disciple, and now we seem to have before us more beloved disciples than we ever imagined before.

So who, according to early Christian sources, might be the follower Jesus loved most? In asking this question, I do not intend to address the broader issue of the role of love in accounts of the proclamation of Jesus or in descriptions of relationships among Jesus and the followers of Jesus. Nor do I seek to trace the widespread use of such words as ἀγαπητός or ⲙⲉⲣⲓⲧ for "loved" or "beloved" and related verbs and similar terms as they are applied to a variety of followers of Jesus as well as the students of other teachers in the world of Mediterranean antiquity. Rather, in this essay I survey the figures who are singled out in early Christian literature—much of which may be dated to the first two centuries CE or may contain traditions deriving from the first centuries—as those favored beyond others among the disciples of Jesus.[2]

1. The Youth Without a Name—or Lazarus

According to the Gospel of Mark, the earliest New Testament gospel, a certain obscure and unnamed νεανίσκος plays a minor role as a youth who wears a linen robe and nothing more and leaves it behind, and so goes streaking through the garden at the time of the arrest of Jesus (14:51–52). A νεανίσκος is also mentioned in the account of the events following the crucifixion, and this νεανίσκος (the same character?) is found in the tomb of Jesus, where he is wearing a white robe and proclaiming Jesus to the women (16:1–8). The latter figure of the νεανίσκος seems not to function as an angel, though Matthew apparently takes him as such (28:1–10) and Luke envisions two angelic men (24:1–11) at the tomb.

Since the announcement by Morton Smith of the discovery in the Judean desert, at the Mar Saba Monastery, of a letter of Clement of Alexandria with references to and quotations from a *Secret Gospel of Mark*, new data on a Markan νεανίσκος—or *the* Markan νεανίσκος— has been made accessible, though the controversy that has swirled

---

[2] The present essay builds on preliminary work in Meyer 2003, 135–148.

around the manuscript has cast a shadow over the discussion.[3] In the past few years two books have been published (Stephen Carlson, *The Gospel Hoax*; Peter Jeffery, *The Secret Gospel of Mark Unveiled*) that offer aggressive challenges to the honesty and integrity of Smith's work, and he has been charged with perpetuating a hoax and a fraud. Meanwhile, other scholars (particularly Scott G. Brown, and now also Allan J. Pantuck) have been busily involved in answering and refuting these charges, and the debate continues. For the sake of this essay, and in recognition of the distinguished career of Morton Smith, I here assume the authenticity of the Mar Saba letter of Clement as well as the *Secret Gospel of Mark*.

Two passages from the *Secret Gospel of Mark* are mentioned in the letter of Clement, and both describe activities of a νεανίσκος. The first fragment, to be placed, according to the letter of Clement, after Mark 10:34, reads as follows:

> And they come to Bethany. This woman whose brother had died was there. She came and knelt before Jesus and says to him, "Son of David, have mercy on me." But the disciples rebuked her. Then Jesus became angry and went with her into the garden where the tomb was. At once a loud voice was heard from the tomb, and Jesus went up and rolled the stone away from the door of the tomb. At once he went in where the youth (ὁ νεανίσκος) was. He reached out his hand, took him by the hand, and raised him up. The youth looked at Jesus and loved him, and he began to beg him to be with him. Then they left the tomb and went into the youth's house (εἰς τὴν οἰκίαν τοῦ νεανίσκου), for he was rich. Six days later Jesus told him what to do, and in the evening the youth (ὁ νεανίσκος) comes to him wearing a linen shroud over his naked body. He stayed with him that night, for Jesus was teaching him the mystery of the kingdom of God. And from there he got up and returned to the other side of the Jordan.[4]

The second, short fragment, to be placed after Mark 10:46a, reads as follows: "The sister of the youth whom Jesus loved (ἡ ἀδελφὴ τοῦ νεανίσκου ὃν ἠγάπα αὐτὸν ὁ Ἰησοῦς) was there, along with his mother and Salome, but Jesus did not receive them."

A case can be made, as I have tried to make such a case elsewhere, that the fragments of *Secret Mark*, if authentic, may reflect a version of

---

[3] On the *Secret Gospel of Mark*, cf. Smith 1973a; Smith 1973b; Smith 1982; Meyer 2003; S.G. Brown 2005.

[4] Unless otherwise indicated, all the translations of primary texts in this essay are my own.

the Gospel of Mark that precedes what we now call canonical Mark.[5] Further, it may be, as I have also argued, that the figure of the νεανίσκος in the Markan tradition (perhaps interpreted to include the story of the so-called rich young ruler, who had kept the commandments "from youth" [ἐκ νεότητος] and is loved by Jesus, according to Mark 10:17–22, the references to the νεανίσκος in the other Markan passages cited, and the fragments of *Secret Mark*) communicates a subplot on discipleship in the Markan tradition. According to the narrative of this subplot, a certain youth, a νεανίσκος, experiences the vicissitudes of discipleship, but he is there in the tomb of Jesus, identifying with Jesus and proclaiming his risen life, at the end of the gospel. He has no name, but he loves Jesus and in turn he is loved by Jesus; he is the unnamed youth "whom Jesus loved." He may function, if my argument is convincing, as a literary figure rather than an historical figure in the Gospel of Mark. The νεανίσκος, beloved of Jesus, is everyman, everywoman, who may hear the gospel, follow Jesus, and be loved.

The parallels between the story of the νεανίσκος in the Gospel of Mark (including the *Secret Gospel of Mark*) and the figure of Lazarus in the Gospel of John have been clear since the initial publication of the *Secret Gospel of Mark*, and from that time it has been suggested that the story of the Markan νεανίσκος preceded the story of the Johannine Beloved Disciple. Morton Smith himself concludes that "there can be no question that the story in the longer text of Mk. is more primitive in form than the story of Lazarus in Jn."[6] Some scholars concur with Smith, some do not. Features of the story of Lazarus in John 11 recall the account of the Markan νεανίσκος, especially from the fragments of *Secret Mark* in the letter of Clement, and Lazarus is said to be loved by Jesus in four passages in the Gospel of John: Lazarus is the one whom Jesus loved (ὃν φιλεῖς, 11:3); Jesus loved (ἠγάπα) Martha, her sister, and Lazarus (11:5); Jesus calls Lazarus our friend (or, our loved one, ὁ φίλος ἡμῶν, 11:11); and those who are around say of Jesus, "Look how he loved him" (ἴδε πῶς ἐφίλει αὐτόν, 11:36). Thus, it might be suggested that the literary figure of the νεανίσκος as a beloved disciple has been historicized as the beloved Lazarus in the Johannine tradition.

---

[5] Meyer 2003, 109–134.
[6] Smith 1973a, 156.

2. John, Maybe the Son of Zebedee, or Perhaps Judas Thomas, or Mary Magdalene

The place and identity of the Beloved Disciple in the Johannine tradition has been discussed by scholars in countless publications, and this is a prominent theme in the present volume. The textual situation concerning the Beloved Disciple in John is made complicated by the presence in the text of Lazarus, said to be loved in John 11, along with a certain unnamed disciple (or disciples?) said to be loved by Jesus, "another disciple," and still other figures. The Beloved Disciple is explicitly mentioned in four passages in the Gospel of John in addition to the Lazarus account.[7]

(1) In the Johannine account of the last supper, when Jesus announces that a disciple will betray him, Peter asks one of the disciples to find out who the betrayer might be, and that disciple addressed by Peter is identified as the Beloved Disciple:

> One of his disciples, whom Jesus loved (εἷς ἐκ τῶν μαθητῶν αὐτοῦ... ὃν ἠγάπα ὁ Ἰησοῦς), was reclining in the bosom of Jesus. Simon Peter beckons to him to ask who it might be of whom he speaks. Leaning thus on the breast of Jesus, he says to him, "Lord, who is it?" (13:23–25)

Jesus proceeds to give indication that Judas is the one who will betray him (13:26).

(2) According to the Johannine passion narrative, several women are standing by the cross, as are two others:

> Jesus, seeing his mother and the disciple whom he loved (τὸν μαθητὴν... ὃν ἠγάπα) standing near, says to his mother, "Woman, look, your son." Then he says to the disciple, "Look, your mother." And from that hour the disciple took her to his own house." (19:26–27)

We shall return to this passage below.

(3) According to John 20:1–2, after the crucifixion Mary Magdalene goes to the tomb of Jesus and discovers that the stone had been moved. The account continues, "So she runs and comes to Simon Peter and to the other disciple, whom Jesus loved (τὸν ἄλλον μαθητὴν ὃν ἐφίλει ὁ Ἰησοῦς), and says to them, 'They have taken the lord from the tomb, and we do not know where they have laid him'" (20:2). Peter and the

---

[7] On the Beloved Disciple in the Gospel of John in general, cf. R.E. Brown 1966; 1970, among numerous other studies.

other disciple (ὁ ἄλλος μαθητὴς, 20:3) run to the tomb, and while the
other disciple reaches the tomb before Peter (20:4), and looks inside,
he himself does not enter until Peter does so. "Then," it is said, "the
other disciple, who came to the tomb first, also entered, and he saw
and believed" (20:8).

(4) The final passage that refers to the Beloved Disciple occurs in the
epilogue to the Gospel of John (chapter 21). There it is maintained that
the risen Christ reveals himself to his disciples and discusses the topic
of love with Peter, and he makes mention of the Beloved Disciple. It is
the Beloved Disciple who initially recognizes Jesus according to John
21:7: "That disciple whom Jesus loved (ὁ μαθητὴς ἐκεῖνος ὃν ἠγάπα ὁ
Ἰησοῦς) says to Peter, 'It is the lord.'" Later, this Beloved Disciple is
linked to the one who is leaning on Jesus at the last supper:

> Peter, turning, sees the disciple whom Jesus loved (τὸν μαθητὴν ὃν ἠγάπα
> ὁ Ἰησοῦς) following, who also was leaning on his breast at the supper,
> and said, "Lord, who is it that is going to betray you?" Peter, seeing him,
> says to Jesus, "Lord, what about him?" Jesus says to him, "If I want him
> to remain until I come, what is that to you? As for you, follow me." So
> this saying spread to the brothers, that this disciple is not to die, but
> Jesus did not say to him that he was not to die, but rather, "If I want him
> to remain until I come, what is that to you?" (21:20–23)

Near the very end of the epilogue, the author or editor of the chapter writes that this Beloved Disciple is in fact the witness who stands
behind the Johannine tradition as an authority figure: "This is the disciple who bears witness concerning these things and who has written
these things, and we know that his witness is true" (21:24).

In his study of the Beloved Disciple traditions, Hans-Martin
Schenke is certainly correct when he observes, "The figure of the
Beloved Disciple is admittedly one of the great puzzles in the mysterious Fourth Gospel."[8] In the history of the scholarly study of the
Johannine Beloved Disciple, attempts have been made to connect the
Beloved Disciple with some historical figure—John son of Zebedee,
of course, and also John Mark, John the presbyter, Matthias, Paul,
Andrew, or some other disciple, including those mentioned here, or
else a Johannine character considered to be the authoritative witness
of the Gospel of John[9]—but Schenke doubts that the issue actually has
to do with any historical figure of a beloved disciple. Schenke surveys

---

[8] Schenke 1986, 114.
[9] Cf. Dunderberg 2006.

other figures who function as beloved disciples—a task we are under-taking here as well—and he concludes that "the Beloved Disciple pas-sages are only a simple fiction of the redactor." He states,

> Reference is made to the alleged Beloved Disciple in the same way as the Pastorals refer to Paul. The function of the Beloved Disciple is to ground the Fourth Gospel (and the tradition of the Christian group in which it originates and has its influence) in the eyewitness testimony of one who was especially intimate with Jesus. This kind of deception may find its explanation and, what is more, its justification, only within a particular historical situation of conflict. The circumstances, however, do not point to a conflict within the group, but rather to a confrontation with another Christian (Petrine) tradition.[10]

Of the other beloved disciples in early Christian literature, Schenke is most intrigued by Judas Thomas, and he proposes that it is Judas Thomas who, as a close disciple and beloved brother of Jesus in the Thomas literature, may have served as the prototype or "historical model" for the Beloved Disciple in the Gospel of John. There are prob-lems with Schenke's proposal, in my estimation, but his theory does address the prominent role of Thomas—doubting Thomas or Thomas the pious Syrian apostle—in the Johannine gospel and the Syrian liter-ary tradition. Further, another beloved brother of Jesus, James the Just, has also been proposed, now by Wilhelm Pratscher, as possibly also being connected to the figure of the Beloved Disciple in John.[11] We shall turn to James the Just as well below.

Esther de Boer, echoing some of the work of Ramon Jusino, pro-vides a different analysis of the Beloved Disciple passages in the Gospel of John and draws an entirely different conclusion.[12] According to de Boer, the best candidate for resolving the question of who the Beloved Disciple is in the Gospel of John must be Mary Magdalene. Though repressive elements of those opposed to the authority of female dis-cipleship may obscure the true role of Mary Magdalene in Johannine tradition, de Boer declares, a close reading of texts central for our understanding of the Beloved Disciple may elucidate who the Beloved Disciple and author of the Gospel of John truly is. For example, in the account of the mother of Jesus and the Beloved Disciple at the cross in John 19, Jesus addresses his mother as "woman," but he never

---

[10] Schenke 1986, 119.
[11] Pratscher 1987, as noted in Dunderberg 2006, 180–187.
[12] Jusino 1998; de Boer 2000.

addresses the Beloved Disciple with a gender-specific vocative. So, if
we read the passage with eyes sympathetic to de Boer's thesis, when
Jesus tells his mother to look at her son, he may mean that Mother
Mary should look at Jesus on the cross, and when he tells the Beloved
Disciple to look at Mary as mother, he may be inviting the Beloved
Disciple Mary Magdalene and Mary the mother of Jesus to find hope
and identity in each other. (The retention of the masculine possessive
pronoun in the phrase "his own house" could simply stem from the
gender of the word μαθητής, or it could reflect complexities in the
editing of the gospel.) As de Boer observes, "The ultimate importance
of the scene in 19:26–27 lies in Jesus' invitation to his mother to look
away from her dying son to find him, alive, in the disciple he loved."
On the basis of such analysis, de Boer sees wide-ranging and provoca-
tive consequences for the study of the Beloved Disciple and her likely
place in the early Christian movement:

> I conclude that Mary Magdalene should be seen as a serious candi-
> date for the identification of the anonymous disciple Jesus loved in the
> Gospel of John. If we indeed look upon her as an important candidate,
> this has consequences for our general perspective on Mary Magdalene.
> She would have had disciples, her testimony would have formed a com-
> munity, her accounts not only of the death and resurrection of Jesus, but
> also of his life and teachings, would have been preserved. But not only
> that, her words would have been canonized and taught through the ages,
> and spread over the world.[13]

3. Mary Magdalene, the Companion of Jesus, along with Her Beloved Friends

Beyond the Gospel of John and the other New Testament texts, the
figure of Mary Magdalene occupies a significant place as a disciple
and follower of Jesus, and she is designated as a disciple whom Jesus
loved more than the other women or the other disciples in a number of
texts. In some of these texts she is plainly understood to be a beloved
disciple.[14]

In the *Gospel of Mary*, the first text of Berlin Gnostic Codex 8502,
Mary (almost always identified by scholars as Mary Magdalene on the
basis of parallels elsewhere) is the central and most significant disci-

---

[13] De Boer 2000.

[14] On Mary Magdalene and the *Gospel of Mary*, cf. Haskins 1993; de Boer 2000;
Brock 2002; King 2003; de Boer 2004; Meyer 2004.

ple of Jesus on the extant pages of the gospel. When the disciples are weeping in grief, it is Mary who stands up, greets them, and offers words of insight and comfort about the savior Jesus: "Do not weep or grieve or be in doubt, for his grace will be with you all and will protect you. Rather, let us praise his greatness, for he has prepared us and made us truly human." The text continues, "When Mary said this, she turned their hearts to the good, and they began to discuss the words of the [savior]" (9). Peter then addresses Mary: "Sister, we know the savior loved you more than any other woman (ⲧⲥⲱⲛⲉ ⲧⲛ̄ⲥⲟⲟⲩⲛ ⲭⲉ ⲛⲉⲣⲉⲡⲥⲱ̄ⲣ ⲟⲩⲁⳉⲉ ⲛ̄ⲟⲩⲟ ⲡⲁⲣⲁ ⲡⲕⲉⲥⲉⲉⲡⲉ ⲛ̄ⲥ̄ϩⲓ̈ⲙⲉ). Tell us the words of the savior that you remember, which you know but we do not, because we have not heard them" (10). Mary responds to Peter by saying, "What is hidden from you I shall reveal to you," and she recounts a special vision of the master Jesus. Following the account of the vision (and a long lacuna), Andrew and Peter, brothers in anger and chauvinism, protest against Mary as a woman. Peter plays the gender card and says about Jesus, "Did he really speak with a woman in private, without our knowledge? Should we all turn and listen to her? Did he prefer her to us?" (17). Such hostility between Peter and Mary Magdalene is also attested in the *Gospel of Thomas* and the *Pistis Sophia*, and it may call to mind the tension between Peter and the Beloved Disciple in the Gospel of John. Eventually, in the *Gospel of Mary*, Levi opposes Peter and defends Mary, and he says, "Peter, you always are angry. Now I see you arguing against this woman like an adversary. If the savior made her worthy, who are you to reject her? Surely the savior knows her well. That is why he has loved her more than us" (ⲉⲧⲃⲉ ⲡⲁⲓ ⲁϥⲟⲩⲟⳉ̄ⲥ̄ ⲛ̄ϩⲟⲩⲟ ⲉⲣⲟⲛ, 18).

In the *Gospel of Philip*, from the Nag Hammadi library, Mary Magdalene is called the companion (ⲕⲟⲓⲛⲱⲛⲟⲥ, ϩⲱⲧⲣⲉ) of Jesus. On one occasion a meditation in the *Gospel of Philip* distinguishes among the three Marys: "Three women always walked with the master: Mary his mother, <his> sister (or, without emendation, her sister), and Mary Magdalene, who is called his companion (ⲧⲉϥⲕⲟⲓⲛⲱⲛⲟⲥ). For Mary is the name of his sister, his mother, and his companion" (ⲧⲉϥϩⲱⲧⲣⲉ, 59). Another time Mary Magdalene is described as the most beloved of the disciples:

> Wisdom, who is called barren, is the mother of the angels. The companion ([ⲧ]ⲕⲟⲓⲛⲱⲛⲟⲥ) of the [savior] is Mary Magdalene. The [savior loved] her more than [all] the disciples, [and he] kissed her often on her [mouth]. The other [disciples]...said to him, "Why do you love her more than all of us?" The savior answered and said to them, "Why do I

not love you like her? If a blind person and one who can see are both in
darkness, they are the same. When the light comes, one who can see will
see the light, and the blind person will stay in darkness." (63–64)

The restoration of lacunae in this passage may be accepted with a
considerable amount of confidence, except for the word "[mouth],"
[ⲧⲁⲡⲣⲟ], which may be restored variously.[15] The reference to kissing
can be interpreted variously, though in the *Gospel of Philip* a ritual kiss
with a spiritual intent may be most likely; note also may be taken of
the additional reference a few pages earlier in the *Gospel of Philip* ("The
perfect conceive and give birth through a kiss. That is why we also kiss
each other. We conceive from the grace within each other," 59).

Other texts likewise highlight the place of Mary Magdalene among
the disciples, though not always in the language of being a beloved disciple. In the *Dialogue of the Savior*, also from the Nag Hammadi library,
Mary is a major dialogue partner (along with the other disciples Judas
and Matthew) with Jesus, and after she utters words of wisdom reminiscent of sayings of Jesus, it is said, "She spoke this utterance as a woman
who understood everything (or, understood completely, 139)." In the
Pistis Sophia Jesus tells Mary that she is exalted above her brothers and
all women on earth, and though she is harshly opposed by Peter, she is
vindicated by Jesus. Jesus pronounces her blessed (ⲧⲙⲁⲕⲁⲣⲓⲁ, 17), and
announces that she is a pure, spiritual woman (or, pure, spiritual one
[feminine], ⲧⲉⲡⲛⲉⲩⲙⲁⲧⲓⲕⲏ ⲛ̄ϩⲓⲗⲓⲕⲣⲓⲛⲉⲥ, 87). At the same time, Jesus in
the *Pistis Sophia* also addresses some of Mary's fellow disciples, including Philip, John, Matthew, and James, as "beloved" (ⲡⲙⲉⲣⲓⲧ), and he
even calls the disciples as a group "my beloved" (ⲛⲁⲙⲉⲣⲁⲧⲉ). There is
enough love for all the disciples in the *Pistis Sophia*.

Lastly, in a song from the Manichaean Psalms of Heracleides in the
Manichaean Psalmbook, Mary is portrayed, poetically, in a scene fash-
ioned after the gently erotic account of Mary at the tomb of Jesus in
John 20:1–18, an account which itself recalls the depiction of a woman
seeking her lover in Song of Songs 3:1–5. In the Manichaean song Jesus
asks Mary to be his messenger, his apostle, the apostle to the apostles:

> Cast this sadness away
> and perform this service.
> Be my messenger to these lost orphans.
> Hurry, with joy, go to the eleven.

---

[15] Possibilities for restoration are suggested in Layton 1989, 1:168–169.

You will find them gathered on the bank of the Jordan.
The traitor convinced them to fish
as they did earlier,
and to lay down the nets
in which they caught people for life.

Jesus adds,

Use all your skill and knowledge
until you bring the sheep to the shepherd.

The song concludes,

Glory to Mary,
because she has listened to her master,
[she has] carried out his instructions
with joy in her whole heart.
[Glory and] triumph to the soul of blessed Mary (ⲧⲘⲁⲕⲁⲣ ⲚⲘⲁⲣⲓⲁ).[16]

4. JUDAS THOMAS THE TWIN

Among the texts that were produced in the rich Syrian heritage of
Thomas Christianity are the *Gospel of Thomas* and the *Book of Thomas*,
both from Codex II of the Nag Hammadi library, and these texts
present Judas Thomas, in contrast to the Johannine figure of doubting Thomas, as an intimate disciple who has few doubts. The *Gospel
of Thomas* refers to Thomas only twice within the text. At the opening
of the text, in the prologue, Thomas is named as the recorder of the
hidden sayings of Jesus and, by implication, the guarantor of the Jesus
tradition. The gospel opens, "These are the hidden sayings that the living Jesus spoke and Judas Thomas the Twin recorded." The designation
of Judas the Twin (in two languages: ⲑⲱⲘⲁⲥ, from Aramaic or Syriac,
and ⲇⲓⲇⲨⲘⲟⲥ, from Greek) rehearses the common preoccupation in
Syrian literature that Judas was the twin brother of Jesus. According
to the New Testament gospels, Jesus had a brother named Judas, and
the Syrian Christian heritage continues this tradition and adds that
Judas is the twin brother. This conviction that Judas is the twin of
Jesus is probably based at least in part on a deeper understanding of
the concept of the spiritual twin known, for example, from the Hymn

---

[16] On references to the beloved in the *Pistis Sophia* and the *Manichaean Psalmbook*,
cf. Meyer 2004, 64–73; and Dunderberg 2006, 180.

of the Pearl in the *Acts of Thomas*. Later in the *Gospel of Thomas*, in saying 13, Thomas is the one, and not Peter or Matthew, who seems to have the correct answer—or no-answer—to the question of Jesus about who he is and what he is like, and Jesus withdraws with Thomas and speaks three unspecified sayings or words to him. This puzzling statement may be intended to prompt a creative response in the reader, who may thereby be encouraged to take the place of Thomas and interact with Jesus and his wise sayings.[17]

The *Book of Thomas* is more overt in identifying Judas Thomas as the Beloved Disciple. The *Book of Thomas* presents sayings of Jesus in dialogue with Thomas as well as a monologue of Jesus. The text begins by referring to the *Book of Thomas* as hidden sayings of Jesus, as with the *Gospel of Thomas*, but in this case Judas Thomas is taken to be the partner in conversation with Jesus and a certain Mathaias is said to be the scribal recorder. Jesus (called the savior) addresses Judas Thomas as "brother Thomas" (ⲡⲥⲁⲛ ⲑⲱⲙⲁⲥ) and "my brother Thomas" (ⲡⲁⲥⲟⲛ ⲑⲱⲙⲁⲥ), and instructs him in wisdom. Jesus says,

> Since it is said that you are my twin (ⲡⲁⲥⲟⲉⲓϣ) and my true friend (ⲛⲁϣⲃⲣ̄ⲙ̄ⲙⲏⲉ), examine yourself and understand who you are, how you exist, and how you will come to be. Since you are to be called my brother (ⲡⲁⲥⲟ(ⲛ)), it is not fitting for you to be ignorant of yourself. (138)

Jesus notes that Judas Thomas may also be described as a person of knowledge, and he says, on Thomas and his quest for knowledge, "So while you are walking with me, though you do lack understanding, already you have obtained knowledge and you will be called one who knows himself" (138).

Hans-Martin Schenke has singled out the passage where Jesus says to Thomas, "You are my twin and my true friend," and he has given it special attention, on account of what he perceives to be its relevance for the tradition of the Beloved Disciple, even in the Gospel of John. Schenke translates the Coptic of this passage back into Greek (ignoring the reference to the twin) as σὺ εἶ...ὁ φίλος μου ὁ ἀληθινός, which he presents in Johannine syntax and style as σὺ εἶ ὃν φιλῶ ἀληθῶς (in the second person singular), or αὐτός ἐστιν ὃν ἐφίλει ἀληθῶς ὁ Ἰησοῦς, "he himself is the one whom Jesus truly loved" (in the third person

---

[17] On Thomas in the *Gospel of Thomas*, the *Book of Thomas*, and other literature, cf. Layton 1989; Meyer 1992; Patterson 1993; Valantasis 1997; Patterson, Robinson and Bethge 1998; Uro 1998; and DeConick 2006.

singular). This, naturally, compares well in Greek with the Johannine statements on the Beloved Disciple.[18]

We need not travel all the way along the path of the Beloved Disciple with Hans-Martin Schenke, however, to appreciate the fact that he has helped to highlight the status of Judas Thomas as a beloved disciple among some Christians in the world of Syrian Christianity.

5. James the Just, the Brother of Jesus—with Peter, and Those Who Are to Come

In *Gospel of Thomas* saying 12, James the Just, leader of the church in Jerusalem, is mentioned, and this brief reference may help us anticipate his more dominant place in texts of the Nag Hammadi codices and Codex Tchacos. In the *Gospel of Thomas* the question of community leadership is raised, and Jesus responds, with a nice Jewish or Jewish-Christian flair, in the attribution of honor due to James, "No matter where you have come from, you are to go to James the Just, for whose sake heaven and earth came into being." While this saying praises James the Just, the next saying (13), placed in juxtaposition to saying 12, seems to shift the focus of importance to Judas Thomas.

The historical person of James the Just was the brother of Jesus and the early leader of the Jerusalem church, as New Testament and early Christian sources indicate, and these factors provide the background for the accounts concerning James in the *Secret Book of James* and the *Revelations of James* (usually entitled the *First* and *Second Revelations of James*).[19] In the *Secret Book of James*, James is coupled with Peter as both are in a conversation with Jesus recorded in a book that, James writes, he composed in Hebrew. Both James and Peter are called beloved (ⲙ̄ⲙⲉⲣⲉⲧ) in the *Secret Book of James* (10), and Jesus says to them that if they do the father's will, "he will love you (plural; ϥⲛⲁⲙⲉⲣⲣⲉ ⲧⲏ̄ⲛⲉ), make you my equal, and consider you beloved (ⲙ[ⲡⲣⲉ]ⲓⲧ) through his forethought, and by your own choice" (5). James himself is made to reflect upon those who will come after, who will also be beloved, when he observes near the end of the text, after the apostles are sent out into

---

[18] Schenke 1986, 123.
[19] On James the Just and the literature on James, cf. Bernheim 1997; Painter 1997; Chilton and Evans 1999; Chilton and Neusner 2001; and Tabor 2006.

the world, "I myself went up to Jerusalem, praying that I might acquire a share with the beloved ones (ⲛ̄ⲙⲡⲣⲉ†) who are to appear" (16).

The *First Revelation of James* consists of a dialogue between Jesus and James on issues of death and a Gnostic understanding of mortality and immortality, with a short account of the martyrdom of James appended at the end. In this text Jesus addresses James as "my brother," as he addresses Judas Thomas in the *Book of Thomas*, but here in the Nag Hammadi version he indicates that their relationship is spiritual: "For not without reason have I called you my brother (ⲡⲁⲥⲟⲛ), though you are not physically my brother (ⲉⲛⲧⲟⲕ ⲡⲁⲥⲟⲛ ⲉⲣⲁⲓ ⲉⲛ̄ ⲟⲩⲁⲏ ⲁⲛ). I know you well. So when I give you a sign, pay attention and listen" (24). (The Codex Tchacos version of Jesus' remarks are as follows: "For not without reason are you called brother [ⲥⲟⲛ], though [you] are not physically a brother [ⲁⲗⲗⲁ ⲛ̄[ⲧⲕ̄] ⲟⲩⲥⲟⲛ ⲁⲛ ⲉⲛ ⲟⲩⲁⲏ]. But you are ignorant concerning yourself, so that [I] shall tell you who I am. Listen" [10].) Nearer the end of the text, James is described as he stops praying, embraces Jesus, and kisses him (31; in the Tchacos version Jesus embraces James, James says, and kisses him [19].)[20]

The *Second Revelation of James*, in which James discourses on Jesus and the nature of salvation, echoes somewhat similar sentiments, with a bit more language of the beloved. According to this text, too, as James recalls, Jesus had addressed James as "my brother" ("Hello, my brother; brother, hello"), and their mother had explained what Jesus meant. James states,

> As I raised my [head] to look at him (Jesus), mother said to me, "Don't be afraid, my son, because he said to you, 'My brother' (ⲡⲁⲥⲟⲛ). You were both nourished with the same milk. That is why he says to me, 'My mother.' He is not a stranger to us; he is your stepbrother (ⲡⲥⲟⲛ [ⲛ̄/ⲉⲁ]ⲡⲉⲕⲉⲓⲱⲧ ⲡⲉ). [I am] not..." (50)

Here the text is unclear, and the Coptic may be read as "he is the brother [of] your father" or "he is the brother [by way of] your father," and the meaning may be that Jesus is the stepbrother, the foster brother, or the cousin of James.[21] A few pages later in the *Second Revelation of James*,

---

[20] The translations of the *First* and *Second Revelations of James* from the Nag Hammadi library are by Wolf-Peter Funk, in Meyer 2007b, 321–342; the translation of *James* (the *First Revelation of James*) from Codex Tchacos, and the translation of the *Gospel of Judas* (below), are from Kasser, Meyer, Wurst and Gaudard 2007 and (in the case of the *Gospel of Judas*) Kasser, Meyer, Wurst and Gaudard 2008.
[21] Cf. the note from Wolf-Peter Funk in Meyer 2007b, 336.

James reports about the time that Jesus kissed him, as in the *First Revelation of James*, and called him beloved. The entire passage, put in the words of James, depicts James as the beloved spiritual brother and disciple of Jesus, and he comes to knowledge and embraces Jesus with what seems to be a spiritual embrace:

> He kissed me on the mouth and embraced me, saying, "My beloved (ⲡⲁⲙⲉⲣⲓⲧ)! Look, I shall reveal to you what the heavens have not known, nor their rulers…My beloved (ⲡⲁⲙⲉ[ⲣⲓⲧ]), understand and know these things, [that] you may come forth from this womb and be as I am. Look, I shall reveal to you what [is hidden]. Reach out your [hand] and embrace me." At once I reached out my [hands], but I did not find him as I thought he would be. After this I heard him say, "Understand, and embrace me." Then I understood, and I was afraid, yet I rejoiced with great joy. (56–57)

6. Judas Iscariot in the *Gospel of Judas*?

There is little love in the *Gospel of Judas*, and strictly speaking no real beloved disciple, unless the love and the beloved are lost in a lacuna. This text now known from Codex Tchacos features Judas Iscariot, though the precise interpretation of his role in the text is disputed among scholars. In any case, whether or not Judas is the prototypal disciple in the *Gospel of Judas*, he is not described as a beloved disciple. Perhaps like Peter in the Synoptic Gospels and particularly the Gospel of Matthew, Judas is the leading disciple in the *Gospel of Judas*, and he has the correct confession of who Jesus is. Like Peter, he too has issues and problems, and if Jesus can turn to Peter in Mark and Matthew and tell him, "Get behind me, Satan," he can refer to Judas in the *Gospel of Judas* as the "thirteenth daimon." Peter denies Jesus, Judas hands him over to the authorities, with similar language in the two instances. In time, Peter ends up in St. Peter's church in Rome and Judas is in the lowest circle of Dante's hell with Brutus and Cassius, yet in their respective texts they are the first among the disciples. But in spite of their prominence, neither one is specifically called a beloved disciple, though Peter has, we have seen, a brush with being beloved in the *Secret Book of James*. They are both awarded considerable status, but they are described in other terms than those of a loved disciple.[22]

---

[22] On Judas Iscariot and the *Gospel of Judas*, cf. Ehrman 2006; DeConick 2007; Kasser, Meyer, Wurst and Gaudard 2007; King and Pagels 2007; Meyer 2007a; Kasser,

Judas Iscariot in the *Gospel of Judas* is the one disciple among the twelve (or thirteen) who spends private time in dialogue with Jesus. The text opens with an incipit that places Judas in the company of Jesus, just before the time of the crucifixion: "The secret word of declaration by which Jesus spoke in conversation with Judas Iscariot, during eight days, three days before he celebrated Passover (or, three days before his passion, 33)." When the disciples assemble, they all have an incorrect profession of who Jesus is, except Judas, who correctly confesses, in Sethian Gnostic terms, that Jesus is the exalted child of the divine. Judas says, "I know who you are and where you have come from. You have come from the immortal aeon of Barbelo. And I am not worthy to utter the name of the one who has sent you" (35). Jesus recognizes "that he (Judas) was reflecting upon the rest (of the things) that are exalted," and so he takes him aside to teach him "the mysteries of the kingdom." Eventually Jesus provides Judas with a cosmological revelation of the creation of the universe and the career of the light of the divine, and that revelation, which dominates the central portion of the *Gospel of Judas*, contains much of the gnosis needed for salvation and enlightenment. Toward the end of the gospel, after Jesus predicts that Judas will sacrifice the man who bears him (the mortal body that the true, spiritual Jesus has been using), he says to Judas, "Look, you have been told everything. Lift up your eyes and look at the cloud and the light within it and the stars surrounding it. And the star that leads the way is your star" (57). The text then comes to a close, with unfortunate lacunae and an understated scene of Judas handing over the mortal body of Jesus to be crucified.

In his essay in the National Geographic edition of the *Gospel of Judas*, Rodolphe Kasser describes what he judges to be a probable reaction among some readers to the figure of Judas in the context of the other disciples in the gospel:

> We smile at the educational dialogues of the "Master" (Rabbi) with his disciples of limited spiritual intelligence, and even with the most gifted among them, the human hero of this "Gospel," Judas the misunderstood—whatever his weaknesses. We also have reasons to smile rather than to moan at the message previously lost to us, miraculously resuscitated, emerging today from its long silence.[23]

Meyer, Wurst and Gaudard 2008; and Scopello 2008. The parallels between Judas as the first of the disciples in the *Gospel of Judas* and Peter as the first of the disciples in the Synoptic Gospels (especially Matthew and Mark) merit further consideration.

[23] Kasser, Meyer, Wurst and Gaudard 2008, 78.

Judas may be seen, within the current discussion of the interpretation of the *Gospel of Judas*, as "most gifted," even something of a "human hero"—for Birger Pearson, "a tragic hero"[24]—in the text. Although he may not be described in the language of love used for a beloved disciple, he may be understood as the foremost of the disciples in the *Gospel of Judas*.

7. Who Is the Beloved Disciple, or Who Are the Beloved Disciples?

After encountering a plethora of beloved disciples in the Gospel of John and other early Christian texts, we come to the realization that the scholarly examination of the figure of the Beloved Disciple has become much more complicated and fascinating with the multiplication of beloved disciples in various gospels and other early Christian texts. The accounts we have surveyed bring forward their several champions as beloved disciples, and we may reasonably suggest that different authors, texts, and communities introduce competing claims about issues of discipleship in early Christian churches, and about the disciple Jesus loved. We may suppose that a given community might be inclined to propose that Jesus loved their favorite disciple most—"Jesus loved our disciple more than yours." Doubtless Hans-Martin Schenke is correct in observing that what is of interest here for the Gospel of John and by extension the other texts and traditions is less any particular historical identity for the disciples as beloved disciples, and much more the issue of the grounding of texts and traditions in what is taken to be authoritative figures professed to be especially close to Jesus. The accounts of beloved disciples in the several early Christian texts are also often intertwined with one another, and the continuities and conflicts in the accounts provide evidence for interaction among textual traditions as noted in the interlocking figures of beloved disciples. How accounts of beloved disciples may relate to one another and influence one another is a subject for subsequent studies on beloved disciples. What the plurality of beloved disciples does point to is the rich diversity of early Christianity seen in the figures of beloved disciples, and this awareness of diversity should govern future explorations of the beloved disciples in the world of the early church.

---

[24] Pearson 2007, 14.

Bibliography

Bernheim, P.-A., *James, Brother of Jesus*, J. Bowden, transl., London: SCM, 1997.

Brock, A.G., *Mary Magdalene, the First Apostle: The Struggle for Authority*, Harvard Theological Studies 51, Cambridge, Mass.: Harvard University Press, 2002.

Brown, R.E., *The Gospel According to John*, The Anchor Bible 29–29A, Garden City, N.Y.: Doubleday, 1966–1970.

Brown, S.G., *Mark's Other Gospel: Rethinking Morton Smith's Controversial Discovery*, Studies in Christianity and Judaism 15, Waterloo: Wilfrid Laurier University Press, 2005.

Carlson, S.C., *The Gospel Hoax: Morton Smith's Invention of Secret Mark*, Waco, Tex.: Baylor University Press, 2005.

Chilton, B. and C.A. Evans, eds., *James the Just and Christian Origins*, Novum Testamentum Supplements 98, Leiden: Brill, 1999.

Chilton, B. and J. Neusner, eds., *The Brother of Jesus: James the Just and His Mission*, Louisville, Ky: Westminster John Knox, 2001.

de Boer, E.A., "Mary Magdalene and the Disciple Jesus Loved," *Lectio Difficilior* 1, http://www.lectio.unibe.ch, 2000.

—— *The Gospel of Mary: Beyond a Gnostic and a Biblical Mary Magdalene*, London: T&T Clark, 2004.

DeConick, A.D., *The Original Gospel of Thomas in Translation, with a Commentary and New English Translation of the Complete Gospel*, Library of Biblical Studies 287, London: T&T Clark, 2006.

—— *The Thirteenth Apostle: What the Gospel of Judas Really Says*, London: Continuum, 2007.

Dunderberg, I., *The Beloved Disciple in Conflict? Revisiting the Gospels of John and Thomas*, Oxford: Oxford University Press, 2006.

Ehrman, B.D., *The Lost Gospel of Judas Iscariot*, Oxford: Oxford University Press, 2006.

Haskins, S., *Mary Magdalen: Myth and Metaphor*, New York: HarperCollins, 1993.

Jeffery, P., *The Secret Gospel of Mark Unveiled: Imagined Rituals of Sex, Death, and Madness in a Biblical Forgery*, New Haven: Yale University Press, 2006.

Jusino, R.K., "Mary Magdalene: Author of the Fourth Gospel?" http://www. BelovedDisciple.org, 1998.

Kasser, R., M. Meyer, G. Wurst and F. Gaudard, eds., *The Gospel of Judas, Together with the Letter of Peter to Philip, James, and a Book of Allogenes, from Codex Tchacos: Critical Edition*, Washington, D.C.: National Geographic, 2007.

—— *The Gospel of Judas*, Washington, D.C.: National Geographic, [2]2008.

King, K.L., *The Gospel of Mary of Magdala: Jesus and the First Woman Apostle*, Santa Rosa, Calif.: Polebridge, 2003.

King, K.L. and E.H. Pagels, *Reading Judas: The Gospel of Judas and the Shaping of Christianity*, New York: Viking, 2007.

Layton, B., ed., *Nag Hammadi Codex II,2–7, Together with XIII,2*, Brit. Lib. Or. 4926(1), and P. Oxy. 1, 654, 655*, 2 vols., Nag Hammadi Studies 20–21, Leiden: Brill, 1989.

Meyer, M., *The Gospel of Thomas: The Hidden Sayings of Jesus*, San Francisco: HarperSanFrancisco, 1992.

—— *Secret Gospels: Essays on Thomas and the Secret Gospel of Mark*, Harrisburg, Pa.: Trinity Press International, 2003.

—— *The Gospels of Mary: The Secret Tradition of Mary Magdalene, the Companion of Jesus*, San Francisco: HarperSanFrancisco, 2004.

—— *Judas: The Definitive Collection of Gospels and Legends about the Infamous Apostle of Jesus*, San Francisco: HarperOne, 2007a.

—— *The Nag Hammadi Scriptures: The International Edition*, San Francisco: Harper-One, 2007b.

Pagels, E.H., *Beyond Belief: The Secret Gospel of Thomas*, New York: Random House, 2003.

Painter, J., *Just James: The Brother of Jesus in History and Tradition*, Studies on Personalities of the New Testament, Columbia: University of South Carolina Press, 1997.

Pantuck, A.J. and S.G. Brown, "Morton Smith as M. Madiotes: Stephen Carlson's Attribution of *Secret Mark* to a Bald Swindler," *Journal for the Study of the Historical Jesus* 6 (2008), 106–125.

Patterson, S.J., *The Gospel of Thomas and Jesus*, Foundations and Facets, Santa Rosa, Calif.: Polebridge, 1993.

Patterson, S.J., J.M. Robinson and H.-G. Bethge, *The Fifth Gospel: The Gospel of Thomas Comes of Age*, Harrisburg, Pa.: Trinity Press International, 1998.

Pearson, B.A., "Judas Iscariot and the *Gospel of Judas*," Institute for Antiquity and Christianity Occasional Paper 51, Claremont: Institute for Antiquity and Christianity, 2007.

Pratscher, W., *Der Herrenbruder Jakobus und die Jakobustradition*, Forschungen zur Religion und Literatur des Alten und Neuen Testaments 139, Göttingen: Vandenhoeck & Ruprecht, 1987.

Schenke, H.-M., "The Function and Background of the Beloved Disciple in the Gospel of John," *Nag Hammadi, Gnosticism, and Early Christianity*, C.W. Hedrick and R. Hodgson, Jr., eds., Peabody, Mass.: Hendrickson, 1986, 115–125.

Scopello, M., ed., *The Gospel of Judas in Context: Proceedings of the First International Conference on the Gospel of Judas Paris, Sorbonne, October 27th–28th, 2006*, Nag Hammadi and Manichaean Studies 62, Leiden: Brill, 2008.

Smith, M., *Clement of Alexandria and a Secret Gospel of Mark*, Cambridge, Mass.: Harvard University Press, 1973a.

—— *The Secret Gospel: The Discovery and Interpretation of the Secret Gospel According to Mark*, New York: Harper & Row, 1973b.

—— "Clement of Alexandria and Secret Mark: The Score at the End of the First Decade," *Harvard Theological Review* 75 (1982), 449–461.

Tabor, J.D., *The Jesus Dynasty: The Hidden History of Jesus, His Royal Family, and the Birth of Christianity*, New York: Simon & Schuster, 2006.

Uro, R., ed., *Thomas at the Crossroads: Essays on the Gospel of Thomas*, Studies of the New Testament and Its World, Edinburgh: T&T Clark, 1998.

Valantasis, R., *The Gospel of Thomas*, New Testament Readings, London: Routledge, 1997.

THE *TRIMORPHIC PROTENNOIA* (NHC XIII,1) AND THE JOHANNINE PROLOGUE: A RECONSIDERATION

Paul-Hubert Poirier
Université Laval

The treatise bearing the postscripted title *Trimorphic Protennoia* (ⲡⲣⲱⲧⲉⲛⲛⲟⲓⲁ ⲧⲣⲓⲙⲟⲣⲫⲟⲥ = πρωτέννοια τρίμορφος), or the *Three Forms of First Thought*, is one of forty-six (or fifty-two if the doublets are taken into account) found in the collection of Coptic papyri discovered at Nag Hammadi, Upper Egypt, in December 1945.[1] Attested to by a single manuscript, the *Trimorphic Protennoia* is manifestly a translation of a lost Greek original. The treatise is the first of two texts which have survived in what remains of Codex XIII of the Nag Hammadi collection. It consists of eight non-folioed and non-numbered leaves, making a total of sixteen written pages of 33–37 lines per page. These leaves are relatively well preserved, apart from the lacunae which affect, to varying degrees, the tops or bottoms of most of the folios.

Before delving directly into the topic of this essay, it may be useful to introduce the treatise itself and to say a few words about its literary character and historical status. The text of the *Trimorphic Protennoia* is divided into three sections, each of them clearly identified by a separate subtitle: "The Discourse of the Protennoia" (42,3); "On Fate" (46,4); "The Discourse of the Manifestation" (50,21). As regards its literary form, the *Trimorphic Protennoia* is essentially a lengthy proclamation by a feminine entity who, using the well-known ἐγώ εἰμι formula, introduces herself at the very beginning of the text as the *prōtennoia*, the "First Thought." In this, the *Trimorphic Protennoia* resembles two other Nag Hammadi texts, namely, *The Thunder: Perfect Mind* (NHC

---

[1] Editions and translations of the treatise: Janssens 1974; Schenke 1974; Janssens 1977; Schenke 1984; Layton 1987, 86–100; Turner 1990; Schenke-Robinson 2003; Poirier 2006; Poirier 2007. For an introduction to and a detailed commentary on the treatise, see Poirier 2006.

VI,2),[2] and the final hymn of the long version of the *Secret Book* (or *Apocryphon*) *of John* (NHC II,1 and IV,1).[3]

The sometimes explicit parallels between our treatise and other Gnostic texts from the Nag Hammadi corpus show that the figure of Protennoia belongs to a wider tradition best represented by the *Secret Book of John*. In fact, this "First Thought," or first emanation, from the Invisible One (*Trim. Prot.* 35,8–9) or the Father (38,8–9), is the second highest principle of the supreme divine hierarchy and should be identified with the power whose emergence from the paternal aeon is described in the *Secret Book* (II 4,10–29; and BG 26,6–27,8, for the short version) and which Gnostic mythology identifies as Barbelo. The *Trimorphic Protennoia* offers a hymnic and poetic account of the manifestation, in three successive stages, of the Invisible Father's First Thought. A complex work, the *Trimorphic Protennoia* makes use of a variety of diverse materials in order to paint a portrait of Protennoia-Barbelo. But, as has been repeatedly observed since 1973, the source to which the text is most indebted is clearly the *Secret Book of John*.[4]

Although even a cursory comparison of the two writings reveals numerous points of contact, the most striking resemblance is to be found when the *Trimorphic Protennoia* is compared to the final hymn of the long version of the *Secret Book of John* (II 30,11–31,27). The *Trimorphic Protennoia* is indeed a reworking, in the form of a revelatory discourse, of the final hymn, combined with other traditions, such as the *descensus ad inferos*.[5] The unknown author of the treatise developed the hymn in two ways: first, by combining its three-part structure with the triad of Father, Mother and Son borrowed from the *Secret Book* itself, and, second, by using the triad of sound (ϩⲣⲟⲟⲩ/φθόγγος), voice (ⲥⲙⲏ/φωνή) and word (ⲗⲟⲅⲟⲥ/λόγος), borrowed from speculations of contemporary logicians and grammarians.[6] By identifying the Son with the Word, the author was able to engage in a polemical reinterpretation of the Johannine prologue, an element not found in the final hymn. We will say more about this later.

---

[2] Ed. and transl. MacRae 1979; and Poirier 1995.

[3] II 30,11–31,27; IV 46,23–49,8, ed. Waldstein and Wisse 1995, 169–175; on the final hymn, see Waldstein 1995; and Painchaud and Barc 1999.

[4] Berliner Arbeitskreis für Koptisch-Gnostische Schriften 1973, 74.

[5] Cf. Poirier 1983; and Poirier 2006, 113–115.

[6] See Poirier 2006, 105–113.

The comparison of the structure of the *Trimorphic Protennoia* with that of the final hymn of the long version of the *Secret Book of John* reveals a structure that is at once simple and complex; simple in terms of the tripartite organisation of the text into three parts related to the triple manifestation of Protennoia, and complex, in that it frequently reformulates and develops the original text in such a way as to disrupt the overall balance achieved in the original. This becomes evident in the first person plural passages (*Trim. Prot.* 36,33–37,3 and 42,22–23) and in the presentation of three descents which, strictly speaking, do not line up well with the treatise's three discourses.[7]

This situation is best explained by the way in which the treatise was composed, that is, on the basis of the long version of the *Secret Book of John*'s final hymn, in combination with references to the myth of the *Secret Book* and other material borrowed from other Gnostic or contemporary sources. Another explanation of the composition of the treatise has, however, been advanced by John D. Turner which presupposes a more or less intricate redactional history. Turner's hypothesis is that the *Trimorphic Protennoia* was originally based on a three-part first person singular aretalogy, to which three successive layers were added: doctrinal passages, explicitly baptismal passages, and Christological passages.[8] While such an explanation is theoretically possible, though unprovable, it does not account for the fact that the *Trimorphic Protennoia* displays, from start to finish, thematic and stylistic influences traceable to the *Secret Book of John*. In addition to the rewriting of the final hymn, this influence is most clearly visible in the *Trimorphic Protennoia*'s frequent use of the explanatory clause ⲉⲧⲉ ⲡⲁⲓ̈ ⲡⲉ, which means "that is." Appearing no less than twenty-one times, the phrase is used to underscore the most significant elements of the text's message.[9] Usually such relatives introduce glosses or terminological equivalents, generally considered to be additions or secondary elements. This is clearly not the case in the *Trimorphic Protennoia*. In the long version (NHC II and IV) of the *Secret Book of John*, no less than thirty clauses introduced by this explanatory relative are to be found. Moreover, four of the relative clauses found in the *Trimorphic Protennoia* have exact parallels in the wording of the

---

[7] Poirier 2006, 13–20.

[8] Turner 1986, 63–71, 74; Turner 1990, 375–384; Turner 2001, 142–151; Turner 2005, 405–412; and Turner's essay in this volume.

[9] On this, see Poirier 2006, 73–78.

long version of the *Secret Book*. Clearly, this stylistic and hermeneutical device is a common characteristic of both the long version of the *Secret Book* and *Trimorphic Protennoia*.

The sheer number of explanatory clauses in both texts, as well as the fact that four of them are identical, suggests a link between the two treatises: either one copied the other or both depend on a common source. Without ruling out the second hypothesis, it appears more likely that one of the texts depends upon the other; namely that the *Trimorphic Protennoia* depends on the *Secret Book*. In support of this conclusion, we can adduce the aforementioned use and development of the *Secret Book*'s final hymn, the presence throughout the *Trimorphic Protennoia* of mythological themes and cosmogonic or anthropogonic episodes drawn from the *Secret Book*, and the fact that the explanatory relatives are better suited to a didactic writing such as the *Secret Book* than to a hymnic composition such as the *Trimorphic Protennoia*. Even though other similarities between this treatise and the long version of the *Secret Book* exist, those already mentioned will suffice to establish a literary relationship between the *Trimorphic Protennoia* and the *Secret Book*, and more precisely to demonstrate that the former seems to be dependant on the latter. The author of the *Trimorphic Protennoia* appropriated the final hymn of the long version of the *Secret Book* and rewrote it, integrating various elements from the *Secret Book*, although in an allusive manner that presupposes the reader's familiarity with the myth. Therefore, the *Trimorphic Protennoia*'s composition and redaction are later than the composition and redaction of the long version of the *Secret Book of John*, on which it obviously depends. The treatise must have been composed in an environment where the *Secret Book* and related works were being read and commented upon, towards the end of the second century at the earliest.

We turn now to the main subject of this essay. The first translators and commentators of the treatise had already remarked the relationship between the *Trimorphic Protennoia* and the Jewish and Christian scriptures.[10] In particular, it was the "stupendous parallels"[11] observed between the Johannine prologue and the third discourse of the Protennoia which first attracted the attention of scholars, as well

---

[10] For an inventory, see Poirier 2006, 85–98.
[11] Colpe 1974, 122: "…die stupenden 'Parallelen' zum Prolog des Johannes-Evangeliums."

as the conclusion drawn from those parallels, namely, that "both texts interpret each other, but it seems at first glance that the light falls more from *Protennoia* onto the Johannine prologue than the reverse."[12] This affirmation has given rise to a heated debate, the history of which we have charted elsewhere.[13] Several lists of parallels between our treatise and the prologue have been drawn up,[14] but in order to facilitate the comparison here, it will be useful to provide our own list, beginning with parallels between the *Trimorphic Protennoia* and certain verses from the prologue, before moving on to a presentation of parallels following the order in which they appear in the treatise. There are actually two ways of evaluating the relevance of those parallels, element by element (for example, the parallel between John 1:14 and *Trim. Prot.* 47,14–15) or considering their order of appearance, in the *Trimorphic Protennoia* or in the prologue.[15]

Prologue → Trimorphic Protennoia

John 1:1 Ἐν ἀρχῇ ἦν ὁ λόγος, καὶ ὁ λόγος ἦν πρὸς τὸν θεόν, καὶ θεὸς ἦν ὁ λόγος	35,33–34 "Existing f[rom the beginning]"
	37,4–5 "That is, the Logos"
	47,15 "Being Logos"
	46,5–7 "I am the [Log]os who is [in the] ineffable [Light], [be]ing in immaculate [...]"
	46,14–15 "I alone am the word, ineffable, immaculate, immeasurable, inconceivable"
John 1:4 ἐν αὐτῷ ζωὴ ἦν	35,12–13 "I am the life of my Epinoia"
John 1:5 τὸ φῶς ἐν τῇ σκοτίᾳ φαίνει	36,5 "[I] shone [down upon the] darkness"
	37,13–14 "And those who are in the darkness, he manifested himself to them"
John 1:6 ἀπεσταλμένος	46,31–32 "Who was sent"

---

[12] Schenke 1974, 733 (transl., Robinson 1981, 650).
[13] Poirier 2006, 83n180.
[14] Compare those of Colpe 1974, 123; Janssens 1977; Evans 1980–1981, 397; and Evans 1993, 50–53.
[15] The English translation of the passages of the *Trimorphic Protennoia* cited in this essay are based on my own edition and French translation (Poirier 2006), with consultation of those by Layton (1987) and Turner (1990).

John 1:9 ῏Ην τὸ φῶς τὸ ἀληθινόν, ὃ φωτίζει — 37,7-8 "Who is a light"

46,32-33 "To illumine those who are in the dar[kn]ess"

47,28-29 "[I] am the light that illumine the all"

John 1:10 ὁ κόσμος δι᾽ αὐτοῦ ἐγένετο — 47,24-26 "[Although] it is I who work in them, but [they thought] that it was by [them] that the All had been created"

John 1:10 ὁ κόσμος αὐτὸν οὐκ ἔγνω — 47,18-19 "And [they] did not know the one who gives me power"

47,24 "None of them knew me"

50,15 "And they did not know me"

John 1:14 ὁ λόγος σάρξ…ἐσκήνωσεν ἐν ἡμῖν — 47,14-15 "I manifested myself to them [in] their tents"

John 1:18 μονογενὴς θεός — 38,23 "God who alone came to existence"

39,6 "God who was begotten"

39,12-13 "The perfect Son, the God who was begotten"

John 1:18 ἐκεῖνος ἐξηγήσατο — 37,18-20 "And the inexplicable teachings he taught them to all those who became Sons of the light"

Trimorphic Protennoia → Prologue

35,12-13 "I am the life of my Epinoia" — John 1:4 ἐν αὐτῷ ζωὴ ἦν

35,33-34 "Existing f[rom the beginning]" — John 1:1 Ἐν ἀρχῇ ἦν…

36,5 "[I] shone [down upon the] darkness" — John 1:5 τὸ φῶς ἐν τῇ σκοτίᾳ φαίνει

37,4-5 "That is, the Logos" — John 1:1 Ἐν ἀρχῇ ἦν ὁ λόγος, καὶ ὁ λόγος ἦν πρὸς τὸν θεόν, καὶ θεὸς ἦν ὁ λόγος

37,7-8 "Who is a light" — John 1:9 ῏Ην τὸ φῶς τὸ ἀληθινόν, ὃ φωτίζει

37,13-14 "And those who are in the darkness, he manifested himself to them" — John 1:5 τὸ φῶς ἐν τῇ σκοτίᾳ φαίνει

37,18-20 "And the inexplicable teachings he taught them to all those who became Sons of the light" — John 1:18 ἐκεῖνος ἐξηγήσατο

38,23 "God who alone came to existence" — John 1:18 μονογενὴς θεός

39,6 "God who was begotten" — John 1:18 μονογενὴς θεός

39,12-13 "The perfect Son, the God who was begotten" — John 1:18 μονογενὴς θεός

46,5-7 "I am the [Log]os who is [in the] ineffable [Light], [be]ing in immaculate [...]"

John 1:1 Ἐν ἀρχῇ ἦν ὁ λόγος, καὶ ὁ λόγος ἦν πρὸς τὸν θεόν, καὶ θεὸς ἦν ὁ λόγος

46,14-15 "I alone am the word, ineffable, immaculate, immeasurable, inconceivable"

John 1:1 Ἐν ἀρχῇ ἦν ὁ λόγος, καὶ ὁ λόγος ἦν πρὸς τὸν θεόν, καὶ θεὸς ἦν ὁ λόγος

46,31-32 "Who was sent"

John 1:6 ἀπεσταλμένος

46,32-33 "To illumine those who are in the dar[kn]ess"

John 1:9 Ἦν τὸ φῶς τὸ ἀληθινόν, ὃ φωτίζει

47,14-15 "I manifested myself to them [in] their tents"

John 1:14 ὁ λόγος σάρξ...ἐσκήνωσεν ἐν ἡμῖν

47,15 "Being Logos"

John 1:1 Ἐν ἀρχῇ ἦν ὁ λόγος, καὶ ὁ λόγος ἦν πρὸς τὸν θεόν, καὶ θεὸς ἦν ὁ λόγος

47,18-19 "And [they] did not know the one who gives me power"

John 1:10 ὁ κόσμος αὐτὸν οὐκ ἔγνω

47,24 "None of them knew me"

John 1:10 ὁ κόσμος αὐτὸν οὐκ ἔγνω

47,24-26 "[Although] it is I who work in them, but [they thought] that it was by [them] that the All had been created"

John 1:10 ὁ κόσμος δι' αὐτοῦ ἐγένετο

47,28-29 "[I] am the light that illumine the all"

John 1:9 Ἦν τὸ φῶς τὸ ἀληθινόν, ὃ φωτίζει

50,15 "And they did not know me"

John 1:10 ὁ κόσμος αὐτὸν οὐκ ἔγνω

In his important review of the facsimile edition of Nag Hammadi Codices XI, XII and XIII, Carsten Colpe was the first to call attention to the relationship between the *Trimorphic Protennoia* and the Johannine prologue. He argues that the treatise gathers, in a manner unlike any previously known text, the main materials of the sapiential speculation which are at work in the prologue, "even though not in the sequence of the Prologue."[16] Our synopsis of the elements common to both texts confirms Colpe's judgment on this point: these elements do not appear on either side in a similar order. This is easily explained as the result of the fact that we have, on the one side, a short text, the prologue, exhibiting a relatively simple structure, and on the other, a much longer text, the composition of which is both complex and loose, in which the parallels to the prologue are concentrated at the beginning (pp. 35–37) and towards the end (pp. 46–50). One has the clear impression that the Johannine elements serve to construct or illustrate

---

[16] Colpe 1974, 122.

the *Trimorphic Protennoia*'s exposition. Nevertheless, even if certain elements common to both texts remain imprecise, others might be best understood as allusions (allusions being defined here as "a device for the simultaneous activation of two texts").[17]

To begin with, the assertion of Protennoia, on p. 47,14–17—"I manifested myself to them [in] their tents (ϲⲕⲏⲛⲏ)"—bears an unmistakable resemblance with the ἐσκήνωσεν ἐν ἡμῖν of John 1:14. But, as J. Helderman has shown, this relationship is not without a polemical intention,[18] insofar as the Protennoia does not establish herself among her own but rather manifests herself "in *their* tents."

The second element which can be seen as an allusion is the title *logos*, "word," or "discourse," attributed to the Perfect Son (37,4–5) and especially to Protennoia herself, in two self-predications (46,5–7.14–15) and in the second part of the affirmation of p. 47 cited above: "I manifested myself to them [in] their tents, being *logos*." To this designation of *logos* must be added those of "God who was begotten" (39,6.13) and of "God who alone came into existence" (38,23), which evoke the μονογενὴς θεός of John 1:18.

The fact that those to whom she manifests herself "in their tents" and whose garments she wore (47,14–17), or those "who watch over their dwelling places" do not recognize Protennoia constitutes a third likely allusion (50,15–16). This lack of recognition stands in sharp contrast with the presence of Protennoia among those who are hers and the recognition she enjoys among them (40,31–32.36; 41,15–16.27–28.32–33; 45,28–29; 49,21–22). The strong emphasis put on those who belong to Protennoia and acknowledge her, and the fact that they are designated as "those who are mine (ⲛⲉⲧⲉ ⲛⲱⲓ̈ ⲛⲉ = οἱ ἐμοί)," contradicts the assertion of the prologue, according to which the Logos "came to what was his own (τὰ ἴδια) and his own (οἱ ἴδιοι) did not accept him" (John 1:11). In the cited passages of the *Trimorphic Protennoia*, we have, so to speak, a negative, polemical, allusion to the prologue.

Finally, among the numerous mentions of the light in the *Trimorphic Protennoia*, the one on p. 46,29–33: "While it (i.e., the Mother) is a sound from a thought, it is also a word (ⲗⲟⲅⲟⲥ) from a voice which was sent to illuminate those who are in the darkness," is an evocation of Luke 1:79 but also of John 1:9: "(The Word) was the true light,

---

[17] Dimant 1988, 409–410.
[18] Helderman 1978, 206–207.

which enlightens everyone, which was coming into the world," as well as John 1:6, even if here the participle ἀπεσταλμένος refers originally to John the Baptist.

On the basis of these parallels, it is possible to state that the *Trimorphic Protennoia* polemically reinterprets the Johannine prologue through the use of allusions intended to convince the reader that the Logos-Protennoia is superior to the incarnated Logos of the Fourth Gospel. The polemical intent of the treatise appears clearly in the self-predication of p. 46,14–15: "*I alone* am the word (λογος), ineffable, immaculate, immeasurable, inconceivable," which relegates the Logos-Jesus of John to the position of a secondary, inferior, figure, who will need to be rescued from the cross by the Logos-Protennoia (50,12–15). A similar polemical intent may be hinted at in the subversive use of the word σκηνή, "tent," which reduces the dwelling (ἐσκήνωσεν) of John 1:14 to a temporary manifestation. Finally, and in marked contrast to the Johannine Logos who was not received by his own people, Protennoia is acknowledged and welcomed by hers.

As we have seen then, the dependence of the *Trimorphic Protennoia* on the long version of the *Secret Book of John* can easily be established on the basis of stylistic, mythological and doctrinal traits common to both writings. Furthermore, the manner in which certain elements common to both texts are treated in the *Trimorphic Protennoia*, i.e., in an allusive and, at times, almost abstruse way, indicates without a doubt the nature of its relationship to the *Secret Book*. The *Trimorphic Protennoia* is essentially a development of the final hymn of the long version of the *Secret Book*, interspersed with elements drawn from elsewhere in that same work. Does this mean that the use of the prologue made by the *Trimorphic Protennoia* is to be explained by its dependence on the *Secret Book*? The answer to this question is negative, simply because in the long version of the *Secret Book*, there is not a single occurrence of the term λόγος nor, in our opinion, any obvious link with the prologue. This is also the case with the final hymn. According to Michael Waldstein's detailed analysis, "despite a striking overall similarity, there are, in fact, no literary contacts between the Prologue and the Monologue (that is, the final hymn) close enough to indicate literary dependence of the Monologue on the Prologue."[19] In

---

[19] Waldstein 1995, 402; see also Nagel 2000, 463: "Zur Verhältnisbestimmung zwischen Prot und dem joh. Prolog ist festzuhalten, daß sich in Prot keinesfalls sichere

his reworking of the final hymn of the *Secret Book*, the author of the *Trimorphic Protennoia*, having constructed the "sound–voice–word" metaphor used throughout the treatise was subsequently led to engage in a polemical reading of the prologue. This had the effect of devaluing the Johannine, and purely Christian, Logos and of elevating the Gnostic Logos.

BIBLIOGRAPHY

Berliner Arbeitskreis für Koptisch-Gnostische Schriften, "Die Bedeutung der Texte von Nag Hammadi für die moderne Gnosisforschung," *Gnosis und Neues Testament: Studien aus Religionswissenschaft und Theologie*, K.-W. Tröger, ed., Gütersloh: Mohn, 1973, 13–76.

Colpe, C., "Heidnische, jüdische und christliche Überlieferung in den Schriften aus Nag Hammadi III," *Jahrbuch für Antike und Christentum* 17 (1974), 109–125.

Dimant, D., "Use and Interpretation of Mikra in the Apocrypha and Pseudepigrapha," *Mikra: Text, Translation, Reading and Interpretation of the Hebrew Bible in Ancient Judaism and Early Christianity*, M.J. Mulder and H. Sysling, eds., Compendia Rerum Iudaicarum ad Novum Testamentum 2.1, Assen: van Gorcum; Philadelphia: Fortress, 1988, 379–419.

Evans, C.A., "On the Prologue of John and the *Trimorphic Protennoia*," *New Testament Studies* 27 (1980–1981), 395–401.

——— *Word and Glory: On the Exegetical and Theological Background of John's Prologue*, Journal for the Study of the New Testament Supplement Series 89, Sheffield: Sheffield Academic Press, 1993.

Helderman, J., "'In ihren Zelten…': Bemerkungen zu Codex XIII Nag Hammadi p. 47:14–18 im Hinblick auf Joh. i 14," *Miscellanea Neotestamentica*, vol. 1, T. Baarda, A.F.J. Klijn and W.C. Unnik, eds., Novum Testamentum Supplements 47, Leiden: Brill, 1978, 181–211.

Janssens, Y., "Le Codex XIII de Nag Hammadi," *Le Muséon* 87 (1974), 341–413.

——— "Une source gnostique du Prologue?" *L'Évangile de Jean: Sources, rédaction, théologie*, M. de Jonge, ed., Bibliotheca Ephemeridum Theologicarum Lovaniensium 44, Leuven: Leuven University Press; Gembloux: Duculot, 1977, 355–358.

Layton, B., *The Gnostic Scriptures: A New Translation with Annotations and Introductions*, Garden City, N.Y.: Doubleday, 1987.

MacRae, G.W., "The Thunder: Perfect Mind (VI,2; 13,1–21,32)," *Nag Hammadi Codices V, 2–5 and VI with Papyrus Berolinensis 8502, 1 and 4*, D. Parrott, ed., Nag Hammadi Studies 11, Leiden: Brill, 1979, 231–255.

Nagel, T., *Die Rezeption des Johannesevangeliums im 2. Jahrhundert: Studien zur vorirenäischen Aneignung und Auslegung des vierten Evangeliums in christlicher und christlich-gnostischer Literatur*, Arbeiten zur Bibel und ihrer Geschichte 2, Leipzig: Evangelische Verlagsanstalt, 2000.

Painchaud, L. and B. Barc, "Les réécritures de l'Apocryphon de Jean à la lumière de l'hymne final de la version longue," *Le Muséon* 112 (1999), 317–333.

Indizien für die Priorität dieses Textes oder der in ihm angenommenen Traditionen gegenüber dem joh. Prolog oder dem Evangelium finden."

Poirier, P.-H., "La *Prôtennoia trimorphe* (NH XIII,1) et le vocabulaire du *Descensus ad Inferos*," *Le Muséon* 96 (1983), 193–204.

—— *Le Tonnerre, Intellect parfait (NH VI, 2), avec deux contributions de W.-P. Funk*, Bibliothèque copte de Nag Hammadi, Section: «Textes» 22, Québec: Les Presses de l'Université Laval; Leuven: Peeters, 1995.

—— *La Pensée Première à la triple forme (NH XIII, 1)*, Bibliothèque copte de Nag Hammadi, Section: «Textes» 32, Québec: Les Presses de l'Université Laval; Leuven: Peeters, 2006.

—— "La Pensée première à la triple forme (NH XIII, 1)," *Écrits gnostiques: La bibliothèque de Nag Hammadi*, J.-P. Mahé and P.-H. Poirier, eds., Bibliothèque de la Pléiade 538, Paris: Gallimard, 2007, 1611–1650.

Robinson, J.M., "Sethians and Johannine Thought: The *Trimorphic Protennoia* and the Prologue of the Gospel of John," *The Rediscovery of Gnosticism: Proceeding of the International Conference on Gnosticism at Yale, New Haven, Connecticut, March 28-31, 1978: Volume Two: Sethian Gnosticism*, B. Layton, ed., Studies in the History of Religions 41 (Supplements to Numen), Leiden: Brill, 1981, 643–662.

Schenke, G., "'Die dreigestalte Protennoia': Eine gnostische Offenbarungsrede in koptischer Sprache aus dem Fund von Nag Hammadi eingeleitet und übersetzt vom Berliner Arbeitskreis für koptisch-gnostische Schriften," *Theologische Literaturzeitung* 99 (1974), 731–746.

—— *Die dreigestalte Protennoia (Nag-Hammadi-Codex XIII)*, Texte und Untersuchungen zur Geschichte der altchristlichen Literatur 132, Berlin: Akademie-Verlag, 1984.

Schenke-Robinson, G., "Die dreigestalte Protennoia (NHC XIII,1)," *Nag Hammadi Deutsch 2. Band: NHC V,2–XIII,1, BG 1 und 4: Eingeleitet und übersetzt von Mitgliedern des Berliner Arbeitskreises für Koptisch-Gnostische Schriften*, H.-M. Schenke, H.-G. Bethge and U.U. Kaiser, eds., Die Griechischen Christlichen Schriftsteller der ersten Jahrhunderte, Neue Folge 12: Koptisch-Gnostische Schriften III, Berlin: de Gruyter, 2003, 807–831.

Turner, J.D., "Sethian Gnosticism: A Literary History," *Nag Hammadi, Gnosticism & Early Christianity*, C.W. Hedrick and R. Hodgson, eds., Peabody, Mass.: Hendrickson, 1986, 55–86.

—— "NHC XIII, 1: Trimorphic Protennoia," *Nag Hammadi Codices XI, XII, XIII*, C.W. Hedrick, ed., Nag Hammadi Studies 28, Leiden: Brill, 1990, 371–454.

—— *Sethian Gnosticism and the Platonic Tradition*, Bibliothèque Copte de Nag Hammadi, Section: «Études» 6, Québec: Les Presses de l'Université Laval; Leuven: Peeters, 2001.

—— "Sethian Gnosticism and Johannine Christianity," *Theology and Christology in the Fourth Gospel: Essays by the Members of the SNTS Johannine Writings Seminar*, G. van Belle et al., eds., Bibliotheca Ephemeridum Theologicarum Lovaniensium 184, Leuven: Leuven University Press / Peeters, 2005, 399–433.

Waldstein, M., "The Providence Monologue in the Apocryphon of John and the Johannine Prologue," *Journal of Early Christian Studies* 3 (1995), 369–402.

Waldstein, M. and F. Wisse, *The Apocryphon of John: Synopsis of Nag Hammadi Codices II, 1; III, 1; and IV, 1 with BG 8502, 2*, Nag Hammadi and Manichaean Studies 33, Leiden: Brill, 1995.

THE JOHANNINE LEGACY: THE GOSPEL AND *APOCRYPHON* OF JOHN

John D. Turner
University of Nebraska-Lincoln

This essay explores the possibility of an intertextual dialogue and a shared history-of-religions background and context for two late first and early second century sectarian movements: Johannine Christianity and Sethian Gnosticism, an early Gnostic movement presently attested in no less than eleven of the fifty-two treatises contained in the fourth-century Coptic codices from Nag Hammadi as well as in several patristic sources. In particular, I suggest that both movements may have originated as non-Christian baptismal sectarian movements that became Christianized during the second half of the first century and gradually came to sustain an increasingly polemical relationship to one another throughout the second century.

Since it is the less-well-known of the two, I begin first with a sketch of the nature and history of the Sethian movement and then move to a discussion of the *Apocryphon of John* and the *Trimorphic Protennoia* as the two Sethian treatises that most clearly sustain close literary contacts with the Johannine gospel and letters. Since the intertextual contacts between these two treatises and the Johannine corpus become most obvious in the prologue of the Fourth Gospel, I then turn to an exploration of points of closest contact between them, namely the *Trimorphic Protennoia* and the Pronoia monologue concluding the *Apocryphon of John*. The remainder of this essay is devoted to a discussion of two other distinctive aspects of the relationship of these two movements, namely the practice and theory of baptism and their common characterizations of revelatory media, which leads to the concluding suggestion that the *Apocryphon of John* was in part intended as a concluding sequel to the Fourth Gospel, and that the Sethian and Johannine movements shared a parallel and interrelated history of development.[1]

---

[1] For a recent, similar but different discussion of this relationship, see Rasimus 2009.

1. SETHIAN GNOSTICISM: CHARACTER AND HISTORY

Most scholars who have touched upon the topic of the intertextual and history-of-religions relationship between the Fourth Gospel and the *Apocryphon of John* have focused attention upon the striking set of conceptual parallels between the Gospel and the Pronoia monologue concluding the longer version of the *Apocryphon*, parallels that are also shared with another Nag Hammadi treatise, the *Trimorphic Protennoia*. In my view, these parallels strongly suggest that these two Nag Hammadi treatises were originally composed in the same environment of late first and early second century Hellenistic Jewish Wisdom speculation as was the Fourth Gospel. These two Nag Hammadi treatises are part of a corpus of eleven Coptic treatises from the Nag Hammadi codices that, together with various patristic testimonies, scholars have classified as "Sethian" or "Classical" Gnostic.[2] This corpus of writings, which share a number of common mythemes, dramatis personae, metaphysical and soteriological doctrines, and ritual and contemplative prescriptions, is sufficiently cohesive as to imply the existence of a sectarian movement of the second through fourth centuries that I and others have called Gnostic Sethianism,[3] owing to the prominent role that the figure of the biblical Seth eventually came to play in their religious thought.[4]

---

[2] These include the *Apocryphon of John* (also in the Berlin Gnostic Codex [BG] 8502), the *Trimorphic Protennoia*, the *Apocalypse of Adam*, the *Hypostasis of the Archons, Thought of Norea, Melchizedek*, and the *Holy Book of the Great Invisible Spirit* (also called the *Gospel of the Egyptians*), and the four Platonizing Sethian treatises *Zostrianos, Allogenes*, the *Three Steles of Seth*, and *Marsanes*. In addition to these, one should also add Cod. Bruc. *Untitled*, and from the recently published Tchacos Codex, the *Gospel of Judas* and perhaps the *Book of Allogenes*.

[3] Schenke 1981, 588–616. Although some scholars doubt the existence of a Gnostic community who called themselves "Sethians," there is in the Nag Hammadi library an abundant literature consistently characterized by sufficiently invariant and coherent set of mythologumena symbolizing the sacred history, rituals, spiritual and worldly experience and polemics with other groups which was written and read by persons who considered themselves to be the contemporary offspring of an ideal "race" or "seed" of Seth, as to warrant the positing of an actual community who habitually identified with the symbolic universe of these treatises. Although it was their opponents rather than the proponents of these views that identified them as "Sethians," this designation is nevertheless heuristically useful. See in general Turner 2001.

[4] See Klijn 1977, *passim*; Pearson 1981, 472–504; Stone 1981, 459–471; Stroumsa 1981, 808–818; Stroumsa 1984, 49–53, 73–80; and Turner 1998a, 33–58. Indeed, the factitive verb phrase of Gen 4:25 "appointed for me" (שת־לי) was etymologized into the Mandaic name Shitīl (שתיל) son of Adam, the "Perfect Plant," or planter of his "plant" (i.e., his seed; cf. the "plant" of the *Gospel of the Egyptians* III 60,15–18 and the "fruit-bearing trees" of the *Apocalypse of Adam* 76,15).

1.1. *The "Sethians"*

Although there is no historical record of any group, Gnostic or otherwise, who actually called themselves "Sethians," during the period 175–475 CE, a number of the fathers of the early church produced antiheretical writings in which they refer to certain revelations and Gnostic groups that either they or their later interpreters called "Sethian": Irenaeus of Lyons (*Adv. haer.* 1.30),[5] <Hippolytus> of Rome (preserved in Pseudo-Tertullian, *Haer.* 2), Epiphanius of Salamis (*Panarion* 26; 39–40), Filastrius of Brescia (*Div. her. lib.* 3), and Theodoret of Cyrrhus (*Haer. fab. comp.* 1.14); of these, Epiphanius—though his testimony is often suspect—is the first to offer any detailed information.[6] Evidently the term "Sethian" was originally coined and used by various church fathers as a convenient designation for certain Gnostic groups whose literature singled out the ancient figure of the biblical Seth to be of signal importance. So while the term "Sethian" does not appear to have been a self-designation, the group or movement to which it referred first received historical treatment as such in the fifth century *Panarion* (39–40) of Epiphanius, bishop of Salamis. Here Epiphanius describes two closely-related Gnostic groups, the Sethians (some of which he says he had met) and the Archontics, and proceeds to describe their

---

[5] Theodoret (ca. 450 CE) identified the "others" (*alii;* i.e., other Gnostics) of Irenaeus' *Adv. haer.* 1.30 as Sethians or Ophites: οἱ δὲ Σηθιανοί, οὓς Ὀφιανοὺς ἢ Ὀφίτας τινὲς ὀνομάζουσιν, *Haer. fab. comp.* 1.14, *PG* 83.364.39. Similarly, he also identified the *gnōstikoi* of *Adv. haer.* 1.29.1 (extant now only in Latin: "*Super hos autem ex his, qui praedicti sunt Simoniani multitudo Gnosticorum exsurrexit*") as Barbeloites: Ἐκ τῶν Βαλεντίνου σπερμάτων τὸ τῶν Βαρβηλιωτῶν, ἤγουν Βορβοριανῶν, ἢ Νααυσσηνῶν, ἢ Στρατιωτικῶν, ἢ Φημιονιτῶν καλουμένων, ἐβλάστησε μύσος (*Haer. fab. comp.* 1.13, *PG* 83.361.35–38), probably based on the prominence of the name "Barbelo" in Irenaeus' summary (in which Seth plays no role) of the theogony and cosmogony underlying the *Apocryphon of John.* The present form of the *Apocryphon*—apparently unknown to Irenaeus—seems to have combined a "Barbeloite" theogony and cosmogony similar to *Adv. haer.* 1.29 with an anthropogony similar to the "Ophite" anthropogony of *Adv. haer.* 1.30, in the process adding the ideas of the heavenly and earthly Seth, the Gnostics as the pneumatic seed of Seth, the four Luminaries as the heavenly dwellings of Adam, Seth, and his seed, and the division of history into four periods demarcated by Barbelo's three salvific interventions.

[6] The earliest main patristic testimonies are Irenaeus' *Adversus haereses* (ca. 175) and the lost *Syntagma* of Hippolytus (ca. 200), on both of which are based the testimonies of Pseudo-Tertullian (225–250), Epiphanius (ca. 375), Filastrius (380/90), and Theodoret (ca. 453). The Sethians described in Hippolytus' *Refutatio* seem quite different than those described in the former sources, and may perhaps be connected with the non-Sethian treatise the *Paraphrase of Shem* (NHC VII,1).

literature and doctrine, in the process no doubt drawing on the heresiological catalogues penned by his predecessors.

Since the publication of the fourth-century Nag Hammadi library, the name "Sethian" has in recent times become a typological category applied by modern scholars to the authors and users of a distinctive group of eleven Nag Hammadi treatises. Many of these eleven treatises refer to a special segment of humanity called "the great generation," "strangers," "another kind," "the immovable, incorruptible race," "the (holy) seed of Seth," "the living and immoveable race," "the children of Seth," and "those who are worthy."[7]

1.2. *A Sketch of Sethian "History"*

In my view, these Gnostic Sethians likely originated as a first century CE fusion of two distinct groups, neither of which had any especial interest in the figure of Seth, whose origins may go back to the first century BCE. The first group is the "*multitudo gnosticorum*," whose mythical theogony and cosmogony is summarized by Irenaeus in *Adv. haer.* 1.29, whom I will designate by the convenient term "Barbeloites." The hallmark of these Barbeloites was a communal rite of baptismal immersion in ordinary water that resulted in an experience of transcendental vision leading to total enlightenment and salvation. This rite, called the "Five Seals," was the instrument of salvation recently conferred by Barbelo, the universal Mother and First Thought of the supreme Invisible Spirit. Together with their self-generated Child Autogenes, the Invisible Spirit and Barbelo formed a supreme trinity of Father, Mother and Child.[8] This Child establishes four angelic Luminaries, one of whom, perhaps acting through the agency of

---

[7] Within these treatises, the phrase "those who are worthy" occurs frequently; the phrases "imperishable (or "holy") seed," "the great generation" and "strangers" occur in the *Apocalypse of Adam*, "the immovable, incorruptible race" and "seed (or "sons")" of the great Seth" occur in the *Gospel of the Egyptians*, "the seed of Seth" and "seed of the perfect (or "immoveable") race" in the *Apocryphon of John*, "the living and immoveable race" and "another kind" in the *Three Steles of Seth*, "the living generations" and "the children of Seth" in *Melchizedek*, "the holy seed (or "children") of Seth," "immoveable [race]," and "living seed" in *Zostrianos*, and the "imperishable seed" in *Marsanes*. The terms "generation," "race," "seed" and "strangers" are all plays on the tradition of Seth's birth as "another seed" (σπέρμα ἕτερον) instead of Abel (Gen 4:25, J source), born in the likeness and image of Adam (Gen 5:3, P source), himself born male and female in the image of God (Gen 1:26–27).

[8] This triadic nomenclature may have been inspired by Plato's Father-Mother-Child triad of principles in *Timaeus* 50d.

Sophia, becomes ultimately responsible for the origin of the world creator who comes to possess a portion of the supreme Mothers' divine light-power by which he fashions the physical cosmos as well as a protoplastic human being to serve as a container for the divine light. Attempting to retrieve her fallen light-power from the world creator's control, the Mother undertakes a series of three descents into the lower world, on the last of which she confers the baptism of the Five Seals enabling her fallen members to be reintegrated into the divine world. The earliest Barbeloite narratives of these descents were set forth as the quasi-hymnic first-person monologues that presently conclude the longer version of the *Apocryphon of John* (II 30,11–31,27) and formed the underlying structure of the *Trimorphic Protennoia*.

Independently of the Barbeloites, who show little interest in the Genesis protology, the second group—which I call "Pre-Sethian Gnostic Revisionists of Genesis 2–9"—seems to have consisted of possibly pre-Christian Jewish exegetes who constructed a mythic narrative based on an elaborate rewriting of Genesis 2–9 that portrayed the origin and subsequent enlightenment of humanity as the work of Sophia, the divine Wisdom. The hallmark of their Genesis interpretation was a radical differentiation between the highest God and an inferior world creator. By the time of the earliest exposition of their views offered by Irenaeus around 180 CE (*Adv. haer.* 1.30), these exegetes, whom Irenaeus identified merely as "*alii*" (i.e., other Gnostics) but were identified as "Sethians or Ophites" by Theodoret in the mid-fifth century, had constructed an elaborate cosmogonical, anthropogonical, and soteriological myth based on an interpretation of the protology of the Mosaic book of Genesis that has much in common with the earliest Enochic literature (Book of the Watchers, Aramaic Levi, Astronomical Book), which maintains that evil has a superhuman and demonic origin, from which theses Gnostics could conclude that Moses' claim that evil originated from the protoplasts' disobedience to the creator must be a lie foisted upon him by the creator, and therefore Moses and the prophets were servants of a deceitful devil (Yaldabaoth). While the absence of the figures of Barbelo, the Four Luminaries, the heavenly Seth and his "seed," and of the sacred baptism of the Five Seals excludes the "Sethian" character of this "Ophite" myth, it nevertheless shares with the second half of the *Apocryphon of John* a striking number of similar mythemes, suggesting that both myths derive from a common parent that was probably composed early in the first half of the second century, and adopted by the author(s) of the *Apocryphon of John* in the second half of the second century.

During the first half of the second century, the Barbeloites evidently amalgamated with certain Christian baptizing groups as fellow practitioners of baptism. In the process, they identified the pre-existent Christ of the Christians with the Autogenes Child of their supreme Father and Mother. This Child was self-generated at Barbelo's request and had been anointed with the Invisible Spirit's very own goodness (or "Christhood," *chrēstia*). At the same time, Jesus—who in the Gospel of Mark had received divine sonship at his own baptism and was identified as the divine Logos in the Fourth Gospel—became regarded as the earthly and masculine guise in which Barbelo had recently appeared as the divine Logos to confer this saving baptism on the Barbeloite community. It would have been these Christian Barbeloites who formulated the myth summarized by Irenaeus in *Adv. haer.* 1.29 and who incorporated a third person narrative sketch of the same myth into the first-person aretalogical speeches of the *Trimorphic Protennoia* (37,3–40,29). During the same period, Irenaeus' account of the "Ophites" in *Adv. haer.* 1.30 (Christ as the "third Male" who with Sophia produced and redeemed Jesus) and *On the Origin of the World* (Christ as Sabaoth's son) show that specifically Christian elements had come to form part of the otherwise strongly Jewish character of the Revisionists' preoccupation with the Genesis protology.

Apparently by mid-second century, there had emerged among the revisionist exegetes of Genesis 2–9 a peculiar interest in the figure of Seth as the paradigm of all persons in whom the divine image was primordially restored after its loss in the figures of Cain and Abel. This morally earnest group of persons—which, in distinction from Gnostic Sethians, I call the "Sethites"[9]—styled themselves as the "worthy ones," the true descendants or "seed" of Seth. They based their sense of a unique role and social status within Judaism upon the sacred history of their primordial enlightenment recently brought to light in the form of certain pillars inscribed by Seth about the events in Paradise (Adam, Eve, Seth and his virtuous seed, the impending destructions by flood and fire). Unlike Moses, Seth was able to learn the first-hand truth about the events in Paradise directly from his father Adam.[10] These

---

[9] For convenience—not for historical reasons—I adopt this designation in the form "Sethites," i.e., Seth-honoring persons, so as to distinguish this group as a *precursor* of the movement that H.-M. Schenke (see note 2 above) had identified by the typological designation "Gnostic Sethians."

[10] See Rasimus 2009.

revelations refocused the rewritings of Genesis already offered by the Revisionists upon the history of the primordial Sethite generations narrated in Genesis 4–9.[11]

In the later second century, the Gnostic Sethianism reflected in the Nag Hammadi codices arose from a fusion of the Christianized "Barbeloites" with those (already-Christianized) Genesis Revisionists who had come to emphasize the Sethite doctrine of the primordial enlightenment and moral superiority of Seth and his seed. It would have been these Christianized Gnostic Sethians who combined the Barbeloite theogony and baptismal soteriology with the "Sethite" anthropogony and sacred history that underlies the *Apocryphon of John*. This fusion of Barbeloite and Sethite mythology may have occurred in the last quarter of the second century, since Irenaeus seems unaware of both the frame story and the special status of Seth and his seed in his version of the *Apocryphon of John*. These Gnostics identified the archetypal, Heavenly Seth with the Autogenes Christ of the Barbeloites as an alternative manifestation of the pre-existent image of God and as the divine savior of Seth's pneumatic seed, the Gnostics. The four Luminaries become the aeonic dwelling places of Adam, Seth, and his seed (both primordial and contemporary) and the history of salvation is divided into dispensations demarcated by the savior's three salvific descents into the lower world. In her third and decisive descent, the Mother causes Christ (or the Logos or Jesus) to appear as the final, contemporary manifestation of the same Seth that had previously rescued his seed from the ancient flood and conflagration sent by the world creator to destroy the earliest humans.[12]

2. THE *APOCRYPHON OF JOHN*

The *Apocryphon of John* is a lengthy dialogue between John, son of Zebedee and the risen Jesus. A text whose underlying doctrinal

---

[11] It is essentially these Sethite versions of the revised Genesis protology that underlie the initial version of the *Apocalypse of Adam*, probably composed during the latter half of the second century, and later reflected in the early third century in the *Three Steles of Seth*.

[12] Gnostic Sethians expressed these doctrines in final version of the *Apocalypse of Adam*, and—even to the point of identifying Seth with Christ—in the *Gospel of the Egyptians*, and went on to superficially "Sethianize" the originally non-Sethite *Hypostasis of the Archons* and *Melchizedek*.

content originally had no specifically Johannine concerns, all four Coptic versions of the *Apocryphon*, both shorter[13] and longer,[14] incorporate that content into a dialogue framework that presupposes John son of Zebedee as the author and direct recipient of Jesus' teaching. In effect, the references to John the Baptist in chapters 1, 2, 4, 5, and 10 of the Gospel of John become understood as references to John son of Zebedee, who in the *Apocryphon* now testifies to the final and definitive *post*-resurrection advent of the divine light into the world. It is therefore likely that the *Apocryphon* was composed after John had become accepted as the author of both the Fourth Gospel and the book of Revelation, a claim first explicitly witnessed—while adducing Polycarp and Papias as also having made such a claim[15]—in Irenaeus' *Adversus haereses* (2.22.5; 3.1.1; 3.3.4; 3.11.1), which also contains the earliest witness to a non-dialogical version of the *Apocryphon*'s main theogony (*Adv. haer.* 1.29). John's questions to the Savior (Jesus) look back to the canonical Gospel and Apocalypse of John, which in effect look forward to the *Apocryphon*, where Jesus deals with matters that remained unanswered in these previous works, such as: how and where the savior originated and was appointed, the nature of the divine world and the supreme Father who sent him, the nature and origin of the lower world and humankind, and the nature of the ultimate destiny of souls, especially those belonging to the unwavering race of the "seed of Seth." This new revelation from the risen Jesus supplements the Gospel and Revelation of John by offering a new, clearly post-resurrection—perhaps even post-ascension[16]—perspective on these earlier Johannine texts.

The soteriological myth of the *Apocryphon of John* seems to have roots in a form of heterodox Jewish speculation on the figure of Sophia, the divine Wisdom of the Hebrew Bible. In the hands of Sethian Gnostics, the biblical functions of Sophia as creator, nourisher, and enlightener of the world were distributed among a hierarchy of feminine principles: (1) an exalted divine Mother called Pronoia or Barbelo, the

---

[13] The so-called short recension (SR): Nag Hammadi Codex III,1 and Papyrus Berolinensis Gnosticus 8502,2.

[14] The so-called long recension (LR): Nag Hammadi Codices II,1 and IV,1.

[15] On the identity of the author of the Fourth Gospel, see also the essays of Hill, Meyer, Mutschler, and Rasimus (Introduction) in this volume.

[16] Depending upon the reading of the shorter version's "I *have* ascended to the perfect aeon" in BG 75,14–15 versus the longer version's "behold, now I am *about* to ascend to the perfect aeon" (II 31,26–27).

First Thought of the supreme deity, the Invisible Spirit; (2) Epinoia, Barbelo's earthly reflection in the primordial Paradise who appears to Adam as the spiritual Eve; and (3) a lower Sophia responsible for both the creation of the physical world and the incarnation of portions of the supreme Mother's divine essence into human bodies. Salvation was achieved by the Mother's reintegration of her own dissipated essence into its original unity.

None of the four versions of the *Apocryphon* is a seamless production. In all versions, the first half contains a very close parallel in Irenaeus' summary of a Gnostic myth in his *Adversus haereses* 1.29, which begins with the emergence of the Mother Barbelo as the supreme Father's First Thought and ends with Sophia's generation of the world creator Yaldabaoth, who boasts of his sole divinity. This section of the *Apocryphon of John* is also roughly parallel to a similar cosmology in the *Trimorphic Protennoia* (36,27–40,29). The second half of the *Apocryphon of John* contains a mythical anthropogony and soteriology that has no parallel in *Adversus haereses* 1.29, but Irenaeus' immediately succeeding chapter (*Adv. haer.* 1.30) goes on to narrate an extremely similar myth that he attributes to certain "other" Gnostics. Beyond materials similar to those found in Irenaeus, the shorter version of the *Apocryphon* also includes a lengthy negative theology on the supreme monadic Father, the Invisible Spirit (BG 23,3–25,7; II 2,33–4,19, paralleled also in the Sethian treatise *Allogenes* NHC XI 62,28–63,25) and a short treatise (BG 64,13–71,2; II 15,16–27,33) on the destiny of four kinds of souls. In addition to these, the longer version of Codices II and IV contain an excerpt from a "Book of Zoroaster" on the creation of the psychic Adam (II 15,13–19,10) and concludes with a three-stanzaed monologue in which the divine mother Barbelo, the First Thought of the supreme Invisible Spirit, narrates her three salvific descents as the divine Pronoia or Providence into the lower world (II 30,11–31,25).

2.1. *The Monologue of Pronoia in the* Apocryphon of John

Although the dialogical framework of the *Apocryphon* puts this Pronoia monologue on the lips of Jesus, its distinctively hymnic style and lack of explicitly Christian content commend it for treatment as a composition in its own right, quite possibly a product of Hellenistic Jewish Wisdom speculation. Indeed, its absence from the shorter versions of the *Apocryphon of John* suggests that it originally circulated apart from any version of the *Apocryphon*.[17] Although the Pronoia monologue by itself evinces no specifically Christian content, its very incorporation into the *Apocryphon of John* as the conclusion of Christ's revelation demands a Christian reading of it. Each of Pronoia's salvific descents narrated in the monologue have clear correspondences with the main narrative's depiction of the Mother Barbelo's three fundamental salvific interventions that serve to punctuate the basic phases of the overall history of salvation narrated in both versions of the *Apocryphon*. Moreover, even though the shorter and longer versions both tell the same story, Bernard Barc and Louis Painchaud have pointed out that the addition of the Pronoia monologue near the end of the main narrative in the longer version led to a basic reworking of the longer version's entire preceding narrative in terms of the monologue's theology.[18] In the following overview of the Pronoia monologue, instances of its impact on the longer version's main narrative will be indicated in italics, while non-italic text represents more or less common agreement in the text of the shorter and longer versions.

2.1.1. *The Transcendent Preexistence of Pronoia*

> I, therefore, the perfect Pronoia of the all, took form in my seed, for I existed first, going on every road. For I am the richness of the light; I am the remembrance of the Pleroma. (*Ap. John* II 30,11–16)

---

[17] By placing the monologue of the essentially feminine figure of Pronoia on the lips of Jesus in the conclusion of the frame story, the longer version of the *Apocryphon of John* secondarily identifies an originally feminine revealer figure with Jesus, even though the main body of the work consistently identifies the preexistent Christ with Autogenes, the son of Barbelo/Pronoia. Thus Jesus himself, not Barbelo/Pronoia, is the one who overcomes the final outbreak of evil. See Waldstein 1995, 369–402.

[18] Barc and Painchaud 1999, 317–333. These changes to the text of the main narrative include: the repeated use (six times compared to once in BG) of the term "Mother-Father" to refer to the "perfect" Pronoia; Pronoia's characterization as "first to come forth" (II 5,11); identifying Pronoia as the source of the divine voice that "came forth" to reveal that "the Man exists and the Son of Man" and caused the aeon of the chief Archon and the depths of the abyss to shake at the appearance of her light in the form of the archetypal First Man (II 14,13–30), as well as identifying Christ's appearance as an eagle upon the tree of knowledge as a manifestation of "the Epinoia from the holy, luminous Pronoia" in order that he might "awaken them from the depth of sleep" (II 23,26–35). The redactor may also have added the account of the withdrawal of Life (Zoë) from Eve (on analogy with the withdrawal of Pronoia from chaos in the monologue) once the chief Archon had noticed her presence in Eve (II 24,8–15).

The self-portrayal of Pronoia echoes that of the divine Wisdom of Jewish Wisdom literature.[19] As the omnipresent creator of everything, Pronoia takes form in her "seed," the fragments of her spiritual substance trapped in humans that inhabit the lower world, bringing them light and knowledge as the memory of their divine origin. As Barc and Painchaud note, the monologue's emphasis on Pronoia's luminosity and primacy is also reflected in the longer version's initial description of the emergence of Pronoia/Barbelo from the Father's light:

> And [his Thought became] actual and revealed herself [and stood at rest and *appeared*] before him [in the brilliance of] his light. This is the *first* [power that] exists prior to the All, [which appeared *from his*] *Thought*. She [is the universal Pronoia]—her light [shines like his] Light—the [perfect] power who is [the] Image of the Perfect, *Virginal, Invisible Spirit*. [*The first power*], *the glory of* Barbelo, the perfect glory in the aeons, *the glory of the revelation*. She glorified the *Virginal Spirit, praising him*, since because of him she had appeared. This is the First Thought, his image. *She became the Womb of all things, since she is prior to them all, the Mother-Father*, the First Man, the *Holy* Spirit, the Triple Male, the Triple Powered, the thrice-named androgynous One, *and the eternal aeon among the invisible things, and the first to come forth*. (*Ap. John* II 4,26–5,11)

2.1.2. *First Descent of Pronoia (II 30,16–21)*

> And I went into the realm of darkness, and I endured till I entered the midst of the prison. And the foundations of chaos shook. And I hid myself from them because of their wickedness, and they did not recognize me. (*Ap. John* II 30,16–21)

In the main narrative of the *Apocryphon* (II 14,13–34), the first descent of Pronoia occurs in response to Sophia's repentance for having brought forth Yaldabaoth, the creator and ruler of the lower world. As a correction of Sophia's abortive act, Pronoia manifests herself as the

---

[19] In such texts as Proverbs 8, Job 28, Sirach 24, and especially Wisdom of Solomon 7, Sophia is regarded as a preexistent divine power, the feminine image, reflection, emanation and breath of the high deity, his instrument in the creation of the world. She is a source of life and light, which she pours forth upon those who seek her. Although a heavenly figure who pervades all things, as God's own breath she covers the primeval earth as a mist like the divine Spirit of Gen 1:2–3, descending from her celestial dwelling to bring wisdom and divine revelation to humankind. Among these she seeks a dwelling, on some accounts successfully finding a permanent earthly dwelling (as Torah and temple in Sirach 24) and on others (*1 Enoch* 42) without success, resulting in her return to her celestial home.

archetypal Man and image of the Invisible Spirit upon the lower waters. The imagery of the longer version's account of this episode has also been influenced by the Pronoia monologue's motifs of the shaking of the foundations of chaos,[20] its contrast between the light of Pronoia and the chief ruler's dark ignorance, and the inability of the lower authorities to fully grasp the presence of the first Man as the true image of the divine:

> And a Voice *came forth from above the exalted aeons*: "Man exists, and the Son of Man." Now the first ruler, Yaltabaoth listened, thinking that the voice came *from his Mother, and he did not realize where it had come from.* And the holy *Mother*-Father, the Perfect One, *perfect Pronoia, the Image of the Invisible One, the Father of all things, the one within whom all things have come into being,* the First Man, {for he} appeared to them [in a human form]. *The entire aeon of the first ruler trembled, and the foundations of the abyss shook, and through the waters that are over matter the lower region [shone] from the [appearance] of his Image that had been revealed.* And when all the authorities and the first ruler gazed in astonishment *they saw the whole of the lower region shining. And through the light,* they saw in the water the pattern of the Image. (*Ap. John* II 14,13–34)

2.1.3. *Second Descent of Pronoia (II 30,21–32)*

> Again I returned, for the second time, and I went about. I came forth from those who belong to the light, which is I, the remembrance of the Providence. I entered into the midst of darkness and the interior of Hades, since I was seeking (to accomplish) my assigned task (οἰκονομία). And the foundations of chaos shook, that they might fall down upon those who are in chaos and might destroy them. And again I ran up to my luminous root lest they be destroyed before the time. (*Ap. John* II 30,21–32)

Pronoia's second descent corresponds to the main narrative's previous episode (II 22,28–23,35; 24,9–17) of the appearance of the luminous Epinoia, hidden in the protoplastic Adam as his true image, to awaken him from the deep sleep of darkness that settled upon him when the first ruler had extracted her from his side and molded her into the figure of

---

[20] Significantly, the initial appearance of Christ to John son of Zebedee at the beginning of the frame story is marked by the same cosmic shaking that occurs upon Pronoia's first descent ("The heavens opened and the whole creation shone, and the world was shaken," II 1,31–33), a motif that probably derives from placing the monologue of Pronoia on the lips of Jesus in the conclusion of the longer version's frame story.

the earthly Eve. Epinoia is thus the spiritual Eve, Life, and the mother of the living, as well as the Tree of Knowledge, awakening the earthly Adam and Eve's thought:

> Then the Epinoia of the Light hid within him (Adam). And the first ruler wished to bring her forth from his rib. Now the Epinoia of the Light cannot be grasped. Though the darkness chased her, it did not grasp her. And he brought forth from him a portion of his power, and he made another molding, with a female form after the likeness of the Epinoia that had appeared to him. And he (the first ruler) brought the portion that he had taken from the power of the Man into the molded figure of femaleness—not as Moses said: "his rib." And he (Adam) saw the woman beside him, and immediately the luminous Epinoia *appeared*, having removed the veil that was over his mind, and he sobered up from the drunkenness of darkness. And he recognized his *likeness* (fem.), and said, "This now is bone from my bones, and flesh from my flesh. Therefore, the man will leave his father and his mother and cleave to his wife, and the two will become one flesh." *For his consort will be sent to him, and "he will leave his father and his mother and cleave to his wife, and the two will become* one flesh." {*For his consort will be sent to him and he will leave his father and mother.*} *Our sister Sophia, who came down in innocence so that she might set right her deficiency*, was therefore named 'Life,' i.e., the Mother of the living, *by the Pronoia of heavenly authority*. And through her *they tasted of the perfect knowledge. I* (i.e., Christ the narrator; SR has Epinoia) *appeared in the form of an eagle on the tree of knowledge, which is the Epinoia from the holy, luminous Pronoia, in order that I might teach them and awaken them from the depth of sleep. For both of them were in a fallen state, and they realized their nakedness. The Epinoia appeared to them as light, awakening their thinking.* (*Ap. John* II 22,28–23,35)

Like the advent of Pronoia, the coming of Epinoia to Adam echoes the Johannine prologue's announcement of the light coming into the world. Just as the prologue states that the darkness has not overcome the light (John 1:5), so also Yaldabaoth, the ruler of the darkness, cannot grasp the luminous Epinoia as if she were a physical object like Adam's rib (Gen 2:21–22). The *Apocryphon* goes on to interpret further details from the Genesis protology: the mystery of marriage in Genesis 2:23–24 is actually union with one's spiritual consort from above; the nakedness of Gen 2:25 (cf. 3:7–21) represents a state of spiritual ignorance raised to conscious thought by being clothed in the light. Neither was it the snake (Gen 3:13) who instructed the protoplasts, but Epinoia appearing as Christ in the form of an eagle, a passage that may be a veiled allusion to traditions identifying Christ with the serpent that stemmed from John 3:13–15, to the effect that that the true revealer is

Christ, an enemy of the serpent: "No one has ascended into heaven but he who descended from heaven, the Son of man. And as Moses lifted up the serpent in the wilderness, so must the Son of man be lifted up, that whoever believes in him may have eternal life."

Again, Pronoia's retreat to her luminous root is reflected in the longer version alone by the episode of her timely extraction of Epinoia from the virgin Eve just before Yaldabaoth attempts to rape her:[21]

> The first ruler saw the virgin who was standing with Adam, *and the living, luminous Epinoia appeared from within her.* And Yaldabaoth filled up with ignorance. *But when the Providence of all things realized this, she sent some beings, and they snatched Life away from Eve.* And the first ruler defiled her and begot from her two children. (*Ap. John* II 24,9–17)

2.1.4. *Third Descent of Pronoia (II 30,32–31,25)*

> Still for a third time I went—I am the light which exists in the light, I am the remembrance of the Providence—that I might enter into the midst of darkness and the interior of Hades, and I filled my face with the light of the completion (συντέλεια) of their aeon. And I entered into the midst of their prison, *which is the prison of the body* (σῶμα). *And I said, "He who hears, let him get up from the deep sleep." And he wept and shed tears, bitter tears he wiped from himself. And he said, "Who is it that calls my name and from where has this hope come to me, while I am in the chains of the prison?" And I said, "I am the Providence of the pure light; I am the thinking of the virginal Spirit* (παρθενικὸν πνεῦμα), *who raises you up to the honored place. Arise and remember that it is you who hearkened, and follow your root, which is I, the merciful One, and guard yourself against the angels of poverty and the demons of chaos and all those who ensnare you, and beware of the deep sleep and the enclosure of the inside of Hades."* And I raised him up and sealed (σφραγίζειν) him in the light of the water with Five Seals (σφραγίς), in order that death might not have power over him from this time on. (*Ap. John* II 30,32–31,25)

Pronoia's ultimately-salvific goal having been temporarily thwarted in her first two descents, first by the ill-prepared wickedness of her potential followers, and second by the impending collapse of the material cosmos they inhabit, her third descent succeeds in guaranteeing the final salvation of her fallen members by raising them from their cosmic prison by means of the baptism of the Five Seals. This pattern of descents is reminiscent of certain Jewish Wisdom poems, according

---

[21] Barc and Painchaud 1999, 328.

to which Sophia/Wisdom attempts to secure a dwelling place in the world she helped to create, sometimes finding an earthly reception, as in Sirach 24, and sometimes not, as in *1 Enoch* 42. The only evidence of possible Christian influence is Pronoia's call to awakening "He who hears, let him get up from the deep sleep," which has a parallel in Eph 5:14: "Awake, O sleeper, and arise from the dead, and Christ shall give you light."[22]

On her third descent into the lower world, Pronoia-Christ, as the only-begotten of the Invisible Spirit "entered into the midst of their prison which is the prison of the body" (II 31,3–4). The longer version (II 19,3–6) emphasizes that this prison is not only the material body, but also the psychic body created by the rulers according to their likeness. The phrase "once more" probably alludes to the distinct accounts of the creation of humanity, taking Gen 1:27 as referring to the psychic body and Gen 2:7 as referring to the material body:

> *And the human appeared, because of the shadow [spark?] of the Light within him.* And his intellect was superior to all those who had created him. When they looked up, they saw that his intellect was superior, and they devised a plan with the entire archontic and angelic company. They took fire and earth and water and mixed them together with the four flaming winds, and beat them together, and created a great disturbance. *And they brought him into the shadow of death, so that they might once again mold him, from the earth and water and fire and wind that are from matter—i.e., the ignorance of darkness and desire and their Counterfeit Spirit—, which is the tomb of the remolding of the body with which the robbers clothed the human, the bond of* forgetfulness (SR: *"matter"*) And he became a mortal human. *It was this one who first descended, and was*

---

[22] Waldstein (1995, 390–391) has noted that the Pronoia monologue exhibits a hymnic structure of three stanzas, whose third stanza contains an elaborate call to awakening (NHC II 31,4–10.14–21, italicized in the above citation) that causes a structural imbalance in comparison to the first two. The secondary character of this material is suggested by a literary seam in II 31,4 (a gloss explaining the "prison" as the body), by the shift to a singular addressee in 31,5–10 from the plural addressees of the first two stanzas (30,11–31,3), and by the shift from the first person singular narrative in the first two stanzas to the style of third person narrative in 31,6–10 and direct address in 31,5–6 and 31,14–21 in the third stanza. The deletion of these additional hundred or so words bring its length more into line with that of the first two. It appears that a redactor has combined two originally independent traditions, (1) a hymnic aretalogy on Pronoia's triple descent and (2) a liturgical fragment containing a call to awakening like the one quoted by Paul in Eph 5:14 ("Awake, O sleeper, and arise from the dead, and Christ shall give you light") and introduced by a gloss explaining that the prison of chaos is the body.

the first separation. But it was the Epinoia of the (SR: *"first"*) *Light that was in him who was to awaken his intellect.* (*Ap. John* II 20,28–21,16)

In the longer version of the *Apocryphon of John*, Pronoia's third descent is narratively equated with the appearance of Christ to John.[23] Just as Pronoia awakens and strengthens the sleeper by bringing knowledge, so also Christ comes in response to the doubting John, giving him the complete revelation of true knowledge in the form of the entire *Apocryphon*:

> And behold, now I shall go up (SR: "I first ascended") to the perfect aeon. I have completed everything for you in your hearing. I have told you everything, so that you may write it down and give it secretly to those who share the same Spirit as you. For this is the secret of the immovable race. (*Ap. John* II 31,25–31)

3. The *Trimorphic Protennoia*

It has often been noted that the Pronoia monologue's pattern of three salvific descents is precisely the same pattern exhibited in the three subtractates of the *Trimorphic Protennoia*, where the Mother Barbelo/Protennoia narrates her three successive earthly descents as Protennoia, the First Thought of the Invisible Spirit. Beginning with George MacRae, this similarity has led several scholars to suspect that there must be a close literary relationship between the Pronoia hymn and the three subtractates of the *Trimorphic Protennoia*.[24] Indeed, careful analysis strongly suggests that some form of the Pronoia monologue probably formed the initial inspiration, if not a direct source, for the original composition of the *Trimorphic Protennoia*. While the Pronoia monologue by itself evinces no specifically Christological content, this was soon acquired: first, by its incorporation into the longer version of the *Apocryphon of John* as the final self-revelatory speech of Christ, who is claimed as the proclaimer of its entire content, and second, by its expansion into the *Trimorphic Protennoia*, where Protennoia appears

---

[23] As Barc and Painchaud (1999, 329–330) note, the monologue's conclusion refers the reader back to the *incipit* prepended to the entire longer version of the *Apocryphon*: "The teaching [of the Savior] and the [revelation] of the mysteries, hidden in silence, [which] he taught to John, [his] disciple" (II 1,1–4).

[24] MacRae 1970, 86–101. For further discussion, see Poirier's essay in this volume, as well as Turner 1990, 374–405; and Turner 2005, 405–412.

as the Logos who descends to reveal himself to those dwelling in darkness, rescue Jesus from the cross, and elevate her seed into the light.

According to the Pronoia monologue, during her first and second descents, Pronoia is apparently not recognized by those she seeks to enlighten. But when the triple-descent motif of the Pronoia monologue was taken up by the *Trimorphic Protennoia*, even though the hostile powers continually fail to recognize her true identity, any conceivable instance of her failure to be manifested to her fallen members was eliminated. Thus on Protennoia's first descent she says: "I cry out in everyone, and they recognize it (the voice), since a seed indwells [them]" (36,15–16):

> I [descended to the] midst of the underworld and I shone [down upon the] darkness. It is I who poured forth the [water]. It is I who am hidden within [radiant] waters. I am the one who gradually put forth the All by my Thought. It is I who am laden with the Voice. It is through me that Gnosis comes forth. [I] dwell in the ineffable and unknowable ones. I am perception and knowledge, uttering a Voice by means of thought. [I] am the real Voice. I cry out in everyone, and they *recognize* it (the voice), since a seed indwells [them]. I am the Thought of the Father and through me proceeded [the] Voice, that is, the knowledge of the everlasting things. I exist as Thought for the [All]—being joined to the unknowable and incomprehensible Thought—I revealed myself— yes, I—among all *those who recognize me*. For it is I who am joined with everyone by virtue of the hidden Thought and an exalted <Voice>, even a Voice from the invisible Thought. And it is immeasurable since it dwells in the Immeasurable One. It is a mystery; it is [unrestrainable] by [the Incomprehensible One]. It is invisible [to all those who are] visible in the All. [It is a Light] dwelling in Light. (*Trim. Prot.* 36,4–33)

> But now I have come down and reached down to Chaos. And I was [with] my own who were in that place. [I am hidden] within them, empowering [them and] giving them shape. And [from the first day] until the day [when I will grant mighty power] to those who [are mine, I will reveal myself to] *those who have [heard* my mysteries], that is, the [Sons] of [the] Light. (*Trim. Prot.* 40,29–41,1)

On her second descent, Protennoia again succeeds in making herself known. She says, "And I hid myself in everyone and revealed [myself] within them, and every mind seeking me longed for me" (45,21–23):

> And I hid myself in everyone and revealed [myself] within them, and *every mind seeking me longed for me*, for it is I who gave shape to the All when it had no form. And I transformed their forms into (other) forms until the time when a form will be given to the All. It is through me that the Voice originated and it is I who put the breath within my own. And

> I cast into them the eternally holy Spirit and I ascended and entered my
> Light. (*Trim. Prot.* 45,21–31)

On her third descent as Logos, Protennoia disguises herself by appearing in the likeness of everyone; no one recognizes her, humans and
cosmic powers alike, until she reveals herself to her own, who immediately receive her:

> (The first time) *I* [*told* all of them about my mysteries] that exist in [the
> incomprehensible], inexpressible [Aeons]. *I taught* [*them* the mysteries]
> through the [Voice that exists] within a perfect Intellect [and I] became a
> foundation for the All, and [I empowered] them. The second time I came
> in the [Speech] of my Voice. I gave shape to those who [took] shape
> until their consummation. The third time *I revealed myself* to them
> [in] their tents as Word and I revealed myself in the likeness of their
> shape. And I wore everyone's garment and I hid myself within them,
> and [*they*] *did not know the one who empowers me.* For I dwell within
> all the Sovereignties and Powers and within the Angels and in every
> movement [that] exists in all matter. And I hid myself within them until
> *I revealed myself* to my [brethren]. And none of them (the Powers) knew
> me, [although] it is I who work in them. Rather [they thought] that the
> All was created [by them] since they are ignorant, not knowing [their]
> root, the place in which they grew. (*Trim. Prot.* 47,5–28)

This failure of the cosmic powers and those who worship them—
perhaps Christians who worship the creator of the lower world—to
recognize Protennoia's identity is especially evident in the final pages
of the *Trimorphic Protennoia.* They narrate the incognito descent of
Protennoia as the divine Logos, hidden in the forms of the various
celestial powers, culminating in her final self-revelation within her
earthly members. In 47,14–15, Protennoia reveals herself to them as
the Logos "in their tents" (cf. John 1:14). Then in *Trim. Prot.* 49,7–8, it
is said that the Archons thought Protennoia-Logos was "their Christ,
while actually she dwells in everyone."

In 49,6–50,20, traditional Christological titles such as Son of God
("Son of the Archigenetor") and Son of Man are polemically interpreted from a Sethian point of view, in a consciously transcenden-
talizing fashion. Protennoia became the "beloved" of the Archons
because since she had temporarily disguised herself as Son of the
Archigenetor until the end of his ignorant decree. Among the "Sons
of Man" Protennoia revealed herself as a Son of Man even though she
is really the Father of everyone. As Logos, Protennoia has put on Jesus
and borne him aloft from the cursed cross into his Father's dwelling
places (cf. John 14:2–3). By implication, the Son of God of the apos-

tolic Christian churches is actually the son of the ignorant world creator; and its Son of Man is only a human among the sons of men:

> [I was] dwelling in them [in the form of each one. [The Archons] thought [that I] was their *Christ*. Indeed I [dwell in] everyone. Indeed within those in whom [I revealed myself] as Light [I eluded] the Archons. I am their *Beloved*, [for] in that place I clothed myself [as] the *Son of the Archigenetor*, and I was like him until the end of his decree, which is the ignorance of Chaos. And among the Angels I revealed myself in their likeness, and among the Powers as if I were one of them, but among the Sons of Man as if I were a *Son of Man*, even though I am Father of everyone. I hid myself within them all until I revealed myself among my members, which are mine…and until I *gather* [together] all [my fellow] brethren within my [*eternal kingdom*]. And I proclaimed to them the ineffable Five Seals in order that [*I might*] *abide in them and they also might abide in me* (John 15:4). As for me, *I put on Jesus. I bore him from the cursed wood, and established him in the dwelling places of his Father.* And those who watch over their dwelling places did not recognize me. I, I am unrestrainable together with my Seed, and my Seed, which is mine, I shall [place] into the Holy Light within an incomprehensible Silence. Amen. (*Trim. Prot.* 49,6–50,20)

Some of these polemical Sethian reinterpretations of "orthodox" Christology in the *Trimorphic Protennoia* seem to depend on key texts from the Gospel of John in order to score their point in any acute fashion. The Johannine prologue's initial claim "In the beginning was the Logos" is countered by showing that what existed in the beginning was not the Logos, but rather the silent divine First Thought, which only later manifested itself as the Logos. This mild polemic is radicalized in the above citation from the third subtractate (*Trim. Prot.* 49,6–50,20) by arguing that the Logos in his incognito descent fooled everyone except his congenital members who recognized him; this theme of mutual recognition between the revealer and "his own" is of course also fundamental to the Johannine literature generally.[25]

---

[25] Cf. John 1:12–14; 10:1–4,14; 14:20; 17:2–23; 1 John 2:3–5; 3:24; 4:6,13; 5:19–20. In the discourse on the good shepherd (John 10:4–5), the voice which the sheep hear and respond to is the voice of their true shepherd who calls them out of the "mixture" of the world. That is, the sheep uniquely recognize their shepherd's voice not on the grounds of habit, but because they are the shepherd's "own"; they share some affinity with the shepherd which enables them to recognize his voice above all others. Jesus' own hear his voice as do all those who are of the truth (18:37; cf. 5:25; 10:4–5,16), but outsiders do not (5:37; cf. 3:8).

The underlying assumption seems to be that an ignorant creator God has fooled the leaders of the Johannine and other churches into teaching others to believe that the Christ was the Son of the world creator. In contrast to the traditional view of John 1:14, Protennoia merely *appeared* as the Logos "in their tents"[26] in the "*likeness* of their shape" but did not *actually* become flesh. In only disguising himself as the Christ of the Johannine community, the Logos was no Son of Man who was lifted up and glorified on the cross, going to prepare a place for the believers; instead, the Logos was the Father of everyone who descended to rescue Jesus from the "cursed"—not redemptive!—cross. In apparent reference to John 14:2–3, it was not Jesus who prepared a dwelling place for his *followers*; instead, it was the Logos who raised *Jesus* aloft and installed him into the aeonic "dwelling places of his Father," not the world creator, but the true Father, the Invisible Spirit (*Trim. Prot.* 50,12–16). In contrast to the Johannine gospel, rather than being the agent of salvation, Jesus is among its recipients. Indeed the Logos did come to confer a baptism, but not a baptism merely conferring the Spirit as in John 3:5 ("Truly, truly, I say to you, unless one is born of water and the Spirit, he cannot enter the kingdom of God"); it was instead a baptism that resulted in immediate rapture into the Light. Rather than having to await the arrival of Jesus or the Paraclete to "draw all people" unto himself (John 3:14; 8:22; 12:32–34), in the *Trimorphic Protennoia*, salvation is immediate: "he received the Five Seals from [the Light] of the Mother, Protennoia…and [he became a light] in Light" (*Trim. Prot.* 48,31–35).

We have seen that, by placing the monologue of Pronoia on the lips of Jesus in the conclusion of its main narrative, the *Apocryphon of John* regards Jesus rather than Barbelo/Pronoia as the one who raises her members into the light. In rather stark contrast, the *Trimorphic Protennoia* makes Jesus the object of redemption rather than its provider. In an apparent parody of John 12:31–32 ("Now is the judgment of this world, now shall the ruler of this world be cast out; and I, when I am lifted up from the earth, will draw all men to myself"), Jesus is

---

[26] "Tents" (σκηνή) may be a gloss on "the likeness of their shape" in *Trim. Prot.* 47,16 in what seems to be conscious opposition to ὁ λόγος σὰρξ ἐγένετο καὶ ἐσκήνωσεν ἐν ἡμῖν of John 1:14). However, the concept of tenting may have been part of the Logos theology of the original aretalogy; cf. Sirach 24:8: τότε ἐνετείλατό μοι ὁ κτίστης ἁπάντων, καὶ ὁ κτίσας με κατέπαυσεν τὴν σκηνήν μου καὶ εἶπεν Ἐν Ἰακωβ κατασκήνωσον καὶ ἐν Ἰσραηλ κατακληρονομήθητι.

indeed raised up by Barbelo/Protennoia rather than his Father, but it is she rather than he who will draw all men to herself.

4. THE JOHANNINE PROLOGUE

The Johannine prologue also manifests an incipient tendency towards periodizing the activity of the Logos into three phases in much the same way that the activity of Pronoia in the Pronoia monologue and the activity of Protennoia in the *Trimorphic Protennoia* are structured: the primordial act of creation and shining into the darkness (John 1:1–5), the initial entrance into the created order which did not recognize him (vv. 9–11), and the incarnation of the Logos in which he finally makes the Father known (vv. 12,14,16,18).[27] Just as in the *Trimorphic Protennoia*, where deliberate Christological interpretation occurs in the third part describing the final descent of Protennoia as the Logos, so also the specifically Christological content of the Johannine prologue occurs in the third part, and in both compositions this shift to Christological content is marked by the concept of the incarnation, the Logos "tenting" among men as Jesus Christ, the unique son of the Father. Unlike Matthew and Luke—or the opinions of the thirteen "kingdoms" of the *Apocalypse of Adam*—the prologue connects the incarnation to the baptism, not the birth of Jesus.

Just as the *Trimorphic Protennoia* seems to polemicize against certain views promulgated in the Fourth Gospel, Elaine Pagels[28] has pointed out that the Fourth evangelist polemicizes against various interpretations of Gen 1:1–3 according to which, on the "first day" prior to the world's creation, the form of the primal human ($\varphi\acute{\omega}\varsigma$) was manifested simultaneously with the appearance of the primordial light ($\varphi\tilde{\omega}\varsigma$). Thus the primordial light is implicitly present in human nature (and vice-versa). With regard to the Genesis account of the creation itself, various exegetes, including Philo, the Hermetic *Poimandres*, the *Gospel of Thomas* (logia 1–3, 17–19, 22, 61, 77, 85), the *Apocryphon of John*, and certain rabbis, interpreted Gen 1:27 as showing that this primordial human form was manifested in two stages: at first, when "God created *adam* in his image," he created a singular being—"in the image of God he created *him*" (Gen 1:27b)—who is also identical with the

---

[27] Cf. Becker 1979, 70; Smith 1999, 48; Keener 2003, 336–337.
[28] Pagels 1999, 477–496.

primordial light of Gen 1:3, but immediately thereafter, Gen 1:27c and Gen 2 depict humankind as a dual species, male and female—"male and female he created *them*" (Gen 1:27c). Likewise, the *Apocryphon of John* (II 4,26–5,11) initially identifies the primordial light as Barbelo, who is "the first Man." Later on in the text (II 14,16–20), after Sophia gives rise to the Archon, the divine voice—which in Genesis says "Let there be light"—again identifies the primordial light by informing the lower authorities that "Man exists, and the Son of Man." Thereupon "the Holy Father appeared to them in human form" and the abyss was shaken by "the light of his image that appeared" (II 14,33; 15,3). Here, the primordial light is both divine and human, and not a few Christian exegetes would have identified that light as the pre-existent Christ.

Against such views, the Johannine prologue (John 1:3) *denies* that the primordial light of Gen 1:1–3 was available through the image of God implicitly present in human nature. The divine image resides exclusively in the Logos, which only ages *later* became manifest in the figure of Jesus. Instead, the primordial light shone into an uncomprehending darkness (John 1:5). Far from being sharing a natural affinity with humanity, when the light came into the world, humans failed to recognize it (1:10), and when it came to "its own," they rejected it (1:11). From the time of its original appearance until the time of John the Baptist, the primordial light failed to penetrate the world's darkness; it manifests its glory, not at the beginning of the cosmos or in primordial humanity, but only when it "became flesh and dwelt among us" in the person of Jesus.

For both the Logos of the Johannine prologue and the figure of Pronoia in the *Apocryphon of John*, the revealer remains unrecognized by the denizens of the lower world, but on the third descent succeeds in being recognized by those who are to be raised into the light. Yet unlike the prologue, Pronoia's failure to be recognized is due, not to the natural opposition of darkness to light or to a rejection on the part of her "own," but to her apparent self-concealment during her first two descents, while on her third descent she clearly announces her presence. In this sense, neither the Johannine prologue nor the Pronoia monologue regards cosmic or cosmogonical manifestation as a path to the salvific knowledge of God.

4.1. *The Transcendent Preexistence of the Logos*

In the beginning was the Word, and the Word was with God, and the Word was God. He was in the beginning with God; all things were made through him, and without him was not anything made that was made. (John 1:1–3)

The *Apocryphon of John* (II 6,10–7,30) identifies the Word with the creative instrumentality of the unique (ⲡⲉϥϫⲡⲟ ⲟⲩⲁⲁⲧ͞ϥ = μονογενής; 6,17) self-generated (Autogenes) Child of Barbelo and the Invisible Spirit, who anointed him with his own goodness or "Christhood" (χρηστία). While he is fully divine and fully perfect, not lacking in any goodness, he is not equal to Pronoia. The Christological relationship is thus defined as one of subordination, while yet insisting that Christ is perfect. Through the Word, the Autogenes Christ creates only the divine realm of aeons structured around the Four Luminaries, having nothing to do with the lower world that originated through the lower mother Sophia.

4.2. *First Descent of the Logos (1:4–5)*

In him was life, and the life was the light of men. The light shines in the darkness, and the darkness has not overcome it. (John 1:4–5)

In the *Apocryphon of John*, these sentences parallel the first descent of the light into the world in the form of the luminous image of the archetypal Man and Son of Man in whose image the lower rulers form the protoplastic Adam. Despite their attempts to capture that light in a mortal soul and material body, the lower rulers could not succeed in overcoming the illumining power of the light. The initial appearance of the image of the archetypal Man also prefigures the subsequent appearance of the Epinoia of light as the spiritual Eve, the mother of the living hidden within Adam (cf. the Johannine "in him was life") to illumine subsequent humanity with a true knowledge of the divine realm.

(There was a man sent from God, whose name was John. He came for testimony, to bear witness to the light, that all might believe through him. He was not the light, but came to bear witness to the light.) (John 1:6–8)

The *Apocryphon of John* understands the John referred to here as the son of Zebedee and not the Baptist, sent to bear testimony to his fellow spirits of the immovable race, who are all the progeny of the Mother's seed caught in the world of darkness.

As is well known, Bultmann also argued that the insertion of references to John the Baptist in verses 6–8 and 15 of the prologue is best explained by regarding it as a hymn originally composed in honor of John the Baptist.[29] As in the Benedictus hymn of Luke 1:76–79, in which Zechariah proclaims John to be the prophet of the Most High who gives his people knowledge of salvation when the light from on high dawns to illumine those dwelling in darkness,[30] the original version of the prologue would have proclaimed John as the definitive advent of the Logos or the divine light and wisdom into this world. Once introduced to the Johannine community and incorporated into the Fourth Gospel, the evangelist would have inserted these verses in order to construe Jesus rather than John as the true light and Logos coming into the world, while the Baptist becomes a mere witness to that event.

4.3. *Second descent of the Logos (1:9–13)*

The true light that enlightens every man was coming into the world. He was in the world, and the world was made through him, yet the world knew him not. He came to his own home, and his own people received him not. But to all who received him, (who believed in his name), he gave power to become children of God; (who were born, not of blood nor of the will of the flesh nor of the will of man, but of God.) (John 1:9–13)

These sentences parallel the *Apocryphon of John*'s story of the second descent of Pronoia (identified with Christ) in the form of the luminous Epinoia who teaches the protoplasts to eat from the tree of knowledge, a figure that the longer version also identifies as Christ. In various episodes, Epinoia comes as the emissary of light to the Mother's seed to enlighten them and combat the rulers of darkness, who continually thwart her work. Like the prologue, she teaches them that their

---

[29] Bultmann 1971, 19–31; *contra* Keener 2003, 333–337. The *Apocryphon of John* construes these as referring to John son of Zebedee.

[30] The portrayal of the deliverer or his forerunner as a light dawning (ἀνατέλλειν, ἀνατολή) or entering the world is also found in the *Testament of Levi* 18 concerning the advent of the messianic priest-king. Besides drawing on the Jewish motif of the descent of the divine Wisdom as presented in Sirach 24 and *1 Enoch* 42, such texts may also draw on the tradition of the eschatological advent of the star and scepter of Num 24:17, often interpreted as referring to the advent of a royal and a priestly Messiah by the Dead Sea sect and others (cf. 1QM 11,6; 1QSb 5,20–25; 4QTest 9–13; CD 7,9–21; also *T. Jud.* 24 and Rev 22:16).

true identity does not belong to flesh and blood nor to sexual desire and reproduction, which are the lies used by the rulers to keep them entrapped in the darkness. Instead, they are the children of God to whom is revealed the true name of God, the Christ: "the Name will be told to those who are worthy of it" (BG 32,18–19; the longer version II 8,27–30 adds that Christ "has been called with a name that is above every name," cf. Phil 2:5–11).

4.4. *Third Descent of the Logos (1:14)*

> And the Word became flesh and dwelt among us, full of grace and truth; we have beheld his glory, glory as of the only Son from the Father. (John 1:14)

In the *Apocryphon of John*, on her third descent into the lower world, Pronoia-Christ, as the only-begotten of the Invisible Spirit "entered into the midst of their prison which is the prison of the body" (II 31,3–4), not only the material body as in both versions, but, for the longer version, also in the super-added psychic body.

Although the *Trimorphic Protennoia* emphasizes that Protennoia as Logos *appeared* in human likeness rather than actually *becoming* flesh, both it and the Pronoia monologue equate Pronoia/Protennoia's third descent into the world with the Johannine prologue's account of Jesus coming in the flesh and thereby invite their readers to consider the entire Fourth Gospel in terms of the Christ's mission to awaken ignorant humanity to a recognition that they are the true children of God who must reject darkness and receive the light, which is Christ himself. In this way all instances of resistance to Jesus' mission in the Gospel of John are to be seen merely as further attempts by the rulers and powers of darkness to oppose the saving work of the divine realm through Christ.

> (John bore witness to him, and cried, "This was he of whom I said, 'He who comes after me ranks before me, for he was before me.'") (John 1:15)

Here, the reference to John is again understood by the *Apocryphon of John* to apply to Jesus' disciple John son of Zebedee, not the Baptist of the Fourth Gospel. And of course, both works emphasizes the pre-existence of Christ before the creation of the world and before the mission of John.

And from his fullness (πλήρης) have we all received grace upon grace. For the law was given through Moses; grace and truth came through Jesus Christ. No one has ever seen God; the only Son, who is in the bosom of the Father, he has made him known. (John 1:16–18)

Both the *Apocryphon of John* (using πλήρωμα) and the Gospel of John (here using πλήρης) agree that the fullness of God is revealed only through Christ's descent into the world, which is what makes both of these texts "Christian." By contrast with Christ, who as the only son of the Father has seen God and brings the full revelation of the truth, Moses did not truly see God as claimed in Exodus (*Ap. John* II 24,9–12; cf. 13,20), and his Torah contains only a clouded version of the truth. Moses has seen only the lower God, and misunderstood what has taken place (cf. "not as Moses said/wrote," *Ap. John* II 13,19–20; 22,22–23; 23,3; 29,6).

Although present evidence is inconclusive, the parallels in imagery and structure between the Pronoia monologue and the Johannine prologue suggest that they may be nearly contemporaneous compositions. If so, the notion of a redeemer's threefold or three-stage descent to rescue those few who recognize him or her from the realm of darkness or chaos to the realm of light was celebrated in the form of various liturgical hymns sometime in the late first century.

Essentially, this scheme of the triple descent of the divine First Thought into this world is a derivative of speculation at home in the Hellenistic Jewish Wisdom schools responsible for the personification of the figure of the divine Wisdom and the development of the myth concerning her role in the creation of the world and in the subsequent enlightenment of mankind as it is found especially in Proverbs (especially 8; 16–18), Sirach (especially 1; 24), Wisdom (especially 9–10), *4 Ezra, 1 Enoch* 42, and in Philo.[31] In this Wisdom tradition, the exalted Sophia was identified with the divine name, glory and Shekinah, and with the revelation of the divine will in the form of the Torah. Sophia was conceived as a radiant light, the effulgence of the most high, who provided enlightenment for all who would seek her instruction. She was the first-born of all creation, and by her the world was established. She was the overflowing source of light and life, a canal of water flowing into a river flowing into a sea, and made her instruction shine forth like the dawn. She made her throne in a pillar of cloud, and she

---

[31] See above, note 19.

covered the earth like a mist, and those who thirsted for her could drink of her. Such images appear also in the early chapters of Genesis, where it speaks of the Spirit hovering over the face of the Tehom, or a mist covering the earth in the Garden of Eden. Having been God's instrument in the creation of the All, she was tirelessly active in the attempt to enlighten its human denizens and save them from peril. It is significant that Wisdom 10:1–6 historicizes Wisdom's salvific activity in the following sequence of visitations: she protected the first-formed father of the world, saved the earth from the flood through Noah and the ark, recognized the righteousness of Abraham amidst the confusion of Babel, and rescued Lot from the fire that descended on Sodom and Gomorrah; the second and fourth of these visitations correspond rather precisely with those attributed to Seth in the Sethian treatises the *Apocalypse of Adam* and the *Gospel of the Egyptians*, while the first corresponds closely with the descent of Pronoia as Epinoia/Eve in the *Apocryphon of John*. Eventually, Sophia desired to seek a place where she might dwell and set up her tent. In *1 Enoch* 42, her seeking is unsuccessful and she twice reascends to heaven among the angels (cf. *4 Ezra* 5:9), while it was only Iniquity who left her abode to dwell like a rain or dew among those whom she did not expect to meet. But in Sirach 24, Sophia's seeking is successful, and she makes her tent among the children of Israel in Zion in the form of the Mosaic Torah.

To judge from the Johannine prologue, the Pronoia monologue and the *Trimorphic Protennoia*, the myth of Sophia's two unsuccessful descents in *1 Enoch* 42 and her successful one in Sirach 24 were combined into a total of three descents into the lower world, two unsuccessful, and the third, successful, resulting in the final awakening and salvation of those who received her. The basic (and perhaps oldest) Sethian texts reflecting such speculation on Sophia, that is, the Pronoia monologue, and the *Trimorphic Protennoia*, are clearly structured around the attempts of the divine First Thought to enter the daily life of a humankind who had become oblivious to her, and to reveal herself and her ultimate source in the higher world. A similar pattern is ascribed to the Logos in the Johannine prologue, but without a clear enumeration of descents, and only a select few respond to the call for enlightenment.

5. Baptism in the Fourth Gospel and the
Apocryphon of John

As we have seen, both the Pronoia monologue of the *Apocryphon of John* and the *Trimorphic Protennoia* portray the salvation brought by Pronoia/Protennoia on her third descent in ritual terms, as enlightenment conferred through the baptismal rite of the Five Seals, in which one is raised up and "sealed in the luminous water." Although the Johannine prologue apparently contains no explicit reference to a baptismal ritual, the coming of the Logos into the flesh nevertheless allows believers to see the "glory" of the Logos who alone has seen the Father. Could it be that this act of seeing is somehow related to a form of baptism?

While we know next to nothing about the baptismal ritual of the Johannine community, one does note a cluster of Johannine baptismal motifs—such as Light, Living Water, the descent of the Spirit upon Jesus reminiscent of the descent of the Logos to become flesh, and the appearance of John as the precursory Voice announcing the advent of the divine light into the world—motifs that are even more explicitly utilized by the "Barbeloite" precursors of Sethianism. These elements were perhaps already associated with the prologue of the Fourth Gospel prior to its incorporation into the Fourth Gospel, no matter whether—on the hypothesis of Bultmann—it may have originated among the disciples of John the Baptist, or whether it may have been an inner-Johannine composition based on the kinds of considerations that later appeared also in 1 John 1:1–3. That is, the prologue may have been introduced into the community either at its inception, or else later on, prepended to some version of the gospel as an appropriate prologue.

Once introduced to the Johannine community and incorporated into the Fourth Gospel, the evangelist would have inserted verses 6–8 and 15 in order to construe Jesus rather than John as the true light and Logos coming into the world, while the Baptist becomes a mere witness to that event: "You sent to John, and he has borne witness to the truth…he was a burning and shining lamp, and you were willing to rejoice for a while in his light" (5:33–35). The evangelist further elaborated this construction of John in 1:19–37 by omitting the tradition of Jesus' baptism by John[32] and having John explicitly deny that

---

[32] Perhaps continuing a tendency to downplay Jesus' baptism by John, as appears in the explanatory dialogue stressing Jesus' superiority to the Baptist prior to the baptism

he is the Christ or Elijah or the prophet (like Moses) and assert both the superiority and priority of Jesus,[33] whom he claims not to have known, but upon whom he has seen the Spirit descend and remain, as well as portraying Jesus' first two disciples as having defected from following John. In this way, John's water baptism has become superceded by a visionary experience of the descent of the Spirit (in this case, upon Jesus, who will in turn enable its future descent on those who believe in him).

Moreover, the Baptist represents a less articulate stage of revelation in preparation for the advent of Jesus as Word: thus Christ appears as the fully articulate Logos who speaks the words of eternal life (6:68), while John the Baptist only appears as a mere "Voice crying in the wilderness" to prepare the way of the Lord (John 1:23; cf. Isa 40:3). Here, the Fourth Gospel's distinction between the Voice and the Logos indeed constitutes a certain parallel with the *Trimorphic Protennoia*. The *Trimorphic Protennoia* presents one with a sort of theology of revelation, in which the First Thought of the Invisible Spirit reveals itself throughout history in increasing degrees of articulateness: first a pure, but not fully articulate Voice which in some sense empowers Protennoia's members; second, a more articulate Speech which gives them shape, i.e., "informs" them; and third, the fully articulate Logos who appears in their own, human, shape.[34]

Interpreted in light of the Sethian salvation history of the *Apocryphon of John*, the First Thought's initial appearance as Voice occurs with Barbelo's revelation to the Archon creator that "Man exists, and the Son of Man," a phrase probably originally referring to the supreme God Man and his Son, the archetypal Adam, in whose image the earthly Adam is made (II 14,13–15). Her second appearance as the feminine Speech of the Voice parallels the appearance of the Epinoia or spiritual Eve, who reveals to Adam his true "shape" or "form" (II 20,14–28; 22,28–23,35). Her third appearance as the masculine and fully articulate Logos grants full enlightenment by means of the Five Seals, the Sethian baptismal

---

in Matt 3:14–15 and in Luke's (3:19–20) prefacing his brief mention of Jesus' baptism in 3:21 by the notice that John had already been imprisoned by Herod Antipas, in effect leaving the administrator of the rite unidentified.

[33] This superiority motif reappears in John 3:25–28; 4:1; 10:40–42.

[34] Nevertheless, in the larger scheme of the Fourth Gospel, the shift from obscurity to clarity rests not so much on this theory of increasingly articulate revelatory media as it does on the key event of the crucifixion: Jesus as revealer speaks in riddles until the point of his glorification on the cross, at which point it becomes clear to the disciples that not only has he come from the Father, but he is also going back to the Father (John 16:25–30).

ritual (II 30,12–31,25).[35] Nevertheless, both the Fourth Gospel and the *Trimorphic Protennoia* clearly associate the Logos with the final, definitive stage of revelation. While the Fourth Gospel distributes the functions of Voice and Word among distinct human figures, the *Trimorphic Protennoia* attributes them to one and the same transcendental being, Protennoia: she is not only the Voice that gave rise to the heavenly Christ who established the Four Lights and the Speech that confuses the Archons as it announces the impending end of their regime, but she is also the Logos who descended to redeem the earthly Jesus from the cross and elevate her seed into the light.

Just as several Sethian texts construe the baptism of the Five Seals as a visionary ascent into the transcendental realm,[36] the Fourth Gospel also interprets baptism as a transcendental event. In contrast to the synoptic accounts, John the Baptist does not baptize Jesus in the ordinary waters of the Jordan, but instead witnesses the descent of the Spirit upon Jesus as the one who will baptize with the Holy Spirit (John 1:33). This Spirit is identified both as the words of Jesus (6:63) and as their future recapitulator (14:26) that will guide his disciples into all truth (16:13). In the Nicodemus dialogue of chapter 3, it seems that the evangelist may have taken a phrase from a traditional Christian liturgy of baptism through which one was initiated into the community ("Unless one is born [from above? again?], he cannot *enter* the Kingdom of God," John 3:5) and transformed it into a form more nearly parallel with the Sethian doctrine of baptism as a visionary ascent: "Unless one is born from above, he will never *see* the Kingdom of God" (John 3:3).[37] In chapters 3 and 4, we learn that while John the Baptist was baptizing at Aenon near Salim, Jesus was in Judea baptiz-

---

[35] Similarly in frg. 5 of Heracleon's commentary on the Gospel of John, the entire series of the prophets is regarded noise (ἦχος), John the Baptist is the Voice (φωνή), while the Savior is the Logos; indeed the Voice is said to become the Logos as a female is transformed into a male. The *Trimorphic Protennoia* may have provided the pre-Christian conceptual background for this theologoumenon: the thing that actually is transformed from female to male is the Wisdom or First Thought of the supreme deity. In *Fug.* 109, Philo considers Wisdom to be the Mother of the Logos. As the Mother of the cosmos, Wisdom speaks with increasing articulation to that cosmos from its creation through its shaping until the point where Wisdom herself takes up residence in the world created through her.

[36] Namely the *Apocryphon of John*, the *Trimorphic Protennoia*, the *Apocalypse of Adam*, the *Gospel of the Egyptians*, *Melchizedek*, *Zostrianos*, and perhaps the *Gospel of Judas*. See Turner 1998b, 63–113; Turner 2006, 941–992; and Sevrin 1986.

[37] John the Baptist's identification of Jesus in 3:31 as "he who comes from above (ἄνωθεν)" echoes Jesus' dialog with Nicodemus about divine birth from above.

ing and making more disciples than John (although the evangelist or a later redactor denies the tradition that Jesus himself baptized; cf. John 3:22–30; 4:1–2). In John 4:14,23, Jesus tells the Samaritan woman at Jacob's well that he dispenses a water that becomes in one who drinks of it a spring welling up to eternal life, and that true worshipers worship the Father in Spirit and truth, a theme echoed again in John 7:38 to the effect that springs of Living Water will flow from the heart of the one who believes in him. Indeed, this Living Water seems to be identical with either the Spirit or Jesus' words or both.

Now in Sethianism, Living Water is frequently mentioned in both theogonical and baptismal contexts and is sometimes directly associated with Jesus. In the *Apocryphon of John* (II 4,19–26), the primal luminosity surrounding the Invisible Spirit is the Living Water from which Barbelo emerges as his First Thought. In the *Trimorphic Protennoia* (46,16–19), the Logos who descends with the Five Seals is the one who pours forth Living Water upon the Spirit below from out of the spring of Living Water, which is identified with Protennoia herself as Voice of the divine First Thought. In the *Gospel of the Egyptians*, Seth appears in the form of the Logos-begotten Jesus bearing the sacred baptism of the Five Seals (III 62,24–64,9). For the (Sethian) *Apocalypse of Adam* (85,22–31), the hidden knowledge of Adam bequeathed to Seth *is* the holy baptism of those born through the Logos and the Living Water in the persons of the imperishable illuminators. Indeed, the latter two treatises (*Gos. Eg.* III 64,10–12; 66,10–11; *Apoc. Adam* 85,30–31) explicitly identify Jesus with the Living Water "Yesseus Mazareus Yessedekeus," surely a barbarization of the name "Jesus of Nazareth."

Just as the Fourth Gospel seems to polemicize—by silence—against the tradition of Jesus' (and perhaps also believers') baptism in ordinary water, the *Apocalypse of Adam* quite clearly regards baptism in ordinary water as a means of enslaving its recipients to the will of the evil powers. The second half of this treatise (77,26–82,19) contains thirteen opinions—the last of which seems to represent the apostolic doctrine of baptism—concerning the origin of the saving Illuminator, who receives nourishment, glory, and power in the beyond, and then "comes (down) to the water"—that is, descends to earth—whereupon he is recognized. But since the author or a later redactor regards such earthly waters as polluted and chaotic, he rejects these opinions in favor of the view that the Illuminator originates from above, where he resides in the light with the "three imperishable illuminators" Yesseus,

Mazareus, Yessedekeus, the Living Water.[38] The incognito descents of the Illuminator are recognized only by those baptized, not in ordinary earthly water, but through a vision of the living water above. The Fourth Gospel also seems to reinterpret John's water baptism in a similar way; as the Illuminator "comes to the water," so John has a vision of the spirit coming upon Jesus, but not as upon one immersed in the earthly baptismal waters of the synoptic story, since according to John 7:38–39, the true baptismal water is the living water of the spirit above. Like the Samaritan woman's confusion of the living water of eternal life that Jesus dispenses with the ordinary water of Jacob's well, the Baptist's use of ordinary water amounts to ignorance: "I myself did not know him; but he who sent me to baptize with water said to me, 'He on whom you see the Spirit descend and remain, this is he who baptizes with the Holy Spirit'" (John 1:33). One is also reminded of the Johannine Nicodemus, who recognizes Jesus only on the basis of his earthly self-manifestation, but, lacking baptismal rebirth in water and spirit, cannot undergo the visionary ascent requisite to entering the kingdom of heaven and seeing Jesus' heavenly origin.

6. REVELATORY MEDIA: VOICE AND WORD

In the Johannine texts so far discussed, the divine Voice serves as an important revelatory medium, sometimes for glorification, sometimes for judgment, and sometimes for both. Thus in the *Apocryphon of John*, on the one hand the voice of the supreme deity glorifies the emergence of his and Barbelo's self-generated:

> And the Holy Spirit completed the divine Self-originate, his Son with Barbelo, so as to have him stand near the great and Invisible Virginal Spirit as the divine Autogenes, the Christ, the one whom he honored with a loud voice. (*Ap. John* II 7,15–21)

On the other hand, in the same work, when the divine Voice of Pronoia announces "Man exists and Son of Man" (II 14,14–15) and she manifests her image in human form, the Voice, whose origin Yaldabaoth is unable to recognize, precipitates a cosmic disturbance:

---

[38] Elsewhere Yesseus Mazareus Yessedekeus ("Jesus of Nazareth is righteous"?) is always a single figure, but is here taken to refer to the three appearances of the Illuminator (*Apoc. Adam* 76,8–9).

The entire aeon of the first ruler trembled, and the foundations of the abyss shook, and through the waters that are over matter the lower region [shone] from the [appearance] of his Image that had been revealed. And when all the authorities and the first ruler gazed in astonishment they saw the whole of the lower region shining. And through the light, they saw in the water the pattern of the Image. (*Ap. John* II 14,24–34)

So also in the *Trimorphic Protennoia*, where Protennoia appears successively as the Voice, Speech and Word of the divine First Thought, her Voice not only conveys revelation, but also judgment:

Then I too revealed my Voice secretly, saying, "Cease! Desist, (you archons) who tread on matter; for behold I am coming down to the world of mortals for the sake of my portion that was in that place from the time when the innocent Sophia was conquered, she who descended so that I might thwart their aim which the one revealed by her appoints." And all were disturbed, each one who dwells in the house of the ignorant light and the abyss trembled. And the Archigenetor of ignorance reigned over Chaos and the underworld and produced a man in my likeness. But he neither knew that that one would become for him a sentence of dissolution nor does he recognize the power in him. (*Trim. Prot.* 40,8–29)

A similar result occurs when Protennoia reveals herself the second time as the Speech of the First Thought to announce the end of the Aeon of the archons:

And the Powers all gathered and went up to the Archigenetor. [They said to] him, "Where is your boasting in which [you boast]? Did we not [hear you say], 'I am God [and I am] your Father and it is I who [begot] you and there is no [other] beside me'? Now behold, there has appeared [a] Voice belonging to that invisible Speech of [the Aeon] (and) which we know not. And we ourselves did not recognize to whom we belong, for that Voice which we listened to is foreign to us, and we do not recognize it; we did not know whence it was. It came and put fear in our midst and weakening in the members of our arms. So now let us weep and mourn most bitterly! As for the future, let us make our entire flight before we are imprisoned perforce and taken down to the bosom of the underworld." (*Trim. Prot.* 43,31–44,14)

A more compressed version of the same scene is offered by Irenaeus' account of certain "other" Gnostics—later identified by Theodoret as "Sethians or Ophites"—in *Adversus haereses* 1.30.6:

Yaldabaoth, becoming haughty in spirit, bragged over all that was beneath him, exclaiming "I am father, and God, and above me there is no one." But when his mother heard him speak thus, she cried out against him, "Do not lie, Yaldabaoth: for the father of all, the first Man, is above you and so is Man the Son of Man." Then, while all of them were disturbed by this new voice and its unexpected proclamation and were seeking the source of the loud voice, so as to distract and seduce them for himself, Yaldabaoth exclaimed, "Come, let us make man after our image."

Similarly in the Fourth Gospel, the revelatory medium of the divine voice conveys both glorification and judgment. Thus in John 12:28–33, after entering Jerusalem to shouts of "Hosanna," Jesus invokes the Father to glorify the Son of Man through his elevation on the cross with the words "Father, glorify thy name." Thereupon the divine voice speaks:

> Then a voice came from heaven, "I have glorified it, and I will glorify it again." The crowd standing by heard it and said that it had thundered. Others said, "An angel has spoken to him." Jesus answered, "This voice has come for your sake, not for mine. Now is the judgment of this world, now shall the ruler of this world be cast out; and I, when I am lifted up from the earth, will draw all men to myself."

In the Gospel of John, those who do not recognize the divine voice are stereotyped as Jews who claim the God of Israel as their Father, but do not recognize the divine voice:

> And the Father who sent me has himself borne witness to me. His voice you have never heard, his form you have never seen; and you do not have his word abiding in you, for you do not believe him whom he has sent. (John 5:37–38)

Nor do they recognize the God whose word Jesus speaks:

> Jesus answered, "If I glorify myself, my glory is nothing; it is my Father who glorifies me, of whom you say that he is your God. But you have not known him; I know him. If I said, I do not know him, I should be a liar like you; but I do know him and I keep his word. (John 8:54–55)

In fact they are devotees, not of God, but of the devil:

> If God were your Father, you would love me, for I proceeded and came forth from God; I came not of my own accord, but he sent me. Why do you not understand what I say? It is because you cannot bear to hear my word. You are of your father the devil, and your will is to do your father's desires. He was a murderer from the beginning and has nothing to do with the truth, because there is no truth in him. When he lies, he speaks according to his own nature, for he is a liar and the father of lies. But, because I tell the truth, you do not believe me. Which of you convicts me of sin? If I tell the truth, why do you not believe me? He who is of God hears the words of God; the reason why you do not hear them is that you are not of God. (John 8:42–47)

Mutatis mutandis, both the Gospel and *Apocryphon* of John characterize the Jews and their leaders as accusing Jesus of being a liar who has
abandoned the traditions of the fathers. In the Gospel:

> He is leading the people astray. (John 7:12)

And in the *Apocryphon*:

> The Pharisee [said to him], ["This Nazarene has greatly] deceived you,
> and he [has filled your ears with lies] and closed [your minds] and turned
> you from the tradition of your ancestors." (*Ap. John* II 1,13–17)

In this case, the representative of the Jews is the Pharisee Arimanios,
clearly a parody on the name of the Zoroastrian evil spirit Ahriman,
whose essential nature is expressed in his principal epithet *Druj*, "the
Lie," which expresses itself as greed, wrath, and envy.

The Johannine understanding of those who reject Jesus' teaching
as children of the devil connects with the *Apocryphon of John*'s entire
portrayal of the powers of darkness who created and rule the lower
world. This lower God is the father of the cosmos whose nature is
shown by his acts of hostility and ignorance. He brought all of humanity into death and desire by fashioning the first human according to
his own image and from the substance of his lower powers, and finally
the flesh. As in the Fourth Gospel, those who reject Jesus are the children of this lower God, not by nature, but because they have not yet
received the true Spirit.

7. THE *APOCRYPHON OF JOHN* AS THE COMPLETION OF THE GOSPEL OF JOHN

As Karen King points out, "The fact that the entire *Secret Revelation
of John* is framed as the return of Christ to complete his revelation
and show the way back to the Divine Realm makes it possible to read
it as the completion of Christ's revelation in the Gospel of John, the
fulfillment of his promise to return and show them the way back to
the Father."[39]

As post-resurrection dialogues, the Coptic versions of the *Apocryphon
of John* are intended to clarify the Fourth Gospel's comparatively more
obscure revelations attributed to a pre-crucifixion savior still veiled

---

[39] King 2006, 237–238. Cf. Nagel 2000, 393–398; and Pleše 2006, 10.

in the flesh. While the Fourth Gospel begins the story only with the appearance of the Logos, the *Apocryphon* starts at its true beginning, with the Invisible Spirit and his First Thought, whose child, the Christ, subsequently requests the appearance of Mind, Will, and Logos. The Fourth Gospel's farewell dialogues between the *pre-crucifixion* Jesus and his uncomprehending disciples Peter, Thomas, and Philip concerning his promised return to the Father are now supplemented by John's *post-ascension* encounter with the very Savior who had indeed already returned to the Father just as he had predicted. The veiled references to the many rooms of his Father's house to which the earthly Savior had promised to take his followers in John 14:2–3 are now clarified in detail, as is the unity between the Father and the Son (John 10:30; 17:11,22): Jesus *is* the Father, Mother and Son. In his capacity as the blessed Mother-Father, Christ had *already* elevated the primordial seed of Seth to the Father's many-roomed house, namely the Four Aeons which he himself had previously prepared *before* this world had ever come to be.

The extreme realized eschatology and transcendentalism of the *Apocryphon of John*, while constituting a tolerable extension of some of the main doctrines of the Gospel's first twenty chapters, strongly contrasts with the doctrine of the Johannine letters, which emphasize the importance of Jesus' fleshly incarnation, his expiatory death on the cross, the sacramental consumption of his flesh and blood, the corporeality of his resurrection body, and his future appearance at the last day to raise up his own. The author or authors of those canonical letters may even have been responsible for various glosses[40] and revisions to the Fourth Gospel that emphasize these same notions. Chapter 21 seems to constitute such a revision, where the sons of Zebedee appear for the first time in the gospel: along with certain other disciples they witness Jesus' "third" resurrection appearance, this time in Galilee, while chapter 20 already narrates three appearances in Jerusalem, one

---

[40] For example, the alternation between realized and futuristic eschatology in chapter 6, where on the one hand, the believer *has* eternal life now (John 6:47,50–51,58); on the other hand, the believer will be "raised up at the last day" (6:39,40,44,54). Similarly, on the one hand, eternal life is received by believing in the Son (6:29,35,40,47,63), while on the other, eternal life can be realized only through eating Jesus' flesh and drinking his blood (6:53–57), alluding to a Eucharistic ritual for whose institution by Jesus the foot-washing scene at the last supper provides no apparent warrant. On such redactions, see Richter 1975, 117–152, but *contra* Anderson 1996, and discussion in Rasimus 2009.

to Mary Magdalene, one to the disciples with Thomas absent, and one to the disciples with Thomas present. Just as the appearance to Mary in chapter 20 seems to be redactionally interrupted in vv. 2–9 portraying a comparative race between Peter and the Beloved Disciple to inspect the empty tomb, so also in chapter 21 Jesus singles out Peter as the leader of the church who is destined for martyrdom, while the Beloved Disciple, who is claimed as the gospel's author, will merely remain alive until Jesus' future parousia.

In contrast with Jesus' future parousia at the end of days envisioned by chapter 21 and the Johannine letters, the *Apocryphon of John* portrays this parousia as occurring in Jerusalem only shortly after the events described in the gospel, and in effect challenges the leadership role John 21 assigns to *Peter* by having the post-ascension Jesus appoint *John* as the teacher of his fellow disciples. In doing so, the *Apocryphon* reasserts the Jerusalem location of the appearances in chapter 20 over against the Galilean location of chapter 21: in answer to John's statement that Jesus had "returned to the place whence he came," the Pharisee Arimanios' taunting response implies that the deceiver Jesus had merely returned to Nazareth of Galilee, whereupon Jesus suddenly appears to John in a mountainous place, not in Galilee—as John 21 and the apostolic Gospel of Matthew have it—but near the Jerusalem temple.

8. A Parallel History of Christological Reflection?[41]

This study has suggested a certain parallelism between the Johannine and Sethian movements, in that both would have originated as non-Christian baptismal sects. The one consisted partly of the disciples of John the Baptist, who were developing a spiritual interpretation of the baptism conferred by their master who—on Bultmann's hypothesis—they believed was manifested among them to bring light into the darkness, as in the Benedictus sung by Zechariah at John's birth (Luke 1:76–79). The other was developing a transcendental baptismal rite as the vehicle of enlightenment conferred by the divine First Thought appearing as the Logos bearing the Five Seals, as in the *Apocryphon of John's* Pronoia monologue. Near the end of the first century, it

---

[41] For a fuller version of the following hypothesis, see Turner 2005, 422–429.

seems that both the prologue and the Pronoia monologue underwent Christianization: the prologue in Johannine Christian circles when it was adopted by the evangelist or his successors and made to refer to Jesus, and the Pronoia monologue in Christianized "Barbeloite" circles when it was construed as the conclusion of Christ's final self-revelation as the divine First Thought to John son of Zebedee.

Sometime in the early to mid-second century, the Johannine letters allow us to detect at least two and perhaps three wings of the Johannine church.[42] Several decades ago, Raymond Brown[43] characterized one wing as represented by the author of the Johannine letters who maintained close contact with the apostolic churches in his insistence on Jesus' advent in the flesh and his future parousia, and the other—more dominant—wing as secessionists from the original community who denied the full humanity of Jesus and downplayed the importance of the earthly life of either Jesus or the believer. The smaller group strove to maintain contact with the apostolic churches and may have facilitated this contact by a subsequent revision of the gospel (such as the addition of chapter 21) to bring its somewhat otherworldly Christology into line with the more dominant apostolic emphasis on the saving significance of Jesus' ministry, death and resurrection as witnessed by the Synoptic Gospels. This group may have succeeded in winning the acceptance of the gospel among such second-century traditionalists as Irenaeus at a time when it was being claimed by Gnostic Christians, including Sethian exegetes like the final redactors of the *Apocryphon of John* and the *Trimorphic Protennoia* as well as Valentinian exegetes such as Heracleon. Given Brown's hypothesis, sometime around the middle of the second century, it is possible that the Sethians behind the *Apocryphon of John* and the *Trimorphic Protennoia* made common cause with the ultra-high Christological thinking of those whom the author of 1 John considered to be secessionists who rejected the propitiatory blood of the cross in favor of the spirit of truth received in baptism, since for them the true advent of Jesus occurred through the spirit, that is the living water of baptism (John 1:33; 3:5; 4:10–14; 7:38–39; 13:5; but *contra* 19:34; 1 John 5:6–8).[44] In effect, they sided with the secessionists in the struggle over the correct interpretation of

---

[42] See Trebilco 2004, 241–271.

[43] Brown 1978, 5–22; Brown 1979, *passim*; Martyn 1979, *passim*; and *contra* Hengel 1993.

[44] See Painter 2002, 302–307; and Trebilco 2004, 289–290.

the gospel, directing themselves against the partisans of the author(s) of the Johannine letters. By casting the Sethian protology, sacred history and soteriology into a dialogue between the risen Jesus and John son of Zebedee, the authors of the *Apocryphon of John* in effect also joined in this struggle.

BIBLIOGRAPHY

Anderson, P., *The Christology of the Fourth Gospel: Its Unity and Disunity in the Light of John 6*, Wissenschaftliche Untersuchungen zum Neuen Testament 78, Tübingen: Mohr Siebeck, 1996.
Barc, B. and L. Painchaud, "La réecriture de l'*Apocryphon de Jean* à la lumière de l'hymne final de la version longue," *Le Museon* 112 (1999), 317–333.
Becker, J., *Das Evangelium nach Johannes*, Ökumensischer Taschenbuchkommentar zum Neuen Testament 4/1, Gütersloh: Gütersloher Verlagshaus, 1979.
Brown, R.E., "Johannine Ecclesiology—The Community's Origins," *Interpretation* 31 (1977), 379–393.
—— "Other Sheep not of this Fold," *Journal of Biblical Literature* 97 (1978), 5–22.
—— *The Community of the Beloved Disciple*, New York: Paulist Press, 1979.
Bultmann, R., *The Gospel of John: A Commentary*, G.R. Beasley-Murray, transl., Oxford: Blackwell, 1971.
Hengel, M., *Die johanneische Frage: Ein Lösungsversuch, mit einem Beitrag von Jörg Frey*, Wissenschaftliche Untersuchungen zum Neuen Testament 67, Tübingen: Mohr Siebeck, 1993.
Keener, C.S., *The Gospel of John: A Commentary*, Vol. 1, Peabody, Mass.: Hendrickson, 2003.
King, K.L., *The Secret Revelation of John*, Cambridge, Mass.: Harvard University Press, 2006.
Klijn, A.F.J., *Seth in Jewish, Christian and Gnostic Literature*, Supplements to Novum Testamentum 46, Leiden: Brill, 1977.
MacRae, G.W., "The Jewish Background of the Gnostic Sophia Myth," *Novum Testamentum* 12 (1970), 86–101.
Martyn, J.L., *History and Theology in the Fourth Gospel*, Nashville: Abingdon, [2]1979.
Nagel, T., *Die Rezeption des Johannesevangeliums im 2. Jahrhundert: Studien zur vorirenäischen Aneignung und Auslegung des vierten Evangeliums in christlicher und christlich-gnostischer Literatur*, Arbeiten zur Bibel und ihrer Geschichte 2, Leipzig: Evangelische Verlagsanstalt, 2000.
Pagels, E.H., "Exegesis of Genesis 1 in the Gospels of Thomas and John," *Journal of Biblical Literature* 118/3 (1999), 477–496.
Painter, J., *1, 2, and 3 John*, Sacra Pagina 18, Collegeville, Minn.: Liturgical Press, 2002.
Pearson, B.A., "The Figure of Seth in Gnostic Literature," *The Rediscovery of Gnosticism: Volume 2: Sethian Gnosticism*, B. Layton, ed., Studies in the History of Religions 41 (Supplements to Numen), Leiden: Brill, 1981, 472–504.
Pleše, Z., *Poetics of the Gnostic Universe: Narrative and Cosmology in the Apocryphon of John*, Nag Hammadi and Manichaean Studies 52, Leiden: Brill, 2006.
Rasimus, T., *Paradise Reconsidered in Gnostic Mythmaking: Rethinking Sethianism in Light of the Ophite Evidence*, Nag Hammadi and Manichaean Studies 68, Leiden: Brill, 2009.
Richter, G., "Präsentische und futurische Eschatologie in 4. Evangelium," *Gegenwart und kommendes Reich*, Schülergabe Anton Vögtle zum 65. Geburtstag, P. Fiedler and D. Zeller, eds., Stuttgart: Katholisches Bibelwerk, 1975, 117–152.

Schenke, H.-M., "The Phenomenon and Significance of Gnostic Sethianism," *The Rediscovery of Gnosticism: Volume 2: Sethian Gnosticism*, B. Layton, ed., Studies in the History of Religions 41 (Supplements to Numen), Leiden: Brill, 1981, 588–616.

Sevrin, J.-M., *Le dossier baptismal séthien*, Bibliothèque Copte de Nag Hammadi, Section: «Études» 2, Québec: Les Presses de l'Université Laval; Leuven: Peeters, 1986.

Smith, D.M., *John*, Abingdon New Testament Commentaries, Nashville: Abingdon, 1999.

Stone, M.E., "Report on Seth Traditions in the Armenian Adam Books," *The Rediscovery of Gnosticism: Volume 2: Sethian Gnosticism*, B. Layton, ed., Studies in the History of Religions 41 (Supplements to Numen), Leiden: Brill, 1981, 459–471.

Stroumsa, G.A., "Aher: A Gnostic," *The Rediscovery of Gnosticism: Volume 2: Sethian Gnosticism*, B. Layton, ed., Studies in the History of Religions 41 (Supplements to Numen), Leiden: Brill, 1981, 808–818.

—— *Another Seed: Studies in Gnostic Mythology*, Nag Hammadi Studies 24, Leiden: Brill, 1984.

Treblico, P., *The Early Christians in Ephesus from Paul to Ignatius*, Wissenschaftliche Untersuchungen zum Neuen Testament 166, Tübingen: Mohr Siebeck, 2004.

Turner, J.D., "Introduction to Nag Hammadi Codex XIII, 1*: Trimorphic Protennoia, 35*,1–50*,24," *Nag Hammadi Codices XI, XII, XIII*, C.W. Hedrick, ed., Nag Hammadi Studies 28, Leiden: Brill, 1990, 371–401.

—— "The Gnostic Seth," *Biblical Figures Outside the Bible*, M. Stone and T. Bergren, eds., Harrisburg, Pa.: Trinity International Press, 1998a, 33–58.

—— "To See The Light: A Gnostic Appropriation of Jewish Priestly Practice and Sapiential and Apocalyptic Visionary Lore," *Mediators of the Divine: Horizons of Prophecy and Divination on Mediterranean Antiquity*, R.M. Berchman, ed., Florida Studies in the History of Judaism 163, Atlanta: Scholars Press, 1998b, 63–113.

—— *Sethian Gnosticism and the Platonic Tradition*, Bibliothèque Copte de Nag Hammadi, Section: «Études» 6, Québec: Les Presses de l'Université Laval; Leuven: Peeters, 2001.

—— "Sethian Gnosticism and Johannine Christianity," *Theology and Christology in the Fourth Gospel: Essays by the Members of the SNTS Johannine Writings Seminar*, G. van Belle et al., eds., Bibliotheca Ephemeridum Theologicarum Lovaniensium 184, Leuven: Leuven University Press / Peeters, 2005, 399–433.

—— "The Sethian Baptismal Rite," *Coptica—Gnostica—Manichaica: Mélanges offerts à Wolf-Peter Funk*, L. Painchaud and P.-H. Poirier, eds., Bibliothèque Copte de Nag Hammadi, Section: «Études» 7, Québec: Les Presses de l'Université Laval; Leuven: Peeters, 2006, 941–992.

Waldstein, M., "The Providence Monologue in the Apocryphon of John and the Johannine Prologue," *Journal of Early Christian Studies* 3 (1995), 369–402.

PTOLEMAEUS AND THE VALENTINIAN EXEGESIS
OF JOHN'S PROLOGUE

Tuomas Rasimus
University of Helsinki & Université Laval

In several studies of the early reception of the Fourth Gospel, it is stated that John's Gospel was first properly accepted and adopted by the Valentinians of whom the first one was Ptolemaeus.[1] Ptolemaeus not only considered the gospel to be apostolic but also wrote a commentary on its prologue some time during the third quarter of the second century. Such statements—based largely on the old paradigm of the early catholic reluctance towards John's Gospel, as well as on Irenaeus' description of a Valentinian "model system"—are in need of correction. Ptolemaeus and the Valentinians do not appear to have been the first Christians to accept the Fourth Gospel as apostolic. Instead, it will be argued in this essay that Ptolemaeus adopted his way of using the Fourth Gospel's prologue as a proof-text for Valentinian theology from an anti-Marcionite Roman discourse from the 150s. This means that the Roman congregations had already accepted the Fourth Gospel by the time Ptolemaeus wrote, and that consequently, Valentinus himself was probably well aware of the gospel. The picture drawn here of Ptolemaeus' use of the Fourth Gospel will be based primarily on his authentic *Letter to Flora*, preserved by Epiphanius (*Pan.* 33.3–7), and secondarily on the Ptolemaean commentary on John's prologue preserved by Irenaeus (*Adv. haer.* 1.8.5), whose ascription to Ptolemaeus himself, however, is only stated in the Latin translation of Irenaeus' text, and is missing from the Greek fragment preserved by Epiphanius. Other examples of Valentinian use of the prologue will be discussed alongside these two primary "Ptolemaean" cases.

---

[1] E.g., Sanders 1943, 55–66, 86; Hillmer 1966, 172; Culpepper 1994, 114–116.

1. Ptolemaeus' *Letter to Flora*

In this didactic letter, which has been classified either as protreptic[2] or isagogic,[3] and which carefully follows the pattern of Greco-Roman public speeches,[4] Ptolemaeus addresses a woman called Flora and discusses the origin and nature of Mosaic Law. In the introduction and narration parts of the letter, Ptolemaeus introduces two erroneous views concerning the origin of both the law and creation that have been put forward by others—views that derive these from the perfect God and the devil, respectively. He then proceeds (in the specification and argumentation parts of the letter) to show with the words of the Lord (according to Matthew) and the apostles (John and Paul) how these views are wrong, and how his own solution, which traces the law and creation back to an intermediate demiurge, is to be preferred as true apostolic teaching. According to Ptolemaeus, the law is not wholly divine, since Moses and the elders have made additions to it; it its thus tripartite.[5] In addition, the divine portion is itself tripartite as it contains sections that are (1) pure but imperfect, like the Decalogue, and these the Savior came to fulfill; (2) mixed with injustice—based on the principle of revenge out of necessity due to the harshness of people—like the "eye for an eye," and these the Savior came to destroy; and (3) symbolic, like ritual laws concerning sacrifice and circumcision, and these the Savior transformed as they were no longer adequate except spiritually. Because the law is thus to an extent imperfect and inadequate but also fights evil, it cannot come from the true God who is good, or the devil who is evil, but from a god that is neither good nor evil but just (δίκαιος)—although harsh in his justice.

---

[2] E.g., Nagel 2000, 294.

[3] Markschies 2000, 229ff.

[4] Dunderberg (2008, 79–80), following Walde's (1996, 971–974) reconstruction of Greco-Roman public speeches, divides the letter into five parts: (1) Introduction (*prooimion/exordium; Pan.* 33.3.1); (2) Narration (*diēgēsis/narratio; Pan.* 33.3.2–7); (3) Specification of the topic (*prothesis/divisio; Pan.* 33.3.8); (4) Argumentation (*pistis/argumentatio; Pan.* 33.4.1–7.7); (5) Conclusion (*epilogos/conclusio; Pan.* 33.7.8–10).

[5] Similar ideas were circulating in the first and second centuries: Philo (*Decal.* 175–176; *Spec.* 2.104; *Mos.* 2.187–191), Justin Martyr (*Dial.* 44), and the author of the Pseudo-Clementine *Homilies* (2.38,43–44,52; 3.39,47,51) likewise detected human additions and/or less valuable parts in the Mosaic Law (that were added, for example, due to the hard-heartedness of the Jews), although they did not necessarily make the exact tripartite division of Ptolemaeus. See Quispel 1966, 16ff.; Fallon 1976; and Dunderberg 2008, 84–87.

Almost all commentators[6] think Ptolemaeus' letter was influenced by the Marcionite schism that began in Rome in the early 140s.[7] It is usually stated that Ptolemaeus wrote against Marcion and his followers when he refuted the view according to which the law and creation are the devil's handiwork.[8] Admittedly, Marcion never said exactly that. Marcion's point was that YHWH cannot be the true God because his law and actions are not characterized by goodness but are driven by warmongering blood-thirst and justice based on revenge;[9] Marcion, nevertheless, never identified YHWH with the devil. Commentators thus usually assume that Ptolemaeus misrepresented Marcion's views here, perhaps in order to make his own solution seem clearer and more plausible.[10] On the other hand, some Gnostics, like the author of the *Apocryphon of John*, did consider YHWH to be the devil.[11] However, some of Marcion's later followers also seem to have pushed their master's argumentation to the conclusion that YHWH was evil;[12] and some heresiologists likewise present Marcion's views in such a manner that it could be easily thought that Marcion's creator god was, in fact, the devil.[13] Ptolemaeus does not specify who the people are who think the law and creation derive from the devil. He is simply

---

[6] E.g., Quispel 1966, 8–40; Lüdemann 1995, 132–137; Markschies 2000, 233–239; Dunderberg 2008, 77–94. Layton (1987, 307) does not mention Marcion in connection with Ptolemaeus' *Letter to Flora*.

[7] Lampe 2003, 241.

[8] See Quispel 1966, 8–40; Campenhausen 1972, 83, 165; Kaestli 1990, 331; Lüdemann 1995, 132–137; and Markschies 2000, 233–239.

[9] Philo had solved the problem of YHWH's occasional nasty behavior, described in the scriptures, by delegating punishments and other lowly activities to subordinate beings, including God's regal power (βασιλικὴ δύναμις), thus preserving the transcendence and goodness of God himself. See *Conf.* 179–182; *Decal.* 176–178; *Abr.* 120–122.

[10] Thus Quispel 1966, 11. Cf. Markschies 2000, 234.

[11] In *Ap. John*, Yaldabaoth plays the roles of both YHWH and the devil. He, for example, issues the false monotheistic claim (II 13,8–9) and breathes into Adam who becomes alive (19,23–32). But he also rapes Eve (24,8–34) and is called "Samael" (11,18)—traits that are attested for the devil in rabbinic sources. See Layton 1987, 307; Pearson 1990, 47–50; and Rasimus 2009a.

[12] Apelles considered the lawgiver to be the devil, while maintaining that a good power of the good God created the world; Marcus considered Marcion's just God evil; and the piece of Marcion's doctrine presented in Hippolytus' *Refutatio*, which assigns the creation to an evil deity (κακὸς δ' ἔστιν, ὡς λέγει, ὁ δημιουργὸς καὶ τούτου τὰ ποιήματα, Marcovich 314.28–29), probably stems from Prepon. See Harnack 1996, 160–196, 332*ff.

[13] Cf., for example, the expression, "author of evils," in Irenaeus, *Adv. haer.* 1.27.2; and Tertullian, *Marc.* 1.2.

refuting a doctrinal position that could apply to Gnostics as well as to radical or misrepresented Marcionites.

Whether Marcionites are included among these opponents or not, Ptolemaeus' own position does seem to be influenced by Marcion's ideas.[14] Ptolemaeus has been characterized as a "moderate Marcionite,"[15] and indeed there are several points of contact between the solutions of Ptolemaeus and Marcion, as Dunderberg has shown:[16] both Ptolemaeus and Marcion (1) regard YHWH as an inferior creator god who is *just* but not good; (2) emphasize the negative aspect of YHWH's justice; (3) point out internal contradictions in YHWH's law; and (4) contrast the teachings of YHWH and the Good God represented by Moses and Jesus, respectively.[17] Clearly, Ptolemaeus' view of YHWH was not as negative as Marcion's, and he also did not deny Christ his role in creation, as did Marcion. But Ptolemaeus appears to have been persuaded by some of Marcion's arguments for distinguishing the just YHWH from the good God, while perhaps at the same time opposing more radical Marcionite views that overly stress YHWH's negative aspects.

Finally, the topic itself of the letter seems to be influenced by the Marcionite schism: the question of the relationship of Mosaic law (and the Jewish scriptures) to the teachings of Jesus and the apostles had become acute due to Marcion's radical solution.[18] All this suggests the strong possibility that the Marcionite schism is to be found in the background of Ptolemaeus' *Letter to Flora*, and that the opponents do include Marcionites.

This, then, brings us to the question of Ptolemaeus' use of John. As noted above, Ptolemaeus uses the words of the Lord and the apostles as proof-texts to support his own position, as well as to abnegate the other two views he considers erroneous. Ptolemaeus cites Jesus from Matthew as his main witness nine times,[19] and the apostles Paul and

---

[14] Quispel 1966, 11; Dunderberg 2008, 87–90.

[15] Löhr 1995, 191.

[16] Dunderberg 2008, 88–89.

[17] Dunderberg (2008, 89) adds that neither Ptolemaeus nor Marcion rejected Mosaic law altogether, as Marcion admitted it is valid for Jews although not for Christians, and Ptolemaeus accepted it with modifications. However, this is not, in my opinion, a very close parallel: most Christians accepted Mosaic Law only with modifications (although usually with smaller ones than Ptolemaeus), whereas the complete denial of its value for Christians was rare.

[18] Campenhausen 1972, 150–165.

[19] Matt 5:21ff. in *Pan.* 33.6.1; Matt 5:38 in *Pan.* 33.6.2; Matt 5:39 in *Pan.* 33.6.3; Matt 11:27 in *Pan.* 33.3.7; Matt 12:25 in *Pan.* 33.3.5; Matt 15:4 in *Pan.* 33.5.7; Matt 5:4–9 in *Pan.* 33.4.13; Matt 19:6,8 in *Pan.* 33.4.4; Matt 19:17 in *Pan.* 33.7.5.

John as secondary witnesses six times: Paul five times,[20] and John once (John 1:3,10–11).[21] Ptolemaeus' allusion to John, specifically to the prologue, occurs towards the beginning of the letter, in the *narratio*, and in a context where he refutes the theory that the creation and law derive from the devil. As proof-texts to counter this opinion, he first cites Matt 12:25 as an authoritative saying of Jesus, and then John 1:10–11 and 1:3 in a somewhat free combination, as another proof-text from an apostle (ἀπόστολος):

> οἰκία γὰρ ἢ πόλις μερισθεῖσα ἐφ᾽ ἑαυτὴν ὅτι μὴ δύναται στῆναι ὁ σωτὴρ ἡμῶν ἀπεφήνατο. ἔτι τε τὴν τοῦ κόσμου δημιουργίαν <αὐτοῦ> ἰδίαν λέγει εἶναι τά τε πάντα δι᾽ αὐτοῦ γεγονέναι καὶ χωρὶς αὐτοῦ γεγονέναι οὐδὲν ὁ ἀπόστολος, προαποστερήσας τὴν τῶν ψευδηγορούντων ἀνυπόστατον σοφίαν, καὶ οὐ φθοροποιοῦ θεοῦ, ἀλλὰ δικαίου καὶ μισοπονήρου· (*Pan.* 33.3.5–6; ed. Holl 1915, 451.12–17).

For our Savior has declared that "A house or city divided against itself cannot stand" [Matt 12:25]. And further, to deprive the liars beforehand of their unfounded wisdom, the apostle says that *"the creation of the world belongs to him"* [John 1:10–11] and that *"all things were made by him and nothing is made without him"* [1:3], that is, by a just God who hates iniquity, not a god of corruption (F. Williams, transl., with modifications; my emphasis).

Two issues need clarification here. First, most commentators have bypassed the references to verses 10–11 of the prologue, noting only the more or less accurate citation of verse 3.[22] But the word ἰδίαν (*Pan.* 33.3.6; Holl 451.14) makes an important allusion to verse 11 of the prologue, where it is stated that "He came to what was his own, and his own people did not accept him (NRSV)" (εἰς τὰ <u>ἴδια</u> ἦλθεν, καὶ οἱ ἴδιοι αὐτὸν οὐ παρέλαβον). This then further suggests that the words

---

[20] 1 Cor 5:7 in *Pan.* 33.5.15; 1 Cor 8:6 in *Pan.* 33.7.6; Rom 2:29 in *Pan.* 33.5.11; Rom 7:12 in *Pan.* 33.6.6; and Eph 2:15 in *Pan.* 33.6.6. As Ptolemaeus seems to have been unable to find Jesus' own words concerning the transformation of the cultic laws, Paul is, in this instance, brought in as the main witness (Rom 2:29; 1 Cor 5:7 in *Pan.* 33.5.11,15).

[21] Nagel (2000, 298) has suggested that Ptolemaeus may also refer to John 1:18 (Θεὸν οὐδεὶς ἑώρακεν πώποτε· μονογενὴς θεὸς ὁ ὢν εἰς τὸν κόλπον τοῦ πατρὸς ἐκεῖνος ἐξηγήσατο) in *Pan.* 33.3.7 ("Father of all, whom none but the only one who knows him has come to make known"; τὸν τῶν ὅλων πατέρα, ὃν μόνος ἐλθὼν ὁ μόνος εἰδὼς ἐφανέρωσε), but this may also be a reference to Matt 11:27 (Πάντα μοι παρεδόθη ὑπὸ τοῦ πατρός μου, καὶ οὐδεὶς ἐπιγινώσκει τὸν υἱὸν εἰ μὴ ὁ πατήρ, οὐδὲ τὸν πατέρα τις ἐπιγινώσκει εἰ μὴ ὁ υἱὸς καὶ ᾧ ἐὰν βούληται ὁ υἱὸς ἀποκαλύψαι) (thus Quispel 1966, 50).

[22] Holl (1915, 451) and Quispel (1966, 48), however, have noted the allusion to verse 11.

τὴν τοῦ κόσμου δημιουργίαν are a paraphrase of verse 10 (John 1:10: ὁ <u>κόσμος</u> δι᾿ αὐτοῦ ἐγένετο). Moreover, Ptolemaeus' apostolic quotation is divided into two parts by the particle τε preceding both parts of the quotation (i.e., 10–11 and 3), and this suggests that also the first part (10–11) is meant to be an actual quotation from John, albeit a free one.

Second, there are textual problems here. Holl, followed by Quispel, emended the word <αὐτοῦ> between the words δημιουργίαν and ἰδίαν. Löhr has suggested that this is unnecessary because the accusative of ἴδιος could replace the genitive of αὐτός as a pronominal subject of the sentence.[23] Whether one accepts his solution or not, a more difficult question is the proper reference of this pronominal subject (whichever), as well as of the two instances of αὐτοῦ in the quotation from John 1:3. Do they refer back to the "Savior" immediately preceding the Johannine quotations, or to the "just God" in the phrase καὶ οὐ φθοροποιοῦ θεοῦ, ἀλλὰ δικαίου καὶ μισοπονήρου a few lines later (Holl 451.17), which appears to be Ptolemaeus' specification of John 1:3? Or, can they refer to both, and what is then the relationship between the Savior and the just God? Markschies suggests that the references are to the Savior but that he is identical with the just God,[24] although this identification is hardly possible in light of the fact that the Savior is said to have come to destroy the just God's law as incongruous with his own nature (*Pan.* 33.5.1; 33.5.7; 33.6.2). One could then accept, with Löhr, that the references are to the just God, and that apparently Ptolemaeus interpreted verses 3 and 10–11 as referring to the creation of the cosmos without the involvement of the Savior.[25] This, however, would be a strange reading for most Christians, including Valentinians. In addition, it seems grammatically more plausible to understand the references to be to the Savior, who has already been mentioned in the immediate context. However, because Ptolemaeus adds that the "all things" of John 1:3 were actually made by the just God, it appears that both the Savior and the just God—who cannot be the same figure, *pace* Markschies—are involved in the creation of the

---

[23] Löhr 1995, 180–182. Cf. Markschies 2000, 240; and Thomassen 2006, 122–123. Löhr understands the reference to be to the demiurge, the just God, a few lines later, while Thomassen and Markschies think the reference can only be to the Savior of the preceding sentence.
[24] Markschies 2000, 239ff.
[25] Löhr 1995, 180–182.

cosmos, according to Ptolemaeus' interpretation of John's prologue. Ptolemaeus does not specify how this is to be envisaged, but other Valentinian sources speak of the Savior-Logos using the demiurge, i.e., the just God, as his instrument in creation.[26] Heracleon—another Valentinian teacher whose genuine fragments show no clear signs of a pleromatic myth—interpreted John 1:3 just this way.[27] In my view, this typical Valentinian distinction between the Savior and the demiurge offers the only reasonable explanation for the passage in *Flora*. In addition, Ptolemaeus' choice of words here may further hint at this kind of two-level interpretation:[28] having changed the γίνομαι of verse 10 to δημιουργία, Ptolemaeus' allusion to verses 10–11 now speaks of the *craftsmanship* (δημιουργία) of the cosmos, while his quotation from verse 3 speaks of the *coming into being* (γίνομαι) of all things.[29]

Ptolemaeus is thus using a paraphrased version of John 1:3,10–11 as an apostolic proof-text to refute an opinion that assigned the creation to the devil because, in Ptolemaeus' reading of the Fourth Gospel, the creation is said to be the Savior's who used the just God as his instrument. As noted above, Ptolemaeus' opponents here have usually been identified as radical Marcionites. These observations become all the more important when we compare this composite reference of verses 3 and 10–11 in *Flora* to Irenaeus' use of a similar composite reference to the prologue as an anti-Marcionite tool (*Adv. haer.* 3.11.1–2). First, Irenaeus cites John 1:1–5 as a general antidote to various heretical doctrines of creation, and then picks out specifically verse 3, stating

---

[26] In most Valentinian cosmogonies, Sophia, of course, participates in the creation as well. For example, in Irenaeus' description of the Valentinian "model system," the demiurge creates through the activity of Sophia who creates through the activity of the Savior (*Adv. haer.* 1.4.5–1.5.3; cf. *Exc. Theod.* 46–49). However, in *Tri. Trac.*, Sophia's role has been assigned completely to the Logos (who is, in that text, different from the Savior), and Heracleon does not explicitly mention Sophia either (although the Samaritan woman of John 4, in most scholars' opinion, stands for Sophia in Heracleon's exegesis).

[27] Heracleon (frg. 1) maintains that the Logos caused the demiurge to create the world, because John 1:3 states that everything was created, not "from whom" or "by whom," but "through whom." See also Thomassen's essay in this volume.

[28] Cf. Pagels 1973, 26, who detects three frames of reference for Valentinian interpretations of John 1:3: (1) "pleromic" as in *Adv. haer.* 1.8.5 and *Exc. Theod.* 6–7; (2) "kenomic" as in *Exc. Theod.* 45.3; and (3) "cosmic" as in *Letter to Flora* and in Heracleon's commentary. See also Kaestli 1990, 348–349.

[29] The Savior is identified as the *first demiurge* in *Exc. Theod.* 47.1 (Πρῶτος μὲν οὖν Δημιουργὸς ὁ Σωτὴρ γίνεται καθολικός). Cf. Irenaeus, *Adv. haer.* 1.4.5 (καὶ διὰ τοῦτο δυνάμει τὸν Σωτῆρα δεδημιουργηκέναι φάσκουσι).

that τὰ πάντα includes the cosmos, and is not restricted to some Valentinian pleroma above it; hence, Christ-Logos is the creator of everything, including our world. Irenaeus then immediately continues by quoting John 1:10–11, and shows that these verses not only qualify τὰ πάντα of verse 3 and thus prove the noted Valentinian reading of verse 3 wrong (for this kind of Valentinian exegesis of the prologue, see below), but also refute Marcion's famous positions that Christ was not the creator of our world, and that in coming to this world, he did not come to his own creation:[30]

> "*All things*," he says, "*were made by Him*" [John 1:3]; therefore in "all things" this creation of ours is (included), for we cannot concede to these men that (the words) "all things" are spoken in reference to those within their Pleroma. For if their Pleroma do indeed contain these, this creation, as being such, is not outside, as I have demonstrated in the preceding book; but if they are outside the Pleroma, which indeed appeared impossible, it follows, in that case, that their Pleroma cannot be "all things": therefore this vast creation is not outside (the Pleroma). John, however, does himself put this matter beyond all controversy on our part, when he says, "*He was in this world, and the world was made by Him, and the world knew Him not. He came to His own (things), and His own (people) received Him not*" [John 1:10–11]. But according to Marcion, and those like him, neither was the world made by Him; nor did He come to His own things, but to those of another (transl., ANF; my emphasis).[31]

Similarly, Ptolemaeus seems to use verses 10–11 not only to qualify his own use of verse 3 (because the craftsmanship of the cosmos is said to belong to the Savior, he must be involved in the creation of

---

[30] Cf. Sanders 1943, 73. Irenaeus repeats the same arguments later in *Adv. haer.* 5.18.2–3, where he again uses John's prologue (1:1–3,10–12,14) against various heretical doctrines of creation. As for Marcion's position that Christ was an *alien* to the world and to humanity, see, e.g., Tertullian, *Marc.* 1.23; *Carn. Chr.* 4. See also Harnack 1996, 118–120.

[31] *Omnia*, inquit, *per ipsum facta sunt*. In omnibus ergo est et haec quae secundum nos est conditio: non enim concedetur eis omnia dici ea quae sunt infra Pleroma ipsorum. Si enim et haec Pleroma ipsorum continet, non extra est tanta ista conditio, quemadmodum ostendimus in eo libro qui ante hunc est; si autem extra Pleroma sunt haec, quod quidem impossibile uisum est, non iam est omnia Pleroma ipsorum: non est ergo extra haec tanta conditio. (11.2) Abstulit autem a nobis dissensiones omnes ipse Iohannes dicens: *In hoc mundo erat, et mundus per ipsum factus est, et mundus eum non cognouit. In sua propria uenit, et sui eum non receperunt.* Secundum autem Marcionem et eos qui similes sunt ei, neque mundus per eum factus est, neque in sua uenit, sed in aliena (ed., Rousseau and Doutreleau 2002, 2:142.30–144.45; original emphasis).

τὰ πάντα together with the just God as well), but also to refute an opinion which had assigned the creation of our world to the devil and thus denied the Savior his role in the creation. It is, moreover, likely that Ptolemaeus' opponents here are, or at least include, radical or misrepresented Marcionites. Thus Irenaeus and Ptolemaeus use the Fourth Gospel's prologue in a strikingly similar manner. This raises the question of the relationship between the two passages. One could assume that the passages are independent of each other—that a similar anti-Marcionite use of John 1:3,10–11 was simply independently invented twice, probably in the same city around the same time (see below)—but the closeness of the parallels makes such an assumption unlikely.

However, there are indications that both Irenaeus and Ptolemaeus have utilized an already established anti-Marcionite use of the prologue, and thus the passages seem to be based on a common source. The very example of Ptolemaeus shows that Irenaeus was not the first one to use John 1:3,10–11 against a doctrinal position that denied the Savior his role in the creation of our world. Moreover, because Irenaeus seems to be unaware of Ptolemaeus' *Letter to Flora* and of its interpretation of John's prologue—he is only aware of the Ptolemaean commentary on the prologue that reads the Valentinian Ogdoad into it (see below)—Irenaeus' anti-Marcionite use of the prologue does not derive from Ptolemaeus. However, Irenaeus has preserved older Roman traditions (e.g., *Adv. haer.* 3.3–4), and it is quite possible that his use of John's prologue here is also based on an older, anti-Marcionite, tradition. This seems especially probable as much of Irenaeus' knowledge of Marcion seems to be based on what appears to be an older catalog of heresies (*Adv. haer.* 1.27.2–4),[32] usually assumed to be the now lost *Syntagma* of Justin Martyr (or an updated version of it), composed in Rome in the middle of the second century;[33] Irenaeus even explicitly cites it, or another, specifically anti-Marcionite treatise by Justin, in

---

[32] The rest of Irenaeus' remarks on Marcion either simply list him and his followers as "heretics" alongside Valentinians and others, or briefly elaborate what has been stated in the catalog-description in *Adv. haer.* 1.27.2–4 (e.g., mutilation of Luke; the doctrine of two Gods, one good, another just; the doctrine of Christ being an alien to the creation).

[33] On Justin's *Syntagma*, see Hilgenfeld 1963, 9–30, 162–341; Wisse 1971, 212ff.; Lüdemann 1995, 113–114.

Adv. haer. 4.6.2.[34] Harnack suggested that the Irenaean passage (*Adv. haer.* 3.11.2) may indicate Marcion's opposition to the Fourth Gospel, but in my opinion, the passage is better understood as an apostolic anti-Marcionite proof-text, which does not in itself necessitate any knowledge of the Fourth Gospel on Marcion's part.[35]

Ptolemaeus, for his part, does not justify his claim that the Gospel of John is an apostolic text. This suggests that the Fourth Gospel had already been accepted as apostolic, at least among the recipient(s) of *Flora*. In addition, and as pointed out above, Ptolemaeus has modified the text of the prologue and given it a new, Valentinian interpretation. This betrays a secondary character of Ptolemaeus' use of the prologue. One could, of course, think that Ptolemaeus was the first one to apply John 1:3,10–11 against a Marcionite position, and that non-Valentinian Christians in Rome were influenced by his innovation and adapted it for their own anti-Marcionite purposes without assuming Ptolemaeus' textual modifications or the Valentinian framework (they also would have detected the paraphrastic allusion to verses 10–11). However, it seems perhaps likelier to assume that Christians in Rome before Ptolemaeus had already applied the Fourth Gospel's prologue—specifically verses 3,10 and 11—against Marcion as an apt apostolic proof-text, and whereas Ptolemaeus adapted such usage into a new, Valentinian context, Irenaeus preserved the usage closer to (or identical with) its original form. While not beyond all doubt, such a scenario seems a reasonable way of explaining the relationship between the two passages.

We can place the composition of Ptolemaeus' *Letter to Flora* in Rome ca. 150 because Justin Martyr, in his *2 Apol.* 2, tells us that a Christian teacher called Ptolemaeus—identical with the Valentinian one as argued below—was martyred in Rome under the prefect Urbicus (144–160) and emperor Antoninus Pius (138–161). Since Justin's *2 Apol.* is an addendum to *1 Apol.*,[36] which can be dated between 148–154 due to its mention of a recent petition to Felix the prefect of Alexandria (*1 Apol.* 29), Ptolemaeus' martyrdom reported in *2 Apol.* can be dated

---

[34] Irenaeus speaks of a *syntagma* against Marcion (*Adv. haer.* 4.6.2) and Justin mentions his *syntagma* against all heresies (*1 Apol.* 62). Lüdemann (1995, 113–114) considers these to be the same text; cf. Lampe 2003, 250n52.

[35] Harnack 1996, 251*.

[36] Lüdemann 1995, 127n39.

to ca. 152.[37] This Ptolemaeus was put to death because the husband of an upper-class woman, who not only was Ptolemaeus' student in Christianity, but who had also divorced her husband due to his immoral behavior, informed the Roman authorities that Ptolemaeus was a Christian (*2 Apol.* 2). Many things in this description match what we learn from *Flora*: (1) Ptolemaeus the martyr died in Rome, and Ptolemaeus the Valentinian almost certainly taught in Rome since Hippolytus identifies him as one of the members of the "Italian" school of Valentinianism (*Ref.* 6.35.5–6);[38] additionally, because the school founder Valentinus himself was active in Rome, the Italian branch of the school was likely situated there as well;[39] (2) the time of the martyrdom falls within the period of Valentinian activity in Rome (ca. 145–185);[40] (3) the name, Ptolemaeus, is the same, and it was not a common one among Roman Christians at the time;[41] (4) both Ptolemaeuses are Christian teachers (διδάσκαλος); (5) both had an apparently upper-class woman as a student;[42] (6) divorce is a prominent theme in both cases; and (7) the theme of revenge (of the lawgiver/former husband) is likewise prominent in both cases.[43]

The identification of the two Ptolemaeuses has not always been accepted,[44] mainly because Justin does not say anything negative about the martyred Ptolemaeus while, at least in his later work *Dialogue with Trypho* (35), he considered Valentinians heretics. However, Justin does not yet include Valentinians among the heretics in *1 Apol.* 26; and as Dunderberg has argued, *2 Apol.*, where the reference to Ptolemaeus occurs, is a defense of Christianity addressed to the pagan emperor. In

---

[37] Lüdemann 1995, 127–128.

[38] On the school-context of Valentinianism, see Lüdemann 1995; Markschies 1997; and Dunderberg 2008.

[39] See, e.g., Irenaeus, *Adv. haer.* 3.4.3.

[40] Lüdemann 1995, 128; Lampe 2003, 239.

[41] Lüdemann 1995, 128–129n46; Lampe (2003, 239n12) counts 13 occurrences in *Corpus Inscriptionum Latinarum.*

[42] In Justin's example, the high-society status is clear, for example, from the fact that she appealed directly to the emperor to postpone her trial due to household affairs—and succeeded (Lampe 2003, 237–238). In Ptolemaeus' case, the status is indicated by the address, "my honorable (καλή) sister Flora"; even though καλή can mean "beautiful"—and this is how Lampe (2003, 240) understands it—it is likelier that it is here used as a status indicator (thus Dunderberg 2008, 90).

[43] For these arguments, see Lüdemann 1995, 128; Lampe 2003, 239–240; and Dunderberg 2008, 90–92. The first one to suspect the common identity of the two Ptolemaeuses was Harnack (see, e.g., 1996, 29–30).

[44] Markschies (2000, 249) and Thomassen (2006, 494) remain skeptical.

such a context, one does not wish to stress internal quarrels, especially when Ptolemaeus offered a suitable example of a high-profile Christian who had friends in high places and who had suffered an unjust but noble martyr's death.[45]

This would then mean that the Roman congregations had accepted and used the Fourth Gospel as apostolic by 150 CE. This goes against the old paradigm according to which the catholic Christians started to use the Fourth Gospel only during the time of Irenaeus. However, there is plenty of evidence suggesting a general acceptance of John's Gospel in Rome at this early date.[46] Among the most important pieces of evidence are:[47] (1) Justin Martyr in Rome knows of it and uses it, as Nagel, Hill and some other scholars before them have already demonstrated;[48] (2) Irenaeus cites older traditions, quite possibly from Rome, according to which the Fourth Gospel was considered apostolic;[49] and (3) the earliest examples of Christian visual arts in the Roman catacombs from the last quarter of the second century contain scenes unique to the Fourth Gospel (e.g., the raising of Lazarus); as many catacombs were church-owned, and consequently their art can be seen as public rather than private, they reflect the already accepted values of the community.[50]

All of this adds up to indicate that the Valentinians were not the first ones to adopt and accept the Fourth Gospel, but it also makes it likely that Valentinus himself knew it. While Valentinus' surviving fragments do not show any clear signs of John,[51] the *Gospel of*

---

[45] Dunderberg 2008, 90–92.

[46] For a thorough evaluation of the evidence, see Nagel 2000; and Hill 2004.

[47] Cf. also the Muratorian fragment—a document containing a list of canonical texts probably from Rome and roughly contemporary with Irenaeus—which not only accepts the Fourth Gospel but also, interestingly, attacks Valentinus and Marcion. See Metzger 1987, 191–201, 305–307; and Hill 2004, 128–138.

[48] Hengel 1989, 12–14; Nagel 2000, 94–116; Hill 2004, 312–351. See also Hill's essay in this volume.

[49] These include the *Gospel Notice* (*Adv. haer.* 3.1.1), whose origin in a Roman community library is suspected by Hengel (1989, 137n5; cf. Mutschler in this volume); and traditions concerning Polycarp in Rome—to which Irenaeus attaches a story of John and Cerinthus that supposedly stemmed from Polycarp and probably originated in Asia Minor (*Adv. haer.* 3.3.4); in addition, Polycarp's *Letter to the Philippians* 7:1–2 contains a clear composite reference to 1 John 4:2–3 and 2 John 7, and thus Polycarp may have also known the gospel, although his allusions to it are not extremely clear (see Grant 1997, 37; Hill 2004, 416–420).

[50] Jensen 2000, 22; Hill 2004, 155–166.

[51] The "Logos" who appeared as a baby to Valentinus according to frg. 7, may or may not be an allusion to John 1:1. Layton's (1987, 239) suggestion that a special

Truth does: the treatise contains several citations and midrashic allusions to the Fourth Gospel, as Williams has demonstrated.[52] Whether the *Gospel of Truth* was written by Valentinus is disputed.[53] Irenaeus mentions that Valentinians have a *Gospel of Truth* (*Adv. haer.* 3.11.9),[54] and Hippolytus then ascribes this observation—together with the Valentinian "model system" of Irenaeus' *Adv. haer.* 1.1–8— to Valentinus himself (Pseudo-Tertullian, *Haer.* 4.6),[55] probably, however, without a historical basis (see below). Nevertheless, the main arguments in favor of Valentinus' authorship are of two types: (1) stylistic comparison between Valentinus' fragments and the *Gospel of Truth* may suggest a common authorship;[56] and (2) the content of the *Gospel of Truth*—describing the aeons as internal aspects of God—corresponds well with Tertullian's statement according to which this was Valentinus' opinion, while Ptolemaeus later externalized the aeons into independent hypostases (*Val.* 4.2).[57] Thus, it remains possible that Valentinus was the author of the *Gospel of Truth*, and that he had utilized the Fourth Gospel.

It is furthermore sometimes suggested that Irenaeus' description of Valentinus' own doctrine (*Adv. haer.* 1.11.1) is dependent on the

---

understanding of John 6:27 ("Do not *digest* [ἐργάζεσθε] the food which perishes, but the food which endures to eternal life, which the Son of Man will give you") lies behind frg. 3, according to which Jesus had a perfect digestion system and thus did not produce excrements seems unlikely.

[52] J. Williams 1988, e.g., 175–187, 199–204.

[53] See Markschies 1992, 339–356; and Thomassen 2006, 424.

[54] The Nag Hammadi treatise does not, properly speaking, have a title, but it begins with the words, "The gospel of truth is joy for those who...," and this *Incipit* can be taken as a title. Thus, e.g., Thomassen 2006, 147. Markschies (1992, 340–343) is more skeptical.

[55] Hippolytus' now lost *Syntagma* is usually thought to have been preserved in a Latin translation as the Pseudo-Tertullian catalog of heresies (Lipsius 1865; Hilgenfeld 1963; Wisse 1981, 568). Hippolytus' *Syntagma* is mentioned by Photius (*Bibliotheca* 121), Eusebius (*Hist. eccl.* 6.22) and Jerome (*Vir. ill.* 61), and what is known of it corresponds almost exactly to the Pseudo-Tertullian heresiology, *Adversus omnes haereses*. Photius says Hippolytus' *Syntagma* consisted of 32 heresies, running from the Dositheans to the Noetians. Pseudo-Tertullian, for its part, consists of about 30 entries (depending on how one wishes to calculate them), and runs from Dositheus to Praxeas. Because the latter taught patripassianism (*Haer.* 8.4; Tertullian, *Prax.*) as did Noetus (Hippolytus, *Contra Noetum; Ref.* 9.7.1–3; 9.10.9–12; 10.27.1–2; Epiphanius, *Pan.* 57), the author of Pseudo-Tertullian may simply have changed the name of the last entry of *Syntagma*. Furthermore, for Hippolytus as the author of *Refutatio*, see Marcovich 1986, 8–17.

[56] Standaert 1976, 259–265. Cf. J. Williams 1988, 4, 205–207; and the critical discussion in Markschies 1992, 339–356.

[57] Cf. Thomassen 2006, 263–266.

Fourth Gospel.[58] This, on the other hand, is unlikely for two reasons. First, the doctrine in question is probably not that of Valentinus, as it does not correspond at all with Valentinus' fragments or Tertullian's statement in *Val.* 4.2.[59] Second, the doctrine contains the usual Valentinian Ogdoad of first aeons, five of whom have names that are found in John's prologue (πατήρ, ἀλήθεια, λόγος, ζωή, ἄνθρωπος). However, this Ogdoad with its "Johannine" names probably had originally nothing to do with the prologue; for example, we have two Valentinian commentaries on the prologue, where the Ogdoad is secondarily brought into an increasingly closer correspondence with the prologue. In fact, there seems to have been a growing tendency among Valentinians to connect their Ogdoad with the prologue of the Fourth Gospel. These commentaries will be investigated next.

2. THE PTOLEMAEAN COMMENTARY ON THE PROLOGUE AND THE VALENTINIAN OGDOAD

Irenaeus considers the Valentinians the most dangerous heretics, and he opens his *Adversus haereses* with a description of the Valentinian "model system" (*Adv. haer.* 1.1–8). It culminates in a commentary on John's prologue, which attempts to show that the Valentinian Ogdoad is alluded to in the prologue. The Valentinian Ogdoad itself describes the first principle—which in some variants is androgynous and thus dyadic—and its expansion into four pairs of divine aeons, which in turn produce additional ones until the divine fullness, the pleroma, is complete with 30 or so aeons. The first Ogdoad consists of four pairs, or syzygies, of male and female aeons that usually, in the various versions of the myth, have similar names. In the case of the model system in Irenaeus, they are: Depth (βυθός)-Silence (σιγή); Mind (νοῦς)-Truth (ἀλήθεια); Word (λόγος)-Life (ζωή); and Man (ἄνθρωπος)-Church (ἐκκλησία). Some of them have additional names, for example, Mind is further identified as μονογενής and ἀρχή (*Adv. haer.* 1.1.1). While the (here dyadic) first principle is unknowable and perhaps in some sense even beyond being, thus anticipating Neoplatonism with the help

---

[58] Hill 2004, 219.
[59] See Markschies 1992, 364–379; and Thomassen 2006, 23–27.

of current Neopythagorean solutions (e.g., Moderatus, Numenius),[60] it produces the next pair of aeons, which in turn produce the next one, and so on, until the Ogdoad is complete. All this takes place beyond and before the lowly separate creator god even comes into being and later arranges our cosmos from matter that had, in the meantime, been produced out of the youngest aeon Sophia's passions and their separation from her by Christ and the Savior (these are two different Christ-figures).

Irenaeus introduces the Ptolemaean commentary as a verbatim quotation (διδάσκουσι...αὐταῖς λέξεσι, λέγοντες οὕτως; Holl 426.1–2). The commentator not only seeks to link the Valentinian Ogdoad to the prologue, but also presupposes a philosophical (a Stoicizing Middleplatonic) scheme of emanations—that is not found in the prologue—that extends all the way from the first principle down to the formation of the material cosmos: the first God (Father) emanated a second principle (Monogenes) which contained all things potentially/seminally (ἐν ᾧ τὰ πάντα ὁ Πατὴρ προέβαλε σπερματικῶς; Holl 426.5–6). This second principle, in turn, emanated a third one (Logos) that contained all things—i.e., all the aeons—actually/essentially (ἐν αὐτῷ τὴν ὅλην τῶν Αἰώνων οὐσίαν; Holl 426.7). This essence was then given form by the third principle, the Logos (ἣν αὐτὸς ὕστερον ἐμόρφωσεν ὁ Λόγος; Holl 426.7–8). Finally—and the commentator expresses this only later when the text of the prologue allows him to discuss events that take place outside the pleroma—another principle, the Savior-Logos, gave form to what lies outside the formed essence, or the pleroma,

---

[60] The first principle in *Adv. haer.* 1.1.1 is described as προών. Similar ideas of the first principle somehow existing beyond being, or having a higher, undetermined being, are also found in Classic Gnostic texts, such as *Ap. John* (BG 24,20–25,1) and especially *Zostrianos* (64,14–16; 74,4–25) and *Allogenes* (49,26–38; 65,32–36), whose Greek versions were read in Plotinus' seminars; cf. the *Chaldean Oracles* frgs. 1, 3–4 Majercik; and Neopythagoreans Moderatus (*apud* Simplicius, *In phys.* 9.230.34–231.27 Diels) and Numenius (frgs. 17, 19–22 des Places). Such ideas also occur in the *Anonymous Parmenides Commentary* (12,29–35; 14,6–25), a text that is almost certainly Middleplatonic and not by Porphyry, as Hadot (1968) maintained. The idea of the first principle's existence beyond being goes ultimately back to Plato (*Republic* 509b; *Parmenides* 137c–142a), but even the renewed stress on this idea cannot be Plotinus' third century invention, elaborated by Porphyry (Hadot 1968). See Bechtle 1999, 77ff.; Corrigan 2000; Turner 2001, 724ff.; Thomassen 2006, 269–314; and Rasimus 2009b.

(πάντα τὰ ἐκτὸς τοῦ πληρώματος δι᾽ αὐτοῦ μεμορφῶσθαι; Holl 427.11–12), i.e., matter.[61]

The commentator understands verse 1 of the prologue to speak of three separate divinities: God, Logos and the Beginning (ἀρχή).[62] Because the Logos was in (ἐν) the Beginning, yet alongside (πρός) God, and because the Logos himself was also a God (θεός), the logical conclusion was that the Beginning in their midst must also be a God; in fact, the commentator seems to have found proof for this in the prologue itself, since he identifies the Beginning with Monogenes, who, in verse 18, is identified as a "God" (μονογενὴς θεός).[63] Verse 2, then, provided for the commentator a "clear" summary of this divine hierarchy, in that these three divinities are mentioned in order, from the third to the first: οὗτος ἦν ἐν ἀρχῇ πρὸς τὸν θεόν (οὗτος refers to λόγος of the preceding verse). Without a clear link to the prologue, however, the commentator proceeds to explain the production of the Beginning from the Father, and of the Logos from the Beginning, with the above-mentioned scheme of emanations. Only in verse 3 does he find something that conforms to his scheme:

---

[61] The distinction between the transcendent and immanent aspects of the Soul or Logos—that here corresponds to the distinction between the Logos and the Savior-Logos—was commonplace in Middleplatonism (Plutarch, de Isis et Osiris 373ab; Albinus, Didaskalikos 10.164,40–165,4; Nicomachus, Theology of Arithmetic 45,6–50,8; Numenius, frgs. 16, 21–22 des Places; Chaldean Oracles, frgs. 50–52 Majercik; see also Dillon 1996, 200, 284, 348–349, 356–359, 374–375, 394–395; and Turner 2001, 363–396, 460–471). That the immanent Logos (or Soul) forms matter/cosmos/nature, is a Stoic concept that many Platonists adopted. The relationships among the first three principles (God-Monogenes-Logos) here, on the one hand, can be seen to anticipate Plotinus, whose Three Hypostases (One-Intellect-Soul, with the Soul also having an immanent aspect in Nature) were already anticipated by the Three Ones of Moderatus (apud Simplicius, In phys. 9.230.34–231.27 Diels). On the other hand, one could also see the God-Monogenes-Logos triad as anticipating the Neoplatonic Procession and Return-scheme, often described as a triad of Being-Life-Mind, where the first principle's hidden/seminal potentiality becomes actualized in Mind via the procession of Life out of Being. See Turner 2001, 407ff., 724ff.; and Rasimus 2009b. Cf. Thomassen 2006, 269–314.

[62] Cf. similar speculations on Gen 1:1 that distinguished among four divinites: God, Beginning, Heaven and Earth. Such speculations were condemned as heresy in rabbinic sources, and Irenaeus says the Valentinians connected them to their first Tetrad (Adv. haer. 1.18.1). See Segal 1977, 74–83.

[63] Many MSS of John 1:18 read μονογενὴς υἱός instead of μονογενὴς θεός. The Greek and Latin of Irenaeus (Holl 426.5; Rousseau and Doutreleau 128.134) suggest that the Ptolemaean commentator used a manuscript that read μονογενὴς θεός. Moreover, the related Valentinian commentary on John's prologue, in Exc. Theod. 6–7, says explicitly that John 1:18 calls Monogenes "God." For the text of John 1:18, see Ehrman 1993, 78–82.

Πάντα δι' αὐτοῦ ἐγένετο, καὶ χωρὶς αὐτοῦ ἐγένετο οὐδ' ἕν· πᾶσι γὰρ τοῖς μετ' αὐτὸν Αἰῶσι μορφῆς καὶ γενέσεως αἴτιος ὁ Λόγος ἐγένετο (ed. Holl).

"All things were made by Him, and without Him was nothing made"; for the Logos was the author of form and beginning to all the Aeons that came into existence after Him (transl., ANF, with modifications; my emphasis).

Verse 3 is interpreted here as relating to the formation of the pleroma, not of the cosmos, as in the *Letter to Flora*. That Valentinian exegetes could see John 1:3 relating to various ontological levels, is further clear from another piece of Valentinian exegesis on John's prologue preserved in Clement's *Excerpts from Theodotus* 45.3, where the creative activity of the Logos concerns the healing of Sophia's passions in the *kenōma*, i.e., the emptiness outside the pleroma.[64]

After the Ptolemaean commentator has thus explained the principle of emanations as well as introduced the three highest gods of the Valentinian pantheon with verses 1–3 (and 18), he proceeds to comment on verses 3c–4a, which, for him, explain the Valentinian concept of syzygy. Since verse 3ab had declared that all things were created by (διά) the Logos, verses 3c–4a now state that what was created in (ἐν) him was Life (ζωή). To the commentator, this means that Life has so much more an intimate relationship to the Logos than the "all things," that Life in him is, in fact, his companion. Even the formation of the "all things," mentioned above (in the emanation scheme), seems to be now delegated to Life, the female aspect and/or syzygy of the Logos, as it is she who gives birth to, manifests and forms the next pair of emanations, Man and Church. This is explained with verse 4b (καὶ ἡ ζωὴ ἦν τὸ φῶς τῶν ἀνθρώπων): Life's illuminating function is understood as formative power (Φῶς δὲ εἶπε τῶν ἀνθρώπων τὴν Ζωὴν διὰ τὸ πεφωτίσθαι αὐτοὺς ὑπ' αὐτῆς, ὃ δή ἐστι μεμορφῶσθαι καὶ πεφανερῶσθαι; Holl 427.4–5). That "Church" (ἐκκλησία) is not mentioned in the prologue, has not prevented the commentator from detecting an allusion to it; for the plural form of ἄνθρωπος is seen to indicate collectivity, i.e., ἐκκλησία (the plural form thus indicates the syzygy in the most intimate manner, the commentator affirms). At this point, the commentator explains that the second Tetrad, i.e., the

---

[64] Cf. Pagels 1973, 26; Kaestli 1990, 348–349.

latter four members of the Ogdoad (Logos-Zoe and Man-Church), are found in the prologue.

The commentator then proceeds to show how the prologue also teaches about the first Tetrad. For him, verses 5 and 14 speak of events taking place outside the pleroma, and specifically of the activity of the Savior who is the "joint fruit" of the pleroma—he is its embodiment immanent in the cosmos. Verse 5 (καὶ τὸ φῶς ἐν τῇ σκοτίᾳ φαίνει, καὶ ἡ σκοτία αὐτὸ οὐ κατέλαβεν) is to be understood as the Savior's imparting form to matter that issued from Sophia's passion. The commentator then proceeds to explain how the Savior in the cosmos, as the embodiment of the pleroma, carried names of the other aeons, such as "Son,"[65] "Truth" and "Life,"[66] as well as "Logos" (1:14). Verse 14, then, specifically contains names that are those of the first four members of the Ogdoad (Father, Grace-Sige, Monogenes, Truth):

> Καὶ ὁ λόγος σὰρξ ἐγένετο καὶ ἐσκήνωσεν ἐν ἡμῖν, καὶ ἐθεασάμεθα τὴν δόξαν αὐτοῦ, δόξαν ὡς μονογενοῦς παρὰ πατρός, πλήρης χάριτος καὶ ἀληθείας.

The commentator's use of the prologue is quite selective (most of the 18 verses are not used at all), and at times quite forced. Irenaeus already pointed out the forced character of the commentary: if John had intended to speak of the Ogdoad, he would have spelled out ἐκκλησία, and would have mentioned the members of the Ogdoad in their proper order, instead of alluding first to the last four and only later to the first four members (*Adv. haer.* 1.9.1). Moreover, the philosophical emanation scheme that the commentator introduces has poor links to the prologue, and is clearly read into it. Finally, in comparison to some other variants of the Valentinian Ogdoad, new names have been given to its eight members here (e.g., μονογενής = ἀρχή, σιγή = χάρις),[67] no doubt to bring the Ogdoad into a closer connection with the prologue.

This assumption gains more strength from the observation that another quite similar Valentinian commentary on the prologue is

---

[65] Some MSS add υἱός to μονογενὴς θεός in John 1:18. See Ehrman 1993, 112n158. But cf. also John 3:16,18; 1 John 4:9.

[66] John 11:25; 14:6. According to the commentator, John 1:4 speaks of the pleromatic Logos, not of the descended Savior.

[67] For example, Ἀρχή and Χάρις as names for Μονογενής and Σιγή are not found in Irenaeus, *Adv. haer.* 1.11.1. Hippolytus' *Ref.* 6.29–36 and *Exc. Theod.* also do not speak of Χάρις as a name for Σιγή.

preserved in Clement's *Excerpts from Theodotus* 6.1–7.3. This short "Theodotian"[68] commentary, however, is not a verbatim quotation but a paraphrase, and the original may have been more extensive. What has survived can be divided into four sections: (1) an exegesis of John 1:1,18 that distinguishes among God, Beginning and Logos (*Exc. Theod.* 6.1–3)—this section is virtually identical with the Ptolemaean speculations; (2) an explanation of the Logos-Life syzygy, based primarily on John 1:3c–4a, but bolstered by John 11:25/14:6 ("I am Life") (*Exc. Theod.* 6.4)—and this section is also no different from the Ptolemaean version; (3) a philosophical scheme of noetic emanation, which, however, is clearly different from the Ptolemaean scheme of "reproductive" emanation: here, the unknown Father wishes to become known, and in his own self-knowing Thought (ἐνθύμησις), he produces the Monogenes Son; the self-knowledge is spiritualized into πνεῦμα γνώσεως, and the commentator explains that it not only binds together Father and Son, but that it is also bound with the πνεῦμα ἀγάπης, which proceeds from the Son and his syzygos Truth, likely to produce the pair Logos-Life already mentioned above (*Exc. Theod.* 7.1–2), although its coming into being is not actually spelled out; this somewhat abrupt break in the description of the noetic emanation—which may be taken as a sign of the selective nature of Clement's paraphrastic description—then shifts the focus to (4) an exegesis on John 1:14,18, which explains that the Savior on earth was not the pleromatic Monogenes, who teaches the other aeons about the Father through knowledge, because it is stated of the Savior on earth that his glory was *as* (ὡς) that of the Monogenes (*Exc. Theod.* 7.3)—this exegesis resembles the Ptolemaean one that treated the Logos become flesh of verse 14 as the Savior who was not identical with any of the other aeons either, but was instead their collective embodiment.

In this commentary, the links to the prologue are not quite as strong as in the Ptolemaean one since ἄνθρωπος and ἐκκλησία are not mentioned at all. The commentary, nevertheless, clearly presupposes the doctrine of the Ogdoad as Monogenes is identified without explanation as νοῦς and ἀλήθεια. However, while in the Ptolemaean commentary

---

[68] This term is used here purely for practical reasons, although the commentary in question probably does not derive from Theodotus himself, perhaps not even from the Eastern school of Valentinianism. Clement introduces the commentary simply as "Valentinian" (*Exc. Theod.* 6.1). For the diverse nature of the material in *Exc. Theod.*, see Sagnard 1948.

known to Irenaeus, seven out of eight members of the Ogdoad had a "Johannine" name, there are only five such members in this version known to Clement (πατήρ, μονογενὴς-ἀρχή, ἀλήθεια, λόγος, ζωή). This again suggests that the Valentinian Ogdoad was gradually brought closer to the Fourth Gospel's prologue since it was found to provide a suitable apostolic proof-text for this aspect of Valentinian theology.[69]

Originally, the Ogdoad probably had nothing to do with John's prologue. Otherwise, we would expect the connection to be clearer; and in any case, the Ogdoad can be explained satisfactorily without any recourse to the prologue. Valentinian mythology is heavily influenced by Middleplatonic and Neopythagorean speculations.[70] The first syzygy is variably named in the different versions, but that the first male principle is sometimes called "Father," is a normal Platonic practice.[71] His alternate name "Depth" is attested in the contemporary *Chaldean Oracles* (frg. 18 Majercik), a collection of Stoicizing Middleplatonic oracular statements, as well as in two probably pre-Valentinian Classic Gnostic documents, *Eugnostos* (V 6,20) and Irenaeus' related description of "Ophite" mythology (*Adv. haer.* 1.30.1).[72]

The first principle's female partner is usually called Silence (Σιγή) but this term is not found in the prologue. However, the term σιγή occurs in the *Chaldean Oracles* (frg. 16 Majercik), and *Eugnostos* (V 15,21; III 88,8–9), as well as in the related *Sophia of Jesus Christ* (III 112,8; 117,17.21) and the *Apocryphon of John* (III 10,15). Dependence on Plato's *Republic* (490b, 509b, 517b) might then explain why the second syzygy, i.e., the first pair of emanations from the first principle, is called Mind and Truth, as van den Broek has suggested.[73] The terms ἀρχή and μονογενής for Mind are likewise not found in all variants of the Ogdoad (e.g., Irenaeus, *Adv. haer.* 1.11.1). Λόγος and ζωή are, admittedly, found in John 1:4, and this verse probably provided the opportunity for Valentinian exegetes to connect the Ogdoad with the prologue. However, the origin of this pair can be better explained as a

---

[69] Cf. Thomassen 2006, 211–218.
[70] See now especially Thomassen 2006, 269–314.
[71] See, e.g., Philo, *Opif.* 7; *Her.* 98; *Chaldean Oracles* frgs. 7, 14 Majercik; Porphyry *apud* Damascius, *De princ.* 2.1.4ff. Westerink-Combès/§43 Ruelle. The appellation goes back to Plato's description of the demiurge (who only in later Platonism was conceived of as a separate entity) in *Timaeus* 28c3.
[72] For the links between *Eugnostos* and Irenaeus' "Ophites," see Rasimus 2009a.
[73] Van den Broek 1996, 117–130.

Valentinian adaptation of Classic Gnostic mythology—Irenaeus (*Adv. haer.* 1.11.1) and the majority of scholars believe that the Valentinians were reformers of earlier Gnostic speculations.[74] In the already mentioned *Eugnostos* and the "Ophite" myth known to Irenaeus, the core structure of the divine hierarchy consists of a series of heavenly Adam and Eve figures.[75] These speculations go back to a Platonizing exegesis of Genesis 1–2 (cf. Philo), where it was sometimes stated that the man of Gen 1:27 was created after the image of God, who was the Logos;[76] since this man (Adam) was androgynous, it was natural to think that his female aspect would be an Eve figure: Ζωή is, of course, Eve's name in the LXX. Adaptation of such Gnostic speculations would well explain the Valentinian interest in syzygies. Moreover, such a background in Genesis speculations—not too different from what is found in Philo—would also explain the final pair of the Ogdoad, i.e., Man and Church: Man (i.e., Adam) himself is here emanated after his archetype Logos, and his female partner Eve can be thought to represent collectivity, expressed by the term ἐκκλησία since Eve is characterized as the "mother of all living" in Gen 3:20. In fact, a somewhat similar idea is present in *Eugnostos* (V 14,18–27; III 86,24–87,8) and the *Sophia of Jesus Christ* (III 111,2–11; BG 111,6–18), where the Ogdoad (likely denoting the upper realm above the seven heavens of the cosmos) is said to consist of ἐκκλησία and ζωή. Instead of basing the derivation of the Valentinian Ogdoad on John's prologue, it makes perhaps better sense to base it on Middleplatonic and Gnostic speculations of the "Ophite" type about the first principles.

While the Valentinian model system itself stems—in the words of Irenaeus—from "Ptolemaeus and his followers whose doctrine is the bud of Valentinus' school" (*Adv. haer.* 1 *praef.* 2), the commentary is ascribed to Ptolemaeus himself. However, because the ascription (*Et Ptolomaeus quidem ita*) is missing from the Greek text preserved by Epiphanius, some scholars have recently raised doubts about the originality of the ascription.[77] Rousseau and Doutreleau, on the other hand, have suggested that Epiphanius dropped the words because he

---

[74] See, e.g., Layton 1987, 217ff.; M. Williams 1996, 33–37; and Dunderberg 2008, 46.

[75] These heavenly Adam and Eve figures are further described in terms of Adam Christology and Sophia speculations. See Rasimus 2009a.

[76] For the opinion that the Logos was the image of God that served as the model for Adam (of Gen 1:26–27), see Philo, *Leg.* 3.96.

[77] Markschies 2000, 249–251; Dunderberg 2008, 198.

presented the model system and the commentary attached to it as the teaching of Valentinus himself, having found the *Letter to Flora* as a representative of Ptolemaeus' own (and different) teaching.[78] Not all scholars have accepted this solution, but the fact—previously not taken into consideration—that Epiphanius, while following Irenaeus' Greek text itself quite faithfully, generally follows Hippolytus rather than Irenaeus in identifying the various "heresies,"[79] speaks in favor of the solution proposed by Rousseau and Doutreleau. Hippolytus, both in his *Syntagma* and *Refutatio*, presents a variant of the model system as the teaching of Valentinus himself.[80] Therefore, the ascription of the commentary in question to Ptolemaeus is probably original to Irenaeus, and not a later addition to the Latin translation.

However, the ascription may not be completely accurate.[81] It may reflect a Valentinian tradition at the time of Irenaeus, according to which Ptolemaeus had written a commentary on John's prologue, while the version preserved by Irenaeus may, in fact, stem from Ptolemaeus' students. Did Ptolemaeus himself then write a commentary on the prologue at all—which could have been elaborated by his students— wishing to show how the apostle John alluded to the Ogdoad? This is related to the question of whether Ptolemaeus himself taught a pleromatic myth or not.[82] The *Letter to Flora* does not explicitly refer to such a myth, but the letter is, on the other hand, only an introductory lesson.[83] Moreover, Tertullian states that Ptolemaeus was, in fact, the

---

[78] Rousseau and Doutreleau 1979, 1:83–85, 218.

[79] For example, Irenaeus' catalog of heresies culminates in three related groups of "Gnostics" *par excellence* (*Adv. haer.* 1.29–31), which he does not properly speaking label; only later heresiologists and copyists of Irenaeus identified these as "Barbelo-Gnostics," "Sethian-Ophites" and "Cainites," respectively. Hippolytus (Pseudo-Tertullian, *Haer.* 2.1–9) describes three groups of "Ophites," "Cainites" and "Sethites," and the first two descriptions are clearly dependent on Irenaeus *Adv. haer.* 1.30–31. However, Hippolytus' account of "Sethites" has no parallel in Irenaeus, and on the other hand, Irenaeus' *Adv. haer.* 1.29 ("Barbelo-Gnostics") has no parallel in Hippolytus. Epiphanius specifically follows Hippolytus—while, however, providing additional details from Irenaeus—in presenting these Gnostic groups in *Pan.* 37–39. Moreover, Epiphanius' description of "Barbelites" in *Pan.* 26 is not based on Irenaeus' *Adv. haer.* 1.29. See Rasimus 2009a. For Epiphanius being heavily dependent on Hippolytus' *Syntagma*, see Lipsius 1865; and Hilgenfeld 1963.

[80] Pseudo-Tertullian, *Haer.* 4.1–6 (a paraphrase of Irenaeus, *Adv. haer.* 1.1–8); Hippolytus, *Ref.* 6.29–36 (a variant of the Irenaean model system known as Version B).

[81] Cf. Lüdemann 1995, 125–126; Thomassen 2006, 215n30.

[82] Markschies (2000) is of the opinion that Ptolemaeus did not teach any pleromatic myth.

[83] Ptolemaeus promises more instruction at the end of the letter (*Pan.* 33.7.9).

inventor of the pleromatic myth (*Val.* 4.2). In heresiological literature, there are basically three different *pleromatic* systems attached to
Ptolemaeus and/or his school: (1) a version of the Valentinian model
system from the school of Ptolemaeus (with the attached commentary
by Ptolemaeus himself) in Irenaeus, *Adv. haer.* 1.1–8; (2) the system
of the "more advanced students of Ptolemaeus" in Irenaeus, *Adv. haer.*
1.12.1; and (3) the teaching of Secundus (Irenaeus, *Adv. haer.* 1.11.2)
which, according to Hippolytus (Pseudo-Tertullian, *Haer.* 4.7), was
what also Ptolemaeus taught; Epiphanius follows this tradition in his
Panarion, and presents the *Letter to Flora*, as well as the Secundian
system, as teachings of Ptolemaeus (*Pan.* 33).

The ascription of the Secundian teaching to Ptolemaeus is likely
erroneous, and goes back to Hippolytus' *Syntagma*, where Hippolytus
assigns the model system from Irenaeus' *Adv. haer.* 1.1–8 to Valentinus
himself. Why he did this, remains unknown, but Irenaeus was certainly
better informed about Valentinians since he was closer in time to the
founders of the school, and had personal information about the school
of Ptolemaeus (*Adv. haer.* 1 *praef.* 2). The system of Ptolemaeus' "more
advanced students"—indicating that the Father had two consorts,
Ἔννοια and Θέλημα—may well be an elaboration or a variant of the
model system, possibly indeed stemming from some of Ptolemaeus'
students.[84] Therefore, that leaves us with the model system itself. There
are, in fact, three versions of the model system preserved in heresiological literature: (1) the so-called "Version A" in Irenaeus, ascribed to
the school of Ptolemaeus; (2) the so-called "Version B" in Hippolytus'
Refutatio 6.29–36, ascribed to Valentinus himself (Hippolytus had
already, in his *Syntagma*, assigned a paraphrase of Version A to
Valentinus); and (3) section C in Clement's *Excerpts from Theodotus*
(43–65), that could thus be called "Version C," and which by virtue
of the (possibly secondary)[85] title is assigned to Theodotus and the
Eastern school of Valentinianism.

The heresiological testimony concerning the origin of the model system, as well as Ptolemaeus' relationship to the pleromatic myth, is thus
diverse. Apart from Tertullian's brief statement (*Val.* 4.2), basically

---

[84] Cf. Thomassen (2006, 17–22, 208–209) who considers *Adv. haer.* 1.12.1 as a variant of the "type B" pleromatology (the model system itself also represents Thomassen's
type B), whose ascription to the Ptolemaeans was probably inherited by Irenaeus from
an earlier heresiological work.

[85] See Markschies 1997, 433–435.

only Irenaeus says that the school of Ptolemaeus taught a pleromatic myth—in fact, two variants of Version A of the model system (*Adv. haer.* 1.1–8; 1.12.1); and that Ptolemaeus himself wrote a commentary on John's prologue connecting the pleromatic Ogdoad with it (1.8.5). In describing the two systems he has assigned to the Ptolemaeans, Irenaeus does mention Ptolemaeus himself, as well as "those around him," i.e., his students (οἱ περί τινα). In the first instance—the model system itself—Irenaeus says he wishes to talk about current heresies, especially about "Ptolemaeus and those around him, whose doctrine is the bud of Valentinus' school";[86] and the second instance—the elaboration by the more advanced students—ascribes the teaching to "the wiser among those around Ptolemaeus."[87] Do these expressions mean that Ptolemaeus himself was still alive and included in the groups in question? Not necessarily, as the οἱ περί τινα (Epiphanius' σύν in the latter instance is likely a modification to Irenaeus' original Greek) can simply take the meaning of someone's students.[88] Furthermore, if Ptolemaeus died in the early 150s, he would no longer be around at the time of Irenaeus, and the expressions would then naturally take the simple meaning, "the followers of Ptolemaeus."

Thus, if none of the pleromatic systems actually described—save the "Ogdoadic" commentary on the prologue—in heresiological literature can be assigned to Ptolemaeus, does it mean that he did not teach a pleromatic myth at all? This is unlikely for several reasons: (1) Irenaeus ascribes the Ogdoadic commentary to Ptolemaeus himself; (2) Irenaeus assigns two variants of the pleromatic myth to Ptolemaeus' own students; (3) Tertullian considers Ptolemaeus to have been the inventor of the pleromatic myth; and, as Thomassen has argued, (4) Ptolemaeus' reputation as one of the greatest Valentinian teachers necessitates that he did invent something—this would tend to exclude the possibility that it was only his students who invented the plero-

---

[86] *Dico autem eorum qui sunt circa Ptolemaeum, quae est uelut flosculum Valentini scolae; Adv. haer.* 1 *praef.* 2 Rousseau and Doutreleau 22.43–45; Epiphanius' Greek: λέγω δὴ τῶν περὶ Πτολεμαῖον, ἀπάνθισμα οὖσαν τῆς Οὐαλεντίνου σχολῆς, *Pan.* 31.9.8 Holl 400.5–6.

[87] *Hi uero qui sunt circa Ptolemaeum scientiores, Adv. haer.* 1.12.1 Rousseau and Doutreleau 180.1; Epiphanius' Greek—which is not identical with the Greek underlying the Latin: Οὗτος τοίνυν ὁ Πτολεμαῖος καὶ οἱ σὺν αὐτῷ ἔτι ἐμπειρότερος ἡμῖν τῶν ἑαυτοῦ διδασκάλων προελήλυθε, *Pan.* 33.1.2 Holl 448.8–9; the reconstructed Greek underlying the Latin: Οἱ δὲ περὶ τὸν Πτολεμαῖον ἐμπειρότεροι; Rousseau and Doutreleau 1979, 181: Fr. gr. 6.1.

[88] Cf. Lüdemann 1995, 124.

matic myth.[89] With Thomassen I thus agree that the best explanation of all the available evidence concerning Ptolemaeus and his followers is that Ptolemaeus did invent the pleromatic myth, which was then elaborated by his students. Given also the fact that the *Letter to Flora* and the Ogdoadic commentary both use John's prologue as an apostolic proof-text for Valentinian theology—a strategy *not* attested in the *Gospel of Truth*, whose author has simply incorporated Johannine themes and language into his own theology—increases the likelihood that Ptolemaeus himself also initiated the process that linked John's prologue to the Valentinian Ogdoad. The other instances of Valentinian exegesis of the Fourth Gospel and its prologue may then be dependent on Ptolemaeus' innovative usage,[90] especially if the *Gospel of Truth* was not written by Valentinus, or at least if it was not written before Ptolemaeus' martyrdom in ca. 152. Ptolemaeus himself, however, may well have adopted the Fourth Gospel as an apostolic proof-text from the anti-Marcionite discourse of the Roman churches in the 150s.

BIBLIOGRAPHY

Bechtle, G., *The Anonymous Commentary on Plato's «Parmenides»*, Berner Reihe philosophischer Studien 22, Bern: Haupt, 1999.

Campenhausen, H. von, *The Formation of the Christian Bible*, J. Baker, transl., Philadelphia: Fortress, 1972.

Corrigan, K., "Platonism and Gnosticism: The Anonymous Commentary on the Parmenides: Middle or Neoplatonic?" *Gnosticism and Later Platonism: Themes, Figures, and Texts*, J. Turner and R. Majerick, eds., Society of Biblical Literature Symposium Series 12, Atlanta: Society of Biblical Literature, 2000, 141–177.

Culpepper, R.A., *John, the Son of Zebedee: The Life of a Legend*, Studies on Personalities of the New Testament, Columbia: University of South Carolina Press, 1994.

Des Places, E., *Numénius: Fragments*, Paris: Société d'édition «les belles lettres», 1973.

---

[89] Thomassen 2006, 263–268.

[90] Theodotus' doctrine and his use of John's prologue (*Exc. Theod.* 41.3; cf. Tertullian's report in *Carn. Chr.* 19 that likewise reads the Valentinian spiritual seed into the prologue; *Exc. Theod.* 41 seems to be attributed to Theodotus himself by the virtue of the singular φησι; cf. Sagnard 1948, 30–31, 145–149; Thomassen 2006, 29) are not only hard to reconstruct, but they are also known only through *Exc. Theod.* preserved by Clement (otherwise, only Theodoret, *Haer. fab. comp.* 1.8, in the fifth century, makes mention of him; cf. Thomassen 2006, 28–38). As a representative of the Eastern school, he probably stayed fairly faithful to Valentinus' own teachings, but Theodotus may, nevertheless, have also been influenced by the Ptolemaean myth and use of John's prologue. Even though the title of *Exc. Theod.* claims that Theodotus was a contemporary of Valentinus, Ptolemaean influence on Theodotus is still possible—especially if Valentinus outlived Ptolemaeus.

Dillon, J., *The Middle Platonists: 80 BC to AD 220*, revised edition with a new afterword, Ithaca, N.Y.: Cornell University Press, 1996.

Dunderberg, I., *Beyond Gnosticism: Myth, Lifestyle, and Society in the School of Valentinus*, New York: Columbia University Press, 2008.

Ehrman, B.D., *The Orthodox Corruption of Scripture: The Effect of Early Christological Controversies on the Text of the New Testament*, Oxford: Oxford University Press, 1993.

Fallon, F., "The Law in Philo and Ptolemaeus: A Note on the Letter to Flora," *Vigiliae Christianae* 30 (1976), 45–51.

Grant, R.M., *Irenaeus of Lyons*, The Early Church Fathers, London: Routledge, 1997.

Hadot, P., *Porphyre et Victorinus*, 2 vols., Paris: Études Augustiniennes, 1968.

Harnack, A. von, *Marcion: Das Evangelium vom fremden Gott: Eine Monographie zur Geschichte der Grundlegung der katolischen Kirche*, ²1924, reprinted Darmstadt: Wissenschaftliche Buchgesellschaft, 1996.

Hengel, M., *The Johannine Question*, J. Bowden, transl., London: SCM; Philadelphia: Trinity Press International, 1989.

Hilgenfeld, A., *Die Ketzergeschichte des Urchristentums*, 1884, reprinted Leipzig: Fues, 1963.

Hill, C.E., *The Johannine Corpus in the Early Church*, Oxford: Oxford University Press, 2004.

Hillmer, M.R., "The Gospel of John in the Second Century," Th.D. dissertation, Harvard University, 1966.

Holl, K., ed., *Epiphanius (Ancoratus und Panarion) I: Ancoratus und Panarion haer. 1–33*, Die griechischen christlichen Schriftsteller der ersten drei Jahrhunderte 25, Leipzig: Hinrichs, 1915.

Jensen, R.M., *Understanding Early Christian Art*, London: Routledge, 2000.

Kaestli, J.-D., "L'exégèse valentinienne du quatrième évangile," *La communauté johannique et son histoire: La trajectoire de l'évangile de Jean aux deux premiers siècles*, J.-D. Kaestli, J.-M. Poffet and J. Zumstein, eds., Le monde de la bible, Geneva: Labor et Fides, 1990, 323–350.

Lampe, P., *From Paul to Valentinus: Christians at Rome in the First Two Centuries*, M. Steinhauser, transl., Minneapolis: Fortress, 2003.

Layton, B., *The Gnostic Scriptures: A New Translation with Annotations and Introductions*, Garden City, N.Y.: Doubleday, 1987.

Lipsius, R.A., *Zur Quellenkritik des Epiphanios*, Vienna: Braumüller, 1865.

Löhr, W., "La doctrine de Dieu dans la lettre à Flora de Ptolémée," *Revue d'histoire et de philosophie religieuses* 75 (1995), 177–191.

Lüdemann, G., "The History of Earliest Christianity in Rome," *The Journal of Higher Criticism* 2 (1995), 112–141.

Majercik, R., *The Chaldean Oracles: Text, Translation, and Commentary*, Studies in Greek and Roman Religion 5, Leiden: Brill, 1989.

Marcovich, M., ed., *Hippolytus: Refutatio Omnium Haeresium*, Patristische Texte und Studien 25, Berlin: de Gruyer, 1986.

Markschies, C., *Valentinus Gnosticus? Untersuchungen zur valentinianischen Gnosis mit einem Kommentar zu den Fragmenten Valentins*, Wissenschaftliche Untersuchungen zum Neuen Testament 65, Tübingen: Mohr (Paul Siebeck), 1992.

—— "Valentinian Gnosticism: Toward the Anatomy of a School," *The Nag Hammadi Library After Fifty Years: Proceedings of the 1995 Society of Biblical Literature Commemoration*, J. Turner and A. McGuire, eds., Nag Hammadi and Manichaean Studies 44, Leiden: Brill, 1997.

—— "New Research on Ptolemaeus Gnosticus," *Zeitschrift für Antikes Christentum* 4 (2000), 225–254.

Metzger, B.M., *The Canon of the New Testament: Its Origin, Development, and Significance*, Oxford: Clarendon Press, 1987.

Nagel, T., *Die Rezeption des Johannesevangeliums im 2. Jahrhundert: Studien zur vorirenäischen Aneigung und Auslegung des vierten Evangeliums in christlicher und christlich-gnostischer Literatur*, Arbeiten zur Bibel und ihrer Geschichte 2, Leipzig: Evangelische Verlagsanstalt, 2000.

Pagels, E.H., *The Johannine Gospel in Gnostic Exegesis: Heracleon's Commentary on John*, Society of Biblical Literature Monograph Series 17, Nashville: Abingdon, 1973.

Pearson, B.A., *Gnosticism, Judaism, and Egyptian Christianity*, Studies in Antiquity & Christianity, Minneapolis: Fortress, 1990.

Quispel, G., *Ptolemée: Lettre a Flora: Texte, traduction et introduction*, Sources chrétiennes 24 bis, Paris: Cerf, 1966.

Rasimus, T., *Paradise Reconsidered in Gnostic Mythmaking: Rethinking Sethianism in Light of the Ophite Evidence*, Nag Hammadi and Manichaean Studies 68, Leiden: Brill, 2009a.

—— "Porphyry and the Gnostics: Reassessing Pierre Hadot's Thesis in Light of the Second and Third Century Sethian Material," *Plato's Parmenides and its Reception in Patristic, Gnostic, and Christian Neoplatonic Texts*, K. Corrigan and J. Turner, eds., Writings from the Greco-Roman World, Atlanta: Society of Biblical Literature; Leiden: Brill, 2009b [forthcoming].

Rousseau, A. and L. Doutreleau, *Irénée de Lyon: Contre les Hérésies: Livre I*, 2 vols., Sources chrétiennes 263–264, Paris: Cerf, 1979.

—— *Irénée de Lyon: Contre les Hérésies: Livre III*, 2 vols., revised edition, Sources chrétiennes 210–211, Paris: Cerf, 2002.

Ruelle, C., ed., *Damascii Successoris Dubitationes et Solutiones: De Primis Principiis, In Platonis Parmenidem*, 2 vols., Amsterdam: Hakkert, 1966.

Sagnard, F., *Clément d'Alexandrie: Extraits de Théodote: Texte grec, introduction, traduction et notes*, Sources chrétiennes 23, Paris: Cerf, 1948.

Sanders, J.N., *The Fourth Gospel in the Early Church: Its Origin & Influence on Christian Theology up to Irenaeus*, Cambridge: Cambridge University Press, 1943.

Segal, A., *Two Powers In Heaven: Early Rabbinic Reports about Christianity and Gnosticism*, Studies in Judaism in Late Antiquity 25, Leiden: Brill, 1977.

Standaert, B., "L'Évangile de vérité: critique et lecture," *New Testament Studies* 22 (1976), 243–275.

Thomassen, E., *The Spiritual Seed: The Church of the 'Valentinians,'* Nag Hammadi and Manichaean Studies 60, Leiden: Brill, 2006.

Turner, J.D., *Sethian Gnosticism and the Platonic Tradition*, Bibliothèque copte de Nag Hammadi, Section: «Études» 6, Québec: Les Presses de l'Université Laval; Leuven: Peeters, 2001.

van den Broek, R., *Studies in Gnosticism and Alexandrian Christianity*, Nag Hammadi and Manichaean Studies 39, Leiden: Brill, 1996.

Walde, C., "Rhetorik (I–V)," *Der Neue Pauly* 10 (1996), 958–978.

Westerink, L. and J. Combès, eds., *Damascius: Traité des premiers principes, volume II: De la triade et de l'unifié*, Paris: Les belles letters, 1989.

Williams, F., *The Panarion of Epiphanius of Salamis: Book I (Sects 1–46)*, Nag Hammadi Studies 35, Leiden: Brill, 1987.

Williams, J., *Biblical Interpretation in the Gnostic Gospel of Truth from Nag Hammadi*, Society of Biblical Literature Dissertation Series 79, Atlanta: Scholars Press, 1988.

Williams, M., *Rethinking "Gnosticism": An Argument for Dismantling a Dubious Category*, Princeton: Princeton University Press, 1996.

Wisse, F., "The Nag Hammadi Library and the Heresiologists," *Vigiliae Christianae* 25 (1971), 205–223.

—— "Stalking Those Elusive Sethians," *The Rediscovery of Gnosticism: Volume 2: Sethian Gnosticism*, B. Layton, ed., Studies in the History of Religions 41 (Supplements to Numen), Leiden: Brill, 1981, 563–576.

HERACLEON

Einar Thomassen
University of Bergen

When Origen wrote his massive commentary on the Gospel of John in the 230s, he had a single precursor in this kind of undertaking, a man called Heracleon. At least, Heracleon is the only previous commentator of John that Origen refers to in his work. Who was Heracleon? Introducing his predecessor for the first time (O. 2.14.100),[1] Origen describes him as "Heracleon, who is said to have been a pupil of Valentinus" (τὸν Οὐαλεντίνου λεγόμενον εἶναι γνώριμον Ἡρακλέωνα). Indeed, Heracleon is often mentioned by Christian writers as a prominent representative of Valentinianism. Clement of Alexandria calls him "the most celebrated of Valentinus' school."[2] Irenaeus mentions him once, briefly,[3] and he also appears in Tertullian[4] and the *Refutatio omnium haeresium.*[5] In the latter source he is said to be a proponent of the "Italian" branch of Valentinianism (6.35.6).[6] That Heracleon was a "Valentinian" is thus a point on which all our sources agree.[7]

---

[1] O. will be used in this essay as an abbreviation for Origen's commentary on the Gospel of John. I use the edition by Cécile Blanc (1970–1996) in the Sources chrétiennes (*Origène: Commentaire sur S. Jean*).

[2] ὁ τῆς Οὐαλεντίνου σχολῆς δοκιμώτατος, *Strom.* 6.71.1.

[3] Irenaeus, *Adv. haer.* 2.4.1. Although Irenaeus tells us nothing more about him, it is noteworthy that Heracleon and Ptolemaeus are the only Valentinians mentioned by name in this passage.

[4] Tertullian, *Val.* 4.2. Like Irenaeus, Tertullian seems to know no more about Heracleon than his name.

[5] In view of the currently mounting doubts about Hippolytus of Rome as the author of this heresiological work (cf. Simonetti 2000), I shall refer to it only by its conventional title *Refutatio*. In it, Heracleon is mentioned as a Valentinian leader three times (6.4; 6.29.1; 6.35.6) (not only once, as Kaler and Bussières mistakenly state [2006, 277]).

[6] For later sources that mention Heracleon (Pseudo-Tertullian, Filastrius, Epiphanius, Theodoret, Praedestinatus, Augustine, Photius), see Brooke 1891, 31–41, whose survey is excellent.

[7] The recent attempt by Kaler and Bussières (2006) to argue that Origen did not consider Heracleon a Valentinian is unconvincing. The phrase "said to have been a pupil" (λεγόμενον εἶναι γνώριμον) does not imply that Origen had any doubts about Heracleon's adherence to Valentinian doctrines. It is the rather stronger claim that Heracleon was a γνώριμος of Valentinus, that is, a pupil or an associate personally

Since he is mentioned by Irenaeus, Heracleon must have been a well-known figure by 180. This fact lends plausibility to the view reported by Origen, that he was a personal associate of Valentinus.[8] Valentinus is said by Irenaeus to have been active in Rome from the 140s to the 160s.[9] It seems that Heracleon also worked in Rome, as is suggested by his attribution to the "Italian school" in the *Refutatio*, as well as by other circumstantial evidence.[10] Nevertheless, it is noteworthy that Heracleon's commentary on John (or any other work by him) is mentioned neither by Irenaeus nor by Clement of Alexandria. Thus it is quite possible that Heracleon wrote this work only towards the end of the second century, as a rather mature man.[11]

Heracleon's commentary on John is known only through the quotations cited by Origen. There are 48 such quotations, of varying length, in Origen's commentary. A couple of additional fragments from other

---

acquainted with the master, that Origen reports as an affirmation made by others. He could obviously have no first-hand knowledge himself of such a matter. (Cf. Brooke 1891, 33: "...the phrase used [γνώριμος] would hardly be natural, unless Heracleon had been a prominent member of the school during the lifetime of Valentinus.") I am inclined to think that what Origen wants to say with this expression is that Heracleon is not only a follower of Valentinus' doctrine but even reported to have been his close associate, which makes him an even more authoritative representative of Valentinianism. The authors' further claim in the article that Origen endeavours to dissociate Heracleon from Valentinianism fails to take into account a number of studies which show that Origen consistently reads Heracleon's anthropology and soteriology on the assumption that he is a proponent of the "Valentinian" doctrine of fixed human natures (Simonetti 1966–1967 [cf. summary pp. 63–64]; Mühlenberg 1975; Aland 1977; Trumbower 1989; Wucherpfennig 2002, 18–21, 163, 254–256, 332–353).

[8] See the preceding note. The statement by Hill (2004, 208n8), that "Heracleon was evidently not a personal disciple of Valentinus" is based on a misinterpretation of Markschies (1997, 430), who only remarks (without supplying arguments) that Heracleon "is not as closely linked to Valentinus as one is generally ready to assume" (cf. also Markschies 1992, 393; Markschies 2003, 336 is more undecided on the issue).

[9] The dates can be deduced from Irenaeus, *Adv. haer.* 3.4.3. See Thomassen 2006a, 417–422.

[10] Ehrman (1993; 1994) has tried to show that Heracleon used a "Western" form of the text of John, but Wucherpfennig (2002, 30–31) considers the text critical evidence inconclusive. Preuschen (1903, ciii) asserted in his introduction to the GCS edition of Origen that Heracleon's Greek contained Latinisms, though he did not provide any examples (cf. Wucherpfennig 2002, 367n38). The possibility that Heracleon was also active for a while in Alexandria, as, among others, Wucherpfennig (2002, 370) suggests, is uncertain.

[11] Cf. Hill 2004, 207–208, though in my opinion Hill relies on this argument from silence rather too confidently.

works by Heracleon have been preserved by other authors.[12] The evidence suggests that his work as a writer was largely, perhaps exclusively, devoted to exegesis; in addition to his commentary on John, he may have composed commentaries on Luke and Matthew as well.[13] As far as we know, Heracleon was the first Christian theologian to write a systematic commentary on an authoritative text.[14]

Commenting on such texts, in order to extract their spiritual meaning, was in itself not a novel pursuit among the Valentinians. The Valentinian Ptolemaeus asserts, in his *Letter to Flora*, that "we shall draw the proofs of what we say from the words of our Saviour, for through these alone are we led without stumbling to the comprehension of that which is" (3.8).[15] Scriptural proof was considered essential. Thus, Irenaeus' report on the doctrine of the Valentinians in the first part of Book 1 of *Against Heresies* includes a series of texts, taken from Matthew, Luke, John and Paul's letters. According to Irenaeus, the Valentinians provided these texts as proofs, claiming that they contained veiled allusions to specific features of their mythology (*Adv. haer.* 1.8.5). Valentinian writings were generally studded with quotations from, or allusions to, the gospels and Paul. By writing commentaries, therefore, Heracleon was in a sense only taking one step further a practice that was already an integral element of Valentinian theological discourse.

Origen's commentary on John, which includes the extant fragments of Heracleon's commentary, is itself incompletely preserved—of the originally at least thirty-two books, only nine have come down to us.[16] The full scope of Heracleon's commentary is therefore unknown. The fragments we have consist of the following:

---

[12] Of these, only frg. 50 is a proper fragment. It is a fairly extensive commentary on Luke 12:8 quoted by Clement of Alexandria in *Strom.* 6.71–73. Frg. 49 (Clement, *Ecl.* 25.1) is a brief report on a remark made by Heracleon about the practice of fire baptism, probably in reference to Matt 3:11. Frg. 51 (Photius, *Epistle* 134) is a vague allusion to the interpretation by "Heracleon and his disciples" of John 1:17, deriving, perhaps, from the lost parts of Origen's commentary.

[13] Cf. the preceding note. It is possible, of course, that Heracleon's comments on Matt 3:11 and Luke 12:8 were made in other works rather than commentaries on these gospels.

[14] Theophilus of Antioch is, however, reported to have written a commentary on the Gospel of Matthew (Jerome, *Comm. Matt.* pref.; cf. *Vir. ill.* 25), which may be contemporary with Heracleon's commentary.

[15] Similarly 7.9: "we can prove all our statements from the teaching (διδασκαλία) of the Saviour."

[16] Books 1, 2, 6, 10, 13, 19, 20, 28, 32.

Frg.	John	Frg.	John	Frg.	John	Frg.	John	Frg.	John
1	1:3	4	1:21	11	2:12	17	4:12–15	41	8:21
2	1:4	5	1:23	12	2:13	18	4:16–18	42	8:22
(51	1:17)	6	1:25	13	2:13–16	19	4:19–20	43	8:37
3	1:18	7	1:26	14	2:17	20	4:21	44	8:43
		8	1:26–27	15	2:19	21	4:22	45	8:44
		9	1:28	16	2:20	22	4:22	46	8:44
		10	1:29			23	4:23	47	8:44
						24	4:24	48	8:50
						25	4:25		
						26	4:26		
						27	4:28		
						28	4:31		
						29	4:32		
						30	4:33		
						31	4:34		
						32	4:35		
						33	4:36		
						34	4:36		
						35	4:37		
						36	4:38		
						37	4:39		
						38	4:40		
						39	4:42		
						40	4:46–53		

From this list it emerges that the preserved parts of Heracleon's commentary essentially cover: (1) a few verses of the prologue, (2) the testimony of John the Baptist, (3) the journey of Jesus to Jerusalem and the cleansing of the temple, (4) the story of the Samaritan woman at the well, (5) the dialogue with the disciples on food and the harvest in John 4:31–38, (6) the story of the healing of the royal officer's son (John 4:46–53), and (7) the dialogue with the Jews in John 8. It is uncertain whether Heracleon's commentary covered the whole text of the gospel,[17] and whether Origen reported all of Heracleon's exegesis even in the extant books of his own commentary.[18] It is difficult to believe that Heracleon did not comment on John 1:1–2, for instance,

---

[17] Origen makes no further references to Heracleon after Book 20 of his commentary.

[18] The refutation of Heracleon's exegesis was surely not Origen's main motive for writing his commentary on John. In fact, Heracleon is often introduced only towards the end of Origen's own discussion of a verse.

and why Origen is silent about his interpretation of these verses (see below) is an open question.

In this essay, the main features of Heracleon's exegesis of the pericopes listed above will be described, before I go on to discuss his perspective on the Gospel of John and his approach to the text in general.

1. The Main Themes of Heracleon's Exegesis

1.1. *The Logos*

Heracleon maintains that the statement "all things were made through him" (John 1:3) means that the Logos was the cause through which the cosmos was made (frg. 1; O. 2.14.100–103). This implies, however, that (1) the Logos was not the cause of the aeon, that is, the transcendent realm (100); and that (2) whereas the work of creation was performed by the demiurge, the Logos was the effective cause which, operating through him, enabled the demiurge to create (102–103).

The Logos is the same as the Saviour, as Heracleon states explicitly in frg. 5 (O. 6.20.108–117, at 108). This is standard Valentinian terminology.[19] The notion that the Saviour-Logos was the formative agent in creation is common Valentinian doctrine,[20] as is the idea that the demiurge is a mere tool wielded by the higher demiurgic power.[21] In fact, Heracleon's interpretation of John 1:3 as a text referring to the demiurgic role of the Saviour-Logos[22] finds parallels in Ptolemaeus' *Letter to Flora* (3.6) and in the *Excerpts from Theodotus* (45.3).[23] Thus,

---

[19] Irenaeus, *Adv. haer.* 1.2.6 (end); *Refutatio* 6.35.4; *Exc. Theod.* 1, 2, 16; *Val. Exp.* 32 (probably).

[20] E.g., Irenaeus, *Adv. haer.* 1.4.5–1.5.2; *Exc. Theod.* 45–47; *Val. Exp.* 35–37. Wucherpfennig asserts that according to the Valentinians, "der Kosmos nicht durch den Logos, sondern durch den Demiurgen geschaffen ist" (2002, 127). This view, which also informs his reading of the fragment and his understanding of Heracleon's relationship with Valentinianism, is seriously inaccurate (as is the statement in Irenaeus, *Adv. haer.* 3.11.2, which Wucherpfennig adduces as evidence). The texts themselves tell us otherwise. It should be added, however, that a demiurgic role is often assigned to Sophia as well, and that in, e.g., Irenaeus' system an attempt has clearly been made to harmonize the respective demiurgic functions of the Saviour and Sophia. See Thomassen 1993, 238–240.

[21] See Thomassen and Painchaud 1989, 395–396.

[22] The point is also made in frg. 22 (O. 13.19.114–118, at 118).

[23] See also Quispel 1966, 77–79; Thomassen 2006a, 123–124.

his exegesis of this verse represents a traditional *topos* of Valentinian exegesis.[24]

In Valentinian theology, the Saviour is brought forth at a particular moment in the salvation narrative.[25] After the passionate and fallen aeon Sophia had repented and turned towards the pleroma for help, the aeons collectively produced and sent forth the Saviour. He healed the passions of Sophia and brought order to the two substances or forces that had come into existence as a result of her passion and her conversion: matter and soul. This organizing activity constitutes his cosmogonic work. Since the Saviour-Logos does not exist from the beginning of the narrative, one wonders how Heracleon may have explained John 1:1–2, and why Origen says nothing about his exegesis of these verses. Perhaps Heracleon contented himself with observing that the Logos existed before the creation of the world. Alternatively, he might have stated at this point that the Saviour-Logos contained within himself the entire divine fullness, as the systematic treatises habitually do when they describe the generation of the Saviour.[26] Neither statement would have been objectionable to Origen.

At any rate, Heracleon interprets τὰ πάντα, "all things," as meaning the cosmos, and he understands the Logos as the transcendent demiurge who provided it with form. The higher realm of the aeon[27] is not included in "all things." Origen at this point accuses Heracleon of

---

[24] There also exists a different exegetical tradition in Valentinianism, which uses John's prologue as proof for the theory of a primordial Ogdoad consisting of the Father/partner + Monogenes/Truth + Logos/Life + Man/Ekklesia (Irenaeus, *Adv. haer.* 1.8.5; *Exc. Theod.* 6–7). Here, Monogenes is identified with the Arche of the prologue, and "the Logos in the Arche" is the male part of the following aeonic syzygy. In Irenaeus, *Adv. haer.* 1.8.5, John 1:3 is then taken to mean that "the Logos became the cause of the formation and the origin of all aeons after him" (See Thomassen 2006a, 211–212, 213–218). This aeon called Logos is not to be confused with the Logos used as a name for the Saviour (as does Quispel 1966, 78; correctly observed by Wucherpfennig [2002, 120n79]—who, however, fails to see the essential identity of Heracleon's exegesis with that of Ptolemaeus and *Exc. Theod.* 45.3).

[25] See especially Irenaeus, *Adv. haer.* 1.2.6; 1.3.1,4; 1.4.5; *Exc. Theod.* 43.2–45.1; *Refutatio* 6.32; *Tri. Trac.* 86–88.

[26] Irenaeus, *Adv. haer.* 1.3.1,4; 1.4.5; *Exc. Theod.* 43.2–3; *Refutatio* 6.32.1–2; *Tri. Trac.* 87,31–36; 88,8–10; *Val. Exp.* 33.

[27] Heracleon's use of ὁ αἰών in the singular is used by Wucherpfennig as an argument for dissociating him from mainstream Valentinianism (2002, 134–139). However, as Wucherpfennig himself notes, the singular form appears both in one of Valentinus' fragments (frg. 5) and in *Tri. Trac.* 74,1–2. The general principle that the same names are regularly used both for the transcendent world as a whole and its individual members was observed long ago by Karl Müller (1920, 179–184).

introducing an arbitrary limitation in his interpretation of the words of the gospel. It may be observed, however, that Origen himself discusses the question of whether certain protological entities might not have come into being through the Logos (O. 2.72–99),[28] giving the impression that this was already a debated issue among the exegetes. Some, he says, are of the opinion that the Holy Spirit did not come into being through the Logos, though he himself holds that it did (73–88). It is clear to Origen, on the other hand, that "the Beginning" in which the Logos "was," and which Origen identifies with the divine Wisdom, must have preceded the Logos, and that since "life" and "light" were "in" the Logos, these attributes could not have come into being *through* him (89–90). Against this background, the exclusion of the aeon from "all things" by Heracleon (who might, as a Valentinian, have argued that the whole transcendent realm in a sense exists "in" the *Archē* = *Monogenēs*), appears rather less extravagant than Origen is making out.

1.2. *The Baptist*

In commeting on the testimony of John the Baptist (John 1:19–34; frgs. 4–10), Heracleon is especially interested in the allegorical meaning of the figure of the Baptist himself. Three aspects of Heracleon's interpretation of the Baptist will be mentioned here. First, Heracleon resolves the contradiction between the Baptist's own denial that he is Elijah or a prophet[29] (John 1:21) and the Saviour's assertion that he is both, in Matt 11:11,13–14.[30] By making a distinction between the Baptist's inward nature—"John himself"—on the one hand, and "the things about him"—his "clothes"—on the other (frg. 5; O. 6.20.112–114), Heracleon can claim that the Baptist was indeed a prophet and Elijah with regard to his outward appearance, while inwardly he was more than a prophet, as the Saviour himself confirmed (Matt 11:9–14; Luke 7:26–28).[31]

---

[28] In fact, it is this discussion that forms the context for introducing the opinion of Heracleon when quoting the first fragment from him in O. 2.14.100–103.

[29] Origen rebukes Heracleon for disregarding the definite article in ὁ προφήτης (John 1:21,25). Ehrman (1993, 107–108) suggests that Heracleon's text may have lacked the article, since it is also absent from certain textual witnesses.

[30] This contradiction also worried Origen; see Wucherpfennig 2002, 203–204.

[31] In paraphrasing the text from the synoptics as μείζονα προφητῶν καὶ ἐν γεννητοῖς γυναικῶν, Heracleon seems to understand μείζονα προφητῶν in the sense

Secondly, Heracleon takes up the self-description of the Baptist as "the voice of one crying in the wilderness" (John 1:23) and explains that the relationship between the Baptist and the Saviour is like that between the φωνή and the λόγος (frg. 5; O. *loc. cit.* 108–111). Moreover, Heracleon asserts, the general class of prophets (πᾶσα προφητικὴ τάξις) is situated at one step down in this hierarchy: they are the "echo" (ἦχος). The tripartition *logos*-voice-echo is a literary commonplace,[32] which was well established in the Valentinian tradition.[33] Heracleon also says that the voice is capable of being turned into *logos*, just as the female can become male and the echo can be changed into voice.

Thirdly, Heracleon sees the Baptist as representing the demiurge (frg. 8; O. 6.39.194–202). When the Baptist proclaims that he is unworthy to untie the thong of Christ's sandal (John 1:27), Heracleon reads this as the demiurge avowing that he is unable to explain and resolve the design regarding the Saviour's flesh (οὐ δύναμαι οὐδὲ διηγήσασθαι ἢ ἐπιλῦσαι τὴν περὶ αὐτῆς οἰκονομίαν [198]).

A similar statement is made in frg. 10 (O. 6.60.306–307). When the Baptist calls Christ "the lamb of God" (John 1:29) and not a full-grown ram, he is speaking, Heracleon explains, with the imperfect understanding of someone who is only a prophet. That is why he refers to the Saviour as an incomplete animal. In contrast, when the Baptist says "who takes away the sin of the world," he speaks in the capacity of someone who is "more than a prophet." In the first case, the Baptist speaks about the Saviour's body, in the second about "him who is in the body." In this fragment, the Baptist speaking as a regular prophet is comparable to the demiurge in frg. 8; both speak only about the body of the Saviour and do not perceive the Saviour's internal nature.

These fragments illustrate several characteristic features of Heracleon's exegesis. First, he seeks to harmonize John and the synoptics,[34] and is concerned to resolve apparent contradictions between the gospels. Second, he pays attention to the precise choice of words (φωνή, ἀμνός, λύειν) and cleverly exploits their semantic connotations. Third,

---

of περισσότερον προφήτου (Matt 11:9; Luke 7:26; cf. frg. 10), although this reading is awkward together with the rest of the phrase.

[32] Wucherpfennig 2002, 224–228.

[33] See Irenaeus, *Adv. haer.* 1.14.2,5. A soteriologically significant distinction between sound and meaning is also made in *Gos. Truth* 23; *Tri. Trac.* 61; 119; 133. Wucherpfennig does not mention the Valentinian parallels.

[34] I.e., Matthew and Luke; there is no evidence that he used Mark.

he allegorizes characters and objects mentioned in the text as types of mythological figures or ideas (John the Baptist = the demiurge; Christ's sandal = his body). These exegetical operations all serve, of course, to justify a specific set of theological ideas. It is not always easy, however, to reconstruct exactly what these ideas are. One of the problems arising concerns the exact relationship between John the Baptist and the demiurge. If the Baptist is a type of the demiurge, may it then be assumed that everything which is said about the Baptist also applies to the demiurge? Does the demiurge have an inner "self" which is superior to his external appearance, just as the inner self of John the Baptist is "more than a prophet" and capable of understanding more of the Saviour than his body? And is the demiurge too like the voice that will become *logos*, viz. the female that will be changed into male?

The problem here is that Valentinian texts normally operate with an ontological hierarchy of matter, soul and spirit. Each of these substances originated in a distinct mental state of Sophia: matter derived from her passion, soul from her repentance and conversion, and spirit from the joy she felt when she saw the Saviour coming towards her. The spiritual seed of Sophia will, after having been incarnated for a while in humans, be redeemed and enter into the pleroma. The "psychic" beings, however, whose essence is soul, and who include both humans and cosmic powers, will attain salvation on a lower level—at least that is what some of the sources seem to say.[35] The demiurge is consistently described in Valentinian texts as a psychic being, and Heracleon clearly adheres to this view, as is shown in particular by frg. 40 (see below). John the Baptist, on the other hand, seems to transcend these categories; he appears to be psychic, like the demiurge, and at the same time spiritual, by virtue of what he is "himself."

No issue has been more discussed by scholars studying the fragments of Heracleon than his views on the categories spiritual, psychic and material, and opinions vary considerably. Some scholars have maintained that Heracleon subscribes to a strict determinism of salvation and perdition according to whether one is born with a spiritual,

---

[35] Irenaeus, *Adv. haer.* 1.7.1,4,5; *Refutatio* 6.32.9; *Exc. Theod.* 34.2; 63.1; 65; *Tri. Trac.* 122 (but *Tri. Trac.* also says that all the saved will eventually be united in the same location [119; 132–133]; cf. Simonetti 1994, 228–239; I am now inclined to think that these apparent contradictions must derive from the use of different sources by the author of *Tri. Trac.*).

psychic or material "nature."[36] Others have concluded that, for Heracleon, the distinctions between the human categories are more fluid,
either in the sense that each person's "nature" is not an inborn quality,[37] or soteriologically, in the sense that humans may be born as
either spirituals or psychics but will nevertheless attain the same kind
of salvation, by the psychics being transformed into spirituals.[38] Yet
other scholars argue that Heracleon does not use the concept of different human natures at all, but that this has been imposed on him
by Origen's report of his views.[39] Although this is not the place to
enter fully into that debate, I would nevertheless like to make the following observations. Heracleon very clearly, in my view, presupposes
and applies the Valentinian theory of three human kinds. However,
he applies it primarily in one context, namely to describe the various responses of humans to the Saviour: there is a spiritual way of
responding to the Saviour, exemplified by the Samaritan woman; there
is also a typically "psychic" way of coming to faith in the Saviour,
exemplified by the "petty king" (this is how Heracleon understands the
"royal officer"); finally there is a "material" way of responding, which
is that of failing to understand and of rejecting the Saviour, exemplified by the Jews in John 8.

Heracleon does not state clearly whether the three kinds of humans
possessed their specific characteristics even before the Saviour arrived.
There is, however, a sense in which all humans were psychics before
that happened, since "the old dispensation" itself, when the world was
under the rule of the demiurge, was essentially psychic. With this common "psychic-ness" as the basis, some humans reacted in a spiritual
way, others in a psychic way and still others in a material way when
the Saviour appeared. As we shall see, Heracleon absolutely rejects the
idea that those who acted in a material way did so because they were
predisposed by nature to do so. In the case of the spiritual response,
Heracleon does not clearly state whether the spirituals were specially
predisposed to receive the Saviour because they possessed a spiritual

---

[36] Sagnard 1947, especially pp. 506–520; Simonetti 1966–1967; Simonetti 1992;
Strutwolf 1993, 114–125; Holzhausen 1998.
[37] Langerbeck 1967, 67–72; Mühlenberg 1975; Aland 1977. Already Heinrici (1871,
144) observed that, "So schwanken trotz der häufig sich wiederholenden Behauptung
der Einzigart det pneumatischen Natur die Grenzen zwischen Pneumatikern und
Psychikern."
[38] Janssens 1959; Pagels 1973; Devoti 1978.
[39] Wucherpfennig 2002, especially pp. 333–357; Dunderberg 2008, 141–144.

seed which the others lacked, although I think this is a distinct possibility. With regard to eschatology, Heracleon never suggests that spirituals and psychics will attain different kinds or levels of salvation.[40] Nor does he state that psychics will eventually become spirituals (which would probably be an incorrect use of terms since, for Heracleon, those categories primarily relate to the various kinds of receptivity to the Saviour rather than to ultimate soteriological states). However, he comes very close to suggesting that psychics will be transformed into spirit by quoting 1 Cor 15:54 in fragment 40.

To conclude by returning to John the Baptist, it seems that the ambiguity of this character arises from the fact that he, as a prophet, is essentially part of the old dispensation, and in that sense psychic, like the demiurge, although he is not necessarily psychic in the sense of not being spiritual. In fact, his being more than a prophet and having a superior inner "self" which is able to perceive the true nature of the Saviour suggest that the Baptist is a spiritual person as well. Thus, because the category of the psychic has a double meaning, and because the Baptist stands at the very point of transition between the old and the new dispensation, Heracleon seems to have been able to conceive of him, exceptionally, as being both psychic and spiritual at once.

1.3. The Descent into the World and the Cleansing of the Temple

Jesus has descended from heaven, according to the Gospel of John; he is from above, sent into the world (3:13,17,31; 8:23, etc.). This idea supplies the framework for much of Heracleon's allegorical interpretation of Jesus' acts in the gospel. Thus, when Jesus "went down" (κατέβη) into Capernaum (John 2:12), this signifies for him the descent of the Saviour into the world (frg. 11; O. 10.11.48). More specifically, Capernaum is the material realm. The Saviour therefore descended into matter, which probably means that he assumed a physical body.[41]

From Capernaum, Jesus made an "ascent" to Jerusalem (John 2:13), which, according to Heracleon, is "the psychic place" (frg. 13; O. 10.33.210–215, at 210).[42] Here, he performed the cleansing of the

---

[40] The passage to this effect in frg. 13 (O. 10.33.211) is fairly clearly a remark by Origen, who misinterprets Heracleon's temple allegory as referring to eschatology (see below, n50).

[41] Cf. Thomassen 2006a, 107–112.

[42] Cf. Thomassen 2006a, 112–115.

temple (John 2:14–17). For Heracleon, this event becomes an image
of the salvific work of the Saviour in the world. More precisely, the
cleansing of the temple means the cleansing of the soul. The traders
in the temple are demons that are cast out[43] by the Saviour (212–214).
The whip used for this purpose Heracleon sees as an image of the
Holy Spirit: it "blows away the wicked." Moreover, Heracleon points
out that the whip must have been equipped with a wooden handle,
which is a type of the Cross (214–215). It was evidently important for
Heracleon to make it clear that the destruction of the demons took
place through the passion[44] of the Saviour on the Cross, which the
Valentinians generally interpret as the power separating spirit from
matter.[45]

Heracleon points out that the gospel uses the word *hieron* to designate the place where the traders were found, and not *naos*.[46] The
former word was chosen "so that it may not be thought that it is
the Calling only, lacking spirit, which elicits help from the Lord." The
"Calling" (κλῆσις) is a common Valentinian name for the psychics,[47]
and Heracleon's insistence on this point indicates that he is taking
issue with the views of some opponent. In fact, the opposing view is
attested by the Valentinian treatise copied by Irenaeus, where it is stated
that "the Saviour . . . came to the psychic, since it possessed free will, in
order to save it" (*Adv. haer.* 1.6.1).[48] What is going on here is internal
Valentinian polemics.[49] Irenaeus' treatise teaches that the spirituals are
saved by nature, just as matter by necessity perishes (1.6.2). Heracleon,
by contrast, emphasizes that the spirituals, no less than the psychics,
need salvation from the Saviour. *Hieron* designates the whole temple

---

[43] This is most explicitly stated in frg. 14: ". . . the powers that were cast out and
destroyed by the Saviour" (O. 10.34.223).

[44] The passion is explicitly referred to in frg. 12 (O. 10.19.117); Thomassen 2006a,
111–112.

[45] Cf. Thomassen 2006a, 66–67, 258–259, 274, 279–280.

[46] Accepting the emendation of τῶν ἄνω to τῷ νάῳ in frg. 13 (O. 10.33.211), for
reasons that will become clear in the following.

[47] Irenaeus, *Adv. haer.* 1.6.4; 1.14.4; *Exc. Theod.* 58.1; *Tri. Trac.* 122. (The usage in
Exc. Theod. 21–22 is different.) The corresponding collective name for the spirituals
is "the Election" (ἡ ἐκλογή).

[48] Thomassen 2006a, 112.

[49] It may be remarked in passing that since Heracleon is here reporting a view
with which he disagrees, it cannot be taken for granted that he subscribes without
reservation to the description of the Calling as "lacking spirit" (χωρὶς πνεύματος), an
expression which has often been referred to in previous discussions about the human
categories in Heracleon.

and not just the inner sanctuary, the *naos*. It includes the forecourt (*pronaos*), where the Levites go, as well as the Holy of Holies, where only the High Priest may enter.[50] By the Levites Heracleon evidently means the psychics, and the High Priest represents the spirituals. Both categories are saved when the Saviour cleanses the temple.

The temple is, as we have seen, the soul. The cleansing of the temple means the purification of the soul through the expulsion of the demons that have taken control over it. Though set in the wider context of the Saviour's descent into the world, the focus in Heracleon's interpretation of this event is on the redemption of the individual human soul—whether that of "spirituals" or that of "psychics." Heracleon apparently acknowledges a distinction between these two categories of humans, but he does not, in this context, draw any soteriological implications from it.[51] Rather, his concern is to stress that the spirituals needed to be redeemed as much as the psychics, by having their souls purified by the Saviour.

1.4. *The Samaritan Woman at the Well*

The episode of Jesus' encounter with the Samaritan woman in John 4 is an exemplary conversion story. This is also how Heracleon treats it.[52] Specifically, the woman is a type of the spiritual person: "She received the faith unreservedly and in accordance with her own nature, for she did not hesitate over what he told her" (frg. 17; O. 13.10.57–66, at 63).

---

[50] Origen has somewhat bungled this part of the fragment, but a satisfactory interpretation has been given by Wucherpfennig (2002, 52): "[Heracleon] claims that **'the temple' is, on the one hand, the Holy of Holies, where only the High Priest enters—** that is where the spirituals end up, I think he is saying—**and, on the other hand, the area of the forecourt, where the Levites are as well,** is a symbol of the psychics, who will attain a salvation outside the Pleroma." (I have distinguished what I regard, following Wucherpfennig, as Heracleon's text from Origen's comments by bold print.) Origen clearly misinterprets Heracleon by taking him to refer to eschatological events, which Origen describes in terms of preconceived ideas about Valentinian eschatology (derived, perhaps, from Irenaeus, *Adv. haer.* 1.7; on the probability that Origen knew Irenaeus' work see Le Boulluec 1977). Heracleon is not, however, concerned with eschatology in this context. Wucherpfennig deserves credit for having solved a problem that has beset all previous studies (and translations) of this fragment and has led to untenable conclusions about Heracleon's eschatological views regarding spirituals and psychics. (I happily retract the statement in Thomassen 2006a, 105n7.)

[51] Cf. the preceding note.

[52] Heracleon's exegesis of this episode is the subject of a lengthy study by Poffet (1985). However, Poffet is more concerned with polemicizing against Heracleon's exegesis than in understanding it on its own terms, and is therefore less helpful for our purposes.

The unhesitating recognition of the Saviour is in fact a characteristic of the spiritual: "The spiritual kind...immediately rushed towards him," the *Tripartite Tractate* states (118), after first having established that humankind is divided into a spiritual, a psychic and a material *genos*.[53] By contrast, hesitation is the typical response of the psychic kind (118–119).[54] The fact that the Samaritan woman did not hesitate is not explicitly stated in John's text, however, and this interpretation clearly represents Heracleon's desire to make the story agree with an established Valentinian *topos* of the spiritual.

Converted, the Samaritan woman abandons the old well, whose water is drunk by animals[55] and leads to corruption;[56] instead, she receives the life-giving water of the Saviour (frg. 17; O. *loc. cit.* 57–61). Her old life had been one of debauchery, and her six husbands represent "all the evil of matter" under which she had suffered (frg. 18; O. 13.11.67–74, at 71).[57] In other words, as in the scene of the cleansing of the temple, the soul of the spiritual person was oppressed and tormented by demons before the Saviour came and set it free. In this case,

---

[53] The theme of immediate recognition recurs in *Tri. Trac.* 133–134 and again in connection with Sophia's response to the Saviour: προδραμεῖν, Irenaeus, *Adv. haer.* 1.4.5; cf. *Exc. Theod.* 44.1. The Samaritan woman and Sophia are quite similar characters (as already Brooke 1891, 42, pointed out), although the Samaritan woman does not have to be considered in the strict sense as a type of Sophia in Heracleon's exegesis, as Sagnard suggests (1947, 502).

[54] Since this seems to be a *topos* in Valentinian thinking about the three human kinds, it is unlikely that the notion of a spiritual *physis* has been introduced by Origen in his report of the fragment, as Wucherpfennig suggests (2002, 338–339).

[55] The animals represent the material forces working on the soul, in other words passions and vices; cf. frg. 20 (O. 13.16.95–97, at 95); cf. Irenaeus, *Adv. haer.* 1.5.4; *Exc. Theod.* 48.3; 50.1; 85.1; *Interp. Know.* (NHC XI,1) 10,36–37; 11,22.26.31–32. The animals are hardly "psychic," as Sagnard asserts (1947, 497).

[56] It has often been assumed, beginning with Origen himself, that Heracleon understands Jacob's well and its water as a metaphor for the "Old Testament" (Loewenich 1932, 85; Wiles 1960, 45; Simonetti 1966–1967, 23–25; Poffet 1985, 23). Since the well brings corruption, and is clearly associated with matter and passions (the Samaritan woman's old life), whereas Heracleon generally has a higher view of Jewish worship and the prophets (they belong to the psychic realm), this is rather unlikely. Nor is there anything in the text that suggests that "Jacob" is an allusion to the demiurge, as Pagels (1973, 87) claims. In this context Heracleon chooses to comment on the animals, not on Jacob (cf. Mühlenberg 1975, 182).

[57] Heracleon probably adds her present partner to the five husbands mentioned in John 4:18 (Janssens 1959, 135n43). Six is the number of matter: frg. 16 (O. 10.38.261; cf. Irenaeus, *Adv. haer.* 1.14.6; Wucherpfennig 2002, 83–84). This is probably because the Hebdomad is associated with the psychic and the Ogdoad with the spiritual (cf. Wucherpfennig 2002, 320–321 [with references to older studies], though he refuses to make the connection).

however, instead of focusing on purification, the theme of the husbands allows Heracleon to introduce another element of Valentinian soteriology: when Jesus says, "You are right in saying, 'I have no husband'" (John 4:17), Heracleon interprets this as meaning that "the Samaritan woman had no husband in the world, for her husband is in the aeon" (frg. 18; 70). The real husband of a spiritual person is her counterpart in the transcendent spiritual realm—her partner, or *syzygos*, often described as an angel, brought to her by the Saviour, who will make her a whole person, filling up the deficiency which has been her life until now.

The conversion is not only an event in the life of the individual, but also signifies, as in the Gospel of John itself, a turning point in the history of salvation. When Jesus tells the woman that, "the hour is coming when neither on this mountain nor in Jerusalem will you worship the Father" (John 4:21), Heracleon applies the familiar Valentinian tripartition model in his interpretation: the mountain is the material realm of the devil and Jerusalem the created world, or, alternatively, the mountain stands for the creation and Jerusalem the creator (frg. 20; O. 13.16.95–97, at 95). In either case, the first is the object of the cult of the Greeks and the second that of the Jews. Both are now superseded, and spiritual human beings will henceforth worship the Father of truth.[58]

The Samaritan woman then becomes a missionary, going into the city and bringing the people to Christ (John 4:28–30). This demonstrates, according to Heracleon, the special role of the spirituals vis-à-vis the psychics: "She returned to the world to announce to the Calling the good tidings of Christ's coming. For it is through the spirit and by the spirit that the soul is drawn towards the Saviour" (frg. 27; O. 13.33.187–192, at 187). This passage provides decisive proof that the Samaritan woman is construed by Heracleon as a type of the spiritual person, as distinct from the psychic.[59] The difference between the two categories as described in this context is the fact that spiritual persons recognize the Saviour immediately, as was shown above, whereas psychics

---

[58] The theme continues in frgs. 21–24.

[59] Thus also Poffet 1985, 103. The attempts in recent scholarship to deny that Heracleon applied the common Valentinian doctrine of three human kinds (Wucherpfennig 2002, especially pp. 333–353; Dunderberg 2008, 141–144) must be considered a blind alley. In fact, Heracleon consistently works with the categories of spiritual, psychic and material in his exegesis, though he seems to have had his own interpretation of their soteriological significance.

need the spirituals to lead them to the Saviour.[60] The idea that the
soul is brought to the Saviour by means of the spirit constitutes a general anthropological and soteriological principle, which is used here,
metaphorically, to describe the relationship between the two categories
of human beings. That relationship is also made clear in frg. 37 (O.
13.51.341): when the gospel says that "many Samaritans from that city
believed in him because of the woman's testimony" (4:39), Heracleon
interprets this as meaning that psychics, who are "from the world,"
came to believe "because of the spiritual church." The word "many"
signifies that there are many psychics, whereas "*one* is the imperishable, uniform and singular nature of the Election."[61] Oneness is,
indeed, considered a mark of the spirit, whereas the soul exists under
the condition of multiplicity and divisibility, as the *Tripartite Tractate*
confirms.[62]

1.5. *The Healing of the Petty King's Son*

The category of the psychic is more extensively discussed in Heracleon's
commentary on the pericope about the βασιλικός and his dying son
in John 4:46–54 (frg. 40; O. 13.60.416–426). The word *basilikos* means
a petty king, Heracleon explains, and it can therefore be taken to
refer to the demiurge (416). His "small and transitory" kingdom is
"the Middle" (416), in other words the psycho-physical cosmos.[63] His
mortally ill son signifies the human being who is proper to the demiurge (416).[64] His being in "Capernaum" means that his soul has been
caught up in matter, causing his sickness. He was "in ignorance and

---

[60] Nothing is said, however, about whether the psychics receive the Saviour differently from the spirituals, once they are brought to him, or whether the salvation they
will attain is of a different kind.

[61] For the terminology Calling/Election, see above, n47.

[62] *Tri. Trac.* 116: "These are such as belong to the single substance, and that is the
spiritual one. The economy, however, is variable, this being one thing, that another."
See also *Tri. Trac.* 122. This dimension of the plurality of the psychics, which does
not consist simply in the fact that they are "many," has been well observed by Aland
(1977, 163n28).

[63] The term "the Middle" is used interchangeably for the demiurge, the Hebdomad
and the region of the soul: Ptolemaeus, *Letter to Flora* 7.4; *Refutatio* 6.32.8; Clement,
Strom. 6.90.3; Irenaeus, *Adv. haer.* 2.14.4. See Thomassen 2006a, 120–121.

[64] ὁ ἴδιος αὐτοῦ ἄνθρωπος can here only mean the category of human beings which
is defined by the fact that they belong to the nature of the demiurge. That nature is,
of course, psychic. Cf. *Tri. Trac.* 105: "The creator himself also sent down souls out
of his own substance, since [he] too has the ability to procreate"; similarly *Refutatio*
6.34.4. However, Heracleon does not state explicitly that psychic humans have a dif-

sins" (416), a condition which leads to death (417–418). The Saviour "descended" (καταβαίνοντος, John 4:51) to him, healed him and gave him life (421).

Heracleon interprets the story as an account of the Saviour's descent into the world to save the human soul. More specifically, the theme is the psychic person: the one who is healed in the story is a human being who belongs to the demiurge (416); his "nature" (φύσις) is indicated by the fact that he is healed at the seventh hour (John 4:52; 424)[65]—the number seven of course alludes to the Hebdomad, which is the domain of the demiurge and the psychic.[66] There are nonetheless important similarities between the petty king's son and the Samaritan woman who typifies the spiritual. Both had led lives of ignorance and sin[67] before the Saviour arrived, that had been dominated by the forces of matter. Both needed the Saviour to redeem them from their condition.[68] What, then, is the difference between them? Heracleon refers to John 4:48, "Unless you see signs and wonders you will not believe," and comments that this remark "is fittingly said to the kind of person whose nature is determined through works, who is persuaded through the senses but does not believe in a word" (419). Here, the difference seems to lie in the way the two categories of persons are brought to believe, rather than in the nature of their faith as such.

---

ferent origin from that of the spirituals (though the sick person is, of course, the demiurge's *son*).

[65] It is fairly clear that φύσις alludes to the specific nature of the psychic also in 420 "to help his son, that it, that kind of nature" (τουτέστιν τῇ τοιᾷδε φύσει), and in 416 "his condition was not in accordance with his nature" (οὐ κατὰ φύσιν), although the latter is also a common expression that simply means being unhealthy (*pace* Wucherpfennig 2002, 278, 295, 352)—Heracleon is here using a *double entendre*. I do not think Aland is quite correct, therefore, when she concludes that only the spirituals have "eine φὺσις im strengen Sinne" (1977, 181; similarly Mühlenberg 1975, 185–186), though the situation is somewhat ambiguous since, on the one hand, the *physis* of the psychics seems to be conceived of by Heracleon in contrast to that of the spirituals and, on the other hand, to refer to the natural propensities of the soul as a component of all human beings.

[66] Barth 1911, 81; Sagnard 1947, 509, 638.

[67] It may, however, be significant that Heracleon does not apply the word "sin" to the Samaritan woman, as Pagels (1973, 88) points out, in spite of Mühlenberg's arguments to the contrary (1975, 173). The Samaritan woman is portrayed more as a victim of the forces of evil than as an active sinner. On the other hand both she and the petty king's son are the victims of ignorance, which is the ultimate cause of sin (Mühlenberg 1975, 178–179).

[68] These similarities have been rightly underlined by Mühlenberg 1975 and Aland 1977.

As previously mentioned, the spirituals distinguish themselves by immediately recognizing the Saviour, whereas the psychics take more time to do so and are led to the faith by the spirituals. In the present case another distinguishing feature is suggested: the psychics need practical demonstrations to be persuaded, and, in fact, the healing wonder in this story serves that precise purpose. It is also said, however, that the demiurge is very ready to believe (εὔπιστος, 422), and, indeed, the soul has a disposition (ἐπιτηδείως) towards salvation (418).[69] The soul as such is not immortal, however, but belongs to the realm of the perishable (417–418). Salvation must therefore take place through a process of total transformation, as described by Paul in 1 Cor 15:53–54: the perishable puts on the imperishable, the mortal puts on the immortal and death is swallowed up in victory (418). This idea of a total replacement is characteristic of Valentinian soteriology.[70] Such a transformation will not, however, be achieved by all psychic beings: Heracleon enters into a discussion as to whether some of them, either among the angels or humans, will perish, and concludes, by adducing scriptural proof (Matthew and Isaiah), that they will (425–426). This is another common Valentinian *topos*: the psychics, in accordance with the nature of the soul, may incline either towards matter and evil or towards goodness and spirit.[71] Thus Heracleon seems, by alluding to 1 Cor 15, to imply that the good psychics, like the demiurge, will be turned into spirit in the process of their salvation. He does not suggest that their salvation will be different from that of the spirituals, but simply notes that the way they attain the faith that will bring them salvation is different.

1.6. *The Children of the Devil*

The dispute between Jesus and the Jews in John 8 gives Heracleon the opportunity to comment on a third type of response to the Saviour: complete rejection. In particular, he explains what the Saviour means

---

[69] In *Exc. Theod.* 56.3 it is said that the psychic has an ἐπιτηδειότης *both* to faith and salvation *and* to unbelief and perdition. Heracleon's use of the term in this context is more optimistic.

[70] This is a recurrent theme in Thomassen 2006a. Specifically, the metaphor of swallowing up in 1 Cor 15:54 (cf. 2 Cor 5:4) is employed in *Treat. Res.* 45 (cf. Thomassen 2006a, 83–84).

[71] Irenaeus, *Adv. haer.* 1.6.1; 1.7.5; 1.8.3; *Exc. Theod.* 56.3; *Refutatio* 6.32.8–9; *Tri. Trac.* 106, 119–122, 130–135.

when he says "you are of your father the devil" (John 8:44). The devil, of course, represents the realm of matter (frg. 20). Just as there are people who are either spiritual or psychic by nature, so too are there those who belong to matter. In this case, however, Heracleon argues that one cannot speak of a *physis*. Commenting on the words "your will is to do your father's desires" (John 8:44), he concludes: "It is because they have loved the desires of the devil and performed them that they become the children of the devil, though they are not such by nature" (frg. 46; O. 20.24.211–219, at 214). In fact, Heracleon explains that there are three different ways of understanding the word "child": one can be a child either by nature (φύσει), by inclination or choice (γνώμη), or by merit (ἀξίᾳ) (215). Since the devil lacks the ability to procreate, being an essentially destructive force (215–216), the child of the devil is one who does his works and thereby becomes like him (216)—in other words "by merit."[72]

Here again Heracleon is working with the Valentinian tripartition of material, psychic and spiritual. According to Irenaeus' presentation of Valentinian doctrine, "they assume three kinds (γένη) of human beings; the spiritual, the choïc and the psychic, corresponding to Cain, Abel and Seth, and by means of these they establish the three natures (τὰς τρεῖς φύσεις)" (*Adv. haer.* 1.7.5).[73] Heracleon evidently takes exception to such a use of the word *physis*, arguing that the idea of a material *physis* is a contradiction in terms: matter has no *physis*. As with the question of the spirituals' need for redemption (frg. 13), Heracleon employs his commentary on John to participate in inner-Valentinian debate. He maintains that no human is material by nature; they become so only through their behaviour.[74] What they were before

---

[72] The second possibility, of being a child by inclination, γνώμη, is also excluded in this case, since that is defined as voluntarily doing the will of another person (215), and the devil has no will, only desires (211); cf. Langerbeck 1967, 69. Doing the works of the devil and becoming like him means performing his desires, as distinct from his will.

[73] Cf. *Exc. Theod.* 54.1: τρεῖς φύσεις. The *Tripartite Tractate* is content with speaking about γένη (cf. 118) rather than φύσεις, though that text also contains a passage that envisages a separate origin for material people (106,2–5).

[74] According to Origen, however, Heracleon says that the words "you are of your father the devil, and your will is to do your father's desires" were spoken "not to those who are by nature (φύσει) children of the devil, the choïcs, but to the psychics who have become sons of the devil by adoption (θέσει)" (213; the translation of θέσει as "by adoption" is that of C. Blanc in her edition). This clearly contradicts Heracleon's argument that the devil does not beget children, and interference from Origen is therefore likely, as Langerbeck has proposed (1967, 69–70; I have not been convinced by

they succumbed to the forces of matter is not clearly stated, though he probably considered them to be psychic.[75]

In principle, the fallen state of the devil's children does not seem to differ from that of the petty king's son who was dying as a result of his sins, or even from that of the Samaritan woman, who had led a life of debauchery until she met the Saviour. Here again, the difference between them lies in the way they respond to the Saviour. The Samaritan woman recognizes him directly from the words he speaks, whereas the petty king needs the proof of a healing miracle to be convinced. The hostile Jews, however, are "unable to hear the words of Jesus and understand what he says" because they are "of the devil's οὐσία" (frg. 44; O. 20.20.168–170, at 168). As was noted above, however, οὐσία should not be understood in terms of φύσις, or a genetic relationship (as Origen wrongly assumes); for Heracleon the word simply means that these people are assimilated to the devil's mode of being because they fulfil his desires and perform his works.[76] Moreover, that οὐσία is defined specifically by their reaction to the Saviour. Thus, all humans have suffered the fate of ignorance, sin and demonic domination as a result of living with a body and a soul; the Saviour came to redeem them all, but they fall into three distinct categories on the basis of how they respond to the offer of redemption, and that is how they manifest their *physis*, or *ousia*.[77]

In conclusion, it may be observed that the various responses to the Saviour occupy a dominant position in Heracleon's commentary on

---

Simonetti's counterarguments [1994, 210–214]). At least the apposition "the choïcs" has very probably been introduced by Origen (who took it from Irenaeus, *Adv. haer.* 1.7.5?)—the term is not attested elsewhere in Heracleon. (Holzhausen 1998, 287, also admits this.) With regard to the rest of the passage, it is very difficult to extract what may have been Heracleon's words from those of Origen. (Wucherpfennig 2002, 349 argues that the whole passage is Origen's.)

[75] The last part of 213 may represent Heracleon's own words (see the preceding note). Cf. also the last part of frg. 40 (O. 13.60.425–426), where the fallen angels and psychic humans are described in terms very similar to the ones used to describe the "children of the devil" in the present fragment.

[76] Langerbeck 1967, 68–69; Wucherpfennig 2002, 347.

[77] For a similar conclusion, see Aland 1977, 181, also 158, 159, though I think it goes beyond our evidence to assert that the different natures of the spiritual and the psychic are not only manifested but even constituted at the moment of confrontation with the Saviour. Cf. *Tri. Trac.* 118, where ambiguity with regard to predetermination remains: "The essences of the three kinds can each be known from its fruit. They were nevertheless not known at first, but only when the Saviour came to them, shedding light upon the saints and revealing what each one was."

John. This is certainly not an alien perspective on the gospel, in which the theme of the reception of the Saviour is evident from the very beginning (cf. John 1:9–13). Heracleon pursues this theme by applying the Valentinian theory of the three human kinds, which he considers to be exemplified by various characters in the gospel's narrative. In addition, he takes the opportunity to offer his own interpretation of that theory and other aspects of Valentinian soteriology, such as the issue of whether the Saviour came to redeem the spirituals as well as the psychics. This suggests that Heracleon is writing primarily for a Valentinian audience. The hermeneutical framework of his interpretation is (his version of) the Valentinian system. At the same time he displays a fair amount of exegetical professionalism: he pays attention to the precise words and phrases occurring in the text he is commenting on, he comments on the appropriateness of the words used for the characters speaking them or their addressees, he supplies historical information relating to the text and he correlates the text of John with the parallel accounts in Matthew and Luke. In these respects he shows himself to be conversant with the craft of the philological commentary of his time.[78]

2. Heracleon's Views of the Gospel of John

2.1. Heracleon's "Canon"

In the remainder of this essay a few general questions raised by Heracleon's treatment of the Fourth Gospel will be discussed, First, what sort of "canon of scripture" did Heracleon assume? Second, in what aspects of the text of the gospel did its authority reside for him? Third, did Heracleon accord a special status to John over against other authoritative texts? Fourth, what did Heracleon's version of the Valentinian system look like, and did his exegesis merely consist in reading that system into the text or was it genuinely informed by the text of the gospel?

First of all, then, what was Heracleon's "canon"? Although he can hardly be supposed to have entertained ideas about a canon of scripture in the same way as fourth century Christian orthodoxy, it is obvious that Heracleon regarded certain texts as "canonical," not only in

---

[78] This has been well demonstrated by Wucherpfennig (2002).

the sense of possessing greater authority than others but also of containing revealed religious truth.[79] His canon comprised, in addition to the Gospel of John, the Gospels of Matthew and Luke, whose texts are alluded to several times in his commentary.[80] As noted above, a passage from Luke (12:8) is the subject of a separate fragment (50; Clement, *Strom.* 4.71–73), which may be an extract from a commentary devoted to that gospel. There is no trace of the Gospel of Mark in the fragments, but this probably reflects the lesser use of that gospel generally during this period rather than a deliberate rejection of it.[81] Heracleon also seems to have used a collection of Paul's letters, including Hebrews.[82]

In addition to these texts, however, Origen states that Heracleon quotes from the *Kerygma Petri* in support of his views (frg. 21; O. 13.17.104). Heracleon seems to have regarded this as an authentic apostolic document, an attitude he shares with Clement of Alexandria.[83] Origen does not accuse Heracleon of using other "apocryphal" texts (unlike Irenaeus' claims related to the Valentinians in general: *Adv. haer.* 1.20.1; 3.11.9).

Finally, Heracleon occasionally refers to the Jewish scriptures, as when he explicitly quotes Isaiah's prophecies about the perdition of some of the sons of the Lord (Isa 1:2,4; 5:6; frg. 40; O. 13.60.426).[84] Heracleon undoubtedly assumes that it is the demiurge who speaks through the prophet, a fact which places this kind of scripture in a different category from that of the apostolic writings.[85]

---

[79] Keefer (2006, 27–29) rightly rejects the view that the Valentinians had no "canonical sensitivity."

[80] Seven allusions to Matt, three to Luke, according to the index in Brooke 1891, 108.

[81] There are at least three certain instances of the use of Mark among Valentinians: Irenaeus, *Adv. haer.* 1.3.3,5; *Exc. Theod.* 85.1.

[82] Cf. Brooke 1891, 108.

[83] The few extant fragments of this writing are found in Clement. For a recent edition and study, see Cambe 2003.

[84] Isaiah is also referred to as prophesying about John the Baptist in frg. 5 (see especially O. 6.21.117).

[85] This distinction needs to be drawn more clearly than Wucherpfennig does, when he speaks about the Bible being a "Gesamtwerk" for Heracleon (2002, 377). On the other hand, it is evident that the demiurge could not have known the true meaning of the words he inspired Isaiah to speak, since the true meaning of the prophecy, i.e. the perdition of a part of the psychics, could only become clear after the advent of the Saviour. Heracleon, therefore, probably assumed that the prophecies ultimately derived from the pre-incarnational Logos-Saviour. (According to frg. 1, the prophets are an "echo" of the Logos.) For Valentinian theories about the spiritual source of the

2.2. *Where does the Authority of the Text reside?*

The question may also be asked whether the authority of the Gospel of John lies in the written text as such or in the figure of the Saviour, whose words and acts are reported in the text. This is an interesting question from the perspective of the process of canonization, because the authority of the words and acts of the Saviour undoubtedly preceded that of the written gospels, whose canonicity was established in the second half of the second century when increasing importance came to be attached to the apostles as writers. So what is the object of Heracleon's commentary? Is it the text of the gospel as such, or is it rather the words and acts of the Saviour reported in it?

An examination of the fragments from this angle reveals that Heracleon comments on the following types of elements in the text of the gospel:

Words spoken by Jesus: 2:19 (frg. 15), 4:13–14 (frg. 17), 4:16 (frg. 18), 4:17–18 (frg. 18), 4:21–22 (frgs. 20, 21, 22), 4:23 (frg. 23), 4:24 (frg. 24), 4:26 (frg. 26), 4:34 (frg. 31), 4:35–38 (frgs. 32, 33, 34, 35, 36), 4:48 (frg. 40), 4:50 (frg. 40), 8:21 (frg. 41), 8:22 (frg. 42), 8:43 (frg. 44), 8:44 (frgs. 45, 46, 47), 8:50 (frg. 48).
Acts performed by Jesus: 2:12 (frg. 11), 2:13 (frgs. 12, 13), 2:14 (frg. 13), 2:15 (frg. 13), 4:40 (frg. 38), 4:47 (frg. 40), 4:51 (frg. 40).
Words spoken by other characters: Jews, priests, Pharisees 1:19–21 (frg. 5), 1:25 (frg. 6), 2:20 (frg. 16), 8:22 (frg. 42); John the Baptist 1:20–21 (frgs. 4, 5), 1:23 (frg. 5), 1:26 (frgs. 7, 8), 1:27 (frg. 8); evil powers 2:17 (frg. 14); the Samaritan woman 4:15 (frg. 17), 4:19–20 (frg. 19), 4:25 (frg. 25); the disciples 4:31 (frg. 28), 4:33 (frg. 30); the people of the city 4:42 (frg. 39); the petty king 4:47 (frg. 40), 4:49 (frg. 40); the servants of the petty king 4:51 (frg. 40).
Acts performed by other characters: Jews, priests, Pharisees 1:19 (frg. 5); the Samaritan woman 4:15 (frg. 17), 4:19 (frg. 19), 4:28 (frg. 27); the disciples 4:27 (frg. 26); the people of the city 4:30 (frg. 27), 4:39 (frg. 37); the petty king 4:50 (frg. 40), 4:53 (frg. 40).
The characters appearing in the narrative: John the Baptist (frgs. 5, 8, 10); priests and Levites (frgs. 5, 6, 7, 13); the traders in the temple (frgs. 13, 14); the Samaritan woman (frgs. 17, 18, 19, 20, 25, 26, 27,

---

prophecies, see *Tri. Trac.* 97,21–23; 100,33–35; 111–114, with the relevant commentary in Thomassen and Painchaud 1989.

30); the disciples (frgs. 26, 28, 30, 35, 36); the petty king, his son and his servants (frg. 40); the Jews (frgs. 41, 42, 43, 44, 45, 46).

Objects, places, institutions etc.: sandal 1:27 (= flesh, frg. 8); Capernaum 2:12 (= matter, frgs. 11, 40); Passover 2:13 (= the passion of the Saviour, frg. 12); Hierosolyma[86] 2:13 (= the psychic region, frg. 13), 4:20–21 (= the creation or the creator, frg. 20); whip 2:15 (= the Holy Spirit and the Cross, frg. 13); temple 2:19–21 (= an image of the Saviour, frg. 16); Samaria [4:4] (= the world, frgs. 26, 31, cf. 28);[87] Jacob's well 4:12–13 (= the old life, frg. 17); animals 4:12 (= material passions, frg. 17, 20); the mountain 4:20–21 (= the devil, matter, evil, frgs. 19, 20); the Jews 4:22 (= images of those in the pleroma, frg. 22); water jug 4:28 (= the ability to receive life and a thought deriving from the power of the Saviour, frg. 27); harvest 4:35 (of the souls of believers, frg. 32); city 4:39 (= the world, frg. 37); two days 4:40 (the present and the future aeon, frg. 38); sickness 4:46 (= being in ignorance and sins, frg. 40); Judea 4:47 (= the Judea above,[88] frg. 40); Galilee 4:47 (= the world, frg. 40).

Words and numbers appearing in the text: δι' αὐτοῦ 1:3 (frg. 1), φωνή 1:23 (frg. 5), λύειν 1:27 (frg. 8); ἀμνός 1:29 (frg. 10); καταβαίνειν 2:12 (frg. 11), 4:51 (frg. 40); ἀναβαίνειν 2:13 (frg. 13); Ἱεροσόλυμα 2:13 (frg. 13); ἱερόν 2:14 (frg. 13); θρέμμα 4:12 (frg. 17); ἅλλεσθαι 4:14 (frg. 17); βρῶμα 4:34 (frg. 31); ἐκ τῆς πόλεως 4:39 (frg. 37); πολλοί 4:39 (frg. 37); παρ' αὐτοῖς 4:40 (frg. 38); βασιλικός 4:46 (frg. 40); σημεῖα καὶ τέρατα 4:48 (frg. 40); ἰδεῖν 4:48 (frg. 40); ἀποθανεῖν 4:49 (frg. 40); χωρεῖν 8:37 (frg. 43); ἐκ τοῦ πατρός 8:44 (frgs. 44, 45, 46); "three" 2:19 (frg. 15); "six" 2:20 (frg. 16), 4:18 (frg. 18); "seven" 4:52 (frg. 40); "forty-six" 2:20 (frg. 16).

Words of the evangelist himself: 1:3 (frg. 1), 1:4 (frg. 2), 1:18 (frg. 3).

---

[86] Ἱεροσόλυμα, the form appearing in John, is distinguished by Heracleon from Ἱερουσαλήμ, of which it is an image. This higher Jerusalem can, in a Valentinian context, only refer to the Ogdoad, the intermediate region between the cosmos and the pleroma; see Irenaeus, *Adv. haer.* 1.5.3; *Refutatio* 6.30.9; 6.32.9; 6.34.3–4; *Tri. Trac.* 92–97, especially 96,36: ΠΟΛΙϹ. (I was probably wrong to doubt this interpretation in Thomassen 2006a, 105n6.) See Barth 1911, 75.

[87] The fact that Heracleon interpreted Samaria as the cosmos is clear from the two fragments cited. Heracleon's commentary is not extant for any verse in the gospel where the name Samaria occurs, but 4:4 ἔδει δὲ αὐτὸν διέρχεσθαι διὰ τῆς Σαμαρείας would surely have invited him to state his interpretation explicitly. (That part of the text was discussed in Origen's lost book 12.)

[88] "Judea above" certainly means the same as Ἱερουσαλήμ in frg. 13 (see n86): this is the Ogdoad from which the Saviour descended into the world.

From this summary it emerges that Heracleon's commentary was by no means restricted to the words spoken and the acts performed by the Saviour. Heracleon evidently regarded the text itself of the gospel as a repository of spiritual truth. This means that he must regard its author as a person uniquely commissioned to convey this kind of knowledge.

Nevertheless, it is probably correct to say that Heracleon pays special attention in his commentary to the words spoken by the Saviour himself, and feels called upon to explain their meaning. Nearly every utterance spoken by Jesus in the parts of the gospel that are covered by the extant parts of his commentary is expounded by Heracleon. There is one notable exception, John 4:32: on this verse Origen explicitly states that Heracleon has made no comment ("frg." 29). In addition, Origen mentions no commentary from Heracleon on Jesus' words in 8:23–24,38–42,45–49, but this may be due to the fact that Origen generally pays less attention to the views of Heracleon from this point onward.

Heracleon's attitude to the words of the Saviour should be understood in the context of the importance attributed to the Saviour's *logoi* generally by the Valentinians. Ptolemaeus' assertion that all certain knowledge is derived from the words of the Saviour was quoted at the beginning of this essay. The Valentinians regarded his teaching activity as an essential part of the Saviour's mission. "He came forward and spoke the word as a teacher," the *Gospel of Truth* proclaims (19; the following pages elaborate the point). He was a teacher of immortality, the *Interpretation of Knowledge* asserts (9), and proceeds to quote a series of sayings of the Saviour.[89] The words of the Saviour have a soteriological effect in themselves: "When the Saviour came, he awakened the soul and enflamed the spark. For the words of the Lord are power" (*Exc. Theod.* 3.1). In fact, the Samaritan woman was "immediately pierced through by the word" when the Saviour spoke to her (ἄρα βραχέα διανυχθεῖσα ὑπὸ τοῦ λόγου (frg. 17; O. 13.10.65). Moreover, the Saviour converted a great many more people through his own words (frg. 38; O. 13.52.349); when they encountered his own words they no longer believed because of the testimony of others but because of the truth itself (frg. 39; O. 13.53.363); some, however, were unable to receive the *logos* (frgs. 43, 44, 45; O. 20.8.54; 20.20.168; 20.23.198).

---

[89] On these texts, see Thomassen 2007, 589–590.

Thus, the crucial soteriological significance of the Saviour's speech makes the words spoken by Jesus in the gospel an object of special hermeneutical interest for Heracleon.

This interest also extends to the Saviour's acts. They too have a profound meaning:[90] His "going down" and his "going up" refer to his movements between the different levels of reality in the course of his salvific mission; his cleansing of the temple signifies the cleansing of the soul; the fact that he stayed with the Samaritans for two days indicates that he dwells with the believers both in this aeon and in the next. In this way, the acts of the Saviour as well are turned into a text which, in addition to its literal meaning, contains a deeper, symbolic significance. This hermeneutical approach to the acts of the Saviour is similar to the exegesis practised by other Valentinians. According to Irenaeus' account, the thirty years when the Saviour did nothing publicly is an allusion to the thirty aeons of the pleroma: this is an example of how, through his acts, the Saviour imparted knowledge about higher things "in a symbolic way, through parables" (μυστηριωδῶς...διὰ παραβολῶν) to "those who are able to understand."[91] Similarly, the passion of the Saviour is interpreted by some as a symbolic (μυστηριωδῶς) representation of the protological events relating to Sophia (Irenaeus, *Adv. haer.* 1.7.2). Heracleon does not apply this kind of pleromatological exegesis. For him, the symbolic significance of the acts of the Saviour always relates to the work of salvation of the Saviour himself in the world. Nevertheless, the hermeneutical principle is basically the same: the principle which is expressed by the formula in the *Gospel of Philip* 67,27: "Everything the Lord did had a hidden meaning."[92]

Closely linked to the acts and words of the Saviour are the various characters he interacts with in the narrative. They are generally regarded as types, personifying various responses to the Saviour in accordance with an established scheme. The Samaritan woman represents the spiritual person, or the spiritual church; the petty king

---

[90] This was well observed by Barth 1911, 53, 70–71.

[91] Irenaeus, *Adv. haer.* 1.3.1. There are further examples in 1.3.2–3.

[92] For the translation and interpretation of this sentence, see Thomassen 2006b. This may be the place to note that Pagels' suggestion that the Valentinians employed "a threefold exegetical schema, according to which the same verse may be interpreted in each of three correlated frames of reference," i.e., the pleroma, the kenoma and the cosmos (Pagels 1973, 26), does not correspond to any exegetical theory articulated in the Valentinian sources themselves.

is the demiurge, his servants are the demiurge's angels and his son is the psychic human being; the hostile Jews[93] of John 8 are persons who have given themselves over to matter and evil; the traders in the temple are evil spirits. Likewise, the words spoken by each of these characters, and the acts they perform, are explained as being typical of, and as demonstrating their respective natures. Finally, Heracleon loses no opportunity to comment on the various objects handled by the characters in the text, on the topographical contexts of the action or on other items mentioned in the course of the narrative, in order to exploit their symbolic potential.

At the same time it should be noted that Heracleon is not exclusively preoccupied with symbolism. For instance, he explains why the Jews sent priests and Levites to question John the Baptist (John 1:19) by saying that these people were particularly concerned with such matters because of their devotion to God (frg. 5). In this case, the interest of Heracleon's comment seems to be simply factual.[94] In most cases, however, Heracleon's factual commentary (the *historikon* in the technical terminology of ancient exegesis) is used to support his allegorical interpretation. This is the case when he explains the Passover of the Jews as "the great feast" (frg. 12), and when he describes the layout of the temple and the categories of people who are allowed to enter its various parts (frg. 13). The allegorical application of factual knowledge is also his main motivation when he comments on the characteristics of prophets (frgs. 6, 19), on the processes of sowing and reaping (frgs. 32–36), and on the topographical characteristics of Capernaum, Judea/Jerusalem and Galilee (frgs. 13, 40). Heracleon evidently takes it for granted that the gospel provides an account of historical events that is factually correct in all details, while at the same time assuming that those events are to be read as an authored text filled with underlying, symbolic meanings.

This conflation of narrative and text is also evident in the cases where Heracleon comments on the actual words used by the evangelist in his narrative (cf. no. 7 in the list above). For example, Heracleon observes that the word κατέβη in John 2:12 was not used idly, for

---

[93] This typology does not concern the Jews collectively, who are generally associated with the category of the psychic (see especially frgs. 20, 21, 22), but only the specific "Jews" who appear in John 8. The malicious Pharisees of frg. 6 also clearly belong to this group.

[94] Cf. Barth 1911, 105–106; Wucherpfennig 2002, 197–198.

there again the beginning of a new *oikonomia* is revealed (frg. 11; O. 10.11.48).[95] Here, the evangelist "reveals" (δηλοῦσθαι) a religious truth by his choice of words, but at the same time, the Saviour himself is revealing this truth by performing an act of symbolic significance.[96] Likewise, the gospel may be considered to contain a deeper meaning when it states that the Samaritans were "many," and that they were "from the city" (John 4:39); that meaning (which is that this is how the psychics are saved) is both revealed by the evangelist in the text through his choice of words, and revealed by the actual events of the story, that is, in the acts performed by the Samaritan citizens. In fact, all the characters in the narrative become, through their words and acts, revealers, in so far as they are elements of the revealing text of the evangelist.

The status of the text of the gospel as revelation in its own right is also evident in the prologue, where the evangelist is explicitly speaking in his own voice, and this is also made an object of exegesis by Heracleon. Thus, in addition to the words and the acts of the Saviour, the words of the evangelist also possesses revelatory authority for Heracleon.

2.3. Is the Gospel of John Special?

Heracleon assumes that the gospel was written by John, a "disciple" (frg. 3 = O. 6.3.3, though he makes no further comment on this fact in the preserved fragments. John, "the disciple of the Lord," is also explicitly named as the author of the gospel in the Valentinian exegesis of the prologue in Irenaeus, *Adv. haer.* 1.8.5. The expression "John, the disciple of the Lord" is also frequently used by Irenaeus, and it is possible that it reflects a (predominantly) Asian tradition that identified the author and "the Beloved Disciple" of the Gospel with John of Ephesus, rather than with John, the son of Zebedee.[97] Be that as it may, the designation "John, the disciple of the Lord" signals a special relationship

---

[95] ἄλλης πάλιν οἰκονομίας ἀρχήν φησι δηλοῦσθαι, οὐκ ἀργῶς τοῦ Κατέ<βη> εἰρημένου. (The word οἰκονομία here probably means a new phase in the history of salvation.)

[96] The ambiguity of the text is reflected in Blanc's translation: "il y a de nouveau là le début de la manifestation d'un autre mystère."

[97] See Bauckham 2006, 459–460, 469.

between this evangelist and Jesus,[98] which may explain why his name is specifically mentioned in quotations from his Gospel. The authors of the other gospels are never referred to by name in the Valentinian sources, and are rarely even brought attention to as writers.[99]

Although many scholars have stated that the Valentinians had a special predilection for the Gospel of John,[100] I do not think this can be demonstrated to be the case. It is easy to see from the various indices available that Valentinians in general used Matthew and Luke at least as much as John.[101] Heracleon himself weaves allusions to the texts of Matthew and Luke into his discussion of passages in John,[102] and, as has already been mentioned, he may have written commentaries on these gospels as well. It may well be a mere coincidence that his commentary on John is so much better documented than his other works.[103] In general, there is no indication that the Valentinians preferred the narrative of John over those of Matthew and Luke (in fact the opposite seems to have been the case), though the prologue was clearly a text that attracted special attention—together with 1 Cor 15, the hymns of Philippians and Colossians, and the announcement story of Luke 1.

---

[98] "Clearly the epithet 'disciple of the Lord' is meant not so much to put John in a group as to distinguish him uniquely. It conveys his special closeness to Jesus, both historically during Jesus' ministry and theologically in his Gospel" (Bauckham 2006, 459, with reference to Mutschler 2004, 699).

[99] At one point, a quotation from the Gospel of Luke is introduced by the words "as the apostle says" (*Exc. Theod.* 74), and the author of the Fourth Gospel is similarly called "the apostle" in Ptolemaeus, *Letter to Flora* 5.15; *Exc. Theod.* 7; see Barth 1911, 29. With the latter designation, a special status for John vis-à-vis the other apostles is no longer maintained (cf. Bauckham 2006, 463–468).

[100] Loewenich 1932, 61, 71; Sanders 1943, 47–66; and many others. The ancient support for this assumption is Irenaeus, *Adv. haer.* 3.11.7 *eo* (sc. *euangelio*) *quod est secundum Iohannem plenissime utentes ad ostentionem coniugationum suarum.* This view has been extensively documented and strongly attacked by Hill 2004, especially pp. 205–222, and, with more caution, Nagel 2000 (summary 476–479). (Irenaeus evidently speaks very selectively, having in mind exclusively, it seems, the exegesis reported by him in *Adv. haer.* 1.8.5.)

[101] See, e.g., the indices in Völker 1932; Simonetti 1993; Evans, Webb and Wiebe 1993; and, not to forget, Barth 1911, 28–38.

[102] In frgs. 5, 10, 13, 33, 40, 46.

[103] As is well known, it was at the request of Ambrose, his sponsor and a previous Valentinian, that Origen incorporated discussion of Heracleon's exegesis into his commentary. Heracleon can hardly have been famous for his commentary on John in particular, since no other ancient writer mentions this work.

2.4. *Exegesis or Eisegesis?*

Finally, questions must be asked about the relationship between the gospel and Heracleon's own ideas. Did the gospel have an impact on Heracleon's thinking, and on that of the Valentinians in general? Or did Heracleon merely read into the text of the gospel tenets of Valentinian theology that had been formed independently of the *Wirkungsgeschichte* of the gospel itself? Or, if there is a commonality of thought between the gospel and Heracleon's ideas, is this commonality attributable to other factors besides the direct influence of the gospel? These questions are best addressed by examining some of the main themes of the gospel.

The Logos. For Heracleon, as for the Valentinians in general, the Logos was not only a name for the Saviour but also the formative power that imposed rationality on the soul-matter complex. This concept of the Logos obviously has roots in Greek philosophy, and Heracleon, like other Valentinians, simply assumed that this was also the meaning of the Logos of John's prologue. This identification was shared by many other Christian theologians, though the Valentinians' interpretation was based on the particular presuppositions implicit in their dualistic ontology, something which led to a need for specifying what was meant by "all things" in John 1:3.

Heracleon does not fail, however, to follow up in his commentary the soteriological role of the Logos which is announced by the prologue. Thus, the Baptist, who enters the scene as a "voice," will be turned into Logos after having recognized the Saviour (frg. 5); the Samaritan woman is "pierced through" (or "nudged very hard") by the Saviour's Logos (frg. 17—*logos* appears to have a double meaning here); salvation and the Logos went forth into the world from the Jewish people (frg. 22; "salvation and the reception of the Logos" are also associated in frg. 33); the Jews of John 8 are incapable of receiving the Saviour's Logos (frgs. 43–46). In these instances, Heracleon is applying in his exegesis a theme that has been prompted by the gospel itself. He is not simply reading into the gospel concepts that derive from other sources, but is expounding the gospel by employing terminology and ideas that are internal to the text.

Christology. Valentinian Christology has often been labelled "docetic." The Gospel of John too has sometimes been said to contain statements that are docetic, or may be interpreted in that way.[104]

---

[104] See, e.g., Hill 2004, 287–288, with references to the literature.

For instance, Jesus announces that "I am not of this world" (8:23, cf. 17:14,16). Although we do not have Heracleon's exegesis of that passage, something similar is implied when he states that Capernaum, the material realm, was alien (ἀνοίκειον) to the Saviour (frg. 11). In my opinion, however, Valentinian Christology in general cannot reasonably be characterized as docetic. In fact, a number of Valentinian texts assert that the Saviour was incarnated in a material body, and that his assumption of human flesh was a soteriological necessity.[105] Heracleon adheres to this view. According to him, the Saviour was incarnated in lowly flesh, symbolized by his "sandal" (frg. 8); the imperfection of his body is indicated by the Baptist calling him a "lamb" (frg. 10); he entered the material realm "Capernaum" (frg. 11); his composition is symbolized by the number forty-six, where six stands for matter and forty for his spiritual component (frg. 16).[106] Moreover, the Saviour suffered a passion (frg. 12), and saved humans by means of his Cross (frg. 13).[107] Thus, the Saviour is a spiritual being who has entered the world carrying a material body.[108] That body is alien to his true nature, but it is not for that reason a "sham."[109] Heracleon clearly has

---

[105] I have attempted to demonstrate this in Thomassen 2006a. The exceptions are the different versions of the Valentinian system found in Irenaeus, in the *Refutatio* and section C of *Exc. Theod.*, which expressly deny that the Saviour assumed anything material, and also that he subjected himself to passion. These sources instead attribute a psychic body to the Saviour.

[106] Frg. 16 constitutes a problem insofar as it actually describes a human being composed of *plasma*, an "inbreathing" and a seed contained in the inbreathing, in other words the familiar Valentinian anthropogonical model based on Gen 2. It is possible, therefore, that the fragment refers to the creation of the first human, as Strutwolf (1993, 158n20) and Holzhausen (1998, 282) argue. On the other hand, the fragment clearly states that the number forty-six is an εἰκόνα...τοῦ σωτῆρος, so if that interpretation is correct, Origen's report of Heracleon's words must be, at best, incomplete. In the context it seems more plausible to understand the temple as a symbol of the incarnated Saviour, whose body is destroyed through his resurrection.

[107] I think it likely that the whip, composed of small cords/the Holy Spirit and a wooden handle is another symbol of the Saviour's body. For the Valentinians, the passion and the incarnation amount to the same salvific act, and the wood of the Cross signifies the matter to which the Saviour was linked trough the incarnation. (See Thomassen 2006, especially pp. 66–68, 90–91, 99, 258–259.)

[108] The statement in *Refutatio* 6.35.6, linking Heracleon to the "Western" Valentinian view that the Saviour's body was psychic, must be misinformed. There is nothing in the fragments that indicates that Heracleon attributed a psychic body to the Saviour, as Strutwolf (1993, 158n20) and Holzhausen (1998, 281n11) assume. It is also noteworthy that Origen never imputes such a notion to Heracleon.

[109] With regard to the exegesis of John 1:29 in frg. 10, Maurice Wiles remarks that "in the principle of its reasoning it is exactly akin to the orthodox two-nature exegesis of the third century" (Wiles 1960, 113–114n6). The fact that Heracleon did not hold a docetist Christology is also stressed by Janssens (1959, 133n36, 140n65), and recognized by Nagel (2000, 337–338).

no problem accepting the idea of the Logos becoming flesh. Although
no exegesis of John 1:14 by Heracleon is reported by Origen, he surely
alludes to that verse in frg. 8 (σάρκα λάβη).

Anthropology. Perhaps the most important guideline followed by
Origen in reporting and criticizing Heracleon's views was his conviction that Heracleon advocated a theory of three fixed human
natures, which Origen assumed to be common Valentinian doctrine.[110]
According to this theory, the spirituals are predestined for salvation
and the material people for perdition, while the psychics will be saved
or perish as a consequence of the way they choose to behave. An individual's nature is an attribute of origin and birth, and not something
that can be acquired.[111] As has been demonstrated, Heracleon's exegesis identifies these three categories of humans in the Gospel of John,
represented by the Samaritan woman, the petty king's son, and the
hostile Jews of John 8. There is no doubt, of course, that Heracleon
is interpreting these characters applying a set of ideas that have not
been derived directly from the gospel. Yet the three episodes in the
gospel are clearly intended as exemplary stories about responses to
Jesus, and Heracleon's interpretation may be seen as an effort to further systematize this intentional aspect of the text, which is natural for
a theologian.

With regard to the question of soteriological determinism, it may
be remarked that the Fourth Gospel itself has not infrequently been
thought to teach some kind of determinism.[112] Thus, the Jews of chapter 8 are said by Jesus to be from below, from this world (8:23), and
to be unable to hear his words because they are not of God but have
the devil for a father (8:33–47). In contrast, Jesus' disciples have been
chosen, and are not of this world (15:19; 17:14,16). It should be noted,
however, that in his discussion of the Jews of John 8 (frgs. 44–46),
Heracleon argues against a deterministic interpretation of their dia-
bolical parentage: if they are called the children of the devil, and thus
are of his *ousia*, it is because they *de facto* perform his evil works and
desires, not because of their distinctive origin. Moreover, although

---

[110] See especially Trumbower 1989, and the other literature cited above, n7.
[111] The clearest expression of this theory occurs in Irenaeus, *Adv. haer.* 1.6–7.
[112] Cf., e.g., Wiles 1960, 107–111; Hill 2004, 280–282. As Trumbower (1989, 138)
states, "John 1:13, 8:21–47, 10:1–30, 11:52, 17:6, and 18:37 can all be read as indicating the pre-determined character of various individuals' responses to Jesus' offer of
salvation." See also Nagel 2000, 328–329.

Heracleon upholds the Valentinian distinction between the spirituals and the psychics, and the idea that the former belong to the Father and the latter to the demiurge,[113] he uses that distinction primarily to describe the different ways through which these categories of people are brought to the Saviour. Thus he is considering both of them in light of the more general perspective provided by the gospel itself: the response of humanity to the appearance of the Logos-Saviour in the world. It is unlikely that Heracleon was brought to tone down the differences between spirituals and psychics as a result of his work with the Fourth Gospel.[114] I think it is more probable that he genuinely disagreed, on theological grounds, with the much more strongly deterministic, and perhaps elitist, interpretation of the anthropological tripartition propounded by those Ptolemaeans whose views are reported by Irenaeus. It is this personal version of Valentinian theology, and not a ready-made dogma, which he brings into his reading of the Fourth Gospel, with the result that his reading is probably less, rather than more, deterministic than the gospel itself.

The System and the Gospel. Being a Valentinian, Heracleon must have presupposed a system akin to the Valentinian systems reported by Irenaeus, the *Refutatio*, the *Tripartite Tractate*, the *Valentinian Exposition* and the various sections of the *Excerpts from Theodotus*. The fragments offer no information about his protological ideas or his version of the myth of the passion of Sophia. In contrast to the examples of Valentinian exegesis reported by Irenaeus, Heracleon seems to have chosen not to use the gospel text to prove these features of Valentinian doctrine. His interest in John's text seems more consonant with perspectives found in the gospel itself: the descent into the world of a saviour that does not belong to it, and his mission to give "life" to those who are able to receive him. Nonetheless, certain aspects of his system can be reconstructed from allusions in the fragments. Thus, there are two main realms: the cosmos and a higher realm from which the Saviour came. The latter is the aeon (frgs. 1, 18), or the pleroma (frgs. 18, 22). The cosmos is subdivided into a material region, which can be described as a cosmos of its own, ruled by the devil (frg. 20, cf. frgs. 44–47), and a psychic region ruled by the demiurge (frg. 40,

---

[113] This distinction emerges from the juxtaposition of frg. 23 τὸ οἰκεῖον τῷ πατρί and frg. 40 ὁ ἴδιος αὐτοῦ (sc. τοῦ δημιούργου) ἄνθρωπος.

[114] Sanders seems to have thought so (1943, 65), but his announced discussion of Heracleon never appeared.

cf. frg. 13). This cosmological framework is Valentinian and has been superimposed on the gospel, though the prominence of the devil in the gospel text may have led Heracleon to pay more attention to this figure than is normal in Valentinian sources.

In addition to these two realms, however, the Valentinians conceived of an intermediate region, usually called the Ogdoad, where Sophia was considered to dwell until she would be restored to the pleroma in the final *apokatastasis*, and from where she and/or the Saviour were thought to carry out their dealings with the cosmos. I think this feature is also evident in Heracleon. The Jerusalem of which the terrestrial Hierosolyma is an image, can hardly be anything but the Ogdoad.[115] "The Judea above" in frg. 40, from which the Saviour descends into the world, surely refers to the same region. Another hint is given by frg. 35 (O. 13.49.324): "The Son of Man above the Place sows; the Saviour, himself also Son of Man, harvests and sends as reapers the angels represented by the disciples, each for his own soul." The "Place" is a name for the demiurge, or his region, the Hebdomad.[116] In fact, it is normally from the Ogdoad above the cosmos that the Saviour and/or Sophia sows the spiritual seed of Sophia into human bodies and souls.[117] Indeed, that is where they were produced, as images of the aeons, and the place from which they were sent down to a life of human incarnation before being integrated into the pleroma. While we do not know the details of Heracleon's ideas about the production of the seed, there is little reason to believe they were substantially different from those found in the known Valentinian systems.[118]

---

[115] See above, n86 and n88.

[116] Cf. *Exc. Theod.* 34, 38, 39, 59.2; *Refutatio* 6.32.7; *Tri. Trac.* 100,29.

[117] This statement needs, however, to be qualified. In Irenaeus, *Adv. haer.* 1.5.6 and *Exc. Theod.* 53.2–5, the context is the anthropogony, and it is Sophia who does the sowing and she clearly does it from the Ogdoad. In *Exc. Theod.* 2 and Valentinus frg. 1, the context is anthropogonical as well, but here the Logos is the sower and it is not said where he sows from. In *Refutatio* 6.34.6 the Saviour (called "the Joint Fruit of the Pleroma") and Sophia do the sowing together, they do it from the Ogdoad, and the context is not the anthropogony: rather, the sowing goes on continuously as new humans are born. The latter version is the one that comes closest to Heracleon's interpretation of the harvest in John 4:35–38 (frgs. 32–36).

[118] It is because the seed is produced outside the pleroma, and for that reason inherently deficient, that they need to be saved and reintegrated into the pleroma. Valentinian sources provide no other explanation for the production of the seed than the notion that it was brought forth by Sophia as images of the Saviour and his angels manifesting the pleroma. What seems likely, however, is that Heracleon attributed the act of sowing the seed into humans to the Saviour-Logos, and not to Sophia. This

Thus, frg. 35, which is a commentary on John 4:36–37 but harmonizes the text with Matt 13:37–38,41, alludes to a substantial feature of the Valentinian system. The Saviour/Son of Man[119] has sown the seed of Sophia into humanity from the Ogdoad,[120] and has himself descended into the world, together with his angels-disciples,[121] to harvest it.

Underlying Heracleon's exegesis, therefore, lies the entire Valentinian system. He obviously takes it for granted that John the disciple was familiar with this system, being one of those spiritual persons whom the Saviour had chosen to pass on to the rest of humanity the knowledge revealed by himself. John's Gospel must therefore contain this knowledge, but it is discernible only if one looks beyond the surface of the text: the characters appearing in it typify attitudes to the Saviour and to the revelation of the truth that can only be understood in the framework of a larger salvation historical narrative; the words spoken and the acts performed by these characters all allude to this meta-narrative, as do the description of the places and artefacts mentioned; the evangelist's choice of words at every point alludes to more than is immediately obvious. It is not unreasonable to suggest that the Fourth Gospel itself, with its prologue and its mysterious saviour figure who is not of this world, invites this kind of meta-narratival reading—a fact which was also widely recognized in the ancient world.[122] From this perspective, and bearing in mind that theology is always a product of the creative interaction of scripture and doctrinal presuppositions constructed from reason, Heracleon's approach is not incompatible with the spirit of the gospel.

---

agrees with Valentinus, frg. 1, and *Exc. Theod.* 2 (cf. Thomassen 2006, 434–435), and may well be the most primitive version of the theme. It is true that Heracleon never mentions the figure of Sophia, but the analogies with other Valentinian sources make it more reasonable to assume that he presupposed some form of the Sophia myth than that he did not.

[119] The title Son of Man has been imported from Matt 13:37,41. It probably indicates that the pleroma, from which the Saviour derives and in whose image the spiritual seed was produced, is conceived as an archetypal Anthropos, as in Valentinus frg. 1, and generally in Valentinianism (Thomassen 2006a, 437–442; this interpretation was already suggested by Janssens 1959, 287).

[120] Again, the question of universalism presents itself. Has the seed been sown into all humans (as, e.g., Aland 1977, 154–155 assumes), or only in a chosen few, the spirituals? Heracleon gives us no answer to this question.

[121] For this idea, see Thomassen 2006a, 49–55, 172–178, 323–325.

[122] See, e.g., Wiles 1960. See also the remarks by Keefer 2006, 41–42.

Bibliography

Aland, B., "Erwählungstheologie und Menschenklassenlehre: Die Theologie des Herakleon als Schlüssel zum Verständnis der christlichen Gnosis?" *Gnosis and Gnosticism: Papers Read at the Seventh International Conference on Patristic Studies (Oxford, September 8th–13th 1975)*, M. Krause, ed., Nag Hammadi Studies 8; Leiden: Brill, 1977, 148–181.

Bauckham, R., *Jesus and the Eyewitnesses: The Gospels as Eyewitness Testimony*, Grand Rapids, Mich.: Eerdmans, 2006.

Blanc, C., *Origène: Commentaire sur Saint Jean: Texte critique, avant-propos, traduction et notes*, 5 vols., Sources chrétiennes 120 bis (2nd ed.), 157, 222, 290, 385, Paris: Cerf, 1970–1996.

Brooke, A.E., *The Fragments of Heracleon*, Texts and Studies 1/4, Cambridge: Cambridge University Press, 1891.

Cambe, M., *Kerygma Petri: Textus et commentarius*, Corpus Christianorum: Series Apocryphorum 15, Turnhout: Brepols, 2003.

Devoti, D., "Antropologia e storia della salvezza in Eracleone," *Memorie della Accademia delle Scienze di Torino*, serie V, 1978, 2:3–83.

Dunderberg, I., *Beyond Gnosticism: Myth, Lifestyle, and Society in the School of Valentinus*, New York: Columbia University Press, 2008.

Ehrman, B.D., "Heracleon, Origen, and the Text of the Fourth Gospel," *Vigiliae Christianae* 47 (1993), 105–118.

—— "Heracleon and the 'Western' Textual Tradition," *New Testament Studies* 40 (1994), 161–179.

Evans, C.A., R.L. Webb and R.A. Wiebe, *Nag Hammadi Texts and the Bible: A Synopsis and Index*, New Testament Tools and Studies 18, Leiden: Brill, 1993.

Heinrici, G., *Die valentinianische Gnosis und Die heilige Schrift*, Berlin: Wiegandt & Grieben, 1871.

Hill, C.E., *The Johannine Corpus in the Early Church*, Oxford: Oxford University Press, 2004.

Holzhausen, J., "Die Seelenlehre des Gnostikers Herakleon," Ψυχή—*Seele—anima: Festschrift für Karin Alt zum 7. Mai 1998*, J. Holzhausen, ed., Beiträge zur Altertumskunde 109, Stuttgart: Teubner, 1998, 279–300.

Janssens, Y., "Héracléon: Commentaire sur l'Évangile selon s. Jean," *Le Muséon* 72 (1959), 101–151, 277–299.

Kaler, M. and M.-P. Bussières, "Was Heracleon a Valentinian? A New Look at Old Sources," *Harvard Theological Review* 99 (2006), 275–289.

Keefer, K., *The Branches of the Gospel of John: The Reception of the Fourth Gospel in the Early Church*, Library of New Testament Studies 332, London: T&T Clark, 2006.

Langerbeck, H., *Ausätze zur Gnosis*, H. Dörries, ed., Abhandlungen der Akademie der Wissenschaften in Göttingen: Philologisch-Historische Klasse 3.69, Göttingen: Vandenhoeck & Ruprecht, 1967.

Le Boulluec, A., "Y a-t-il des traces de la polémique antignostique d'Irénée dans le Péri Archôn d'Origène?" *Gnosis and Gnosticism: Papers Read at the Seventh International Conference on Patristic Studies (Oxford, September 8th–13th 1975)*, M. Krause, ed., Nag Hammadi Studies 8, Leiden: Brill, 1977, 138–147.

Loewenich, W. von, *Das Johannes-Verständnis im zweiten Jahrhundert*, Beihefte zur Zeitschrift für die neutestamentliche Wissenschaft und die Kunde der älteren Kirche 13, Giessen: Töpelmann, 1932.

Markschies, C., *Valentinus Gnosticus? Untersuchungen zur valentinianischen Gnosis mit einem Kommentar zu den Fragmenten Valentins*, Wissenschaftliche Untersuchungen zum Neuen Testament 65, Tübingen: Mohr (Paul Siebeck), 1992.

—— "Valentinianische Gnosis in Alexandrien und Ägypten," *Origeniana Octava: Origen and the Alexandrian Tradition: Papers of the 8th International Congress:*

Pisa, 27–31 August 2001, 2 vols., L. Perrone, ed., Bibliotheca Ephemeridum Theologicarum Lovaniensium 164, Leuven: Leuven University Press / Peeters, 2003, 1:331–346.

Mühlenberg, E., "Wieviel Erlösungen kennt der Gnostiker Herakleon?" *Zeitschrift für die neutestamentliche Wissenschaft und die Kunde der älteren Kirche* 66 (1975), 170–193.

Müller, K., "Beiträge zum Verständnis der valentinianischen Gnosis I–IV," *Nachrichten von der königlichen Gesellschaft zu Göttingen: Philologisch-Historische Klasse* (1920), 179–242.

Mutschler, B., "Was weiß Irenäus vom Johannesevangelium? Der historische Kontext des Johannesevangeliums aus der Perspektive seiner Rezeption bei Irenäus von Lyon," *Kontexte des Johannesevangeliums: Das vierte Evangelium in religions- und traditionsgeschichtlicher Perspektive*, J. Frey and U. Schnelle, eds., Wissenschaftliche Untersuchungen zum Neuen Testament 175, Tübingen: Mohr Siebeck, 2004, 695–742.

Nagel, T., *Die Rezeption des Johannesevangeliums im 2. Jahrhundert: Studien zur vorirenäischen Aneignung und Auslegung des vierten Evangeliums in christlicher und christlich-gnosticher Literatur*, Arbeiten zur Bibel und ihrer Geschichte 2, Leipzig: Evangelische Verlagsanstalt, 2000.

Pagels, E.H., *The Johannine Gospel in Gnostic Exegesis: Heracleon's Commentary on John*, Society of Biblical Literature Monograph Series 17, Nashville: Abingdon, 1973.

Poffet, J.-M., *La méthode exégétique d'Heracléon et d'Origène, commentateurs de Jn 4: Jésus, la Samaritaine et les Samaritains*, Paradosis 28, Fribourg: Éditions universitaires, 1985.

Preuschen, E., *Origenes Werke, Bd. 4: Der Johanneskommentar*, Die griechischen christlichen Schriftsteller der ersten drei Jahrhunderte 10, Leipzig: Hinrichs, 1903.

Quispel, G., *Ptolemée: Lettre a Flora: Texte, traduction et introduction*, Sources chrétiennes 24bis, Paris: Cerf, 1966.

Sagnard, F., *La gnose valentinienne et le témoignage de saint Irénée*, Études de philosophie médiévale 36, Paris: Vrin, 1947.

Sanders, J.N., *The Fourth Gospel in the Early Church: Its Origin & Influence on Christian Theology up to Irenaeus*, Cambridge: Cambridge University Press, 1943.

Simonetti, M., "Eracleone e Origene," *Vetera Christianorum* 3 (1966), 111–141, and 4 (1967), 23–64.

—— *Testi gnostici in lingua greca e latina*, Scrittori greci e latini, Rome: Fondazione Lorenzo Valla / Mondadori, 1993.

—— "Eracleone, gli psichici e il Trattato Tripartito," *Ortodossia ed eresia tra I e II secolo*, M. Simonetti, ed., Armarium 5, Soveria Manelli: Rubbettino, 1994, 205–243.

—— *Ippolito: Contro Noeto*, Biblioteca Patristica 35, Bologna: EDB, 2000.

Strutwolf, H., *Gnosis als System: Zur Rezeption der valentinianischen Gnosis bei Origenes*, Forschungen zur Kirchen- und Dogmengeschichte 56, Göttingen: Vandenhoeck & Ruprecht, 1993.

Thomassen, E., "The Platonic and the Gnostic 'Demiurge,'" *Apocyphon Severini presented to Søren Giversen*, P. Bilde et al., eds., Aarhus: Aarhus University Press, 1993, 226–244.

—— *The Spiritual Seed: The Church of the "Valentinians,"* Nag Hammadi and Manichaean Studies 60, Leiden: Brill, 2006a.

—— "*Gos. Philip* 67:27–30: Not 'in a mystery,'" *Coptica—Gnostica—Manichaica: Mélanges offerts à Wolf-Peter Funk*, L. Painchaud and P.-H. Poirier, eds., Bibliothèque Copte de Nag Hammadi: Section «Études» 7, Québec: Les Presses de l'Université Laval; Leuven: Peeters, 2006b, 925–939.

—— "From Wisdom to Gnosis," *Colloque international:* «L'Évangile selon Thomas et les textes de Nag Hammadi», L. Painchaud and P.-H. Poirier, eds., Bibliothèque Copte de Nag Hammadi: Section «Études» 8, Québec: Les Presses de l'Université Laval; Leuven: Peeters, 2007, 585–598.

Thomassen, E. and L. Painchaud, *Le Traité Tripartite (NH I, 5)*, Bibliothèque Copte de Nag Hammadi: Section «Textes» 19, Québec: Les Presses de l'Université Laval, 1989.

Trumbower, J.A., "Origen's Exegesis of John 8:19–53: The Struggle with Heracleon over the idea of Fixed Natures," *Vigiliae Christianae* 43 (1989), 138–154.

Völker, W., *Quellen zur Geschichte der christlichen Gnosis*, Sammlung ausgewählter kirchen- und dogmengeschichtlicher Quellenschriften, Neue Folge 5, Tübingen: Mohr Siebeck, 1932.

Wiles, M.F., *The Spiritual Gospel: The Interpretation of the Fourth Gospel in the Early Church*, Cambridge: Cambridge University Press, 1960.

Wucherpfennig, A., *Heracleon Philologus: Gnostische Johannesexegese im zweiten Jahrhundert*, Wissenschaftliche Untersuchungen zum Neuen Testament 142, Tübingen: Mohr Siebeck, 2002.

INFLUENCE AND INTERPRETATION OF THE GOSPEL OF JOHN IN ANCIENT CHRISTIANITY: THE EXAMPLE OF *EUGNOSTOS* (NHC III,3 AND V,1)

Anne Pasquier
Université Laval

The text entitled *Eugnostos* appears in two codices of the Coptic Nag Hammadi library: Codex III (70,1–90,13) and Codex V (1,1–17,18), the latter version being more recent than the former. *Eugnostos* has been subject to subsequent rewritings and reorganizations, the most striking of which is the *Sophia of Jesus Christ*, a text that exists in two analogous copies written in Coptic, as well as in Greek fragments.[1] Furthermore, many citations have been preserved in certain excerpts from a "Valentinian Letter," copied by Epiphanius in his *Panarion* 31.5.1–8.[2] Did the author of *Eugnostos* III know of the Fourth Gospel? Possibly, but there are no explicit citations, and only a few verbal reminiscences. The Codex V version does, however, try to establish express ties with the Johannine prologue, an interesting detail in itself. Thus, this version belongs to an interpretative tradition that developed during the second and third centuries CE, especially in Alexandria.[3] My objective is to examine the possible connections between the Gospel of John and the different versions of *Eugnostos*, and to explore especially the ways the Codex V version has integrated and interpreted Johannine passages.

The author of *Eugnostos* announces a transcendent God—unheard of by all men including the wise—and opts for the rhetorical genre of

---

[1] One of the versions of *The Sophia of Jesus Christ* follows *Eugnostos* immediately in Codex III (90,14–119,18), while the other one is contained in the Berlin Codex 8502 (77,8–127,12). The Greek fragments are to be found in the *Oxyrhynchus Papyrus* 1081 (no. 1064 of the A. van Haelst catalogue). *Soph. Jes. Chr.* has integrated the text of *Eugnostos* in a new frame: a revelation dialogue between the risen Christ and his disciples.

[2] *Eugnostos* has also influenced the Manichaean doctrine of the five intellectual members of the primordial Man. See now *The Seventh Letter of Ktesiphon* (Berlin P. 15998).

[3] For the Gospel of John having explicitly influenced both versions of *Soph. Jes. Chr.*, see Pasquier 2009 (part 2, chapter 5).

epideictic discourse, or "praise rhetoric," in order to reveal his presence. The use of philosophical terms, the concise nature of the style, as
well as the hymnic and solemn tone of the treatise, confer to the text
the qualities of a dogmatic celebration. These characteristics are comparable to those found in the "Sacred Speech,"[4] a literary genre widespread in Middleplatonic writings. *Eugnostos* is no doubt intended for
an audience sensitive to the philosophical or theological-philosophical
thought and doctrines. The author uses language that is philosophical
as well as hymnic to further the teachings of the two divine Principles
that reign over the all, the spiritual universe. One finds great coher-
ence in the organization and structure of the text, whose description of
events unfolds from what is hidden to what is manifested, and whose
main principle is that what is invisible can be found in what is visible—a principle accessible only through a revelation.[5] In other words,
the identity of this otherwise unknown God and his spiritual world
is revealed only at the end of the revelation, and this is possible only
because this God has manifested himself in the visible world.

The text relates the appearance of an "illuminating light," a "beginning" of the revelation and of knowledge. At first hidden in the unbegotten Father, this light, spilling forth from infinity, reveals itself through
the figure of the Immortal Man. This Man also receives the name
of "Self-Begetter Man" or "Self-Father Man" (*Eugnostos* III 77,14–15;
V 6,19–21), as well as the "Only-begot[ten], the Only [Son] (*monogenēs*)"
(V 5,22–23), and the "perfect [Only-]be[gotten]" (III 77,2). The Son is
also named "Father" in that he stands at the origin of salvation and
revelation. He is the first Man of the "beginning" or of the intelligible
world (III 85,9–10; 86,13–14; V 13,8–9). Having at first been hidden,
he then manifests and unveils himself: after that of "Man," he assumes
the title of "Son of Man" and then that of "Savior." He is also identified
with Wisdom, who in turn is called "Truth" (*Alētheia*), "Love" (*Agapē*)
and "Faith" (*Pistis*).

This doctrine is a form of Christianity characterized by Hellenistic
Judaism and by a spiritualized pagan religion that can be compared to

---

[4] See Pasquier 2000, 25–32. This literary genre is well described by Hadot 1968,
1:457–461. For example, there are traces of it in Albinus, *Didaskalikos* 10; and
Iamblichus, *De mysteriis* 8.2.

[5] Following the classical rhetorical tradition, the structure of *Eugnostos* III can be
expressed as follows: *exordium* (70,1–71,18), *narratio* with *propositio* (71,18–74,12),
probatio (74,12–90,4) and *peroratio* (90,5–11).

Hermeticism. By allegorical interpretation and the treatment of certain themes such as the divine throne and the celestial temple, *Eugnostos* is, in fact, very close to Hellenistic Judaism. In the Codex III version, the revelation is not based on the texts of the New Testament, but mostly on the first three chapters of Genesis to which a spiritual interpretation is given.[6] From the unknown and hidden to the manifested and revealed, this interpretation illustrates how the scriptures are directed towards the revelation of the Savior and of the church.

There are some indications in *Eugnostos* that point to the origin and date of the text.[7] In fact, *Eugnostos* is without a doubt *the* text taking up most explicitly the Philonic doctrine of the divine attributes (*dynameis*) or names.[8] The important place that is granted to the figure of Wisdom, as well as the type of allegorical exegesis that the text expounds, strongly suggest an Alexandrian background, and enable us in all probability to locate the text's composition in this very city.

Moreover, there are literary parallels that allow us to date the text. *Eugnostos* contains a classification of intellectual movements, which is certainly borrowed from an older source, but which the author integrates into his/her own theological doctrine. The same list is mentioned by Irenaeus in his *Adversus haereses* 2.13.2, in reaction against Valentinians who had used it to establish their doctrine of the spiritual world.[9] This is an important clue for dating and locating *Eugnostos* since the list in question is a central theme in the text, and has influenced the author's teaching as a whole. We can deduce from this fact that a version of *Eugnostos* was known to Irenaeus, and this allows us to date the text prior to 180 CE. Another interesting literary parallel occurs in a section on negative theology that directly follows the *exordium* in *Eugnostos*, and which greatly resembles a passage found in the first chapter of the *Apology* of Aristides the Athenian.[10] The

---

[6] *Eugnostos* refers to the Old Testament texts in an atomistic manner. Throughout the text, one finds many key terms from and allusions to Gen 1–3 and other Jewish sources. This manner of reference supposes that the implied readers were able to understand not only the allusions and the key terms, but also the original context where they occur.

[7] See Pasquier 2009 (part 2, chapter 3).

[8] See below, n. 19.

[9] See Rousseau and Doutreleau 1982, 1:236–240, 366–370. According to *Eugnostos*, the unbegotten Father and his image, the celestial Man, possess mind, thought, reflections, deliberations, and inner logos or word (*nous, ennoia, enthymesis, phronēsis, logismos*) (III 73,8–11; 78,5–9; V 3,10–15; 7,6–9).

[10] See van den Broek 1988, 202–218.

latter is usually thought to date from 124–140 CE.[11] Two hypotheses can therefore be formulated: either *Eugnostos* and Aristides' *Apology* each in their respective ways incorporated a source that probably circulated during the first quarter of the second century, or, simply put, one was directly influenced by the other. Whichever solution is adopted, this parallel allows us, in all probability, to place *Eugnostos* in the first half, if not the first quarter, of the second century CE.

More precisely, I personally believe that *Eugnostos* could have been written in Alexandria during the period that immediately followed the Jewish revolt of 115–117 CE, in an environment where it was customary, at the time, to interpret the Christian message within the framework of Judeo-Hellenistic Wisdom speculation.[12] It is from this very type of background that traces of Gnostic systems or Gnostic Christianity emerged, and the intended audience of *Eugnostos* also seems to have consisted of Christians coming from such a social and cultural context. *Eugnostos* propounds a particular form of Christianity, inspired by a Philonic tradition whose very appeal might have lain in the fact that it did not introduce an abrupt change from the conceptual framework of Hellenistic Judaism.[13]

1. A Brief Comparison with the Fourth Gospel

Although *Eugnostos* III does not explicitly use the Fourth Gospel as a scriptural source, it does share several important themes with this Gospel such as the "Son of Man" and the "name of God," a name which expresses the essence of his revelation by the Son. As in the Gospel of John, the Son of Man in *Eugnostos* also constitutes a link between heaven and earth since his authority is conferred upon him by God (John 5:27; *Eugnostos* V 9,7–9).[14] Above all, the Son of Man in *Eugnostos* is identified with the main figure of Christianity. In contrast to the figure of the Son of Man in Jewish apocalyptic, the Son of Man in *Eugnostos* has already revealed himself as the Savior. However,

---

[11] See Pouderon et al. 2003, 32–39; Alpigiano 1988, 7–48.

[12] The Jewish revolt of 115–117 CE in Alexandria almost destroyed the Jewish community, thus permitting Christianity to surface. Although Alexandrian Christianity already existed, it had not distinguished itself properly from the local Jewish community. See Jakab 2004, 53–64; Modrzejewski 1997, 307–312.

[13] See Pasquier 2007b, 571–613.

[14] Two pages (79–80) are missing from the Codex III version.

although there are several important concepts in *Eugnostos* III that have Johannine parallels, these concepts were probably drawn from sources other than the Fourth Gospel.

The title of Son of Man in the Fourth Gospel seems to imply a celestial status, as its origins lie in the Danielic Son of Man (John 3:13; 5:27; 6:62).[15] This is also the case in *Eugnostos*, which was possibly also inspired by Daniel. In Dan 7:13–14, authority, glory and sovereign power were bestowed upon the one who was "like a son of man." The eternal kingdom will then be given to the saints of the Most High (Dan 7:18,22,27). The word "saints," as used in Daniel, most often refers to angelic creatures (cf. Dan 7:10). However, it is also plausible that the expression "saints of the Most High" refers to angels as well as to members of the Israelite nation, the faithful ones who will be acclaimed during the judgment to come. On the other hand, the kingdom of the Son of Man in *Eugnostos* is identified with the church which replaces Israel: the angels "created" by him are named "church of the saints" and the "lights without shadow" (*Eugnostos* III 81,5–6; V 9,13–17).

Furthermore, the Gospel of John and *Eugnostos* III did in all probability draw from the contemporary Jewish tradition. It was a Jewish trend at the end of the first century CE to compare the figure of the Son of Man to that of the Messiah and to combine their respective functions. However, the complexity and opacity of the Jewish texts— *1 Enoch* 37–71; *4 Ezra* 7:29; 13:3; and *2 Baruch* 53:8–11; 73:1—is in itself a considerable problem. The most explicit among these texts, *1 Enoch*, suggests the existence of the Man, and not only the vague figure presented as the likeness of man, as in the dream of Daniel or even in *4 Ezra*; and this Man is identified with the redeeming Messiah (*1 Enoch* 38:2–3; 45:3,4). The two other texts also reveal the vision of a redeeming Messiah associated with the light. In *4 Ezra* 7:29, this Son of Man is called "my Son" or "my servant the Messiah."

Eugnostos, in fact, might have been influenced by the Ethiopian version of *1 Enoch* where the Son of Man manifests himself in the Second Parable, chapter 46. In *1 Enoch*, his "name" was proclaimed even before the creation of all things (48:3), he is described as being the "light" of the nations (48:4), and the "wisdom" of the Lord of spirits revealed

---

[15] How much the fourth evangelist drew upon earlier traditions where this figure had already undergone reinterpretation is a matter of debate (Ashton 2007, 240–276).

him to the saints and the just; it is by his "name" that they will be "saved" and that they will gain "life" (48:7). This Son of Man is seated upon a glorious "throne" and it is through him that the saints will obtain their everlasting "dwelling" (62:2,3,5; 71:16). These designations all appear in *Eugnostos* when the celestial Man reveals himself as the Son of Man and Savior, to give Life to the members of the church (see, for example, *Eugnostos* III 76,18–19; 77,3–4.9–13; 81,1–18). The use of the theme of glory is constant throughout the text in expressing the manifestation of God's power and authority, which are inextricably linked to his revelation.

However, this identification between the Son of Man and the Messiah was already complete in the Synoptic Gospels, which indicates that they possibly were the inspiration behind the Gospel of John and *Eugnostos*.[16] As is the case with the canonical gospels, the expression itself became a title,[17] and, in *Eugnostos*, the influence of Matthew particularly is felt: the Son of Man "receives his authority from his [Father]" (*Eugnostos* V 9,7–9; cf. *Soph. Jes. Chr.* III 104,22–23; BG 99,16–18).[18]

Another important motif can also be found in the Gospel of John: that of the divine name (17:6,12: "your name which you gave me"; cf. 5:43; 10:25; 17:26). This is also an essential theme in *Eugnostos*, wherein this name bestows salvation. In *Eugnostos*, the celestial Man, as knowledge of the unbegotten Father who is designated "He-Who-Is" (Exod 3:14; *Eugnostos* III 71,13–14), reveals the primordial denomination: Divinity and Kingship (III 77,9–13; 77,23–78,3; V 6,14–18; 6,29–7,2).

This Gnostic text exhibits an old Christological model according to which the Son is the name of God and the dawning of a new day. This doctrine of the Son-Name can also be observed in the *Gospel of Truth* (39) and in the *Shepherd of Hermas* (*Similitude* 9.14.5). The theology of the name, present in certain books of the Bible, is applied to the celestial Man. The name then becomes a description of his divinity. Such a theology, strongly Jewish in essence, presupposes speculations associated with the problem of divine manifestation, reflections which

---

[16] However, in the Synoptic Gospels, the title "Son of Man" refers to the future, celestial role of Jesus.

[17] It is difficult to say whether the expression has become an actual title in *1 Enoch* as in the New Testament texts. See de Viviès 2002, 286; and Coppens 1983, 128–138.

[18] It seems that *Eugnostos* has linked Matt 28:18 ("all authority has been given to me") with Matt 11:27 ("all has been given to me by my Father"). Cf. also Matt 26:29. The expression "The kingdom of the Son of Man" (*Eugnostos* III 81, 13–14) also seems to derive from Matt. The same expression also occurs in *Gospel of Mary* 9,9–10.

relate to the two principal names given to God in the Hebrew Bible, *Elohim* and YHWH, which are translated by *kyrios* and *theos* in the Septuagint.

However, *Eugnostos* is, above all, intricately linked to the teachings of Philo of Alexandria who applies a double name (associated with a double power) to God's *Logos*:[19] "the Father of the universe, who in the sacred scriptures is called by his proper name, I am that I am; and the beings on each side are those most ancient powers... one of which is called his creative power, and the other his royal power. And the creative power is God... and the royal power is the Lord" (*Abr.* 121; Yonge, transl.). In fact, Philo maintains that the two powers are unified because God is the *Logos* (*Cher.* 27–28). Philo's probable influence on the author of *Eugnostos* therefore implies that the latter also identifies the celestial Man with the *Logos*. However, *Eugnostos* III never describes him explicitly as such, in contrast to *Eugnostos* V (17,11).

The motif of the divine name, as applied to a celestial being, is present in Judaism and is undeniably the source that inspired the Fourth Gospel and *Eugnostos*. Although it is difficult to establish or even perceive a direct influence from one to the other, parallels can be drawn between the *Apocalypse of Abraham*, which is usually dated to the end of the first century CE, and the Gospel of John and *Eugnostos*.[20] In the tenth chapter of this apocalypse, Abraham heard a divine voice speaking: "Go, Yaoel of the same name, through the mediation of my ineffable name." Yaoel is an angel sent by God to Abraham "in the likeness of a man" (cf. Dan 7:13), and on whom he has bestowed the authority of his name. Yaoel also says of himself: "I am Yaoel... a power through the medium of his ineffable name in me" (*Apoc. Ab.* 10:4,5,8; Rubinkiewicz, transl.). The name itself, "Yaoel," is the result of the fusion of the two divine names, YHWH and El.[21] The name had also been given to the people of God: in *4 Ezra* 4:25, the divine name is bestowed upon Israel.

To understand the teachings conveyed by *Eugnostos*, we must undeniably refer to the writings of Philo, an author who identifies the "beginning" of Gen 1:1 with the firstborn *Logos*, named "Principle,"

---

[19] For Philo (*Cher.* 27; *Plant.* 86–90; *Mut.* 11–31; *QG* 1.57; *Mos.* 2.99–100), the name "God" stands for God's creative power (*poiētikē*), and the name "Lord" for his royal one (*basilikē*).

[20] See Caquot and Philonenko 1987, cxxxvii.

[21] See Segal 1977, 68.

"Name of God," "Man in the image of God," "Seer" and "Israel" (*Conf.* 146–147). One aspect in particular deserves further investigation, since it later on influenced the exegesis of the Johannine prologue, put forth by the Valentinians, Clement of Alexandria and Origen. According to Philo, the divine name conceals itself in the divine reason or intellect since only the divine reason itself, where the Ideas or the Platonic Forms reside, can house God's powers (*Opif.* 20). In *Eugnostos*, the archetypal Man, bearer of God's name, is endowed with an intellect that displays an inner *logos* which contains in itself the spiritual world's plenitude. As a mirror and image of the unbegotten Father, he has an intellect "which is specific to him." From this intellect, comparable to a monad, emerges, like a dyad, a thought (*ennoia*) "according to his likeness" (III 78,6–9; V 7,6–9); from this, following the model of derivation of numbers, originate myriad intellectual powers that take the form of reflections and deliberations. As the Father, Man is first of all presented as the intelligible archetypical cosmos.

According to Claude Panaccio's study, the oldest straightforward references to the expression *logos endiathetos* (inner logos), as distinguished from the *logos proforikos* (spoken logos), date back to the first century CE. Other than a single mention made by a barely known author, Heraclitus, the references are mainly concentrated in Philo's works.[22] Although Philo does not make any allusions to a typology such as found in *Eugnostos*, our understanding of the Gnostic point of view owes much to him because this psychology is related to metaphysics of a theological nature. Philo connects the *logos endiathetos* to the cosmological *logos*, which is the intelligible paradigm of the universe, while the outer *logos* represents the inherent order of the sensible creation.

2. Influence of the Gospel of John on *Eugnostos* III?

When it comes to the title Son of Man, the concept of the *Logos* or the theme of the divine name, the Gospel of John does not seem to have inspired *Eugnostos* III. The gospel never specifies the name that could simply designate God as he reveals himself.[23] Despite this, the

---

[22] Panaccio 1999, 63ff.

[23] However, in John 5:22–27, the Son has received a double power: to give life and to judge; this is not unlike Philo's doctrine of the divine name.

likelihood of some Johannine influence on *Eugnostos* III, nevertheless, is conceivable, even if it is difficult to pinpoint exactly. Thus, it is possible that even the author of this version of *Eugnostos* may have known the Johannine gospel. For instance, Man the Son of Man is described as being the "Light which illuminates," a designation which in itself is reminiscent of the creation of light in Gen 1:3, as well as in Gen 1:14–15, where it is written that the great light was created to illuminate the earth. However, the fact that he is presented as a spiritual star is also suggestive of John 1:5 ("the light shines in the darkness") and especially John 1:9 ("the light...which illuminates all men"). Thanks to his arrival as Savior, "Life" has been generated in each member of the church (*Eugnostos* III 87,7–8; John 1:4). Other expressions, like "the [Only-]be[gotten]" (*monogenēs*) (*Eugnostos* III 77,2 = V 5,22–23: "The Only-begot[ten], the Only [Son]"), could also have been taken from the Fourth Gospel. Nevertheless, as mentioned above, the Codex III version of *Eugnostos* is not based upon the writings of the New Testament, but particularly upon the first three chapters of Genesis of which a spiritual interpretation is given. *Eugnostos* III can therefore be considered to belong to an important tradition, that of hexaemeral literature, which takes its founding principles from Gen 1–3 with its genealogies, and which generated Christian commentaries on it with spiritual aims as early as the second century CE. The author of *Eugnostos* III borrows elements from Greek allegory as well as Jewish traditions to construct his/her own exegesis.

The text's simple structure and the absence of explicit Christian citations emphasize the ancient character of *Eugnostos* III. There is indeed only one set of writings, those which will later become the Old Testament, that is authoritative for Christians during the first half of the second century CE. Moreover, it is, in fact, among other reasons, this same ancient character of *Eugnostos* that may have prompted the rewriting of the text, visible in the Codex V version. *Eugnostos* III would thus be representative of an older environment than that in which the Codex V version was developed, of a milieu where it was still possible to rely almost solely on the Jewish scriptures to establish and nurture a given doctrine.[24]

---

[24] I think this explains why such writings are later, in the Nag Hammadi library, placed side by side with texts that are explicitly Christian.

This means that even though *Eugnostos* III may have been influenced by the Gospel of John, the author does not necessarily consider it to be a proof-text in the rhetorical sense, or even a sacred writing. At the very most, perhaps it is possible to detect one of the first attempts at exploiting or using the Fourth Gospel in *Eugnostos* III, but at this point we can only put forth hypotheses concerning this complex and delicate issue. It rather seems as if the Gospel of John and *Eugnostos* III delved into shared traditions that were drawn, for the most part, from Judaism. As it has already been surmised, even if a considerable number of key notions are common to both *Eugnostos* III and the Fourth Gospel, it is uncertain whether one necessarily borrowed these from the other.[25]

Whatever its source of inspiration, *Eugnostos* suggests a theological vision and a Christology that differ from those found in the Fourth Gospel. The presentation and organization of a text are an expression of its values, its vision of the world and its theological horizon. John includes the figure of the Messiah in a gospel genre, in a "life" account directed towards the Passion, even if this Passion is seen as an exaltation and a glorification. In spite of the fact that his objective was not to record the story itself, but to interpret it, the historical figure of Jesus remains the evangelist's central focus and starting point. The Gospel aspires towards forging of a link between the historical Jesus and the title "Son of Man," which he is given and which indicates his celestial origin. The reasons for the descent and ascent of the Son of Man are therefore understandable.[26] Wayne Meeks has emphasized how everything in this particular gospel occurs on earth, even if the figure of the Son of Man demonstrates that Jesus does in fact belong to another world.[27] This Jesus reveals that the Word of God became flesh, which also leads to a new vision of God.

In *Eugnostos*, the names and characteristics applied to the Savior are essentially those of a glorious being. The titles "Man" and "Son of Man" are paramount and refer undoubtedly to a being from above. Most importantly, as is the case with numerous Gnostic texts, the figure of the Son of Man, under the influence of Platonism, is reinterpreted following that of the archetypical Man whereas this is not the

---

[25] For example, the terms "Truth" and "Beginning" as designations for the Son.
[26] See Ashton 2007, 240–276.
[27] Meeks 1972, 50.

case in the Gospel of John. Moreover, following the Philonic tradition (cf. *Opif.* 134–135), *Eugnostos* differentiates the man of Gen 1:26–27 from the one in Gen 2:7 (made from "dust" and "fathered" on earth) (*Eugnostos* III 70,3–6). We know that the interpretation of the dual account of creation in Genesis allowed—still under the influence of Platonism—several interpreters, among them Philo of Alexandria, to mark a distinction between an incorruptible spiritual and celestial man, created in God's image, and a worldly man who is corruptible. This celestial Man becomes the Savior in *Eugnostos*, and he indeed appears as such. *Eugnostos* does not place any emphasis on the historical figure of Jesus, or on his death, but rather emphasizes the inner enlightenment of the church. This very church constitutes the Savior's body: his celestial figure does indeed encompass within himself God's people, which lends him characteristics similar to the Jewish figure of the Son of Man, himself a half-individual, half-collective figure.

This same doctrine is presented in the Codex V version which, however, is more explicit in its incorporation of certain aspects of the Gospel of John, especially in reference to the prologue. This version of *Eugnostos* thus prefigures the Valentinian exegesis known to us through indirect sources. Valentinus' students gave preference to the gospel's prologue because of the Hellenic attributes apparent in the language.[28]

3. An Interpretative Tradition of the Gospel of John: The Codex V Version

The omissions and explicative scholia introduced in *Eugnostos* V sometimes break with *Eugnostos* III's more linear form. More didactic, this new version transforms the succinct and hymnic form of its source, probably because it was not intended for the same audience, but maybe also because the text itself, during its circulation, lost its primary purpose.[29] Furthermore, the author of *Eugnostos* V explicitly uses excerpts from texts that later became known as the New Testament to support

---

[28] In the rest of the gospel, there has occurred a Hellenization of language but not of the message.

[29] *Eugnostos* III seems to be linked to a ritual setting, more precisely to a baptismal one; see Pasquier 2009 (part 2, chapter 3).

his teachings.[30] These excerpts are introduced as citations rather than simple allusions. One interesting factor is the author's desire to establish an unequivocal connection with the Johannine prologue (John 1:1,9; *Eugnostos* V 5,19–29).

The first Man or celestial Man, as described in *Eugnostos* V, has within himself the Wisdom named "Truth." Although both versions of *Eugnostos* allocate a similar task to the Wisdom that concerns the spiritual knowledge that will be received by those who are saved, *Eugnostos* III describes the archetypical Man's wisdom as *one* undeniable truth. This concept is particularly indebted to Platonism and Judaism in that it means the eternal reality as revealed to men. According to the Wisdom of Solomon, this truth is understood solely by those who have faith in God: it is identical to the design elaborated by God for the wise (Wis 4:17).[31] In the Codex V version of *Eugnostos*, "Truth" becomes a denomination or a designated entity.

The name "Truth," given to the female counterpart of the Principle (*archē*) or of the *monogenēs* Son, is, according to Irenaeus (*Adv. haer.* 1.1.1), a Valentinian concept: "This Mind they also call Only-begotten, Father and Beginning of all things. Truth was emitted at the same time he (Mind) was" (Unger and Dillon, transl.).[32] The Valentinians themselves probably borrowed the name from the Gospel of John in which "Truth" is almost considered as one of Christ's names (John 14:6). In addition, if the Son's spouse is called "Truth," it is because the Son is "full of grace and truth" (John 1:14).

After the description of the Son's self-manifestation in the Unbegotten Father or "Pre-Principle," he is told to manifest himself *ad extra*, which reveals him as the Principle of salvation and knowledge: "Now… c[a]me forth another Principle, with [the] Only-[be]gotten, Wholly Unique begotten [Son]…Father who [sprin]gs up from himself—wh[o] is [the] Principle (or Beginning: *archē*) [in] which the Logos dwe[lls]" (cf. John 1:1). This Principle radiates inexpressible, illuminating Light (cf. John 1:9) (*Eugnostos* V 5,19–29).

---

[30] For example, at the end of the *exordium*, and at the conclusion of the text—i.e., in strategic passages—quotations from the New Testament are introduced; *Eugnostos* V 2,12–13; 17,15–17: "For [to] everyone who has, more will be added" (Matt 13:12 = Matt 25:29).

[31] See Dodd 1953, 177.

[32] Transl. Unger and Dillon 1992, 23. See also, e.g., *Adv. haer.* 1.12.1,3; 1.11.1; 1.15.1.

Line 22 of the Codex V version has the Greek term *monogenēs*, that is, the "unique son," and the immediately preceding Coptic [x]ⲡⲟ ⲟⲩⲁⲁϥ has the same meaning. The purpose of this redundancy is undoubtedly to highlight, for the readers, the connection that links it to the Johannine gospel, a text that *Eugnostos* V considers essential to the argumentation (John 1:14,18; 3:16).

There are some similarities between this interpretation and the one attributed to the Valentinians by Clement of Alexandria (*Excerpts from Theodotus* 6.1–4) and Irenaeus. In his *Adversus haereses* 1.8.5, Irenaeus presents the Valentinian exegesis as follows:

> Since, then, he speaks of the first origin (of things), he (John) does well to start his doctrine with the Beginning, that is with the Son and the Word. He writes as follows: *In the Beginning was the Word, and the Word was with God, and the Word was God. He was in the Beginning with God.* First, he distinguishes these three: God, Beginning, and Word. Then he unites them in order to show the emission of each one singly, namely of Son and Word, and the union of Son to Word, and of both to the Father. For the Beginning is in Father and from Father; but Word is in Beginning and from Beginning.[33]

This exegesis then gives rise to the aeonic couples, found, for example, in Irenaeus' *Adv. haer.* 1.1.1: the Son is Intellect and Truth, *Logos* and Life, and the spiritual Man and the church.

Such a distinction between two aspects of the Son, who is simultaneously intellect and logos, i.e., the inner logos and the uttered logos, is found in the *Gospel of Truth*. In the *exordium* (*Gos. Truth* 16,31–17,4), the Son is presented as a thought that eternally inhabits the mind of the Father, that is, as *logos endiathetos* (latent reason), before being uttered with a view to salvation. Many of the notions expressed in the *exordium* are used again near the end of the text (37,7–15): "While they were still depths of his Thought, the uttered Word revealed them. Now a Mind that speaks, which is a silent Word and Grace, is called 'Thought,' since they were in it before being revealed. It came about then that it was uttered, when the will of him who willed desired it."[34]

The philosophical doctrine of the double *logos*, i.e., the inner *logos* differentiating itself from the uttered *logos*, was used for the interpretation of the Johannine prologue. Apart from the Valentinians, it is easy

---

[33] Transl. Unger and Dillon 1992, 44.
[34] Transl. Pasquier.

to notice ties with the interpretations by Clement of Alexandria and Origen. What Clement himself briefly describes in his *Exc. Theod.*,[35] Origen details in his *Commentary on St. John*, exposing in this work the major part of his theory on *"epinoiai*," that is the miscellaneous denominations given to Christ in the Bible.[36] Following in the footsteps of the Valentinians, Origen does indeed distinguish, in the Johannine prologue, many of the important names by which Christ reveals himself to humankind for the sake of salvation, such as intellect, truth, *logos* and life. The one *logos*, according to Origen, constitutes a complex unity, a plurality that we are able to distinguish by our mind, with many of these roles existing for the sake of our sanctification. This *Logos* is a unitary mediator who in himself constitutes a multitude of goods.

This subtle and elaborate theory has been the subject of many studies to which we can refer.[37] *Epinoiai* are "notions of reality." C. Blanc, in her edition of Origen's *Commentary on St. John*, notes that the definition most often given to the word *epinoiai* is "aspect ou attribut de l'objet pensé."[38] We can therefore surmise that *epinoiai* are at once subjective and objective. They are thoughts concerning the Son, but these have a corresponding objective reality. They demonstrate a hierarchy of aspects of Christ. These designations do not, however, affect Christ's unitary nature because he is the beginning as well as the end, although he is not the same, depending on the different attributes used (*epinoiai*).

As stated previously, the laconic expression and style found in the Codex III version of *Eugnostos*, which are due to its literary genre as well as the fact that this version builds its argumentation by resorting mainly to the writings of the Jewish scriptures, both explain the rewriting that materialized as *Eugnostos* V. This rewriting is also an attempt at making the original text more accessible and better adapted to a new context, and these transformations also indicate a change in the intended audience. The author of *Eugnostos* V writes for an audience that is familiar with the Alexandrian tradition of *epinoiai*,

---

[35] *Exc. Theod.* 7.3; 8.1–4; 12.3; 13.1.

[36] Origen's two most important texts on *epinoiai* are *Comm. Jo.* 1–2; and *Princ.* 1.2.

[37] Crouzel 1980, 131–150; Letellier 1991, 587–611; Simonetti 1993, 123–127; Wolinski 1995, 465–492. For the doctrine of *epinoiai* in Gnostic texts, see Pasquier 2003, 355–365.

[38] Blanc 1996, 82.

which consists of establishing distinctions between the Son's denominations, especially as described in the Johannine prologue.[39] Moreover, *Eugnostos* V is more concerned with clarifying the Son's unique role in the revelation of knowledge.

The Codex III version seems to have been composed for an audience more attuned to Judaism since as much emphasis is placed on the notion of community as on the Savior himself. The Savior, in fact, is described as being constituted by the congregation of those who are saved in him, which makes him a corporative entity.[40] On the other hand, Codex V seeks to singularize him, and it stresses his superiority in accordance with the Valentinian interpretation that is reported by Irenaeus (*Adv. haer.* 1.1–2); it then became necessary to add other titles to those of "Man" and "Son of Man," titles that highlight a Semitic vision which is collective in nature.

The Codex V version, nevertheless, conserves the text of its source with the genealogies borrowed from Genesis, whereas in the Valentinian versions known to Irenaeus and Clement of Alexandria, the description of the "first genesis" of spiritual nature, as Irenaeus presents it, is only depicted and explained through the Johannine prologue. In other words, a text of Christian origin—the Fourth Gospel—is the cornerstone for the description of the spiritual world and the rendering of salvation. On the other hand, the exegesis of Genesis, instead, is considered to be a teaching relative to the physical creation, even if this knowledge attests to the existence of the invisible spiritual seed in the molded Adam described in Gen 2:7 (*Adv. haer.* 1.5.5ff.; 1.7.2; *Exc. Theod.* 47.1–50.3). The version detailed in *Eugnostos* V should probably be placed in between: it does indeed reflect the Valentinian point of view, one which is later than the one established in the Codex III version, but it does seem to predate the versions known to Clement and Origen.

---

[39] This tradition is perhaps a legacy from Philo who distinguished the several powers in the *Logos* from the various Biblical divine names.

[40] The Savior is the manifestation of the archetypal Man, bearer of God's name, who is endowed with an intellect that displays an inner *logos*, which in turn contains in itself the plenitude of the spiritual world. In the Savior, then, resides a thought that represents the church (*ennoia*), and which will appear at the time of salvation with its different members. In such a view, Man is a corporate personality who is dependent on all the members. For the links between *Eugnostos* and the "Ophite" doctrine described by Irenaeus, see Rasimus 2009.

4. Hypotheses Concerning the Links between the Gnostic Myth and the Gospel of John

Eugnostos presents a "masculine" Savior united with a "feminine" church. What does it mean? The true image of God is revealed as double, masculine and feminine (Gen 1:26). Unity, separation and reunification of the couple is the way in which the myth of the androgyne will unfold. With this myth, the history of salvation is related. It takes place in three "aeons" or stages. From hidden to manifest, the Son is revealed under several aspects: First appearing as Man, he then assumes the title of Son of Man, and finally that of the Savior.

The first aeon, called "Unity and Rest," belongs to the immortal Man, who is the first androgynous Man of the Beginning, or of the intelligible world (*Eugnostos* III 85,9–10; 86,13–14; V 13,8–9). The first androgynous moment is one of a union of two realities that are hidden but whose names will be unveiled in the course of the manifestation. The first one to come forth from the world of plenitude of the *Anthrōpos* is the Son of Man named "Adam." However, the disclosure of the first name in this process of revelation not only manifests a difference between the masculine and the feminine, but it also leads to an unavoidable, gradual downgrading in the course of the unfolding of the divine reality.

In fact, a second aeon that belongs to the Son of Man then appears. It is the "middle" aeon or the second day, marking a departure from plenitude (*Eugnostos* III 85,11–13; 86,10–13; V 13,9–11). The unity is broken due to "the deficiency of the feminine part" (III 85,8–9; V 13,7). "Deficiency," however, brings salvation in its wake. This second, female element in the androgynous *Anthrōpos* must first be saved so that it can become manifest (as the church, i.e., a community of the saved). Therefore, the Son of Man appears as the Savior in order to bring about salvation. He then reveals the church, who has as one of its names "Life" (*Zoe* or Eve). This further shows the church's relationship with the Son of Man, who is Adam. But the duality of the name of the church—divided into the two parts (*meros*) of "church" and "Life"—also shows its lack of completion (III 87,2–5; V 14,20–25).

To the extent the church has appeared, thanks to the coming of her salvation, she is named "Life," and this discloses her union with Adam, i.e., the Son of Man. However, since some of the church's members are not yet gathered together, the church can also be called the mother of those she gives birth to spiritually; she is so named "in order that she manifest that by a woman Life came about" (III 87,5–7; V 14,25–27). The definition of the church named "Life" is a reference back to Gen 3:20, where Eve is designated as the mother of the living; to her corresponds Adam, the Son of Man, the *Anthrōpos* representing the whole or the perfect Man. As an intermediary between his pleromatic aspect (that of Principle-Intellect) and the church that is the worldly realization of his thought (*ennoia*), the Son of Man is engaged in a downgrading process because, as long as salvation remains unfinished, he is not complete either. Thus it is in gathering together the church that he will manifest the androgynous Man of the Beginning, the pleroma. Such a doctrine may have influenced the Valentinian exegesis of John's prologue. In fact, the Valentinian concept of syzygies may arise from this kind of exegesis of masculine and feminine genealogies.

It is not possible to exclude the existence of some form of Johannine influence on *Eugnostos* III. However, if, as it seems, the two texts draw their inspiration from different Jewish traditions, how can the gradual rapprochement of *Eugnostos* to the Fourth Gospel be understood? Rudolf Bultmann, in his studies on the Gospel of John, was correct in his assumption that there exist similarities between the Fourth Gospel and Gnostic texts, and that the latter exploit an essentially mythological language.[41] However, his hypothesis, in which the fourth evangelist had based his writings on a pre-Christian Gnostic text, stripping it of its mythological references, does not hold today. By studying the manuscripts that have reached us, there does not seem to exist any pre-Christian documents that would portray the figure of a Savior who descends to earth and ascends back to the heavens. Furthermore, in my opinion, the first "Gnostics" seem to have appeared only at the beginning of the second century CE.

If we come back to *Eugnostos* in particular, we rather seem to find ourselves in a Christian and Judeo-Hellenic milieu or background. The Christians, submerged in this Judeo-Hellenic environment, passed down Philo's works and the particular exegesis they contained, a fact that allows us to better understand how *Eugnostos'* doctrine could have been developed. At the base of it all could lie Philo's conceptual structure as it constitutes an interpretation of the double narrative of man's creation found in Genesis. As asserted by this interpretation,

---

[41] Bultmann 1925, 100–146; Bultmann 1971.

there exists an incorruptible man, God's very image (Gen 1:26–27), and this one is distinct from the man shaped out of earth (Gen 2:7). This in itself implies the existence of "creators" that are different, or the existence of an inferior Power that helped shape the man of Gen 2:7. It is from within this molded man that the Spirit springs forth, thereby allowing the incorruptible man, God's image, to be born.

Likewise, by analyzing Gen 1:27, Philo describes the *Logos*, God's firstborn, using the expressions "Principle," "Name of God" and "Man in the image of God" (*Conf.* 146–147). The author of *Eugnostos* identified this celestial Man with the Savior. This connection, on the other hand, had been made very early: it is already found in Paul's 1 Corinthians (15:47–49 on the celestial and the earthly man).

The role played by the other Jewish traditions is also important. Because of his status as a celestial being and due to his standing as half-individual, half-collective, in some sources, the Son of Man was integrated as a figure of importance.[42] His title is particularly significant in Gnosticism as it is often associated with the celestial Man as well as with Wisdom, representing the Spirit.[43] All of these figures that can be closely tied to the notions of the chosen people or the community seem to have influenced Gnostic theology in one way or another. Since the Jewish Son of Man is the celestial symbol of a chosen community, and the latter remains on earth, the constant descending and ascending movements are easily understood. In any case, the relation between the Son of Man and the Messiah had already been established in the Synoptic Gospels.

It is thus possible, with such a framework in mind, to understand how the Christian message could have been thus interpreted, and how the Jewish figure of the Son of Man could have been picked up and assimilated. From the hidden to the manifest, *Eugnostos* indeed presents an overview in which the archetypical Man is identified with the Savior who represents the pleroma. *Eugnostos* does incorporate the notion of a community preexisting in the divine Thought or in the divine Name. The fact that this community has to manifest itself and needs to be saved, justifies the dynamism associated with

---

[42] See, for example, *1 Enoch* 71:14.
[43] For a catalog of the majority of these references, one can readily consult the work by Borsch (1970).

the descent and the further glorification of the Savior. The Son of Man reveals himself from the primordial Man, so that he can generate an inner illumination within the molded man. Thus, little by little, he restores the pleromatic harmony of all the members of the church in this world. To this is then added the Jewish myth of Wisdom who descends to earth and represents the community where, being united with man, she takes on a human form, so to speak.

If the Gospel of John and *Eugnostos* each underwent parallel evolutions based on diverse Jewish and, eventually, Christian traditions, it follows that the Gnostic myth was ultimately constituted independently from and before being influenced by the Johannine gospel.[44] However, is it not possible to think that the fourth evangelist could have known and have been influenced by such an emerging myth, modifying it thereafter? Such a myth need not have been a pre-Christian Gnostic one, as Rudolf Bultmann thought, but instead a Christian one, perhaps containing the kinds of mythological elements that we encounter in *Eugnostos*. The Gospel of John could, in turn, have had an impact on certain Gnostic currents and played a role in the elaboration of their respective ideologies, teachings and works. There can, however, only exist hypotheses, with all certitudes having been drowned in the mass of unanswered questions relating to Gnosticism.

BIBLIOGRAPHY

Alpigiano, C., *Aristide di Atene: Apologia*, Biblioteca Patristica 11, Firenze: Nardini Editore, 1988.
Ashton, J., *Understanding the Fourth Gospel*, Oxford: Oxford University Press, ²2007.
Blanc, C., *Origène: Commentaire sur Saint Jean: Tome I (Livres I–V)*, Sources chrétiennes 120, Paris: Cerf, ²1996.
Borsch, F., *The Christian and Gnostic Son of Man*, Studies in Biblical Theology 2/14, London: SCM, 1970.
Bultmann, R., "Die Bedeutung der neuerschlossenen mandäischen und manichäischen Quellen für das Verständnis des Johannesevangeliums," *Zeitschrift für die Neutestamentliche Wissenschaft* 24 (1925), 100–146.
—— *The Gospel of John: A Commentary*, G.R. Beasley-Murray, transl., Oxford: Blackwell, 1971.
Coppens, J., *Le Fils d'homme vétéro- et intertestamentaire*, Bibliotheca Ephemeridum Theologicarum Lovaniensium 61, Leuven: Leuven University Press / Peeters, 1983.

---

[44] The most ancient fragment of the Fourth Gospel (a passage from John 18) known to us may be dated between 94–127 CE, and is of Egyptian provenance: Papyrus Rylands 457 or P52.

Crouzel, H., "Le contenu spirituel des dénominations du Christ selon le Livre I du Commentaire sur Jean d'Origène," *Origeniana Secunda: Second colloque internationale des etudes origéniennes, Bari, 1977*, H. Crouzel and A. Quacquarelli, eds., Quaderni di 'Vetera Christianorum' 15, Rome: Edizioni dell'Ateneo, 1980, 131-150.

de Viviès, P., *Apocalypses et cosmologie du salut*, Paris: Cerf, 2002.

Dodd, C.H., *The Interpretation of the Fourth Gospel*, Cambridge: Cambridge University Press, 1953.

Hadot, P., *Porphyre et Victorinus*, 2 vols., Paris: Études Augustiniennes, 1968.

Jakab, A., *Ecclesia Alexandrina: Évolution sociale et institutionnelle du christianisme alexandrin (IIe et IIIe siècles)*, Christianismes anciens 1, Bern: Lang, ²2004.

Letellier, D., "Le Logos chez Origène," *Revue des Sciences philosophiques et théologiques* 75 (1991), 587-611.

Meeks, W., "The Man from Heaven in Johannine Sectarianism," *Journal of Biblical Literature* 91/1 (1972), 44-72.

Modrzejewski, J.M., *Les Juifs d'Égypte de Ramsès II à Hadrien*, Paris: Quadrige / Presses Universitaires de France, ²1997.

Panaccio, C., *Le discours intérieur: De Platon à Guillaume d'Ockham*, Paris: Seuil, 1999.

Pasquier, A., *Eugnoste: Lettre sur le Dieu Transcendant (NH III, 3 et V, 1)*, Bibliothèque Copte de Nag Hammadi, Section: «Textes» 26, Québec: Les Presses de l'Université Laval; Leuven: Peeters, 2000.

—— "La doctrine des dénominations de Dieu dans le valentinisme: Comparaison avec Origène," *Origeniana Octava: Origen and the Alexandrian Tradition: Papers of the 8th International Congress: Pisa, 27-31 August 2001*, 2 vols., L. Perrone, ed., Bibliotheca Ephemeridum Theologicarum Lovaniensium 164, Leuven: Leuven University Press / Peeters, 2003, 1:355-365.

—— "Eugnoste," *Écrits gnostiques: La Bibliothèque de Nag Hammadi*, J.-P. Mahé and P.-H. Poirier, eds., Bibliothèque de la Pléiade, Paris: Gallimard, 2007, 571-613.

—— *Eugnoste (NH III, 3 et V, 1): Lettre sur le Dieu transcendant*, vol. 2, Bibliothèque copte de Nag Hammadi, Section: «Textes» 33, Québec: Les Presses de l'Université Laval; Leuven: Peeters, 2009.

Pouderon, B. and M.-J. Pierre, *Aristide: Apologie: Introduction, textes critiques, traductions et commentaire, avec la collaboration de B. Outtier et M. Guiorgadzé*, Sources chrétiennes 470, Paris: Cerf, 2003.

Rasimus, T., *Paradise Reconsidered in Gnostic Mythmaking: Rethinking Sethianism in Light of the Ophite Evidence*, Nag Hammadi and Manichaean Studies 68, Leiden: Brill, 2009.

Rousseau, A. and L. Doutreleau, *Irénée de Lyon: Contre les heresies: Livre II: Édition critique*, 2 vols., Sources chrétiennes 293-294, Paris: Cerf, 1982.

Rubinkiewicz, R., "The Apocalypse of Abraham," *The Old Testament Pseudepigrapha: Volume 1: Apocalyptic Literature and Testaments*, J.H. Charlesworth, ed., Garden City, N.Y.: Doubleday, 1983, 681-705.

Segal, A., *Two Powers in Heaven: Early Rabbinic Reports about Christianity and Gnosticism*, Studies in Judaism in Late Antiquity 25, Leiden: Brill, 1977.

Simonetti, M., *Studi sulla cristologia del II e III secolo*, Studia Ephemeridis Augustinianum 44, Roma: Institutum Patristicum Augustinianum, 1993.

Unger, D., *St. Irenaeus of Lyons: Against the Heresies: Volume 1: Book 1*, with further revisions by John J. Dillon, Ancient Christian Writers 55, New York: Paulist Press, 1992.

van den Broek, R., "Eugnostus and Aristides on the Ineffable God," *Knowledge of God in the Graeco-Roman World*, R. van den Broek, T. Baarda and J. Mansfeld, eds., Études preliminaries aux religions orientales dans l'empire romain 112, Leiden: Brill, 1988, 202-218.

Wolinski, J., "Le recours aux *'EΠINOIAI* du Christ dans le Commentaire sur Jean d'Origène," *Origeniana Sexta: Origène et la Bible: Actes du Colloquium Origenianum Sextum: Chantilly, 30 août—3 septembre 1993*, G. Dorival and A. Le Boulluec, eds., Bibliotheca Ephemeridum Theologicarum Lovaniensium 118, Leuven: Leuven University Press / Peeters, 1995, 465–492.

Yonge, C., ed., *The Works of Philo*, New updated edition, Peabody, Mass.: Hendrickson, 1993.

"THE ORTHODOX GOSPEL": THE RECEPTION OF JOHN IN THE GREAT CHURCH PRIOR TO IRENAEUS

Charles E. Hill
Reformed Theological Seminary

1. INTRODUCTION: THE MYTH OF ORTHODOX JOHANNOPHOBIA

In some areas of Johannine studies it has not been unusual to see the word "Johannine" in company with words like "Gnostic," "Valentinian," or "heterodox." The relationship of the Fourth Gospel itself, or some of its presumed sources, to emergent Gnosticism is a theme which has inspired a number of different approaches. But where there has been more of a consensus is in the idea of Gnostic or heterodox reception of John in the second century. One scholar says, "the gnostics adopted it as their special gospel."[1] Another speaks of the "omnipresence" of John among the Valentinians,[2] and another says it is well known that in the second century John "was much the preserve of heretics."[3]

Being the Gnostics' "special gospel" would naturally mean that John would encounter difficulties among the orthodox.[4] Scholars have often commented on "The nearly complete silence of the record during the crucial decades of the early second century,"[5] with regard to John and the orthodox. The reason for this silence is thought to go beyond the obvious differences with the synoptic accounts. As Raymond Brown wrote, "The Great Church...was at first wary of the Fourth Gospel because it had given rise to error and was being used to support error."[6] T.E. Pollard says, "second-century writers hesitated to use

---

[1] Charlesworth 1995, 382.
[2] Poffett 1990, 320, "Une différence fondamentale entre les écrits de la Grande Église et ceux des Valentiniens. D'un côté, une absence de citations johanniques claires, et cela même lorsque la pensée est très proche, par exemple chez Ignace d'Antioche; de l'autre côté, une omniprésence des textes du quatrième évangile."
[3] Trevett 1992, 197.
[4] On the use of terms like "orthodox" and "catholic" in preference to forms prefixed by "proto-," see Hill 2004, 3–10.
[5] Culpepper 1994, 131.
[6] Brown 1979, 146–147.

St John's Gospel because gnostic use of it made them either suspicious of its orthodoxy or afraid that to use it might give the impression that they were allying themselves with Gnosticism."[7] Not only this, but the Fourth Gospel is believed to have engendered open hostility among some orthodox writers, the chief (and virtually the only) examples of which are Gaius of Rome, writing in the early third century, and a nebulous group dubbed "the Alogi" by Epiphanius of Salamis. According to James H. Charlesworth, "Many pre-Nicene critics did not consider it reliable and authentic; it was tainted by the interpretations found in Heracleon's Ὑπομνέματα [sic]. Other Valentinians and numerous gnostics almost caused the GosJn to be cast into the rubbish heaps of condemned literature."[8]

In this view, we owe John's rescue from the rubbish heaps largely to the efforts of one man, Irenaeus of Lyons, who is said to have rehabilitated it and set it alongside three other gospels as "apostolic" witnesses to the truth.[9]

The foundation for this paradigmatic approach to the early reception of John is the 1934 landmark study of Walter Bauer, *Rechtgläubigkeit und Ketzerei im ältesten Christentum*,[10] the thesis of which was that what the church would later call heresy was the primitive and dominant form of Christianity in many places and for a long time, until the Roman ecclesiastical hierarchy could carry through its program of imperial expansion. Until its translation into English in 1971, Bauer's book did not receive nearly the attention among English-speaking scholars that it was to receive after that watershed publishing event. But one aspect of his study managed to slip through the language barrier early on, namely, his views on the reception of John's Gospel. A copy of *Rechtgläubigkeit und Ketzerei* made its way into the hands of a young Cambridge student named Joseph N. Sanders, whose prize-winning student essay of 1939 was published in 1943 as *The Fourth Gospel in the Early Church*. This modest monograph of 87 pages came to have a huge influence in English-language, Johannine scholarship. Embraced by C.K. Barrett, Raymond Brown and a host of other scholars, and enhanced by a 1966 Harvard Th.D. thesis by Melvyn Hillmer, what I have affectionately called the Orthodox Johannophobia Paradigm,

---

[7] Pollard 1970, 25.
[8] Charlesworth 1995, 407.
[9] E.g., Sanders 1943, 66; Culpepper 1994, 123.
[10] Bauer 1934.

came to dominate the landscape, with regard to the understanding of the early reception of John, though not quite completely.[11]

Recently, the grave weaknesses of this paradigm have been exposed in various ways by a number of studies.[12] It is quite true that at some point in the second century, Gnostic and Valentinian Christians were indeed using John, the latter in particular. Several studies of John's legacy among Valentinians and Gnostics are contained in the present volume. But the Valentinians took over virtually all of the books currently used by their contemporaries in the "great church" in Rome,[13] and the relationship between Gnostics and this gospel was not always as congenial as supposed.[14] Meanwhile, the presence of the Fourth Gospel as an important fixture in "orthodox" church life before Irenaeus has, until recently, gone under-appreciated. It will be the purpose of this essay to highlight the use of the Fourth Gospel among Irenaeus' predecessors in the mainstream of orthodox Christianity, summarizing, reworking, and updating portions of my 2004 book, *The Johannine Corpus in the Early Church*. Before doing so, however, some important issues of method must gain our attention.

2. Identifying the Use of a Johannine Text

Some of the disagreement about the use of John in authors prior to Irenaeus, particularly orthodox authors, has been engendered by the problem of identifying literary citations, allusions or echoes. How may we tell if a secondary author is actually using an earlier text?

There is no standard answer or even approach to this question. One recent treatment simply urges scholars to state their methodology, while being careful and cognizant of what they are doing.[15] At the outset I should say that the particular history of scholarship on the reception of John necessarily affects the goals I have in the investigation. Because the consensus of scholarship has been that early orthodox writers and churches either did not know the Fourth Gospel, until

---

[11] For a fuller accounting of the history of research, see Hill 2004, 13–55.

[12] Hengel 1989; Röhl 1991; Hengel 1993; Nagel 2000; Hill 2004. In the meantime, other, more nuanced approaches to the early life of the Johannine gospel have been teased out by others.

[13] E.g., van Unnik 1955.

[14] See Röhl 1991; Hill 2004, 205–293.

[15] Gregory and Tuckett 2005.

perhaps just before Irenaeus, or that they knew but avoided it or used it with genuine theological reservations, the first thing I am looking for is good evidence that an author was familiar with the written gospel. I am not so much concerned whether we conclude that the author "quotes" John, paraphrases it, alludes to it, or echoes its thoughts, but rather, first of all, whether we can say with any kind of assurance that the author knows the Gospel of John (assuming its existence in virtually the same form as we have in the earliest surviving papyri). Ascertaining knowledge of "Johannine oral tradition" which might have predated the written gospel and theoretically continued to circulate after the gospel was written (insofar as this might be discoverable), while very valuable in other respects, will not suffice here, for it will not tell us about the reception of John as a written gospel.

Second, if there is a strong possibility or probability that the author knew John, I am interested in whether or not we can say that the author has appropriated John in a positive way, as an authority in some sense. This may or may not reflect a use of John as "scripture" or as "canonical." Such determinations are often notoriously difficult, particularly in the earliest sources, and the attempt to make them often entails assumptions and debatable definitions on our part. For our purposes, particularly in dealing with the earlier sources, it will be enough if we can get a sense that an author is using John in a positive way or in a critical way.

The object then is to find evidence of "literary knowledge" of John, evidence of the existence and use of John's written gospel and not simply of oral tradition. This seems a very narrow focus, but on the other hand, I am not defining literary knowledge in a very narrow way. "Literary knowledge" or "literary dependence" may be indirect. I am not necessarily assuming that the author has a copy of the Gospel of John, as such, in his possession as he writes, to which he may refer back to check for the precision of his citation. He may or may not. The author may have read (or heard) the gospel or passages from it recently and be citing from memory. He may actually have memorized portions long ago and be citing from memory. Many have inferred the existence of "intermediate" sources of various kinds, for instance, a notebook or "testimonia book" of citations extracted from the gospel and perhaps other sources; or a gospel harmony of the sort produced by Tatian, which it has been suggested that Justin might have used; or a catechetical or liturgical sourcebook of some kind. Scholars are sometimes willing to ascribe to an author knowledge of one of these sources before ascribing to him knowledge of the Gospel of John itself. While I think it is rather unlikely that a second-century church leader would have had access *only* to a source dependent upon John and not also be familiar with the gospel itself, even if this were the case, I would still regard this as evidence of the knowledge and use of John. The theorized intermediate source assumes the prior existence and use of the gospel, if not on the citing author's part then on the part of the one who put together the notebook, catechism, liturgical book, or gospel harmony. It is only if this alternative source is not truly inter-mediate but rather independent of the Gospel of John, and if its use by the citing author was unaccompanied by a knowledge of the written gospel, that we may say that John is not referenced and no witness to John exists.

Sometimes scholars theorize that a given author might not know a written gospel firsthand but only through hearing it read. In this case, one might say the author knows John's Gospel only "orally." Yet I still conceive of this as a *literary* dependence (though indirect), as pub-lic reading assumes the use of a written text and not simply unwrit-ten oral tradition. Be this as it may, all the authors considered here, I would argue, knew of John's Gospel not simply by public reading, but by personal reading.

Now to the stickier matter of Johannine sources and oral tradition. Helmut Koester's early work on the synoptic material in the Apostolic Fathers,[16] in effect established a preference among many scholars for regarding synoptic parallels in the Apostolic Fathers as reflecting a knowledge not of the written gospels but of their written or oral sources, or later derivatives from common origins. He argued that one should not claim another author's knowledge of one of the Synoptic Gospels unless one could show that the parallel entailed Matthew's, Mark's, or Luke's final "redactional" material, words peculiar to the finished forms, as opposed to proposed earlier forms, of the gospels. Koester's approach is generally seen as an advance on less sophisti-cated methods used previously which gave scant consideration to synoptic materials not derived directly from the finished Synoptic Gospels. Koester's approach, on the other hand, has been criticized for being too restrictive; as often assuming particular, unproven theories of gospel composition and redaction; and for assuming the continuing

---

[16] Koester 1957.

viability of pre-synoptic sources long after the publication and circulation of Matthew, Mark, and Luke.[17]

One of Koester's students, Melvyn Hillmer, sought in his much-
quoted 1966 Harvard dissertation[18] to extend Koester's methodology,
as much as was applicable, to the study of the reception of John. He
argued that in those cases in which explicit quotation formulae or
explicit attribution are lacking, "it is necessary to determine whether
the writer shows knowledge of material or characteristics which are
peculiar to the evangelist. If a writer has parallels only with material
contained in John's sources or the traditional material in the gospel
then there is no proof that he has used the Fourth Gospel."[19] The precise contents, however, of John's "sources" or "traditional material"
are not always self-evident to all scholars, and attempts to establish
them sometimes involve debatable assumptions about the composition history of the gospel. Hillmer at least allows that the presence of
"material or characteristics peculiar to the evangelist" will tip the scales
toward regarding the material as indicating a use of the gospel. I take
it that these could include stories unique to John but more especially
attributes of John's particular theology and literary style.

In any case, this "redactional" criterion, however precisely understood, has become bedrock for many investigators. Another of
Koester's students, Arthur Bellinzoni, in his recent examination of the
possible use of Luke in the Apostolic Fathers,[20] proposes three criteria for determining whether an author is borrowing from a gospel:
first, accessibility, that is, the gospel must have been accessible to the
author in question; second, textual distinctiveness, that is, the sort of
distinguishing redactional characteristics Koester and Hillmer have
delineated; and third, rate of recurrence, that is, the case for use of a
document is strengthened by the presence of multiple apparent paral-

---

[17] For a recent treatment of Koester's views and subsequent developments, see
Gregory and Tuckett 2005. With regard to Justin's possible use of non-canonical collections of Jesus' sayings, see Skarsaune 2007, 67.

[18] Hillmer 1966.

[19] Hillmer 1966, 6. See also from the introduction, "In order to establish definitely
that the written gospel has been used it is necessary to have either explicit quotation
formulae or some indication that the written gospel is being cited, or else it is necessary to prove that parallels are with material in the gospel which has been written by
the author himself or which reflects characteristics of his work."

[20] Bellinzoni 2005, 50–51.

lels in the secondary work—even though a lack of recurrence cannot necessarily disqualify the possibility.

It is well to remember that those in the second century who engaged in literary borrowing from John were not conscious of the importance of quoting only "redactional" material and avoiding "traditional" material when quoting. Thus we must keep in mind that in cases in which we might judge that borrowed material reflects only traditional and not redactional material, our level of confidence about the source may not correspond at all to the actual historical facts of the use, or non-use, of John.

Distinguishing literary indebtedness to John's Gospel from indebtedness to "Johannine tradition," whether this is taken to mean oral tradition, a hypothetical earlier edition of the gospel, or a hypothetical written source used by the author(s) of John is, of course, not an easy business. The gospel ostensibly claims to be written by an eyewitness who recorded what he saw and heard (21:24–25). To the extent that events and speeches recorded in John really happened, we may allow the possibility that stories about them circulated independently of the Fourth Gospel.[21] But as we all know, judgments differ widely among scholars as to the historicity of the material in John. If the Johannine "Sondergut" is adjudged highly, how far is that tradition likely to have spread before the gospel was written, in what form did it exist, and how long and in what form did it survive after the circulation of the written gospel? And if it is not adjudged highly, this creates certain problems for assuming its early and widespread circulation. If the distinctively Johannine traditions do not reflect historical events and speeches but owe their origins to a localized community formed much later, or to a set of individual teachers in that later community, it is somewhat problematic to assume the early, wide reach and acceptance of these traditions while at the same time holding that the community which produced them was sectarian in outlook and somewhat removed from more mainstream Christians, and that the gospel produced at length by his community was avoided or rejected by those who had accepted its traditions in oral form. If Christians far and wide from early on

---

[21] Gregory and Tuckett (2005) say, John "is a narrative that purports to report events and discourses in the life of Jesus...Therefore the possibility may not be excluded altogether that such events and discussions may have circulated in oral traditions quite independent of these written texts, or on [sic] sources which may have been used both by the authors of either text and also by others."

were somehow familiar with distinctively "Johannine" traditions, and accepted them, it would seem that whenever the written Johannine gospel appeared these Christians might have been prepared to receive it favorably.

Perhaps the best we can do, without pleading for an individual theory on Johannine composition history, is to ask in each case whether it is possible or relatively likely that the material in question could have passed to the secondary writer as part of oral tradition about Jesus apart from the written gospel.

Finally, something should be said about the standards and techniques of literary borrowing in antiquity. Often when a scholar concludes a given author's "silence" with regard to John, a particular view of quotation standards and techniques is being invoked. That is, it is often assumed that it was the unwavering ideal of ancient authors to reproduce the underlying text with exact verbal precision. Thus any significant deviation is taken to signify that the borrowed source, if there was one, was something other than the Fourth Gospel. In my 2004 monograph I argued, however, that authors in our period often did not have the same standards of precision in citing earlier written sources that we do. While precise citation did of course occur, it was far from the universal practice, and standards clearly could vary even within the work of a single author. I cited in particular the work of the classical scholar John Whittaker in this regard, who wrote a very important article on the subject in 1989.[22] Since 2004, Sabrina Inowlocki has published a number of studies[23] of the citation practices of ancient authors, including examples from Plato, Aristobulus, Cicero, Porphyry, the Corpus Hermeticum, and in particular the Jew Josephus and the Christian Eusebius.[24] She concludes, very much in line with Whittaker, that

> The changes brought by an author to the cited passage vary substantially. They generally consist in the omission or addition of words, in gram-

---

[22] Whittaker 1989.

[23] See Inowlocki 2005a; Inowlocki 2005b; Inowlocki 2006.

[24] Many other studies could be cited. See, e.g., on Plutarch's use of Plato, Hershbell 1986, 240, "Although some of these divergences are possibly due to the condition of the extant manuscripts of Plutarch, and some to variation in the manuscripts of Plato he used, it seems clear that Plutarch was not always accurate in his quotations, and that he sometimes added or deleted words, or substituted equivalent words or phrases for those used by Plato." He also speaks of Plutarch's "paraphrases or 'quasi-quotations' of the 'Timaeus'" (240).

matical changes, in the combination of citations, and in the modification of the primary meaning of the quotation. These changes may be
deliberate, which means that they are made by the citing author specifically in order to appropriate the content of the citation. They may also
be accidental. If deliberate, the changes result from the author's wish
to adjust the citation to his own purposes, to "modernize" the stylistic
expression of a more ancient writer, or to adapt the grammar of the cited
text to that of the citing text. It may be noted that deliberate changes do
not always stem from the citing author's eagerness to tamper with the
primary meaning of the passage, as modern scholars often suspect and
harshly condemn.[25]

This being the case, we may accept that if other factors point to the
use of an earlier source (in this case John), certain variations from
the precise wording of the potential source may not be sufficient in
themselves to disqualify the thesis of literary borrowing. This will not
have probative value; it will not enable us to be certain of a potential
use, but it will force us to be more careful before rejecting such a conclusion because of discrepancies due to omission, addition, variation
of word order, grammatical change, substitution, and lack of regard
for the original context. These are all well attested features of citation
practice in the period which concerns us.

   I also adopt a more inclusive set of criteria than some. Since I am
trying to assess the probability of a given author's knowledge of the
written Gospel of John (and secondarily, the author's attitude towards
it), I seek to allow contextual or circumstantial factors to play their
parts. I believe such an approach is historiographically superior to
one which focuses solely on the "textual" features (sometimes quite
restricted, at that) of a text. All scholars work with some such assumptions. To give a simple illustration, let us imagine that exactly the same
"Johannine-sounding" phrase shows up in Ignatius of Antioch and in
an anonymous Christian letter from the fifth century. Let us say further
that the phrase does not correspond perfectly with its Johannine parallel, but it is a fairly striking or peculiar phrase none the less. Most of us
would deem it inherently more likely that it signifies actual knowledge
of John in the fifth-century letter than in Ignatius. This has nothing to
do with purely textual factors—the exact form of the words, the length
of the parallel material, the respect or lack of respect for the original
context—but is simply due to contextual factors, for we know that the

---

[25] Inowlocki 2006, 40.

Gospel of John was widely-used and respected as scripture by virtually all Christian groups in the fifth century, while we might not be ready to make the same assumption about all Christians writing ca. 110–117 CE. We may see how contextual factors may affect our evaluations in some of our authors below.

3. CATALOGUE OF ORTHODOX USERS

I have elsewhere catalogued twenty-two pre-Irenaean Christian sources which may be regarded as within the orbit of "orthodox Christianity" (some more clearly than others) and which, I argue, either certainly or very probably knew the Fourth Gospel and used it in a positive way.[26] These are: *Epistle of Vienne and Lyons*; Hegesippus; Athenagoras; the Christian interpolator of the *Sibylline Oracles*; Theophilus of Antioch; Claudius Apollinarius of Hierapolis; Melito of Sardis; the Christians opposed by Celsus; Tatian; the *Gospel of Peter*; Justin Martyr; the *Martyrdom of Polycarp*; the *Ad Diognetum*; *Epistula Apostolorum*; *The Shepherd of Hermas*; the Long Ending of Mark; the *Odes of Solomon*; Aristides; Papias of Hierapolis; Polycarp; Ignatius; Papias's Asian elders; and the elder John.

To re-examine each of these adequately is out of the question in this essay. Instead I have selected eight for closer examination, touching only briefly upon a few of the others. Some of these eight are selected because of the importance of their witness to the Fourth Gospel, others because they have suffered relative neglect in scholarship, others for a combination of reasons. Treating some of these works allows me to respond to some who have interacted with my interpretations of the evidence of particular authors.

3.1. Epistle of Vienne and Lyons

We begin with a source that was close to Irenaeus and surely well known to him. The *Epistle of Vienne and Lyons* was written in the wake of anti-Christian pogroms in Vienne and Lyons in the year 177. The churches there sent a letter to the outside Christian world, addressed to "the brethren in Asia and Phrygia, who have the same faith and hope of redemption." The letter was also carried to the bishop of Rome

---

[26] Hill 2004.

personally by a presbyter named Irenaeus, who some suggested might also have been its author. Whoever wrote the letter wrote in the first person plural, ostensibly on behalf of the churches of the two cities. The letter was evidently signed by a number of the martyrs and confessors. This letter, as well as the several letters from individual martyrs and confessors which were sent out along with it, thus represents the witness of Irenaeus' own Christian community previous to his writing of *Adversus haereses*.

In reflecting on its experience of suffering, this community regarded that experience as a fulfillment of the prediction of Jesus recorded in John 16:2.

> When this rumour spread all men turned like beasts against us, so that even if any had formerly been lenient for friendship's sake they then became furious and raged against us, and there was fulfilled that which was spoken (τὸ... εἰρημένον) by our Lord, that the time will come when "whosoever killeth you will think that he doeth God service (ὅτι ἐλεύσεται καιρὸς ἐν ᾧ πᾶς ὁ ἀποκτείνας ὑμᾶς δόξει λατρείαν προσφέρειν τῷ θεῷ)" (*EpV&L* 5.1.15).[27]

Here the author appears to invoke the words of Jesus in John 16:2, "They will put you out of the synagogues; indeed, the hour is coming when whoever kills you will think he is offering service to God." There are, however, certain minor differences between this apparent citation of John and the MSS of John, which read, ἔρχεται ὥρα ἵνα πᾶς ὁ ἀποκτείνας ὑμᾶς δόξῃ λατρείαν προσφέρειν τῷ θεῷ.[28] First, there is a question as to when the author intends his quotation to start. It is possible that his words ὅτι ἐλεύσεται καιρὸς ἐν ᾧ constitute an indirect citation and that the direct citation begins only with πᾶς. Or, this all may be part of what he considers a direct (but inexact) citation of the Lord's words. In any case, his ὅτι ἐλεύσεται καιρὸς ἐν ᾧ ("that the time will come when...") represents the substitution of a future indicative, ἐλεύσεται, for John's futuristic present indicative ἔρχεται, and a substitution of καιρὸς ἐν ᾧ for John's ὥρα ἵνα. Beginning with the word πᾶς, however, the only difference with John is in the substitution of the future δόξει for the aorist subjunctive δόξῃ, in keeping with the change he has already made by eliminating the ἵνα. It is conceivable that these changes could reflect the precise wording of the author's

---

[27] Greek text and English translations of *EpV&L* are from Lake 1926.
[28] The only pertinent variation in the MSS is the omission of ὑμᾶς in B.

source, and thus that his text of John differed from the text which has survived in manuscripts or that it came from an alternative source. But the direct quotation repeats eight words exactly and changes only the mood and tense of a ninth, and the verbal changes here and in the possibly indirect quotation are simply the kinds of changes we often see in the secondary use of a text by a later author in antiquity. Not only is the meaning not distorted but the citing author still preserves a substantial amount of material that is distinctive to John, among known possible sources. He attributes the saying to Jesus, and it is attributed to Jesus in the only known source which has this material, the Gospel of John, which we know was in circulation by this time. The author clearly accepts these words as a real prediction of the historical Jesus. He obviously believes they constitute an authentic prophecy, for he believes the words are coming to pass before his eyes.[29] By his informal introduction of this prophecy as something "spoken by our Lord," he seems to assume that the recipients of the letter are already familiar with the prediction.

Yet, what the author of the epistle has altered from the text of John is instructive. His substitutions for John's futuristic present and his elimination of John's ἵνα plus the subjunctive amount to changing stylistic elements that we would call distinctively Johannine. Here, therefore, the chief criterion of Koester, Hillmer, and Bellinzoni fails us, for these are certainly distinctive, Johannine redactional elements and it is precisely these that the author chooses to change—perhaps precisely because they were so distinctive.

Another, more complex Johannine allusion occurs when the endurance of a Christian named Sanctus is praised, who held "firm in his confession, refreshed and strengthened by the heavenly spring of water of life which proceeds forth from the body of Christ (ὑπο τῆς οὐρανίου πηγῆς τοῦ ὕδατος τῆς ζωῆς τοῦ ἐξιόντος ἐκ τῆς νηδύος τοῦ Χριστοῦ)" (EpV&L 5.1.22). Even though there are several differences in vocabulary, this seems to be a combined use of three Johannine texts, corresponding mainly to John 7:38, "as the scripture has said, out of his heart shall flow rivers of living water (ποταμοὶ ἐκ τῆς κοιλίας αὐτοῦ ῥεύσουσιν ὕδατος ζῶντος)," combined interpretatively with Rev 22:1, "Then he showed me the river of the water of life (ποταμὸν ὕδατος ζωῆς), bright as crystal (λαμπρὸν ὡς κρύσταλλον), flowing from the

---

[29] Cf. Irenaeus, Adv. haer. 3.24.1.

throne of God and of the Lamb" (cf. also John 19:34). From Rev 22:1
comes the notion of a heavenly living water, and the idea that this
heavenly living water flows from the body of Christ relates to John
7:38. But the author has also substituted πηγή for ποταμός used in
both John 7:38 and Revelation 22:1. This substitution seems adequately explained by supposing that the author has also consciously
or unconsciously combined these texts interpretatively with John 4:14,
"but whoever drinks of the water that I shall give him will never thirst;
the water that I shall give him will become in him a spring (πηγή) of
water welling up to eternal life."

The practice of combining references is well known in both non-
Christian[30] as well as Christian sources. In the present case we evidently are witnessing the influence of an exegetical tradition. Readers
of the Fourth Gospel, then as they do now, must have easily made the
connection (as I recall doing, years ago when I first began to read John
closely) between the living water that Jesus promised the Samaritan
woman in John 4:10–15 and the water which would flow from Jesus'
heart (κοιλία) in 7:38, water which the Johannine author immediately
interprets for the reader as signifying the Holy Spirit (7:39). The author
of the *EpV&L* is also familiar with an exegetical linking of this theme
from the Johannine gospel with the figure of the river of the water of
life from Revelation 22:1, which flows from the heavenly throne. That
this is indeed a traditional exegetical linking is impressively confirmed
by Irenaeus, who is familiar with the same combination of Johannine
texts. He similarly refers to the Holy Spirit as "that most limpid fountain which issues from the body of Christ (*de corpore Christi prec-
edentem nitidissimum fontem*)" (*Adv. haer.* 3.24.1). Even though the
expression is not the same and the verses are combined in a different
way, again we seem to have the mingling of the same passages, John
4:14 and 7:38 with Rev 22:1. The Holy Spirit as flowing water proceeding from the body of Christ comes from John 7:38. But here too,
as in *EpV&L*, rather than *fluvium* or *flumen*, reflecting an underlying
ποταμός which is used in both John 7:38 and Rev 22:1, we have the
word *fons*, the typical Vulgate translation of πηγή in the LXX and the
NT, the word used in John 4:14 for the water that Jesus gives, which
wells up to eternal life. We also have an apparent reflection of Rev

---

[30]   Whittaker 1989, 90–92; Stanley 1992, 281; Inowlocki 2006, 46.

22:1 in the mention of that fountain as "most limpid" (*nitidissimum*),[31] corresponding to λαμπρὸν ὡς κρύσταλλον, "clear as crystal" in Rev 22:1. This points, again, to an exegetical tradition of comingling these Johannine verses into a single concept: the Holy Spirit as luminous, living water, flowing from the heavenly body of Christ. This would seem to bespeak a fairly longstanding use of the Gospel of John and the Revelation of John in the Christian preaching which formed the background of the author.

Another passage in the letter is remarkable for its containing apparent allusions to three Johannine sources. A man named Vettius Epagathus, it says, "was called the 'Comforter of Christians,' but had the Comforter in himself, the spirit of Zacharias which he had shown by the fullness of his love when he chose to lay down even his own life for the defence of the brethren, for he was and he is a true disciple of Christ, and he follows the Lamb wheresoever he goes" (*EpV&L* 5.1.10). Vettius is called the παράκλητος of the Christians because he had τὸν παράκλητον "in himself, the Spirit of Zacharias..." This comparison of Vettius with Zecharias is apparently related in the author's mind both to the Zechariah of 2 Chr 24:20–21 (called "the elder Zecharias" in *EpV&L* 5.1.9) who was clothed with the Spirit of God, who gave his testimony and then was brutally martyred, and to the later Zechariah, the father of John the Baptist, who was also said to have walked in the commandments and ordinances of the Lord blameless (5.1.9; Luke 1:6). The point here is that the author equates the "Spirit of Zacharias," that is the Holy Spirit (cf. both 2 Chr 24:20 and Luke 1:67) with ὁ παράκλητος. This use of the term παράκλητος for the Holy Spirit invokes the promise of Jesus in John 14:16–17,26; 16:7 to send ὁ παράκλητος to his disciples. In accord with the words of 1 John 3:16, which the author has clearly adapted for this purpose, Vettius showed the fullness of his love by choosing to "lay down even his own life for the defence of the brethren."[32] The "Johannine" tribute to Vettius extends to the appraisal of his position in the afterlife, as it is said, in the words of Revelation 14:4, that he "follows the Lamb where-

---

[31] Lewis and Short 1879, "I. *shining, glittering, bright, polished, clear* (class.; syn.: splendidus, lautus)." The Vulgate uses *splendidus* for λαμπρός in Rev 22:1.

[32] ὃ διὰ τοῦ πληρώματος τῆς ἀγάπης ἐνεδείξατο, εὐδοκήσας ὑπὲρ τῆς ἀδελφῶν ἀπολογίας καὶ τὴν ἑαθτοῦ θεῖναι ψυχήν; 1 John 3:16: ἐν τούτῳ ἐγνώκαμεν τὴν ἀγάπην, ὅτι ἐκεῖνος ὑπὲρ ἡμῶν τὴν ψυχὴν αὐτοῦ ἔθηκεν· καὶ ἡμεῖς ὀφείλομεν ὑπὲρ τῶν ἀδελφῶν τὰς ψυχὰς θεῖναι (cf. John 15:13, μείζονα ταύτης ἀγάπην οὐδεὶς ἔχει, ἵνα τις τὴν ψυχὴν αὐτοῦ θῇ ὑπὲρ τῶν φίλων αὐτοῦ.)

soever he goes."[33] This very distinctive phrase thus places Vettius in the company of the 144,000 chaste and spotless ones redeemed from the earth, who now worship before the throne (cf. *Mart. Pol.* 14:1–2; *5 Ezra* 2:38–40). It would appear that the author and his community are steeped in the Johannine literature. And again, he seems to assume that the recipients of the report will catch his Johannine allusion when he jumps from ὁ παράκλητος as "Advocate," probably the name given to Vettius by the governor,[34] to ὁ παράκλητος as Jesus' name for the Holy Spirit in the Gospel of John.

Later in his account the author speaks of those who denied Christ and did not repent, as "sons of perdition" (οἱ υἱοὶ τῆς ἀπωλείας) (*EpV&L* 5.1.48). While one might imagine such a term of opprobrium to have been a commonplace, without any particular textual referent, it is interesting that its only occurrence in the NT is in John 17:12 (ὁ υἱὸς τῆς ἀπωλείας). That this Johannine passage is behind the phrase here is made more likely not only from the other instances of apparent Johannine borrowing, but because the author is referring here not simply to unbelievers or opponents but to those who denied Jesus. In John 17:12, "son of perdition" refers to Judas, the archetypal denier of Jesus.

One could try to argue that all these apparent Johannine allusions derive not from direct or indirect literary knowledge of the written gospel but rather from Christian tradition known only orally. But in this Christian setting in Gaul in 177 CE, which obviously contained literate Christians, that seems extremely unlikely. It is much easier to agree with William Frend who has remarked, "Clearly the Fourth Gospel and the Apocalypse were two of the main sources of inspiration to the writer."[35] I only add that the First Letter must have been known as well.

The witness of the *EpV&L* is interesting for several reasons. First, whether Irenaeus was its author or not, it shows that the Fourth Gospel was in use, along with the Apocalypse of John and at least the first Johannine Epistle, along with several more NT texts, among these churches in Gaul before Irenaeus wrote his major works. When embarking on the writing of *Adversus haereses* a few years later,

---

[33] See Hill 2001, 138.
[34] Lawlor and Oulton 1954, 2:155.
[35] Frend 1981, 19.

Irenaeus certainly had no need to introduce or defend this gospel to his own Christian communities in Gaul. There is no reason to assume that he was aware of doing anything controversial among his fellow orthodox believers, whether they be in Gaul, in Asia Minor, in Rome, or elsewhere, when he used John's Gospel in *Adversus haereses*.

In fact, the epistle strongly suggests that Christian communities in Phrygia and Asia, as well as the church in Rome, were familiar with these books of the Johannine corpus as well. The Christian communities in Gaul were composed of many Asian and Phrygian transplants, some of whom, like Irenaeus, may have sojourned in Rome on the way. We know that there was a significant contingent of Christians from Asia Minor in Rome in the second century, and it is possible that these Asians now in Gaul may have first sojourned in Rome and may have been part of a Roman mission in Gaul. In any case, the connections with both Asia Minor and Rome are important. The churches in the letter stress a unity of their faith and hope with the churches in Asia and Phrygia whom they address (*EpV&L* 5.1.3), and they call Eleutherus of Rome "father" and speak of him as one to whom they were accustomed ("once more and always") to greet by letter (5.4.2). This denotes a relationship of longstanding, as suggested also by the fact of Irenaeus' commission from the churches in Gaul to deliver the letter personally to the bishop. The strong connections of fellowship both with Rome and with Asia and Phrygia are *prima facia* evidence that Christians with such cross-regional affiliations might also have shared much the same authoritative texts. It is unlikely that these young churches, certainly planted among those Irenaeus calls "barbarians" in the recent past, would have instituted the use of written Christian authorities unknown or unacceptable to the mother churches from whom they came and from whom they perhaps were still receiving support. At the very least this demonstrates that when he used the Fourth Gospel in *Adversus haereses* Irenaeus was not trying to engineer a takeover from his Valentinian opponents, nor did he need to mount a defense for it among orthodox Christians. It already had standing among the churches in Gaul and the correspondence renders it very likely for Asia, Phrygia, and Rome, prior to the 180's.

As it happens, the use of John in Asia Minor prior to the writing of the *Epistle of Vienne and Lyons* may be corroborated fairly copiously from several earlier authors, as we shall see. In the 160s we have record of an earlier phase of the quartodeciman controversy in which both Melito of Sardis and Apollinarius of Hierapolis participated. While apparently taking different sides of the issue (this is debated by some), each author uses the Fourth Gospel as authoritative. We shall point to earlier examples in more detail below.

3.2. The Christians Opposed by Celsus[36]

The next author we examine is neither an orthodox nor a heretical writer, but an unbeliever. The anti-Christian apologist Celsus, in his treatise *The True Word* written sometime between 160 and 180, is apparently "the first pagan to set out to write a whole treatise against Christianity."[37] Everything we know about Celsus and his book comes from Origen's *Contra Celsum* written probably about 248. Where Celsus wrote his book is a matter of uncertainty; most scholars have favored either Rome or Alexandria.

Wherever he was, Celsus knew at least several Christian books which were clearly closely associated with the form of Christianity he was mainly attacking. Among these was the Gospel according to John. Some have voiced skepticism that Celsus could have had access to Christian scriptures, assumed to be hard to come by,[38] but this is contradicted by strong evidence. First, Celsus, by his own words, is aware of and fully accepts the common notion that "the disciples of Jesus wrote such accounts regarding him" which portrayed his suffering and death (*Cels.* 2.16). Indeed, he has his fictional Jewish opponent of Christianity claim explicitly to have taken his information about Christianity "from your own books (ἐκ τῶν ὑμετέρων συγγραμμάτων)" (2.74 cf. 2.77), and this is naturally taken as a thinly veiled claim of Celsus' own. That he made use of these books is sufficiently clear, secondly, from Origen's testimony. Origen says that Celsus "endeavours to cast reproach upon Him from the narratives in the Gospel (ἐκ τῶν γεγραμμένων ἐν τῷ εὐαγγελιῷ)" (*Cels.* 2.34). He attests that Celsus "makes numerous quotations from the Gospel according to Matthew,"[39] while he charges that Celsus omits other texts from the gospels which would have hurt his case (*Cels.* 1.34). Origen notes that Celsus "extracts from the Gospel [this time it is John] even passages

---

[36] See Hill 2004, 309-311.
[37] Frede 1999, 133.
[38] Lona 2005, 36.
[39] ἐκ τοῦ παραθέμενον αὐτὸν πολλὰ ἀπὸ τοῦ κατὰ Ματθαῖον εὐαγγελίου. Greek from Borret 1967–1976. The verb παρατίθημι is sometimes used for quotation, as in Apollonius Dyscolus, the second-century grammarian, *De pronominibus* 52.7; 89.22.

which are incorrectly interpreted"[40] (*Cels.* 2.36). Again Origen alleges that Celsus "extracts[41] from the gospel narrative those statements on which he thinks he can found an accusation" (*Cels.* 2.37).

Origen certainly knew what it was to extract statements from books for the purpose of composing your own, and he knew the gospel narratives quite well enough to recognize Celsus' use of them. Alexander is certainly correct, then, to observe that "Celsus is the first pagan writer to show indisputable independent knowledge of the gospels as texts…"[42] We need not suppose, of course, that Celsus had read these books either carefully or sympathetically. There is every reason to acknowledge Origen's charges that Celsus' reading was selective and for the purpose of spotting difficulties he could exploit. From Origen's expressions it would appear that Celsus followed what was evidently a common custom. Having obtained copies of Christian gospels, Celsus made extracts of certain passages as they were read out by a servant, or else the roles were reversed. These extracts then became Celsus' tools of reference as he wrote his books against the Christians.[43] The third reason for concluding Celsus' familiarity with the gospels comes from the actual evidence of his knowledge as preserved by Origen. We confine ourselves here to the evidence for his knowledge of John.

Origen says that Celsus, who believed it to be self-evident that "the body of a god is not nourished with such [earthly] food," was "able to prove from the Gospel narratives (ἀπὸ τῶν εὐαγγελικῶν γραμμάτων) both that He partook of food, and food of a particular kind" (*Cels.* 1.70). From Origen's comments it is evident that these gospel narratives included John's reference to Jesus thirsting "near the well of Jacob,"[44] and drinking from the water of that well (John 4:6–7). Celsus also mocks Jesus by implicitly charging that the water which flowed from the body of Jesus—something recorded only in John's Gospel—

---

[40] φέρων ἀπὸ τοῦ εὐαγγελίου οὐδε καλῶς ἑρμηνευομένας λέχεις.

[41] ἐκλαβὼν λέχεις, "extracting words" or "expressions." See also 1.40,58; 2.24,32,33,50–51,55; 6.16.

[42] Alexander 2005, 233.

[43] Much as Origen assumes was the case with Plato, who, he alleges, "quoted" (ἐκτεθεῖσθαι) things "from a perusal of our prophetic writings" (*Cels.* 6.19). See the interesting account of his uncle's practice given by Pliny the Younger, *Letters* 3.5, and the discussion in Inowlocki 2006, 34–35.

[44] παρὰ τῇ πηγῇ Ἰακώβ. In Hill 2004, 309, I suggested that Celsus' knowledge of Jesus eating a piece of fish after his resurrection likely signaled his familiarity with John 21:13. While that may be true, the language, I now realize, is more directly related to Luke 24:42–43.

was like the watery ichor supposed to belong to the immortal bodies of the gods (*Cels.* 2.36, cf. *Iliad* 5.340). Origen criticizes Celsus, then, for extracting "from the Gospel even passages which are incorrectly interpreted," in this instance, John's testimony in John 19:34–35 that when Jesus' side was pierced "there came thereout blood and water." In another passage Celsus refers to Jesus after his resurrection, showing "the marks of his punishment, and how his hands were pierced with nails" (*Cels.* 2.55; 2.61), a comment clearly based on the account in John 20:24–29, as Origen in fact attests (*Cels.* 2.61). Celsus apparently knows another detail from the Gospel of John, a challenge by some Jews that Jesus exhibit some unmistakable sign that he was the Son of God, from a meeting which is said to have taken place "in the temple." This seems to refer to the incident recorded in John 10:22–26, when Jesus was accosted "while walking in the temple, in the portico of Solomon" at the feast of the Dedication. Celsus' Jew is also familiar with the Christian title of Logos for Jesus (*Cels.* 2.31). This does not necessitate his knowledge of John 1:1,14, particularly if he was in any way familiar with the writings or teachings of Christian apologists like Justin.[45] Yet because Celsus' Jew appears to be referring throughout to testimonies derived from the gospels,[46] this probably tips the balance towards John as the specific source of information.

There is every reason to affirm, then, that Celsus had access to a copy of John's Gospel and used it indiscriminately along with the Gospels of Matthew and Luke (and perhaps Mark) as a source for information about Jesus and what Christians believed about him. There is even one text whose meaning is debated but which some have taken to indicate Celsus' awareness of a four-fold gospel canon (*Cels.* 2.27).[47] It is not necessary that one draw this conclusion, however, in order to recognize that Celsus was well aware of Christian reliance upon their gospels and that he himself faced no great obstacles in obtaining at least the three mentioned above. Had he obtained his own copies? Had he simply made extracts from copies borrowed from an unsuspecting Christian, a former Christian, or from a well-stocked library? We do not know. But we must conclude that Celsus at some time had in his possession copies of Christian gospels which he considered the

---

[45] Lona 2005, 144.

[46] His next objection has to do with the genealogies in Matthew and Luke (*Cels.* 2.33).

[47] Hengel 1993, 28n48. See also the note *ad loc.* in Chadwick 1965.

Christians' "own books" (2.74 cf. 2.77), among which was what we know as the Gospel of John.

If we could be certain either that Celsus was a Roman, or had based his knowledge of orthodox Christians from what he had observed while in Rome, this would be particularly striking evidence of the failure of Bauer's thesis that the Roman church, a bastion of orthodoxy, was suspicious of and opposed to the Gospel according to John, throughout the second century. In any case, Celsus' knowledge of the contents of John and other gospels as written accounts, and not simply as oral traditions, is important for attesting to the association of these written gospels together and as sources of the faith and teaching of the Christians as Celsus sees them. Celsus shows how John's Gospel was (a) available, (b) commonly associated both with the synoptics ("your own books," 2.74 cf. 2.77) and (c) with the great church which he was opposing, and this at a time before Irenaeus wrote, and in a locality, whether Rome or Alexandria, far distant from Lyons. He supplies further evidence that Irenaeus had no need to "defend" the Gospel of John to his orthodox peers.

3.3. *Justin Martyr*

As the *Diatessaron* of Tatian the Assyrian is treated elsewhere in this volume, Tatian's contribution will not be covered here, except to say that the importance of John's Gospel in the composition of the *Diatessaron*, and the recognition of John as reflecting orthodox impulses, is enlightened by a look at its role in the writings of Tatian's teacher, Justin.[48]

Did Justin know the Fourth Gospel? The votes of scholars are divided.[49] Some find little or no reason to think Justin knew John, or they find that he may have used it but only with caution. Here I shall look at portions of his writings which I believe demonstrate not only that Justin knew and used John but that it was one of the gospels he designated "the apostolic memoirs," which he says were used in ser-

---

[48] That is, whatever purpose Tatian had in producing the *Diatessaron*, and whatever theological tendencies it may have exhibited (traces of encratism have been suggested), its acceptance and inclusion of the Fourth Gospel cannot be explained (*pace* Bauer 1971, 206–207; Barrett 1978, 125; Brown 1979, 148) as merely a result of his turn towards heterodoxy. It was simply the continuation of his practice already signified in his orthodox *Oratio* and a reflection of the practice of his teacher Justin.

[49] See Hill 2004, 313.

vices of Christian worship in Rome alongside the prophetical writings of the OT (*1 Apol.* 67.3).

Justin's only "quotation" of John, or rather, of Jesus in John, occurs in a well-noted section of his *First Apology*, where he seeks to inform the rulers about "the manner in which we dedicated ourselves to God when we had been made new through Christ" (*1 Apol.* 61.1). He proceeds to speak of the Christian baptismal practice as he knows it in Rome:

> Then they are brought by us where there is water, and are regenerated in the same manner in which we were ourselves regenerated. For, in the name of God, the Father and Lord of the universe, and of our Saviour Jesus Christ, and of the Holy Spirit, they then receive the washing with water. For Christ also said, "Except ye be born again, ye shall not enter into the kingdom of heaven" (ἂν μὴ ἀναγεννηθῆτε, οὐ μὴ εἰσέλθητε εἰς τὴν βασιλείαν τῶν οὐρανῶν).[50]

The close correspondence to John 3:3,5 is obvious, though there are certain verbal discrepancies. Justin has "kingdom of heaven," and John has "kingdom of God." And instead of John's two distinct words, "born" (γεννάω) and "again" (ἄνωθεν), Justin uses a single compound word, "reborn" (ἀναγεννάω). Because of the variations, Helmut Koester believes the words attributed to Christ by Justin are not beholden to the Fourth Gospel at all, but are derived instead "from the free tradition" preserved in a current baptismal liturgy, and this in a more original form than appears in John.[51] In this, Koester is echoing the earlier conclusions of his students, Bellinzoni and Hillmer.[52] Never mind that no baptismal liturgy, current or not, has been produced which reflects these forms of the saying attributed to Christ.

And whatever else we may say about these differences, they are just the kind of alterations that scholars such as Whittaker and Inowlocki observe in citations by authors of the period. Substitutions of synonymous or near synonymous words, either for the sake of clarity or for an emphasis that the citing author wants to make, or for reasons

---

[50] The Greek of *Dial.* is from Marcovich 1997; of *1 Apol.* is from Wartelle 1987.

[51] Koester 1990, 258, 361–362 (reiterated recently in Koester 2005, 31). Koester also alleges that the Johannine "you cannot see" of John 3:3, instead of "you cannot enter" in Justin, is more evidence of a discrepancy between the John and Justin's source (Koester 1990, 258). John 3:5, however, also has "you cannot enter."

[52] Bellinzoni 1967, 136–137, "Justin has independently preserved a liturgical baptismal text in a form older than that found in John and that John's text is probably based on the same or on a similar tradition"; cf. Hillmer 1966, 54–58.

inexplicable, are among the common alterations that authors make to their cited texts without, in their views, distorting those texts. In the case of his substitution of "reborn" (ἀναγεννηθῆτε) for John's "born again" or "born from above" (ἐὰν μή γεννηθῇ ἄνωθεν), it is quite possible that Justin simply felt that ἀναγεννάω would be less perplexing to his pagan audience than the expression "born from above."[53] At any rate, he had already adopted ἀναγεννάω as his term for regeneration through baptism, using it three times in the first part of the paragraph,[54] thus, this modification of John 3:3,5 is in keeping with this chosen theological vocabulary. Tatian would soon use the same lexical modification of John 3:3 or 3:5, "I too, in imitation of the Word, having been begotten again (ἀναγεννηθείς)" (*Orat.* 5.3).

The divergences between Justin's οὐ μὴ εἰσέλθητε εἰς τὴν βασιλείαν τῶν οὐρανῶν and John's οὐ δύναται εἰσελθεῖν εἰς τὴν βασιλείαν τοῦ θεοῦ (John 3:5) may be due, as some have suggested, to a conscious[55] or unconscious conflation, with Matthew 18:3 (οὐ μὴ εἰσέλθητε εἰς τὴν βασιλείαν τῶν οὐρανῶν).[56] It is a natural enough slip for those well acquainted with the similar saying in Matthew. It is even possible that βασιλείαν τῶν οὐρανῶν is what appeared in Justin's text of John, as even the original scribe of Codex Sinaiticus wrote βασιλείαν τῶν οὐρανῶν in his copy of John 3:5.[57] According to Romanides,[58] all citations of John 3:3–5 before Origen, have "kingdom of heaven" instead of "kingdom of God."

Thus the differences between Justin's citation and the surviving texts of John are not such as make it necessary to posit another source for Justin besides John. Moreover, it is perhaps helpful to remember that Justin is only claiming to quote Jesus here, not John. That is, Justin, one might say, accurately quotes Jesus (in reproducing his meaning), though he does not, from a text-critical standpoint, accurately quote

---

[53] Pryor 1992, 165.

[54] 61.3,4. He also uses the noun ἀναγέννησις in 61.3; 66.1 and in *Dial.* 138.2. Cf. τὸ μυστήριον τῆς πάλιν γενέσεως ἡμῶν in *Dial.* 85.7. Ἀναγεννάω may have been, as Romanides (1958–1959, 127) thinks, a technical term for the baptismal rite in Justin's day. But it at least was the term Justin had adopted.

[55] Whittaker 1989, 89.

[56] Romanides 1958–1959, 131–132; Pryor 1992, 165, "surely by the second century, texts such as Matthew 18:3 and John 3:3, 5 would have been understood baptismally with a resulting fusing of texts!"

[57] See Swanson 1995, 28.

[58] Romanides 1958–1959, 130–131.

the text of John—just as he often does not accurately quote the texts of the Synoptic Gospels, or even the LXX.[59]

But could the appearance of this saying of Jesus in *1 Apol.* 61.4 be the result of its survival through the "free tradition," without Justin's knowledge of the written gospel? For this to be the case one must posit the survival of the story in Rome in about 150, and this is only part of the difficulty. The other part is the assumption that this free tradition was accessible to Justin apart from the written gospel which all agree was in existence and circulating well before this time. If *1 Apol.* 61.4–5 represented the only place in Justin's writings where a familiarity with John seems to surface, one might perhaps be tempted to hold these two suggested solutions in equilibrium. But it is not the only place, even in the same context.

Completely ignored in the treatments of this saying of Jesus by Koester, Hillmer, and Bellinzoni are the words which immediately follow it in Justin's apology (61.5): "Now, that it is impossible for those who have once been born to enter into their mothers' wombs, is manifest to all," words which echo the reply of Nicodemus in John 3:4: "How can a man be born when he is old? Can he enter a second time into his mother's womb and be born?"[60] Did the baptismal tract postulated by these scholars contain a denial of the possibility of re-entering one's mother's womb as well?[61] Did this part, too, survive till 150 in the "free tradition" apart from the gospel context? Or, did Justin and the Johannine author each come up with the thought of

---

[59] When Justin cites the Greek OT in *1 Apol.*, he sometimes cites from a shorter form which Skarsaune (2007), argues comes from a Christian testimonia source. These citations from scripture often condense (by omission), interpolate, and combine materials. See Skarsaune 2007, 59–60. In *Dial.* 32.1, the citation of Gen 49:10–11 exhibits "several significant deviations from the LXX text" (Skarsaune 2007, 55). The deviations include the substitution of words, changes in the forms of verbs, and the omission of whole lines (possibly by homoteleuton). What is most striking is that Justin specifically claims here to be reproducing the words of Moses "literally" or "in these very words" (εἶπεν αὐτολεξεὶ οὕτως)!

[60] ὅτι δὲ καὶ ἀδύνατον εἰς τὰς μήτρας τῶν τεκουσῶν τοὺς ἅπαξ γεννωμένους ἐμβῆναι, φανερὸν πᾶσιν ἐστι (*1 Apol.* 61.5); πῶς δύναται ἄνθρωπος γεννηθῆναι γέρων ὤν; μὴ δύναται εἰς τὴν κοιλίαν τῆς μητρὸς αὐτοῦ δεύτερον εἰσελθεῖν καὶ γεννηθῆναι (John 3:4).

[61] Certainly there is no correspondence in any text cited as a parallel baptismal text by Bellinzoni (Hippolytus, *Ref.* 8.10; *Apos. Con.* 6.15; Pseudo-Clementine *Hom.* 11.26; Pseudo-Clementine *Recogn.* 6.9).

re-entering one's mother's womb independently?[62] I find each of these suggested solutions to be more difficult than the suggestion that in both his paraphrastic citation of Jesus' words in John 3:3,5 and in his echo of the Johannine record of Nicodemus' objection in John 3:4 Justin is simply dependent upon John's written gospel.[63] John's Gospel was certainly in existence and available by this time; the correspondence here is substantial in content, in wording, and in length. The fact that Justin does not quote John with exact verbal precision, in this case, has very little relevance.

Justin also knows details contained only in John's account of Jesus' baptism (*Dial.* 88.7). Justin observes that while some supposed that John the Baptist was the Christ, he himself "cried to them, 'I am not the Christ, but the voice of one crying; for he that is stronger than I shall come, whose shoes I am not worthy to bear.'" Koester correctly points out, "The answer 'I am not the Christ' has a parallel only in the Gospel of John; the continuation of the Baptist's answer in Justin ('but the voice of a crier') also recalls the text of the Fourth Gospel."[64] It looks in fact like Justin, in summarizing the account in John 1:20–23, has simply skipped from the Baptist's denial "I am not the Christ" (1:20) to his affirmation, "but 'the voice of one crying'" (1:23), where he is quoting Isa 40:3. Koester denies that this signifies Justin's knowledge of the Fourth Gospel, however, preferring the explanation that Justin simply "developed the answer of the Baptist on the basis of Luke's text [Luke 3:15] and the Isaiah prophecy [Isa 40:3]."[65] Luke 3:15 says, "As the people were in expectation, and all men questioned in their hearts concerning John, whether perhaps he were the Christ (μήποτε αὐτὸς εἴη ὁ χριστός)..." Koester's explanation would mean that both Justin and John independently, from the crowds' musing "whether perhaps he were the Christ" (Luke 3:15), put the words "I am not the Christ (οὐκ εἰμι ὁ χριστός)" into the Baptist's mouth, and then both independently excerpted words from Isa 40:3 and placed them too in the mouth of the Baptist (none of the Synoptic Gospels

---

[62] Culpepper 1994, 113: "The protest that one cannot literally be born again can be made any time such metaphorical language is used. Here too, Justin need not be citing John 3:3–5." This seems to me to be a stretch.

[63] Thus also Grant 1998, 59; cf. Wartelle 1987, 290; Barnard 173n370.

[64] Koester 1990, 391.

[65] Koester 1990, 391.

has the Baptist citing Isa 40:3 in regards to himself). I find this rather hard to believe.

From a significant battery of texts not considered by Koester, we may also surmise that John's prologue played a formative role in Justin's understanding of Christ as the Word of God, God's Monogenos, "begotten after a peculiar manner" (1 Apol. 22.2; 23.2), and as having become flesh. As I have summarized elsewhere:[66]

> While John's Gospel may not have been the only influence on Justin's 'Logos Christology', the connections with John's presentation are numerous and have convinced many that it was a key source, or the key source, for his understanding of Jesus' eternal deity (1 Apol. 5.4; 10.6; 60.7; 63.15; 2 Apol. 6.3, 4–5) and incarnation (1 Apol. 21.1; 22.2; 23.2; 32.10; Dial. 63.2). Justin uses the word λόγος a few times early in his first apology in the sense of 'reason'. He introduces another meaning, as a title for Jesus Christ as a divine being, in chapter 5, speaking of 'Reason Himself (αὐτοῦ τοῦ Λόγου), who took shape, and became man (μορφωθέντος καὶ ἀνθρώπου γενομένου), and was called Jesus Christ' (1 Apol. 5.4). This certainly recalls the Prologue of the Fourth Gospel, where Jesus Christ is called ὁ λόγος, and specifically it recalls John 1:14 (καὶ ὁ λόγος σὰρξ ἐγένετο), the first time the title is used in connection with the incarnation.[67] Justin elsewhere refers to this Word as divine (θεῖοις, 1 Apol. 10.6), as God (θεός, 1 Apol. 63.15), both reminiscent of John 1:1, ἐν ἀρχῇ ἦν ὁ λόγος...καὶ θεὸς ἦν ὁ λόγος. Justin describes the Logos as τῷ παρὰ θεοῦ Λόγῳ (1 Apol. 60.7), the Fourth Gospel says ὁ λόγος ἦν πρὸς τὸν θεόν (1:1); ὡς μονογενοῦς παρὰ πατρός (1:14); ὁ ὢν παρὰ τοῦ θεοῦ (6:46). In the second apology he speaks similarly, and refers to the creation of the world through the Son (2 Apol. 6.3, 4–5). Justin knows the Logos as God's only proper or rightful Son (ὁ μόνος λεγόμενος κυρίως υἱός, cf. John 1:14, δόξαν ὡς μονογενοῦς παρὰ πατρός, who was with him (συνών, cf. John 1:1, 2 ἦν πρὸς τὸν θεόν)[68] at the beginning (τὴν ἀρχήν, cf. John 1:1, 2, ἐν ἀρχῇ), through whom God created all things (δι᾽ αὐτοῦ πάντα ἔκτισε, cf. John 1:3, πάντα δι᾽ αὐτοῦ ἐγένετο). John is not quoted, but Justin's words are but a paraphrase of the Fourth Gospel's teaching about the Logos from its Prologue. Several times Justin speaks of the Word's becoming man or becoming flesh (e. g., 1 Apol. 21.1; 22.2; 23.2; 32.9, 10; 63.2) in terms which, given Justin's penchant for varying the wording of his sources and of his own expressions, appear as permutations of John 1:1, 13, 14, 18. One example is 1 Apol. 32.10, 'And the first power after God the Father and Lord of all

---

[66] Hill 2006b, 155–156. For a more detailed consideration of this material, see Hill 2004, 316–325. None of this material is treated in Koester 1990.

[67] Wartelle 1987, 244.

[68] Cf. also Dial. 62.4, συνῆν τῷ πατρί.

is the Word, who is also the Son; and of Him we will, in what follows, relate how He took flesh and became man (σαρκοποιηθεὶς ἄνθρωπος γέγονεν)'. Of this passage Wartelle says, 'Ce texte semble bien être écrit avec le souvenir précis du Prologue de l'*Évangile de Jean*'.[69]

References to Christ's being "produced without sexual union" (*1 Apol.* 21.1), literally, "without mixing," i.e., of bloods (cf. *Dial.* 54.2; 63.2), and "becoming man according to His will" (*1 Apol.* 23.2; cf. *Dial.* 3.2) appear to go back to the so-called "Western" reading of John 1:13, or to the Christological interpretation which may have given rise to it, which substitutes the singular pronoun and verb for the plural and therefore understands "who was born, not of bloods nor of the will of the flesh nor of the will of man, but of God" as a reference to Jesus, not to Christians. There is one passage in the *Dialogue* which apparently gives the source of this teaching about the Word becoming flesh:

> For I have proved that he was *monogenes* (μονογενής) to the Father of all things (τῷ πατρὶ τῶν ὅλων), begotten of him in a peculiar manner as Word and Power, and later become man through the virgin, as we have learned from the memoirs.[70] (*Dial.* 105.1, cf., 100.2,4)

Here we seem to have a clear assertion that Justin's source for his beliefs about Christ's pre-existence and his incarnation was (or at least included) the *Apostolic Memoirs*. That is, he claims he is not basing this teaching on oral tradition, on liturgical or catechetical manuals, *testimonia* sources, or, ultimately, on rudimentary gospel harmonies, but on a written text or texts which he considers to belong to these *Memoirs*, books he elsewhere says were written by Jesus' apostles and their followers (*Dial.* 103.8). Because the only *known* writing which could possibly have provided him with this kind of information about the pre-existence of Jesus as "only-begotten" of the Father is the Gospel according to John, it would seem that we have a "smoking-gun" reference to John (John 1:14,18; 3:16). John Pryor has argued, however, that what Justin attributes to the *Memoirs* should be restricted to the mention of the virgin birth alone. He argues that since Justin says he has demonstrated his case, if Justin is relying on John, we should find "evidence of *direct* dependence on John 1 in the argument of the

---

[69] Wartelle 1987, 271.
[70] Μονογενὴς γὰρ ὅτι ἦν τῷ πατρὶ τῶν ὅλων οὗτος, ἰδίως ἐξ αὐτοῦ λόγος καὶ δύναμις [θεοῦ] γεγενημένος, καὶ ὕστερον ἄνθρωπος διὰ τῆς παρθένου γενόμενος, ὡς ἀπὸ τῶν Ἀπομνημονευμάτων ἐμάθομεν, προεδήλωσα (my translation).

earlier chapters."[71] Pryor finds no such evidence, while finding on the other hand that Justin does use Matthew and Luke in chapter 78 in demonstration of Christ's birth from a virgin.

A problem with Pryor's argument, however, is that Justin does not say here that he has "proved" his assertion "from the *Memoirs*," only that he and others have learned something from the memoirs. The plural "we" in, "as we have learned from the *Memoirs*," refers not to Justin and Trypho, and therefore not to what he and Trypho have agreed to, but to Justin and other Christians.[72] What is Justin saying he has proved? The sentence asserts that he has proved "that he was *monogenes* to the Father of all things." Then follow two subordinate clauses describing by adjectival participles this figure who is *monogenes* to the Father as "begotten (γεγεννημένος) of him in a peculiar manner as Word and Power, and later become (γενόμενος) man through the virgin." In saying that he has proved this one to be the Only-begotten to the Father of all things, he is evidently referring to the discussion recorded earlier in chapters 61–62. Neither there nor anywhere else previously in the *Dialogue* has he used the word μονογενής itself,[73] but in 61–62 he "proved" from scripture that

> God begat (γεγέννηκε) before all creatures a Beginning…since he was begotten of the Father by an act of will (ἐκ τοῦ ἀπὸ τοῦ πατρὸς θελήσει γεγεννῆσθαι)…the Word (ὁ Λόγος) of Wisdom who is Himself this God begotten of the Father of all things (ἀπὸ τοῦ πατρὸς τῶν ὅλων γεννηθείς),[74] and Word, and Wisdom, and Power, and the Glory of the Begetter (τοῦ γεννήσαντος)…(61.1–3).[75]

---

[71] Pryor 1992, 156–157 (his emphasis). Recognizing the reference to John are Grant 1998, 58; and Ferguson 2002, 302–303. Hofrichter (1992, 194) acknowledges that the title *monogenes* relates to the prologue of John, but thinks Justin relied on a form of the Johannine prologue which was still independent of the Fourth Gospel. It is hard to see how this could be, if indeed Justin relates it to the *Memoirs*.

[72] ἐμάθομεν in 105.1; συνήκαμεν in 81.3; and νενοήκαμεν in 75.1; 100.1, all refer to something Justin and other Christians have learned, understood, or perceived from the scriptures, but which cannot be attributed to Trypho and his friends.

[73] The word has arisen from the Greek translation of Ps 22:20, but the fact that Justin instinctively understands this as a Christological title is instructive. In *1 Apol.* 23.2 he had said "that Jesus Christ is the only proper Son who has been begotten by God (μόνος ἰδίως υἱὸς τῷ θεῷ γεγέννηται)." This too would seem to reflect John's μονογενής.

[74] Cf. Μονογενής…τῷ Πατρὶ τῶν ὅλων οὗτος in *Dial.* 105.1.

[75] In *Dial.* 62.4 Christ is called the γέννημα of God.

Justin went on to "prove" this by citing texts from the Jewish scriptures, Prov 8:21–36, Gen 1:26,28 and 3:22, not from the *Memoirs*; and indeed, in *Dial.* 63.1 Trypho pronounces that "This point has been proved to me forcibly, and by many arguments, my friend." Since Justin could not, however, prove from the Jewish scriptures that this being, the *monogenes* of the Father, had been born of the virgin of Isa 7:14, he finally resorts to testimonies from Matthew and Luke (though without naming them) in *Dial.* 78. When Justin says he has "proved" these things, then, he seems to have in mind the entire postulation ("that he was *monogenes* to the Father of all things, begotten of him in a peculiar manner as Word and Power, and later become man through the virgin"), which he has proved through the Jewish scriptures and the Gospels of Matthew and Luke. This means that when he says he has *learned* of these things from the *Memoirs* he must also have in mind the entire postulation.

Even if one could restrict Justin's reference to the *Memoirs* to his statement in the second subordinate clause about Christ being born of a virgin, this statement would still likely reflect his knowledge of John. This is because he is not speaking simply about the miraculous birth of a child from a virgin, but about a divine figure, the Only-begotten of the Father, "becoming man through the virgin." The accounts of Jesus' birth in Matthew and Luke speak about a virgin conceiving apart from the participation of a human father; Matthew's goes so far as to say that the child was "of the Holy Spirit" (1:20, ἐκ πνεύματός ἐστιν ἁγίου, cited in *Dial.* 78.3). They do not speak of a pre-existent being becoming man through the virgin. Both the description of this divine personage and the description of his "becoming man" are given in language which elsewhere shows the imprint of John's prologue on Justin's formulations.[76] Even that Justin says he learned from the *Memoirs* about the Only-begotten of God "having become man through the virgin" is still as much as saying that John's Gospel was one of the *Memoirs*.

---

[76] Christ's "becoming man" (ἄνθρωπος γέγονεν) through the virgin in 105.1 is specified as his "having become flesh by God's will, to be born man by the virgin (κατὰ τὴν βουλὴν τοῦ θεοῦ σαρκοποιηθέντα αὐτον...διὰ τῆς παρθένου γεγεννῆσθαι ἄνθρωπον)" in 87.2, reflecting the wording of John 1:14 (σὰρξ ἐγένετο). Cf. "having taken flesh" (σαρκοποιηθείς), *1 Apol.* 32.10. Justin's understanding of this "becoming man" or "being made flesh" had been stipulated in *Dial.* 63.2 as being unique, "since his blood did not spring from the seed of man, but from the will (ἐκ θελήματος) of God," reflecting the Christological application of John 1:13 (cf. *Dial.* 78.2; *1 Apol.* 21.1; 22.2; 23.2; 32.9,10).

The conclusion that John was one of Justin's Apostolic Memoirs, is confirmed by a study of the matters which he refers to as being found in "the Acts which took place under Pontius Pilate," as I have detailed elsewhere.[77] In three places in the *First Apology* (35.9; 38.7; 48.3), Justin refers the emperor and the senate to something he calls "The Acts which took place under Pontius Pilate," as if to a set of records. Despite some attempts to do so, it is apparent that these "acts" cannot be related to later apocryphal Pilate literature, such as the *Acts of Pilate* now contained in the *Gospel of Nicodemus*.[78] Though his Latin loanword in Greek letters (*acta*; ἄκτων) gives these records an official sound, it is impossible to conceive of them as official Roman documents chronicling the activities of Pontius Pilate, for they allegedly narrate Jesus' birth and growth to manhood, his healing of those afflicted with various physical handicaps and diseases and his raising of the dead (*1 Apol.* 48.3), the gainsaying, denial and torture of him by his persecutors, their setting him on a judgment seat, his crucifixion, the soldiers' using nails to affix his hands and feet to the cross, and their casting of lots for his vesture. The many details all but demand that Justin is here referring, by another name, a name tailored to the apologetic occasion, to the gospels in use by him and other Christians in Rome at the time.[79] That the Christian gospels could receive such an appellation is evident both from the title of Luke's second volume, the Acts of the Apostles (which we know was in use at least from the time of Irenaeus), and from comparison with how both Papias and apparently Ignatius speak of the contents of the gospels (see below).[80] That Justin is indeed referring to these gospels under the name of "Acts which took place under Pontius Pilate," may be ascertained from two sets of passages in the *First Apology* and the *Dialogue with Trypho*. In *1 Apol.* 35 and 38, Justin claims that the emperor may read of the fulfillment of Ps 22:16 and 18 ("They pierced my hands and feet" and "They parted my garments among them, and cast lots upon my vesture") in the "Acts which took place (τῶν...γενομένων) under Pontius Pilate." But in *Dial.* 104 he attests to Trypho that the fulfillment of Ps 22:15c–18 "is written to have taken place (γενόμενον) in the *Memoirs*

[77] For the argument in greater detail, see Hill 2007.

[78] See Koester 1990, 42; Wartelle 1987, 273, on 35.9.

[79] Koester (1990, 41–42) argues that these are instead "gospel materials," by which he apparently means materials which pre-date the written texts known as gospels.

[80] See Hill 2007, 90–91.

of his apostles." It is the same with Ps 22:7, "They spake with their lips, they wagged the head, saying, 'Let Him deliver Himself.'" In *1 Apol.* 38 Justin refers the reader to the "Acts" for the fulfillment, while in *Dial.* 101.1–4 he refers Trypho to the *Memoirs of the Apostles.*

The point to make here is that in material which he attributes to the "Acts," Justin includes details known only through the Fourth Gospel. All of these, then, are "redactional" elements unique to John, among known gospels. First, there is Justin's mention of the judgment seat at the trial of Jesus. Justin believes that Isa 58:2, "They now ask of me judgment, and dare to draw near to God," was fulfilled when, during Jesus' trial, the Jews sat Jesus down on the judgment seat (αὐτόν ἐκάθισαν ἐπὶ βήματος, *1 Apol.* 35.4). It is only in John's Gospel that we read of a βῆμα on which Jesus could have sat: "When Pilate heard these words, he brought Jesus out and sat down on the judgment seat at a place called The Pavement, and in Hebrew, Gab'batha." Justin has apparently read ἐκάθισεν of John 19:13 as referring not to Pilate but to Jesus. This is an exegetical tradition known also to the author of the *Gospel of Peter* (the Akhmim Fragment) 3:7, who also has Jesus rather than Pilate seated, but who substitutes the words καθέδραν κρίσεως, seat of judgment, for John's βῆμα.[81]

Then there is Justin's exegesis of Ps 22:16, "They pierced my hands and my feet," which he says has reference to "the nails (ἥλοι) of the cross which were fixed in his hands and feet" (*1 Apol.* 35.7). The Synoptic Gospels do not mention Jesus' being held to the cross by nails (as opposed to rope or leather, which were used with many crucifixion victims); among early gospels, only John and the *Gospel of Peter* mention them. This is, of course, a detail of Christ's crucifixion which might have been widely known without reference to any written narrative. But in *1 Apol.* 38.7 Justin tells his readers specifically that they can learn about this fulfillment of Ps 22:16 from a written source, alluding to the source mentioned in chapter 35, "the Acts which occurred under Pontius Pilate." And, as pointed out above, in *Dial.* 104 Justin claims that the piercing predicted in Ps 22:16 "is written to have taken place in the memoirs of his apostles." This, again, points to the identity of the *Memoirs* and the "Acts," and it means not only that Justin knew

---

[81] On the relationship between the Gospel of John, *Gos. Pet.* and Justin, see Koester 1992, 396–397; Hill 2004, 306–309, 330–332; and on *Gos. Pet.* and Justin, see now Foster 2007, who argues convincingly that Justin was not dependent upon *Gos. Pet.*

a written account which mentioned the nails of the crucifixion, but that such a source was one of the *Memoirs of the Apostles.*

Further details concerning the casting of lots for Jesus' garment, in fulfillment of Ps 11:18 (John 19:24) in *1 Apol.* 35.5,8; 38.4; *Dial.* 97.3, and Justin's mention of Jesus healing some who were afflicted "from their birth" (ἐκ γενετῆς in *Dial.* 69.6, cf. John 9:1,19,20,32), also point to the same conclusion.[82] Justin has relied on John's written gospel for his knowledge of Jesus' crucifixion, and this gospel must have been one of the *Memoirs of the Apostles.*

Walter Bauer contended that "the gospel of John has left no noticeable impression on Justin," and that Justin simply reflected the caution towards this gospel which was typical of the Roman church "right up to almost the end of the second century—a mood that manifests itself through silence and through explicit rejection."[83] On the contrary, when Justin is read carefully, we see that John has figured prominently in Justin's understanding of the divine Christ, the Only-begotten of the Father of all, and his being made flesh, and in Justin's knowledge of the events of Christ's life and his teaching. He is familiar with elements which are scattered throughout the gospel, which also speaks against his being dependent simply upon tradition or upon pre-Johannine sources.

A number of scholars have thought that Justin's words in *Dial.* 103.8, that the *Memoirs* were composed by "Jesus' apostles and their followers," imply his acceptance of four Gospels, two written by apostles, two by followers of apostles.[84] In any case, it seems we must conclude that John was one of the Gospels which Justin calls the *Memoirs of the Apostles.* As such, John was evidently read from, on occasion, in the weekly meetings of Roman Christians for worship on Sundays (*1 Apol.* 67.3) and was expounded like the prophets and other Gospels. Not only does this conclusion follow from the evidence of Justin's writings, it also helps explain how John would soon function alongside the three Synoptic Gospels as the basis of Tatian's *Diatessaron*, how Celsus could associate it with other writings of the great church, how it figured in the correspondence between the churches in Gaul, Asia Minor, and Rome in the ensuing decades, and how by the dawn of

---

[82] Hill 2007, 92–93.
[83] Bauer 1971, 206, 208.
[84] Most recently, Skarsaune 2007, 72. See his list of scholars.

the third century, paintings based on the contents of this Gospel could be found among the earliest surviving forms of Christian art in the Roman catacombs.[85]

All of this tends to show the bankruptcy of Bauer's thesis that an attitude of caution towards John characterized the Roman church of the second century, culminating in the vocal opposition by Gaius in the early third century, who allegedly "sensed in the gospel of John a spirit of heresy with which his Roman-ecclesiastical attitude could not be reconciled."[86] The fairly complex issues surrounding Gaius are beyond the scope of this essay,[87] but it is right to point out that more recent study has called into question whether Gaius ever criticized John at all[88] (though he probably did criticize the Apocalypse). And if Gaius or anyone in Rome in his day leveled the charges against John's Gospel that are attributed by Epiphanius to the "Alogi" (*Pan.* 51.3.1–6)[89] and attributed in medieval Eastern sources to Gaius, it is clear, first of all, that the charges would have had to do with discrepancies with the synoptics, not with a supposed gnosticizing tendency in John.[90]

---

[85] See Hill 2004, 155–166. Among the earliest examples are apparent representations of the raising of Lazarus (John 11); the Samaritan woman at the well (John 4); the healing of the paralytic (John 5:1–9); and the Good Shepherd (John 10:1–19, among other places). That these images cannot simply be attributed to heterodox groups is shown, first, by the fact that there are literary attestations of the popularity of the stories they represent in second-century orthodox sources, second by the fact that the images often appear alongside images from the OT or from other gospel texts—whoever commissioned them also accepted scriptural texts received by the great church in Rome, third by their appearance in portions of the Catacomb of Callistus, which is known to have been owned and administered by the Roman church (Hippolytus, *Trad. ap.* 34; *Ref.* 9.7; 9.12.14; cf. Tertullian, *Apol.* 39.5–6). The catacomb images were part of "the gradually emerging public 'face' of a religion that was developing its identity—and making it visible…the art's content reflected the faith and values of the whole Christian community" (Jensen 2000, 22).

[86] Bauer 1971, 208. Bauer's reading of the situation has been followed by many scholars.

[87] See Hill 2004, 172–204.

[88] Brent 1995; Hill 2004, 183–190.

[89] "Alogi" (unreasoning) is the name Epiphanius says he gives to a group who criticized the Apocalypse and Gospel of John and attributed them to Cerinthus. Several scholars, including Smith (1979) and Culpepper (1994), have concluded that there never was such a group but that Epiphanius was speaking about Gaius and Gaius alone. In my opinion, Brent (1995) is probably closer to the mark, who thinks that Epiphanius is amalgamating criticisms from various quarters and assigning them all to a single group he has constructed for the purpose.

[90] The only possible basis for such a conjecture is the later charge (by Epiphanius) that the Alogi, and then (by the Syrians Ebed Jesu and Dionysius bar Salibi) that Gaius, attributed both the Apocalypse and the Gospel to Cerinthus. The earliest wit-

Secondly, such criticism, if it came from orthodox quarters, clearly proved to be quite ephemeral and ineffective in the face of what must by this time have been a very longstanding practice of using John as an authoritative gospel. The evidence collected above from the Gallican correspondence, the possible witness of Celsus, the witness of both Tatian and now Justin at the midpoint of the second century show how misguided Bauer was in his influential evaluation of the fortunes of John. But the evidence from Justin for the use of John for exposition in worship in Rome in the mid-second century implies that it was no recently accepted gospel, but must have held an important place in Rome and among the orthodox for some time previous.

3.4. *The* Epistula Apostolorum

The author of the *Epistula Apostolorum* is unknown, but he was an orthodox Christian almost certainly writing in Asia Minor during the time of Polycarp, possibly as early as the second decade of the second century, but perhaps more likely in the decade or so preceding 150.[91] The use of John's Gospel in this work is substantial. Schmidt said "in keiner der uns überlieferten Schriften des 2. Jahrhunderts eine derartig starke Benutzung des Johannes-evangeliums hervortritt wie in der vorliegenden."[92] As a rough indicator, the edition in *New Testament Apocrypha* gives fifty-three separate references to John, five to 1 John. This work also helps confirm in a number of ways the relationship of Justin Martyr to John as delineated above.

Because its indebtedness to the written gospel is not really controversial, I shall not take time to establish it here, but rather only illustrate it. As it was with Justin Martyr, the prologue of the Fourth Gospel was a crucial datum for this author's understanding of the incarnation of

---

ness to this attribution (Gaius himself, in Eusebius, *Hist. eccl.* 3.28.2 and Dionysius of Alexandria, in Eusebius, *Hist. eccl.* 7.25.2) concern only the Apocalypse and not the Gospel, and this was most likely based on Cerinthus' alleged chiliasm, not his docetism. The most extensive study of the problem, Smith 1979, 324–327, concludes that Gaius never attributed John to Cerinthus.

[91] For demonstration of these conclusions, see Hill 1999; and Stewart-Sykes 1997.

[92] Schmidt 1919, 224–225. Hengel believes that the *Ep. Apost.* "shows as well that at that time the authorship was already attributed to John, the beloved disciple and apostle" (Hengel 1989, 12; cf. Hengel 1989, 20, 74; Hill, 1997). This identification has to do with the wide use of John and the placement of John at the head of the apostle list in *Ep. Apost.* 11 (a list which also includes Nathanael, who is only mentioned in the Fourth Gospel).

the Word of God. In *Ep. Apost.* 3.2 the author declares that, "the Word
which became flesh [John 1:14] through the holy virgin Mary…was
born not by the lust of the flesh but by the will of God [John 1:13]…"
This shows that he too is familiar with the Christological application of
John 1:13 and shows the importance of John 1:14, "the Word became
flesh" (also *Ep. Apost.* 14.5; 39.16, cf. 21.2). It exemplifies the background for Justin's use of the same Johannine concepts (e.g. *Dial.* 63.2).
The author refers to Jesus' turning the water into wine at the wedding
in Cana (*Ep. Apost.* 5.1–3; John 2:1–11). He knows Jesus' "new commandment; love one another" (John 13:14; *Ep. Apost.* 18.5). Also like
Justin, he knows the Johannine post-resurrection appearance of Jesus
in which he invites his disciples to inspect his crucifixion wounds (*Ep.
Apost.* 11.9; 23.1 cf. John 20:27). When the disciples express wonder-
ment at what they have seen and heard, they are told, "Much more
blessed are they who have not seen and (yet) have believed" (*Ep.
Apost.* 29.6 Copt.), in these circumstances a rather obvious echo of
John 20:29.

The *Epistula* is familiar with passages throughout the Fourth
Gospel, which is good evidence for its acquaintance not with an early
"signs source" or another hypothetical source for the Fourth Gospel,
but the Fourth Gospel itself in the first half of the second century in
Asia Minor. Its deep indebtedness to John (not to mention 1 John
and Revelation) is a problem for the typical Orthodox Johannophobia
Paradigm argument, a problem which certainly cannot be averted by
a claim that it came to him through Gnostic influence.[93] The work
sets itself conscientiously and even aggressively against all docetic tendencies, insisting on Christ's being "in the flesh" not only during the
crucifixion, but also after the resurrection. As an anti-docetic work
which relies heavily on John for its Christology, the *Epistula* is a fitting
indicator of the Asian background for both Justin and Irenaeus, and
also of the milieu of Polycarp and Papias. It is also earlier than any
writing which can confidently be attributed to Heracleon, Ptolemaeus,
or Valentinus.

---

[93] Hillmer's statement (1966, 171), that the work is "strongly influenced by
Gnosticism" seriously overstates the evidence and misses the overt apologetic import
of the work. See Hill 1999, 24; and Hill 2004, 372.

3.5. Polycarp of Smyrna

While there are plausible traces of Polycarp's knowledge of the Johannine gospel in his *Letter to the Philippians* (particularly 5:2; 7:1), there is nothing clear enough to command assent.[94] From this lack of compelling evidence in Polycarp's single, short epistle (or double, if one follows the theory of Harrison),[95] Koester says "it is certain that he did not know the Gospel of John," not when he wrote the letter, and not ever.[96] But clearly, such "certainty" would require us to know a great deal more than the contents of *Philippians* can tell us. On the other hand, since it is commonly, though not unanimously, thought that the letter shows Polycarp's familiarity with 1 John 4:2–3 (possibly 2 John 7 as well) in 7:1,[97] Robert Grant thinks that, "Such an echo of the Epistle suggests that he knew the Gospel as well…"[98] From a purely textual point of view, of course, Polycarp's knowledge of 1 John still says nothing one way or another about his knowledge of the gospel. Grant may be of this opinion because of the difficulty of imagining a situation in which the Johannine letters are known but the gospel is not. In a case such as this, in which we have textual uncertainty, contextual factors may contribute something to a historical judgment of the probabilities on the issue.

These contextual factors have to do with the presence or absence of evidence for the use of John in contemporary or earlier authors which might inform us of the milieu of Polycarp. We have already seen that within Polycarp's lifetime the *Ep. Apost.*, in Asia Minor, makes profound use of this gospel to combat docetism. Earlier material from

---

[94] Here I accept the criticism of Michael Holmes of my own overstatement in Hill 2004, 420. I should not have said that the plausible traces "give us a reasonable assurance that Polycarp indeed knew and valued the Fourth Gospel" at the time when he wrote to the Philippians. They give us, I believe, a reasonable assurance that he *could* have known this gospel at that time, but they are not of a nature to assure us that they could not have come from Polycarp's interaction with the author of the gospel (Holmes 2005, 199) or indeed, from other sources. Holmes' approving citation of Grant's statement that *Phil.* 5.2 shows that "'Polycarp could have quoted from the gospel' but chose not to" (Holmes 2005, 198n42), however, is misleading because Polycarp most often does not "quote" but rather intermingles the words of his sources with his own.

[95] Harrison 1936. Hartog's recent study (2002, 169) determines that this hypothesis "is not necessary at all" and if claimed, the second letter would be best dated before 120 CE.

[96] Koester 1995, 135; cf. Koester 1995, 138.

[97] E.g., Hartog 2002, 189; Holmes (2005, 224) calls it "very probable."

[98] Grant 1997, 37.

Ignatius and Papias' elder is yet to be considered. There are also other second-century materials closely related to Polycarp himself.

One of these is the written account of Polycarp's martyrdom written by one Marcianus. There is a possible Johannine allusion in Polycarp's prayer in 14:2 where he mentions his expectation concerning "the resurrection of eternal life (εἰς ἀνάστασιν ζωῆς αἰωνίου)," recalling John 5:29, εἰς ἀνάστασιν ζωῆς, with the characteristic Johannine αἰώνιος added. In the narrative itself, the author relates how Polycarp's martyrdom was a martyrdom "in accordance with the gospel" (1:1), and marks out a number of coincidences between circumstances surrounding the capture and death of Polycarp, and the accounts of the Lord's passion as recorded in the gospels. In 8:1 Marcianus tells his readers that when "the hour came" (τῆς ὥρας ἐλθούσης, cf. the climactic ἐλήλυθεν ἡ ὥρα, John 17:1) for Polycarp's departure, "they set him on an ass (cf. John 12:14, etc.), and led him into the city on a 'great Sabbath day'" (John 19:31). John's is the only account to mention "the great Sabbath" (John 19:31) in connection with Jesus' death.[99] The fact that the many points of correspondence are spread out in more than one gospel, and the fact that their recognition depends on his readers' familiarity with the gospel events in question, suggests that the written gospels, including John, are being used in the Smyrnaean community at the time of Polycarp's death.

Irenaeus' testimony, repeated in at least three publications over a period of many years, is that Polycarp saw, heard and was ordained by John the apostle.[100] In one place he claimed he could remember how Polycarp "reported his intercourse with John and with the others who had seen the Lord, how he remembered their words..." (in Eusebius, *Hist. eccl.* 5.20.6). His description of Polycarp's relationship with apostles is laced with Johannine language, though it contains no actual reference to Polycarp using the Fourth Gospel. But in *Adv. haer.* 4.27–32 Irenaeus repeats and elaborates the oral, anti-Marcionite teaching of an unnamed elder, a disciple of apostles, which he had memorized. Many factors combine to show that this disciple of apostles is in fact

---

[99] Also mentioned in chapter 21 and in the *Martyrium Pionii* 2.1; 3.6. See Buschmann 1998, 167–169.

[100] Irenaeus, *Adv. haer.* 3.3.4; *Letter to Florinus* and *Letter to Victor* in Eusebius, *Hist. eccl.* 5.20.6 and 5.24.16, respectively.

Polycarp.[101] There is one place in this material which reflects the elder's knowledge of the Fourth Gospel. In *Adv. haer.* 4.31.1, while defending the saints of the old covenant against Marcionite slander, Irenaeus cites the words of the elder, who said that we should "'give thanks concerning them to God, because at the coming of our Lord he forgave them their sins.' For he also used to say that they gave thanks for and rejoiced in our salvation." Irenaeus' use of John 8:56 and its interpretation in the earlier part of book 4 show that this is an allusion to Jesus' words in John 8:56, "Your father Abraham rejoiced to see my day, and he saw it and was glad."[102] The import is that Irenaeus had learned his interpretation of John 8:56 from the apostolic elder, Polycarp. This instruction probably took place sometime between about 140 and 154.

An excellent, though in the nature of the case not fully conclusive, argument can be made that the so-called *Epistle to Diognetus* is actually the transcript of a speech given by Polycarp before a Smyrnaean nobleman named Diognetus.[103] If this work is by Polycarp, the use of John in his teaching at some point near the middle of the second century is manifest.[104] Just one pair of allusions must suffice here. The author speaks of God sending his Son, and "when he sent him, he did so as one loving, not judging (ἔπεμψεν ὡς ἀγαπῶν, οὐ κρίνων)" (7:5), and later says, "For God loved (ἠγάπησε) men...to them he sent his one and only Son (πρὸς οὓς ἀπέστειλε τὸν υἱὸν αὐτοῦ τὸν μονογενῆ)" (10:2). The conceptions and the language are surely indebted to John 3:16–17, "For God so loved (ἠγάπησεν) the world that he gave his only Son (τὸν υἱὸν τὸν μονογενῆ)...For God sent (ἀπέστειλεν) the Son into the world, not to condemn (οὐ...ἵνα κρίνῃ) the world, but that the world might be saved through him" (cf. John 12:47; 1 John 4:9).

Thus, while judgments may continue to differ on the likelihood that Polycarp knew the Fourth Gospel at the time of writing to the Philippians (we can, of course, not be "certain" that he did or did not know it), there is other evidence to make it extremely likely that he did in fact use this gospel in the course of his ministry. And even if one

---

[101] For the evidence and the significance of the identification, see Beatrice 1990; and Hill 2006a, 7–94.

[102] Hill 2006a, 61–64.

[103] Beatrice 1990; Hill 2006a, 97–165. For the archeological proof of a Smyrnaean city ruler named Diognetus and his grandson of the same name in the time of Polycarp, see Hill 2006a, 160–165.

[104] For the evidence, see Hill 2004, 361–366.

chooses to reject all this evidence, if the author of the *ad Diognetum*
is someone else, if Irenaeus' apostolic presbyter is someone else, these
sources and the allusions in the *Martyrdom* remain as witnesses to the
influence of John among the orthodox, all most likely in Asia Minor,
in the period of Polycarp's life. These factors, along with analyses of
the *Apology* of Aristides, the letters of Ignatius and the fragments of
Papias (see below) would at least constitute contextual factors which
should help the historian to render a judgment on the probability that
Polycarp knew John's Gospel at the time he wrote to the Philippians.

3.6. *Aristides of Athens*

Almost always overlooked in discussions of the early testimony to John
is the apologist Aristides of Athens. The *Apology* of Aristides survives
entire in a fourth- or fifth-century Syriac translation, and in part in
a fifth-century Armenian version (chapters 1–2), two fourth-century
Greek fragments (chapters 5.3–6; 15.6–16.1) found at Oxyrhynchus,
and a very valuable Greek paraphrase of almost the entire work incorporated into the tenth-century *Life of Barlaam and Joasaph* 26–27 by
one Euthymius in Bithynia.[105] Eusebius states that this apology was
presented to Hadrian (*Hist. eccl.* 4.3.3), and this is borne out by the
title in the Syriac version, and the address of the Armenian.[106] This
probably occurred when Hadrian visited Athens in 125 and was there
initiated into the Eleusinian mysteries.

As is typical of Christian apologists of the early period, Aristides
does not cite his written authorities explicitly to unbelievers who

---

[105] See Wolff 1937. On the relative accuracy of the Syriac and the Greek of *Barlaam*,
the Greek fragments of an ancient recension discovered at Oxyrhynchus have provided a trustworthy guide. After a close comparison with the first of these fragments
Grenfell and Hunt (*Oxyrhynchus Papyri* 15, no. 1778) reported that the Syriac version tends to expand, *Barlaam* to contract, but that each is essentially faithful to the
original. Milne (1924, 75) affirmed this conclusion after studying the second fragment,
finding in the Syriac eight amplifications and two omissions: "On the whole, however,
the Syriac gives a tolerably close rendering, although it does not appear to reproduce
the terseness and austerity of the Greek."

[106] The address in the Syriac goes on to mention Antoninus Pius (138–161 CE).
Grant (1998, 38–39) suggested an original apology to Hadrian was reworked and
presented again to Antoninus Pius. Pouderon, Pierre and Outtier (2000, 181–182),
however, show that the Armenian and the Syriac go back to a common Eastern redaction, and argue that because the Armenian is consistent in referring to Hadrian in
both the title and the address, the reference to Antoninus is due to the Syrian scribe's
confusion.

did not hold them to be authoritative. And yet, it seems clear that Aristides knows a plurality of authoritative Christian gospels (15.1 Greek; 2.4 Syriac). He makes bold to exhort the emperor to *read* about the Christian teaching in what he calls "the gospel."

Greek of *Barlaam*	Syriac
15.1 And if you would read, O King, you may judge the glory of his presence from the holy gospel writing,[107] as it is called among themselves.	2.4 This is taught in the gospel, as it is called, which a short time ago was preached among them; and you also if you will read therein, may perceive the power which belongs to it.

Aristides here refers to "the gospel," which, though it may have been "preached" among Christians, is here in about 125 assumed to be available in written form and known by the name of "gospel" to Christians. The singular "gospel," as we know from a period even later than this, can be used when the witness of plural gospels is in view,[107] and this seems to be the case here, as Aristides will mention details of the life of Christ which cannot have come from any single gospel known to us.

There are excellent reasons for thinking that one of the gospels which Aristides had in mind was the Gospel according to John. In a very brief catalogue of biographical facts about Jesus, Aristides states that Jesus "was pierced by the Jews, and he died and was buried" (2.5 Syriac).[109] John's is the only account of the crucifixion known up to this time to record the piercing (John 19:34).[110] Of course, a detail such as this could have been learned by tradition and not have come directly from any written gospel.[111] Yet two factors should be borne in mind. First, apart from possibly the allusion to Zech 12:10, "when they look on me,

---

[107] Ἐκ τῆς παρ' αὐτοῖς καλουμένης εὐαγγελικῆς ἁγίας γραφῆς. The word ἁγίας, as it is not attested in the Syriac or Armenian, is probably not original (Pouderon, Pierre and Outtier 2000, 176).

[108] See *Dial.* 10.2; 100.1; Irenaeus, *Adv. haer.* 3.5.1; 3.11.7. On the use of the singular "gospel" in *Dial.* 10.2; 100.1, Barnard (1967, 57) says, "This seems to refer to a *collection* of written memoirs as is the case with Irenaeus and many subsequent writers."

[109] The agreement of the Syriac and Armenian shows ἐκκεντέω must have been in the original, though the Greek of *Barlaam* has simply "through the cross" (15.1). Pouderon, Pierre and Outtier (2000, 191) conclude that the author who adapted the apology to his new context in *Barlaam* ignored the verb ἐκκεντέω because "le mot était ignoré des formules de foi en usage au xᵉ siècle" when he worked.

[110] Pouderon, Pierre and Outtier (2000, 191) say that this "évoquit nécesairement Jn 19,37."

[111] Or from a post-gospel testimonia source, such as Justin may have used.

on him whom they have pierced" in Rev 1:7, the piercing of Jesus is evidently only attested in works which are much later than and dependent on the Fourth Gospel (*Sib. Or.* 8.296; Apollinarius of Hierapolis; Irenaeus, *Adv. haer.* 3.22.2; 4.33.2; 4.35.3; *Acts of John* 97; Clement, *Exc. Theod.* 61.3).[112] Second, and most significantly, this reference to a detail recorded only in John occurs in chapter 2[113] of the apology, in precisely the context in which Aristides informs the reader that his information about Jesus comes from "the gospel, as it is called." And this is not a reference to the unwritten, oral gospel proclamation, for this gospel is something which he enjoins the emperor to read for himself to ascertain whether what Aristides is saying is true.[114] Presumably, if the emperor could not find an account of the piercing in this "gospel," Aristides' truthfulness would be in jeopardy. There is thus every reason to believe that here Aristides is repeating a distinctive aspect of the crucifixion of Jesus which he had read in a gospel which his words suggest would have been available in Athens for the emperor to peruse if he so chose.

A familiarity with the Fourth Gospel seems to underlie another portion of chapter 2. Here Aristides speaks of Jesus Christ as "having come down from heaven" (ἀπ' οὐρανοῦ καταβάς). This kind of language is not found in the Synoptic Gospels but is very Johannine, echoing, as Titus Nagel points out, two Johannine passages, John 3:13, ὁ ἐκ τοῦ οὐρανοῦ καταβάς, and John 6:38, ὅτι καταβέβηκα ἀπὸ τοῦ

---

[112] Cf. Justin, who several times cites Zech 12:10, the text which John 19:37 says was fulfilled by this event (ὄψονται εἰς ὃν ἐξεκέντησαν). The verb used in the most common LXX tradition (κατορχέομαι) does not mean "pierced" but "treated despitefully."

[113] The editor who incorporated the apology into *Barlaam* transferred this section to a later part of his dialogue, now numbered chapter 15. The Syriac and Armenian have the original placement.

[114] The information Aristides gives in chapter 2 cannot all have come from only one of our gospels (canonical or non-canonical). He mentions that Jesus was confessed as Son of God Most High (*Barlaam* ὁ υἱὸς τοῦ θεοῦ τοῦ ὑψιστοῦ), a title found only in Mark 5:7 and Luke 1:32; 8:28; not in Matthew or John. He then mentions Jesus' descent from heaven and birth through a Hebrew virgin. The descent from heaven is explicit only in John. The virgin birth is recounted only by Matthew and Luke. Then comes the mention of the piercing, the burial (not in *Barlaam*), the resurrection after three days, and the ascension to heaven. The "piercing," if it comes from a written gospel, must come from John and the ascension could come from any but Mark (even from Mark if he had the long ending, 16:19). At minimum this seems to require Luke and John, but it is hard to exclude Matthew, and even Mark cannot be ruled out. All this Aristides refers to "the gospel," which he alleges the emperor can read.

οὐρανοῦ.[115] Aristides also mentions in the same context Jesus' "assuming flesh" (σάρκα ἀνέλαβε).[116] While this also could be explained as a Christian commonplace, it is highly relevant that this statement too occurs in the section in which Aristides encourages the emperor to "read" about these things in "the gospel." And the only gospel to contain such language is, of course, the Gospel according to John 1:14. As he repeats in chapter 16,

Greek of *Barlaam*	Syriac
And that you may know, O King, that in saying these things I do not speak at my own instance, if you deign to look into the writings of the Christians, you will find that I state nothing beyond the truth.	Take, then, their writings, and read therein, and lo! you will find that I have not put forth these things on my own authority, nor spoken thus as their advocate; but since I read in their writings I was fully assured of these things as also of things which are to come.

In addition to the above evidence, there are two portions of the Greek of *Barlaam*, not reflected in the Syriac, which contain probable allusions to John. The author says in chapter 15 that God made all things "through the only-begotten Son (ἐν υἱῷ μονογενεῖ) and the Holy Spirit," which seems, in part, ostensibly based on the theology of John 1:3,14 and is reminiscent of Justin. This Greek version also contains a reference to Jesus' voluntary death on the cross (διὰ σταυροῦ θανάτου ἐγεύσατο ἑκουσίᾳ βουλῇ), which may well be based on John 10:17,18. We may conclude from a comparison with the Oxyrhynchus Greek fragments that there are places where the Syriac omits something from the original and where the Greek of *Barlaam* preserves the original better than the Syriac. Thus it is quite possible that these reflections of the teaching of John go back to the original, but lacking support from the Syriac, we cannot be entirely confident of this.

Aristides the Athenian philosopher emphasizes the textual authorities of Christianity in a way which is quite remarkable for the time and for the newly flourishing apologetic "genre." It is highly significant, then, that John's Gospel was apparently known to him and included in the designation "gospel," referring to a written account or accounts

---

[115] Nagel 2000, 118–119.

[116] In the Syriac, "And it is said that God came down from heaven, and from a Hebrew virgin assumed and clothed himself with flesh." Pouderon, Pierre and Outtier (2000, 189) indicate that the Armenian has "prendre chair" (*marmin arnul*).

of Jesus the Messiah in common use among Christians. It is no less significant that Aristides seems to imply, as Justin will later do, that the Christian written "gospel" was so readily accessible that the emperor could be expected, at least rhetorically, to be able to secure a copy of his own.

3.7. *Ignatius of Antioch*

J.N. Sanders illustrates a tendency among some scholars to want it both ways with regard to Ignatius and John when he states, "one cannot say with any certainty that Ignatius knew our Fourth Gospel,"[117] and later in the same publication uses Ignatius to exemplify "the reluctance shown by the early Church to accept the Fourth Gospel as Scripture."[118] But how can Ignatius have been reluctant to accept a gospel he never knew? If we judge that Ignatius did not know the Fourth Gospel, we at least cannot at the same time use him as evidence of orthodox Johannophobia. Since many have found as little or less evidence of Mark and Luke and scarcely if any more of Matthew in Ignatius, the evidence for orthodox Johannophobia will be about the same as for orthodox Marcophobia, Lukophobia, and Mattheophobia.

Regarding Ignatius, the goals of investigation and questions of method become particularly acute, though in the history of research such goals and questions have often operated at the level of unstated assumption. Many scholars are seeking implicitly or explicitly to answer the question of "direct literary dependence" and to answer that question will only accept what they call "conclusive proof."[119] Usually this seems to mean explicit or exact quotation, in forms that cannot be paralleled anywhere else.[120] If the only question worth answering is that of direct literary dependence, if all we are interested in is conclusive proof, and if the test employed is exact quotation of a substantial amount of unique Johannine material, the results will be predictably negative. Hence, many have pronounced a lack of "conclusive proof" of Ignatius' use of the Gospel of John.

But in the nature of the case, given Ignatius' letters are what they are—letters written not only "on the road" but in captivity and surely

---

[117] Sanders 1943, 14.
[118] Sanders 1943, 85.
[119] Sanders 1943, 14; Haenchen 1984, 7; cf. Schoedel 1985, 185.
[120] Rathke 1967, 39–40.

apart from whatever "writing library" he might have had in Antioch—
perhaps the question of direct literary dependence, the ideal of conclusive proof, and the standard of exact quotation are not very realistic.
Even under the best of conditions, exact citation of a substantial
amount of earlier text may not have been Ignatius' ideal.[121] But in
Ignatius' circumstances setting up these standards amounts to stack-
ing the deck in favor of a particular conclusion.

In my 2004 monograph, I noted six places in the letters of Ignatius
which potentially show his knowledge of John's Gospel. Even more
recently Paul Foster has treated the question of Ignatius' possible use
of NT writings, including John.[122] He is consciously building on Inge's
treatment of a century earlier[123] and comes to more reserved conclusions than his predecessor. He examines only the instances which Inge
thought showed the most probable contact with John. Foster contrasts
his and Schoedel's negative conclusions with my own more positive
ones, though he quite fairly points out that we really have two different
goals: his is to determine whether Ignatius "uses John" in his letters,
mine to determine Ignatius' knowledge of John. "Use" here seems to
assume a conscious and direct borrowing of Johannine material.

Earlier in his essay, Foster had stated that the inaccuracy in
Ignatius' references to earlier sources "is due to the pragmatic factors surrounding the composition of his epistles," noting also that "It
is highly unlikely that Ignatius had access to the texts he cited while
being taken to Rome."[124] But when assessing the Johannine parallels
the angle of approach seems to change. Inge had concluded that "on
the whole direct literary dependence seems much the most probably
hypothesis." Foster dissents from Inge's conclusion here, but in dis-
senting, Foster seems to be accepting Inge's framing of the question as
that of "direct literary dependence." Here, despite what had been said
earlier,[125] Foster's negative assessment seems to bring in the idea again

---

[121] Whittaker 1989.

[122] Foster 2005.

[123] Inge 1905.

[124] Foster 2005, 161. On this observation by earlier scholars, see Hill 2004, 426–
427.

[125] Cf. also Foster 2005, 165, writing of Ignatius' knowledge of 1 Cor 1:18,20 in *Eph.*
18:1, "Hence, once again, there is an inexact quotation of material from 1 Corinthians,
probably reflecting the fact that while being transported in Roman custody Ignatius
did not have access to a copy of 1 Corinthians. None the less, he knew its contents
well enough to paraphrase the epistle at certain points, at times with quite a high correspondence with its actual vocabulary."

of Ignatius writing his letters with a copy of John's Gospel in front of him, checking to make sure he has copied the words correctly.

3.7.1. Romans 7:2

The first of the two passages Foster cites is *Rom.* 7:2:

> My lust has been crucified, and there is no fire of material love in me; but water living (ὕδωρ δὲ ζῶν) and speaking in me, speaking to me from within, "Come to the Father (Δεῦρο πρὸς τὸν πατέρα)."

Because Ignatius' reference to "living water" concerns spiritual water and not physical water, he is certainly closer to John 4:10 and 7:38 than to the use of the phrase in Hellenistic literature generally or in *Didache* 7:1–2, where it simply means "running water."[126] These other parallels, then, are of no real value. The fact that this "living water" seems to stand for the Spirit, also signifies an element in common with John.[127] For Foster, however, the Johannine parallel is virtually neutralized by noting a parallel with *Odes of Solomon* 11:6–7, which also speaks of living water speaking: "And speaking waters touched my lips from the fountain of the Lord generously. And so I drank and became intoxicated, from the living water that does not die." This provides a parallel to the notion of living water also "speaking," a concept not present in John. Few, however, would posit that Ignatius is actually dependent upon the *Odes*, which most seem to date later than Ignatius,[128] but both could be indebted to ideas not uncommon in the Syrian Christian milieu. This certainly does not rule out Ignatius' knowledge of John as a source for the notion of the Spirit as "living water,"[129] though this short phrase by itself seems quite insufficient to allow us to conclude that it reflects such knowledge.

---

[126] So also Schoedel 1985, 185.

[127] The fourth-century author of the long recension wrote ἀλλάμενον, "welling up," instead of λαλοῦν, "speaking," which would be a rather more clear indication of indebtedness to John 4:14 ("but whoever drinks of the water that I shall give him will never thirst; the water that I shall give him will become in him a spring of water welling up [ἀλλάμενου] to eternal life"). Lightfoot in fact regarded ἀλλάμενον as the most probable reading, suggesting that the λαλοῦν "might very easily suggest itself to a scribe from the following λέγον" (Lightfoot 1981, II:2:225). Lightfoot points to the popularity of the motif of the "living waters welling up," from John 4:14, later in the second century among Naassenes, Sethians, and in Justin the Gnostic, as referred to in Hippolytus, *Ref.* 5.9,19,27.

[128] For the various views on this see Hill 2004, 380–383.

[129] Note again the allusions to the living water of John 4:14; 7:38 in *EpV&L* and Irenaeus cited above.

In their treatments of *Rom.* 7:2, Inge, Schoedel, and Foster all stop with the term "living water" which Ignatius says spoke in him.[130] But what the inner voice urged Ignatius, to "Come to the Father' (Δεῦρο πρὸς τὸν πατέρα), that is, to come to the Father not by way of conversion but by way of death,[131] also has strong links to Johannine thought and language. The construction πρὸς τὸν πατέρα occurs sixteen times in the NT, of which ten are in the Johannine gospel and two in 1 John.[132] In the Apostolic Fathers, the phrase occurs only once more, in *1 Clem.* 62:2, where it refers to "thoughts toward the Father." None of the non-Johannine instances uses the phrase to depict belief in "coming" πρὸς τὸν πατέρα through death, as Ignatius does. On the other hand, of the ten uses of the phrase πρὸς τὸν πατέρα in John, eight (13:1; 14:12, 28; 16:10,17,28; 20:17*bis*) refer to Jesus' going or ascending πρὸς τὸν πατέρα in connection with his death and resurrection (the two epistolary passages refer to Jesus' heavenly presence "with the Father").[133] For instance, John 16:28, "I came from the Father and have come into the world; again, I am leaving the world and going to the Father (πρὸς τὸν πατέρα)." John also contains Jesus' unique claim in 14:6 that his followers can come πρὸς τὸν πατέρα only through him. Thus it is not simply the phrase, but the idea of coming to the Father through the instrumentality of death, which links Ignatius to John's teaching.

Thus in *Rom.* 7:2, the living water speaking in Ignatius and commanding him to endure to the end and so come to the Father through death, marries two Johannine concepts expressed in Johannine terms. But one should not stop with *Rom.* 7:2 and fail to see that the immediately following verse contains further Johannine parallels. It is even possible that Ignatius' mention of the Johannine "living water" has triggered the thought of the Johannine "living bread" (ὁ ἄρτος ὁ ζῶν, John 6:51) which he now goes on to reference.

---

[130] Kieffer (1992, 2236), on the other hand, characterizes the connection, "Si on reçoit de Jésus l'eau vive qu'il a promise en Jn 4,10 et 7,38, on peut le suivre chez le Père."

[131] For Ignatius' expectation of "attaining God" through death, see Hill 2001, 85–90.

[132] The four remaining passages are Luke's two references to the prodigal son's return "to my father," in each case followed by a pronoun (Luke 15:18,20); and two references in Ephesians which speak of access "to the father" in prayer (2:18; 3:15).

[133] On the material in John see de Boer 2005.

3.7.2. Romans 7:3

> I take no pleasure in the food of corruption (τροφῇ φθορᾶς), nor in plea-
> sures of this life. I desire the bread of God (ἄρτον θεοῦ), that is, the flesh
> (σάρξ) of Christ who is of the seed of David; for drink I desire his blood
> (πόμα θέλω τὸ αἷμα αὐτοῦ), which is incorruptible love.

Ignatius' words in these two statements are very reminiscent of the
"Bread of Life" dialogue in John 6:22–58. Ignatius says he takes no
pleasure in the "food of corruption" (τροφῇ φθορᾶς); Jesus says in
John 6:27 not to work for "food which perishes" (τὴν βρῶσιν τὴν
ἀπολλυμένην)—the same concept but expressed in different words, as
we might expect from someone who did not have a copy of the gospel
in front of him but who was familiar with its teaching.

Ignatius says what he desires instead is "the bread of God, that is,
the flesh of Christ" (cf. "the bread [of God]" in *Eph.* 5:2); Jesus allu-
sively calls himself "the bread of God" in John 6:33. John 6:33 represent the only occurrence of the term ἄρτος θεοῦ in the NT or the
LXX.[134] It is possible, of course, that Ignatius is familiar with such a
phrase simply from common Christian Eucharistic theology, quite
apart from a familiarity with John's Gospel. But a few things should
be kept in mind.

First, Ignatius' words here do not occur in a Eucharistic context (cf.
Phld. 4:1; *Smyrn.* 7:1) but a martyrological one. Also, Ignatius specifies
that by the bread of God he means the flesh of Christ. John 6:51–56
repeatedly identify the living bread, the bread that Jesus gives, with
the σάρξ of Jesus. The synoptic and Pauline passages which recount
the Last Supper all identify the bread of that supper with Jesus' σῶμα,
not with his σάρξ. After mentioning his desire for the flesh of Christ,
Ignatius says he desires Christ's blood. Jesus in John 6:53 pronounces
that those who do not eat his flesh and drink his blood do not have
eternal life. This pairing of the concepts of eating Jesus' flesh and
drinking his blood, repeated four times in John 6:53–56, is also unique
to John among the gospels.

Schoedel, who comments on some but not all of these links between
Ignatius and John, believes they do not add up to "literary depen-
dence." If he is speaking of direct literary dependence, I would agree.
Ignatius was certainly not copying from a text of John's Gospel as

---

[134] In both John and Ignatius both nouns are anarthrous (Kieffer 1992, 2236).

he wrote to the Romans. But "indirect literary dependence" does not seem to be considered by Schoedel.

It seems we must say that Ignatius is familiar with Jesus' Bread of Life discourse in some form. Did this come to him through only oral means, or through a lost written source used by the author of the Fourth Gospel? If this were the only portion of John Ignatius knew, we might have to leave the question open. But we have seen already from *Rom.* 7:2 that Ignatius also seems familiar with other portions of John's Gospel outside the Bread of Life discourse. The greater the number of credible points of familiarity with disparate portions of the gospel, the more difficult, it seems to me, it is to explain them all on some basis other than knowledge of the Fourth Gospel. And there is yet more material to consider.

3.7.3. Philadelphians *7:1*
The other Ignatian text treated by Foster is *Philadelphians* 7:1.

> For even if some wished to deceive me according to the flesh, neverthe-less the Spirit, being from God, is not deceived. For it "knows whence it comes and whither it goes (οἶδεν γὰρ πόθεν ἔρχεται καὶ ποῦ ὑπάγει)," and it proves the secret things.

This has a clear and very close resemblance to Jesus' words in John 3:8, "The wind [or spirit] (πνεῦμα) blows where it wills, and you hear the sound of it, but you do not know whence it comes or whither it goes (οὐκ οἶδας πόθεν ἔρχεται καὶ ποῦ ὑπάγει); so it is with every one who is born of the Spirit" (cf. also 8:14). Here would seem to be just what the seekers for certainty of direct literary dependence are looking for. Five exact same words, πόθεν ἔρχεται καὶ ποῦ ὑπάγει, in exactly the same sequence, including two verbs in exactly the same form, same tense, voice, mood, person, number.[135] In addition to the five-word phrase, each author has a form of the word οἶδα, John in Jesus' denial that his opponents "know" whence the Spirit comes and whither it goes, and Ignatius in an affirmation that the Spirit itself does "know" whence it comes and whither it goes. Each author also

---

[135] Foster (2005, 166) argues for Ignatius' knowledge of 1 Cor 4:4 (ἀλλ᾽ οὐκ ἐν τούτῳ δεδικαίωμαι) in *Rom.* 5.1 (ἀλλ᾽ οὐ παρὰ τοῦτο δεδικαίωμαι), on the basis of a five-word correspondence where "only two of the words agree exactly," concluding, "There can be little doubt that Ignatius is drawing, from memory, on the wording of 1 Corinthians."

relates the subject of this phrase to nothing else than the Spirit of God. Moreover, one would certainly have to place this phrase in the category of Johannine "redactional material" as it is distinctive to John among all known, early gospels. Not only this, but it relates to a particularly Johannine theme which runs through the Fourth Gospel,[136] the theme of the mystery of "whence Jesus is" and "whither he is going" (cf. John 7:27–28; 8:14,23; 9:29–30; 13:3; 19:9). Distinctive redactional material is just what Koester, Hillmer, and Bellinzoni require before acknowledging dependence upon a NT source.

In spite of this, some have found it easier to believe that Ignatius got the phrase from an unknown Gnostic source,[137] or from an unwritten and otherwise unknown saying of Jesus,[138] or, as Koester conjectures, from a "traditional theological maxim... perhaps deriving from a liturgical context."[139] For Foster, the high level of verbal correspondence is not yet convincing because of "the way the phrase is used in a manner so different from the Johannine context."[140] But is the manner so different? True, Ignatius is not talking about the mysterious working of the Spirit in regeneration, as Jesus is in John. Ignatius is instead talking about the Spirit's work in himself when he uttered "inspired" words to the Philadelphians when in their midst, words which, as he later learned, were prophetic in nature, seeming to presuppose divine foreknowledge of the church's situation. When recalling this event to the Philadelphians and wishing to attribute the words he spoke that day to the divine Spirit, he simply describes that Spirit with a phrase which Jesus used with reference to the Spirit, memorably and uniquely in the Gospel of John. The two contexts are different, though not so entirely different. It is not as though the being which "knows whence it comes and whither it goes" is a snake, a centurion, or a runaway

---

[136] Other aspects of this theme were picked up by the author of the Egerton Gospel (1 verso 20); see Hill 2004, 304.

[137] Wetter 1917–1918. The "parallels" in Marcus the Valentinian in Irenaeus, *Adv. haer.* 1.21.5 and in the *Exc. Theod.* 78 used by Wetter and cited by Hillmer (1966, 11–12), besides being much later, differ from both John and Ignatius to a wide extent. The phrase found in John and Ignatius hardly qualifies to be a called a "technical gnostic phrase," as Hillmer would have it. See also Nagel 2000, 241–243.

[138] Von der Goltz, as mentioned by Richardson 1935, 74.

[139] Koester 1990, 258; cf. Sanders 1943, 13; Hillmer 1966, 12, "an element of the free tradition regarding the coming of the Saviour and his departure familiar to both writers."

[140] Foster 2005, 184. Also impressed by the differences in context is Mitchell 2006, 32.

slave; Ignatius is talking, like Jesus in John, about the Holy Spirit. And in any case, I have trouble seeing why this amount of difference in context should matter very much.[141] Robert Grant's words about Ignatius and Paul are equally applicable to Ignatius and John and bear repeating: "he can take Pauline expressions and use them in contexts of his own. Such usage is hardly surprising. Ignatius, in fact, could not have used Pauline expressions in Pauline contexts."[142]

Schoedel finds in *Phld.* 7:1 "the strongest possibility in Ignatius of a dependence directly on the Fourth Gospel" but in the end is non-committal because of "the absence of other positive evidence of such dependence."[143] I find myself in disagreement with him about the supposed absence of positive evidence. But again it is worth noting that Schoedel appears to be thinking in terms of direct literary dependence, which ought to be dismissed as a red herring. It seems hard to deny that the best explanation for the expression in *Phld.* 7:1 is that Ignatius was familiar with the Gospel according to John. But *Romans* 7:2,3 and *Philadelphians* 7:1 are still not the only passages worthy of consideration in Ignatius.

3.7.4. Magnesians 7:1–8:2
In *Magnesians* 7:1–2 Ignatius writes,

> Just as then the Lord did nothing without the Father (ὁ κύριος ἄνευ τοῦ πατρὸς οὐδὲν ἐποίησεν), being united with Him (ἡνωμένος ὤν), whether through himself or through the apostles, so you do nothing without the bishop and the presbyters...Let all run together as unto one temple of God, as to one altar, to one Jesus Christ, who came forth from one Father, remaining with the one, and returned (to him) (τὸν ἀφ᾽ ἑνὸς πατρὸς προελθόντα καὶ εἰς ἕνα ὄντα καὶ χωρήσαντα).

Shortly thereafter, in *Magnesians* 8:2, he continues,

> On this account they [i.e., the prophets] were persecuted, being inspired by his grace, to persuade the disobedient that God is one, who manifested himself through Jesus Christ his Son, who is his Word proceeding from silence (λόγος ἀπὸ σιγῆς προελθών), who in all respects pleased the one who sent him (ὃς κατὰ πάντα εὐηρέστησεν τῷ πέμψαντι αὐτόν).

---

[141] I dare say that one could find as much difference between the contexts of Paul in 1 Cor 4:4 and Ignatius in *Rom.* 5:1, though Foster regards Ignatius as indebted to Paul at this point none the less.

[142] Grant 1963, 324.

[143] Schoedel 1985, 206.

Here again we seem to have a cluster of Johannine allusions. What draws our attention first here is the apparent double allusion to a single passage, John 8:28–29. That Jesus, negatively, did nothing without the Father and, positively, always did what was pleasing to the Father are concepts distinctive to the depiction of Jesus in John's Gospel. The denial is repeated three times in John (5:19,30;[144] 8:28), and the affirmation appears only in 8:29; the full expression occurs thus only in 8:28–29.

> So Jesus said, "When you have lifted up the Son of man, then you will know that I am he, and that I do nothing on my own authority (ἀπ' ἐμαυτοῦ ποιῶ οὐδέν) but speak thus as the Father (ὁ πατήρ) taught me.[29] And he who sent me is with me (καὶ ὁ πέμψας με μετ' ἐμοῦ ἐστιν); he has not left me alone, for I always do what is pleasing to him (ὅτι ἐγὼ τὰ ἀρεστὰ αὐτῷ ποιῶ πάντοτε)."

Ignatius invokes the concept but splits it up, so to speak, so that the full concept may seem to act as an *inclusio* for the section *Magn.* 7:1–8:2. When the echoes of John 8:28–29 are placed together we find six of the same or nearly the same words: πατήρ; ποιῶ; οὐδέν; πέμπω (in the form of an aorist substantive participle, "the one who sent" Jesus); τὰ ἀρεστά...ποιῶ / εὐαρεστέω;[145] and πάντοτε / κατὰ πάντα. In addition to these, Ignatius' phrase "without the Father" (ἄνευ τοῦ πατρός) in this context is certainly equivalent in meaning to Jesus' "from myself" (ἀπ' ἐμαυτοῦ). And the subject in both accounts, Jesus, is the same. It seems to me that this is a rather remarkable set of concurrences to which neither Inge, nor Schoedel, nor Foster, has called attention.

---

[144] John 5:19, "So Jesus said to them, 'Truly, truly, I say to you, the Son can do nothing of his own accord (οὐ δύναται ὁ υἱὸς ποιεῖν ἀφ' ἑαυτοῦ), but only what he sees the Father doing. For whatever the Father does, that the Son does likewise.'" John 5:30, "'I can do nothing on my own (οὐ δύναμαι ἐγὼ ποιεῖν ἀπ' ἐμαυτοῦ οὐδέν). As I hear, I judge, and my judgment is just, because I seek not my own will but the will of him who sent me (τοῦ πέμψαντός με).'"

[145] The compound form of the verb εὐαρεστέω is used in the NT only in Hebrews (11:5,6; 13:16); it is used five or six times in the Apostolic Fathers (*1 Clem.* 41:1 [MSS CLS]; 62:2 [*bis*]; *Magn.* 8:2; Pol. *Phil.* 5:2; Herm. *Vis.* 3.1.9; *Sim.* 8.3.5); in no case except in *Magn.* 8:2 does it refer to Jesus. Nor is the adjective εὐαρέστος used to refer to Jesus or to what he did. The uncompounded verb ἀρέσκω is used 16 times in the NT and 12 times in the Apostolic Fathers with Jesus as subject only in Rom 15:3, where Paul says Christ did not please himself. The uncompounded adjective ἀρεστός used in John 8:29 occurs elsewhere in the NT only in Acts 6:2; 12:3; and 1 John 3:22. Only in John 8:29 does it refer to what Jesus did. Thus, only in John 8:29 and in Ignatius, *Magn.* 8:2 is a form of this word group used of Jesus doing what was "pleasing" to the Father.

Consider in particular Ignatius' use of the verb πέμπω in the aorist substantive participle to refer to the Father as "the one having sent" Jesus. This use of this form of πέμπω can be found nowhere in the NT except in John,[146] where it occurs no less than 25 times![147]

Moreover, between the echo of John 8:28–29b in *Magn.* 7:1 and the echo of John 8:29c in *Magn.* 8:2, there are other Johannine concepts. The idea of Jesus being one with the Father is distinctive to John among the gospels, and his remaining one with the Father during his time on earth, as we saw, reflects John 8:29a–b, "And he who sent me is with me, he has not left me alone." The conception of Jesus as the Word is of course Johannine.[148] His coming forth from the Father and then returning to him is also distinctively Johannine, as one sees in John 13:3; 16:28. John and Ignatius use different compounds of ἔρχομαι for Jesus' going forth from the Father, but this is understandable, particularly if Ignatius is not writing with a copy of John before him for reference. Again, besides what seems to be a clear use of at least one Johannine passage, there is a cluster of apparent Johannine allusions or echoes.

We have examined here a number of passages which, I believe, indicate Ignatius' knowledge of John's Gospel. There are other possible ones,[149] including one mentioned by Allen Brent in two recent publications. Concerning *Eph.* 17:1, "For this reason the Lord received perfumed ointment on his head in order that he might breathe incorruption into the Church," Brent observes, "Ignatius will interpret the significance of Jesus' anointing by an unknown woman shortly before his death [Matt. 26.7; Mark 14.3] in the light of Christ's breathing into the apostles in this passage [i.e., in John 20.21–22]."[150] Ignatius' reference to the Lord receiving ointment on his head, even Schoedel acknowledges, is based on Ignatius' knowledge of the story "in a form close to that of Matthew (26:7; cf. Mark 14:3) where the oil is poured

---

[146] The verb in the future indicative is used for the father in the parable of the wicked tenants in Luke 20:13, which is an oblique reference to the divine Father.

[147] The author of the *ad Diognetum* (Polycarp?) uses the verb in the aorist indicative eight times in 7:2–6 for God's sending of his Son, but this passage too is dependent upon John (Hill 2004, 363).

[148] For the idea of the Word proceeding "from silence" see Schoedel 1985, 121; and Hill 2004, 435–437.

[149] See in particular *Phld.* 9:1–2 (John 10:7,9; 14:6; 8:30–59; 17:20–23); *Smyrn.* 1:1–2 (John 20:25), and the detailed treatment of these and other places in Nagel 2000, 216–251.

[150] Brent 2007, 38–39, also 86. See also Brent 2006, 436.

'on Jesus' head' and not (as in Luke 7:38 and John 12:3) on his feet."[151] It seems reasonable that Ignatius has another event in the life of Christ in mind for Jesus' breathing on the church, and the only one recorded in any gospel is that recorded in John 20:22, "And when he had said this, he breathed on them (ἐνεφύσησεν), and said to them, 'Receive the Holy Spirit...'"

Ignatius is the recipient of substantial Johannine tradition. Is it more likely that at least some of this tradition reached him through the written Johannine gospel, or that all of it reached him through other means?[152] Several factors lead me to think he must have known the written gospel. First, though the length of the parallels is not great, there is a relatively high number of them.[153] If we deny Ignatius' knowledge of John's Gospel, this means we must imagine that the contents of several of the speeches now recorded in that gospel must have come to Ignatius from some other route(s). Second, the level of specific lexical correspondence in some of them, particularly the exact correspondence with five consecutive words of Jesus in John 3:8 in *Phld.* 7:1 but also the several echoes in *Magn.* 7:1–8:2, is also impressive. Third, and closely related to the second, is the fact that so much of the borrowed Johannine material appears to be "redactional," going beyond mere acquaintance with stories which might have been passed on orally, or concepts which might have been communicated in Christian teaching or preaching, to a knowledge of distinctive terms and literary themes of the written gospel. Fourth, the close parallels relate to many different portions of John and are not restricted to one or two, making the supposition of oral tradition that much less likely. Fifth, the fact that the Johannine material often occurs in clusters has been underappreciated by scholars but would seem to indicate that when Ignatius' mind starts on a Johannine phrase, this often triggers other Johannine words or concepts, just the sort of thing we might imagine from one

---

[151] Schoedel 1985, 82.

[152] Some have posited that Ignatius instead knew the author of the gospel. While this certainly cannot be ruled out, at least not on chronological grounds, to account for all the parallels would demand that he had heard orally and mentally retained substantial portions of the teaching that ended up in widely separated sections of the written gospel.

[153] It is interesting that even J.N. Sanders (1968, 33) later acknowledged this: "...there are many resemblances in thought and language to the FG, though nothing that can be called a quotation...There are so many of these passages in Ignatius that it seems reasonable to suppose that he knew the FG."

who is not referencing his borrowed materials in his study, but is writing "on the go." The three criteria outlined by Bellinzoni: accessibility; the presence of redactional material; and the repetition of material from the same source, are more than adequately met in Ignatius.

Another factor has yet to be mentioned. Ignatius' use of the term "gospel," in all but one instance, seems to function, if not exactly as a title, as a reference to the content[154] of a written work or works.[155] For example,

> But the gospel has something exceptional, the coming of the Saviour, our Lord Jesus Christ, his passion and the resurrection. For the beloved prophets made proclamation pointing to him, but the gospel is the perfection of incorruption. (*Phld.* 9:2)

> It is fitting...to give heed to the prophets, and especially to the gospel, in which the passion is made clear to us and the resurrection is accomplished. (*Smyrn.* 7:2)

The way Ignatius pairs "the gospel" with "the prophets" and the way he refers to elements from the story of Jesus as being "in" the gospel, suggest that he is not just a precursor of later Christian usage, but a witness to the early associations of this word with the books now known as gospels.[156] This textual consciousness forms part of the background for his use of concepts, words, and phrases which he has in common with the Fourth Gospel, and shows that it is by no means improbable that one of the "gospel" documents so referenced is John.

3.8. *Papias of Hierapolis*

Papias of Hierapolis in Asia Minor wrote his *Exposition of the Lord's Oracles* in five books perhaps as early as before 110, perhaps as late as the early 130's. Papias is famous among scholars of early Christianity for two main things. First, he recorded tradition from an elder (almost certainly named John) about the origins of the Gospels of Matthew and Mark which is preserved for us by Eusebius (*Hist. eccl.* 3.39.15–16). Second, he made a statement about written and oral sources for his

---

[154] Much as does the word "law" in John 1:17; Acts 7:53; Rom 6:14,15; 10:4; Gal 3:17; Eph 2:15; Heb 9:19.

[155] The singular "gospel" was often used to denote plural written works throughout the second century (Aristides, *Apology* [15.1 Greek; 2.4 Syriac]; *Ep. Apost.* 1; Justin, *Dial.* 10.2; 100.1; *2 Clem.* 8:5; Theophilus, *Ad Autol.* 3.12; Irenaeus, e.g., *Adv. haer.* 1.7.4; 3.5.1; 4.34.1).

[156] See Hill 2005.

traditions (3.39.3–4) which has confused readers ever since Eusebius excerpted it for his *Ecclesiastical History* (if not before)!

Papias recorded tradition he had learned from an elder, evidently many years previous to his writing, about the origins and literary characters of Matthew and Mark (*Hist. eccl.* 3.39.15–16), but in these excerpts there is nothing about Luke or John. Bauer believed John was omitted by Papias because it "apparently belonged to the long-winded prattle in which the great masses took pleasure...the Fourth Gospel [was suspect], no doubt, because of its content, origin, and the friends it had made."[157] Yet despite the fact that the excerpts mention only Matthew and Mark, others have noted that there are a few indications from Papias' surviving fragments and from reports by Irenaeus about the exegesis of the elders, most probably derived from Papias' books, that Papias must indeed have used John's Gospel. Irenaeus cites an exegetical tradition of certain "elders, the disciples of the apostles" which referred to Jesus' saying recorded in John 14:2, "In my Father's house are many mansions" (*Adv. haer.* 5.36.2).[158] If this is not from Papias' book, it "yields additional and independent testimony to the same date and character as that of Papias."[159]

A number of scholars including Lightfoot, Hengel, Culpepper, Grant, and Bauckham,[160] have argued for Papias' knowledge of John's Gospel from the order and identities of the disciples named in an introductory section of Papias' book cited by Eusebius in *Hist. eccl.* 3.39.4: "but if ever anyone came who had followed the presbyters, I inquired into the words of the presbyters, what Andrew or Peter or Philip or Thomas or James or John or Matthew, or any other of the Lord's disciples had said..." The disciples Andrew, Philip, and Thomas are prominent only in John and the order in which they appear (excepting Matthew at the end) here mirrors the order in which they are introduced in John 1:40 and 21:2 and is contrary to any synoptic list. Hengel and Bauckham believe that Papias not only used John but must have said something about John's Gospel, but that Eusebius has edited it out because it contained something he did not agree with.

---

[157] Bauer 1971, 187.
[158] On this see Hill 2004, 407–408.
[159] Lightfoot 1893, 197.
[160] Lightfoot 1893, 194–198; Hengel 1989, 17–21; Bauckham 1993, 45–53; Culpepper 1994, 111–112; Grant 1997, 35; Bauckham 2006, 417.

But it might be that Eusebius did not repeat in 3.39.15–16 what Papias said about John because he had already given it earlier in his book, though without attribution of his source. In an earlier article I presented evidence that Eusebius has in fact paraphrased Papias' comments on John (and Luke), when he refers to an earlier written source (κατέχει λόγος, "a record preserves") while cataloguing the writings of John the apostle in 3.24.5–13.[161] The full evidence cannot be repeated here. The argument will instead be briefly summarized, and then parts of it will be revisited in a response to Richard Bauckham, who has recently commented on it at some length.

First, we know that Irenaeus and Eusebius knew Papias' account of the origins of the gospels, and links between the material explicitly attributed to Papias in 3.39.15–16 and statements about gospel origins in later writers indicates that in all probability other writers also knew this account. Some of the authors who apparently knew Papias' words about the writing of Mark and Matthew also speak in ways similar to one another about Luke and John. This could suggest that, if indeed Papias wrote about Luke and John, he might also be the source for these later writers on these gospels as well. Indeed, we find that there are several parallels between their testimonies about Luke and John and the material Eusebius cites from his written source about Luke and John in *Hist. eccl.* 3.24.

Second, the account in 3.24 is linked to Papias by close similarities in both the concerns and the wording of the material Eusebius attributes to Papias later in 3.39.15–16. These include (a) that each gospel had its origin in the preaching of one or more apostles, (b) that the evangelists wrote at the request of others, (c) that a form of the word "recollections" associated these gospels with the firsthand reports of the Lord's personal disciples, (d) a concern for the different degrees or types of "order" or "arrangement" of the materials in the gospels, and (e) the attempt to find an "endorsement" for each gospel from another accepted, textual authority.

Alternatives to Papias as the source are also considered, but none comes near to satisfying the relevant data as well as does the *Exposition of the Lord's Oracles* by the bishop of Hierapolis. Accepting the bulk of the account in 3.24.5–13 (in particular, 3.24.5–7,11) as coming from Papias' book would explain much of the tradition concerning the four

---

[161] Hill 1998; repeated and augmented somewhat in Hill 2004.

gospels which occurs in later writers who used Papias' work, such as
Justin, Irenaeus, the author of the *Muratorian Fragment*, Clement,
Origin, and Victorinus of Pettau. The material recorded in *Hist. eccl.*
3.24.5–16 seems to provide a missing link.

All of this would mean not only that these gospels were known
to the elder in the very early years of the second century, but that
they were already held in high esteem. They were already credited to
apostles or to followers of apostles (anticipating Justin). Efforts were
also being made to provide accounts of their origins and to deal, at
least summarily, with some of the difficulties posed by having multiple authoritative accounts of Jesus' words and deeds which did not
always entirely match each other. Because it is nearly certain that the
elder who passed this information on to Papias is his "elder John," this
would mean that whoever "John" was to whom the Fourth Gospel was
being attributed, he was not John the elder.

The most extended interaction with the thesis which I have seen so
far in English[162] is that of Richard Bauckham in his recent book, *Jesus
and the Eyewitnesses*.[163] Bauckham acknowledges that "a good case"
has been made for the proposal, but also says that he doubts if it can
be sustained.[164] He offers no reasons why the case cannot be sustained,
but instead offers six "qualifications" of it. The first two qualifications
have to do with the fact that in 3.24.5–13 Eusebius is not quoting his
source verbatim but giving a paraphrase, and in at least one section
(3.24.8–10) breaks in with his own comments, which may still reflect
something of the substance of the source, but contain noticeably his
own thoughts. These points I affirmed in the original essay,[165] and they
do not affect the argument that the source Eusebius is using and paraphrasing is Papias.

The third of Bauckham's qualifications has to do with Eusebius' use
of φασί ("they say") in the course of his reporting on what the source
says. Bauckham acknowledges that Eusebius is working with a written
source in 3.24.5–7 when saying "a record holds" (κατέχει λόγος), but
he says it is not clear that the use of φασί in 3.24.7 and 11, in apparently referring back to this source, can indeed refer to a written source.

---

[162] The recent work by Norelli 2005, which contains a lengthy reply, has come into
my hands unfortunately too late to be responded to here.
[163] Bauckham 2006, 433–437.
[164] Bauckham 2006, 433.
[165] See, e.g., Hill 1998, 593–594, 599.

Here he is simply mistaken.[166] But he is right, on the other hand, to surmise that Eusebius could be using "they say" because he is reporting Papias' (written) words, who was himself passing on oral reports. "If the author of the source in 3.24.6–8, 11, is Papias, then Papias could be citing what he had heard that the elders had said or what he had heard that John the Elder had said."[167] This "qualification," then, only supports the identification of Eusebius' source as Papias, and simply stresses that the information goes back to a time before Papias wrote, to some time which must be quite close to the turn of the first/second centuries.

Another of Bauckham's qualifications concerns a conclusion I drew from the identification,[168] and does not really touch the proposal to identify the source of 3.24.6–15 as Papias. This means that only two of Bauckham's six qualifications remain, and propose any significant difficulties. To these we now turn.

The first concerns what the unattributed source in 3.24.5 and the attributed Papian fragment in 3.39.16 say about Matthew. Bauckham thinks that what Eusebius records from his anonymous source in 3.24.5–6 could not be part of the same account which Eusebius attributes to Papias in 3.39.16 (he acknowledges that it could have come from another context in Papias' work).[169] On the contrary, I think they would fit together quite well. Bauckham observes that one of the concerns reflected in 3.39 is "the issue of order in the Gospels," whereas the only point of agreement between the two sources is the assertion "that Matthew wrote in Hebrew." There is no reason, however, why these two concerns might not have been combined in the same account. In 3.24.5–7 Eusebius is only repeating enough of the source's information on Matthew (Mark and Luke too) as will provide the necessary background for relaying its tradition on John, which is the subject at hand. It is quite reasonable to suppose that his source in 3.24.5–13,

---

[166] See Hill 2004, 387–388n93.
[167] Bauckham 2006, 435.
[168] This conclusion has to do with Papias' view of the authorship of the Fourth Gospel, which, Bauckham charges, is invalid. Here too, I believe Bauckham is mistaken. The import of the fragment surely is that its source believed the author of the gospel was the apostle John, but what is even more certain is that it rules out John the elder as the author of the gospel, because he is apparently the source of Papias' tradition and speaks of another John as author of the gospel. This, of course, directly contradicts Bauckham's own thesis about the authorship of John.
[169] Bauckham 2006, 435.

whose aim clearly was to give information about the origins of each of these gospels, did so in order, and the information Eusebius quotes about Matthew and Mark in 3.39.15–16 (which stresses that Mark did not give things in order but that Matthew did) would fit well after the information he so briefly summarizes in 3.24.6 before the information on John in 3.24.7.

The most substantial difficulty Bauckham claims to find with the identification of the two sources has to do with the problem of "order" in the gospels. I shall deal with it in more depth because it will also give the reader a better idea of the nature of the evidence for identifying Eusebius' source on the origin of John's Gospel as Papias.

Bauckham recognizes that both Papias in 3.39.15 and Eusebius' source in 3.24.5–13 share concern for "order,"[170] but believes that the solution each source gives to the problem is different, even that they are "quite inconsistent," and that this is then "strong evidence against" identifying the sources.[171] He claims then that "in order to save the attribution to Papias we have to speculate about what the source itself said and how Eusebius has altered it."[172] This unfortunately gives the reader a distorted impression about the actual argument and itself relies on Bauckham's own theories (which are by no means devoid of speculation!) about what Papias "must be inferred" to have said about John.

The difference between the two accounts, as relates to order, is, according to Bauckham, as follows:

> The solution to the difference in order between the Gospels that Papias must be inferred to have offered is that John's Gospel does follow a correct chronological order, while the other Gospels (at least Mark and Matthew) do not. In *Hist. eccl.* 3.24.5–13 the solution is quite different. The four Gospels are reconciled without an admission that any of them is not "in order." John is said to have confined himself to filling in the gap left by the Synoptics at the beginning of their accounts of Jesus' ministry. They narrated only what happened after John the Baptist was put in prison, whereas John narrated what occurred before John the Baptist was put in prison. Eusebius is evidently wholly content with this solution to the whole issue of differences in order between the Gospels.[173]

---

[170] Bauckham 2006, 435.
[171] Bauckham 2006, 436.
[172] Bauckham 2006, 436.
[173] Bauckham 2006, 436.

What Papias said about Mark in 3.39.15 was that Mark set things down as he (Peter) remembered them; he did not make "an ordered arrangement" (σύνταξιν)[174] and did not put things "in order" (τάξει) but wrote as Peter remembered, tailoring his speeches to his hearers' needs (χρείας) (*Hist. eccl.* 3.39.15). Papias, or rather, the elder he is quoting, seems to be responding to some criticism from somewhere about Mark's lack of "order" (τάξις) and Bauckham believes the comparison is being made to John. This may be so, but we may only think this from inference or "speculation," for nowhere in the account which Eusebius relates in 3.39.15–16 is John mentioned. In fact, this section does say that one gospel writer did make an "ordered arrangement" (συνετάξατο) and that writer is Matthew, not John. It is, I believe, quite true that in the tradition from the elder repeated by Papias all the gospels are being considered with respect to the question of literary arrangement (τάξις), but this means not only Mark and John. Matthew's Gospel would apparently be preferred to Mark's in terms of "orderly arrangement." The unnamed source Eusebius uses in 3.24.5–13 definitely focuses on John's preservation of the beginnings of Jesus' ministry—omitted from the other gospel accounts—and not on the chronological "order" of events in the rest of the gospel story (though, as Bauckham observes, issues of chronology might have been mentioned in portions of the accounts Eusebius omits). But the issue of an author's τάξις or the lack of it cannot be restricted to matters of chronology.[175] It can refer to various matters having to do with literary skill in composition. Even the omission of important material is a matter of "order," as Quintillian indicates in a quote mentioned by Bauckham himself: if an author's "order" is faulty, he might "repeat many things, omit many things."[176]

But elsewhere in his book, Bauckham acknowledges something different about what may be inferred about Papias' view of John's "order." Bauckham has argued, correctly, I think, that the author of the *Muratorian Fragment* is dependent at points on Papias' account of

---

[174] This is how Bauckham (2006, 203, 214) translates the noun σύνταξις; he translates the verb συγκατατάξαι "to put into properly ordered form" when referring to Papias' description of his own work in *Hist. eccl.* 3.39.3 in Bauckham 2006, 218.

[175] See, e.g., Stewart-Sykes 1995, who shows that τάξις does not in the first place refer among historians to chronological order (though it may include it) but literary arrangement, "the task of ordering a series of events into a narrative" (490).

[176] Quintillian, *Institutio Oratoria* 7, preface 3, cited by Bauckham, 2006, 219n56, from Schoedel.

the gospels, particularly on what Papias must have said about John.[177]
After citing a version of 1 John 1:1–3, the author of the *Muratorian Fragment* says of John, "Thus he professes himself not only an eyewitness and hearer but also a writer of all the miracles of our Lord in order." Bauckham writes,

> That John was not only an eye- and earwitness but also wrote "all the miracles of the Lord in order" (*per ordinem*) corresponds to Papias's assertion that *Mark* "neither heard the Lord nor accompanied him and did not write in order (*taxei*)" what Jesus said and did. Because John, unlike Mark, was an eyewitness he was able to write "in order." Moreover, the order that the Muratorian Canon validates in this way is that of the Lord's miracles, referring to the most obvious way in which the Gospel of John appears to insist on chronological order: in specifying the first two "signs" as the first and second of a sequence (2:11; 4:54)...Such a statement is the kind of claim we have already concluded that Papias probably made about the Gospel of John.[178]

Bauckham thus acknowledges that Papias' (or his elder's) reference to Mark's "order" concerns the very thing he denies that it concerns when critiquing my proposal to identify Eusebius' source in 3.24.5–13 as Papias. In the *Muratorian Fragment* (echoing Papias), John's writing "all the miracles of the Lord in order" most likely reflects, as Bauckham says, John's ordering of Jesus' first two "signs" in sequences in John 2:11 and 4:54. Here is what Eusebius says in 3.24.7–8,11–12:

> After the three Gospels which had been previously written had already been distributed to all, and even to himself, they say (φασί) that he welcomed them and testified to their truth, but that there was therefore only lacking to the Scripture (or writing) the account concerning things which had been done by Christ at first (περὶ τῶν ἐν πρώτοις) and at the beginning (καὶ κατ' ἀρχήν) of the proclamation. (8) The record (ὁ λόγος) is certainly true...[After some comments of his own, Eusebius returns to the account.] (11) Now they say (φασί) that on account of these things, the apostle John was exhorted to hand down (παραδοῦναι) in the Gospel according to himself the time passed over in silence by the first evangelists and the things which had been done by the Saviour at this time (that is, things before the imprisonment of the Baptist), and that he signified this when saying "this beginning of marvels (ταύτην ἀρχήν...παραδόξων) did Jesus" [John 2:11], and then by calling to mind

---

[177] Bauckham 2006, 427.
[178] Bauckham 2006, 427. Again, "Thus it is likely that the last paragraph...is closely dependent on Papias"; "...as far as order is concerned, John is superior. This confirms that this latter point comes from his source, Papias" (428).

(or remembering, μνημονεύσαντα) the Baptist in the midst of the acts of Jesus as still then baptizing at Aenon near Salem, plainly indicating this when he says "for John was not yet cast into prison" [John 3:24].[179] (12) Thus John in the Scripture (or writing) of the Gospel according to him hands down (παραδέδωσιν) the things done (πραχθέντα) by Christ when the Baptist had not yet been cast into prison, but the other three evangelists call to mind (or remember, μνημονεύουσιν) the things after the Baptist had been shut up in prison.

This forms a remarkable coincidence with the *Muratorian Fragment*'s statement that John wrote "all the miracles of our Lord in order," and a remarkable coincidence with what Bauckham had said Papias "must have said" about John. In the context of stating that John's account recorded events before the arrest of the Baptist, the report used by Eusebius commented on John's ordering of the miracles, "and that he signified this when saying "this beginning of marvels (ταύτην ἀρχήν...παραδόξων) did Jesus" (John 2:11) before reporting that John was still not imprisoned in John 3:24.

One more rather uncanny detail seems to confirm that the author of the *Muratorian Fragment* knew the material Eusebius cited anonymously in 3.24.5–13. In reporting his source in the latter passage, Eusebius cites John 2:11, but does so in a peculiar way. Instead of John's "this beginning of signs (σημείων)" Eusebius writes, "this beginning of marvels (παραδόξων)." No surviving text of the gospel has this substitution. Eusebius may have made the substitution himself, but it is significant that in his two other uses of this verse he follows all the manuscripts of John's Gospel in using σημείων. It is more likely that Eusebius, instead of finding his copy of John's Gospel and looking up its wording, simply reproduced the wording of his source, which had substituted the word παραδόξων for σημείων. It is most telling, then, that when the *Muratorian Fragment* in the text cited above speaks about John "writing all the miracles of our Lord in order," instead of using the word *signum*, which normally translates σημεῖον and which the Vulgate uses in John 2:11 and 4:54 and everywhere else in John

---

[179] This entire sentence in 3.24.11 is related in indirect speech as the contents of what "they say." This clearly refers the reader back to the source in 3.24.6–7. Bauckham raises the possibility that the source only consisted of the material in 3.24.6–7, and then bases his rejection of the identification of Eusebius's sources as Papias on this restriction. But the content of 3.24.11 (relating as they do to what he had introduced in 3.24.5–7), Eusebius' use of "they say," and the indirect discourse all link this material to Eusebius' written source.

for σημεῖον, the Fragmentist uses the word *mirabilium*, the word used by the Vulgate to translate παράδοξος in Luke 5:26 and elsewhere. Apparently the underlying Greek of the *Muratorian Fragment* had παραδόξων not σημείων. It strikes me as unlikely that this same substitution should show up both in the *Muratorian Fragment*, at a point where it appears to know Papias' account, and in Eusebius' unnamed source, unless that source was Papias.

In conclusion, I do not regard Bauckham's "qualifications" as carrying any weight against the identification of Eusebius' source in *Hist. eccl.* 3.24.5–13 as Papias. If we accept this identification the implications are significant for understanding not only the early afterlife of the Fourth Gospel, but for the four gospels as a group. If we do not accept this identification, it is still highly probable, from Papias' apostle list and from the tradition of the elders cited by Irenaeus, that both Papias and the generation before him in Asia Minor were using this gospel.

4. Conclusion

Was John "the Gnostics' special Gospel"? How close did the orthodox come to consigning this gospel to the flames as condemned literature? From even our very limited study here, we would have to say: not very close.

Contrary to what has been the prevailing paradigm for the study of Johannine community history, there is every reason to believe that from very early on John was quite valued by those churches considered Irenaeus' predecessors, in Syria, Asia Minor, Achaia, Rome, Gaul, and in Egypt. John rather quickly became closely associated with the "great church" and was widely regarded as one of its written authorities, as is evident in Aristides, *Ep. Apost.*, Justin and Celsus. It might even with good reason be dubbed "the orthodox gospel" even in the period before Irenaeus. Not that it was the most used gospel among the orthodox—from our present state of knowledge that honor would have to go to Matthew. But while John shared with Matthew and other gospels its role of providing the churches with authoritative accounts of Jesus' life on earth, his miraculous signs, and his teaching, for use in preaching, catechizing, and liturgy, John also played a special role. Yes, it provided some of the best-loved stories about Jesus: the turning of the water into wine, the encounters with Nicodemus and with the woman at the well, the bread of life discourse, the raising of Lazarus, the encounter with Thomas after the resurrection (and more). But beyond this and in a way unparalleled by any other gospel it clarified orthodox Christology for churches in the line of Irenaeus' predecessors. Thus, more than any other gospel it was useful in apologetic contexts with Jews and with pagans for instruction about the pre-existent deity of the Word, his fellowship with the Father, his part in the creation of "all things." More than any other gospel it was used in polemical contexts with pagans and with Christian docetists of various kinds for instruction about the Word's becoming flesh, his partaking of earthly food and drink, his suffering in the flesh and his rising in the flesh. Its usefulness in this orthodox undertaking is mirrored in the Gnostic context in the attempts to "silence" John's witness to the Word's becoming flesh and suffering in the flesh (e.g., *Trim. Prot.* 47,13–19; *Acts of John* 101.8–9).

From a time very early in the second century it is clear that materials which appear uniquely or almost uniquely in the Fourth Gospel were in use among the mainstream or "apostolic" churches, those associated with Ignatius and his addressees, and elders of the generation preceding Papias. It is not quite clear just when we can say with certainty that these evidences owe their existence to written materials or to what we call the Gospel of John. But the apparent awareness of written gospels in Ignatius, the clear references to gospel writings in Aristides, and the definite knowledge of named, written gospels in Papias, if he is indeed Eusebius' source in *Hist. eccl.* 3.24.5–13, all speak for a very early influence of the gospel itself, preparing the way for its use in Rome in services of worship in Justin's day. In any case, the Fourth Gospel soon became a mainstay among the orthodox. As such it might be read by any who could obtain a copy, who were interested in finding out about Christianity for friendly purposes (Aristides), unfriendly purposes (Celsus), or simply for purposes of curiosity (Trypho; Aristides' and Justin's recommendations to the emperor). In this sense, little has changed from then till now.

BIBLIOGRAPHY

Alexander, L., "The Four among pagans," *The Written Gospel*, M. Bockmuehl and D.A. Hagner, eds., Cambridge: Cambridge University Press, 2005, 222–237.

Barnard, L.W., *Justin Martyr*, Cambridge: Cambridge University Press, 1967.

Bauckham, R., "Papias and Polycrates on the Origin of the Fourth Gospel," *Journal of Theological Studies New Series* 44 (1993), 24–69.

—— *Jesus and the Eyewitnesses: The Gospels as Eyewitness Testimony*, Grand Rapids, Mich.: Eerdmans, 2006.

Barrett, C.K., *The Gospel according to John: An Introduction with Commentary and Notes on the Greek Text*, Philadelphia: Westminster John Knox, ²1978.

Bauer, W., *Rechtgläubigkeit und Ketzerei im ältesten Christentum*, Tübingen: Mohr Siebeck, 1934.

—— *Orthodoxy and Heresy in Earliest Christianity*, R.A. Kraft and G. Krodel, eds., Philadelphia: Fortress, 1971.

Beatrice, P.F., "Der Presbyter des Irenäus, Polykarp von Smyrna und der Brief an Diognet," *Pléroma Salus carnis: Homenaje a Antonio Orbe, S.J.*, E. Romero-Pose, ed., Santiago de Compostela: Publicationes Compostellanum, 1990, 179–202.

Bellinzoni, A.J., *The Sayings of Jesus in the Writings of Justin Martyr*, Supplements to Novum Testamentum 17, Leiden: Brill, 1967.

—— "The Gospel of Luke in the Apostolic Fathers: An Overview," *Trajectories through the New Testament and the Apostolic Fathers*, A.F. Gregory and C.M. Tuckett, eds., Oxford: Oxford University Press, 2005, 45–68.

Borret, M, *Origène: Contra Celse: Introduction, texte critique, traduction et notes*, 5 vols., Sources chrétiennes 132, 136, 147, 150, 227, Paris: Cerf, 1967–1976.

Brent, A., *Hippolytus and the Roman Church in the Third Century: Communities in Tension before the Emergence of a Monarch-Bishop*, Supplements to Vigiliae Christianae 31, Leiden: Brill, 1995.

—— "The Enigma of Ignatius of Antioch," *Journal of Ecclesiastical History* 57 (2006), 429–456.

—— *Ignatius of Antioch: A Martyr Bishop and the Origin of Episcopacy*, London: T&T Clark International, 2007.

Brown, R.E., *The Community of the Beloved Disciple*, New York: Paulist Press, 1979.

Buschmann, G., *Das Martyrium des Polykarp übersetzt und erklärt*, Kommentar zu den Apostolischen Vätern 6, Göttingen: Vandenhoeck & Ruprecht, 1998.

Chadwick, H., *Origen: Contra Celsum*, Cambridge: Cambridge University Press, 1965.

Charlesworth, J.H., *The Beloved Disciple: Whose Witness Validates the Gospel of John?* Valley Forge, Pa.: Trinity Press International, 1995.

Culpepper, R.A., *John, the Son of Zebedee: The Life of a Legend*, Columbia: University of South Carolina Press, 1994.

—— *The Gospel and Letters of John*, Nashville: Abingdon Press, 1998.

de Boer, M.C., "Jesus' Departure to the Father in John: Death or Resurrection?" *Theology and Christology in the Fourth Gospel: Essays by the Members of the SNTS Johannine Writings Seminar*, G. van Belle et al., eds., Bibliotheca Ephemeridum Theologicarum Lovaniensium 184, Leuven: Leuven University Press / Peeters, 2005, 1–19.

Ferguson, E., "Factors Leading to the Selection and Closure of the New Testament Canon: A Survey of Some Recent Studies," *The Canon Debate*, L.M. McDonald and J.A. Sanders, eds., Peabody, Mass.: Hendrickson, 2002, 295–320.

Foster, P., "The Epistles of Ignatius of Antioch and the Writings that later formed the New Testament," *The Reception of the New Testament in the Apostolic Fathers*, A.F. Gregory and C.M. Tuckett, eds., Oxford: Oxford University Press, 2005, 159–186.

—— "The Relationship between the Writings of Justin Martyr and the So-Called *Gospel of Peter*," *Justin Martyr and His Worlds*, S. Parvis and P. Foster, eds., Minneapolis: Fortress, 2007, 104–112, 198–200.

Frede, M., "Origen's Treatise *Against Celsus*," *Apologetics in the Roman Empire: Pagans, Jews, and Christians*, M. Edwards et al., eds., Oxford: Oxford University Press, 1999, 131–155.

Frend, W.H.C., *Martyrdom and Persecution in the Early Church: A Study of a Conflict from the Maccabees to Donatus*, Oxford: Blackwell, 1965, reprinted Grand Rapids, Mich.: Baker Book House, 1981.

Grant, R.M., "Scripture and Tradition in St. Ignatius of Antioch," *Catholic Biblical Quarterly* 25 (1963), 322–335.

—— *Irenaeus of Lyons*, The Early Church Fathers, London: Routledge, 1997.

—— *Greek Apologists of the Second Century*, Philadelphia: Westminster John Knox, 1998.

Gregory, A.F. and C.M. Tuckett, "Reflections on Method: What Constitutes the Use of the Writings that later formed the New Testament in the Apostolic Fathers," *The Reception of the New Testament in the Apostolic Fathers*, A.F. Gregory and C.M. Tuckett, eds., Oxford: Oxford University Press, 2005, 61–82.

Grenfell, B.P. and A.S. Hunt, *The Oxyrhunchus Papyri* 15, London: Egypt Exploration Society, 1922.

Haenchen, E., *John 1: A Commentary on the Gospel of John Chapters 1–6*, R.W. Funk, transl., Hermeneia, Philadelphia: Fortress, 1984.

Harrison, P.N., *Polycarp's Two Epistles to the Philippians*, Oxford: Oxford University Press, 1936.

Hartog, P., *Polycarp and the New Testament: The Occasion, Rhetoric, Theme, and Unity of the Epistle to the Philippians and its Allusions to New Testament Literature*, Wissenschaftliche Untersuchungen zum Neuen Testament 2.134, Tübingen: Mohr Siebeck, 2002.

Hengel, M., *The Johannine Question*, London: SCM, 1989.

—— *Die johanneische Frage: Ein Lösungsversuch, mit einem Beitrag von Jörg Frey*, Wissenschaftliche Untersuchungen zum Neuen Testament 67, Tübingen: Mohr Siebeck, 1993.

Hershbell, J.P., "Plutarch's 'De animae procreatione in Timaeo': An Analysis of Structure and Content," *Aufstieg und Niedergang der römischen Welt*, Part 2, Principate, 36.1, H. Temporini and W. Haase, eds., Berlin: de Gruyter, 1986, 234–247.

Hill, C.E., "The Identity of John's Nathanael," *Journal for the Study of the New Testament* 67 (1997), 45–61.

—— "The *Epistula Apostolorum*. An Asian Tract from the Time of Polycarp," *Journal of Early Christian Studies* 7 (1999), 1–53.

—— *Regnum Caelorum: Patterns of Millennial Thought in Early Christianity*, Cambridge: Cambridge University Press, ²2001.

—— *The Johannine Corpus in the Early Church*, Oxford: Oxford University Press, 2004 [Corrected, paperback edition, 2006].

—— "Ignatius, 'the Gospel' and the Gospels," *Trajectories through the New Testament and the Apostolic Fathers*, A.F. Gregory and C.M. Tuckett, eds., Oxford: Oxford University Press, 2005, 267–285.

—— *From the Lost Teaching of Polycarp: Identifying Irenaeus' Apostolic Presbyter and the Author of* Ad Diognetum, Wissenschaftliche Untersuchungen zum Neuen Testament 186, Tübingen: Mohr Siebeck, 2006a.

—— "The Fourth Gospel in the Second Century: The Myth of Orthodox Johannophobia," *Challenging Perspectives on the Gospel of John*, J. Lierman, ed., Wissenschaftliche Untersuchungen zum Neuen Testament 2.219, Tübingen: Mohr Siebeck, 2006b, 135–169.

—— "Was John's Gospel among Justin's *Apostolic Memoirs*?" *Justin Martyr and His Worlds*, S. Parvis and P. Foster, eds., Minneapolis: Fortress, 2007, 88–84, 191–193.

Hillmer, M.R., "The Gospel of John in the Second Century," Th.D. dissertation, Harvard University, 1966.

Hofrichter, P., "Logoslehre und Gottesbild bei Apologeten, Modalisten und Gnostikern. Johanneische Christologie im Licht ihrer frühesten Rezeption," *Monotheismus und Christologie: Zur Gottesfrage im hellenistischen Judentum und im Urchristentum*, H.-J. Klauck, ed., Quaestiones Disputatae 138, Freiburg: Herder, 1992, 186–217.

Inge, W.R., "Ignatius," *The New Testament in the Apostolic Fathers*, by a Committee of the Oxford Society of Historical Theology, Oxford: Oxford University Press, 1905, 63–83.

Inowlocki, S., "La pratique de la citation dans le *Contre Apion* de Flavius Josephus," *Ktema: civilizations de l'Orient, de la Grece et de Rome antiquities* 30 (2005a), 371–393.

—— "'Neither Adding nor Omitting Anything': Josephus' Promise not to Modify the Scriptures in Greek and Latin Context," *Journal of Jewish Studies* 56/1 (2005b), 48–65.

—— *Eusebius and the Jewish Authors: His Citation Technique in an Apologetic Context*, Leiden: Brill, 2006.

Jensen, R.M., *Understanding Early Christian Art*, London: Routledge, 2000.

Kieffer, R., "Les premiers indices d'une réception de l'évangile de saint Jean," *The Four Gospels 1992: Festschrift Franz Neirynck*, 3 vols., F. van Segbroeck et al., eds., Leuven: Leuven University Press, 1992, 3:2225–2238.

Koester, H., *Synoptische Überlieferung bei den apostolischen Vätern*, Texte und Untersuchungen zur Geschichte der altchristlichen Literatur 65, Berlin: Akademie-Verlag, 1957.

—— *Ancient Christian Gospels: Their History and Development*, Philadelphia: Trinity Press International, 1990.

—— "Ephesos in Early Christian Literature," *Ephesos: Metropolis of Asia Minor: An Interdisciplinary Approach to its Archaeology, Religion and Culture*, H. Koester, ed., Harvard Theological Studies 41, Valley Forge, Pa.: Trinity Press International, 1995, 119–140.

—— "Gospels and Gospel Traditions in the Second Century," *Trajectories through the New Testament and the Apostolic Fathers*, A.F. Gregory and C.M. Tuckett, eds., Oxford: Oxford University Press, 2005, 27–44.

Lake, K., *Eusebius: The Ecclesiastical History*, Volume 1, The Loeb Classical Library, Cambridge, Mass.: Harvard University Press, 1926.

Lawlor, H. and J.E.L. Oulton, *Eusebius, Bishop of Caesarea: The Ecclesiastical History and the Martyrs of Palestine: Translated with Introduction and Notes*, 2 vols., 1927, reprinted London: Society for Promoting Christian Knowledge, 1954.

Lewis, C. and C. Short, *A Latin Dictionary*, Oxford: Clarendon Press, 1879.

Lightfoot, J.B., *The Apostolic Fathers: Clement, Ignatius, and Polycarp: Revised Texts with Introductions, Notes, Dissertations, and Translations*, 5 vols., [2]1889–1890, reprinted Grand Rapids: Baker Book House, 1981.

—— *Essays on the Work Entitled* Supernatural Religion: *Reprinted from* The Contemporary Review, London: MacMillan, [2]1893.

Lona, H.E., *Die* Wahre Lehre *des Kelsos: Übersetzt und erklärt*, Kommentar zu frühchristlichen Apologeten 1, Freiburg: Herder, 2005.

Marcovich, M., *Iustini Martyris: Dialogue cum Tryphone*, Patristische Texte und Studien 47, Berlin: de Gruyter, 1997.

Milne, H.J.M., "A New Fragment of the *Apology* of Aristides," *Journal of Theological Studies* 25 (1924), 73–77.

Mitchell, M.W., "In the Footsteps of Paul: Steps along the Road to Canon in Ignatius of Antioch," *Journal of Early Christian Studies* 14/1 (2006), 27–45.

Nagel, T., *Die Rezeption des Johannesevangeliums im 2. Jahrhundert: Studien zur vorirenäischen Auslegung des vierten Evangeliums in christlicher und christlich-gnostischer Literatur*, Arbeiten zur Bibel und ihrer Geschichte 2, Leipzig: Evangelische Verlagsanstalt, 2000.

Norelli, E., *Papia di Hierapolis: Esposizione degli oracoli del Signore: I frammenti: Introduzione, testo, traduzione e note*, Milano: Paoline Editoriale Libri, 2005.

Pollard, T.E., *Johannine Christology and the Early Church*, Cambridge: Cambridge University Press, 1970.

Poffet, J.-M., "Indices de réception de l'Évangile de Jean au IIe siècle, avant Irénée," *La communauté johannique et son Histoire: La trajectoire de l'évangile de Jean aux deux premiers siècles*, J.-D. Kaestli, J.-M. Poffet and J. Zumstein, eds., Paris: Labor et Fides, 1990, 305–321.

Pouderon, B., M.-J. Pierre and B. Outtier, "À propos de l'Apologie d'Aristide. Recherches sur un prototype commun aux versions syriaque et arménienne," *Revue des sciences religieuses* 74 (2000), 173–193.

Pryor, J., "Justin Martyr and the Fourth Gospel," *The Second Century* 9 (1992), 153–169.

Rathke, H., *Ignatius von Antiochien und die Paulusbriefe*, Texte und Untersuchungen zur Geschichte der altchristlichen Literatur 99, Berlin: Akademie-Verlag, 1967.

Richardson, C.C., *The Christianity of Ignatius of Antioch*, New York: Columbia University Press, 1935.

Röhl, W.G., *Die Rezeption des Johannesevangeliums in christlich-gnostischen Schriften aus Nag Hammadi*, Europäische Hochschulschriften, Reihe 23/428, Frankfurt am Main: Lang, 1991.

Romanides, R.S., "Justin Martyr and the Fourth Gospel," *The Greek Orthodox Theological Review* 4 (1958–1959), 115–134.

Sanders, J.N., *The Fourth Gospel in the Early Church: Its Origin and Influence on Christian Theology up to Irenaeus*, Cambridge: Cambridge University Press, 1943.

—— *A Commentary on the Gospel According to St. John*, edited and completed by B.A. Mastin, New York: Black, 1968.

Schmidt, C., *Gespräche Jesu mit seinem Jüngern nach der Auferstehung*, Texte und Untersuchungen 43, Leipzig: Hinrichs, 1919.

Schoedel, W.R., *Ignatius of Antioch: A Commentary on the Letters of Ignatius of Antioch*, Philadelphia: Fortress, 1985.

Skarsaune, O., *The Proof from Prophecy: A Study in Justin Martyr's Proof-Text Tradition: Text-Type, Provenance, Theological Profile*, Novum Testamentum Supplements 66, Leiden: Brill, 1987.

—— "Justin and His Bible," *Justin Martyr and His Worlds*, S. Parvis and P. Foster, eds., Minneapolis: Fortress, 2007, 53–76, 179–187.

Smith, J.D. Jr., "Gaius and the Controversy over the Johannine Literature," Ph.D. dissertation, Yale University, 1979.

Stanley, C.D., *Paul and the Language of Scripture: Citation Technique in the Pauline Epistles and Contemporary Literature*, Cambridge: Cambridge University Press, 1992.

Stewart-Sykes, A., "TAXEI in Papias: Again," *Journal of Early Christian Studies* 3 (1995), 487–492.

—— "The Asian Context of the New Prophecy and of *Epistula Apostolorum*," *Vigiliae Christianae* 51 (1997), 416–438.

Swanson, R., ed., *New Testament Greek Manuscripts: Variant Readings Arranged in Horizontal Lines Against Codex Vaticanus: John*, Sheffield: Sheffield Academic Press, 1995.

Trevett, C., *A Study of Ignatius of Antioch in Syria and Asia*, Studies in the Bible and Early Christianity 29, Lewiston, N.Y.: Mellen, 1992.

van Unnik, W.C., "The 'Gospel of Truth' and the New Testament," *The Jung Codex: A Newly Recovered Gnostic Papyrus*, F.M. Cross, ed., London: Mowbray, 1955, 79–129.

Wartelle, A., *Saint Justin: Apologies: Introduction, texte critique, traduction, commentarie et index*, Paris: Études Augustiniennes, 1987.

Wetter, G.P., "Eine gnostische Formel im vierten Evangelium," *Zeitschrift für die neutestamentliche Wissenschaft* 18 (1917–1918), 49–63.

Whittaker, J., "The Value of Indirect Tradition in the Establishment of Greek Philosophical Texts or the Art of Misquotation," *Editing Greek and Latin Texts:*

Papers given at the Twenty-Third Annual Conference on Editorial Problems: University of Toronto 6–7 November 1987, J.N. Grant, ed., New York: AMS, 1989, 63–95.

Wolff, R.L.,"The Apology of Aristides—A Re-examination," *Harvard Theological Review* 30 (1937), 233–247.

THE *DIATESSARON* AND THE SECOND-CENTURY
RECEPTION OF THE GOSPEL OF JOHN

Nicholas Perrin
Wheaton College

For some time now it has been widely assumed that in the earliest decades of its reception the Gospel of John remained strictly the domain
of heterodox forms of Christianity. According to this line of thinking,
it was not until Irenaeus' heyday towards the end of the second century that the Fourth Gospel, overcoming the hurdle of proto-orthodox
suspicions, made any substantive inroads into the "great church"—
all this largely due to Irenaeus himself. It is, I suspect, little coincidence that those who have subscribed to this reconstruction have also
granted only limited significance to Tatian's four-fold gospel harmony,
the *Diatessaron*. Because Tatian's harmony (ca. 173 CE) incorporated
John alongside the Synoptic Gospels *and* preceded Irenaeus' writings
by roughly a decade, it is impossible to grant much evidentiary weight
to the *Diatessaron* without also diminishing the watershed significance
normally attached to the bishop of Lyons's endorsement of John. One
may be forgiven for wondering whether it is merely out of defer-
ence to the dominant paradigm, which I have just outlined, that the
Diatessaron's use of John has been regarded as somehow subsidiary to
the moment of Irenaeus,[1] explained by Tatian's lapse into heresy (constituting him as the exception who proves the rule of proto-orthodox
aversion to John),[2] or simply ignored.[3]

---

[1] See, e.g., Haenchen 1984, 14; and Culpepper 1994, 122. A variation of this
involves the view that Tatian's harmonization of the gospel traditions implied—at
least in Tatian's eyes—a low view of their authority: see Campenhausen 1972, 175;
Gamble 1985, 30–31; and Petersen 2004, 66–68. I have argued elsewhere (Perrin 2003)
that this simply misunderstands the nature of ancient Jewish harmonization, which
presupposed rather than preempted the authority of the source texts. So also, in the
case of Tatian, Merkel 1971, 90–91.

[2] Bauer 1996 [1934], 206–207; Barrett 1978, 125; Brown 1979, 141.

[3] Schnackenburg 1968; Lindars 1982; Poffet 1990; Zumstein 1990; Keefer 2006.
Tatian is only fleetingly mentioned in Wiles (1960, 98–99), all of which is quite a
departure from Sanders (1943, 32) who in connection with Tatian's *Oratio* writes,
"This is almost the beginning of orthodox interpretation of the Fourth Gospel."

In this essay I wish to argue that the current scholarly marginaliza-
tion of the *Diatessaron*, within the larger discussion of John's reception
in the second century, stands in need of revision: contrary to widespread belief, Tatian's harmony can actually tell us quite a bit about
the Fourth Gospel and its reception in the pre-Irenaean church. My
argument consists of two parts. In the first part I wish to show that on
examining the sequence of the pericopae (insofar as it can be reconstructed on the basis of the witnesses), it becomes clear that Tatian
assigns a rather high value to the Fourth Gospel. One might even go so
far as to say—and here I move onto more controversial ground—that
in the *Diatessaron* the Fourth Gospel acquires a kind of hermeneutical privilege unshared by the Synoptic Gospels. In the second part, I
argue that on considering the earliest testimony to Tatian's theological
shift, it becomes apparent that the Assyrian's high estimation of John
cannot be credibly attributed to his change of views. If the two parts
of my larger argument together prove valid, this has implications for
our understanding not only of Tatian, but also, more broadly, of the
second-century church and its reception of John.

1. The Sequence of the *Diatessaron* and the Hermeneutical Value of the Fourth Gospel

The task of weaving together four gospels into one unified and chronologically ordered account is a difficult one by any standard. It doesn't
require much imagination to realize that anyone thoughtfully setting
about such an undertaking would face a number of interpretive deci-
sions which would on the one side impinge on the organization and
emphases of the harmony's final form, and on the other side presuppose certain judgments regarding the gospels, along with a willingness
to discriminate among them. Where finitude requires that one and only
one gospel speak at a given juncture or in cases where two or more
gospels appear to give conflicting accounts, like William Styron's character Sophie, the harmonist must choose for one beloved and against
another. The basis for such choices may not always be entirely patent to
later readers. But where one gospel is chosen at the expense of another,
it is sometimes possible to discern implicit evaluative judgments on the
part of the harmonist. This, I would argue, is just the case at several
points when we consider the sequence of the *Diatessaron* and the role
of the Fourth Gospel within that sequence.

Unfortunately, we possess no extant manuscripts of Tatian's famed text.[4] Despite its immense popularity in the Syrian church (indeed, precisely on account of its popularity), the gospel harmony was systematically eradicated in the fifth century so as to remove any competition with the "separated gospels" that have come down to us in the Old Syriac (OS^c, OS^s). We do, however, have a vast array of textual witnesses, spanning centuries and vast geographical distances. Since these Diatessaronic witnesses betray the impress of the now-lost gospel harmony in differing degrees, and since there are sometimes considerable differences between these witnesses, it bears stating that when we are contemplating the original wording of the *Diatessaron*, we are—as is sometimes the case of text criticism—dealing in the realm of the highly provisional.

When it comes to reconstructing the original sequence of the first major gospel harmony, we are on somewhat firmer ground. Largely retracing the path laid by the fourth-century *Commentary* of Ephraem, the nineteenth-century giant Theodor Zahn was able to set down a sequence he considered likely.[5] When shortly thereafter the Arabic Harmony came to be published, it only served to confirm Zahn's hypothesized sequence, and with very little exception.[6] Between the Arabic Harmony and Ephraem, the sequence of the so-called Eastern family of Diatessaronic witnesses comes to light with striking clarity. While this sequence disagrees at points with the sequence of Codex Fuldensis, the earliest Latin witness and the chief representative (along perhaps with the Tuscan Harmony) of the so-called Western family, scholars generally presume that the shared sequence of the Arabic Harmony and Ephraem reflects the sequence of Tatian himself.[7] In

---

[4] The recent suggestion of Koltun-Fromm (2008) that Tatian was not in fact the author of the *Diatessaron*, as intriguing as it may be, strikes me as relying on a level of skepticism towards tradition that, if applied evenly to all early church history, would render the patristic corpus as mere smoke and mirrors. Moreover, the author crucially assumes, wrongly in my view (see discussion below), that the *Oratio* was written after Tatian's break from Rome.

[5] Ephraem's *Commentary* finds its best attestation in two twelfth-century Armenian manuscripts, translations of which were published in 1876. Whether or not Harnack (1881, 475) was the first to seize upon the potential of using Ephraem's order to reconstruct the order of the *Diatessaron*, Zahn (1881) was the first to lay out a detailed reconstruction of the latter, which, according to Petersen (1994, 122), "many connoisseurs regard... as unsurpassed."

[6] J.H. Hill 1894, 15.

[7] So, e.g., Petersen (1994, 178) who follows F.C. Burkitt (1924).

the twentieth century, building afresh on the major harmonies descendent from the Diatessaronic tradition, Louis Leloir has refined Zahn's sequencing further.[8] To the best of my knowledge, Leloir's work has gone unsurpassed: grateful for this groundwork, we are able to reconstruct the original sequence of the *Diatessaron* with a fair degree of certitude, especially where Eastern and Western families agree.

From the beginning of the gospel harmony, it becomes clear that Tatian's ordering of pericopae speaks to a high view of John. As commences the Fourth Gospel (John 1:1), so commences Tatian's gospel harmony: "In the beginning was the Word and the Word was with God and the Word was God."[9] Not only does the *Diatessaron* begin on a Johannine note, it appears to close on one as well: "There are, however, many other things which Jesus did, which if every single one of them were written down, I suppose that not even the very world would contain those books which would have to be written" (John 21:25).[10] That the Fourth Gospel provides the bookends of Tatian's harmony is significant, for it virtually goes without saying that there is something intrinsically programmatic about the beginning and ending of a composition. As is well known in the study of literary forms, the narrative frame provides the context against which the remainder is to be understood; it sets the stage and pulls closed the curtain, and as such is hermeneutically determinative. Tatian's life of Christ inescapably becomes the story of the "Word" who was "with God and was God," a story which closes with the same whimsical editorializing found at the end of the Fourth Gospel. By beginning and ending as it does, the *Diatessaron*, as Tatian is doubtlessly well aware, does more than lend its seal of approval to the Gospel of John; it implicates the Johannine text as a kind of hermeneutical lens through which Christ is to be understood.[11]

---

[8] Leloir 1956.

[9] This is clearly the case on both external and internal grounds. Aphrahat (*Demonstrations* 1.10) cites John 1:1 as the start of "the Gospel of our Saviour," doubtlessly the *Diatessaron*. As for textual witnesses, important Middle Dutch (aside from Utrecht), Middle High German, and Latin sources speak for the Western family; the Arabic Harmony and Ephraem secure John 1:1 as Tatian's starting point as well. Whilst the text of Codex Fuldensis begins with Luke 1:1–4, its *capitularia* (table of contents), which begins with John 1:1, betrays that at this point the text of Fuldensis has been tampered with. See Zahn 1881, 73–74, 113–114.

[10] Apparently convinced by the Arabic alone, Leloir (1956, 213) judges that Tatian ended with this verse.

[11] It will not do to suggest that the insertion of John 1:1–4 at the beginning was more or less an arbitrary choice, as if to say, "Well, where else might he have put it?"

The shaping force of the Fourth Gospel is further borne out on considering the way in which Tatian arranges subsequent pericopae. Zahn has already made this point on the surmise that Tatian has arranged his chronology according to the order of the Johannine Passovers.[12] Generally speaking, when Tatian considers the synoptic material, he prefers to follow the order of Matthew against Mark and Luke.[13] On comparing Tatian's reordering of Markan and Lukan material, it is clear that Tatian is more interested in preserving the order of the former.[14] But of all the evangelists, the one whose order is least disrupted is none other than John.[15] This last point should not be overpressed since one would expect fewer disagreements to settle in the case of John. However, interestingly, among the few places where John and Matthew are in conflict, Tatian can be found giving preference to the former by relocating the latter.

An instance of this can be gleaned from the witness of the Arabic Harmony and Codex Fuldensis, where the Calling of the Four Disciples (Matt 4:18–22//Mark 1:16–20) is moved to a point shortly before the description of the early Galilean ministry (Matt 4:12–16//Mark 1:17).[16] While the decision to transpose the pericope against their Matthean order is rather mystifying at first glance, it appears that Tatian is actually trying to resolve a conflict between Matthew and John. Matthew

---

We have to reckon with the fact that the author of the *Diatessaron* and the *Oratio* (among other no longer extant works) was far too well trained a rhetorician to have been oblivious to the significance of this move. While I might in some sense agree with Wiles ("we need to beware of thinking of... [Tatian] as setting out to interpret the [Fourth] Gospel" [1960, 99]), at the same time, we must guard against the opposite error which fails to see that placement of material *is* interpretation. Similarly, Zahn 1881, 261; Head 1992, 130–131, 137; and Nagel 2000, 72.

[12] See discussion in Zahn 1881, 249–261, partially summarized as follows: Tatian "hat seine Schema vom Gang der öffentlichen Wirksamkeit Jesu, wie gezeigt wurde und eigentlich selbstverständlich ist, sowie jemand den Versuch einer Verarbeitung aller vier Evangelien macht, hauptsächlich aus Johannes gewonnen. Zwischen dem ersten und dritten Passa nach der Taufe Jesu verläuft eine zwei-jährige Wirksamkeit. Sowohl den Anfangspunkt, als auch das die Grenzscheide der beiden Jahre bildende Passa und die das zweite Jahr in drei ungleiche Abschnitte theilenden Feste der Laubhütten und der Tempelweihe und die auf diese Feste fallenden Besuche Jerusalems: also mit einem Wort das ganze chronologische Fachwerk hat er aus Johannes" (261).

[13] J.H. Hill 1894, 27; Leloir 1956, 210.

[14] According to J.H. Hill (1894, 30–31), this is particularly noticeable in the middle section of Luke (9:51–19), where dislocations relative to Matthew and Mark are innumerable.

[15] J.H. Hill (1894, 30–31) finds that the number of dislocations of John is about half that of Matthew or Mark.

[16] The passage is omitted in Ephraem.

has Jesus beginning his Galilean ministry *after* John the Baptizer is arrested (Matt 4:12); this in turn is followed by the calling of the four fishermen (Matt 4:18–22). Meanwhile, John shows Jesus beginning his Galilean ministry *before* John's arrest (John 3:22–26; 4:1–3). By moving the call of the four disciples to a point prior to John's imprisonment, Tatian seems to have made his favorite Synoptic Gospel bow out to John in the interest of chronological accuracy.[17]

Another conflict between John and the synoptic tradition occurs in connection with the Anointing at Bethany. Matthew and Mark agree that this anointing (Mark 14:3–9//Matt 26:6–13) follows Jesus' Triumphal Entry into Jerusalem (Mark 11:1–10//Matt 21:1–9). John, however, makes the anointing (John 12:1–8) take place before the Triumphal Entry (John 12:12–19). Perhaps with added inducement from John's chronological markers (John 12:1,12), Tatian follows the fourth evangelist (anointing then entry) against the combined testimony of the first and second evangelists (entry then anointing). Again, the synoptic material gives right of way to the Johannine text. When forced to choose between John on the one side and Matthew and Mark on the other, Tatian opts for the former.

In Matthew, the Healing of the Leper (8:2–4) follows on the heels of the Sermon on the Mount (Matthew 5–7), yet for some reason the *Diatessaron* skips right over this pericope to the Healing of the Centurion's Servant (Matt 8:5–13). Tatian then reinserts the Healing of the Leper between the Healing of the Syro-Phonecian Woman (Matt 15:21–28//Mark 7:24–30) and Jesus' Healings on the Mountain (Matt 15:29–31).[18] Mark has the parallel story of the leper much earlier in Jesus' ministry (Mark 1:40–45), and had Tatian here been impressed by Mark's order, he would have surely inserted it between Jesus' Praying in a Solitary Place (Mark 1:35–39) and the Healing of the Paralytic (Mark 2:1–12).[19] Like Mark, Luke also has the Healing of the Paralytic (Luke 5:17–26) immediately following the Healing of the Leper (Luke 5:12–16). But even though Luke's order is corroborated by Mark, the

---

[17] As convincingly argued by Zahn 1884, 249–250, followed by J.H. Hill 1894, 30.

[18] This is at least the case in the Eastern witness. Codex Fuldensis keeps the Healing of the Leper immediately after the Sermon on the Mount, but this probably was done so as to conform Tatian's text to Matthew.

[19] This is all the more surprising seeing that Mark, somewhat uncharacteristically, chronologically links the Healing of the Paralytic to the Healing of the Leper with the phrase "a few days later" (Mark 2:1).

third evangelist too is ignored by Tatian at this point. What might have swayed the author of the *Diatessaron* to relocate the Healing of the Leper against the witness of all three Synoptic Gospels?

The short answer, it seems, is John. Mark implies that when the leper came to Jesus (Mark 1:40), it was the midst of Jesus' tour of the "next towns" (Mark 1:38) scattered "throughout all Galilee" (Mark 1:39). Luke also pinpoints Jesus' healing of the leper in "one of the towns" (Luke 5:12), presumably, given the surrounding Lukan context, within Galilee. Tatian seems to have associated this stint in Galilee with the Galilean visit recorded in John 4:43–45, which in his *Diatessaron* immediately precedes the Healing of the Leper (Matt 8:2–4 parr.). Tatian moves the Healing of the Leper to the end of John 4, it seems to me, in order to connect this healing with the Healing at the Pool of Bethesda (John 5:1–15). Because Tatian's juxtaposition of passages was sometimes driven by thematic resemblances (not just chronological sequence), and because these two accounts have some striking similarities, not least their both being centrally concerned with the question of willingness (whether on the part of Jesus in Mark 1:40 or on the part of the suppliant in John 5:6), I find that the Johannine Healing at the Pool story had an overwhelming gravitational pull on the synoptic Healing of the Leper. Not insignificantly, Tatian's interest in grouping the two passages together prompts him to disrupt the trajectory of the triple tradition rather than move the Johannine material.

These examples are merely illustrative of the way in which John's Gospel influenced Tatian's ordering of his harmony. They are not meant to imply that there are no occurrences whereby John's material is transposed for the sake of conforming to the synoptic record. Indeed there are. The clearest example of one such transposition is in the Cleansing of the Temple. Over the centuries readers of John have struggled as to whether John's temple cleansing was meant to be the same event depicted by the triple tradition at the end of Jesus' ministry or whether there were in fact two cleansings. Tatian opts for the former option. Consequently, he moves the Johannine account (John 2:12–22), along with the meeting with Nicodemus, to a relatively later point in his story. Thus if we surmise a gospel's weightiness on the basis of its gravitational pull, the pull is by no means unidirectional.

This suggests that for Tatian the Fourth Gospel was no mere supplement to the story of Jesus. Rather, in John the author of the *Diatessaron* found an account which was faithful in its theological reflection and credible as a historical record. There is not the slightest indication that Tatian considered the Fourth Gospel any less reliable than the first three gospels. On the contrary, John seems to have been the foundation stone on which the building blocks of synoptic material were laid; it was also the edifice around which these same synoptic materials would be forced to bend. At the same time, it would go beyond the evidence to say that in Tatian's eyes the authority of John outstrips that of the synoptics. For the author of the *Diatessaron*, John is a kind of *primus inter pares*.[20]

2. The Fourth Gospel and Tatian's Heresy

Having established Tatian's high view of the Gospel of John, it remains to be shown whether his appreciation might be connected with his alleged lapse into heresy.[21] After all, if Tatian came to use John as scripture only as a result of the heterodox outlook he acquired late in life, this would certainly confirm that the Fourth Gospel was, as late as the 170s, *en vogue* among the Gnostics but, correspondingly, unfashionable among the proto-orthodox. In this case too we could only suppose that Irenaeus' endorsement of John was indeed something of a breakthrough if not a complete *volte-face* within the great church tradition. On the other hand, if Tatian's appropriation of John cannot be convincingly linked to his theological turn, but can be better explained by influences within the proto-orthodox trajectory, then this too has implications, which point in a very different direction. For reasons I hope to make clear, the latter path seems to make far more sense of the available evidence.

Like so many events in second-century history, Tatian's turn to heresy is shrouded in obscurity, at least in the details. We do, however, have as a starting point certain remarks first handed down by Irenaeus:

---

[20] It may be that John came close to sharing this status with the First Gospel. This would at any rate fit quite well with the early church's predilection for the apostolic evangelists.

[21] I am quite aware that categories of "heresy" and "(proto-)orthodoxy" risk anachronism. At the same time, it is clear the great church maintained such categories, as the rite of excommunication implies, even if these categories were themselves quite fluid. I use the terms here and throughout for the sake of concision.

Springing from Saturninus and Marcion, those who are called Encratites (self-controlled) preached against marriage... Some of those reckoned among them have also introduced abstinence from animal food, thus proving themselves ungrateful to God, who formed all things. They deny, too, the salvation of him who was first created. It is but lately, however, that this opinion has been invented among them. A certain man named Tatian first introduced the blasphemy. He was a hearer of Justin's, and as long as he continued with him he expressed no such views; but after his martyrdom he separated from the Church, and, excited and puffed up by the thought of being a teacher, as if he were superior to others, he composed his own peculiar type of doctrine. He invented a system of certain invisible Aeons, like the followers of Valentinus; while, like Marcion and Saturninus, he declared that marriage was nothing else than corruption and fornication. But his denial of Adam's salvation was an opinion due entirely to himself.[22]

While rumor would circulate among later church fathers that Tatian was the founder of Encratism (Eusebius, *Hist. eccl.* 4.29.6), the bishop of Lyons makes no such claim. Instead, according to Irenaeus, the author of the *Diatessaron* joined the Encratites and subsequently won them over to his belief in Adam's perdition. Although Tatian is said to have shared, while he was attached to the Encratite community, an interest in invisible Aeons with the Valentinians and negative views on marriage with Marcion and Saturninus, Irenaeus emphasizes that the doctrine regarding Adam originated with Tatian himself. The bishop's account seems to suggest that "this blasphemy" was the precipitating cause of conflict with the church at Rome, the unsatisfactory resolution of which culminated in Tatian's separation at some point after the death of his mentor, Justin Martyr († 163–168 CE). According to Eusebius, Tatian's break with the Roman church occurred about 172 CE, a date which admirably fits the evidence.[23]

To be sure, it is quite possible and indeed probable that Irenaeus' remarks are tinted with exaggeration—proto-orthodox criticism of the lapsed was seldom understated. At the same time, there must be some substance to the bishop's words, for it is clear that Tatian and the church do part ways and that in a time when the Roman church was relatively tolerant.[24] It is at any rate not unlikely that the author of the *Diatessaron* became increasingly sympathetic with the very sects

---

[22] Irenaeus, *Adv. haer.* 1.28.1 (transl., ANF 1:353).
[23] See discussion in Petersen 2005, 129–134.
[24] See Lampe 2003, 385–396.

mentioned by Irenaeus, and therefore there is no *a priori* reason to rule out the possibility that Tatian's high view of John evolved out of these sympathies. Of course, saying that something is "possible" is not the same thing as saying that it is "likely." The likelihood that Tatian's high view of John derived from Marcion, Saturninus and Valentinus must be assessed on the evidence.

Before turning to this issue, it bears considering Tatian's goals in composing his *Diatessaron*. The question has been taken up in depth by Tjitze Baarda, who, after noting Tatian's chastisement of Greek historians who muddle their facts and live at ease with their contradictions, summarizes the *Diatessaron's raison d'être* as follows:

> The *Diatessaron* was a careful attempt to create *one* historical account of the words and deeds of Jesus, as far as they could be reconstructed on the basis of the memoirs of the apostles contained in the various gospels, predominantly those which later on received canonical status. The basic idea of the harmony was that the truth becomes visible in unity and harmony. The sources contained discrepancies and contradictions, but by using historical methods the historian could demonstrate that one universal biography of Jesus could be created which solved the διαφωνία of the sources in the συμφωνία of a harmony.[25]

Baarda's conclusion is persuasive; it fits everything we know about the composer of the *Diatessaron*.[26] While certain Christians, like the later Origen and those of the Alexandrian school, remained impervious to apparent discrepancies between the gospels, as these difficulties only underscored the necessity of a "spiritual" (as opposed to literal) reading of the scriptures, Tatian was cut from a different hermeneutical cloth. Convinced that truth must exhibit a thoroughgoing unity, the history behind the gospels—precisely because the gospels were true— also had to exhibit the same kind of unity. Certainly, the *Diatessaron* was born partially out of scholarly inquisitiveness, but the Assyrian had a very practical apologetic concern as well. In drawing up his gospel harmony, Tatian was in essence seeking to assure his faithful readers of the factual trustworthiness of the four gospels despite the occasional appearance of discord, which was especially emphasized by the opponents of proto-orthodoxy.

---

[25] Baarda 1989, 133–154; see 142–143, quote on p. 154.
[26] See Elze 1960, 34–40.

Among those whom Tatian would have had in the forefront of his mind were the Marcionites. As the Marcionites saw it, the gospels were far from harmonious; in fact, they flatly contradicted one another.[27] Sharing Tatian's assumption that the gospels' truthfulness depended on their consonance, but parting ways with the Assyrian's conviction that the four-fold gospels were historically reconcilable, the Marcionites saw the disagreements among the gospels as decisively undermining their usefulness for faith and practice. Not much later than the middle of the second century, when Justin's church was using a plurality of "Memoirs" and Marcion was singling out the Third Gospel and only the Third Gospel as authoritative, Marcionites must have searched intently for gospel difficulties so as to provide grist for their polemical mills.[28] With this same debate showing no signs of cooling in his time, Tatian would have simply conceived his project as part and parcel of this conversation, that is, as a means of refuting the hugely successful Marcionites. So, even if the Assyrian eventually came to share Marcion's negative views on marriage, this does not necessarily mean that he saw himself as having been influenced by the Pontic shipbuilder (Irenaeus only says that Tatian's view was "like [that of] Marcion"); much less does it imply that Tatian's view of scriptures was somehow positively shaped by the Marcionite movement. On the contrary, like Justin (his mentor) before him and Rhodon (his student) after him, Tatian, in composing the *Diatessaron*, appears to be joining a larger effort to head off Marcion's criticism of the four-fold gospel. While it hardly bears stating since, as is well known, Marcion had already decisively rejected John, Tatian could hardly have acquired his fondness for John from Marcion.

---

[27] A fine example of the later Marcionites' biting criticism can be found in the *Dialogue of Adamantius* 1.7 (van den Sande Bakhuyzen 1901, 14):

ΜΕΓ. Διαφωνοῦσι τὰ εὐαγγέλια καὶ ἄλλα καὶ ἄλλα λέγουσιν, ὅθεν φαίνεται φάλσα.

ΑΔ. Ἄλλον καὶ ἄλλον Χριστὸν εὐαγγελίζονται; ἐν τούτῳ οἴει διαφωνεῖν;

ΜΕΓ. Οὔκ, ἀλλ᾽ ἀντίκειται.

Meg.: The gospels disagree; some say one thing, while others another thing. All of from which appear falsities.

Ad.: Do they preach one Christ and then another Christ? Is it in this respect you say that they disagree?

Meg.: No, rather they contradict each other.

[28] Marcion's student, Apelles, likely picked up on the Greek penchant for teasing out inconsistencies and turned it against his proto-orthodox foes. See Harnack 1924, 1:361.

But even if Tatian always lined up with the proto-orthodox in their practical insistence (against Marcion) on multiple authoritative gospels, this does not rule out the possibility that it was the movement initiated by Valentinus,[29] who in Irenaeus' account of Tatian's apostasy is mentioned alongside with Saturninus,[30] that ultimately induced the Assyrian to include John in the harmony. After all, as has been pointed out elsewhere, the Valentinians (like Tatian) also seem to have been especially attracted to John.[31] In this case, it was Tatian's commitment to the plurality of the gospels that led him to compose his harmony, but it was his accession to Valetinianism that led him to include John.

Despite the initial persuasiveness of this reconstruction, it is not, in my mind, fully persuasive. When we consider Tatian's goals in composing the *Diatessaron* and the hermeneutical disposition which those goals reflect, which I have discussed above, and when we consider, by contrast, the "spiritual" exegesis so characteristic of the Valentinian school (including Valentinus, Theodotus, Ptolemy, and Heracleon), it becomes clear that any theory that explains Tatian's use of John simply by the Valentinians' use of the same gospel is woefully inadequate. Such a theory founders because it fails to realize that while for the Valentinians the appropriation of John alongside the Synoptic Gospels was intrinsically unproblematic, in the mind of Tatian, who was constrained by theological necessity to maintain the historical compatibility of the gospels, the idea of *adding* John (again, on the assumption that he was persuaded to do so only through his contact with the Valentinians) would have been fraught with difficulties. In other words, it is patently unlikely that the Valentinians could have persuaded Tatian to accept John since they were apparently not able to win him over to their hermeneutic, a hermeneutic which for the Valentinians was the only means of rendering the Fourth Gospel as admissible in the first place.

---

[29] Given the larger argument of Markschies 1992, I will leave open the possibility that Irenaeus is confounding the views of Valentinus with those of his more extreme followers.

[30] It makes no sense to consider Saturninus as an advocate for John as there is no evidence that he used the Fourth Gospel. It is even possible that this disciple of Menander never even knew the text existed. See Braun 1959, 293; and C.E. Hill 2004, 224.

[31] Irenaeus, *Adv. haer.* 3.11.7. Baarda (1989, 150) sees this shared privileging of John as possible grounds for linking Tatian's use of John with Valentinus.

A more likely explanation for Tatian's use of John lies closer to hand in Justin Martyr. While earlier investigation of Justin has indeed emphasized the apologist's reticence to use the Fourth Gospel, more recent scholarship, while not necessarily denying this reticence, is at least calling its significance into question. It is, I believe, now becoming increasingly clear that Justin did use the four now-canonical gospels and speaks of normative Christianity as habitually using the same four.[32] Moreover, if Tatian sat at Justin's feet, and if Justin knew and used John authoritatively, then it makes most sense to suppose that Tatian's attachment to the Fourth Gospel came not through heterodox influence but by way of Justin.[33] When Tatian defects from the proto-orthodox ranks after the death of his master, he takes his high view of John with him.

This explanation is confirmed in light of Charles Hill's illuminating discussion of Tatian's *Oratio ad Graecos*. Here Hill reminds us that Tatian quotes authoritatively from the Fourth Gospel at more than a handful of places (*Orat.* 4.1–2 [= John 4:24], *Orat.* 5.1 [= John 1:1], *Orat.* 13.1–2 [= John 1:4,5], *Orat.* 19.4 [= John 1:3]).[34] It can be maintained that Tatian's use of John found its impetus in his heretical turn if and only if the *Oratio* was subsequent to that turn. The evidence seems to indicate otherwise. There are two factors in particular that point in this direction. First, as W.L. Petersen points out, Tatian's apology seems to have been written fairly close to the time of his conversion (cf. *Orat.* 35.2), that is, probably at some point in the late 150s.[35] Secondly, as Hill remarks, the wording of *Oratio* 19 would lead us to believe that Justin was in fact still alive at the time of the document's writing.[36] The bulk of evidence then leads us, along with a fairly sizable contingent of scholars, to locate the *Oratio* fairly early in Tatian's career, and therefore, well before his break from the great church. This means that Tatian had already—long before the *Diatessaron* was probably even conceived—authoritatively cited John in a proto-orthodox

---

[32] The argument of Stanton 2003 is particularly persuasive.
[33] On the evidence for Justin's influence on Tatian see Lampe 2003, 285–291; and Hunt 2003, 116–122.
[34] C.E. Hill 2004, 223.
[35] See C.E. Hill 2004, 299, where he cites Petersen 1994, 73n120. On the dating of Tatian's conversion, see Petersen 2005, 134.
[36] C.E. Hill 2004, 299.

context.[37] Again, this leads us to suppose that Tatian inherited his high view from Justin's community at some point in the 150s.

This still leaves unresolved the question as to why Tatian is more forthright in his use of the Fourth Gospel, at least compared to Justin. I have argued above that in Tatian's eyes John occupied a 'first among equals' status. This does not seem to have been the case with Tatian's teacher. How is Tatian's more direct and more explicit use of John to be explained? I think we can begin by recalling that the period in which Tatian wrote his gospel harmony is also a time in which we detect a certain defensive posture in regards to the Fourth Gospel. In this connection, we might think of the *Muratorian Fragment* or Irenaeus' remarks. I quote them both below:

> The fourth of the Gospels is that of John, one of the disciples. To his fellow disciples and bishops, who had been urging him to write, he said, "Fast with me from today to three days, and what will be revealed to each one let us tell it to one another." In the same night it was revealed to Andrew, one of the apostles, that John should write down all things in his own name while all of them should review it. And so, though various elements may be taught in the individual books of the Gospels, nevertheless this makes no difference to the faith of believers, since by the one sovereign Spirit have been declared all things in all the Gospels: concerning the nativity, concerning the passion, concerning the resurrection, concerning life with his disciples, and concerning his twofold coming...[38]

> And therefore the Gospels are in accord with all these things, among which Christ Jesus is seated. For that according to John relates His original, effectual, and glorious generation from the Father, thus declaring, "In the beginning was the Word, and the Word was with God, and the Word was God." Also, "all things were made by Him, and without Him was nothing made." For this reason, too, is that Gospel full of all confidence, for such is His person.[39]

Judging by the language of both texts ("All things in *all* the Gospels" and "that Gospel is *full of all confidence*" [italics added]), it appears that some either from within or without the church have been leveling charges against John's credibility. It can hardly be a coincidence that about the same time Celsus, as cited by Origen, is voicing his

---

[37] See bibliography provided by C.E. Hill 2004, 299. See also Hunt 2003, 3.
[38] *Muratorian Fragment*, lines 9–23, as translated by Metzger (1987, 305–307) with slight modification.
[39] Irenaeus, *Adv. haer.* 3.11.8 (transl., ANF 1:428).

complaints in regards to Christians who are repeatedly revising their gospels:

> After this he says that some believers, as though from a drinking bout, go so far as to oppose themselves and alter the original text of the gospels three or four or several times over, and they change its character to enable them to deny difficulties in face of criticism.[40]

While there are different ways to understand Celsus's words (for example, as referring to fast and loose copying practices among Christians), I take it that the famed opponent of Christianity is referring to the plurality of now-canonical gospels (explaining why he says that they have been made over "three or four times").[41] His criticism, which roughly dates to the time of the *Diatessaron*'s composition, concerns the discrepancies between the gospel accounts; it was a criticism which naturally could have been partially, maybe even largely, averted by the church's dropping the Fourth Gospel. Assuming that these kinds of arguments against Christianity and its prized texts were already in the air before the 170s, we now have an important backdrop for Tatian's project. In this case, it would be mistaken to think of the *Diatessaron* as having been created in a vacuum; rather, it was composed, at least in part, to confirm in the face of gainsayers both the appropriateness of multiple gospels and the appropriateness of John itself. As such, Tatian's harmony is more than a synthesis of the gospels for the curious and perplexed; it is an *apologia* for four-fold gospel and, therefore too, for the Fourth Gospel itself.

3. Conclusion

In the preceding discussion, I have attempted to establish two points. First, I have sought to show that on examination the *Diatessaron*'s sequence betrays a high view of the Fourth Gospel on the part of its author. Not only is the Gospel of John on par with the synoptics, it is in some sense the backdrop against which the other three are to be understood. Second, taking up the argument that Tatian's high view of John was only a result of his turn to heterodoxy, I have considered the sectarians associated early on with Tatian's break from the great

---

[40] Origen, *Cels.* 2.27.1–5 (Chadwick 1953, 90).
[41] So too Merkel 1971, 12.

church. When the evidence is weighed, it appears that none of the sus-
pects can be convincingly charged with smuggling John's Gospel into
Tatian's thought-world. Instead, Tatian fell heir to the Fourth Gospel
while under Justin and Justin's proto-orthodox church. The added
emphasis which Tatian lays on John, at least when he is compared to
his mentor, can be partially explained as the Assyrian's contribution
to a broadly based apologetic for the Fourth Gospel. Seeing that this
takes place after Tatian's break from Rome, it appears that this defense
of John fell across sectarian (proto-orthodox and heterodox) lines.

Although all we have left of Tatian's *Diatessaron* is its wake of textual witnesses, it continues to speak. From it we learn then that the
Fourth Gospel had its late-second-century defenders arising from
theologically diverse quarters; we learn too that if there was a swell-
ing wave of Johannine approval within the sea of second-century
Christianity, that wave was already taking recognizable shape at least
a generation before the bishop of Lyons set pen to paper. In light of
the former point, perhaps it is time to discard the assumption that
the orthodox Irenaeus and the lapsed Tatian could not have agreed,
for all their mutual misgivings, on the authority of John within the
four-fold canon. Perhaps too, in light of the latter point, it is time
to ask ourselves whether Irenaeus' validation of the Fourth Gospel is
anywhere as innovative or significant as it has typically been made
out to be. Sometimes the lines of history, by which historians mark
out epochal turning-points and discrete movements, are more sharply
defined than reality warrants.

BIBLIOGRAPHY

Baarda, T., "ΔΙΑΦΩΝΙΑ—ΣΥΜΦΩΝΙΑ: Factors in the Harmonization of the Gospels,
    Especially in the Diatessaron of Tatian," *Gospel Traditions in the Second Century:
    Origins, Recensions, Text and Transmission*, B. Aland and W.L. Petersen, eds., Notre
    Dame, Ind.: University of Notre Dame Press, 1989, 133–156.
Barrett, C.K., *The Gospel according to St. John: An Introduction with Commentary and
    Notes on the Greek Text*, Philadelphia: Westminster, ²1978.
Bauer, W., *Orthodoxy and Heresy in Earliest Christianity*, R.A. Kraft and G. Krodel,
    eds., Philadelphia: Fortress, 1971, reprinted Mifflintown, Pa.: Sigler, 1996.
Braun, F.-M., *Jean le théologien et son Évangile dans l'Église ancienne*, Études Bibliques,
    Paris: Librairie Lecoffre / Gabalda, 1959.
Brown, R.E., *The Community of the Beloved Disciple*, New York: Paulist Press, 1979.
Burkitt, F.C., "Tatian's Diatessaron and the Dutch Harmonies," *Journal of Theological
    Studies* 25 (1924), 113–130.
Campenhausen, H.F. von, *The Formation of the Christian Bible*, Philadelphia: Fortress,
    1972.

Chadwick, H., *Origen: Contra Celsum*, Cambridge: Cambridge University Press, 1953.

Culpepper, R.A., *John, the Son of Zebedee: The Life of a Legend*, Studies on Personalities of the New Testament, Columbia: University of South Carolina Press, 1994.

Elze, M., *Tatian und seine Theologie*, Forschungen zur Kirchen- und Dogmengeschichte 9, Göttingen: Vandenhoeck & Ruprecht, 1960.

Gamble, H.Y., *The New Testament Canon: Its Making and Meaning*, Guides to Biblical Scholarship, New Testament Series, Philadelphia: Fortress, 1985.

Haenchen, E., *John 1: A Commentary on the Gospel of John Chapters 1-6*, R.W. Funk, transl., Hermeneia, Philadelphia: Fortress, 1984.

Harnack, A. von, "Tatian's Diatessaron und Marcion's Commentar zum Evangelium bei Ephraem Syrus," *Zeitschrift für Kirchengeschichte* 4 (1881), 471–505.

—— *Die Mission und Ausbreitung des Christentums in den ersten drei Jahrhunderten*, 2 vols., Leipzig: Hinrichs, ⁴1924.

Head, P.M., "Tatian's Christology and its Influence on the Composition of the Diatessaron," *Tyndale Bulletin* 43 (1992), 121–137.

Hill, C.E., *The Johannine Corpus in the Early Church*, Oxford: Oxford University Press, 2004.

Hill, J.H., *The Earliest Life of Christ Ever Compiled from the Four Gospels, being the Diatessaron of Tatian, Literally Translated from the Arabic Version and Containing the Four Gospels Woven into One Story*, Edinburgh: T&T Clark, 1894.

Hunt, E.J., *Christianity in the Second Century: The Case of Tatian*, London: Routledge, 2003.

Keefer, K., *The Branches of the Gospel of John: The Reception of the Fourth Gospel in the Early Church*, Library of New Testament Studies 332, London: T&T Clark, 2006.

Koltun-Fromm, N., "Re-Imagining Tatian: The Damaging Effects of Polemical Rhetoric," *Journal of Early Christian Studies* 16 (2008), 1–30.

Lampe, P., *From Paul to Valentinus: Christians at Rome in the First Two Centuries*, M. Steinhauser, transl., Minneapolis: Fortress, 2003.

Leloir, L., "Le Diatessaron de Tatian," *L'Orient syrien* 1 (1956), 208–231.

Lindars, B., *The Gospel of John: Based on the Revised Standard Version*, New Century Bible Commentary, Grand Rapids, Mich.: Eerdmans, 1982.

Markschies, C., *Valentinus Gnosticus? Untersuchungen zur valentinianischen Gnosis mit einem Kommentar zu den Fragmenten Valentins*, Wissenschaftliche Untersuchungen zum Neuen Testament 65, Tübingen: Mohr (Paul Siebeck), 1992.

Merkel, H., *Die Widersprüche zwischen den Evangelien: Ihre polemische und apologetische Behandlung in den Alten Kirche bis zu Augustin*, Wissenschaftliche Untersuchungen zum Neuen Testament 13, Tübingen: Mohr (Siebeck), 1971.

Metzger, B.M., *The Canon of the New Testament: Its Origin, Development, and Significance*, Oxford: Clarendon Press, 1987.

Nagel, T., *Die Rezeption des Johannesevangeliums im 2. Jahrhundert: Studien zur vorirenäischen Aneignung und Auslegung des vierten Evangeliums in christlicher und christlich-gnosticher Literatur*, Arbeiten zur Bibel und ihrer Geschichte 2, Leipzig: Evangelische Verlagsanstalt, 2000.

Perrin, N., "Hermeneutical Factors in the Harmonization of the Gospels and the Question of Textual Authority," *The Biblical Canons*, J.-M. Auwers and H.J. de Jonge, eds., Bibliotheca Ephemeridum Theologicarum Lovaniensium 163, Leuven: Leuven University Press / Peeters, 2003, 599–605.

Petersen, W.L., *Tatian's Diatessaron: Its Creation, Dissemination, Significance and History in Scholarship*, Supplements to Vigiliae Christianae 25, Leiden: Brill, 1994.

—— "The Diatessaron and the Fourfold Gospel," *The Origins and Transmissions of the Earliest Gospels—The Contribution of the Chester Beatty Gospel Codex P⁴⁵*, C. Horton, ed., Journal for the Study of the New Testament Supplement Series 258, London: T&T Clark, 2004, 50–68.

—— "Tatian the Assyrian," *A Companion to Second-Century Christian 'Heretics,'* A. Marjanen and P. Luomanen, eds., Supplements to Vigiliae Christianae 76, Leiden: Brill, 2005, 125–158.

Poffet, J.-M., "Indices de réception de l'Évangile de Jean au IIe siècle, avant Irénée," *Communauté johannique et son histoire: La trajectoire d'évangile de Jean aux deux premiers siècles*, J.-D. Kaestli, J.-M. Poffet and J. Zumstein, eds., Le monde de la Bible, Geneva: Labor et Fides, 1990, 305–326.

Roberts, A. and J. Donaldson, *The Ante-Nicene Fathers*, 10 vols., 1885–1887, reprinted Peabody, Mass.: Hendrickson, 1994.

Sanders, J.N., *The Fourth Gospel in the Early Church: Its Origin and Influence on Christian Theology up to Irenaeus*, Cambridge: Cambridge University Press, 1943.

Schnackenburg, R., *The Gospel According to St. John*, Herder's Theological Commentary on the New Testament, London: Burns & Oates, 1968.

Stanton, G., "Jesus Traditions and Gospels in Justin Martyr and Irenaeus," *The Biblical Canons*, J.-M. Auwers and H.J. de Jonge, eds., Bibliotheca Ephemeridum Theologicarum Lovaniensium 163, Leuven: Leuven University Press / Peeters, 2003, 353–370.

van de Sande Bakhuyzen, W.H., *Der Dialog des Adamantius: ΠΕΡΙ ΤΗΣ ΕΙΣ ΘΕΟΝ ΟΡΘΗΣ ΠΙΣΤΕΩΣ*, Leipzig: Hinrichs, 1901.

Wiles, M.F., *The Spiritual Gospel: The Interpretation of the Fourth Gospel in the Early Church*, Cambridge: Cambridge University Press, 1960.

Zahn, T., *Forschungen zur Geschichte des neutestamentlichen Kanons und der altkirchlichen Literatur*, Erlangen: Deichert, 1881.

Zumstein, J., "La communauté johannique et son histoire," *Communauté johannique et son histoire: La trajectoire d'évangile de Jean aux deux premiers siècles*, J.-D. Kaestli, J.-M. Poffet and J. Zumstein, eds., Le monde de la Bible, Geneva: Labor et Fides, 1990, 359–374.

JOHN AND HIS GOSPEL IN THE MIRROR OF IRENAEUS OF LYONS: PERSPECTIVES OF RECENT RESEARCH

Bernhard Mutschler
Evangelische Hochschule Ludwigsburg

In Memory of Birgit Michaela Rettich-Mutschler (1967–2008), my beloved wife, mother of our three children

The last fifteen years have seen the development of a new interest in the relationship between the Gallic bishop, Irenaeus of Lyons, and some of the main New Testament authors he frequently quotes.[1] In the case of the Gospel of John, however, monographic contributions have been rare.[2] In this summary, I would like to present some aspects of how the recent research has seen John and his gospel in the mirror of Irenaeus of Lyons. Subdivided into three parts, this essay presents (1) a historical perspective, (2) a literary perspective, and (3) a theological perspective.

1. What Irenaeus Reveals about John— A Historical Perspective[3]

After collecting the information Irenaeus gives about John (1.1), we will ask from which sources these details were derived, and whether they are trustworthy or not (1.2).

---

[1] See Noormann 1994 (*Corpus Paulinum*); Bingham 1998 (Gospel of Matthew); and Mutschler 2004a (*Corpus Johanneum*). Research on Irenaeus and Luke-Acts, especially the Gospel of Luke, is still wanting. It would also be desirable to see an investigation into the reception of 1 Peter and the figure of the disciple Peter, and, of course, a study on Irenaeus and the Gospel of Mark, which has been nearly completely neglected in this regard.

[2] For a lucid and prominent treatment, see Lewis 1908; Loewenich 1932; and Ciani 1955. A short history of modern research is found in Mutschler 2004a, 4–8.

[3] For a brief summary, see Mutschler 2006, 501–503.

1.1. *Irenaeus about John*

It was observed already long ago that the church father[4] of the second century knows more details about the fourth evangelist than he does about the other three.[5] To show this concretely, Irenaeus mentions Matthew 16 times by name, Mark 7 times, and Luke 31 times (altogether 54), while he mentions John alone about 60 times.[6] Peter is mentioned almost as often (46 times), and among the New Testament authors only Paul, naturally, is named more often than John by Irenaeus (approximately 120 times).[7] For Irenaeus, John is the *discipulus Domini* par excellence, *the* disciple of the Lord. All combinations of *Dominus* and *discipulus* are, in fact, exclusively reserved for John![8]

Certain other remarkable observations can be made, too.[9] The most common form of the formula, "disciple of the Lord," in Greek is, Ἰωάννης ὁ τοῦ Κυρίου μαθητής and in many cases Irenaeus continues with φησί (or *inquit, ait, meminerit, dicens, dixisset,* εἰρήκει).[10] Eleven explicit quotations from the Fourth Gospel, 2 John and Revelation, are thus similarly, although not stereotypically, introduced. However, the formula *discipulus Domini* was not invented by Irenaeus; he probably took it over from his traditions in Asia Minor[11] or—in the case of *Adv. haer.* 3.1.1—Rome.

The formula, ὁ τοῦ Κυρίου μαθητής, is not, in fact, found in the Fourth Gospel (nor in other parts of the New Testament). (Irenaeus, for his part, does not use the Johannine expression, "disciple whom Jesus loved," which appears five times in the Fourth Gospel.)[12] It is, however, fairly easy to see how the formula was developed out of the

---

[4] Kraft 1991, 69: "der erste katholische Kirchenvater"; Campenhausen 1965, 7: "ein wahrhaft ökumenischer Kirchenvater."

[5] Hoh 1919, 33: "vom vierten Evangelisten ungleich mehr und spezielleres weiß als von den übrigen drei."

[6] Mutschler 2006, 501; similarly Mutschler 2004a, 696. Reynders 1954, 2:88, 92, 175, 185, 192–193, 237; Reynders 1958, 8, 10.

[7] Mutschler 2006, 501. Cf. Reynders 1954, 2:21, 41, 88, 231, 237; Reynders 1958, 10.

[8] Irenaeus, *Adv. haer.* 1.8.5 (twice); 1.16.3; 2.2.5; 2.22.3; 2.22.5; 3.1.1; 3.3.4; 3.11.1 (twice); 3.11.3; 3.16.5; 3.16.8 (*eius* instead of *Domini*); 3.22.2 (αὐτοῦ instead of τοῦ Κυρίου); 4.20.11; 4.30.4; 5.18.2; 5.26.1; 5.33.3; 5.35.2; *Ep. Vict.* (Eusebius, *Hist. eccl.* 5.24.16). See the critical edition of Rousseau, Doutreleau et al. 1965–1982.

[9] For a comparison chart, see Mutschler 2004a, 163; and in detail ibid., 154–172.

[10] Mutschler 2004a, 164–166.

[11] Either presbyters as in Irenaeus, *Adv. haer.* 2.22.5; 4.30.4; 5.33.3; or Polycarp and his listeners, as in *Adv. haer.* 3.3.4.

[12] John 13:23; 19:26; 20:2; 21:7,20; Ruckstuhl and Dschulnigg 1991, 162 (= C 61).

Gospel of John. Μαθητής is used 78 times in John, more than in any other gospel or corpus in the Bible.[13] In the post-Easter perspective and post-Easter terminology, a "disciple of Jesus" becomes consequentially a "disciple of the Lord," a *discipulus Domini*.

For the sake of completeness, some earlier occurrences of the formula in the plural should also be mentioned here: (1) Acts 9:1 reports that Saul still raged "against the disciples of the Lord."[14] (2) Half a century before Irenaeus, Papias of Hierapolis mentions especially "Aristion and the elder John, (both) disciples of the Lord."[15] And (3) the *Martyrdom of Polycarp* refers generally to "disciples and imitators of the Lord."[16]

As for the singular formula itself, one may ask whether Irenaeus employs it so often in order to stress John's discipleship—which from a historical perspective is somewhat problematic—or in order to bolster the authority of the *youngest* gospel by attributing an apostolic origin to it. We may ask more precisely: Did Irenaeus want to emphasize the youngest gospel's origin amidst the Lord's circle of disciples? Be that as it may, the bishop of Lyons does not use the formula *discipulus Domini* incidentally, but addresses with it either a traditional or a scriptural topic: "Johannes ist in allen Fällen ein Gewährsmann von ganz besonderem Gewicht, der Schriftzitate oder Traditionen mit der Autorität dieses einzigartigen und besonderen Status als ὁ τοῦ Κυρίου μαθητής bzw. ὁ μαθητής τοῦ Κυρίου verbürgt."[17]

A further significant detail is that Irenaeus' only explicit use of the formula in the plural (*discipuli* or μαθηταί) is not traced back to a disciple, but to the Lord himself.[18]

So, it is not just any disciple, from whom the Fourth Gospel stems according to Irenaeus. It is "the disciple of the Lord," who "leaned upon His breast," as Irenaeus points out twice.[19] These are allusions to

---

[13] Morgenthaler 1973, 118. Ἀπόστολος, e.g., is used only once, in John 13:16.

[14] Εἰς τοὺς μαθητὰς τοῦ κυρίου (Acts 9:1).

[15] ...ἤ τις ἕτερος τῶν τοῦ κυρίου μαθητῶν ἅ τε Ἀριστίων καὶ ὁ πρεσβύτερος Ἰωάννης τοῦ κυρίου μαθηταί (Papias frg. 3 Holmes = frg. 5 Körtner and Leutzsch = frg. 2.4 (134,23–24) Funk and Bihlmeyer = 290,23–24 Lindemann and Paulsen; in Eusebius, *Hist. eccl.* 3.39.4).

[16] Μαθητὰς καὶ μιμητὰς τοῦ κυρίου (*Mart. Pol.* 17:3).

[17] Mutschler 2004a, 168.

[18] *Quemadmodum Dominus ait discipulis* (Irenaeus, *Adv. haer.* 4.9.1 [Matt 13:52]). For the plural, μαθηταί, see Mutschler 2004a, 162n51.

[19] Ὁ καὶ ἐπὶ τὸ στῆθος αὐτοῦ ἀναπεσών, Irenaeus, *Adv. haer.* 3.1.1 with frg. gr. 1:9–10 (Eusebius, *Hist. eccl.* 5.8.4); *ipse est in cuius pectore recumbebat ad cenam* (Irenaeus, *Adv. haer.* 4.20.11).

John 13:25 and/or 21:20,[20] and show a decisive and unique closeness between John and the Lord. This implies again that, for Irenaeus, John is "the" disciple, and correspondingly Christ is his "teacher" (*Iohannis magister*, ὁ τοῦ Ἰωάννου διδάσκαλος).[21] This is the only time Christ is explicitly called the teacher of a single disciple.

Moreover, John is sometimes called an apostle, either together with others[22] or alone.[23] Although Paul is normally "the apostle" for Irenaeus,[24] the term is not restricted exclusively to Paul, unlike *discipulus Domini* is for John. John belongs to the group of those "who have seen the Lord,"[25] and therefore is one of the eyewitnesses of Jesus.[26] But this is of course self-evident for "the disciple of the Lord," who "leaned upon His breast."

Two further details from Irenaeus, however, cannot be based on the Gospel of John or the New Testament. (1) John was alive "until the time of (the emperor) Trajan"[27] (who reigned from January 28, 98 CE),[28] and lived in Ephesus, the capital of Asia Minor, as Irenaeus attests several times.[29] According to Martin Hengel, the Johannine testimonies about Ephesus are older than anything reported of the geographical provenance of the other gospels.[30] (2) In the Roman Bath of Ephesus, John once met Cerinthus—and fled hastily, because he

---

[20] Ἀναπεσών...ἐπὶ τὸ στῆθος (John 13:25); καὶ ἀνέπεσεν...ἐπὶ τὸ στῆθος αὐτοῦ (John 21:20); Mutschler 2004a, 155–156; Mutschler 2004b, 705–706; Mutschler 2006, 96–98.

[21] Irenaeus, *Adv. haer.* 1.9.2 with frg. gr. 1:1016 (Epiphanius, *Pan.* 31.28.7); Normann 1967, 137–152, 178–179.

[22] Irenaeus, *Adv. haer.* 2.22.5; 3.3.4 with frg. gr. 5:28 (Eusebius, *Hist. eccl.* 4.14.7); 3.12.5; 3.12.15; 3.21.3; 4.35.2; Irenaeus, *Ep. Vict.* (Eusebius, *Hist. eccl.* 5.24.16).

[23] Irenaeus, *Adv. haer.* 1.9.2–3. with frg. gr. 1:1017.1029 (Epiphanius, *Pan.* 31.28.8; 31.29.1). For more details, see Mutschler 2004a, 169; Mutschler 2004b, 699–700.

[24] Reynders 1954, 2:32, 231; Noormann 1994, 39–58.

[25] Τῶν ἑορακότων τὸν Κύριον, *Ep. Flor.* (Eusebius, *Hist. eccl.* 5.20.6).

[26] Τῶν αὐτοπτῶν, *Ep. Flor.* (Eusebius, *Hist. eccl.* 5.20.6).

[27] Μέχρι τῶν Τραϊανοῦ χρόνων, *usque ad Traiani tempora*, Irenaeus, *Adv. haer.* 2.22.5 with frg. gr. 1:4 (Eusebius, *Hist. eccl.* 3.23.3); 3.3.4 with frg. gr. 6:3–4 (Eusebius, *Hist. eccl.* 3.23.4).

[28] Kienast 1990, 122: Trajan was emperor until August 7, 117 CE.

[29] Irenaeus, *Adv. haer.* 3.1.1 with frg. gr. 1:10 (Eusebius, *Hist. eccl.* 5.8.4); 3.3.4 (twice) with frg. gr. 5:20 (Eusebius, *Hist. eccl.* 4.14.6); and frg. gr. 6:1–2 (Eusebius, *Hist. eccl.* 3.23.4); Mutschler 2004b, 697.

[30] Hengel 1993, 99: "daß *sie jedenfalls älter sind als alles, was wir über die geographische Herkunft anderer Evangelien erfahren.*" For the role of Ephesus as the place of the "Johannine school" (*johanneische Schule*), see ibid., 288–306; Heckel 2004, 633–635.

feared that the Bath would collapse with such a heretic, an "enemy of the truth," within its walls.[31]

Irenaeus does not report enough details for a full biography of John, but what he does report is more exact than anything he says of the other three evangelists, as I have pointed out elsewhere: "Es ist… ungleich mehr und sehr viel genauer als alles, was Irenäus über die anderen, früheren drei Evangelisten zu berichten weiß."[32]

To sum up, in Irenaeus' view, the author of the Fourth Gospel is unique in his relationship to the Lord. He is mentioned much more frequently than the other evangelists; he is "the" disciple of the Lord, who "leaned upon His breast"; and an "apostle," who was still alive in Asia Minor when Trajan became emperor. He must have been quite old at the end of the first century—probably the last survivor of the apostles' generation.[33]

1.2. Irenaeus' Sources and Reliability

Irenaeus' sources about John are of course another question. First, it is of great importance that Irenaeus "of Lyons" himself grew up in and emigrated from Asia Minor. Therefore he knew witnesses who knew "John" in or around Ephesus. Irenaeus mentions Papias of Hierapolis,[34] Polycarp of Smyrna,[35] and, in particular, a group of anonymous "presbyters."[36] He also refers to people who had had

---

[31] Irenaeus, *Adv. haer.* 3.3.4 with frg. gr. 5:19–24 (Eusebius, *Hist. eccl.* 4.14.6). Irenaeus traces this incident, which seems legendary, back to "listeners to Polycarp" whom he clearly distinguishes from the bishop of Smyrna himself.

[32] Mutschler 2004a, 245; similarly Mutschler 2004b, 723.

[33] Pier Franco Beatrice and Charles E. Hill have recently tried to identify the "presbyter," mentioned in the fourth book of *Adversus haereses*, with Polycarp (Beatrice 1990, 179–185; Hill 2006, 7–94; see Irenaeus, *Adv. haer.* 4.27–32; cf. 1.24–31; 3.18–23; 4.27–39). Such a hypothesis had been explicitly denied by Adolf von Harnack (1958, 2/1:386) and Hans Freiherr von Campenhausen (1963, 216n82). However, a thorough re-examination of such a hypothesis could lead to some very interesting historical results. See my forthcoming study on *Polycarp and Belief.*

[34] Irenaeus, *Adv. haer.* 5.33.4 with frg. gr. 28:1–3 (Eusebius, *Hist. eccl.* 3.39.1).

[35] Irenaeus, *Adv. haer.* 3.3.4 with frg. gr. 5:19–21 (Eusebius, *Hist. eccl.* 4.14.6); 5.33.4 with frg. gr. 28:1–3 (Eusebius, *Hist. eccl.* 3.39.1); *Ep. Flor.* (Eusebius, *Hist. eccl.* 5.20.6); *Ep. Vict.* (Eusebius, *Hist. eccl.* 5.24.16).

[36] Irenaeus, *Adv. haer.* 2.22.5 with frg. gr. 1:1–4 (Eusebius, *Hist. eccl.* 3.23.3); 5.33.3.

personal contact with John,[37] as well as to "listeners to Polycarp."[38] Apart from these people who belong to a "younger generation of witnesses," Irenaeus relies in a general manner on "the church of Ephesus" as a "true witness of the tradition of the apostles."[39] Possibly "the church of Ephesus" is more or less equivalent to the anonymous "presbyters."[40]

Of course, Irenaeus did not himself know John and the apostles (Irenaeus' older generation of witnesses),[41] but they were known by the "presbyters," Polycarp, and Papias, all of whom Irenaeus knew. Thus, the chain of witnesses between Irenaeus and the Lord is short.[42] Moreover, this is the only case of a concrete linkage between a church father and a New Testament author.

The connection to the church of Ephesus may also be more significant than Irenaeus discloses, as the bishop grew up in the Ephesus region and came from there to Lyons.[43] Ephesus was not just the home of Irenaeus, but also the city where John—and before him Paul—had lived and worked. Therefore Irenaeus' rhetorical aim seems clear: With a connection to the church of Ephesus, he increases his own importance and strengthens his own position.[44]

While Irenaeus mentions the older Papias and the younger "listeners to Polycarp" only once, it seems that Polycarp, the bishop of Smyrna, was in fact his main source about the Christian past.[45] In his letter to Florinus, Irenaeus styles himself as a disciple of the second generation after John:

---

[37] Τῶν κατ᾽ ὄψιν τὸν Ἰωάννην ἑωρακότων, Irenaeus, Adv. haer. 5.30.1 with frg. gr. 24:29–30 (Eusebius, Hist. eccl. 5.8.5).

[38] Οἱ ἀκηκοότες αὐτοῦ, Irenaeus, Adv. haer. 3.3.4 with frg. gr. 5:19–21 (Eusebius, Hist. eccl. 4.14.6).

[39] Ἡ ἐν Ἐφέσῳ ἐκκλησία…μάρτυς ἀληθής ἐστιν τῆς τῶν ἀποστόλων παραδόσεως, Irenaeus, Adv. haer. 3.3.4 with frg. gr. 6:2–4 (Eusebius, Hist. eccl. 3.23.4).

[40] "The presbyters" are mentioned twice in connection with John, but more than twenty times altogether in the works of Irenaeus. See Preuschen 1905, 101–107; Lewis 1908, 42; Reynders 1954, 1:90; 2:252, 295; Reynders 1958, 28.

[41] Irenaeus mentions John nine times, but the "apostles" only four times. See Mutschler 2004b, 707n67 (nos. 1, 3, 4, 9 for the apostles; 1–9 for John).

[42] For a graphic scheme see Mutschler 2004b, 708; for the whole context, see ibid., 704–714.

[43] Mutschler 2004b, 711: "beredtes Schweigen…das mannigfache Verbindungen nach Ephesus—ältere wie gegenwärtige, biographisch veranlaßte wie dienstlich begründete—voraussetzt."

[44] Mutschler 2004b, 714.

[45] Mutschler 2004b, 711, 715; and ibid., 722: "Polykarp scheint die wichtigste Einzelpersönlichkeit gewesen zu sein, die Irenäus theologisch geprägt hat und mit der er persönlich Umgang hatte."

For while I was still a boy I knew you (sc. Florinus) in lower Asia in Polycarp's house when you were a man of rank in the royal hall and endeavouring to stand well with him. I remember the events of those days more closely than those which happened recently, for what we learn as children grows up with the soul and is united to it, so that I can speak even of the place in which the blessed Polycarp sat and disputed, how he came in and went out, the character of his life, the appearance of his body, the discourses which he made to the people, how he reported his intercourse with John and with the others who had seen the Lord, how he remembered their words, and what were the things concerning the Lord which he had heard from them, and about their miracles, and about their teaching, and how Polycarp had received them from the eyewitnesses of the word of life, and reported all things in agreement with the Scriptures.[46]

When one evaluates the historical data delivered by Irenaeus, one is inclined to agree with Paul Hartog that "Polycarp may have had a few stories of a (brief?) childhood connection with John, and Irenaeus, for his part, may have remembered only little of the material."[47] But this conclusion seems to be too cautious. If the flashback in Irenaeus' letter is taken seriously, Irenaeus emphasizes explicitly that he remembers "the events of those days" very well, "for what we learn as children grows up with the soul and is united to it." His observations are detailed and do not appear to be based only on one single day or on a short period of time. Obviously, Polycarp remembered John mainly as an eyewitness of the Lord, for he "had seen the Lord" and "what were the things concerning the Lord." This means that for Polycarp John is mainly interesting as a link to the Lord. Nonetheless, John is the only apostle, the only eyewitness, and the only of the four evangelists who is mentioned here *by name*. It is clear that Polycarp—who was about sixty years younger than John—did not stay in John's company for decades or even for several years. However, if this had been only a *brief* "childhood connection," Polycarp would likely not have told his memories to the next generation several decades later.[48] Therefore, I claim that Polycarp, as well as Irenaeus, knew more than "a few

---

[46] *Ep. Flor.* in Eusebius, *Hist. eccl.* 5.20.5–6; transl., Lake 1992, 497, 499.
[47] Hartog 2002, 41.
[48] Μετὰ τὴν Ἰωάννου συναναστροφὴν ὡς ἀπήγγειλεν, *Ep. Flor.* (Eusebius, *Hist. eccl.* 5.20.6).

stories." They probably remembered much better and more precisely than younger people do in our media-overblown times.[49]

For my assessment of the sources in general, and especially concerning Polycarp, two different yet related circumstances are of basic importance. (1) A modern evaluation of the Polycarp-Irenaeus tradition depends to a high degree on the coincidental transmission of texts. Had we not received the fragment of the letter to Florinus transmitted in Eusebius' *Ecclesiastical History*, we would not know any details about the means and the intensity of the transfer of traditions. Thus, in using that fragment, we respect and interpret an ancient source— and are far from an *argumentum ex silentio*. (2) Irenaeus refers to the *argumentum traditionis* in contexts that can be very different from each other. But each time he replies to a concrete conflict in his time: He is challenged by and shapes theology in conflict ('*Theologie in Auseinandersetzung*').[50] He does not argue for the sake of arguing (*l'art pour l'art*). In other words: The bishop needs an actual reason for appealing to his traditions concerning the past. He is not a historian, but a bishop who is obliged to respond to the actual challenges of his community and church, to the theological debates of his time.[51]

Therefore it is clear that we gain insight into the historical traditions about John rather incidentally than systematically, let alone completely. Had Irenaeus been inclined to fill up, fabricate, or forge traditions, he would have done it more effectively and with "better" results. Some gaps could have been closed easily, more obviously, and more convincingly. But this would have been a disservice to his aims, in Lyons as well as in Rome or Asia Minor. Although certain modern scholars have disputed Irenaeus' reliability,[52] he was not accused of lying in his time—and he would not have risked that for any reason. Irenaeus probably knew some details about John and his gospel, which we do

---

[49] Mutschler 2004a, 245. A clear example is recently given by Teufel 2008, 85, about her father, the New Testament scholar Prof. Ernst Käsemann (July 12, 1906–February 17, 1998): "Von manchen besonders eindrücklichen Erlebnissen hat mein Vater im Lauf der Jahre mehrfach erzählt. Dabei fiel auf, daß sich die Erzählungen über die Zeit hin nicht im geringsten veränderten. Inzwischen sind Dokumente über manche der von ihm berichteten Vorgänge zugänglich. Sie stimmen mit seinen Berichten bis in kleinste Details überein. Insofern scheint der Gedanke, daß einschneidende Ereignisse von Menschen über Jahrzehnte in unveränderter Weise tradiert werden können, nicht abwegig."

[50] Mutschler 2004b, 713, with eight concrete examples.

[51] Mutschler 2006, 496–497.

[52] E.g., Brox 1966, 148: "'Auffüllung der Fakten'"; similarly Hartog 2002, 35–41.

not and cannot know today for several reasons. An interesting detail is that he presents the Ephesian John as "talking," but Paul as "writing."[53] I have elsewhere analyzed the trustworthiness of Irenaeus' historical traditions about John and his gospel in more detail,[54] and as far as I can see, the bishop delivers reliable and trustworthy information.

2. How Irenaeus Uses the Fourth Gospel— A Literary Perspective

In this section, we will discuss the Fourth Gospel as an integral part of a group of writings written by John (2.1), and as part of a four-gospel canon (2.2). In addition, we will see that Irenaeus provides by far the most references to the Gospel of John in the second century (2.3), and, in contrast to other second-century authors, he provides explicit quotations (2.4).

2.1. *The Fourth Gospel as Part of the* Corpus Johanneum *and the Question of its Authorship*

As we have seen, the author of the Fourth Gospel receives authorization from both sides of his Gospel, as it were: from the Lord, upon whose breast he once leaned, and from Polycarp, who later spoke to a young Irenaeus about John's time in Ephesus. Thus John is, in a historical perspective, in a frame,[55] and is at the same time part of a chain of transmission that leads from the Lord via John and Polycarp to Irenaeus.

There is no question in Irenaeus' mind that the Gospel "according to John" (ΚΑΤΑ ΙΩΑΝΝΗΝ) is written by John.[56] The *inscriptio* of the Fourth Gospel and the Gospel itself belong inseparably together since the moment of publication.[57] Martin Hengel therefore calls the Gospel inscriptions *"part of the Gospels as originally circulated."*[58]

---

[53] Mutschler 2004a, 245: "Jedoch stellt sich Irenäus...den ephesinischen Johannes—ganz im Gegensatz zu Paulus—fast ausschließlich 'redend' und nicht 'schreibend' vor." Ibid., 268: "meist sprechend, nicht schreibend."

[54] Mutschler 2004b, 714–723; and in brief ibid., 738–740 (nos. 11–19).

[55] Mutschler 2004a, 248.

[56] Irenaeus, *Adv. haer.* 3.11.7; 3.11.9; Mutschler 2006, 249–254, 273–279.

[57] Hengel 1984, 51; Hengel 1993, 33; Hengel 2003, 23; see also Mutschler 2004b, 731.

[58] Hengel 1993, 205n1: "Teil des Werkes." Hengel 2000, 48–56, especially p. 50.

According to Irenaeus, the same John wrote not only the Gospel, but also the book of Revelation. This was "not long ago, but almost in our generation, near the end of the rule of Domitian."[59] Furthermore, John composed 1 John and 2 John, which Irenaeus considers as one letter (*epistola*);[60] but this is how he occasionally deals with 1 and 2 Corinthians, too.[61] Irenaeus neither mentions nor uses the very short and private epistle 3 John.[62] In any case, it is absolutely clear for Irenaeus that—unlike the current consensus[63]—all these writings are works of one and the same author: John,[64] "the disciple of the Lord," who "leaned upon His breast."

2.2. *The Fourth Gospel as Part of the Four-Gospel Canon*

The Fourth Gospel is not only a part of a *Corpus Johanneum* consisting of at least four writings, but also of the four gospels.[65] In the *Evangeliennotiz*, John is clearly the fourth of the gospels:[66]

> Matthew also issued a written Gospel among the Hebrews in their own dialect, while Peter and Paul were preaching at Rome, and laying the foundations of the Church. After their departure, Mark, the disciple and interpreter of Peter, did also hand down to us in writing what had been preached by Peter. Luke also, the companion of Paul, recorded in a book the Gospel preached by him. Afterwards, John, the disciple of the Lord, who also had leaned upon His breast, did himself publish a Gospel during his residence at Ephesus in Asia. (transl., ANF)

The concluding *Johannesnotiz* concentrates the well-known data about his gospel: Ἔπειτα Ἰωάννης, ὁ μαθητὴς τοῦ Κυρίου ὁ καὶ ἐπὶ

---

[59] Οὐδὲ γὰρ πρὸ πολλοῦ χρόνου ἑωράθη, ἀλλὰ σχεδὸν ἐπὶ τῆς ἡμετέρας γενεᾶς, πρὸς τῷ τέλει τῆς Δομετιανοῦ ἀρχῆς (Irenaeus, *Adv. haer.* 5.30.3 with frg. gr. 26:5–6 in Eusebius, *Hist. eccl.* 5.8.6); Mutschler 2004b, 701. According to modern research, Revelation and John are not written by one and the same author. See, e.g., Frey 1993, 421, 424.

[60] Irenaeus, *Adv. haer.* 3.16.5; 3.16.8; Mutschler 2006, 312–325, 349–357.

[61] *In ea epistula quae est ad Corinthios* (Irenaeus, *Adv. haer.* 3.13.1); Mutschler 2006, 353, 500.

[62] Mutschler 2004a, 61–63; Mutschler 2004b, 702.

[63] See, e.g., Mutschler 2004b, 731–737, 741–742; Pokorný and Heckel 2007, 578–584.

[64] Mutschler 2004a, 249–250; Mutschler 2004b, 700–702; Mutschler 2006, 500–501.

[65] A brief summary is found in Mutschler 2006, 503–504.

[66] Irenaeus, *Adv. haer.* 3.1.1 with frg. gr. 1 (Eusebius, *Hist. eccl.* 5.8.2–4); for the Fourth Gospel passage, see Mutschler 2004a, 155–158; Mutschler 2004b, 700–701; Mutschler 2006, 95–100.

τὸ στῆθος ἀναπεσὼν καὶ αὐτὸς ἐξέδωκεν τὸ εὐαγγέλιον ἐν Ἐφέσῳ τῆς Ἀσίας. Not only through the explication "in Asia," which is not functional from an Asian perspective, but also for several other reasons it is conceivable to think that the *Evangeliennotiz* originally comes from Rome.[67] It seems to be a list from a library, probably from an archive of the Roman community.[68] The list was developed between 120 and 135 CE.[69] It is the officially accepted information about the formation of the four gospels, at least in the churches of Gaul, Rome and Asia Minor,[70] and it reflects an old opinion of the chronological order, which starts with the Gospel of Matthew.[71] Thus the *Evangeliennotiz* is Irenaeus' "literarhistorische Basiserklärung" at the beginning of the third book of *Adversus haereses*, which itself begins with scripture-based arguments.[72]

The order of the gospels in the *Evangeliennotiz* is the canonical one: Matthew-Mark-Luke-John. This is striking, because Irenaeus normally uses the order Matthew-Luke-Mark-John.[73] Both orders begin with an apostolic author (Matthew) and end with another one (John); the canon of the four gospels therefore has an apostolic frame or *conclusio*. This goes well with the fact that most of the pre-Constantine papyri of the gospels belong to either John (15) or Matthew (12).[74] The gospels that were traced back to disciples of the apostles[75] stand in the middle, as today. John, in his final position, is an apostle as well as a disciple, but not a disciple of an apostle. He is "the disciple of the Lord." In *Adv. haer.* 3.11.8, the unique order John-Luke-Matthew-Mark conforms to the symbols in Rev 4:7.[76]

---

[67] Thornton 1991, 12–20, 40–62; Mutschler 2004a, 158–161; Mutschler 2004b, 705.

[68] Thornton 1991, 40, 45: "Eine 'bibliothekarische Liste' aus dem 'römischen Gemeindearchiv.'"

[69] Thornton 1991, 62.

[70] Mutschler 2004a, 161; Mutschler 2004b, 740; Mutschler 2006, 95.

[71] Mutschler 2006, 66, 79. For the predilection for the primacy of the Gospel of Matthew from very early on, see Köhler 1986, *passim*.

[72] Mutschler 2004a, 170; Mutschler 2006, 79.

[73] Irenaeus, *Adv. haer.* 3.9.1–11.7; 3.11,7; 4.6.1; Campenhausen 2003, 229n242: "Irenäus geläufigste Reihenfolge"; Mutschler 2004a, 217: "geläufigste Reihenfolge bei Irenäus"; Mutschler 2006, 65–80, especially pp. 66, 71–74.

[74] Mutschler 2004a, 237.

[75] Mutschler 2006, 34–35.

[76] Mutschler 2006, 67, 79, 254–264.

In the same passage (*Adv. haer.* 3.11.7–9), Irenaeus vehemently and elaborately defends the four-gospel canon:[77] He defends it against several attempts at manipulation or abuse by specific groups;[78] he shows that the harmony of the number of *four* gospels conforms to the universal harmony in nature and salvific history;[79] and he attacks several groups who do not agree with the four gospels.[80] The word *evangelium* denotes a single gospel as well as the canon of four gospels.[81] For "the Gospel" is given "under four aspects, but bound together by one Spirit": τετράμορφον τὸ εὐαγγέλιον, ἑνὶ δὲ Πνεύματι συνεχόμενον.[82] This is an impressive way to deal with the "problem" that four different gospels were passed down.[83]

2.3. *The Reception of the Fourth Gospel in Figures*

Although it is quite difficult to determine exactly how many times Irenaeus quotes from or alludes to one of the Synoptic Gospels, it is evident that he does so more often in the cases of Matthew and Luke than John.[84] More than half of his references to the New Testament relate to these three gospels.[85] The Gospel of Mark receives (not unexpectedly) the least attention.[86]

Within the four New Testament *Corpora*, the Johannine writings are the ones to which Irenaeus refers least.[87] On the other hand, the

---

[77] Mutschler 2006, 249–280.

[78] Irenaeus, *Adv. haer.* 3.11.7; Mutschler 2006, 249–254.

[79] Irenaeus, *Adv. haer.* 3.11.8; for the Gospel of John, see Mutschler 2006, 254–273.

[80] Irenaeus, *Adv. haer.* 3.11.9; for the Gospel of John, see Mutschler 2006, 273–280.

[81] Mutschler 2006, 256–257.

[82] Irenaeus, *Adv. haer.* 3.11.8 with frg. gr. 11:11; Mutschler 2006, 257–258.

[83] Around the same time, Tatian, the disciple of Justin Martyr, composed his artificial "Gospel through the four" (τὸ διὰ τεσσάρων εὐαγγέλιον, i.e., the *Diatessaron*), an *Evangelienharmonie*. There is also the larger question of Irenaeus' biblical reception, involving the (later so-called) Old and New Testaments, but such a study would exceed the scope of this essay. See Mutschler 2004a, 32–100, 223–242; ibid., 274: "Faktisch hält sich Irenäus fast vollendet an die Grenzen des sich bildenden zweigeteilten christlichen Kanons, wie er im Alexandria des vierten Jahrhunderts belegt ist"; and Mutschler 2006, 504–506.

[84] Matthew: 247 quotations and 231 allusions; Luke: 166 quotations and 144 allusions; John: 110 quotations and 127 allusions. Mutschler 2004a, 71.

[85] 1025 references out of 1932. Mutschler 2004a, 71–72.

[86] 18 quotations and 12 allusions. Mutschler 2004a, 71.

[87] Synoptic Gospels: 722 times; *Corpus Paulinum*: 698 times; Luke-Acts: 454 times; *Corpus Johanneum*: 309 times. Mutschler 2004a, 72–74, 228–229.

bishop related probably more intensely to the Fourth Gospel than to the Gospel of Matthew or to the *Corpus Paulinum*.[88] Within the *Corpus Johanneum*, the gospel gets cited by far the most.[89] The greatest part of the references to the Fourth Gospel are found in *Adversus haereses* 3–5, where Irenaeus discusses scriptural proof.[90] Related to the length of the writings, the Fourth Gospel is given a greater than average reception,[91] just ahead of Luke's Gospel.

Compared with authors before and shortly after him, Irenaeus refers to the Gospel of John more often than others, including Clement of Alexandria.[92] In absolute figures, Irenaeus' writings contain many more references to the Fourth Gospel (324) than those of earlier authors combined (138), among them Ignatius, Justin, Tatian, Melito, Athenagoras, Theophilus, Ptolemaeus and Heracleon.[93] Even all the (preserved) authors of the second century together (including post-Irenaean ones) contain fewer references to the Fourth Gospel (298) than Irenaeus.[94] Individually, Irenaeus refers to the Fourth Gospel at least ten times more often than any other author before him.[95] This concerns especially the references to the prologue,[96] and it gives already a clear hint of Irenaeus' theological direction. We will, however, first take a closer look at how Irenaeus' references are distributed within the Fourth Gospel, and then at the nature of his references.

More than one-third of the references are made to the prologue (John 1:1–18). Almost half of the references concern the rest of the first half of the gospel, John 1:19–12:50. And only every fifth reference is to John 13:1–21:25.[97] Thus the prologue seems to be very important for Irenaeus, in contrast to the second half of the gospel. Especially

---

[88] 23.6% of the text of the Fourth Gospel is referred or alluded to. See Mutschler 2004a, 255–256.

[89] 237 out of 309 references. Mutschler 2004a; 71–72, 234–235.

[90] Irenaeus, *Adv. haer.* book 1 (37 references), book 2 (22), book 3 (79), book 4 (45), book 5 (39); *Epid.* (15). Mutschler 2004a, 71. For a more detailed description, see ibid., 80–98, 188–191. For a scheme, see ibid., 234.

[91] It occupies the tenth position in the list of twenty-four. Mutschler 2004a, 76.

[92] 11.7% of the total NT references in Irenaeus *versus* 9.4% in Clement. Mutschler 2004a, 101.

[93] Mutschler 2004a, 210. For the pre-Irenaean period see Nagel 2000, *passim*, with a Johannine table ibid., 543–549.

[94] Mutschler 2004a, 212.

[95] Mutschler 2004a, 210–211.

[96] Mutschler 2004a, 212.

[97] See Mutschler 2004a, 192, for exact numbers and ibid., 178–186, for more details.

chapters 6, 9, 10, 13 and 16 are under-represented, while chapters 18 and 21 are extremely under-represented.[98] Of the prologue, especially the verses John 1:1–3, 14 and 18 are prominent.[99] If one takes a closer look at the Irenaean text, even more references can be found, most of them, however, being mere allusions.[100] Nonetheless, predominantly they tend to lead in the same direction.[101] This means that there is more Johannine language and theology in Irenaeus than has been previously observed.[102] Johannine language does not simply pervade Irenaeus' thoughts. It is itself the language of Irenaeus' theology.[103]

2.4. *Irenaeus Quotes the Fourth Gospel Explicitly and Closely*

Irenaeus refers to the Fourth Gospel not only more often than any author before him, but also more explicitly and more closely. For example, the only explicit and close quotation before Irenaeus can be found in Theophilus of Antioch,[104] while Irenaeus has at least 104 of them.[105] This means that of all the references to the Fourth Gospel in Irenaeus (324), every third one is explicit. In introducing some of his quotations of the Fourth Gospel, Irenaeus has "the Lord" speaking 31 times, John 16 times, his gospel 4 times, John *in* his gospel 3 times, and scripture 2 times.[106] Irenaeus is therefore by far the most comprehensive and most meticulously[107] working exegete of the Fourth Gospel before Origen, although Irenaeus wrote no philological commentary on the gospel.[108]

---

[98] Mutschler 2004a, 192–193, 213, 251–252 (scheme).

[99] Vv. 10–12 are also fairly prominent. See Mutschler 2004a, 192, 213, 252–253 (scheme).

[100] For *Adv. haer.* 3 (ca. 90 references), see Mutschler 2004a, 201–206, 208–210.

[101] Mutschler 2004a, 206–210, 214–216.

[102] Mutschler 2004a, 215: "dass noch einmal mehr johanneische Sprache und Theologie in den irenäischen Texten steckt, als durch die Angaben in der Sources Chretiennes-Ausgabe deutlich wird."

[103] E.g., Mutschler 2004a, 219.

[104] Nagel 2000, 477: "das einzige gekennzeichnete Wortlautzitat aus dem vierten Evangelium findet sich bei Theophilus von Antiochien."

[105] Mutschler 2004a, 196, 211.

[106] Mutschler 2004a, 197.

[107] Mutschler 2004a, 195–196.

[108] Mutschler 2004a, 211.

3. How Irenaeus Interprets the Gospel of John—
A Theological Perspective

Next, after having sketched the theological challenge in Irenaeus' time (3.1), we will take a look at *Adversus haereses* 3 as a "Johannine book" (3.2). Then, *Adversus haereses* 3.11.1–6 will be briefly investigated both as a particularly Johannine section (3.3), and as an Irenaean network of Johannine texts from the prologue (3.4). Finally, the Fourth Gospel will be examined as the theological backbone of Irenaeus, and Irenaeus will be viewed as *the* Johannine theologian until Origen (3.5).

3.1. *The Theological Challenge in the Time of Irenaeus*

The main provocation for Irenaeus at the end of the second century CE was the Gnostic challenge, representing, however, only a part of the broader heterodoxy of his time. Specifically, Irenaeus focuses on the so-called Valentinians.[109] Besides the Valentinians, he considers Marcion (and his followers) and various other Gnostics as his main target. In fact, these three opponents are mentioned together several times.[110] But the Valentinians can be taken *pars pro toto* as Irenaeus affirms: "For they who oppose these men (the Valentinians) by the right method, do [thereby] oppose all who are of an evil mind; and they who overthrow them, do in fact overthrow every kind of heresy."[111] Mainly four areas of doctrine pose an extreme theological challenge for Irenaeus:

(1) How should scripture and tradition be related, and which one has priority? What constitutes a scripture? How many gospels and which ones should be included in scripture? And what is the status of the Old Testament books?

(2) What is the relationship between God, creation and redemption? Is there continuity in the salvation history? Is the same God responsible for creation and salvation, or is there a demiurge who is opposed to the true God?

---

[109] *Qui sunt a Valentino*, is a formula; see Mutschler 2006, 192n318. The Valentinians are "totally in error," *nihil recte dicentes* (Irenaeus, *Adv. haer.* 3.11.7); Mutschler 2006, 250–252.

[110] Mutschler 2006, 295n3.

[111] Irenaeus, *Adv. haer.* 4 *praef.* 2; Mutschler 2006, 498.

(3) Did the mediator become flesh, or was he in any way separated from matter? How do God and mankind come together in the redeemer Christ?

(4) Is there a salvation of the flesh (*salus carnis*)? The answer to this question is closely related to Christology and cosmology.

Thus, the main theological challenges belong either to the hermeneutical field (1) or to the correlation between God, world, man, redeemer (Christ) and salvation (2–4). To put the question in more general terms: How is the tension between the Christian doctrine and the Platonic philosophy to be resolved?[112]

3.2. Adversus Haereses *3 as a Johannine Book*

Almost exactly one third of Irenaeus' references to the Fourth Gospel occur in Book 3 of *Adversus haereses*.[113] Therefore it makes very good sense to focus on that important book,[114] which is also perhaps the best structured of the five books.[115] In short: *Adversus haereses* 3 is a "Johannine book."[116]

Questions of scripture and tradition are treated as a matter of principle in the first five chapters of book 3.[117] The subsequent chapters deal with the one true God who is the maker of heaven and earth.[118] The second large part of the third book discusses Christology: one and the same Jesus Christ, true man and true God for our salvation.[119] Finally, Irenaeus states again the contrast between the church—her preaching and belief—and the heretics.[120]

It is impossible to examine all or even most of the references to the Fourth Gospel in this essay. Therefore, let us take a look at the

---

[112] Mutschler 2006, 497–500.
[113] Mutschler 2004a, 136–138, 194; Mutschler 2006, 507.
[114] Mutschler 2006, 7–8.
[115] Mutschler 2006, 8: "vielleicht das am besten strukturierte und gelungene Buch des Theologen und Schriftstellers Irenäus"; ibid., 508: "eine von Irenäus sorgfältig komponierte, gut verständliche und planvoll gestaltete Einheit." For details, see Mutschler 2006, 13–63, 508–518.
[116] Mutschler 2006, 507.
[117] Mutschler 2006, 15–25, 508–509.
[118] See Mutschler 2006, 25, 46, 510–514.
[119] Mutschler 2006, 46–57, 514–517.
[120] Mutschler 2006, 58–63, 517–518.

highest concentration of Johannine references within Irenaeus' works: *Adversus haereses* 3.11.1–6.

3.3. Adversus Haereses *3.11.1–6 as a Particularly Johannine Section*

The greatest concentration of allusions to and quotations from the Gospel of John is found in *Adversus haereses* 3.11.1–6. Irenaeus shows in 3.9.1–3.11.6 that all four gospel writers confess and witness one and the same God, as do Moses and the prophets.[121] Because there is no possibility for separation between creation and incarnation, it is the one God who made everything through his Word (John 1:3). And this is exactly the same Word who "was made flesh, and dwelt among us" (John 1:14).[122] Irenaeus emphasizes John 1:14, and insists explicitly that "according to the opinion of none of the heretics was the Word of God made flesh."[123] This means that John 1:14 functions as a *shibboleth* in Christology! Here the whole theological challenge for Irenaeus and his time is either won or lost.[124]

In bridging the gap between the creator and that God whose Word was made flesh, Irenaeus employs the figure of John the Baptist: The latter is "more than a prophet" because he not only announced the Word of God becoming flesh but also "saw Him when He came, and pointed Him out, and persuaded many to believe on Him, so that he did himself hold the place of both prophet and apostle (transl., ANF)."[125] Irenaeus thus proves that the creator and the one whose Word was made flesh are the same.

According to our section, Christ took matter from the earth to make wine out of water in Cana (John 2), and he took "the loaves which the earth had produced" to satisfy the gathered multitude (John 6); both are also the elements of the Lord's Supper.[126] John 1:18 shows that Father and Son belong inseparably together and that the visible son

---

[121] Mutschler 2006, 34–42, 153.

[122] Irenaeus, *Adv. haer.* 3.11.1–2; Mutschler 2004a, 218–219; Mutschler 2006, 176–199.

[123] Irenaeus, *Adv. haer.* 3.11.3; Mutschler 2004a, 219–220; Mutschler 2006, 199–217.

[124] Mutschler 2004a, 220: "Fleischwerdung aber bedingt im theologischen Denken des Irenäus Leidensfähigkeit, diese wiederum bedingt sowohl die Möglichkeit als auch den Fleischlichkeit einschließenden Realismus des Heils."

[125] Irenaeus, *Adv. haer.* 3.11.4; Mutschler 2004a, 221; Mutschler, 2006, 218–221.

[126] Irenaeus, *Adv. haer.* 3.11.5; Mutschler 2004a, 221–222; Mutschler 2006, 222–235.

"declares to all the Father who is invisible" as he did, e.g., to Nathanael and Peter.[127]

The main questions of this particularly Johannine section are: (a) Is there one single God, or is there a distinction between God and a distinct maker? (b) What is the identity of the maker? (c) What role does matter take in the whole process of salvation? And above all: (d) Who is Christ and how is he connected to these questions? The greater theological areas (*loci*) are thus theology, creation/cosmology, soteriology, and Christology. Soteriology is closely connected with anthropology, pneumatology, ecclesiology, and eschatology in other parts of Irenaeus' work. These main theological fields (*loci*) can be sketched with the help of a triangle:

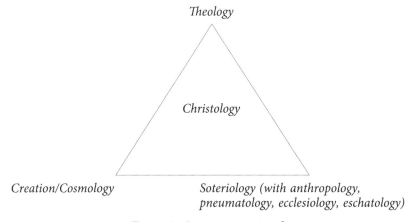

Figure 1: Controversy triangle

The question of Christ (Christology) is placed in the center of the triangle due to its central role: All theological questions meet in Christology like roads of the city leading to its center.[128]

A comparison with the Gnostic challenge for the church in Irenaeus' period shows that all corners of the triangle and its center deal with issues that are under controversy:[129] God, creation, redemption and Christ, or, alternatively: God, creation, incarnation and salvation. This means that Irenaeus answers the theological and Gnostic challenge in

---

[127] Irenaeus, *Adv. haer.* 3.11.6; Mutschler 2004a, 222; Mutschler 2006, 235–247.
[128] See Mutschler 2004a, 260.
[129] Mutschler 2004a, 260.

his Johannine chapters. It is hoped that the greater question of the controversy between the Gnostics (e.g., the Valentinians) and the church (Irenaeus) can be examined more clearly with the help of our triangle. We may thus call it a "controversy triangle."

3.4. *The Prologue of John (1:1–18) as an Irenaean Network of Johannine Texts*

A complementary look at the specifically Johannine chapters in Irenaeus' writings deals with those verses that Irenaeus quoted most often. It has to be remembered that more than one-third of the references to the Fourth Gospel are to its prologue, John 1:1–18.[130] As noted above, a closer look at the prologue shows that especially the verses John 1:1–3, 14 and 18 are quoted and alluded to more often than other verses of the prologue.[131]

For example, the expression *Verbum Dei* ("the Word of God," John 1:1ff.) is used about 100 times in *Adversus haereses*, and 29 of those occur in Book 3.[132] Ten literal quotations of John 1:3 occur in *Adversus haereses*,[133] while some 60 references to John 1:14 can be identified.[134] In fact, John 1:14 is by far the most cited verse of the Fourth Gospel in Irenaeus' writings.[135] It is also striking that Irenaeus emphasizes the first half of the verse very strongly (σὰρξ ἐγένετο, *incarnatus*),[136] while pre-Irenaean and Gnostic literature remains inarticulate concerning the incarnation.[137]

Many of the references to John 1:1–18 are not distributed equally in Irenaeus' writings—far from it. In addition, they are very often connected to each other. Therefore we can call them a network of Johannine texts.[138] Most of these combinations are again found in the third book of *Adversus haereses*.[139]

---

[130] Mutschler 2004a, 192.

[131] Mutschler 2004a, 252.

[132] Mutschler 2004a, 178–179, 202–203; Mutschler 2006, 148–149n189.

[133] Mutschler 2006, 150nn197–198.

[134] Mutschler 2004a, 252; Mutschler 2006, 156n22.

[135] Mutschler 2004a, 252.

[136] Mutschler 2004a, 219–220; Mutschler 2006, 155–156.

[137] Nagel 2000, 480; Mutschler 2004a, 261.

[138] According to Bingham 1998, 301, Irenaeus has "a tendency to understand Matthean passages within a network of biblical texts."

[139] Mutschler 2004a, 220, 257–258.

No other combination (network) of Johannine or any other biblical texts is so favored by Irenaeus as that of John 1:1–3,14,18.[140]
Combinations of these verses occur quite seldom in Justin, Clement of
Alexandria or Tertullian.[141] Irenaeus refers to these verses even more
often than Justin, Clement and Tertullian together.[142] This shows that
these verses are extremely important for Irenaeus, since they are at
the forefront of his writings and theology. These verses, too, can be
arranged in a triangle:

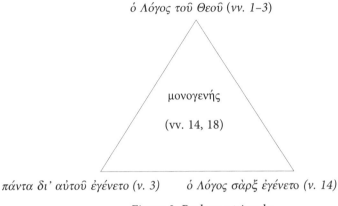

Figure 2: Prologue triangle

Of course, themes, verses and catchwords could be arranged in other
types of figures as well.[143] But it is nonetheless clear that we are dealing
with a "Prologue triangle," or a "Johannine triangle," or simply a basic
"theological triangle of Irenaeus." To understand the triangle better, it
is necessary to consider that incarnation (John 1:14) in the Irenaean
context very often has a soteriological aura: A *pro*-structure is inherent in the topic of incarnation.[144] If this fact is taken into account, it
becomes obvious that the "Prologue triangle" fits well with the triangle
dealing with the main theological fields in the controversy between

---

[140] Mutschler 2004a, 258.
[141] Mutschler 2004a, 259n89.
[142] 75 vs. 53 references. See Mutschler 2004a, 259n90.
[143] Mutschler 2004a, 261.
[144] See Mutschler 2006, 156: "Theologisch ist dem Inkarnationsgeschehen eine
pro-Struktur inhärent," e.g., *pro nobis, pro salute nostra, pro hominibus, propter hom-
inem.*

the Gnostics and the church (Irenaeus), our "controversy triangle."[145] To state it explicitly: Irenaeus' exegesis of the prologue responds to the main Gnostic challenges.[146] The prologue is a firm foundation on which Irenaeus stands in repudiating the Gnostic positions.

3.5. The Fourth Gospel as Irenaeus' Theological Backbone—Irenaeus as the Johannine Theologian of the Second Century

If the view outlined above is correct, then some inevitable conclusions follow:

(1) The bishop of Lyons takes the Gnostic challenge of his time as a theological one, which means that it poses both an exegetical and a systematic challenge. He responds to it in a unique way with the aid of the Fourth Gospel, especially with its prologue, John 1:1–18.

(2) Within the Johannine Corpus, the Fourth Gospel becomes essential for his response to the challenge, although in terms of bare numbers, Irenaeus refers to the other three New Testament Corpora (Synoptic Gospels, Paul, Luke-Acts) more.

(3) The "theological triangle of Irenaeus" is a Johannine one with Christology in its center. It corresponds exactly with the "controversy triangle" with the Valentinians (who stand *pars pro toto* for the Gnostics).

(4) Irenaeus' exegesis of the prologue focuses on Christology (connected with the theme of the unity of God). Therefore, Irenaeus refers mostly to John 1:1–3,14,18. In the same vein, he interprets John 1:13 exclusively from a Christological point of view.[147]

(5) Verses such as John 1:3 and 1:14 have the character of a *shibboleth* for accurate (i.e., biblical) theology or a litmus test for heretics.[148] If theological statements taken from the Fourth Gospel are the steadfast foundation of Irenaeus' theological accents, especially

---

[145] Mutschler 2004a, 261: "Das skizzierte 'theologische Dreieck' des Irenäus ist also zugleich ein antignostisches und letztendlich auch eine Art theologisches Gerüst des Johannesprologs."

[146] Mutschler 2004a, 260: "zu allen vier Bereichen eine richtungsweisende Antwort."

[147] Irenaeus, *Adv. haer.* 3.16.2; 3.19.2; 3.21.5; 3.21.7; 5.1.3; Mutschler 2004a, 263; Mutschler 2006, 302–306, 428–432, 451–459.

[148] Mutschler 2004a, 263.

concerning creation, incarnation and salvation, it is the Fourth Gospel that functions as *the theological backbone* of the bishop.[149]

(6) Because Irenaeus himself came from Asia Minor to Gaul, he underlines his Johannine foundation impressively for historical reasons.

(7) If Irenaeus provides his readers with genuine and obviously old traditions about the Fourth Gospel, and if verses of that gospel guide the theological debate with his opponents,[150] then the bishop of Lyons can be said to practice Johannine theology. In other words: He is *a Johannine theologian*.[151]

(8) Significant reasons for this thesis are especially the following: (i) the appellation "the disciple of the Lord" for John; (ii) the use of Johannine key sentences such as John 1:3 or 1:14 as theological shibboleths or dogmatic guard-rails; (iii) the foundational meaning of Johannine words and statements for incarnational Christology; and (iv) the use of an unrivalled network of Johannine texts.[152] None of these four items has strong parallels in other authors of the second century.[153]

(9) Although Irenaeus restricted himself to "applied" exegesis[154] and did not write a full or even selective commentary on the Gospel of John, he is not only *a* Johannine theologian, but even more: Irenaeus of Lyons is *the* Johannine theologian until Origen. Because Irenaeus should always be read while keeping his opponents in mind,[155] he in fact proceeds with a—pardon the anachronism—"method of correlation" (Paul Tillich).

(10) In retrospect, Irenaeus became *the* exegete, systematic theologian, and interpreter of the Fourth Gospel for the whole century;[156] and the Gospel of John served as the foundation and theological backbone in his controversy against the Gnostics.

---

[149] Irenaeus' anthropology and soteriology are mainly Pauline, while his Jesus traditions are based mostly on the Gospels of Matthew and Luke. Mutschler 2004a, 269.

[150] Mutschler 2006, 519: "Bilanziert man diesen Umgang mit der gnostischen Herausforderung, dann wird sie mehr als zur Hälfte in den großen Zügen johanneisch repliziert."

[151] Cf. the title of Mutschler 2004a, *Irenäus als johanneischer Theologe*.

[152] Mutschler 2004a, 268–269.

[153] Mutschler 2004a, 269: "Blickt man über Irenäus hinaus, so sind *alle vier johanneischen Argumente*—einzeln oder im Verbund—*für keinen anderen Autor des zweiten Jahrhunderts charakteristisch als für Irenäus.*"

[154] Van Rompay 1997, 106–107; Mutschler 2004a, 263.

[155] Mutschler 2004a, 266.

[156] Mutschler 2006, 520.

BIBLIOGRAPHY

Beatrice, P.F., "Der Presbyter des Irenäus, Polykarp von Smyrna und der Brief an Diognet," *Pléroma: Salus carnis*, Festschrift A. Orbe, E. Romero-Pose, ed., Santiago de Compostela: Publicaciones Compostellanum, 1990, 179–202.

Bingham, D.J., *Irenaeus' Use of Matthew's Gospel in Adversus Haereses*, Traditio Exegetica Graeca 7, Leuven: Peeters, 1998.

Brox, N., *Offenbarung, Gnosis und gnostischer Mythos bei Irenäus von Lyon: Zur Charakteristik der Systeme*, Salzburger patristische Studien 1, Salzburg: Pustet, 1966.

Camelot, T., *Ignace d'Antioche, Polycarpe de Smyrne: Lettres, Martyre de Polycarpe: Texte grec, introduction, traduction et notes*, Sources chrétiennes 10, Paris: Cerf, ²1958.

Campenhausen, H. von, "Polykarp von Smyrna und die Pastoralbriefe," *Aus der Frühzeit des Christentums: Studien zur Kirchengeschichte des ersten und zweiten Jahrhunderts*, Tübingen: Mohr Siebeck, 1963, 197–252.

—— "Irenäus und das Neue Testament," *Theologische Literaturzeitung* 90 (1965), 1–8.

—— *Die Entstehung der christlichen Bibel*, Mit einem Nachwort von Christoph Markschies, Beiträge zur Historischen Theologie 39, Reprinted edition of 1968, Tübingen: Mohr (Paul Siebeck), 2003.

Ciani, P., *Ireneo e il IV Vangelo*, Aversa: Macchione, 1955.

Frey, J., "Erwägungen zum Verhältnis der Johannesapokalypse zu den übrigen Schriften des Corpus Johanneum," M. Hengel, *Die johanneische Frage: Ein Lösungsversuch mit einem Beitrag zur Apokalypse von Jörg Frey*, Wissenschaftliche Untersuchungen zum Neuen Testament 67, Tübingen: Mohr (Paul Siebeck), 1993, 326–429.

Funk, F. and K. Bihlmeyer, eds., *Die Apostolischen Väter: Neubearbeitung der Funkschen Ausgabe von Karl Bihlmeyer: Erster Teil: Didache, Barnabas, Klemens I und II, Ignatius, Polykarp, Papias, Quadratus, Diognetbrief*, Sammlung ausgewählter kirchen- und dogmengeschichtlicher Quellenschriften 2/1, 1, Tübingen: Mohr (Paul Siebeck), ³1970.

Harnack, A. von, *Geschichte der altchristlichen Literatur bis Eusebius*, 4 vols., 2nd enlarged edition, Leipzig: Hinrichs, 1958.

Hartog, P., *Polycarp and the New Testament: The Occasion, Rhetoric, Theme, and Unity of the Epistles to the Philippians and its Allusions to the New Testament Literature*, Wissenschaftliche Untersuchungen zum Neuen Testament 2.134, Tübingen: Mohr Siebeck, 2002.

Heckel, U., "Die Einheit der Kirche im Johannesevangelium und im Epheserbrief: Ein Vergleich der ekklesiologischen Strukturen," *Kontexte des Johannesevangeliums: Das vierte Evangelium in religions- und traditionsgeschichtlicher Perspektive*, Wissenschaftliche Untersuchungen zum Neuen Testament 175, J. Frey and U. Schnelle, eds., Tübingen: Mohr Siebeck, 2004, 613–640.

Hengel, M., *Die Evangelienüberschriften: Vorgetragen am 18. Oktober 1981*, Sitzungsberichte der Heidelberger Akademie der Wissenschaften, Philologisch-historische Klasse 1984/3, Heidelberg: Winter, 1984.

—— *Die johanneische Frage: Ein Lösungsversuch mit einem Beitrag zur Apokalypse von Jörg Frey*, Wissenschaftliche Untersuchungen zum Neuen Testament 67, Tübingen: Mohr (Paul Siebeck), 1993.

—— *The Four Gospels and the one Gospel of Jesus Christ: An Investigation of the Collection and Origin of the Canonical Gospels*, London: SCM, 2000.

—— "Die vier Evangelien und das eine Evangelium von Jesus Christus," *Theologische Beiträge* 34 (2003), 18–33.

Hill, C.E., *From the Lost Teaching of Polycarp: Identifying Irenaeus' Apostolic Presbyter and the Author of Ad Diognetum*, Wissenschaftliche Untersuchungen zum Neuen Testament 186, Tübingen: Mohr Siebeck, 2006.

Hoh, J., *Die Lehre des hl. Irenäus über das Neue Testament*, Neutestamentliche Abhandlungen 7/4-5, Münster: Aschendorff, 1919.

Kienast, D., *Römische Kaisertabelle: Grundzüge einer römischen Kaiserchronologie*, Darmstadt: Wissenschaftliche Buchgesellschaft, 1990.

Köhler, W.-D., *Die Rezeption des Matthäusevangeliums in der Zeit vor Irenäus*, Wissenschaftliche Untersuchungen zum Neuen Testament 2.24, Tübingen: Mohr (Paul Siebeck), 1987.

Körtner, U. and M. Leutzsch, *Papiasfragmente: Hirt des Hermas*, Schriften des Urchristentums 3, Darmstadt: Wissenschaftliche Buchgesellschaft, 1998.

Kraft, H., *Einführung in die Patrologie*, Darmstadt: Wissenschaftliche Buchgesellschaft, 1991.

Lake, K., *Eusebius: The Ecclesiastical History*, Vol. 1, The Loeb Classical Library 153, 1926, Reprinted Cambridge, Mass.: Harvard University Press, 1992.

Lewis, F., "The Irenaeus Testimony to the Fourth Gospel. Its Extent, Meaning, and Value," *Historical and Linguistic Studies in Literature Related to the New Testament*, Issued under the Direction of Biblical and Patristic Greek, Second Series: Linguistic and Exegetical Studies 1, Chicago, 1908, 451–514.

Lindemann, A. and H. Paulsen, eds., *Die Apostolischen Väter: Griechisch-deutsche Parallelausgabe auf der Grundlage der Ausgaben von Franz Xaver Funk/Karl Bihlmeyer und Molly Whittaker mit Übersetzungen von Martin Dibelius und Dietrich-Alex Koch*, Tübingen: Mohr (Paul Siebeck), 1992.

Loewenich, W. von, *Das Johannes-Verständnis im zweiten Jahrhundert*, Beihefte zur Zeitschrift für die neutestamentliche Wissenschaft 13, Gießen: Töpelmann, 1932.

Morgenthaler, R., *Statistik des Neutestamentlichen Wortschatzes*, 1958, Reprinted Zürich: Gotthelf, 1973.

Mutschler, B., *Irenäus als johanneischer Theologe: Studien zur Schriftauslegung bei Irenäus von Lyon*, Studien und Texte zu Antike und Christentum 21, Tübingen: Mohr Siebeck, 2004a.

—— "Was weiß Irenäus vom Johannesevangelium? Der historische Kontext des Johannesevangeliums aus der Perspektive seiner Rezeption bei Irenäus von Lyon," *Kontexte des Johannesevangeliums: Das vierte Evangelium in religions- und traditionsgeschichtlicher Perspektive*, Wissenschaftliche Untersuchungen zum Neuen Testament 175, J. Frey and U. Schnelle, eds., Tübingen: Mohr Siebeck, 2004b, 695–742.

—— *Das Corpus Johanneum bei Irenäus von Lyon: Studien und Kommentar zum dritten Buch von Adversus Haereses*, Wissenschaftliche Untersuchungen zum Neuen Testament 189, Tübingen: Mohr Siebeck, 2006.

Nagel, T., *Die Rezeption des Johannesevangeliums im 2. Jahrhundert: Studien zur vorirenäischen Aneignung und Auslegungsgeschichte des vierten Evangeliums in christlicher und christlich-gnostischer Literatur*, Arbeiten zur Bibel und ihrer Geschichte 2, Leipzig: Evangelische Verlagsanstalt, 2000.

Noormann, R., *Irenäus als Paulusinterpret: Zur Rezeption und Wirkung der paulinischen und deuteropaulinischen Briefe im Werk des Irenäus von Lyon*, Wissenschaftliche Untersuchungen zum Neuen Testament 2.66, Tübingen: Mohr (Paul Siebeck), 1994.

Normann, F., *Christos Didaskalos: Die Vorstellung von Christus als Lehrer in der urchristlichen Literatur des ersten und zweiten Jahrhunderts*, Münsterische Beiträge zur Theologie 32, Münster: Aschendorff, 1967.

Pokorný, P. and U. Heckel, *Einleitung in das Neue Testament: Seine Literatur und Theologie im Überblick*, Tübingen: Mohr Siebeck, 2007.

Preuschen, E., *Antilegomena: Die Reste der außerkanonischen Evangelien und urchristlichen Überlieferungen*, Gießen: Töpelmann, ²1905.

Reynders, B., *Lexique comparé du texte grec et des versions latine, arménienne et syriaque de l'« Adversus haereses » de Saint Irénée*, 2 vols., Corpus Scriptorum Christianorum

Orientalium 141/142—Subsidia 5/6, Leuven: Imprimerie Orientaliste Durbecq, 1954.

—— *Vocabulaire de la „Démonstration" et des fragments de Saint Irénée*, Chevetogne: Édition de Chevetogne, 1958.

Rousseau, A., L. Doutreleau et al., eds., *Irénée de Lyon: Contre les heresies*, 10 vols., Sources chrétiennes 100.1–2, 152–153, 210–211, 263–264, 293–294, Paris: Cerf, 1965–1982.

Ruckstuhl, E. and P. Dschulnigg, *Stilkritik und Verfasserfrage im Johannesevangelium: Die johanneischen Sprachmerkmale auf dem Hintergrund des Neuen Testaments und des zeitgenössischen hellenistischen Schrifttums*, Novum Testamentum et Orbis Antiquus 17, Göttingen: Vandenhoeck & Ruprecht, 1991.

Teufel, E., "Grußwort," *Dienst in Freiheit: Ernst Käsemann zum 100. Geburtstag*, J. Adam, H.-J. Eckstein and H. Lichtenberger, eds., Theologie interdisziplinär 4, Neukirchen-Vluyn: Neukirchener Verlag, 2008, 83–86.

Thornton, C.-J., *Der Zeuge des Zeugen: Lukas als Historiker der Paulusreisen*, Wissenschaftliche Untersuchungen zum Neuen Testament 56, Tübingen: Mohr (Paul Siebeck), 1991.

van Rompay, L., "Antiochene Biblical Interpretation: Greek and Syriac," *The Books of Genesis in Jewish and Oriental Christian Interpretation: A Collection of Essays*, J. Frishman and L. van Rompay, eds., Traditio Exegetica Graeca 5, Leuven: Peeters, 1997, 103–123.

JOHANNINE ECHOES IN EARLY MONTANISM

Turid Karlsen Seim
The Norwegian Institute in Rome & University of Oslo

This essay is being written at the Norwegian Institute in Rome, which is situated on Gianicolo near the church and catacombs of San Pancrazio and not far from Via Aurelia. In antiquity this was an area where immigrants lived, especially various groups coming from the East. Epigraphic evidence tells us that many of them originated in Asia Minor, and there is also a tradition, however historically unreliable, that St. Pancras himself was a Phrygian orphan martyred at the age of fourteen on the Via Aurelia during the Great Persecution in the early fourth century. Epigraphic and literary evidence also seems to suggest that Montanism survived in Greek-speaking immigrant centers just outside of the Aurelian walls of Rome, long after it was rooted out of Rome's mainstream Christian communities.[1] One of them was centered around Via Aurelia, not far from where I am sitting as I write.

Proximity to possible Montanist survivors in Rome in the fourth and fifth century may create an ambience for writing about their movement, but they were probably in many ways different from Montanists some hundred years earlier. In fact, in the late second century, the label Montanism, which names the movement after its founder Montanus, was not yet invented. It is hostile and late, a heresiological classification coined as far as we know, not until the fourth century. In the third century the movement was by some called the Cataphrygian heresy (Eusebius, *Hist. eccl.* 5.16.1; 5.18.1),[2] but in the movement itself they spoke of the New Prophecy being not so much concerned about provenance as about the prophetic activity which they rightly regarded as their hallmark.[3] However, most modern commentators conveniently

---

[1] Tabbernee 1997, 454–462.

[2] For further discussion of this term, see Tabbernee 2007, xxx.

[3] It has been suggested that the adjective "new" was added to the original self-designation "The Prophecy" for polemical purposes by the movement's ecclesial opponents; cf. Kraft 1955, 249. Paulsen (1978, 47) interprets *nea* as a delimitation over against the prophecy of the OT but as including the NT prophecy with which the Montanists claimed to be in continuity.

tend to use Montanism and New Prophecy interchangeably, as do I in this essay.

Before addressing the role Johannine traditions may have played in the early phase of the Montanist movement, it is necessary to dwell on some preliminary questions concerning the sources available, and the historical and methodological framework, in order to show the vulnerability of any attempt at answering most questions about early Montanism. Cautiousness is not least called for given the limitations imposed by the fact that the sources to the New Prophecy movement are few and fragile, often woven into contexts of hostile contamination. We know from Hippolytus' *Refutatio* 8.19.1 that the new prophets and prophetesses produced writings but these did all perish with the movement itself.[4] The exception is several treatises written by Tertullian during his Montanist period (207–220). The most comprehensive reports by opponents are preserved by Eusebius (263–340) in his *Ecclesiastical History* 5 and by Epiphanius (315–403) in his *Panarion* 48. Eusebius draws on two earlier sources for his presentation of the Cataphrygian heresy. The oldest and most extensive is the so-called Anonymous, who is said to go back to thirteen years after the death of Maximilla, one of the three original prophets and who probably died as the last of the three. The other source is Apollonius, slightly younger but most probably also from the late second century or at the turn of the century. Epiphanius does not identify his sources but the oldest and most important (*Pan.* 48.1–13) may be late second or early third century, and it converges with Eusebius' account. From these sources and a few others, nineteen prophetic oracles have been distilled, of which fourteen are considered to be authentic and five to be questionable.[5] In current research epigraphic sources and archeological findings have become increasingly important but unfortunately they do not yield much for the topic of this essay.[6]

Montanism originated in the mid-160s in the remote mountainous area of Phrygia,[7] when a man, Montanus, together with two women,

---

[4] The authorship of the *Refutatio* has been disputed by Brent 1995; see also Tabbernee 2007, 73–74.

[5] There are several collections of sources to Montanism: de Labriolle 1913; Aland 1960 (the last pages); and most recently Heine 1989.

[6] A major collection and interpretation of inscriptions was published 1997 by William Tabbernee. For the discovery in Phrygia of the site of Pepouza, see Tabbernee and Lampe 2008.

[7] This is today generally agreed against the information of Epiphanius who assumes the mid 150s.

Maximilla and Priscilla, began to speak prophetically in the spirit. They and their followers were not what Robin Lane Fox calls "intellectual heretics,"[8] and it is today broadly acknowledged that the Montanists but for a few exceptions conformed to a mainstream position on controversial doctrinal issues such as Christology or Trinitarian theology. The point of contention was their prophetic activity; only in their acceptance of the Spirit's new words did they part from other Christian groups.[9] It is all the more interesting that this core area of conflict is where Johannine traditions may have been most influential as an authoritative frame of reference.

Some scholars have entertained the idea that the New Prophecy was an intrusion of pagan revelatory ecstasy and have sought to explain Montanus by paganizing him. Robin Lane Fox claims that this is to surrender to his ancient critics and their wish to belittle his appeal, which is all the easier because his Phrygian context already regularly was scorned by critics who lived in the older Greek cities.[10] From a different perspective David E. Aune makes a similar observation deeming paganization of the origin of the New Prophecy as replicating the ancient polemic.[11] He argues that prophets and their revelation played an integral role within early Christianity until the beginning of the second century. Thereafter the inevitable forces of institutionalization banished prophets from their role as leaders and marginalized the revelatory significance of their proclamations.[12] It is, however, not unlikely, that Christianity in Asia Minor in some places may have kept a prophetic tradition at least in cherished memory developing also chains of prophetic succession.[13]

---

[8] Fox 1986, 405.

[9] Cf., i.a., Paulsen 1978, 35: "Hat man sich erstmal von dem Zwang befreit, den Montanismus als innovatorische Häresie zu verstehen, so wird man weder in seiner Eschatologie, noch in dem Insistieren auf der Prophetie, weder in den etischen Mahnungen, noch in der Gemeindeverfassung *a priori* neuartige Züge und Motive erkennen können" (my italics). Indeed, this is what the early source of Epiphanius in *Pan.* 48.1–3 also clearly states. See also Marjanen 2005.

[10] Fox 1986, 405. See also Stewart-Sykes 1997.

[11] Aune claims that Eusebius and his anonymous source model the early Montanist prophets after Lucian's satire on the prophet Alexander of Abonuteichos (cf. Aune 1983, 313). Tabbernee (2007, 122–123) points to the surprising absence in the pre-Constantinian anti-Montanist polemics of any cultic aberrations; they attacked Montanism not because they believed it to be syncretistic, but because to them it was a form of Christianity inspired by an evil spirit intent on perverting the church.

[12] Aune 1983, 189.

[13] See Kraft 1955, 255, 263.

This living tradition of prophecy in Asia Minor is by some being further connected to the presence in the same region of Johannine traditions. Thus Alistair Stewart-Sykes claims that "the roots of Asian Christian Prophecy lie in the tradition of the Fourth Gospel," and that "Montanism simply was a branch of the same tree as Melito of Sardis and the *Epistula apostolorum.*" Hence Montanism had, at least at an early stage in Phrygia, much in common with other Asian prophecy, and its appeal to earlier Asian prophecy, including the apostle John, was not without reason.[14] Also David E. Aune finds that all the major features of early Montanism, including the behavior associated with possession trance, are derived from early Christianity, not least from Johannine traditions: "Montanism is particularly closely associated with the Gospel of John and the Apocalypse of John: their emphasis on the Paraclete was drawn from the former, and their preoccupation with the New Jerusalem…was gleaned from the latter." The New Prophecy attached itself to Jesus' promise for the future in the Gospel of John that the Spirit/Paraclete would "teach… all things" and "guide… into all truth" (John 14:26; 16:13).[15] It is this Paraclete they referred to as the One who speaks through the new prophets. Hence the Montanists had a legitimate source for their claim in the Gospel of John and authentication both for the prophetic mode as the way in which the Spirit speaks and the newness of its content as an advancement in truth. These major points in their view of the Spirit were both critically countered but not necessarily labeled as heretical by their opponents—even if that happened increasingly.[16]

Many commentators have made similar sweeping statements about the Johannine dependence and rhetorical presence in Montanism from its very beginning, assuming that the Montanists spoke in the name of the Paraclete and thus depended on John's Revelation for their eschatology and the particular terminology of the Paraclete passages in John's Gospel for accreditation of their prophetic activity. The

---

[14] Stewart-Sykes 1999, 4.

[15] Aune 1983, 313.

[16] Aune (1983, 189) claims that since Montanism was labeled a heresy, prophets and their revelations were thereafter carefully controlled and held in low esteem or even rejected as heresy. He draws the conclusion that in early Christianity, as in Judaism, the gradual decline of prophetic activity is attributable to social rather than theological factors.

overall image has therefore been that the New Prophecy movement was steeped in Johannine language and ideas.[17]

One possible marker of a Johannine echo is the use of the first person ἐγώ εἰμι in some of the early and most likely original prophetic oracles. Do they have any affinity to similar sayings in the Gospel of John? This form of speech should not be mistaken, as many no doubt enjoyed doing at the time, to imply that the prophets claimed to be the person who spoke in or through them nor that all the three divine persons were heard to speak in an undifferentiated way. The "I" form is in fact common in possessed speech, and conforms to the type David E. Aune has designated "oracles of self-commendation" whose function it is, as a preface to a longer prophetic speech, to legitimate the prophetic spokesperson as a reliable source of divine revelation. Even if it is unusual that the inspired speech is attributed to God, it is not unknown (cf. Rev 1:8; 21:5–8).[18]

M.E. Boring has in a series of articles pursued evidence of the impact prophetic oracles and activity have had on the portrayal of Jesus in the gospels, and his article on the Gospel of John has influenced studies on Montanism, even if he himself does not make the connection.[19] Boring finds that the portrayal of Jesus and the Paraclete in the Gospel of John bears witness to prophetic activity in the Johannine community, probably being regarded as a manifestation of the presence of the Paraclete in their midst. This presence was identified as a speech charisma with

---

[17] See, i.a., Kurt Aland, who in his influential 1960 article, in fairly general terms claims that: "Der Zusammenhang der Apokalypse mit der Montanistischen Enderwartung ist ja... offensichtlich. Aus ihm stammen ganz deutlich die einzelnen eschatologischen Vorstellungen... soweit sie uns noch bekannt sind. Die Beziehung zum Johannesevangelium... ist allein schon darin gegeben, dass Montanus sich als Paraklet bezeichnet. Wo in den Quellen die Aufgabe des Paraklets geschildert wird, wird stets das Johannesevangelium zitiert und auf johanneischer Formeln zurückgegriffen" (pp. 131–133), and he quotes (132) S.A. Fries: "Der Montanismus lebte von johanneischen Ideen und Begriffe." Aland finds further support in Bludau (1925) who addresses the silence in early sources about the Gospel of John saying: "Dieses Schweigen ist nicht mit der relativ späten Entstehung des Evangeliums zu erklären sondern: das Johannesevangelium ist in so starken Masse von ketzerischen Bewegungen in Anspruch genommen wurden, dass es dem Abendland verdächtig war." In later Montanism, when it was clear that the apocalyptic events foreseen by the early prophets did not take place, eschatology became less important even if later catastrophes led to eschatological revivals (Aland 1960, 118).

[18] Aune 1983, 315. Also Kraft (1955) points to the apocalyptic context for this form of prophetic saying.

[19] Boring 1979. Aune (1983, 240–244) has a critical assessment of Boring's work on the Synoptic Gospels.

which "an identifiable group" was endowed. Thereby a chain of revelation is established in some similarity to that in Revelation 1:1–3 but with one link less, since there is no mediating angel. The Spirit and prophet together are conceived of as one functioning entity.

Alistair Stewart-Sykes advances Boring's proposal even further to say that the portrayal of Jesus as an enthusiastic prophet in the Fourth Gospel, may perhaps illustrate the prophetic practice of the author of the gospel.[20] He also mentions that the apocalypse certainly is the product of a visionary prophet whose use of the "I" form, however, is restricted to sayings of Christ in the visions. With some caution he suggests that the "I" form in these cases marks speeches of a Christian prophet speaking under the inspiration of the Paraclete—much in the same way as it happens in the introductory formula employed by the New Prophets. He concludes: "Thus the Johannine community, itself familiar with the activities of prophets (and false prophets according to 1 John 4:1) would recognize the depiction of an enthusiastic prophet in the Fourth Gospel readily enough."[21] This is unfortunately building a conclusion by laying one hypothesis on top of another. Given the scarcity of source material, such a risky procedure is understandable but the result is subject to a high degree of uncertainty.

Also Christine Trevett finds Boring's proposal "suggestive" and exploits it in more general and cautious terms: "If the New Prophecy *was* a revival of prophetism which had been known in Asia Minor Christianity and which had itself coloured the portrayal of the Johannine Paraclete, then we do not have to look far for explanation of why the work of the Three and the activity of the Paraclete should have become linked." She then adds that "in Rome such an association may well have been less obvious and debate ensued."[22] The addition is part of her ongoing argumentation with Ronald E. Heine and his alternative interpretation of early Phrygian Montanism relative to Montanism in Rome. Heine's position is that "the Paraclete passages were not used by the Montanists in the earliest known debate between

---

[20] Stewart-Sykes 1999, 5–6.
[21] Against Hill (1979) who mistakenly identifies enthusiastic inspiration and mantic delivery. The denial by one of Epiphanius' unnamed sources that enthusiastic prophecy ever took place, he also takes to indicate that the source either is later than the second century, from a period when such prophecy had come under attack, or that it is not Asian (Stewart-Sykes 1999, 7).
[22] All citations from Trevett 1996, 93.

them and their ecclesiastical opponents in Phrygia."[23] He points to the fact that the early sources on Montanism in Phrygia neither mention the Gospel of John nor the Paraclete, and he wants to explain why they came to play an important role when the New Prophecy had to defend its case in Rome.

The New Prophecy was present in Rome in a remarkably short time after it first appeared in Phrygia, and before the turn of the century it was well established in the metropolis.[24] We are confident about this early presence in Rome because of a conflict which, according to Eusebius (*Hist. eccl.* 2.25.5–7; 6.20.3), involved the status of Johannine writings. Towards the very end of the second century, a man from Asia Minor, named Proclus, clearly an adherent to the New Prophecy came under some attack of the Roman presbyter Gaius. Little is known about the content of the dispute but among the issues addressed were probably prophetic succession, eschatology, and the legitimacy of "new scriptures."[25] It also appears that Gaius denied apostolic authorship to the Gospel of John.[26] He did this, not on theological but on literary-historical grounds, proving in detail the many historical discrepancies and contradictions between the Gospel of John and the Synoptic Gospels. According to Eusebius (*Hist. eccl.* 3.28.1–2), Gaius accredited the Book of Revelation to the heretic Cerinthus, and a twelfth century Syrian source says that he also referred the authorship of the gospel to Cerinthus. Around 200 CE, Gaius presented his arguments in a *Dialogue with Proclus*, of which some fragments are

---

[23] Heine has developed this idea in two articles (Heine 1987, 4; Heine 1989a), the second being a short version of the first. His 1992 article follows the same contextually diversified approach.

[24] For further discussion of dating, see Tabbernee 2007, 37–38, who concludes with a date in the early to mid 170s.

[25] This episode features in much of the secondary literature on Montanism; see more recently Butler 2006, 23–24; Trevett 1996, 55–56, 131, 139–140; and Culpepper 1994, 120–122. Tabbernee (2007, 68–70, 127) plays the conflict down to an intellectual, if passionate, dialogue on important issues that took place face-to-face. Lampe (2003, 381) sees it as an example of the fractionation into house communities, so that around 200 CE there were, according to Pseudo-Tertullian, two distinctly marked Montanist groups in Rome, one influenced by modalist monarchianism under a certain Aeschinus (known also from Hippolytos and Jerome) and a group tending towards Logos theology under Proclus.

[26] In his essay in this volume, Charles E. Hill admits that Gaius may have criticized the Apocalypse, but calls into question whether he ever criticized (the Gospel of) John. However, most important to Hill is the fact that the criticism "proved to be quite ephemeral and ineffective."

known. Since a man of some standing in the churches in Rome saw a possible line of attack in refuting not just the way in which Montanist used certain Johannine traditions but indeed the two Johannine writings themselves, their authority does not seem to have been beyond challenge in Rome towards the end of the second century—even if his attack in the end cost him dearly.

Gaius was challenged by Irenaeus (*Adv. haer.* 3.11.9,12), an advocate for the Gospel of John, who in this case performed the balancing act of condemning both those who removed one of the four gospels and those who added to them. After a critical comment on Marcion, Irenaeus continues:

> Others for sure, in order to nullify the gift of the spirit which has been poured out on the human race in accordance with the Father's good pleasure in the most recent times, do not receive that form which is the Gospel according to John, in which the Lord promised to send the Paraclete. These reject at the same time both the Gospel and the prophetic Spirit. They are miserable indeed since they certainly do not wish that there be false prophets, but they remove the prophetic gift from the church (*Adv. haer.* 3.11.9).[27]

Gaius also provoked Hippolytus who in 204/5 wrote his *Defense of the Gospel of John and Revelation*, which Epiphanius used (*Pan.* 51.3.1–2) to construct a sectarian group (including Gaius) whom he labeled the *Alogi*. There is, however, no reason to connect Gaius with such a group—both the name and the sect itself may never have existed.[28]

Gaius' attempt at discrediting the Gospel of John and the Book of Revelation indicates that to second century followers of Montanus in Rome as represented by Proclus, Johannine traditions/writings probably were used to support and defend their New Prophecy.[29]

---

[27] Tabbernee (2007, 36) holds that Irenaeus is not particularly speaking in defense of the New Prophecy but simply maintaining the prudent and orthodox position of the Gallic churches on prophetic gifts and the nature of prophecy against those who would deny prophecy altogether.

[28] Tabbernee (2007, 68–69) calls them "figments of Epiphanius' fertile imagination," and even if he did not completely invent them, "any alleged link to Gaius or to their 'anti-Montanism' is spurious."

[29] The same applies to the later fourth-century information provided by Jerome in his *Epistula XLI ad Marcellam*, which says that a follower of Montanus sent to Marcella a collection of texts from the Fourth Gospel to show how the promised Paraclete was present in the Montanist movement. Another fourth-century source of significance is the *Dialexis* or *Dialogue Between a Montanist and an Orthodox*, where the dialogue form is used to denounce the errors of Montanism. In this text the Montanist refers to dominical sayings from the Gospel of John such as John 10:30 and 14:9–11. The *Dialexis*

However, beyond this we know only vaguely how they were interpreted and used also in the case of Proclus. A comment in Pseudo-Tertullian distinguishes between the followers of Proclus and the followers of Aeschinus—both belonging to the New Prophecy. Both groups are said to agree that, while the apostles had the Holy Spirit, the New Prophets had the Paraclete who revealed more in Montanus than Christ revealed in the gospel. Since this, together with a mention in Hippolytus' *Refutatio*, is the first explicit statement that the Montanists referred to the source of their prophecies as the Paraclete, Ronald E. Heine draws the conclusion that this is how, where and when the Montanist claim to the Paraclete had its beginning. He therefore maintains that the appeal to the Paraclete passages in John's Gospel belongs to a distinctively Roman development within the Montanist movement which in turn influenced the North-African branch, in casu Tertullian. Hence the earliest and most abundant appearance of references to the Paraclete is in the Montanist writings of Tertullian whereas the earliest sources about the Phrygian prophets do not mention any Montanist appeal to the Paraclete, and those passages that do, Heine deems to be suspect or late. In Rome the question of contestation was whether there could be prophets after the time of the apostles. The New Prophecy in Rome therefore had to justify its "newness," that is, the validity of post-apostolic prophecy. They found the support they needed in the passages about the Paraclete in John's Gospel. In the Phrygian context, however, the church at large had not and did not deny the possibility of prophetic gifts and activity. There the argument concerned the ecstatic or mantic nature of the New Prophecy and also whether the Montanist prophecy was false.

Ronald E. Heine's interpretation is a praiseworthy attempt at a contextual interpretation of the New Prophecy, branching it out into two diverse expressions: Phrygia/Asia Minor and Rome together with Carthage/North Africa. His observation that there is none or only scarce mention of the Paraclete in the early Phrygian material is undeniable and he is not alone in commenting on this. This, however, also applies to the early Roman material. His argumentation therefore depends on his reconstruction of an assumed Montanist

---

shows that in the fourth century people believed that Montanus used the Gospel of John; however, the most prominent dispute is not over John but concerns Paul's teaching.

counter-strategy to a certain line of critique in Rome and on an
exclusive association of both Irenaeus and Tertullian with Rome—
denouncing their connections with Asia Minor and knowledge about
the situation there.

One might in fact equally well assume that the Montanists in Rome
came under this kind of attack from Gaius precisely because they
traditionally used the Gospel of John and the Book of Revelation or
Johannine traditions to support their prophetic activity. There seems
to be hardly any doubt that the founding New Prophets in Phrygia
had eschatological expectations, however imminent, and that they
entertained ideas about Jerusalem attached to the Phrygian towns
of Pepouza and Tymion. Whether Jerusalem was the name already
given to Pepouza,[30] or whether they expected the heavenly Jerusalem
to descend on the mountain between Pepouza and Tymion, does
represent a significant difference. Both options, however, might
imply the Book of Revelation as a frame of reference even if the
latter is a stronger echo than the former. In one of the authentic
oracles assigned to Maximilla, she declares: "After me there will no
longer be a prophet(ess), but the end." This may simply indicate
that these first prophets lived in a context where expectations of an
imminent end were alive and perhaps common without any particular influence of the Book of Revelation. However, in a famous
oracle attributed to Priscilla, an echo of Revelation is easily heard,
when she says: "Having assumed the form of a woman, Christ came
to me in a bright robe and put wisdom in me, and revealed to me
that this place is holy, and that it is here that Jerusalem will descend
from heaven."[31] Furthermore, the recent archeological discovery
of the sites of Pepouza and (tentatively) Tymion, appears to have
strengthened the eschatological connotations to Rev 21: "Believing
that (according to a literalistic interpretation of Rev 21:1–2,9–10) the
New Jerusalem would be able to be seen descending out of heaven
(cf. Rev 3:8) from (not on) 'a great high mountain' (Rev 21:10),
Montanus found such a mountain in his own native region."[32] It

---

[30] This is the position of Trevett (1996, 100) who argues that the primary reference is
the mention of Jerusalem in the letter to Philadelphia in Rev 3, rather than Rev 21.

[31] Quoted from Heine 1989b. In a footnote to the last oracle, he notes that its authenticity has recently been questioned, and that Tertullian may not have known it, and
never spoke of the end involving Pepouza.

[32] Tabbernee 2007, 115–118, especially p. 116. After discovering the site of Pepouza
and Tymion (see n6 above) the particular local conditions have made him change his

therefore seems that a convincing case can be made for the eschatological scenario that the Phrygian New Prophets were influenced by
the prophetic Revelation which they attributed to the apostle John.

While accepting some of Ronald E. Heine's observations, Christine
Trevett insists that John's Gospel played a formative role also in the
East. Her method is based on a strategy of reversal: she interprets the
polemic and the biblical passages used by the opponents as mirroring
Montanist positions and use of scripture—even when there is no direct
indications that they themselves did use this language. In referring to
Eusebius' report in *Hist. eccl.* 5.1,3–4 on the (possibly Montanist) martyrs of Gaul, she claims that what she calls "paraclete language" deliberately echoes language that was meaningful to the Prophets.[33] In a
detailed discussion, she further points to the fact that Epiphanius' early
source (*Pan.* 48.11.3–4; 48.13.5) echoes and directly appeals to some
sayings of Jesus in the Gospel of John, including John 16:14 about the
Paraclete. According to Trevett this clearly presupposes a corresponding Montanist claim since otherwise there would have been "no need
for comparison between the promised Paraclete which glorifies *Christ*
and the figure of Montanus, whose prophetic words ("I am the Lord
God…") seemed self-glorifying."[34] This shadow- or echo-reading is, of
course, possible but it works only by implication, and I found myself
not being persuaded by it—even more so since *Pan.* 48.1–13 provides
a blend of many passages of equal standing from a variety of New
Testament writings.

In lack of particular evidence, Trevett reverts to ideas about Asia
Minor as a region where any inbreaking of prophetism would have
been associated with the Paraclete due to the emphases of John's
(Asian) Gospel.[35] With prophecy in decline, the sudden surge of activity which the New Prophecy represented could not but be associated
in some minds with the promised Paraclete. So the lack of discussion of the Paraclete in Asian sources should not be taken to mean
that the two came to be associated only in Rome. Rather the Paraclete
scarcely figures in Asian sources because the conjunction of Paraclete

---

mind. He no longer believes, as he suggested in an earlier publication, that Montanus'
reason for naming Pepouza "Jerusalem," was organizational (reviving Acts 1) rather
than eschatological.

[33] Trevett 1996, 64.
[34] Trevett 1996, 64–65. She is, however, more cautious on p. 129.
[35] See above, p. 347.

and prophetism was taken for granted, and the Asian debate centered instead on form, function and criteria for testing the prophecies or the spirits, so as to discredit them. Trevett concludes that Montanus, Priscilla and Maximilla were prophets and functioned as Paracletic figures. However, when she proceeds to describe their teaching, references to the Gospel of John or other Johannine writings are significantly absent.[36]

Trevett tries to compensate for this silence with another circumvention or generalization: The New Prophets appealed to sources which envisaged a new order such as the one they themselves established—including a public, ministerial and sometimes priestly activity of women. Trevett mentions four such sources: John's Gospel which looked to the Paraclete as the source of "all truth"; apocalyptic writings which were radically critical of their own age of compromise; Galatians 3:28 (only in later sources); and Joel 2:28–29 (as also quoted in Acts 2:16–21).[37] This list is interesting in that it may help demonstrate how various passages/sources contribute in various ways. However, Trevett is not able to concretize the use of John's Gospel much beyond her conjecture that "the 'truth' into which the promised Paraclete would lead (as the prophets saw it) was surely not constrained so as to fit into catholic modes of male priestly activity and lay (and female) inactivity"[38]—which of course hermeneutically is nothing but speculation even if it reflects the actual participation of women in some Montanist ministries. It is only the Joel citation which may be said explicitly to support women's prophecy as part of the eschatological scenario. As far as I can see, the Paraclete passages and the promise of further advancement in truth simply warranted novelty—without going into concretizations or details. As a reception of the Gospel of John this is compelling but also remarkably limited, and it does not support the image of a movement immersed in Johannine traditions.

Since the sources leave so much in darkness, it is difficult to conclude anything definitively. However, whereas Christine Trevett tends to overstate her case into conjectures, Ronald E. Heine turns silence into denial. A middle ground seems to be that incidents and polemic preserved in antagonistic sources both in Rome and Asia Minor may be taken to indicate that writings or rather traditions assigned to the

---

[36] Trevett 1996, 92–94.
[37] Trevett 1996, 195.
[38] Trevett 1996, 195–196.

apostle John were important to the early New Prophecy movement not only in Rome but also in Asia Minor. In Rome Gaius confronted the Montanist Proclus by challenging the authority most likely of both John's Gospel and his Revelation, that is, Johannine writings and traditions more broadly. In the East it appears that John's prophetic Revelation was important and that what is now John's First Letter may have played a role as the spirits were tested.

One should constantly bear in mind that for the followers of Montanus all writings/traditions attributed to John served as a coherent complex.[39] Tertullian, in his *Adversus Marcionem*, clearly identifies John the prophet/seer of revelation with the apostle John who also wrote the gospel and is identical with the elder of the epistles. Hence they moved freely between the various writings/traditions assigned to the apostle John and interpreted them as illuminating one another. Revelation was seen as bearing witness to the fact that John himself had been a prophet who in ecstasy had communicated new revealed insights.[40] Most likely there has been a fluctuation between oral tradition, memorized text and written documents. Echoes and single sayings leave open the question as to whether they reflect knowledge of particular written texts or simply are due to a living oral tradition— or perhaps both. The existence of written documents did not mean that oral traditions ceased, and texts were orally performed so that most people in the Christian communities related to texts by hearing them read or simply memorized and, in the case of the gospels, often also harmonized.[41] Thus they might refer to the apostle John, his Gospel, Letter or Revelation, without ever having seen a copy of any of these writings.

In a short but critical examination some years back, F.E. Vokes contested the general claim that the New Prophecy had a strong Johannine flavour.[42] I find his observations acute. He points to the fact that in Eusebius' report there is no reference to the Paraclete and none to the Fourth Gospel apart from the introduction provided by Eusebius him-

---

[39] Cf. Culpepper 1994, 89: "…once the Epistles and Apocalypse were accepted along with the Fourth Gospel as the work of the apostle, references of the elder and the seer were mingled indiscriminately with references to the apostle." This was well established by the end of the second century (Culpepper 1994, 131–32).

[40] In order to remain within this frame of mind, I prefer, in this essay, to speak of the Gospel of John rather than the Fourth Gospel—despite the title of the volume.

[41] See Graham 1987.

[42] Vokes 1968.

self. Epiphanius has ample references to the Old Testament prophets and quotations from many parts of the NT but no particular Johannine emphasis, while Hippolytus (*Ref.* 8.19) says that the Montanists thought that the Paraclete came in Priscilla and Maximilla and that Montanus was a prophet above them who learned more from them than from the law, the prophets and the gospel. There is, however, no further reference to scripture in the passage. Finally, Pseudo-Tertullian writes that the Montanists as far as he knew, held that whereas the Holy Spirit was in the apostles, the Paraclete said more and greater things to Montanus than Christ set forth in the gospel (*Haer.* 7.2). The point at this stage is not to review one more time the discussion about the role references to the Paraclete may have played in the Montanist movement but to note how little else there is which seems to be informed by John's Gospel. Is this any different in the one source known to us which makes great use of the term Paraclete, namely Tertullian?

The New Prophecy arrived in North Africa at latest by the turn of the second to the third century, probably by way of Rome but also from direct contact with Asia Minor.[43] Tertullian most probably became engaged with the New Prophecy in 207/8.[44] Jerome later states that Tertullian "lapsed into the doctrine of Montanus" (*Vir. ill.* 53), simply assuming that involvement with the New Prophecy meant breaking off from the church at large. However, recent scholarship seems to agree that at this early stage and perhaps particularly in Carthage, supporters of the New Prophecy had not left or been made to leave the church but formed a charismatic group or circle within it.[45]

In his later writings Tertullian appears as a strong theological voice of the New Prophecy. It may be unusual and extreme, but it is not "heretical." Whereas some claim that the influence of Montanism profoundly affected Tertullian's understanding of spirit and church, others hold that it brought little change to his theological outlook but that his tone and style became more strident. The influence of the New Prophecy primarily confirmed the ascetic views which he already held on martyrdom, marriage, fasting and forgiveness of sins.[46]

---

[43] Cf. that Trevett's (1996, 67) main interest in Tertullian "is to discover whether his version of the Prophecy bore much relation to that in Asia Minor."

[44] In his 1985 postscript which is included in the updated reprint of his 1971 book on Tertullian, Barnes pulls back from his previous position, which had an earlier date.

[45] Tabbernee 1997, 54–59; Tabbernee 2007, 62–66; Butler 2006, 25–26.

[46] Cf., i.a., Osborn 1997.

Tertullian speaks frequently of the Paraclete and he also refers to Montanus, Maximilla and Priscilla, or the Three. The earliest reference to the New Prophecy is found in *Adversus Marcionem*. Some Montanist scholars read such references primarily with a view to establishing earlier sources and citations of "pure" Montanist material such as oracles—thus applying an insular approach and supporting that much of Tertullian's writings express his individual, idiosyncratic profile with limited representative value for the movement as such. Kurt Aland examines whether Tertullian changed his mind when he became a Montanist but more importantly he asks why earlier views which Tertullian continued to uphold, should not be counted as Montanist.[47]

Despite their early third-century origin, I have chosen to take account of some parts of the earliest writings from Tertullian's Montanist period, among them one where a prophetic oracle is included. My approach is, following Aland, to read Tertullian's texts not only as containing some Montanist references or oracles but to regard Tertullian as *a* representative of the New Prophecy and the one who has left us with the most comprehensive sources still extant. However idiosyncratic, they are not hostile. The question may well be less about how Montanism influenced Tertullian and more about how Tertullian's own personality is reflected in his writings and came to shape what is remembered as Montanism.[48] A caveat is therefore also called for when it comes to how reliable Tertullian is as a source to any form of Montanism other than his own. However, "making due allowances for the nature of Tertullian's 'Montanist' works, it is still possible to see how at least one adherent of the New Prophecy in the pre-Constantinian era answered the charges of pseudo-prophecy, novelty and heresy."[49]

These examples from Tertullian make possible longer lines of argumentation. Thus echoes from scripture are sometimes heard

---

[47] Aland 1960, 120. Being concerned with stages of development, he points to Tertullian's detachment from the original, earliest Phrygian prophecy in that Pepouza and expectations of the New Jerusalem are simply not mentioned. However, Tabbernee (2007, 130, 155–56) claims that in *Adversum Marcionem* 3.24.4 (probably from 208 CE) Tertullian refers to the "city which the apostle John had seen," and also that the only extant fragment from his *De ecstasi* may indicate that he "accepted the validity of Montanus' prophecy concerning the impending judgment" (Tabbernee 2007, 155).

[48] Dunn (2004) holds that all of Tertullian's Montanist works are dated 206–211 CE, and that, except in the case of *Ad Scapulam*, there is no work written after 206 that does not display characteristic Montanist indicators.

[49] Tabbernee 2007, 132.

more distinctly, or it becomes clear that the oracle has a function in relation to an exegetical or hermeneutical reflection. In *De fuga in persecutione* 9, probably from the year 209, Tertullian cites two oracles within the same context. There is nothing in the oracles themselves that indicates a Johannine resonance. They are concerned with martyrdom and are often read as evidence that followers of the New Prophecy were encouraged not just to suffer but to seek martyrdom.[50] Tertullian does not name the prophet who uttered them, but many interpreters attribute them to Montanus himself.[51] It has also been claimed that the content at least of one of them indicates that they were uttered by women and probably also primarily addressed to women.[52] However, Tertullian may equally well refer to them as authentic though contemporary revelations of the Paraclete by one of the local prophet(esse)s active in Carthage, as suggested by William Tabbernee.[53] He also shows how Tertullian a year later, in *De anima* 55.5, again quotes part of one of the two oracles, this time probably from memory. In *De anima* the oracle is attributed to the Paraclete, not the "Spirit" as before, which may simply mean that there to his mind is no distinction between the two terms; they may be used interchangeably.[54] This is all the more likely since, in *De fuga in persecutione* 9, the two oracles conclude a hermeneutical exercise concerning the status of "the command to flee from city to city"— implicitly referring to Matt 10:23 as part of the Galilean commission of the Twelve. Tertullian argues that in the teaching of the apostles themselves this command was not renewed, and it also goes against their example as they never fled. This is explicitly applied to Paul and also to John, who has already been implied as the one who wrote his letters to the churches in confinement on an island because he confessed and did not fly. He taught that we must lay down our lives for one's brethren (John 15:13). In his Revelation he has heard the doom of the fearful, and in his letters the exhortation is accordingly that "there is no fear in love, but perfect love casts out fear; for fear

---

[50] For this discussion, see Tabbernee 2007, 201–260. Generally, he contests the idea that the Montanists encouraged voluntary martyrdom.
[51] See Tabbernee 2007, 213n35.
[52] Jensen 1996, 148.
[53] Tabbernee 2007, 213–214.
[54] Tabbernee 2007, 213–214.

has to do with punishment"—the fire of the lake, no doubt—"and whoever fears has not reached perfection in love" (1 John 4:18–19). This passage shows how the assumption that the apostle John wrote the Gospel, the Letter and the Revelation, allows a free flow of reference and thought between these writings. Also seeking the council of the Spirit brings approval of what the Spirit has already uttered about not being fearful and letting down one's life. Hence in this case the specificity of the oracle, which has no apparent allusion to any Johannine passage, is yet supported by the references to John, proving that the Spirit does not do more than approve the word of the same Spirit exhorting not flight but *martyrium*. The Paraclete calls to martyrdom and denounces those who flee (*De fuga in persecutione* 9.4; 11.3).

In *De monogamia* 2.1–4, no oracle is cited but it is an interesting example of the hermeneutical function which the Johannine echoes serve. Tertullian states that those who reproach the (Montanist) practice of monogamy with heresy also have to deny the Paraclete "for no other reason than that they consider him to be the instigator of a new discipline, and one that is too harsh indeed for them." Tertullian's first point is therefore to discuss whether the Paraclete has taught things that may be considered new *adversus catholicam traditionem* and also burdensome. Now, he says:

> The Lord himself has addressed each issue. For when he says: "I have still many things which I would say to you, but you cannot bear them yet; when the Holy Spirit has come, he will lead you into all truth" (cf. John 16:12–13), he asserts sufficiently indeed that the Spirit will inform fully of things which can both be considered to be new, in that they have never been made known before, and sometimes burdensome, in that they had not been made known for that very reason (*Mon.* 2.2).

He then adds that this is not a carte blanche for anything new and burdensome to be ascribed to the Paraclete, and lists the criteria by which an *adversarius spiritus* should become apparent. The Paraclete, having had many things to teach fully conferred upon him by the Lord, positively proves himself by bearing testimony to Christ himself, that he is such as we believe, together with the whole order of God the creator. He will glorify Christ (cf. John 16:14) and cause things to be remembered about him, and when he has taught those things about the primitive rule of faith, he will reveal many things belonging to the discipline. Finally Tertullian, returning to John 16:12–13, repeats that these revelations "come from no other Christ than him who said that he had also many other things which the Paraclete would teach fully, and that when these teachings (such as monogamy) are burdensome, they 'are no less burdensome to the present (recipients) than they were to those who at that time could not yet endure them.'" Later in *Mon.* 14.7, he adds that "any one can bear them now, since he who gives power to bear them is present." However, when it comes to the conduct actually prescribed by the Paraclete, he draws almost exclusively on other apostolic writings, such as Paul's 1 Corinthians.

The hermeneutical pattern is extremely clear and it constantly repeats itself: the passages about the Paraclete in John 16 and also John 14 are of crucial importance in that they represent a springboard for launching a new and burdensome discipline for mature Christians. The concretization of this discipline does not challenge the fundamental rule of faith. It is sometimes supported by a host of other textual references but—not surprisingly given the issues involved—hardly ever from the Gospel of John. Indeed, the content of the oracles shows that the Paraclete spoke on disputed issues of conduct; he is the "determiner of discipline." Theologically, this supports the idea that the New Prophecy provided an extension of Tertullian's initial theme of divine economy. Beyond the rule of faith which is perfect and complete and which declares the oneness of God and the saving work of Christ, there is scope for novelty because the grace of God continues to advance until the very end.[55]

Tertullian's use of Johannine writings thus supports the profile we have seen throughout. He may be theologically more elaborate and advanced; the eschatology is less in focus but references to the Paraclete are abundant. His interest in John is primarily related to the crucial and almost repetitious role the Paraclete plays both in his hermeneutics and his understanding of divine economy and progressive revelation. In order to support Tertullian's moral strictness, the Paraclete was important as the determiner of discipline through prophetic oracles, but for further defense of the strict moral conduct the oracles sought to impose, other New Testament writings were in actual fact more important and suitable.

In conclusion, the Johannine sayings by Jesus about Holy Spirit/ Paraclete were important to the self-understanding of the New

---

[55] Osborn 1997, 213.

Prophecy—most probably already in its early Phrygian beginning even if the Johannine term Paraclete is not used in still extant sources until a generation or two later. Christ's promise according to the apostle John of a Holy Spirit/Paraclete that should lead further into the truth was regarded as being fulfilled in a prophetic activity which was challenged first as to its source and later also as to its post-apostolic novelty. The dominical sayings about the Paraclete helped counter both lines of opposition, as did the fact that the same apostle had himself been a prophet having visions and hearing heavenly voices. The Montanists' reception of the Gospel of John therefore cannot be seen in isolation from their use of the other traditions they also attributed to the apostle John, especially the Revelation. The time and traditions of the apostle(s) were rendered due honor at the same time as their authority also allowed the Montanists to honor the New Prophecy as being in continuity with this normative time precisely because the newness of their oracles was a witness to the promised advancement in truth. Yet, beyond the pleas to the Paraclete, however significant, specific references to the Gospel of John are remarkably scant and almost absent in what is left of Montanist sources.

BIBLIOGRAPHY

Aland, K., "Bemerkungen zum Montanismus und zur frühchristlichen Eschatologie," *Kirchengeschichtliche Entwürfe: Alte Kirche, Reformation und Luthertum, Pietismus und Erweckungsbewegung*, Gütersloh: Mohn 1960, 105–148.

Aune, D.E., *Prophecy in Early Christianity and the Ancient Mediterranean World*, Grand Rapids, Mich.: Eerdmans, 1983.

Barnes, T.D., *Tertullian: A Historical and Literary Study*, Oxford: Clarendon Press, ²1985.

Bludau, A., *Die ersten Gegner der Johannesschriften*, Biblische Studien 22, Freiburg: Herder, 1925.

Boring, M.E., "The influence of Christian prophecy on the Johannine portrayal of the Paraclete and Jesus," *New Testament Studies* 25 (1979), 113–123.

Brent, A., *Hippolytus and the Roman Church in the Third Century: Communities in Tension Before the Emergence of a Monarch Bishop*, Supplements to Vigiliae Christianae 31, Leiden: Brill, 1995.

Butler, R.D., *The New Prophecy & "New Visions": Evidence of Montanism in The Passion of Perpetua and Felicitas*, Patristic Monograph Series 18, Washington, D.C.: Catholic University of America Press 2006.

Culpepper, R.A., *John, the Son of Zebedee: The Life of a Legend*, Minneapolis: Fortress, 1994.

de Labriolle, P., *Les sources de l'histoire du Montanisme: textes grecs, latins, syriaques*, Collectanea Friburgensia 24, Fribourg: Librairie de l'université; Paris: Leroux, 1913.

Dunn, G.D., *Tertullian*, The Early Church Fathers, London: Routledge, 2004.

Graham, W.A., *Beyond the Written Word: Oral Aspects of Scripture in the History of Religion*, Cambridgde: Cambridge University Press, 1987.

Fox, R.L., *Pagans and Christians*, Perennial Library, San Francisco: Harper & Row, 1986.

Heine, R.E., "The Role of the Gospel of John in the Montanist Controversy," *Second Century* 6 (1987), 1–19.

—— "The Gospel of John and the Montanist Debate in Rome," *Studia Patristica* 21, E. Livingstone, ed., Leuven: Peeters, 1989a, 95–100.

—— *The Montanist Oracles and Testimonia*, Patristic Monograph Series 14, Macon, Ga.: Mercer University Press, 1989b.

—— "Montanus, Montanism," *The Anchor Bible Dictionary*, vol. 4, Garden City, N.Y.: Doubleday 1992, 898–902.

Hill, D., *New Testament Prophecy*, Atlanta: John Knox, 1979.

Jensen, A., *God's Self-Confident Daughters: Early Christianity and the Liberation of Women*, Louisville, Ky.: Westminster John Knox, 1996.

Kraft, H., "Die altkirchliche Prophetie und die Entstehung des Montanismus," *Theologische Zeitschrift* 11 (1955), 249–271.

Lampe, P., *From Paul to Valentinus: Christians at Rome in the First Two Centuries*, M. Steinhauser, transl., Minneapolis: Fortress, 2003.

Marjanen, A., "Montanism: Egalitarian Ecstatic 'New Prophecy,'" *A Companion to Second Century Christian 'Heretics,'* A. Marjanen and P. Luomanen, eds., Supplements to Vigiliae Christianae 76, Leiden: Brill, 2005, 185–212.

Osborn, E., *Tertullian, First Theologian of the West*, Cambridge: Cambridge University Press, 1997.

Paulsen, H., "Die Bedeutung des Montanismus für die Herausbildung des Kanons," *Vigiliae Christianae* 32 (1978), 19–52.

Stewart-Sykes, A., "The Asian Context of the New Prophecy and of Epistula Apostolorum," *Vigiliae Christianae* 51 (1997), 416–438.

—— "The Original Condemnation of Asian Montanism," *Journal of Ecclesiastical History* 50 (1999), 1–22.

Tabbernee, W., *Montanist Inscriptions and Testimonia: Epigraphic Sources Illustrating the History of Montanism*, Patristic Monograph Series 16, Macon, Ga.: Mercer University Press, 1997.

—— *Fake Prophecy and Polluted Sacraments: Ecclesiastical and Imperial Reactions to Montanism*, Supplements to Vigiliae Christianae 84, Leiden: Brill, 2007.

Tabbernee, W. and P. Lampe, *Pepouza and Tymion: The Discovery and Archeological Exploration of a Lost Ancient City and an Imperial Estate*, Berlin: de Gruyter, 2008.

Trevett, C., *Montanism: Gender, Authority and the New Prophecy*, Cambridge: Cambridge University Press, 1996.

Vokes, F.E., "The Use of Scripture in the Montanist Controversy," *Studia Evangelica* 5, Texte und Untersuchungen zur Geschichte der altchristlichen Literatur 103, Berlin: Akademie-Verlag, 1968, 317–320.

INDICES

A. *Index of Modern Authors*

B. *Index of Ancient Sources*

OLD TESTAMENT

OLD TESTAMENT APOCRYPHA

OLD TESTAMENT PSEUDEPIGRAPHA

QUMRAN

NEW TESTAMENT

Nag Hammadi and Related Codices

Nag Hammadi Codices

Manichaean Texts

Other Ancient Authors and Texts

C. Index of Subjects

SUPPLEMENTS TO NOVUM TESTAMENTUM

ISSN 0167-9732

Recent volumes in the series

100. Jackson-McCabe, M.A. *Logos and Law in the Letter of James.* The Law of Nature, the Law of Moses and the Law of Freedom. 2001. ISBN 90 04 11994 9
101. Wagner, J.R. *Heralds of the Good News.* Isaiah and Paul "In Concert" in the Letter to the Romans. 2002. ISBN 90 04 11691 5
102. Cousland, J.R.C. *The Crowds in the Gospel of Matthew.* 2002. ISBN 90 04 12177 3
103. Dunderberg, I., C. Tuckett and K. Syreeni. *Fair Play: Diversity and Conflicts in Early Christianity.* Essays in Honour of Heikki Räisänen. 2002. ISBN 90 04 12359 8
104. Mount, C. *Pauline Christianity.* Luke-Acts and the Legacy of Paul. 2002. ISBN 90 04 12472 1
105. Matthews, C.R. *Philip: Apostle and Evangelist.* Configurations of a Tradition. 2002. ISBN 90 04 12054 8
106. Aune, D.E., T. Seland, J.H. Ulrichsen (eds.) *Neotestamentica et Philonica.* Studies in Honor of Peder Borgen. 2002. ISBN 90 04 126104
107. Talbert, C.H. *Reading Luke-Acts in its Mediterranean Milieu.* 2003. ISBN 90 04 12964 2
108. Klijn, A.F.J. *The Acts of Thomas.* Introduction, Text, and Commentary. Second Revised Edition. 2003. ISBN 90 04 12937 5
109. Burke, T.J. & J.K. Elliott (eds.) *Paul and the Corinthians.* Studies on a Community in Conflict. Essays in Honour of Margaret Thrall. 2003. ISBN 90 04 12920 0
110. Fitzgerald, J.T., T.H. Olbricht & L.M. White (eds.) *Early Christianity and Classical Culture.* Comparative Studies in Honor of Abraham J. Malherbe. 2003. ISBN 90 04 13022 5
111. Fitzgerald, J.T., D. Obbink & G.S. Holland (eds.) *Philodemus and the New Testament World.* 2004. ISBN 90 04 11460 2
112. Lührmann, D. *Die Apokryph gewordenen Evangelien.* Studien zu neuen Texten und zu neuen Fragen. 2004. ISBN 90 04 12867 0
113. Elliott, J.K. (ed.) *The Collected Biblical Writings of T.C. Skeat.* 2004. ISBN 90 04 13920 6
114. Roskam, H.N. *The Purpose of the Gospel of Mark in its Historical and Social Context.* 2004. ISBN 90 04 14052 2
115. Chilton, B.D. & C.A. Evans (eds.) *The Missions of James, Peter, and Paul.* Tensions in Early Christianity. 2005. ISBN 90 04 14161 8
116. Epp, E.J. *Perspectives on New Testament Textual Criticism.* Collected Essays, 1962-2004. 2005. ISBN 90 04 14246 0
117. Parsenios, G.L. *Departure and Consolation.* The Johannine Farewell Discourses in Light of Greco-Roman Literature. 2005. ISBN 90 04 14278 9
118. Hakola, R. *Identity Matters.* John, the Jews and Jewishness. 2005. ISBN 90 04 14224 6
119. Fuglseth, K.S. *Johannine Sectarianism in Perspective.* A Sociological, Historical, and Comparative Analysis of Temple and Social Relationships in the Gospel of John, Philo, and Qumran. 2005. ISBN 90 04 14411 0 (in preparation)
120. Ware, J. *The Mission of the Church.* in Paul's Letter to the Philippians in the Context of Ancient Judaism. 2005. ISBN 90 04 14641 5

121. Watt, J.G. van der (ed.) *Salvation in the New Testament*. Perspectives on Soteriology. 2005. ISBN-13: 978 90 04 14297 8, ISBN-10: 90 04 14297 5
122. Fotopoulos, J. (ed.) *The New Testament and Early Christian Literature in Greco-Roman Context*. Studies in Honor of David E. Aune. 2006.
    ISBN-13: 978 90 04 14304 3, ISBN-10: 90 04 14304 1
123. Lehtipuu, O. *The Afterlife Imagery in Luke's Story of the Rich Man and Lazarus*. 2006. ISBN 978 90 04 15301 1
124. Breytenbach, C., J.C. Thom and J. Punt (eds.) *The New Testament Interpreted*. Essays in Honour of Bernard C. Lategan. 2006. ISBN 13: 978 90 04 15304 2;
    ISBN 10: 90 04 15304 7
125. Aune, D.E. & R. Darling Young (eds.) *Reading Religions in the Ancient World*. Essays Presented to Robert McQueen Grant on his 90th Birthday. 2007.
    ISBN 978 90 04 16196 2
126. Pennington, J.T. *Heaven and Earth in the Gospel of Matthew*. 2007.
    ISBN 978 90 04 16205 1
127. Petersen, S. *Brot, Licht und Weinstock*. Intertextuelle Analysen johanneischer Ich-bin-Worte. 2008. ISBN 978 90 04 16599 1
128. Hultin, J.F. *The Ethics of Obscene Speech in Early Christianity and Its Environment*. 2008. ISBN 978 90 04 16803 9
129. Gray, P. and G.R. O'Day (eds.) *Scripture and Traditions*. Essays on Early Judaism and Christianity *in Honor of Carl R. Holladay*. 2008. ISBN 978 90 04 16747 6
130. Buitenwerf, R., H.W. Hollander and J. Tromp (eds.) *Jesus, Paul, and Early Christianity*. Studies in Honour of Henk Jan de Jonge. 2008. ISBN 978 90 04 17033 9
131. Huizenga, L.A. *The New Isaac*. Tradition and Intertextuality in the Gospel of Matthew. 2009. ISBN 978 90 04 17569 3
132. Rasimus, T. (ed.) *The Legacy of John*. Second-Century Reception of the Fourth Gospel. 2010. ISBN 978 90 04 17633 1

brill.nl/nts